PHILOSOPHY IN GEOGRAPHY

THEORY AND DECISION LIBRARY

AN INTERNATIONAL SERIES
IN THE PHILOSOPHY AND METHODOLOGY OF THE
SOCIAL AND BEHAVIORAL SCIENCES

VOLUME 20

PHILOSOPHY IN GEOGRAPHY

Edited by

STEPHEN GALE

University of Pennsylvania, Philadelphia, Pa., U.S.A.

and

GUNNAR OLSSON

Nordic Institute for Studies in Urban and Regional Planning,
Stockholm, Sweden

D. REIDEL PUBLISHING COMPANY

DORDRECHT : HOLLAND / BOSTON : U.S.A.

LONDON : ENGLAND

Library of Congress Cataloging in Publication Data

Main entry under title:

Philosophy in geography.

(Theory and decision library)
Includes bibliographies and index.
1. Geography—Philosophy. I. Gale, Stephen.
II. Olsson, Gunnar.
G70.P46 910'.01 78–21037
ISBN 90–277–0948–3

Published by D. Reidel Publishing Company,
P.O. Box 17, Dordrecht, Holland

Sold and distributed in the U.S.A., Canada and Mexico
by D. Reidel Publishing Company, Inc.
Lincoln Building, 160 Old Derby Street, Hingham,
Mass. 02043, U.S.A.

Printed in The Netherlands

TABLE OF CONTENTS

Preface   vii

Introduction   ix

J. M. BLAUT/Some Principles of Ethnogeography   1

ANNE BUTTIMER/Erewhon or Nowhere Land   9

MICHAEL F. DACEY/A Framework for Examination of Theoretic Viewpoints in Geography   39

MICHAEL DEAR/Thirteen Axioms of a Geography of the Public Sector   53

STEPHEN GALE and MICHAEL ATKINSON/On the Set Theoretic Foundations of the Regionalization Problem   65

REGINALD G. GOLLEDGE/Reality, Process, and the Dialectical Relation Between Man and Environment   109

PETER GOULD/Signals in the Noise   121

DAVID HARVEY/Population, Resources, and the Ideology of Science   155

LESLIE J. KING/Alternatives to a Positive Economic Geography   187

DAVID LEY/Social Geography and the Taken-For-Granted World   215

BERNARD MARCHAND/Dialectics and Geography   237

ERIC G. MOORE/Beyond the Census: Data Needs and Urban Policy Analysis   269

GUNNAR OLSSON/Social Science and Human Action or on Hitting Your Head Against the Ceiling of Language   287

JOHN S. PIPKIN/Problems in the Psychological Modelling of Revealed Destination Choice   309

DAVID RUSSELL/An Open Letter on the Dematerialization of the Geographic Object   329

ALLEN J. SCOTT/Land Use and Commodity Production   345

ERIC S. SHEPPARD/Spatial Interaction and Geographic Theory   361

W. R. TOBLER/Cellular Geography   379

YI-FU TUAN/Space and Place: Humanistic Perspective   387

MICHAEL J. WOLDENBERG/A Periodic Table of Spatial Hierarchies   429

Unconventional Name Index   457

Reference List   459

INDEX OF NAMES   461

INDEX OF SUBJECTS   469

PREFACE

In any edited volume most credit is due to the individual authors. The present case is no exception and we as editors have done little apart from serving as coordinators for a group of friends and colleagues. For once, the responsibilities are shared.

We feel that the collection gives a fair representation of the activities at the frontier of human geography in North America. Whether these premonitions will be further substantiated is of course to be seen. In the meantime, we take refuge in Vico's saying that "doctrines must take their beginning from that of the matter of which they treat". And yet we also know that new treatments never lead to final ends, but rather to new doctrines and to new beginnings.

It is also a pleasure to acknowledge those publishers and authors who have given permission to reprint copyrighted materials:

Association of American Geographers for Leslie J. King's 'Alternatives to a Positive Economic Geography', *Annals of the Association of American Geographers*, Vol. **66**, 1976;

Edward Arnold (Publishers) Ltd. for Yi-Fu Tuan's 'Space and Place: Humanistic Perspective', in Christopher Board *et al.* (eds.), *Progress in Geography*, Vol. **6**, 1974;

Economic Geography for David Harvey's 'Population, Resources, and the Ideology of Science', *Economic Geography*, Vol. **50**, 1974;

Institute of British Geographers for David Ley's 'Social Geography and the Taken-for-Granted World', *Transactions of the Institute of British Geographers*, Vol. **2**, 1977; and

North-Holland Publishing Company for Allen J. Scott's 'Land Use and Commodity Production', *Regional Science and Urban Economics*, Vol. **6**, 1976.

STEPHEN GALE and GUNNAR OLSSON
Philadelphia and Ann Arbor,

March 1977

INTRODUCTION

I. THE ECLECTICISM OF DISCIPLINARY CHANGE

Within the scientific community, change is often foreshadowed by an increased concern with philosophical and methodological issues. We find that traditions, principles, and alliances — the very theoretical and epistemological presuppositions of an area of inquiry — come to be questioned and scrutinized. Radical transformations of purpose and substance are proposed. Of equal significance are the moves for modifications in the structure of arguments.

For the historian of science, changes in a discipline are usually viewed as parts of an intellectual evolution. But for those who toil daily in the garden, change is rarely seen as a clear, systematic shift in a paradigm. More often, it is experienced as a series of disputes which involve the nature of observation and evidence, the effects of existing theoretical presuppositions, and the efficacy of alternative modes of inference. Rarely is there a grand rejection of a theory or a line or inquiry; even more rarely is there a conclusive resolution of a dispute. The fundamental questions remain much the same, even though the methodologies gradually may shift as the ongoing dialogue between intellectual communities continues.

It is in the spirit of this conception of scientific change that the essays in the present volume were collected. Our approach is natural, since modern geography has undergone an almost continual transformation of purpose, language, and methodology. There has been a clear movement from the early concerns with discovery and mapping, via the social Darwinism, human ecology, and geo-politics around the first world war, to the current involvement in cultural, economic, environmental, and regional issues. And yet, geography has exhibited an eclecticism that defies conventional codification even though there has prevailed a synthetic attitude and a tendency to focus on broad concerns with man's social and environmental relationships rather than on the visibility of singular theories. The daily work is marked by an awareness of competing modes of thought and perhaps even by the importance of maintaining the viability of the conflict.

Since in the mid 1950's, when James and Jones published *American*

Geography: Inventory and Prospect,[1] there have been only scattered attempts to trace the development of the philosophy of geographic thinking.[2] In part this is a result of the diverse subject matter and of a general feeling that the so-called 'quantitative revolution' of the 1960's had exorcised philosophy from the legitimate concerns of the discipline. But even during that period, it gradually became clear that the changing relations among individuals, the sciences, and society once again necessitated philosophical and methodological reevaluation. It is the purpose of the present volume to provide an exposition of some recent creative and critical activities within North American geography.

It is obvious that no collection can portray the dynamic plot which characterizes a discipline's actors and their respective motivations and relationships. Instead, we have had to use the more indirect, selective means of soliciting manuscripts from those geographers who had exhibited more or less developed philosophic concerns in their previous work. In addition, most of the authors had some direct or indirect connections with the 'quantitative' movement of the last decade. But not even these biases could prevent geography's acknowledged eclecticism from appearing. Indeed we have come to believe that the diversity may be an extremely healthy sign although we appreciate that it may be frustrating to those who believe only in unified approaches to well-defined problems. What is found in the collection is therefore not one but several themes and not only one but several methodologies. In one form or another, we expect that they may all survive. Some might even turn into the types of research programs that the late Imre Lakatos regarded as the real substance of scientific appraisal. It is our hope that the collection itself will serve as an intellectual touchstone capable of generating further development.

The disciplinary diversity and eclecticism is further underscored by our attitude toward editing the papers. Except for minor adjustments, the articles were left untouched. Moreover, we have chosen to publish the papers in alphabetical order rather than in traditional groupings. On closer inspection, we believe that this ordering is not as artificial as it may first seem. Indeed, we arrived at it in frustration after failing in our attempts to impose any of the usual frameworks on the collection.

By choosing the alphabetical approach we wish to emphasize that the variability and change in a discipline are difficult to contain within conventional classifications. At the same time we discovered that in this way we could offer four books in one, simply by furnishing alternative 'Tables of Organization'. Each of these books can be read on its own, but the richer message is in the number of ways that the individual papers can be tied to the others.

Even though each Table contains exactly the same essays, they form rather different intellectual mosaics. None is neutral as the various orderings all reflect our own ideologies of what is now and what ought to be in the future. The three non-alphabetical orderings can be entitled as follows.

A.   *Geometric Forms and Social Relations: Essays on the Problem of Geographic Inference*

B.   *Thought and Action: Geographic Perspectives on Functional Attitudes*

C.   *Objective Certainty and Subjective Ambiguity: Analytical and Phenomenological Approaches in Geography*

The three volumes clearly reflect a number of traditional questions albeit ordered under somewhat novel categories. Taken together, the three frameworks could provide a focus for critical attention and a basis for assessing the various trends in the discipline. Of equal importance, however, is the understanding which we hope may emerge from reflection on the categories themselves. One such reflection is in Table I and another is contained in the Unconventional Name Index and Reference List on pp. 457–459.

Both the alphabetical and the substantive frameworks derive from a complex and on-going debate within the geographic community. However, since much of the existing literature is diffuse and spread through a variety of publications, the full dimensions of the discussions have not always been clear even to the participants themselves. It is therefore necessary to provide a historical dimension to our selection of themes and to indicate why we believe that our particular categorial frameworks are capable of illuminating past, present and future trends within the discipline.

II. GEOMETRIC FORMS AND SOCIAL RELATIONS: ESSAYS ON THE PROBLEM OF GEOGRAPHIC INFERENCE

Throughout its history, geography has been closely tied to the use of maps both as representational devices and as analytical tools. Gradually, however, it became apparent that maps cannot in and of themselves provide a sufficient basis for a scientific discipline. The attitude began to spread that the collection and presentation of spatial data may lead to an understanding neither of the

TABLE I

Characterization of papers

Author	Geographical perspective		Functional perspective		Methodological perspective		Total number of entries
	Form	Relations	Thought	Action	Analytical	Phenomenological	
Blaut		X	X			X	3
Buttimer		X	X	X		X	4
Dacey	X		X		X		3
Dear		X		X		X	3
Gale	X	X	X	X	X		5
Golledge	X	X	X			X	4
Gould	X	X	X		X	X	5
Harvey		X	X	X		X	4
King	X	X	X	X	X	X	6
Ley		X	X	X		X	4

Table 1 (continued)

Author	Geographical perspective		Functional perspective		Methodological perspective		Total number of entries
	Form	Relations	Thought	Action	Analytical	Phenomenological	
Marchand	X	X	X		X	X	5
Moore		X		X	X		3
Olsson		X	X	X	X	X	5
Pipkin	X	X	X		X		4
Russell	X	X	X	X	X	X	6
Scott	X	X		X	X		4
Sheppard	X	X	X		X		4
Tobler	X		X		X		3
Tuan		X	X			X	3
Woldenberg	X		X		X		3

distributions themselves nor of the generating processes. The need was acutely felt for the development of some sort of general theory. Two traditions emerged, but both took the map as its starting point. The difference was that one approach attempted to discover the spatial or purely geometric laws which were 'embedded' in the observed distributions, while the other aimed at the identification and refinement of the behavioral process laws of which the distributions were spatial manifestations.

Out of these conflicting attitudes came an articulated understanding of what has been called the geographic inference problem of form and process. Those who viewed geography as applied geometry asked whether the map was a function of particular geometric laws. Those who thought of geography as only another social science discipline, searched for the laws of human inter-actions as these manifested themselves over distance. The central methodo-logical issue was whether a mapped distribution is primarily an instance of geometric spatial laws or of laws of human behavior. Does the description of spatial distributions lead only to knowledge of spatial forms or does it con-stitute a basis of the discovery of laws of human behavior as well?

Inference and method are of course highly interrelated and in the late 1950's and early 1960's the geographers' interest in theory was paralleled by the adoption and application of quantitative techniques. It was at this stage that an increasing number of writers began to refer to geography as a kind of applied geometry whose major task was to find models of geometric axioms and theorems. It was frequently assumed that the geometric laws were both positive and normative; the 'is' of spatial analysis was held to be the same as the 'ought' of spatial planning. Planning was often equated with the design of optimal spatial patterns, which in the extreme were conceived as geometric representations of the efficiency conditions of neoclassical economic theory. Social equity and spatial efficiency were thought of as two sides of the same descriptive/prescriptive coin.

At its root, the question was one of the positive characterization of spatial phenomena. Were spatial phenomena to be discussed primarily in terms of their geometric representations or were they to be tied to the behavioral presuppositions of human decision making? Throughout, geographers recog-nized the importance of spatial considerations, but one school searched for instances of geometric laws, while the other showed more concern with human behavior. But embedded in these different attitudes was a crucial inference problem; is it possible to reason from form to process, from process to form? What is cause and what is effect? And so it was that by the mid-1960's the geographic inference problem had become a central philosophic

TABLE II

Geometric form and social relations: Essays on the problem of geographic inference

---

PART I: GEOGRAPHY AS SPATIAL FORM

MICHAEL J. WOLDENBERG / A Periodic Table of Spatial Hierarchies
W. R. TOBLER / Cellular Geography
MICHAEL F. DACEY / A Framework of Examination of Theoretic Viewpoints in
Geography

PART II: GEOGRAPHIC INFERENCE IN THEORY

LESLIE J. KING / Alternatives to a Positive Economic Geography
REGINALD GOLLEDGE / Reality, Process, and the Dialectical Relation Between
Man and Environment
PETER GOULD / Signals in the Noise
DAVID RUSSELL / An Open Letter on the Dematerialization of the Geographic
Object

PART III: GEOGRAPHIC INFERENCE IN PRACTICE

STEPHEN GALE and MICHAEL ATKINSON / On the Set Theoretic Foundations
of the Regionalization Problem
JOHN S. PIPKIN / Problems in the Psychological Modelling of Revealed Destination
Choice
ERIC G. MOORE / Beyond the Census: Data Needs and Urban Policy Analysis
ERIC S. SHEPPARD / Spatial Interaction and Geographic Theory
ALLEN J. SCOTT / Land Use and Commodity Production
BERNARD MARCHAND / Dialectics and Geography

PART IV: GEOGRAPHY AS SOCIAL RELATIONS

MICHAEL DEAR / Thirteen Axioms of a Geography of the Public Sector
DAVID HARVEY / Population, Resources, and the Ideology of Science
J. M. BLAUT / Some Principles of Ethnogeography
ANNE BUTTIMER / Erwhon or Nowhere Land
YI-FU TUAN / Space and Place: Humanistic Perspective
DAVID LEY / Social Geography and the Taken-For-Granted World
GUNNAR OLSSON / Social Science and Human Action or On Hitting Your Head
Against the Ceiling of Language

---

and methodological question within the discipline. Not only was geography
supposed to yield insights into the laws of spatial behavior, but into the
methodological issues of form and process reasoning as well. The problem was
thus characterized both in terms of conventional statistical inference and in
terms of interpreting pictorial representations. What kind of information is

actually contained in a map or a picture? Is it geometrical, behavioral or a combination of the two?

The geographic literature from the past two decades can in many ways be seen as a reflection of these inferential concerns and attitudes. The present volume is no exception and in Table II we have attempted to order the papers accordingly. Roughly speaking, Woldenburg, Tobler, and Dacey present various versions of the geography as geometry argument; King, Golledge, Gould and Russell, spend considerable time on the theoretical implications of the geographic inference problem itself; Gale and Atkinson, Pipkin, Moore, Sheppard, Scott and Marchand examine some of its practical planning consequences; while Dear, Harvey, Blaut, Buttimer, Tuan, Ley and Olsson argue that geography should focus mainly on the analysis of behavioral processes and social relations.

III. THOUGHT AND ACTION:
GEOGRAPHIC PERSPECTIVES ON FUNCTIONAL ATTITUDES

The attitudes to the spatial inference problem has led to a number of distinct lines of reasoning. The spatial or 'geography as geometry' school, has remained rather orthodox, while the 'behavioral geography' school, has undergone some remarkable changes during the last decade. Aspects of this development are inherent in the different attitudes toward the relations between thought and action on the one hand and to the concepts of certainty and ambiguity on the other.

To see this better, it may be helpful to ask what it means to behave. What role do the laws of ideal types of individual and social behavior play in the explanation and prediction of spatial patterns? Clearly, these are central questions to anyone concerned with the spatial consequences of behavioral laws. Equally clearly they are complex. The complexity, however, is rooted in more than the nature of behavior. For just as explanation and prediction must ultimately be confronted by problems of prescription and instrumentality, representation and observation become confronted with questions of language. Is it ever possible to observe and describe something which is not already inherent in the analytical language itself?

In the last decade, it has become increasingly clear that the different methodological approaches to the issues of geographic inference also imply very different concepts of man. On the one hand there is the conception of man as a mechanistic being whose actions are representable through geometric laws, while, on the other hand, there is the alternative position that man is a non-mechanistic constantly evolving being. The former line resulted in what has been called a 'spatialization of geographic thought'. When extended from theory into the realm of action, the former line suggests that individual and aggregate decisions can be effected through changes in the spatial location of human enterprises; spatial structure became paramount while human social behavior was regarded as a primary consequence. Conversely, the latter orientation treated changes in individual and social behavior not as by-products of spatial manipulation, but as directly dependent on modifications of individual attitudes and social belief structures. What initially appeared as a methodological question concerning the structure of inference, thus became an issue of profound intellectual and political import. If the point is to change the world, should one modify behavior through manipulations of spatial arrangements or vice versa? And which approach is more moral?

To see these issues more clearly it may be helpful to order our papers within the categorial framework of thought and action. The debate can in fact be characterized in very straight-forward philosophical terms. Most succinctly, the question is whether a form of extensional calculus can represent the entities of geographic description or whether some richer phenomenological reasoning modes are necessary. A traditional dualism thus resurfaced in the debate over geographic methodology. In the process, the spatial inference problem has changed from the initial concern with the relationship between space and behavior and into an issue of the representability of thought and observation. The question is classical and asks whether it is possible to understand any phenomenon except through a detailed and empathic presentation of the scene on which the real drama occurred. The problem deals not only with the meaning of meaning, but with the meaning of rules.

Just as the papers can be ordered through the categories of spatial form and behaviorial process, they can be seen in terms of thought, meaning, and action as in Table III. The issue is whether geography must limit itself to the characterization and representation of thoughts and observations or whether it can also be translated into the realm of action. Whatever the answer, it will have direct political and social implications. Among the present papers, those by Dacey, Tuan, Woldenberg, Tobler, Pipkin, Sheppard, Golledge, Marchand, and Blaut may be seen as variations on the theme that geography is an intellectual enterprise, distinguished by its special way of constructing and reconstructing thought. The extreme alternative to that theoretical approach is represented by the papers by Moore, Dear, and Scott which see geography as

TABLE III

Thought and action: Geographic perspectives on functional attitudes

PART I: GEOGRAPHY AS THOUGHT

MICHAEL F. DACEY / A Framework for Examination of Theoretic Viewpoints in
    Geography
YI-FU TUAN / Space and Place: Humanistic Perspective
MICHAEL J. WOLDENBERG / A Periodic Table of Spatial Hierarchies
W. R. TOBLER / Cellular Geography
JOHN S. PIPKIN / Problems in the Psychological Modelling of Revealed Destination
    Choice
ERIC S. SHEPPARD / Spatial Interaction and Geographic Theory
REGINALD GOLLEDGE / Reality, Process, and the Dialectical Relation Between
    Man and Environment
BERNARD MARCHAND / Dialectics and Geography
J. M. BLAUT / Some Principles of Ethnogeography

PART II: GEOGRAPHY AS THOUGHTS
TO CHANGE THE WORLD

LESLIE J. KING / Alternatives to a Positive Economic Geography
PETER GOULD / Signals in the Noise
DAVID LEY / Social Geography and the Taken-For-Granted World
ANNE BUTTIMER / Erewhon or Nowhere Land
GUNNAR OLSSON / Social Science and Human Action or On Hitting Your Head
    Against the Ceiling of Language
DAVID RUSSELL / An Open Letter on the Dematerialization of the Geographic
    Object
DAVID HARVEY / Population, Resources, and the Ideology of Science
STEPHEN GALE and MICHAEL ATKINSON / On the Set Theoretic Foundations
    of the Regionalization Problem

PART III: GEOGRAPHY AS ACTION

ERIC G. MOORE / Beyond the Census: Data Needs and Urban Policy Analysis
MICHAEL DEAR / Thirteen Axioms of a Geography of the Public Sector
ALLEN J. SCOTT / Land Use and Commodity Production

directly relevant to action. Finally, King, Gould, Ley, Buttimer, Olsson, Russell, Harvey, and Gale and Atkinson try to view thought and action in a more integrated fashion, such that the concepts and methods of reasoning are examined in terms of their effect on action.

IV. OBJECTIVE CERTAINTY AND SUBJECTIVE AMBIGUITY: ANALYTICAL AND PHENOMENOLOGICAL APPROACHES IN GEOGRAPHY

In the categorial frameworks discussed thus far, the tension of form and process yielded to the deeper tension between thought and action. The latter reflects the apparent demands on the intellectual community to remain removed from the world in which ideas are put into practice. Traditionally, this has been typical of much academic reasoning, but the close ties with planning have made the problem more acute in geography than in many other disciplines. Geography deals with reality, but as long as geographers contribute directly to the practice of planning, the tension cannot itself remain solely an academic issue. Thus it now turns out that the initial problem of form and process involves not only an inferential but a political issue. It is not an issue of conventional political categories, however, but of alternative conceptions of man. If man is a machine, then we could obviously limit ourselves to the search for analytical laws characterized by the certainty of closed concepts. But if man is conceived as a richer, searching being, then he can be understood only through empathic accounts in which ambiguity and open concepts play crucial roles. It follows that different conceptions of man have their counterparts in different modes of reasoning. Should it be formal, analytic, objective and certain? Or should it be informal, phenomenological, subjective and ambiguous? Those geographers who stressed the search for geometric laws have tended in the former direction, while the behaviorists have been most inclined to move in the latter.

Table IV is an attempt to order the papers of the volume along this dimension. The works by Tobler, Sheppard, Woldenberg, Pipkin, Gale and Atkinson all fall towards the analytic end of the spectrum. But others have maintained that formalized methods too easily yield to the fallacy of misplaced concreteness. Their argument has been that natural language provides the most appropriate reasoning mode and that it should be used more freely both in description and in prescription.

The papers by Dear, Golledge, Harvey, Blaut, Tuan, Buttimer, and Ley present various sides of this debate; many of them have indeed been deeply involved in the gradual rejection of the analytical approach. Perhaps most significantly, however, much of the geographic literature has recognized the need for a more circumspect view of the problem of translation. It has clear counterparts in the philosophical literature itself and it is represented here by King, Moore, Gould, Marchand, Russell, and Olsson.

TABLE IV

Objective certainty and subjective ambiguity: Analytical and phenomenological
approaches in geography

PART I: GEOGRAPHY AS
FORMAL/ANALYTICAL REPRESENTATION

W. R. TOBLER / Cellular Geography
ERIC S. SHEPPARD / Spatial Interaction and Geographic Theory
MICHAEL J. WOLDENBERG / A Periodic Table of Spatial Hierarchies
JOHN S. PIPKIN / Problems in the Psychological Modelling of Revealed Destination
   Choice
STEPHEN GALE and MICHAEL ATKINSON / On the Set Theoretic Foundations
   of the Regionalization Problem
ALLEN J. SCOTT / Land Use and Commodity Production
MICHAEL F. DACEY / A Framework for Examination of Theoretic Viewpoints in
   Geography

PART II: GEOGRAPHY AND THE
PROBLEM OF TRANSLATION

LESLIE J. KING / Alternatives to a Positive Economic Geography
ERIC G. MOORE / Beyond the Census: Data Needs and Urban Policy Analysis
PETER GOULD / Signals in the Noise
BERNARD MARCHAND / Dialectics and Geography
DAVID RUSSELL / An Open Letter on the Dematerialization of the Geographic
   Object
GUNNAR OLSSON / Social Science and Human Action or On Hitting Your Head
   Against the Ceiling of Language

PART III: GEOGRAPHY AS
DIALECTICAL/PHENOMENOLOGICAL REASONING

MICHAEL DEAR / Thirteen Axioms of a Geography of the Public Sector
REGINALD GOLLEDGE / Reality, Process, and the Dialectical Relation Between
   Man and Environment
DAVID HARVEY / Population, Resources, and the Ideology of Science
J. M. BLAUT / Some Principles of Ethnogeography
YI-FU TUAN / Space and Place: Humanistic Perspective
ANNE BUTTIMER / Erewhon or Nowhere Land
DAVID LEY / Social Geography and the Taken-For-Granted World

V. CONCLUSION

Categorial frameworks become meaningful only within their own historical and intellectual contexts. The three examples we have chosen in this Introduction reflect the idiosyncratic approach to geography. Although most social sciences have their own special cases of the inference problem, these have rarely been tied so closely to the questions of thought and action as in geography. Indeed for most other disciplines, questions of action are of only minor importance since few of them have fashioned any direct extensions of their theoretical work. In contrast, geography has been linked so closely with planning that the question of thought and action has had a profound impact on its history.

But if the grappling with form and process led to issues of thought and action, the struggle with thought and action has led to questions of certainty and ambiguity. These can best be understood in relation to the attempts of taking us beyond natural language and into formal reasoning. This aspect of the debate may not yet have been particularly well represented by geographers even though it is present throughout the literature. What is important to recognize, however, is that seemingly substantive issues are always part of a set of methodological predilections. It is only by recognizing these connections that the history and progress of the discipline can be measured.

It should finally be stressed that the past several decades have moved towards a view of inquiry and action in which language plays a central role; observations, concepts, and reasoning modes are taken to be directly dependent on their linquistic presuppositions. To some extent this development can be traced to debates within philosophy itself, but for the most part it seems to be a response to the practical problems of inquiry. How are the observer and the observed related? How are concepts formed and used? What is the relationship between inference procedures and problem types? How are praxis and action connected to understanding? How much of what we say is what we want to say and how much is it determined by the categorial frameworks of the language we use? How is our methodology related to our conception of man, and our conception of man to our methodology? Can we say anything which is not already in the particular language we are using?

STEPHEN GALE and GUNNAR OLSSON

NOTES

[1] James, P. E. and Jones, C. F.: 1954, *American Geography: Inventory and Prospect*, Syracuse University Press, Syracuse.
[2] For exceptions, see Glacken, C. J.: 1967, *Traces on the Rhodean Shore*, University of California Press, Berkeley; Harvey, D.: 1969, *Explanation in Geography*, Edward Arnold, London; Davies, W. K. D. (ed.): 1972, *The Conceptual Revolution in Geography*, University of London Press, London; and Olsson, G.: 1975, *Birds in Egg*, Geographical Publications, No. 15, Ann Arbor, Michigan.

J. M. BLAUT

SOME PRINCIPLES OF ETHNOGEOGRAPHY

I

Geography is a belief-system. This says nothing about the truth of its statements. True or false, they are *believed in*.

The belief-status of a statement is a very different thing from the truth-status of that same statement. The former is an ethnographic fact. It emerges from the analysis of a social process (when we ask how beliefs come to be acquired) and a psychological process (when we ask about their cognitive content). Truth-status is a judgment made by human beings; hence the truth-status of a statement cannot be fully ascertained until we also know its belief-status. The process of *verification*, the use of scientific method, is only a part, and often only a small part, of the process of *validation*, the process by which a statement comes to be accepted; receives a social license; enshrines itself as a belief.

II

The fashion these days is to attach the prefix 'ethno-' to a word — as in 'ethnobotany', 'ethnomedicine', etc. — when we want to signify the fact that our concern is with the scientific belief-system which is characteristic of a particular group, or when we want to compare or theorize about such systems. Thus we speak of 'Hanunóo ethnobotany', 'Subanun ethnomedicine', and so on; and thus, also, we speak of 'the study of ethnobotany', meaning not 'the study of botany', but the study across cultures (and classes) of *beliefs* about botany (Conklin, 1957; Blaut, *et al.*, 1959; Frake, 1962). When we gather together all those 'ethnos' which are suffixed by the name of a science, we get, quite naturally, *ethnoscience* (Sturtevant, 1964). And the study of ethnoscience has proven itself, in the decade or so of its existence, to be a very powerful, and just possibly revolutionary, field of endeavor, an approach to the study of empirical beliefs, or cognition, which is peculiarly reliable and peculiarly free of ethnocentrism.

1

Assume, for the sake of my argument, that geography is a distinguishable set of scientific beliefs in all groups. Necessarily, then, there is an *ethnogeography* (Knight, 1971). I contend that the study of ethnogeography is well worth pursuing; and in this paper I outline some of the principles which underlie its pursuit.

III

The subject matter of ethnogeography is the set of all geographical beliefs held by the members of a definite human group at a definite time. The group may be a culture, a subculture, a class, a profession, an age-group, or whatever. The set of beliefs is more or less ordered: it forms a *belief-system*. Each such system is examined, in ethnogeography, from at least three points of view: What are its properties — its contents, structure, and dynamics? How does it interact with other aspects of the group's culture — how is it *bound* to that culture? And what does it do for (and to) our theories about geographical cognition in general?

In principle, there is an ethnogeography of every human group — a point worthy of emphasis. There is a Hanunóo ethnogeography. There are ethnogeographies of Puerto Rican tobacco farmers and ancient Greek philosophers. There is an Association-of-American-Geographers ethnogeography. This last is in some ways the most intriguing one of all. It is the ethnogeography of ourselves, the ethnogeography of our textbooks, lectures, and articles: our runes and stelae.

IV

'Belief-system' is an awkward expression, but necessary. It is not possible to isolate the unit-particular of study, the isolated belief, except in the context of a containing belief-system. We encounter here a methodological problem which has already given ethnoscience a certain amount of difficulty (Tyler, 1969, 16). The most useful methodology thus far applied in this field is an adaptation of structural linguistics (Conklin, 1962). In linguistics, the identification of elementary units (morphemes, lexemes, etc.) is not very difficult; and, working at this level, ethnoscience has produced some fine studies, notably some descriptive, taxonomic, historical, and comparative analyses of ethnoscientific systems (Berlin and Kay, 1969; Friedrich, 1970; Murton,

1973). But, in social reality, the effective unit of communication and perhaps cognition is not a morpheme, a word, or even a 'concept': it is an assertion of belief — something at least comparable to the linguist's 'kernel sentence' and the logicians 'statement' (or 'proposition'). Logicians in effect concede this to be true when they transliterate a simple logical formula. Instead of merely asserting, for instance, that "Some s's are a's", they decompose the formula into two statements, each necessary: (1) "There is an s", such that (2) "Some s's are a's". Hence "s", a concept which enters discourse as the subject of a proposition, is already the object of an existence-proposition, "There *exists* an s . . . " (either logically or empirically). Therefore, the elementary unit of belief is already a complex entity, something on the level of a complete sentence or proposition. We can call it a *belief-statement*. But even this entity is an elementary unit only in principle, not in (typical) methodological practice. The signification of any belief-statement encountered, say, in a geography textbook is always a function of the context, the belief-system described in that textbook. Still more graphic examples come from ethnogeographic fieldwork. I ask a farmer to explain, for instance, soil erosion. He offers a belief-statement. I ask "Why is that true?" He replies, "Because . . . " And thus we descend a chain of connected statements, finally arriving — as the last step — at the elementary beliefs. In sum: the notion of belief-systems, at various levels of complexity, is the more central concept in ethnogeography; the ultimate particles of belief (like the ultimate particles of physics) are end-products of research, the results primarily of disaggregation, not aggregation.

An entire ethnogeography is a belief-system. But it cleaves naturally into subsystems, which can simply be called *theories*. Thus, in AAG-ethnogeography, there is 'theory of map projections', 'theory of settlement forms', and the like; and, in the ethnogeography of Puerto Rican tobacco farmers, there is 'theory of soils', 'theory of marketing', and its like. There must also be theories, complex belief-systems, dealing with salient but unique events: e.g., 'theory of the discovery of America'. (We can dismiss without comment the strangely persistent notion that subject matters are not theoretical but 'historical' if they happen only once, since this notion merely confuses a theory with its empirical instances.) A theory is a belief-system in which the component beliefs are closely interwoven. To some extent they are connected by a tight relation which can be called *argument*. The paradigm for this sort of connection is logical implication, but the relation is typically somewhat less precise, a matter of reasonable inference: "Since we believe P, it seems reasonable also to believe Q".

The theories which comprise an ethnogeography are not quite that tightly connected to each other. However, they are connected, and thus we can rightly consider an ethnogeography a definite system. Among the forms of connection, the loosest one of all, and perhaps the typical one at the level of entire theories and their interconnections, is the relation of *compatibility*. This merely confirms the fact that two belief-statements or theories can co-exist peacefully in the same ethnogeography: they are not cognitively or culturally dissonant (Blaut, 1970). The relation of compatibility of course reflects a social judgment, not a logical one. It proves to be an important aspect of the process by which hypotheses acquire belief-licenses. Various other things being equal, a new hypothesis is admitted to belief-status if it is compatible with existing beliefs, and denied this status if it is not. More generally, the process by which a belief is licensed, the process of validation, involves three sorts of judgment. One is scientific verification. The second is a judgment of compatibility with existing beliefs. The third is a matter of deter-mining whether the candidate-belief does or does not fit into the non-cognitive portion of a group's culture: into the group's values and, more generally, interests. Does it *conform*?

V

Long ago John Dewey asserted the principle that scientific beliefs are judged by their utility — are validated by practice (Dewey, 1916). This principle is best stated in negative form: beliefs (or rather, candidate-beliefs) are *not* validated by a group unless the group finds them to be useful. I use 'group' rather than 'culture', because in most cases the belief-holding reference group is not an entire culture but a social segment of a culture. (Every group possesses a culture: not every group *is* a culture.) The beliefs constituting the ethnogeography of an elite group (or a group which adheres to, identifies with, and receives its awards from an elite) will be those beliefs which the elite finds useful — or, more precisely, those beliefs which it finds unharmful, which do not contravene its interests. This connection between beliefs and social practice can be referred to as the *binding* — culture-binding, class-binding, etc. — of a belief-system. However, the binding of cognitive pro-cesses, like scientific beliefs, and non-psychological processes in culture, which I describe as practice, occurs through a mediating process, convention-ally called 'evaluation', or 'values', and aggregated into a *value-system*. The belief-system and the value-system are relatively distinct; they interact in what Tolman (1951) nicely calls a 'belief-value matrix'. The interaction between the two systems is to a certain extent reciprocal: goals which a group's belief-system declares to be positively unrealizable will not, in general, be sought. But, for our purposes, the primary relation is the influence of values on beliefs, not vice-versa. We may say that, in general, a hypothesis will not be licensed as a belief unless it is *conformal* to a group's value-system.

Among the three sorts of judgment passed on a candidate-belief – verifiability, compatibility, and conformality – this last one appears to be the only essential judgment. A geographical hypothesis can, and often does, gain acceptance without empirical verification. In most such cases, however, its acceptance reflects a judgment of compatibility: a model, for instance, is built out of 'reasonable' assumptions, reasonable because they 'fit' the existing belief-system. But I find it hard to conceive of a situation in which a hypothesis will be accepted as a belief if the interests of the belief-holding group will be significantly damaged thereby; and I am sure that this is true for AAG-ethnogeography as it is for that of any other group of natives. Note, however, that I have not reified the notion of values into something separate and distinct from culture, something *sui generis*, a cause uncaused. Values are simply the psychological expression of a group's interests; they are the medium, more or less transparent, through which practice filters into cognition, or belief. They are goal-preferences, or what Dewey called 'agendas for action' – not windows to the soul.

VI

Thus far I have merely listed some (not all) of the principles which seem, at present, to underlie the study of ethnogeography. It remains only to list some of its uses, as follows:

(1) Among current approaches to the general and cross-cultural study of geographical cognition, ethnogeography possesses certain unique and built-in safeguards against ethnocentrism, the most serious of all obstacles to reliable knowledge in this field. To begin with, ethnocentrism is itself a focus of study, i.e., central to this approach is a concern with the binding between culture and belief. Secondly, ethnogeography – in common with all branches of ethnoscience – departs from the axiomatic position that the scientific beliefs of any one group are quite as scientific, quite as theoretical, as those of any other group. This axiom allows us to compare all ethnogeographies on a common scale, with a common set of methods and principles; and it buries once and for all the innately ethnocentric idea of a 'primitive mind', of

'pre-scientific thought'. And, finally, ethnogeography allows us to examine geographical beliefs as they are expressed in natural language (and other symbol-systems). Hence it puts into our hands the tools of modern linguistics which has already freed itself to a large extent from ethnocentrism, e.g., it has long since abandoned simple linguistic relativism and the distinction between 'primitive' and 'civilized' languages, and has formulated both its basic theory (Chomsky, 1973) and methodology (Conklin, 1962) in terms of culturally universal categories.

(2) While it would be wrong to make too grandiose a claim for the reliability of an approach like ethnogeography, which rests primarily on the methods of ethnographic linguistics and semantics, it is nonetheless true that these methodologies provide rather exact information. Most of the data for this kind of analysis are concrete, artifactual records, either written or at least tape-recordable. A linguistic text can be examined with rather sharp methodological instruments. And — returning to our former point — the results of linguistic and semantic analysis gain added reliability precisely because they are not tainted with ethnocentric errors or, rather, are much less tainted than the alternative approaches, such as 'perception research' and 'cross-cultural psychology' (in which *we* test *their* cognition according to *our* rules, using *our* language and *our* questionnaires or clever tests).

(3) But the most useful virtue of ethnogeography must surely lie in the fact that we train it upon ourselves: examine our own beliefs and their cultural and social bindings. It is worth speculating what will happen to geographical theory (ours) after it has been exposed to ethnogeographical analysis. What will become, for instance, of diffusion theory after we have shown how strongly conformal it is to European culture and the interests of the European elite: how it proves that progress in general is a matter of passively accepting what European culture has to offer and how it denies the genius of inventiveness to non-Europeans (and the European poor). By the same token: What will happen to our conformal theories of economic development, of 'modernization', theories which invariably argue that prosperity is a matter of accepting West-European capital (and control), and to the profit of West-European countries and their corporations? What will happen to theoretical geography in general when we discover that its models are as much bound to culture (and class) as are the products of empirical research — and perhaps more so, since model-selection is surely the most ethnocentric of all endeavors in a science like ours in which a given universe of data will fit any of a number of models and the choice of one model is, at heart, a value-judgment? I am raising these questions, not answering them, but I assert that ethnogeography

can do our culture-bound profession a great deal of good, though it may cause some pain.

Department of Geography
University of Illinois at Chicago Circle

BIBLIOGRAPHY

Berlin, B. and Kay, P.: 1969, *Basic Color Terms: Their Universality and Evolution*, University of California Press, Berkeley and Los Angeles.
Blaut, J. M. *et al.*: 1959, 'A Study of Cultural Determinants of Soil Erosion and Conservation in the Blue Mountains of Jamaica', *Social and Economic Studies* 8, 403–420.
Blaut, J. M.: 1970, 'Geographic Models of Imperialism', *Antipode* 2, 69–85.
Chomsky, N.: 1973, 'Introduction', in A. Schaff, *Language and Cognition*, McGraw-Hill, New York.
Conklin, H.: 1957, *Hanunóo Agriculture*, Food and Agriculture Administration, Rome.
Conklin, H.: 1962, 'Lexicographical Treatment of Folk Taxonomies', *International Journal of American Linguistics* 38, 119–141.
Dewey, J.: 1916, 'The Logic of Judgments of Practice', in his *Essays in Experimental Logic*, University of Chicago Press, Chicago.
Frake, C.: 1962, 'The Ethnographic Study of Cognitive Systems', in T. Gladwin *et al.* (eds.), *Anthropology and Human Behavior*, The Anthropological Society of Washington, Washington, D.C.
Friedrich, P.: 1970, *Proto-European Trees*, University of Chicago Press, Chicago.
Knight, C. G.: 1971, 'Ethnogeography and Change', *Journal of Geography* 70, 47–51.
Knight, C. G.: 1974, *Ecology and Change: Rural Modernization in an African Community*, Academic Press, New York.
Murton, B. J.: 1973, 'Folk Classification of Cultivated Land and Ecology in Southern India', *Proceedings of the Association of American Geographers* 5, 199–202.
Sturtevant, W.: 1964, 'Studies in Ethnoscience', *American Anthropologist* 66, 99–131.
Tolman, E. C.: 1951, 'A Psychological Model', in T. Parsons *et al.*, *Toward a General Theory of Action*, University of Chicago Press, Chicago.
Tyler, S. A.: 1969, 'Introduction', in S. A. Tyler (ed.), *Cognitive Anthropology*, Holt, Rinehart and Winston, New York.

ANNE BUTTIMER

EREWHON OR NOWHERE LAND

I. INTRODUCTION

Throughout a century of Western social thought, mankind's perennial enquiry into the where, when, and how of life has yielded a rich legacy of speculation. From the ebullient satire of Butler's *Erewhon*, (Butler, 1872) and the idealism of utopian fiction, the angry critique of Existentialist and Marxist philosophy and the resounding protest of popular song, evidence abounds that the human spirit remains undaunted in its desire to not only grasp the course of events but also to ameliorate and control the conditions of life. The increasing rate and complexity of change in our day renders the challenge to rationality so overwhelming that at times it becomes difficult to pause, reflect, and evaluate the latent assumptions and implications of scholarly effort. Barriers to communication between separate worlds of scholarship, too, prevent the flow of insight between different specialized perspectives, or the restoration of harmony between the YIN and the YANG of human reason.

The folkways of *Erewhon*, under the satirical gaze of Butler, all appeared internally consistent, albeit absurd, because of the 'unreason' governing this strange land. The roles assumed by professors of Hypothetics, Evasion, and Inconsistency, within their Colleges of Unreason, the use of currency from Musical Banks, and the ubiquitous assent to the expertise of Straighteners — all add up to a picture of one particular society somewhere. Butler's account could have served not only as entertainment for readers in England, but also as a mirror which Erewhonians could have used to gaze at the absurdity of their own life styles, values, and social organization. How fascinating it would be if a contemporary Butler could look in a similar way at our Colleges of Unreason, our speculative games in hypothetics and straightening! Planners, psychiatrists, landscape arthitects and social workers today could be seen as having roles analogous to those of Erewhon's 'Straighteners'. The role of academic geographers, other social scientists and philosophers, could be seen as analogous to those of 'Professors' in the Colleges of Unreason. Role systems and values are no doubt very different, the separation of professor and

9

S. Gale and G. Olsson (eds.), Philosophy in Geography, 9–37. All Rights Reserved.
Copyright © 1979 by D. Reidel Publishing Company, Dordrecht, Holland.

straightener roles is not so clearly defined, nor do we speak exclusively for one culturally circumscribed world like Erewhon. Today we seek universal principles governing behavior everywhere and blueprints for planning which might be applicable anywhere. Could the contemporary geographer and would-be planner find himself satirized in the Beatles' cry:

> "He's a real nowhere man
> sitting in his nowhere land
> making all his nowhere plans
> for nobody . . . "?

One of the profound differences between the 'unreason' of either end of our century appears to lie not only in the manner in which the where, how, and why of life is posed, but also in our conceptions of the 'who'. Do we speak of somebody, living somewhere, or of anybody, anywhere? Have we, social scientists involved in applied work, ever seriously considered what life might be like in the rationally-designed environments which our disciplines have taught us to imagine and prescribe? And if we had been assigned to them, with little or no discretion over the choice or the design, what would the impact be on our attitudes and perceptions of life?

As repeated evidence of ecological and political crisis join a gnawing sense of personal and collective failure to cope, scholars engage so eagerly in the quest for rational understanding that they become less open to hear such satire. Why, at this time, question whether or how reason may address itself to these issues? Something of the naïveté of a child, the vision of a poet, or the wit of a novelist, would be needed to question, for instance, whether the geographer could plan wisely for the organization of space or the management of ecological systems. Yet, as the pace of analytical and programmatic effort gains momentum, it may be crucially important to pause and reflect critically upon the nature and direction of our applied endeavors.

This paper outlines some general themes for a critical look at the geographer's involvement in applied work: to sound a note of YANG amidst the resounding YIN of contemporary 'rationality'. Adopting a Butler-style perspective on contemporary Erewhon, it focuses first on some of the metaphors used in applied geography as expressions of the 'professor's' desire to combine his efforts with those of the 'straightener'.[1] Recognizing the positive intent and reasonable success of much applied work, it raises some questions concerning its logical and practical rationale, as well as the short- and long-term consequences of a managerial approach toward the amelioration of environmental problems. Next it explores the myth of 'rationality' and the peculiar sets of social and ideological influences which tend to shape both the language and style of the geographer's engagement in problem resolution. Thirdly, it examines some of the philosophical premises which underlie contrasting perspectives on an ideal social and physical order.

A critical look at the record to date can benefit from the categories of philosophy and sociology of knowledge, but these do not necessarily point toward a direction for future effort. To clear the ground for a more logically-defensible and practically relevant applied geography, there are legacies of thought and practice to be transcended. One needs emancipation not only from ideological and institutional influence, but also a clearer understanding of the geographer's potential role in elucidating problems. Unwittingly perhaps, geographers appear to have assumed the anthropocentric bias characteristic of Western philosophy and social sciences generally, and an implicit faith in scientific rationality. There appears to be a need, in the applied sphere particularly, for a kind of geography which regards man as part of the biosphere as a whole; a geography which refuses to base its identity solely on the criteria appropriate to other disciplines. There is also a need to evoke the conscious engagement of people in coping with issues which touch their lives, and the best intentioned efforts of specialized academic and planning elites have often prevented rather than encouraged this. A critical examination of role and appropriate domain of effort is needed if we wish to assume practical relevance to society.

I.1. *Utopia for Erewhon*

Revisting Erewhon, one century later, Butler might have remarked on the profound changes evident within its Colleges of Unreason. Professors, for a variety of reasons, are more involved in the practical affairs of society. Straighteners, now more numerous and functionally specialized, are obviously failing in their duties as counsellors, therapists, and monitors of social life. More rational ideas and guidelines are needed in order to cope with the unprecedented nature and volume of ecological and social crises.

Each type of professor rallies his own brand of Hypothetics to the task of ameliorating Erewhon life. Some share visions of efficient and comprehensive administrative systems, others speculate on ways whereby the production and distribution of material goods and services could be organized more efficiently. Theories are advanced to show how social relationships and interactions might be better streamlined and rationally harmonized. Prophets of doom warn of ecological catastrophe and propose measures which could help restore equilibrium and sustained yield of national resources. The specialization of expertise which by now characterizes academic life has led to much keener insight into particular facets of social life and its environmental context, but it has also created enormous difficulties in communicating across disciplinary boundaries, thus militating against the prospect of ever reaching an integrated perspective on problems or their resolution. A cacaphony of monologues serves to confuse rather than elucidate the real world anxieties and hopes of people. While diversity of perspectives marks an impressive advance in knowledge, the lack of a common language prevents professors from reaping the full fruits of specialized endeavor.

Geographers, of course, argue that they possess special skills to deal with manifold phenomena. Sensitive to the straighteners' challenge, they had always endeavored to gain a more comprehensive grasp of the connections between physical and human processes. *De facto*, however, the thrust of applied geographic concern had not only been limited by the restricted vision of subdisciplinary specialization but it had also become imbued with the anthropocentric bias of related disciplines. The concerns of other occupants of the biosphere – animals, plants, resources, technology – had been relegated almost exclusively to specialized and separated disciplines, and rarely if ever had the language of interdisciplinary or cross-disciplinary effort been sensitive to any other sphere of being except human or ecological 'systems'.

Philosophers and others watch this movement with a mixture of cynicism and guarded optimism. They offer fresh insight into the philosophical premises underlying the ideas and practices of various disciplines, and remark about ways in which ideology and politics often influence the nature and direction of professors' work. As ever unrivalled masters in the art of sitting-on-the fence, however, they often leave the applied geographer in a worse state of confusion than when he had begun. Overwhelmed by the urgency of immediate problems he has difficulty grasping either the full meaning of philosophical critique or constructing a more comprehensive and logically defensible overall framework for applied work. To illustrate some features of the contemporary American geographer's approach to applied research let us focus more specifically on some of the standard metaphors used in his contribution to the general discourse. These metaphors can best be appreciated in the context of the ideal social and physical order which is deemed desireable.

I.2. *Geographic Perspectives: Diagnosis and Therapy*

Within the ideal vision commonly held in the mid 20th century, peace and justice for all is to be guaranteed by scientifically-based research and planning. Equal opportunities to material welfare are to be available to all individuals and rational programming of economic and social life is to guarantee general harmony with the society. Many geographers feel they have much to offer on the feasibility of various strategies which could help achieve such an order. To gain a perspective on inequalities within existing levels of social well-being, for example, they offer 'gap maps': summary documentation on the spatial dimensions of various problems which were to be 'straightened'. Further, they offer special insight into the mechanisms whereby inequalities come to be, i.e., inefficiencies in delivery of services, 'non-rational' location of jobs, schools, and housing and other aspects of everyday life. If only straighteners could be convinced of the rationality involved in central place systems, they could experiment with alternative models of locational efficiency, and thus hopefully reduce inequalities. On the general question of social justice however, geographers remain divided and this often leads to conflicts over values, ideological orientation, and even some of the philosophical foundations of their work. Some argue for revolution within the capitalist system which had dominated this land for at least a century; some spell out reformist strategies without even questioning the fundamental structure of society; others argue that nothing short of radical demolition of existing structures would ever suffice to guarantee a route toward justice. A look at each of these metaphors: 'inequality', 'inefficiency', and 'injustice', illustrates some dimensions of the problems faced by the applied geographer today.

I.2.1. *Inequality*. By mid-century, a considerable bank of data was available to allow geographers to document spatial variations in social well-being within society. For example, they could offer some useful insight into pressing issues of poverty by plotting the spatial distribution of income within the entire population.

The implicit solution to poverty is simply to transfer 'income' from the 'have' regions to the 'have not', i.e., to reduce the gaps on the welfare map. This solution had already been applied in other contexts with a reasonable measure of success. Why not apply this relatively straightforward procedure, then, to other spheres of social inequality, e.g., housing, education, health and retail services? In fact, their professional association begins compiling a whole atlas of such gap maps to indicate their corporate support for this venture.

From the fence, however, come voices of protest and philosophical misgiving. First, questions are raised concerning the methodology of using aggregate measures of welfare over such wide and diverse regions as administratively defined areas and census tracts. What was the value of an index of average income for a total district where obvious differentials existed? Secondly, queries emerge about the feasibility of such solutions as fiscal transfer, bussing of schoolchildren, or legal proscriptions against prejudicial housing codes. The geographer should become aware of the economist's hypothetics — the political scientist's too — before he could assume that structural and spatial solutions could thus be harmonized. More seriously, however, comes the criticism of language: what precisely was meant by 'poverty'? Surely people varied in their definitions of what constituted well-being — poverty was a relative rather than an absolute state — and also would not the capacity to earn currency be a more important measure of wealth or poverty than a record of bank deposits? Other social scientists come to the geographer's . defense, elaborating on the need (not only on methodological but moral grounds) for standard definitions of poverty and minimal standards of pro- vision. The debate takes various directions, and indeed minimal standards for welfare are eventually defined at least for the benefit of census takers and civil servants. Misgivings still abound, however, from both within and without the geographer's world. How was this equalization of welfare to be achieved? Was it to be administered by a 'straightener' elite equipped with the social scien- tist's rational blueprint? What relationship could or should exist between those who plan, and those for whom plans were made? What role could or should individuals play in creating and implementing social change? Was there a qualitative difference between planning policy at a national and local scale? These questions probe to the heart of taken-for-granted folkways deeply anchored within society as a whole, and they challenge geographers and straighteners to question both their conventional roles and the myriad ways in which their ideas and practices had become inextricably bound up with economic, technological, and political interests.

Some geographers dismiss such distractions and press on with unabated zeal to find more incisive analytical tools to examine problems. After all, evi- dence abounded from socialist societies that redistribution of wealth had actually succeeded in reducing inequalities. Others heed the methodological cautions and revise their procedures; several become more explicit in their ideological stances. A great number do agree that their 'gap maps' merely scratched the surface of social problems and they rally disciplinary expertise toward the task of elucidating processes responsible for causing such inequal- ities.

I.2.2. *Inefficiency*. If the gaps on spatial inequality maps could be regarded as somehow stemming from inefficiencies in certain underlying systems, then a fresh perspective could perhaps be gained on the issue of social injustice. A whole range of tools from the geographer's arsenal could be applied to this task, e.g., assessing systems of service provision, transport networks, job opportunities, and access to market. To solve problems of inequality, one had merely to restore, or infuse some rationality into 'spatial systems'. For if spatial systems were made to function efficiently, then everyone would behave rationally, support his appropriate node in the spatial hierarchy of services, and not have to wander about in search of alternatives.

Voices from the fence again come to temper the geographer's enthusiasm. Look at the evidence, it is argued: Garden City and New Town plans, concrete jungles and White Elephants all originally planned on the basis of good spatial models and theory, and the results have not been impressive. Besides, what justification does the geographer offer for assuming that there is a connection between the efficiency of spatial systems and the quality of human life? What if some of the key ingredients of human happiness are not reduceable to a metric which can be accomodated in spatial models? What, again, if it is the very efficiency of spatial systems which produces inequality, and thereby militates most against the quality of human life?

Questions such as these provoke more fundamental enquiry into the implicit ideals sought in studies of both equality and efficiency. Was the 'geographic' utopia one in which all men would have access to an equal share of material welfare, and all systems were operating efficiently? But were these two conditions compatible? In some cases, it could be argued, these two objectives were at odds with one another — that it was the very efficiency of spatial systems which contributed most toward polarization of wealth and increasing levels of inequality. Centralized economic and social opportunity, growth poles, and rational networks of communication could be regarded as 'systems of spatial domination'. Was there something inherent in geographic models themselves which made them particularly amenable to application in 'imperializing' contexts, favoring the 'supplier's' view of services rather than the client's, the investor's perspective rather than the consumer's? Decentralization plans for hospitals, social welfare, services or schools appear to have been based on the criteria of 'supply efficiency' — optimal allocation of personnel, equipment, and service outlets. They have not always been sensitive to the nature, quality and location of probable demand. Could it be because the focus of both analysis and therapy had rested on ROLES, aggregate measures of population, rather than on individual persons, that the 'planned' service failed to satisfy people in their total everyday situations? The impasse was more than methodological; there were issues here of a moral and ideological character, and these generated heated debate over what one actually meant by 'social justice'.

I.2.3. *Injustice.* For the applied geographer, willing to adopt legal definitions of justice, metaphysical and ethical problems scarcely arose. The meaning of terms such as 'equality' and 'efficiency', rights and responsibilities, could be logically derived from publicly affirmed norms and standards. Disturbing evidence from their own actual practice, however, coupled with a growing confidence in confronting philosophical questions, begins to generate much debate over the nature of society generally, its ideological underpinnings, and the justification for having such an elite as planners and applied social scientists at all. What if an ideal social order were to involve more than a full complement of material goods and security against environmental hazards? The capacity to allow individual human beings to grow creatively, to be concerned about one another and about their environments: how could one plan for such situations? Few would question the desireability of minimal standards of material provision, but how were facilities and opportunities to be redistributed? Was one to invite or compel the underprivileged to adopt a life-style and ethic which had already made the affluent ones less than happy? Could people be trusted to draft their own course toward 'development?'

A painful realization dawns on the socially-conscious geographer. He begins to realize the extent to which spatial models had sometimes been used to impose a rational structure on social life which left little room for human becoming except at the price of buying into an alien system of values, behavior and world view. Spatial models promised efficiency and they had often vindicated themselves; what had not been specified was efficiency for whom, and what were the social costs or inefficiencies for the powerless. Having elucidated various structural (political, economic, technological) foundations for social injustice, was one then to deduce that solutions must also be construed in structural terms? Once identifying a capitalist system as arch villian, for example, should one argue for revolution to abolish the market and set up some kind of socialist structure? In this more 'spatially just' economy of the future, could inequalities be reduced (even eliminated by force?), would inefficiencies in spatial systems be intolerable, and could an omniscient 'people' be in charge?

The validity of these and other claims for the best strategy toward overall social reform could only be argued on theoretical or ideological grounds:

evidence from both socialist and capitalist societies remained equivocal. In so many varied political situations, would-be managers of the social order had only limited success in harnessing the 'efficiencies' of production elites for the welfare of society at large. Zealots of structural reform from Rousseau and Ebenezer Howard, to Monnet and Doxiadis, had spent their energies on the architecture of political systems to the neglect of one vital ingredient, viz., human individuals whose lives were to be organized and influenced by these systems. The story of revolutions through history revealed again and again that structural change does not necessarily bring about a change in social dispositions, in the perception or quest for social injustice. Structural reform could, of course, facilitate and precipitate changes in behavior: legal prescriptions and proscriptions could remove or add constraints on opportunities. History, however, suggested that 'have' privileges are not easily ceded to 'have nots' and the skills developed by powerful elites to circumvent legal constraints were by now public knowledge.

To varying degrees, then, each of the geographer's metaphors evokes not only issues of logic and methodology, but also triggers worries over their metaphysical and ethical implications. Justifications for the use of terms such as 'inequality', 'inefficiency', or 'injustice' could not even begin without a specification of the 'utopia' toward which applied research was directed. The nature and dynamics of this ideal is in turn deeply influenced by the sociological and political context in which applied research is actually practiced, as becomes clear when one examines the characteristic roles assumed, and the interests which are served in the process. First, let us examine some competing 'utopian' views of social and environmental order in terms of their fundamental assumptions about life, knowledge, and planning. For there is a peculiar sense of 'self fulfilling prophecy' about the models cultivated within particular social sciences; no matter how we may protest about the detached attitudes of the Ivory Tower, our ideas do actually shape the realities we study. And all metaphors of truth – be they mystical scientific, or poetic – bear public consequences with profound ethical importance for contemporary life.

II. CONTRASTING SCENARIOS OF UTOPIA

Two countervailing themes emerge from recent scholarly writing on the ideal order for society and environment. On the one hand one hears the case for more rationally-ordered monitoring systems to guide and police technology and life styles. On the other hand one hears the plea for an environment which allows for freedom and creativity for the individual. At the risk of understating or diminishing the range and diversity of contemporary effort, one could propose a bi-polar continuum of stances ranging from optimal levels of rational order at one extreme to maximum levels of individual freedom on the other. Like any polarity, this is an artificial construct, designed to highlight contrasts, and to provoke an awareness of the logical foundations and extensions of existing stances. In a very general sense, one might label one pole as that of the positive scientist, and the other is that of the existentialist. The capacity of this schema to accomodate the literature is limited; its aim is rhetorical, designed to open the way for discovering forgotten elements, and intended as an invitation to improve communication among those who are concerned about the practical significance of scholarly effort. What is lost in terms of accuracy may be a justifiable price to pay for improved clarity on the general directions toward which our literature points.

At each pole of our continuum, elaborate scenarios are often sketched, and arguments rallied on both sides. Certain basic contrasts in their fundamental ideological and moral premises, however, make it difficult to evaluate and judge between these seemingly conflicting visions of the ideal order. Perhaps the question to raise is not whether they are compatible or reconcilable, but rather whether there is a perspective on mankind and world which might enable both to discern more clearly where the appropriate arena for their efforts might lie.

To highlight contrasts between the two poles of our continuum, one could outline a stereotypical set of goals which reflect their respective visions of the ideal social order. In the existentialist scenario, self-aware and responsible persons are actively engaged in creating communities and caring for their own environments (Wild, 1963; Winter, 1966; Teilhard de Chardin, 1965; Fromm, 1968). The flowing of individual personalities assumes primary importance; the order and dynamics of social systems are evaluated in terms of personal growth among community members. In the positive scientist's scenario the social order is managed and directed by rationally-designed administrative systems; crises and conflicts are contained, techno-structures controlled; individual needs and behavior are accomodated through well programmed feedback mechanisms (Bell, 1969; Toffler, 1972).

The gulf between these two visions of an ideal social order seems enormous. The human geographer, too, may often feel caught in the tensions between these two extremes (Mercer and Powell, 1972; Samuels, 1971; Entrikin, 1975, 1976). Our traditional concern for the earth as home of man, however, should ideally place us in a position to offer some contribution toward better communication across the gulf. It could be argued, from a geographic viewpoint, that as long as utopia is conceived in purely anthropocentric terms, that there will be an inevitable impasse in the debate between 'systems' and 'persons'. Our perspective should challenge minds to examine the relationship between the role of humans as creators of and actors within socio-technical systems on the one hand, and their role as part of nature on the other. To transcend the difficulties created by disciplinary specialization may be extremely difficult within our present institutional settings, but it may very well be the *sine qua non* for developing a language and perspective on knowledge of the biosphere as a whole. Without an integrated perspective on knowledge. how can one apply bits of know-how to practical planning (Giddens, 1974)? The route toward developing such a perspective needs to be cleared not only of administrative constraints, but also of the philosophical and conceptual undergrowth which litters our present language and separate endeavors.

II.1. *Rational and Irrational Man*

To begin such ground-clearing one has to appreciate the fundamental philosophy of knowledge and action which underlies the positions held at either end of our continuum. What existentialism offers fundamentally is a perspective on the quality and meaning of human life in the concrete everyday world. Its epistemological foundations stem largely from the phenomenological critique of objectivism and scientific theory, so it speaks of lived experience in the language of meaning, and tries to make values explicit (Jasper, 1956, 1957; Spiegelberg, 1960). The present is seen as emanating from a history, and projected toward a future. Positive science, by contrast, seeks order and measurement in explaining systems operative within the physical and social world (Braithwaite, 1960; Hempel, 1965; Carnap, 1966). Though not explicitly concerned with meaning in the full existentialist sense, it does investigate ordered meaning, i.e., the internal consistency and logic of systems and organizations. It is fundamentally a 'scientific' perspective, emphasizing objectivity, and striving in its use of the scientific method at least, to become 'value free' (Chase, 1962; Myrdal, 1969). Its focus rests primarily on the dynamics of present processes and structures, though it does also claim a predictive function. Explanation may involve references to antecedent processes, but the verification of its postulates, and the validity of its assumptions, depend upon conventionally accepted rules, or to calculations based on the tangibly measureable data of present and past experience. Assertions about practical application usually take the form of extrapolation from existing trends; it has to make assumptions concerning the variability or stability of other conditions in the future (Braithwaite, 1960; Arendt, 1968).

When these contrasting perspectives on knowledge are applied to planning, or to future projection, important contrasts become evident in the manner in which 'value' issues are resolved, and also in assumptions about the manner in which individuals may exercise discretion over the process of change. For the positive social scientist, individuals are usually conceptualized in terms of aggregates – groups labelled and classified according to the methodological requirements of particular research models. Policy formulation, on the other hand, tends to construe populations in terms of roles, sectors, and demographic types, manipulable within the framework of a rational social order. In contrast to this, the existentialist sees individuals as conscious human subjects who have a right and responsibility to choose their own future. Individual persons become free in responding creatively to ambiguous situations, in becoming consciously engaged in shaping their own lives and milieux. Freedom, in this view, involves more than the elimination of external constraint; it also demands a measure of self-awareness which enables a person to transcend his own situation and evaluate it. Positive scientists have indeed tried to accommodate considerations of value differences (Kohler, 1959; Myrdal, 1969; Scheibe, 1970). As observable phenomena, values have been considered as objectively measureable data which should be included as variables in testing particular hypotheses and developing theory. It is recognized also that values not only influence definition of problems, but also the models used in projecting planning strategies (Gouldner, 1962; Langer, 1965; Olsson, 1971, 1972; European Cultural Foundation, 1971). Hence comes the increasingly convincing argument for more pluralistic models for social policy, and a more diversified base for democratic participation in decision-making and management (Fromm, 1968; Illich, 1971).

There are many limitations in each of these polarized perspectives which make their relevance as guides for geographic enquiry seriously questionable. The objectivist and 'rational' underpinnings of positive science derive from the peculiar philosophical traditions which have influenced Anglo–American social science (Passmore, 1968). Philosophy of science has become virtually identical with epistemology (ways of knowing) as distinct, and often divorced from metaphysical and ethical concerns (Carnap, 1966).

Whereas tremendous gains have been achieved in logical precision and the internal consistency of particular methods and models of analysis, little tangible guidance is available in evaluating the human implications of particular types of logic, rationality, and objectivity as guides for our perceptions of social reality (Brown, 1969, Bortoft, 1971). Despite the enormous strides made in analytical precision and in the verification of descriptive statements, epistemology *per se* has difficulty in supplying criteria to guide the leap of faith between empirical-descriptive statement and normative prescriptive ones (Carnap, 1966; Hempel, 1965).

Each position contains, no doubt, a germ of truth, and valid methods whereby that version of truth is to be articulated. Taken separately, however, each can lead to exaggerated conclusions about the feasibility of particular planning strategies. The existentialist position is particularly valuable as critique and caution to the rational planner, but in itself it either refuses to make judgement about the ethical and logical dimensions of normative projection, or else implicitly assigns this to the area of personal or ideological choice (Entrikin, 1976). With some exceptions, there is a tendency among existentialists to absolutize individual freedom and the capacity for responsible choice, and to overlook the enormous managerial challenges of designing systems of production, exchange, and organization at the collective level.

Both traditions share an anthropocentric bias; future is seen primarily in human terms, whether one emphasizes managerial efficiency of socio-technical systems on the one hand, or the freedom for individuals on the other. This bias has found ideological and institutional support in most Western societies, whether of a laissez-faire capitalist-type or of a more centrally organized socialist one. The domination of nature, it has been argued, is part and parcel of the genesis of scientific methodology (Leiss, 1974; Schroyer, 1975).

II.2. *Rationality's Challenge: to be 'straightened' or 'tamed'?*

The volume of literature which has emphasized contrasts between phenomenology and positive science has perhaps clouded our ability to grasp their common denominators (Husserl, 1954; Wild, 1963; Mercer and Powell, 1972). At the core of each stance lay an implicit faith in objectivity. Yet the ultimate goal of rational knowledge, in most Western intellectual traditions, was ideally one of emancipation, i.e., the rules and discipline which guided enquiry were intended to set the mind free to explore and elucidate reality in a logically defensible and/or experientially grounded manner. It is not surprising that in recent years, the overwhelming challenge of applying knowledge to action and planning has brought scholars from both traditions to an appreciation of common problems, and a concerted attempt to reach solutions. A critique of knowledge and action has to incorporate more than simply the logic and acuity of cognitive processes for it is now observed that both the logic and methodology of scientific enquiry are intimately conjoined with the human interests which they serve (Habermas, 1974. See also, Gadamer, 1975 and Goulet 1971.).

The directions set by Husserl, i.e., to become aware of those 'filters' through which the mind screens its perceptions of reality, and to aim at arriving at a state of pure objectivity, has offered a valuable critique of 'objectivism', *a priori* models, and procedures of positive science (Husserl, 1931, 1954; Pivcevic, 1970; Spiegelberg, 1960). Few, however, still cling to the hope of achieving a state where one may be certain of having grasped the 'essences' of things, and, in fact, hermeneutical scholars freely admit that any interpretation of 'fact' is inevitably influenced by preconceptions (Ricoeur, 1971; Palmer, 1969; Kockelmans, 1975). Joining the long line of scholarship which for a century or so has pursued a *Verstehen* approach to knowledge, they have probed into the whole area of meanings, values, and ideas, which have characterized the human record (Dilthey, 1954, 1957; Martindale, 1968). They do not rely on *a priori* theory or the testing of lawlike hypotheses; rather they attempt to unmask the meanings expressed in human behavior and action, following a method analogous to the literary interpretation of texts (Palmer, 1969; Kockelmans, 1975). Hermeneutical knowledge is always mediated through the categories of the interpretor's pre-understanding. Hence if he does not simultaneously become aware of his own meaning world, he will fail to unmask the meanings underlying the situations he studies (Tuttle, 1969). There is an obvious trap here: for the language through which he can gain and eventually articulate such understanding may simply be a different version of knowledge — a different language and a different understanding from that of the positive scientist (Bortoft, 1971). How is one to evaluate the appropriateness of different forms of language in the arena of knowledge in use, if one has not clarified the appropriate language for the communication of knowledge itself? There is a vital need for this kind of interpretative elucidation of human meaning when one considers applied scientific work. It serves the 'practical' human interest, i.e., it can yield insight into the rules whereby theory may be applied in practice (Habermas, 1971; Marcuse, 1972).

Theory, hypothetico-deductive procedures, and the testing of hypotheses belong to the domain of the empirical–analytical sciences. The fundamental goal of this type of enquiry is technical: it is essentially concerned with 'know how' rather than 'know what'. Under specified conditions, these procedures may arrive at law-like statements which may have predictive power.

But the application of such theoretical knowledge to planning still depends upon the *a priori* rules established to direct the relationship between theory and practice within a particular setting (Habermas, 1971).

Both types of enquiry are thus needed in the attempt to make geographic knowledge relevant to the resolution of planning problems. One could argue that much of the confusion and *gaucheries* of applied social science has stemmed from a confusion of 'technical' and 'practical' interests. This kind of confusion can be better understood when one considers the manner in which ideology and political vested interest have often co-opted and channelled scholarly work. Strong views have been expressed for instance, on the growing tendency for so-called 'objective science' to become manipulated toward ideologically defined ends, especially those of technological rationality. Philosophers from a variety of stances have endeavored to emancipate rationality, in the literal sense of the term, from the constraints of social context, or methodological naïveté; to restore it to *reason*, to shield it from the dangers of political manipulation and epistemological confusion (Gadamer, 1975; Heidegger, 1971).

To restore order within rationality's empire may be a laudable and necessary step in the direction of ground clearing for the applied geographer. As long as its central aim is to write a recipe for more logically based knowledge of facts, and the ingredients for a more controllable blueprint for human management of environments, however, it may still remain caught in an anthropocentric trap. As with the geographer's own metaphors, the language which provides categories for a critique of the present or past may not be adequate for the formulation of an alternative way (Bortoft, 1971).

Could one not conceive of 'taming' rather than 'straightening' of rationality? To use Heidegger's words, a straightened rationality would still belong with the *Herrschaftswissen* (literally 'knowledge of overlordship') which has characterized Western science, and might simply further the compelling drive which humans betray to control and manipulate nature for their own ends (Heidegger, 1967). Technologically sophisticated societies have been shaped and influenced by the same attitude toward knowledge as they demonstrate in their attitudes toward things and toward other human beings as well. The hubris of Western man, in Heidegger's view, has robbed things of their wholeness; in trying to dominate the earth, they rob it of its integrity and thus distort it. The opposite of *Herrschaftswissen* is *Bildungswissen* (knowledge of meaning and creativity); it demands an attitude of *Gelassenheit* a tenderness in our perspectives on things, letting them be and become. If such an attitude is lacking, is it any wonder that we are constantly surprised by the often

'irrational' and anarchistic way in which knowledge itself may grow? We trust
in the logic and power of operationalized enquiry, systems of deduction and
theory, rather than in the charisma and insight of bright individuals. Yet it is
clear from history that great advances in knowledge have almost invariably
come about from the inspiration and insight of particular scholars. In the
light of such considerations, should one not look again at our institutional
structures, subdisciplinary specialization, and rules whereby scientific knowledge is applied in practice? Does our sociological context tend to bury rather
than promote individual creativity in scholarship, and open, caring engagement in discussion with people actually involved in environment issues?
Perhaps the most fundamental challenge which critical philosophy can offer
to applied geography is this: there is an intimate connection between our
ways of approaching knowledge and its relationship to action on the one
hand, and the syndrome of attitudes and behavior between people and
environments which characterize contemporary society. The hope is that
once having grasped the ideological and institutional influences which have
surrounded our thoughts and practices to date, we may be in a better position
to evaluate the appropriateness of particular methods and directions for geographic effort in the future.

III. COLLEGE OF UNREASON

III.1. *Myth of the 'Intelligentsia'*

To deal adequately with the complex ways in which social institutions and
the roles assumed by scientists influence thought and practice one would have
to survey a very broad spectrum of the sociology of knowledge (Mannheim,
1936, 1952; Mills, 1958; Gouldner, 1962; Berger and Luckman, 1967).
Mannheim, writing in the 1930's, remarked on the inevitable tensions
between what he labelled ideological and utopian forms of thought during
periods of social change (Mannheim, 1936). Ideological thought, in his view,
tends to justify the *status quo* and the existing power position of dominant
social classes; it could be used as an instrument of social oppression by power
elites. Utopian thought, on the other hand, tends to interpret reality in terms
of a projected future, and to justify radical changes; it could be used as an
instrument of fundamental reform or revolution. Mannheim envisioned only
one group who could be sufficiently detached from the existing social order
as to be able to make a radical critique of the present, and invent scenarios

for alternatives; this was the 'intelligentsia' whose ideas could be used as bases for rational social planning.

Though the pace and complexity of social change may be even more dramatic in our day, this tension between ideological and utopian forms of thought may be more apparent than real. While there is a discernible tension in most Western societies between the values of social egalitarianism on the one hand, and the exigencies of industrial capitalism on the other, a substantial portion of pure and applied social sciences appears to be closely aligned to technological process (Habermas, 1971, 1974; Marcuse, 1968). Could one suggest that ideology and utopia have converged in recent scenarios for future environments? Marcuse, critical of the Weberian concept of 'rationality' and cynical about the role of 'intelligentsia' lies pointed to this (con) fusion:

> the very concept of technical reason is perhaps ideological. Not only the application of technology but technology itself is domination (of nature and men) – methodical, scientific, calculated, calculating control. Specific purposes and interests of domination are not foisted upon technology 'subsequently' and from the outside; they enter the very construction of the technical apparatus. Technology is always a historical-social project: in it is projected what a society and its ruling interests intend to do with men and things. Such a 'purpose' of domination is 'substantive' and to this extent belongs to the very form of technical reason (Marcuse, 1968, p. 223).

Marcuse, among others, has argued that rationality, in the service of technology, can no longer perform the emancipatory, detached, function envisioned by Weber (Weber, 1949, 1958). Rather it serves as 'rationalization' in the Freudian sense of the term, i.e., justification of the *status quo* (Habermas, 1971). This is because the rationality of science and technology is essentially one of control; it is a rationality of domination (Marcuse, 1972; see also Leiss, 1974). He is perhaps foremost in articulating the political content of 'technical reason', and has elaborated on the political mechanisms which contribute toward a persistence of this situation within so-called democratic societies today.

III.2. *Folkways of Applied Scholarship*

How many geographers were aware, when first they tried to offer their expertise in applied situations, that such constraints were to be confronted? Sociology of knowledge, by focussing on the ways in which context and language actually mold the articulation of ideas, can sometimes give the impression of overemphasizing the media, and ignoring the intentions and motivations underlying the message. Many geographers have indeed been stirred by a sense

of concern and responsibility to help alleviate problems and forestall processes which threatened to destroy the quality of life and environments
(Griffin, 1965; Zelinsky, 1970; Wolpert, 1976). Once embarked upon this
course, did they not find themselves surrounded by a complex sociological
situation where institutionally defined roles, funding sources, and even the
medium of print set boundaries and direction for the articulation of their
efforts? A great deal of the direction and volume of applied research today
is shaped by the practical and technical interests of sponsors, which in turn
tend to favor the promotion of existing (ideological and economic) conditions. Though most problems are many-faceted, the actual intellectual
exploration of them does not promote dialogue among different stances or
feedback between planners and those for whom they plan.

Consider, for example, some typical features of academic involvement: the
multidisciplinary team organizing a symposium on a particular problem.
Through a variety of 'objective' stances, the issue is dissected into several discrete parts, individual human experiences converted to aggregate estimates,
and some kind of 'whole' picture is sought through the assembly of specialized parts. The value and success of such a meeting would probably be judged
in terms of the ideas presented, the practicability and/or political feasibility
of its conclusions, perhaps even on the nature and number of committees
appointed to explore new avenues of research. The question of whether the
process itself – the physical assembly of concerned scholars – had sparked
insight or openness to dialogue with alternative stances would hardly be considered as measures of success. 'Proceedings' may be published which are
really 'preceedings': they are often the homework preparation of discussion
rather than a record of the discussion itself. How much more provocative it
would be if there were evidence of dialogue initiated not only among different 'invited' stances, but also between the official contributors and other
participants who did not have a prepared script? From the vantage point of
eliciting active engagement from various sectors of society, the critical
criterion of success should surely be not one of discerning which positions are
logically defensible, 'right', or 'wrong', but rather whether or how they invite
dialogue? The print industry itself is a medium ill suited to provoking any
kind of dialogue. It serves to assemble a *smörgasbord* of position statements,
each illustrating and promoting a distinct type of 'know how' rather than a
concerted effort to elucidate the 'what'. The lag which often occurs between
the actual experience of environmental crisis and the time when printed
reports are finally published, gives many academics the feeling of being *post
facto* commentators on issues, or else weak-voiced prophets of doom.

Consultant reports, whether or not academics are involved, may be delivered more speedily, albeit at greater expense to the decision maker. Many academics deplore the poor quality of research which often lies hidden beneath the glossy pages of such reports, and scoff empirically about the 'token' or 'rubber stamp' character of the exercise. Yet in most urgent situations, academic geographers do not have the time, energy, or data required to do thoroughly scientific research before risking an opinion or estimate. If we have done our homework on grounding our geographic models in real life situations, why should we lack the confidence to make intuitive judgements when necessary without compromising truly 'academic' standards? As long as various contributors may hide behind the facade of print and feasibility reports, there is little room for sharing such intuitive leaps in the dark, partially grounded opinions – let alone engaging in the discussion of values, ethics, and hopes for problem resolution with the people who are involved in the problem.

The basic assumption underlying our conventional exercises is that intellectual discourse over issues will lead to some kind of solution. Conflicts may be resolved by bright ideas, particularly if these can be couched in practical policy statements. A second assumption is that what is written in rational language will ultimately lead to action; and this usually involves a faith in institutional means for promoting social change. Both assumptions virtually ignore and often prevent the potential input of gifted individuals – gifted in the sense of grasping problems in a comprehensive way and committed to living with the solutions. And more seriously still, from an intellectual point of view, they may allow little room for discovery in the process.

To recognize the ways in which rationality has been abused in the past does not suggest that it should be abandoned; should it not rather suggest that rationality should be channelled more appropriately, i.e., orientated toward discovery rather than validation of knowledge? The 'intelligentsia' myth and the ethic of scholarly objectivity and detachment, laudable in its own right, has unfortunately led to an elitism and redundancy of effort which actually robs society of that very precious interplay of insight and responsibility which is required today in the face of environmental and social crisis. How reasonable or even rational is it to justify – ethically or pragmatically – the situation where an elite assumes the role of articulator and arbitrator for society in general? Weberian rationality has inspired the erection of tightly-knit research bureaucracies, each with clear lines of specialization, but this has often led to a stifling of individual freedom and creativity. When an elite abrogates responsibility for the analysis and planning of the social order does it not tend to deaden initiative rather than elicit an awareness of the scope for involvement which individuals could assume for their own collective future? Even in situations where the 'intelligensia', cooperating with an efficient managerial elite, has designed blueprints for society based on majority opinion, there is still the pragmatic challenge of making such plans effective. Almost every Western society since World War II has had its share of failure in implementing such plans. The managerial spirit would remain undaunted by such questions: they merely pose a challenge to its executive and manipulative and political skills, and there would be little difficult to find a behavioral scientist to provide models for the task.

IV. EREWHON REVISITED: A ROLE FOR THE GEOGRAPHER?

The desire to ameliorate social conditions and to protect the fabric of life for future generations is no doubt a positive feature of contemporary geography. If we are to fully appreciate Heidegger's critique of *Herrschaftswissen*, however, and wish to cultivate a more concerned, caring, approach to knowledge and action, it would serve well to evaluate our present endeavors in this light.

On purely logical grounds, there are serious limitations in our present approaches to the modelling of both spatial and ecological systems as bases for prognoses or planning policy. The complexity of contemporary problems demands insight and direction from fields of knowledge and experience far beyond the scope of existing social science methodology. The geographer, in his disciplinary role, may be well equipped to analyse several dimensions of problems, to specify what needs to be done in order to redress imbalances, to streamline spatial systems of service, or to revamp administrative systems. But to claim that such structural or mechanical changes will inevitably bring about social justice is at best an exaggeration.

Social justice, however defined, involves moral judgements concerning the quality and ordering of social life. It is presumptuous to assert that general standards for social justice can be subsumed entirely under the rubric of spatial equality or the efficiency of spatial systems. Justice involves the whole person, not just journey to work, take-home pay, or the sum total of material conditions which the external observer may wish to 'equalize'. It also involves the social environment, and the types of interaction which occur among persons, 'nature', and technology. A definition of justice which does not incorporate each is not only inadequate, but may be destructive as well.

While there is no doubt much pedagogical value in spatial models of inequality and inefficiency, it should be observed that the logic underlying a critique of the present may not be unequivocally relevant in projecting about alternatives. Such global assessments, based on external criteria, ignores the question of whether it is possible to reach an objective measure of what constitutes 'poverty', or 'welfare', and to what extent the rational efficiency of servicing systems may influence the human experience of well-being. These models are characteristically pertinent to the description and manipulation of systems extraneous to individual experience. Their value emphases derive from the prerequisites of systems generally, be they biological, technological, or cybernetic. They impinge upon, and constrain human behavior, but they do not EXPLAIN it. What may be far more helpful is an explanation − eludication − rather than partial attempts at scientific 'explanation'. We have come to recognize the extent to which most of the *status quo* systems modelled by spatial analysts have become imbued with the values of industrial growth and managerial efficiency, and how poorly they elucidate the values or interests of client or consumer populations. With increasing levels of specialization, both in technology and in the executive and consultant caste system which controls it, the language and dynamics of such systems are further and further removed from those who may be most affected by them (Goulet, 1971).

A more fundamental critique, from a geographic viewpoint, could be addressed to the 'humanist' trap, and our failure to consider the quality of 'justice' in whole earth terms (Lovelock, 1975; Heidegger, 1967). Our characteristic discourse echoes the ideological legacy of eighteenth century European Enlightment, and the faith in mind-over-matter which has generated economic, technological, and political systems which prove insensitive to nature and the human body. How many of our spatial models, for instance, assume *ceteris paribus*, a featureless plane rather than the living surface of the earth? May one validly persist in the taken-for-granted assumption in ecological models that the whole orchestra of natural milieux can be subsumed under the rubric of 'environmental factors', expressed in categories suitable for systems analysis and systems management?

The more one probes into the sociological, political, and philosophical dimensions of applied scholarship, the more it becomes obvious that ethical questions need to be elucidated also (Winter, 1966). Each of the stances assumed on knowledge, action, and the utopian order, is supported by a particular ethic of its own. These ethical imperatives, be they oriented toward scholarly standards, *status quo* maintenance, economic growth, social equality, or personal growth, lend motivation and energy to each participant's contribution, but they also often underlie fixed opinions, intransigent to discussion or compromise. To deal with conflicts merely on the level of ideas, 'know how', or political fiat, ignores the power of ethically grounded opinions. Should the geographer assume a relativist stance on such conflicts of ethic, and trust in the political process to arbitrate between them? Recent political history does not augur well for this. Should he pretend that ethical conviction is a purely private affair and acquiesce in the 'intelligentsia' stance on knowledge and action?

Without denying the autonomy and importance of personal belief and ethics, could one not strive toward a more general ethical horizon on earth life as a whole, which could guide discussion on environmental issues (Teilhard de Chardin, 1965; Ferkiss, 1969)? The challenge is surely not to judge among existing ethical stances, but rather to elicit an awareness of their environmental implications. Having suffered repeatedly through history from the blinding effects of one ethical tyranny after another, should we not be now in a better position to admit the limitations of inherited norms, and listen to one another as we endeavor to formulate a wider vision on earth life as a whole? Wherein, then, might the contribution of geography lie?

The answer depends on the particular geographer's mode of construing the world, his image of the ideal social order, and his understanding of the strengths and limitations of his discipline's research potential. Our metaphorical language in applied geography tends to reveal a Cartesian world view, a managerial perspective on social life, and a tendency to extrapolate from partial analyses of discipline-defined problems to blueprints for societal planning as a whole. If one were to recapture a more fundamental definition of geography, however, one might begin to sense a path beyond the historically conditioned practices which guide our present task.

The overall task of geography has often been cited in terms as broad as the drama of human life within its total environmental setting. If the goals of human existence are seen to be the fulfillment of human potential, then state of *becoming* should be more important than *state of being*. If such human becoming can be construed as part of total becoming within the biosphere, then our time-worn geographic perspective may in fact be one of the most valuable contributions possible toward the resolution of social and ecological issues. A perspective this broad does not immediately specify a workable research programme for any one discipline, but it could provide a framework for multidisciplinary approaches on major issues. For example, many problems could be construed in terms of the juxtaposition in space and time of groups who have unequal opportunities to choose and exercise discretion over their environments. One could investigate what environmental forces impede or facilitate the interests, or life projects, of such groups (Hägerstrand, 1974a). At the interface between societies and their environments one finds more than simply the tension between human beings and 'spatial systems': one finds the juxtaposition in space and time of highly complex systems of forces, each operating according to its own appropriate direction and rhythmicity. Humans bring with them a history, collective memories, as well as images and anticipations which guide their actions within changing environments. Natural systems have their own internal dynamic and ecological prerequisites, which are often brashly ignored by the rationally defined functional systems superimposed upon them. To gain a grasp of this complexity, or to offer hope to manage it wisely, one gets little help from specialized disciplinary research which separates and atomizes each of its components. It is not an encyclopedic atlas of juxtaposed distributions which is needed, but rather a method to enable us to appreciate the *relational* problems and consequences of such juxtaposition in space and time. Case studies which reveal the interpenetration of these multidimensional processes within particular situations may be a far more valuable contribution than debates over scientific respectability or ideological orthodoxy.

This does not mean, of course, that we ignore the quest for general propositions, and analyses of general processes which lead to environmental crises. A focus on values, for example, could yield insight into the directions of particular policy orientations, and help predict and forestall outcomes deemed undesireable. Having reached some assessment of the values which operate within our own institutional and 'market' contexts as applied geographers, for example, we could begin to assess the values which guide other institutions and systems, particularly those which are likely to have the most profound influence on the future. An effort could be made to identify those institutions which are likely to impinge upon the everyday time–space horizons of urban populations, e.g., media, communications facilities, commercial and educational institutions, and examine (a) their probable effect upon opportunities and choices for individuals, and (b) the kind of knowledge and attitudes about environment which these institutions propagate and their behavioral consequences. Existing models provide some tools whereby these features of the functional environment may be elucidated, (Hägerstrand, 1974b), but we have not, by and large, begun to explore the bio-ecological consequences of certain styles of organizing functional environments. Rationality mediated through institutions and technology tends to impose a clock/calendar time scheduling on systems of employment, retail, transport and administrative service and eventually on industrial and agrarian livelihoods as well. This eventually leads to a human use of space and time which may be grossly out of synchronization with the natural rhythmicity of biological and physical time, with severe consequences for human and ecological health (Fischer, 1968; Luce, 1973). The 'hurry sickness' and TYPE A Behavior for which the medical world treats (and blames) the victim could perhaps be elucidated in terms of those everyday environments whose space–time routines are so badly synchronized with the natural physiological rhythms (Friedman and Rosenman, 1975). Could we not examine contemporary *genres de vie* in terms of their temporal as well as spatial characteristics, focussing, not only on their functional 'efficiency', and the values and images which characterize their perspectives, but especially on the ways in which they succeed or fail in orchestrating their activities with the natural rhythmicity and dynamics of air, water, earth and seasons?

A retrospective and critical study of the evolution of technology and society could yield valuable insight if it were formulated in this comprehensive manner. If one is convinced that political revolution is the only road to salvation, there are many interesting experiences of the twentieth century which could be re-examined. Efforts to move toward a rational utopia founded upon an egalitarian social philosophy, could be studied in Scandinavia and elsewhere. Similarly, efforts to achieve anarchist and libertarian social reform in Civil War Spain as well as revolutionary social change in the context of China or Cuba in the twentieth century deserve critical study. It is ironic how eager we are to draft blueprints for the future and at the same time how unwilling we seem to be to look at past experiences. Our spatial and ecological models, derived in large part from an effort to shape our discipline according to the style of systematic social and natural sciences, remain often insensitive to time, development, and the inextricable connections of place and rhythmicity within life as a whole.

Ultimately, perhaps the most important role for geographers might emerge from its evocative and pedagogical efficacy. If we succeed in achieving a measure of critical insight into our own situations, and how appropriate our ways of thinking may be to elucidate them, we could begin to devise methods to help individuals to become aware of their own life situations, to understand the dynamics of those systems which surround them (Richards, 1975). Pedagogical efforts proposed in the late 'sixties and early 'seventies, e.g., learning webs, grass roots dialogue and networks of self-educating groups (Illich, 1971; Freire, 1970) may have now had enough time to yield data on the feasibility of such strategies. The aim, in general terms, was to initiate and promote discussion and engagement from a wide spectrum of people on issues related to environments. In this model of learning, change was envisioned not only on the part of participants, but also in the content, style, and structure of planning (Fromm, 1968). Could we not now find evidence of the strengths and limitations of these approaches? Even if one notices more complacency rather than militancy over environmental issues, this would still not mean that the 'consciousness raising' approach was an irrelevant one; rather it might suggest that it did not address itself to a sufficiently wide audience. Why should consumers, tenants, and clients be the only target for such a pedagogical program? Could it not be argued that it is the managerial sector (and its academic consultants) which have a more serious need for 'consciousness raising'? Instead of decrying our existing links with the so-called establishment, then, should we not consider the content of our message and eventually discover media more appropriate for communicating it?

The applied geographer's role, like that of philosopher or social scientist, can only be envisioned within the larger framework of processes leading toward awakening responsibility among various sectors of society. Does this role of provocateur, or facilitator of such a movement, not require that we eventually allow the 'objects' of our research to become 'subjects' of their own individual and collective lives? We may have expertise to offer at various stages of this effort, but to imagine that we can write the script, set the stage, and manage the production, seems not only pretentious, but could also be destructive of that very creativity from all actors which this period of history demands.

Revisiting Erewhon today leaves little doubt that enormous structural changes may be needed in order to redress imbalances of power and wealth. Its Colleges of Unreason need emancipation from the stifling effects of functional specification and cooptation by ideological or technological interests. External reform, however, needs to be matched by an even more pervasive revolution within the minds and hearts of individual people, be they regarded as playing a consumer, straightener, professor, or managerial roles. Structural reform and legislated social justice meted out to hungry automatons so they may be 'straightened' to fit 'rational' folkways, belongs to a Cartesian, managerial view of society. An appeal for internal renewal and creativity within human individuals implies an existential view of society where people can create as well as accumulate, acquire as well as inherit, learn to grapple with environmental problems rather than have them resolved for them by some intellectual or managerial elite. But it may also imply a fundamental renewal with the Colleges of Unreason: the old Hypothetics provide primarily 'autopsy' language to describe problems; in fact, the various brands of unreason which they have perpetuated have now become incarnate on the lived landscape. The first step to take in becoming more 'relevant' to society, then, is to deal with the basic homework on what we take for granted about reason and unreason, knowledge and action.

The geographer's success in contributing toward a whole earth perspective depends upon the breadth of his vision and the depth of his empathy for the manifold social and bio-ecological roots and directions within the human prospect. The value of our achievement may well lie in demonstrating potential paths for concerted action, rather than the discovery of uniquely 'spatial' or 'geographical' solutions to problems. In this quest, the more we arouse social, political and environmental consciousness among all potential actors in the planning process, the more we ourselves and our discipline may learn the art of creative becoming.

Graduate School of Geography
Clark University

NOTES

[1] The relationship between academic geography and actual planning endeavors within European schools often contrast sharply with those prevailing in American contexts. References here are primarily made to American experience.

BIBLIOGRAPHY

Arendt, H.: 1968, *Between Past and Present*, The Viking Press, New York.

Berger, P. L. and Luckman, T.: 1967, *The Social Construction of Reality*, Doubleday, New York.

Bell, D. (ed.): 1969, *Toward the Year 2000: Work in Progress*, Beacon Press, Boston.

Bortoft, H.: 1971, 'The Whole, Counterfeit and Authentic', *Systematics* 9, 43–73.

Braithwaite, R. B.: 1960, *Scientific Explanation. A Study of the Function of Theory*, Harper, New York.

Brookfield, H. C.: 1969, 'On the Environment as Perceived', in C. Board *et al.* (eds.), *Progress in Geography* I, Edward Arnold, London, pp. 51–80.

Brown, G. S.: 1969, *Laws of Form*, George Allen and Unwin, London.

Butler, S.: 1872, 1901, *Erewhon and Erewhon Revisited*; References are to the Modern Library Edition, New York, 1927.

Carnap, R.: 1966, *An Introduction to the Philosophy of Science*, Basic Books, New York.

Cavell, S.: 1964, 'Existentialism and Analytic Philosophy', *Daedalus* 93, Summer, 946–974.

Chase, S.: 1962, *The Proper Study of Mankind*, Harper and Row, New York.

Dilthey, W.: 1957, *Philosophy of Existence: Introduction to Weltanschaungslehre*, Brookman Association, New York.

Dilthey, W.: 1972, 'The Rise of Hermeneutics', *New Literary History* 3, 229–261.

Dubos, R.: 1965, *Man Adapting*, Yale University Press, New Haven.

Entrikin, J. N.: 1975, 'Science and Humanism in Geography', Unpublished Ph.D. Dissertation, University of Wisconsin, Department of Geography, Madison, Wisconsin.

Entrikin, J. N.: 1976, 'Contemporary Humanism in Geography', *Annals of the Association of American Geographers* 66, 615–632.

European Cultural Foundation: 1971, *Citizenry and City in the Year 2000*, Deventer, Kluwer.

Ferkiss, V. C.: 1969, *Technological Man: The Myth and the Reality*, Braziller, New York.

Fischer, R.: 1968, 'Biological Time', in J. T. Fraser (ed.), *The Voices of Time*, Allen Lane, The Penguin Press, London.

Freire, P.: 1970, *Pedagogy of the Oppressed*, Herder, New York.

Friedman, M. and Rosenman, R. H.: 1975, *Type A Behavior and Your Heart*, Fawcett Publications, Connecticut.

Friedrichs, R. W.: 1970, *A Sociology of Sociology*, Oxford University Press, New York.

Fromm, E.: 1968, *The Revolution of Hope: Toward Humanized Technology*, Harper and Row, New York.

Gadamer, H. -G.: 1975, *Truth and Method*, Seabury Press, New York.

Giddens, A.: 1974, *Positivism and Sociology*, Heinemann, London.

Gouldner, A. W.: 1962, 'Anti-Minotaur: The Myth of a Value-free Sociology', *Social Problems* 9, 199–213.

Goulet, D.: 1971, *The Cruel Choice: A New Concept in the Theory of Development*, Atheneum, New York.

Griffin, D. W.: 1965, 'Some Comments on Urban Planning and the Geographer', *The Professional Geographer* XVII, 4–6.

Habermas, J.: 1971, *Knowledge and Human Interests*, Beacon Press, Boston.

Habermas, J.: 1974, *Theory and Practice*, Beacon Press, Boston.

Hägerstrand, T.: 1974a, 'The Domain of Human Geography', in R. Chorley (ed.), *Progress in Geography*, Cambridge University Press, New York.

Hägerstrand, T.: 1974b, 'The Impact of Transport on the Quality of Life', Lunds Universitets Kulturgeografiska Institution, Lund.

Heidegger, M.: 1967, *Vorträge und Aufsätze*, Pfullingen, Neske.

Heidegger, M.: 1971, *Poetry, Language, Thought*, Harper and Row, London.

Hempel, C. G.: 1965, *Aspects of Scientific Explanation and Other Essays in the Philosophy of Science*, Free Press, Glencoe, Illinois.

Husserl, E.: 1931, *Ideas: General Introduction to Pure Phenomenology*, Macmillan, New York.

Husserl, E.: 1954, *The Crisis of European Philosophy* 6, Nijhoff, The Hague.

Illich, I.: 1971, *Deschooling Society*, Harper and Row, New York.

Illich, I.: 1973, *Tools for Conviviality*, Harper and Row, New York.

Jasper, K.: 1956, 'Reason and Existence', in W. Kaufmann (ed.), *Existentialism from Dostoevsky to Sartre*, Meridian Books, New York, pp. 158–232.

Jasper, K.: 1957, *Man in the Modern Age*, Doubleday, Garden City, New York.

Jencks, C.: 1971, *Architecture 2000: Predictions and Methods*, Praeger Publishers, New York.

King, L. J.: 1976, 'Alternatives to a Positive Economic Geography', *Annals of the Association of American Geographers* **66**, 293–308.

Kockelmans, J. J.: 1975, 'Toward an Interpretative or Hermeneutic Social Science', *Graduate Faculty Philosophy Journal* **5**, 73–96.

Kohler, W.: 1959, *The Place of Value in a World of Facts*, Meridian, New York.

Langer, S.: 1965, 'The Social Influence of Design', *University* **25**, 7–12.

Lefebvre, H.: 1974, *La Production de l'Espace*, Editions Anthropos, Paris.

Leiss, W.: 1974, *The Domination of Nature*, Beacon Press, Boston.

Lovelock, J.: 1975, 'The Gaia Hypothesis', *New Scientist* **6**.

Luce, G.: 1973, *Body Time: Physiological Rhythms and Social Stresses*, Pantheon, New York.

Mannheim, K.: 1936, *Ideology and Utopia*, Routledge and Kegan Paul, London.

Mannheim, K.: 1952, *Essays on the Sociology of Knowledge*, Oxford University Press, New York.

Marcuse, H.: 1968, *Negations: Essays in Critical Theory*, Beacon Press, Boston.

Marcuse, H.: 1972, *Studies in Critical Philosophy*, Beacon Press, Boston.

Martindale, D.: 1968, 'Verstehen', in D. Sills (ed.), *International Encyclopedia of the Social Sciences* **16**, Macmillan Company, New York.

Mayer, H. M.: 1954, 'Geographers in City and Regional Planning', *Professional Geographer* **VI**, 7–12.

Mercer, D. and Powell, J. M.: 1972, *Phenomenology and Other Non-Positivistic Approaches in Geography*, Monash University Publications in Geography.

Mills, C. W.: 1958, *The Sociological Imagination*, Prentice-Hall, Inc., Englewood Cliffs, New Jersey.

Myrdal, G.: 1969, *Objectivity in Social Research*, Random House, New York.

Nagel, E.: 1953, 'On the Method of Verstehen as the Sole Method of Philosophy', *Journal of Philosophy* **50**, 154–157.

Olsson, G.: 1971, 'Correspondence Rules and Social Engineering', *Economic Geography* **47**, 545–54.

Olsson, G.: 1972, 'Some Notes on Geography and Social Engineering', *Antipode* **IV**, 1–22.

Palmer, R. E.: 1969, *Hermeneutics*, Northwestern University Press, Evanston, Illinois.

Passmore, J.: 1968, *A Hundred Years of Philosophy*, Penguin Books, Baltimore, Maryland.

Pivcevic, E.: 1970, *Husserl and Phenomenology*, Hutchinson University Library, London.

Polanyi, M.: 1969, *Knowing and Being*, University of Chicago Press, Chicago.

Richards, P.: 1975, 'Alternative Strategies for the African Environment – Folk Ecology as a Basis for Community Orientated Agricultural Development', in P. Richards (ed.), *African Environment*, International African Institute, London.

Ricoeur, P.: 1971, *Conflict of Interpretations*, D. Ihde (ed.), Northwestern University Press, Evanston, Illinois.

Ricoeur, P.: 1973, 'The Model of the Text: Meaningful Action Considered as Text', *New Literary History* **5**, 91–117.

Samuels, M. S.: 1971, *Science and Geography: An Existential Appraisal*, Unpublished Ph.D. Dissertation, Department of Geography, University of Washington, Seattle.

Sartre, J. P.: 1956, *Being and Nothingness*, Philosophical Library, New York.

Sartre, J. P.: 1963, *Search for a Method*, A. A. Knopf, Inc., New York.

Scheibe, K. E.: 1970, *Beliefs and Values*, Holt, Rinehart and Winston, New York.

Schroyer, T.: 1975, *The Critique of Domination*, Beacon Press, Boston.

Spiegelberg, H.: 1960, *The Phenomenological Movement: A Historical Interpretation*, M. Nijhoff, The Hague.

Teilhard de Chardin, P.: 1964, *The Future of Man*, Harper, New York.

Teilhard de Chardin, P.: 1965, *Building the Earth*, Dimension Books, Wilkes-Barre, Pennsylvania.

Thompson, W. L.: 1971, *At the Edge of History*, Harper, New York

Toffler, A. (ed.): 1972, *The Futurists*, Random House, New York.

Tuttle, N. H.: 1969, *Wilhelm Dilthey's Philosophy of Historical Understanding: A Critical Analysis*, E. J. Brill, Leiden.

Weber, M.: 1949, *The Methodology of the Social Sciences*, The Free Press, Glencoe, Illinois.

Weber, M.: 1958, *The Protestant Ethic and the Spirit of Capitalism*, Scribner, New York.

White, G.: 1972, 'Geography and Public Policy', *Professional Geographer* **XXIV**, 101–104.

Whorf, B. L.: 1956, *Language, Thought and Reality*, J. B. Carroll (ed.), M.I.T. Press, Cambridge, Massachusetts.

Wild, J.: 1963, *Existence and the World of Freedom*, Prentice-Hall, Inc., Englewood Cliffs, New Jersey.

Winch, P.: 1958, *The Idea of a Social Science*, Routledge and Kegan Paul, London.

Winter, G.: 1966, *Elements for a Social Ethic*, Macmillan, New York.

Wolpert, J.: 1976, 'Opening Closed Spaces', *Annals of the Association of American Geographers* **66**, 1–13.

Zelinsky, W.: 1970, 'Beyond the Exponentials', *Economic Geography* **46**, 498–535.

MICHAEL F. DACEY

A FRAMEWORK FOR EXAMINATION OF
THEORETIC VIEWPOINTS IN GEOGRAPHY[1]

My discussion concerns the nature of a model that purports to classify theoretic viewpoints in geography. Though the model has a simple structure, it has clarified for me some methodological aspects of geographic research. It has also identified several basic research problems that evidently have not been previously recognized.

My discussion will have the following structure. First, I will examine the need and possible uses of a classification of theoretic approaches to geography. Second, I will define the model and illustrate some applications. Finally, I will identify some of the more interesting results generated by the model.

I. BACKGROUND

Discussions and controversies on the methodological basis of geographic research frequently evolve around dichotomies and dualities: ideographic–nomothetic, universality–uniqueness, deterministic–stochastic, behavioral–morphological, explanation–description, inductive–deductive.

I am not convinced that distinctive attributes of methodologies are revealed by such dichotomies. Some of these are specious in that the two parts are not incompatible, the two parts fail to encompass a multiplicity of alternatives or one of the two parts encompasses all viable alternatives. Others seem only to be a consequence of semantic confusion. Other dichotomies appear valid but fail to distinguish critical methodological issues.

The philosophy of science literature also utilizes numerous dichotomies to draw distinctions between scientific methods. While I am not qualified to evaluate the validity or utility of these dichotomies, I have not found them useful in structuring geographic research.

Within a single discipline, it is frequently only subtle differences that distinguish alternative approaches to problems so that it is not surprising that a single dichotomy is too crude a model to comprehend the distinctive elements of alternative theoretical formulations in geography. The need may be for a

39

S. Gale and G. Olsson (eds.), Philosophy in Geography, 39–52. All Rights Reserved.
Copyright © 1979 by D. Reidel Publishing Company, Dordrecht, Holland.

more refined model that takes into account a larger range of methodological components.

II. USES OF A MODEL

Before attempting to construct a new model, there is need to identify its intended uses and the criteria appropriate for its evaluation.

The basic use of the model is to distinguish alternative trends in contemporary geographic theory. In addition to this use, I shall try to construct a model that is useful for understanding the role of theory in the design and interpretation of empirical research. It would also be useful if the model contributed to the identification of types of analytic techniques that are required for the continued development of geographic theories, without regard to the methodological biases of these theories.

The need is for a model that exposes and integrates the distinctive features of current theoretic viewpoints in geography. My search for types of models that could be adapted to the structure of contemporary geography was not notably successful.

The only suitable model that I located was developed by Wallace (1969) to explain the methodological structure of contemporary sociology. Extensions and generalization of this model will be used to structure the methodologies of geography and several other social science fields.

Before identifying elements of the model, several underlying assumptions are clarified. I shall also try to establish the domain to which statements of the model pertain.

Every classification has its limitations. One limitation is that it magnifies certain differences, ignores others and may delude us into believing that the former are more real than the latter. Worse, the assumed dimensions of the classification scheme may be erroneous in that they rest on unfruitful premises or unreliable observations. However, it is not claimed that the distinctions made by the model are more valid than others but simply they are not less valid, they are not grossly contradicted by observations and they are useful for understanding the role of theory in research.

A second limitation is the requirement that every observation be placed into one part of each dichotomy. This may force us to distort observations to fit the classification. This risk will be somewhat negated by using the model to classify only idealized methodologies, or 'isms', rather than classifying existing theories or the methodological works of particular theorists. As a general rule, concrete theories or works are sufficiently moderated in their arguments that they are inadequate for paradigms for class types. The differences among theories are mainly differences of emphasis. However, in application of the model, the chief concern is not on these similarities but rather to focus upon the differences among theories in conceptual emphasis.

III. UNDERLYING ASSUMPTIONS

Some discussions of methodologies attempt to identify the conceptual frameworks that competing theories resemble. The present model is instead motivated by attempts to respond to the following type of questions: "What kinds of direct observations and analysis does each theory imply?" By placing the stress on observations indicated by theory, as well as the empirical generalizations based on these observations and the analytic tools used for the study of these observations, it is possible to construct a model that suggests conclusions about both theories and the design and interpretation of empirical research.

The term 'theory' is taken to mean any set of symbols (symbolic construct) that is claimed verifiably to represent and make intelligible specified classes of phenomena in one or more of their relationships. A theory is said to be 'of' a particular class of phenomena whenever the theory offers an explanation of phenomena in that class. An explanation of phenomena in a class occurs when that class is treated as the explanandum or dependent variable, regardless of the nature of the independent variables.

The model does not use phenomenological differences in explananda to differentiate theories. This is because all scientific theories require both an explanandum and an explanans and two quite different theories might be equally interested in the same class of phenomena if one is interested in it as an explanandum while the other is interested in it as explanans. There is, however, a critical distinction between these kinds of theoretic interest, and the following model classifies theories on the basis of the distinction between how the explanandum is defined and how it is explained.

IV. STRUCTURE OF THE MODEL

The model classifies theories of a phenomenon X, so that X is the explanandum of theories described by the model. Each theory specifies relations

MICHAEL F. DACEY

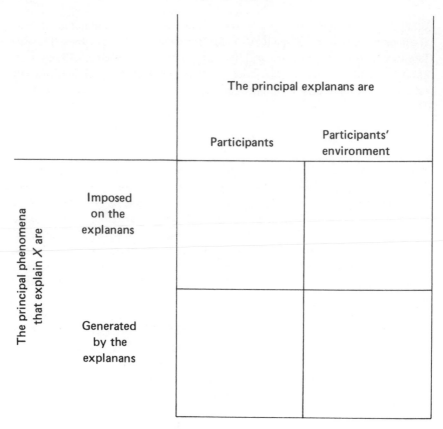

Fig. 1. Basic property space described by the model.

between X and elements recognized by the theory. In many social science theories these elements include humans or human institutions, and to reflect this humanistic quality of the explanantia, the elements are referred to as 'participants in the theory' or, simply, 'participants'. Despite this suggestive terminology, the model itself makes no assertions concerning the attributes of participants, which are described only by the theory in which they occur.

Consider a theory that explains X. The relation of X to theory is treated as being one of two types. The explaining elements of one type of theory stress conditions that are *imposed on* either the participants of the theory or on the universe that environs these participants. In this type of theory the viewpoint is that X reflects relations with participants that are 'determined'

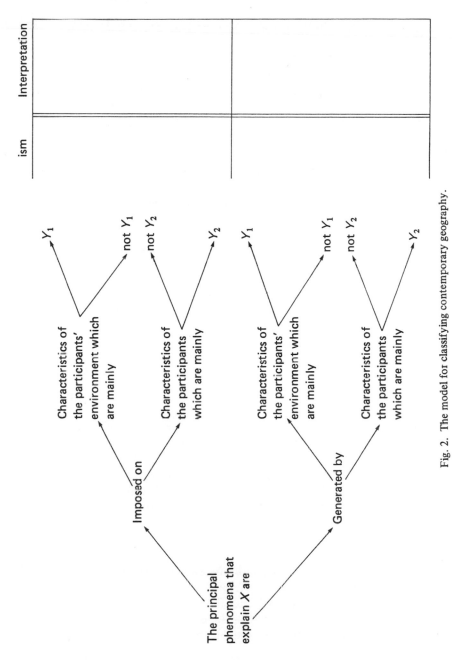

Fig. 2. The model for classifying contemporary geography.

or 'controlled' by conditions that are temporally prior or logically more primitive.

The explaining elements of a second type of theory stress conditions that are *generated by* either the nature of the participants of the theory or the nature of the universe that environs these participants. In this type of theory the viewpoint is that X reflects relations with participants that are 'self-determining' or 'free-willed'.

Figure 1 displays the property space identified by this partitioning of explaining elements of a theory.

An additional dimension is added to the model by placing a second dichotomy on the nature of the explanantia of a theory. Denote the dichotomy for participants' environment by Y_1 and for participants by Y_2.

Figure 2 displays the basic model, which is read from left to right. The model contains three parameters: the explanandum X and the sentential constants Y_1 and Y_2. Associated with each class is an ism which serves to characterize the class but is not a formal element of the model. The use of isms is meant to convey that the classes are idealized types of theories and theoretical viewpoints, which are more extreme in their formulation than are concrete theories or formulated theoretical viewpoints. Also, the interpretation of each class is not a component of the model, though the interpretations may provide a useful frame of reference.

V. USE OF THE MODEL

Before considering applications of the model, it needs to be noted that there does not explicitly exist a model for geography or for any other academic discipline. This situation occurs because the model classifies theories that explain X and this explanandum is a phenomenon. If a group agrees that some phenomenon X_S is the principal explanandum of an academic discipline X, then the classification of theories of X_S may be viewed by this group as a classification of S.

The specification of the explanandum X does not determine the classification of theories. The selection of the sentential variables Y_1 and Y_2 may affect the classification and probably biases the selection of the isms associated with each of the eight classes. Although the isms are not properly part of the model, it seems highly likely that the selected terminology will evoke psychological reactions in at least some readers.

Criteria are needed to guide the specification of X, Y_1, Y_2 and the eight isms. While the order of specification is probably not critical, it may be more productive to specify the components of the model in left to right order so that X is set first while the isms reflect the selections for Y_1 and Y_2.

The following assumptions underlie the selection of the explanandum. (1) The model has little relevance to a particular explanandum unless it occurs as a dependent variable in several or more competing or complementary theories. (2) The study of a model is productive only when these several theories are largely the product of workers in a common academic discipline. (3) The utility of the model is greatest for an explanandum that is the central focus of a large, diverse group of researchers, such as characterize most disciplinary and some interdisciplinary efforts.

Each explanandum examined in this study has been selected because it appears to be the central focus of several theories used in a social science field. Moreover, it is assumed that the explanandum is similarly defined in each of these theories. However, verification of this assumption requires detailed content analyses of these theories.

The criteria for specifying Y_1 and Y_2 are even more fuzzy. What are needed are variables that produce eight classes which, on one hand, include and distinguish the major, competing theories of X and, on the other hand, correspond to existing theories of X. These conditions evidently suggest that the model has little utility for an X if there exist only two or three theories of X and, unless the dimensions of the model are increased, if there exist more than eight theories of X. In the ensuing applications of the model the specification of Y_1 and Y_2 has proceeded largely by trial, error and subjective evaluation.

Once X, Y_1 and Y_2 are set, there remains the sensitive task of identifying the ism terminology. While this terminology is external to the model, it should be suggestive of the fundamental conceptual emphasis of each class of the model. One difficulty is that the terminology has resorted to some barbaric expressions, such as demographism. However, most of the other isms are listed in *Webster's Third New International Dictionary* and the dictionary definitions approximate class characteristics.

VI. APPLICATIONS

Although my interest in the model is its application for the classification of geographic theories, it may be advantageous to first experiment with other disciplines.

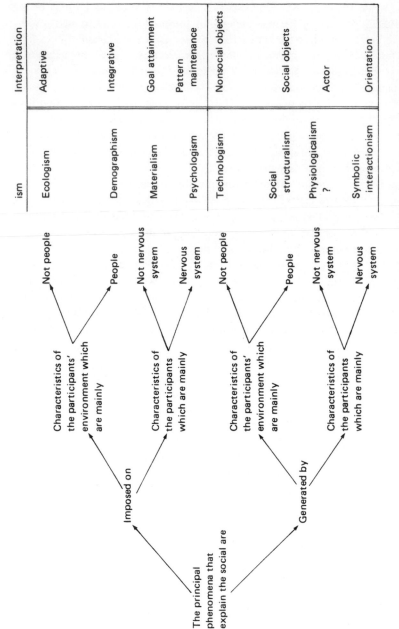

Fig. 3. The model with X = social, Y_1 = people, Y_2 = nervous system; adapted from Wallace (1969), Figure 2.

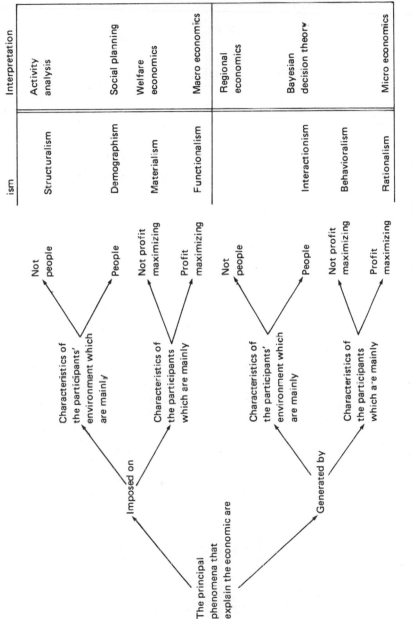

ism	Interpretation
Structuralism	Activity analysis
Demographism	Social planning
Materialism	Welfare economics
Functionalism	Macro economics
	Regional economics
Interactionism	
Behavioralism	Bayesian decision theory
Rationalism	Micro economics

Fig. 4. Interpretation of the model for X = economic, Y_1 = people, Y_2 = profit maximization.

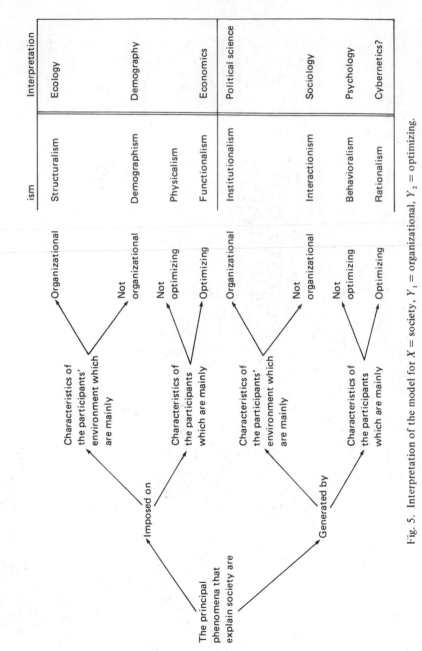

Fig. 5. Interpretation of the model for X = society, Y_1 = organizational, Y_2 = optimizing.

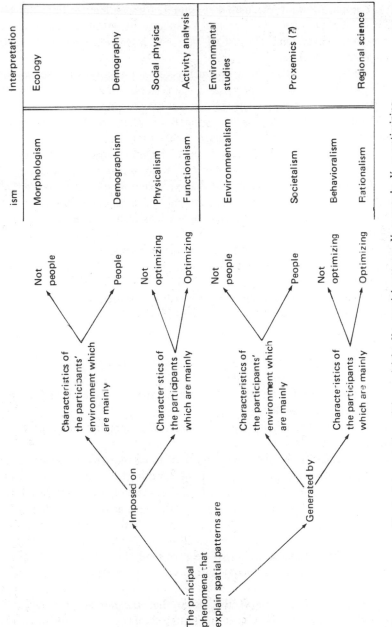

Fig. 6. Interpretation of the model for X = spatial patterns, Y_1 = people, Y_2 = optimizing.

The application of the model, Figure 3, to sociology utilizes the terms given by Wallace (1969), which has X replaced by social, Y_1 by people and Y_2 by nervous system. The list of isms and interpretations are essentially those given by Wallace.

Evidently the explanandum of much economic theory is the economic. If so, the model of Figure 4 proposes a classification of economics by putting X = economic, Y_1 = people and Y_2 = profit maximizing.

Presumably the model may be applied to other social sciences, but my knowledge of these fields is too meager to even attempt a classification.

If it as agreed that the society is the focus of social science theory, then the model generates a broad classification of social science theories. The model of Figure 5 uses 'society' for the explanandum of social science theory and equates Y_1 and Y_2 with organizational and optimizing. Notice that two interpretations are provided for one class while anthropology and geography are academic fields missing from the nearly complete list of social science fields. History is also missing, but it may not be a social science.

The application of the model that will be examined in detail is defined by X = spatial pattern, Y_1 = people and Y_2 = optimizing (Figure 6). To the degree spatial patterns are the explanandum of geographic research, this model proposes a classification of geographic theories.

VII. ANALYSIS OF THE MODEL

First, I note some of the things not accomplished by the model or by this examination of the model.

It does not generate the typical division of geography: urban geography, cultural geography, etc.

Many of the dichotomies frequently used to categorize geographic research are not identifiable or are devoid of meaning in the context of the model: inductive–deductive, deterministic–stochastic, ideographic–nomothetic, etc.

A critical assumption is that spatial patterns serve as the common explanandum of numerous geographic theories. Although the explanation of spatial patterns seems to be a prevailing objective of the contemporary geographic literature, other explananda might be proposed. For example, it might be profitable to examine the model with areal differentiation as the explanandum.

Next, I will note some of the issues that the model seems to clarify. Although I will frequently refer to upper-half theories and lower-half theories, these halves refer only to positions in Figure 6 and do not convey a value assignment.

The research topics of classical and continuing interest in geography seem to be covered by the upper-half theories. In contrast, the topics covered by bottom-half theories have been only of spasmodic but intense interest. Examples include environment determinism in the post World War I period, the rationalistic models of the late 1950's that were engendered by the infusion into geography of regional science axioms and techniques, and the behavioralism that currently dominates geographic studies.

This interpretation suggests that the continuing schism in geographic theories may be between the 'generated by' and 'imposed on' approaches.

This distinction between the two kinds of theories evidently has implications to empirical analysis. The tools and techniques of analysis that are currently available are evidently designed to handle morphological relations of the 'imposed on' type. Possibly, the lower-half theories have floundered because of inability to describe and analyze relations that have the explanandum of a theory generated by attributes of the participants of a theory.

If this interpretation is valid, the development of lower-half theories is inhibited by lack of suitable methods and tools of analysis. If so, the current effort in behavioral aspects of geography is probably misdirected.

This interpretation is reinforced by the observation that the work in the early sixties was focused upon theories of the rational type. Research effort directed by this class of theories was not terminated because all the interesting problems were solved. I suspect that this effort was aborted because of inadequate analytic ability. While one currently developing trend is to research directed by behavioral theories, the model suggests that the changing emphasis is only from participants that are optimizing to participants that are not optimizing. Because there is little reason to anticipate that there is much difference between the analytic and relational problems arising in rational and behavioral theories, current behavioral research may fail because of inability to handle the same analytic problems that stymied the development of rational theories.

The preceding observations are based on a critical assumption: the analytic methods used to establish relationships between explanandum and explanantia for 'imposed on' types of theories are unsuitable for establishing relationships for 'generated by' types of theories. If this is a valid assumption, it poses the problem of what types of tools are required for investigation of 'generated by' theories.

The relations established by upper-half theories are generally morphological

relations. In contrast, the task of lower-half theories is to relate spatial structures to largely non-spatial atrributes of participants or participants' environments. The inherent natures of these two kinds of relations seem to present
geography with challenging problems.

While morphological relations have proved easier to identify, the utility of
morphological relations is seldom recognized. This may be the reason the
upper-half theories have had little impact on the making and evaluation of
policy. Possibly, the current political, social and environmental climate is one
that can profitably utilize morphological relations. The problems associated
with ghettos, poverty, pollution and congestion are to a significant extent
problems of spatial concentration. Although geographers claim particular
competence in the analysis of spatial structure and spatial relations, it remains
for geography to demonstrate that theories of morphological relations can
contribute to the solution of the contemporary social and economic problems.

The task confronting lower-half theorists seems equally challenging. While
some geographers fluently argue the need to relate attributes of participants
and their environment to morphological structures, the establishing of actual
relations has proved elusive. I am not at all convinced that available social
science theories are capable of relating non-spatial attributes of participants
and their environment to spatial patterns. At the least, the geographic literature contains few, if any, verifiable relations of this kind. One unavoidable
question concerns the existence of an empirically verifiable theory that
relates non-spatial attributes of the elements of a theory to spatial patterns.
The challenge to a lower-half theorist is first to demonstrate the theory's
existence and then to demonstrate its application.

Department of Geography
Northwestern University

NOTES

[1] The support of the National Science Foundation, Grant GS-1627 is gratefully acknowledged.

BIBLIOGRAPHY

Wallace, W. L. (ed.): 1969, *Sociological Theory: an Introduction*, Aldene, Chicago.

MICHAEL DEAR

THIRTEEN AXIOMS OF A GEOGRAPHY OF
THE PUBLIC SECTOR

> Modern urban man is born in a publicly financed
> hospital, receives his education in a publicly sup-
> ported school and university, spends a good part of
> his time travelling on publicly built transportation
> facilities, communicates through the post office or
> the quasi-public telephone system, drinks his public
> water, disposes of his garbage through the public
> removal system, reads his public library books,
> picnics in his public parks, is protected by his
> public police, fire and health systems; eventually
> he dies, again in a hospital, and may even be buried
> in a public cemetery.
>
> MICHAEL B. TEITZ (1968, p. 36)

Decisions made in the public sector affect almost all aspects of our lives. The
welfare of future generations depends upon those decisions now being made.
It is odd, therefore, that the spatial outcomes of public sector decisions do
not form a more prominent focus in contemporary geographic theory. The
purpose of this essay is to correct this imbalance, by outlining a framework
for the study of a geography of the public sector. Four themes are pursued:
preliminaries; pattern; process; and theory and methodology. Together, they
define the thirteen principal axioms of a public sector geography.

I. PRELIMINARIES

I.1. *Focus*

A geography of the public sector is concerned with the spatial outcomes of
decision-making by all institutions which are publicly accountable.

I.2. *The State*

The most important of these institutions is the State itself, since it is the

53

S. Gale and G. Olsson (eds.), Philosophy in Geography, 53–64. All Rights Reserved.
Copyright © 1979 by D. Reidel Publishing Company, Dordrecht, Holland.

major source of the outcomes we wish to consider. However, concern might also extend to quasi-public bodies, such as nationalized industry or utility companies. It is important to distinguish between the 'State' *per se*, and the 'political system' of any society. The State is a collection of institutions, including government, administration, the police, and the judiciary. In contrast, the political system is best envisaged as the superstructure of the State, including the political parties and pressure groups which vitally affect the operation of the political process, and hence, of the State itself (cf. Miliband, 1973, pp. 46–51).

If the State is to become an endogenous variable in geographical analysis, it is vital that comparative analyses of spatial outcomes under different State systems be undertaken. In western capitalist society, which is based upon private property and private enterprise, there is considerable ambiguity in the State's role. At least five different interpretations have been suggested, viewing the state alternatively as (i) supplier of public goods and services; (ii) facilitator of the market mechanism; (iii) social engineer, intervening to achieve its own policy objectives; (iv) arbiter among competing social groups; and (v) agent on behalf of a ruling elite (Clark and Dear, 1976). In contrast, the basis of socialist systems is State ownership and control of enterprise. Yet even in this potentially less ambiguous setting, considerable variation in the State role may be observed. For example, the Russian State bureaucracy has been equated with the bourgeoisie under capitalism, since it acts to extract the economic surplus from workers and thereby delivers social and economic privileges to itself. Under this 'state capitalist' system, social inequality persists (Lane, 1971). Moreover, it is precisely this kind of State structure which the People's Republic of China is trying to avoid.

I.3. *Spatial Outcomes*

The spatial outcomes from State decisions derive from two sources: (i) policies for the regulation of society; and (ii) the provision of public goods and services.

Strategies of social regulation are a major concern in the proposed paradigm. At the most fundamental level, these strategies act to preserve such basic institutions as private property. Around these institutions, a more pragmatic edifice of administrative and legal machinery has been constructed. For present purposes, the most significant set of regulatory policies are those contained in the machinery of land use planning legislation. Bourne (1975) has recently shown how different State systems can lead to fundamentally differing planning philosophies, with predictable consequences upon patterns of land use development.

In many ways, the provision of public goods and services has a more immediate impact upon public welfare. The precise nature of the spatial outcome will depend upon the reason for intervention. Three reasons are normally considered: the existence of external effects in production or consumption (e.g., the incidence of air pollution); the existence of other market failures (e.g., monopoly); and the development of preferred standards for community life (e.g., a preference for more urban parkland). In all cases, the private market would tend not to produce in a socially optimum manner. As a consequence, a wide range of goods and services are provided by the State, including pure public goods (an air pollution control monitor) and merit goods (a library system).

I.4. *Public Facilities*

An important agent in the delivery of public goods and services is the public facility system. Three facility types have been recognized: 'service', where the consumer travels to the facility to obtain the good (e.g., schools); 'despatch', where the good is taken to the consumer from the facility (e.g., fire stations); and 'utility', where the good is distributed to the consumer via some network mode (e.g., pipe, cable), and where some attenuation of capacity, as the consumer is approached, is required (cf. Teitz, 1968).

Since the mere presence of public facility in a neighbourhood can mean the difference between availability and non-availability of a particular good or service, the redistributive potential of the facility system is clearly significant.

II. PATTERN IN PUBLIC SECTOR GEOGRAPHY

II.1. *Direct Impact*

The majority of public decisions will ultimately acquire some geographical dimension, such as a concentration of public housing sites. In examining the patterns of these spatial outcomes, we are first interested in the direct impact of the decision; i.e., in those welfare consequences which are directly intended by the decision-makers. In a study of the school, street, and library systems in Oakland, California, Levy *et al.* (1974) discovered that public decisions produced three typical patterns in spatial outcomes. These were:

(1) *'the more, the more'* which describes the tendency to allocate most funds to those areas which have already received a majority of previously available resources;

(2) *compensation* in which the very poorest neighborhoods receive extra resources; and

(3) *resultants* which are the patterns which no-one intends (see Axiom II.2).

Given that society's resources are not infinite, it is clear that when one group gains from a public program, some other group loses. Moreover, given the cradle-to-the-grave ramifications of public decisions, the global impact of these decisions upon human welfare is hard to underestimate.

II.2. *Indirect Impacts*

In addition to their direct impact, most public policy decisions have a range of direct welfare consequences which were largely unforeseen by decision-makers. These indirect impacts are due to unanticipated side-effects (i.e., the externalities) of the decision. For example, a policy to rehouse residents from a demolished slum neighborhood might have the effect of destroying old friendships and community ties.

Three groups of external effect seem particularly significant in generating the indirect impacts of public decisions: user-associated; neighborhood-associated; and jurisdictional (Dear, 1976). User-associated externalities are borne by those people who in some way participate in a public decision (i.e., they also share in the direct benefits of the program). For example, those people relocated by an urban renewal scheme suffer the inconvenience of removal; or, those obliged to live in public housing might feel stigmatized as a consequence. Conversely, neighborhood-associated externalities affect those who are not part of the decision or its associated program. Thus, people in the vicinity of an urban park may never actually visit the park, although their property values might rise because of its proximity. Finally, jurisdictional spillovers arise because it is often difficult to confine the impact of a government's decision to within its own jurisdictional boundaries. Hence, when recreational facilities in one jurisdiction are used by residents of another, and this use goes unpriced, a jurisdictional spillover is said to have occurred. The incidence of such effects is particularly significant when inter-jurisdictional cooperation is required to finance large-scale, multi-jurisdictional programs (e.g., for regional waste-disposal).

An important question in public decision-making is the extent to which decision-makers are (un)aware of the full consequences of their choices. Harvey (1973, p. 58) has suggested a high degree of awareness, in that ". . . much of what goes on in a city (particularly in the political arena) can be interpreted as an attempt to organize the distribution of externality effects to gain income advantages". There is sufficient evidence of 'slippage' in current public policy-making (in the form of pay-offs, kick-backs, bribery, etc.) to lend at least some credence to this suggestion.

III. PROCESS IN PUBLIC SECTOR GEOGRAPHY

So far, I have argued that decisions by publicly accountable institutions, particularly the State, have a major impact on human welfare through regulatory policies, provision of public goods and services, and location of public facilities. Any geography of the public sector ought to focus on the pattern of direct and indirect spatial outcomes of public decision-making. However, we cannot stop at description of patterns; we must also strive to explain those patterns, and to expose the *processes* through which they are achieved.

III.1. *Decision Agents*

From the outset, it has to be recognized that decision-making in the public sector is much more complex than in the private sector. The first major source of this increased complexity is in the number of agents party to each decision. Four participant groups may be recognized initially: government, consumer, community, and supplier. Let us consider these in turn.

Government (as one part of the State) is responsible for the specific decisions on regulatory policy, or for the delivery of public goods and services. These decisions may occur at national, regional, or local levels. Since government consists of a body of elected officials, it is motivated (in part at least) to protect the welfare of its constituents. In this concern, it is influenced by special interest groups, by constituency pressures, and by its internal political composition. Consequently, a government's decision criteria are multi-dimensional and are often complicated by the fact that there is a relatively short time between achieving office and seeking re-election.

In many decisions on public policy, the opinions of consumers (the client group) carry least weight. This is especially the case when the potential client group is poor, or in a minority. It is particularly acute for the handicapped consumers (e.g., the mentally retarded), who are unable to voice their demands, and have to rely on an advocate group. However, not all client groups can be regarded as 'victims' in the decision process. The construction industry always seems to have a large voice in the preparation of housing legislation, for example.

The voice of the client group is often lost in the many voices which derive from the wider community. Its members elected the government under whose auspices the public good is being delivered, or legislation drafted. Although not a consumer of the good, the community frequently has an effective veto power on decisions regarding it. It is sometimes useful to distinguish between the 'impacted' community, and the community 'at large'. For example, a community group which feels the negative impact of a sewage treatment plant in its neighborhood may be in conflict with the community at large, which recognizes the city-wide benefits of the plant.

Finally, the supplier/producer of the public good is also party to the decision calculus. Suppliers can be private or public agents. The former are attracted by the profit motive, and are usually subcontracted to the government. However, where profits are not possible, government itself generally takes over the role of supplier.

III.2. *Market Organization*

For any public good or service, government is faced with a choice between *production* of the good, including its manufacture and distribution, or accepting responsibility for its *provision* at public expense (usually by contracting with a separate agency for its production). The provision option has many advantages, at least in theory. It avoids long-term commitment of public monies, and encourages competition amongst potential contractors, thereby ensuring an efficient, responsive, low-cost service. It also provides an important means for dealing with the spillover issue, in that arrangements for cooperative provision are likely to be more easily achieved than arrangements for cooperative production (Ostrom *et al.*, 1961).

An important organizational question concerns the point at which public production stops and private provision begins. There is, of course, considerable political bias against public production in capitalist societies. Where it does occur, the power of decision-making (with respect to the given good or service) is generally delegated to that political unit whose boundaries are coterminous with the good's market area. Hence, defence responsibilities are normally vested at the national level, while local fire protection arrangements are generally delegated to the neighborhood or town level. One major difficulty with this appealing arrangement is that market areas rarely coincide with political boundaries. The myriad of potential scales and organizations between national and local levels is testimony to the problem of coping with the resultant jurisdicational spillovers.

The problem of deciding the level at which decision-making discretion is to be delegated is complicated by the difficulties of obtaining true estimates of the effective *demand* for public goods and services. Consumers rarely possess the resources to back their demands — either financially, or in terms of political skill. Hence, demand for public goods is often ineffective, or even non-existent. Decisions with respect to the provision of such goods therefore have to be made on different criteria (see below). Under these circumstances, the absence of a traditional *supply* side response is hardly surprising.

The difficulties of market organization for a set of public facilities under these circumstances have been described by Teitz (1968, pp. 43–44). Consider the case of a good with zero direct cost, and no individual choice, such as a fire protection service. Here, the spatial form of the service (and hence, the incidence of its benefits) are determined by technical considerations, such as minimum operating size, and maximum permissible response time. The latter criterion argues for at least some degree of facility dispersion, while the former limits dispersion because of the technical need to operate above some minimum size. When consumer choice is significant, a different set of considerations emerge. Thus, in a library system, the larger facility has a greater stock of books, and therefore attracts more consumers. Demand is then regulated by the travel cost that consumers have to bear in obtaining service. In this example, the attractions of size have to be offset against the advantages of accessibility. As Teitz points out, the facility system is able to generate demand for its services by organizing itself appropriately. However, in doing so, its costs will rise.

In summary, market organization for delivery of public goods and services requires the simultaneous resolution of questions of demand; supply; production/provision; size, spacing and number of facilities; and welfare impacts. We should not be surprised if optimality in public decisions is an impossible concept.

III.3. *Decision Criteria*

What, then, are appropriate criteria for decision-makers in the public sector? The redistributive nature of the majority of public decisions, and the accountability of decision-makers, have forced attention away from traditional *efficiency* concerns. Although such considerations as cost-effectiveness, etc., are still important, they are frequently subordinated to *equity* goals in decision-making. Equity criteria are based upon the notion that some groups in society are worse off than others, and that the difference between the groups is worth diminishing. Little systematic research investigation on equity in spatial outcomes has been undertaken. The study by Levy *et al.* (1974) is indicative of the complexity of the research task. They suggest three possible equity criteria in the provision of public services:

(1) *market equity* in which public resources are distributed according to the revenues received;

(2) *equal opportunity* where an equal dollar amount in resources is distributed, on a per capita basis, irrespective of tax contributions; and

(3) *equal results* where, ultimately, the quality of streets, libraries, etc., in all neighborhoods shall be equal.

All three criteria are, to a certain degree, 'fair'. However, market equity and equal opportunity will tend to perpetuate existing social inequalities while the equal results alternative has greater redistributive capacity.

Judgements on the degree of redistribution preferred by any society clearly require something beyond a simple statement of equity alternatives. They involve instead some consensus on the relative merits of the potential recipients of the benefits of the redistributive policies. In short, an exogenous theory of justice is implied. Most contemporary treatments of *social justice* seem to focus on Rawls' (1971) contractual model of justice. Miller (1976) has recently recognized three criteria in social justice: to each according to his rights; to each according to his dessert; and to each according to his need. Moreover, he suggests that attempts to accomodate all three criteria simultaneously (such as in Rawls) are doomed to failure. Harvey (1973) has explicitly considered social justice in spatial systems, and favors Runciman's weak ordering of social justice, based upon three principles:

(1) *need* which represents the minimum standard of quantity or quality of life;

(2) *merit* which allocates more to those faced with special difficulties in contributing to production; and

(3) *contribution to the common good* where talents beneficial to all society warrant special reward.

The problems of operationalizing any of these criteria are immense, and we are once again forced to consider the political basis of public program decision criteria.

III.4. *Power*

Power is a key concept in explaining the spatial outcomes which derive from the decision process in the public sector. Each of the decision agents have qualitatively differing degrees of power. Government, for example, has the *power* to initiate public sector programs, and even has recourse to the use of *force* in the face of non-compliance with its wishes. Community power, on the other hand, is much more limited. It is only when large scale urban social movements arise that community power is strongly felt, since it then begins to resemble aspects of a class struggle (Castells, 1976). The central point, however, is simply that a differing distribution of power is the determining factor of many spatial outcomes, and the major force in generating systematic social conflict over those outcomes.

IV. THEORETICAL AND METHODOLOGICAL CONSIDERATIONS

I have deliberately postponed any discussion on theory and methodology in a geography of the public sector until now. This is because I believe that most geographers would agree with the thrust of the arguments presented up to this point. It is when an attempt is made to link these propositions into a single coherent paradigm that dissent may be anticipated. I present my paradigmatic overview in this final section of the paper in order to emphasize that the study of public sector geography is not contingent upon acceptance of my personal viewpoint. (Indeed, it would be advantageous if dissenters pursued their own lines of thought into the nature of a geography of public sector.) With this caveat, let us consider the implications of the preceding propositions.

IV.1. *Theory*

The theoretical basis of a public sector geography has its origins in the sociological theory of conflict. At the macro-level, the paradigm addresses those structural dimensions which cause conflict, and which regulate the process of conflict (e.g., private property relations). At the micro-level, concern focusses upon the specific cause of conflict and its redistributive impact (e.g., the loss of property due to urban renewal).

The focus of conflict theory is change, and the coercion of some members of society by others, in a process of dissent. Conflict theorists consider the social structure to be constituted by force and constraint. This is in strong contrast with the more traditional consensus view of society, which is characterized by stability, coordination and integration. It conceives of society in terms of a functionally integrated system, held in equilibrium by certain patterned and recurrent processes (Dahrendorf, 1959, Ch. V).

The movement in social theory away from consensus models and toward conflict models of society has not, in general, been appreciated in geographical theory. The majority of geographical models still assume the existence of some equilibrium state; this is especially true of those models which have been absorbed from economics, including most land use models. Now, I am not advocating the rejection of equilibrium approaches in favor of an exclusive application of a conflict model. Society appears to have elements of conflict and consensus, and there is no intrinsic criterion for preferring one theoretical approach over the other. However, the existing equilibrium models seem to be singularly ill-equipped for dealing with the complex problems raised in public sector geography (e.g., the absence of traditional demand and supply categories, and decision-making by multiple agencies on the basis of equity or social justice criteria). Moreover, given the propositions developed in this paper, my personal belief is that future efforts ought to concentrate more upon those explanations which include conflict, constraint, and change. They may be less elegant than equilibrium explanations, but they are more likely to be relevant and realistic in dealing with real-world problems.

IV.2. *Methodology*

The future potential of a paradigm of public sector geography seems to depend crucially upon a revolution in geographic method. In the post-quantitative era, we seem unaccustomed to thinking in anything other than mathematical or statistical terms. The unfettered flexibility of verbal thinking often has to be learned again. As Galbraith has remarked, the predominance of mathematical methods often leads to an atrophy of judgement and intuition, and to the exclusion of the mathematically inconvenient from consideration. Let me emphasize immediately that I am not advocating a return to the dark days of the pre-quantitative era; mathematical and statistical methods have an integral role in the development of a public sector geography. What I am suggesting is that we are looking for original explanations on freshly-observed relationships, and flexibility is the keynote in these early explorations. Unfortunately, as Marx so vividly states (in *The Eighteenth*

Brumaire of Louis Napoleon): "The tradition of all the dead generations weigh like a nightmare on the brain of the living".

The methodological flexibility which I advocate could initially be channelled into four directions. First, and most straightforwardly, there is a need for the development of case studies in conflict, especially in the use of 'scenarios' to evaluate potential conflict outcome (Wolpert *et al.*, 1972). Secondly, there is a need for the development of heuristic models for comparative analysis of conflict outcomes. These models focus upon the common structural dimensions of any conflict situation (Dear, 1976). Of course, such efforts could proceed simultaneously with the development of pure methodological analyses for public sector problems. These include, for instance, analysis of the conflict dimensions of the external effects of public programs (Dear *et al.*, 1977). Finally, new methodological insight might be encouraged by the development of what Seley (1973) has called 'middle-level' theory — implying the evaluation of conflict theories in other disciplines for their relevance in geography.

IV.3. *Philosophy and Ideology*

Most geographers are still overly concerned with the appearance of society, instead of considering the social foundation upon which that society is based. This typically leads to a concern with pattern, and rarely with process. It is a throwback to the old positivist traditions in geographic thinking — a position long held to be untenable in philosophy, but still clung to in geography and economics (cf. Hollis and Nell, 1975).

My belief is that the ultimate answer to every geographical problem is a political question (to paraphrase Joan Robinson). Any geography of the public sector, with its concern for the distribution of public program benefits, etc., must focus upon the structural foundations of society. The thrust of its questioning is toward the material (especially economic) basis of society, and particularly the processes by which it determines the superstructure of social, legal and administrative institutions.

Since these assertions summarize the historical materialist approach to social theory, it follows that any geography of the public sector cannot avoid being a Marxist geography — in the sense of providing a fundamental critique of the social order of capitalist societies. However, this does *not* necessarily imply a socialist geography, which I take to be dedicated toward working for a radical alteration in social relations. I have no doubt that many scholars will take umbrage at my philosophical inconsistency, in suggesting that conservative methodologies, liberal idealists, marxists, socialists and others can co-exist peacefully under the public sector geography rubric. But these are early days for our paradigm, and I have little doubt that the explanatory power of certain models will prove themselves as time passes.

Department of Geography
McMaster University

BIBLIOGRAPHY

Bourne, L. S.: 1975, *Urban Systems: Strategies for Regulation*, Clarendon Press, Oxford.

Castells, M.: 1976, 'Theoretical Propositions for an Experimental Study of Urban Social Movements', in C. G. Pickvance (ed.), *Urban Sociology: Critical Essays*, Tavistock Publications, London.

Clark, G. and Dear, M.: 1976, 'Theory of the State in Urban Spatial Processes', Paper presented at the annual meeting of the Regional Science Association, Toronto.

Dahrendorf, R.: 1959, *Class and Class Conflict in Industrial Society*, Stanford University Press, California.

Dear, M.: 1976, 'Spatial Externalities in Locational Conflict', *London Papers in Regional Science* 7 (forthcoming).

Dear, M., Fincher, R. and Currie, L.: 1977, 'Measuring the External Effects of Public Programs', *Environment and Planning*, (forthcoming).

Harvey, D.: 1973, *Social Justice and the City*, Johns Hopkins Press, Baltimore.

Hollis, M. and Nell, E.: 1975, *Rational Economic Man: A Philosophical Critique of Neo-Classical Economics*, Cambridge University Press, London.

Lane, D.: 1971, *The End of Inequality?: Stratification Under State Socialism*, Penguin Books, Harmondsworth.

Levy, F. S., Meltsner, A. J. and Wildavsky, A.: 1974, *Urban Outcomes*, University of California Press, Berkeley.

Miliband, R.: 1973, *The State in Capitalist Society*, Quartet Books, London.

Miller, D.: 1976, *Social Justice*, Clarendon Press, Oxford.

Ostrom, V., Tiebout, D. M. and Warren, R.: 1961, 'The Organization of Government in Metropolitan Areas', *American Political Science Review* 55, 831–842.

Rawls, J.: 1971, *A Theory of Justice*, Harvard University Press, Cambridge.

Seley, J.: 1973, 'Paradigms and Dimensions of Urban Conflict', unpublished Ph.D. dissertation, University of Pennsylvania, Philadelphia, Pa.

Teitz, M. B.: 1968, 'Toward a Theory of Urban Public Facility Locations', *Papers, Regional Science Association* XXI, 38–51.

Wolpert, J., Mumphrey, A. J. and Seley, J.: 1972, 'Metropolitan Neighborhoods: Participation and Conflict Over Change', Commission on College Geography, Resource Paper No. 16, Association of American Geographers, Washington, D.C.

STEPHEN GALE AND MICHAEL ATKINSON

ON THE SET THEORETIC FOUNDATIONS OF
THE REGIONALIZATION PROBLEM

> Given a set of objects — they may be animals, plants
> people, central places or almost anything of interest
> in a research project — then the taxonomic problem
> in simplest terms is to arrange the objects into a
> system of classes on the basis of some measure-
> ments on the objects. The result is a classification.
> If the objects are areal units then the classification
> has produced 'regional types'. If, however, the
> arrangement of areal units has been carried out so
> as to allocate only contiguous areal units to the
> same class as 'region' then the solution is a regional-
> ization.
>
> SPENCE and TAYLOR (1970, p. 3)

I. INTRODUCTION[1]

1. It is one of the peculiarities of current practice in geography that, in the study of 'quantitative methods', far less attention has been given to the 'quantitative' part than to 'methods'. 'Quantitative' is assumed, roughly, to have something to do with numbers, numerically distinguished constructs, or measures in general; and with this assumption being made, a variety of numerically-based methods are simply adopted for use in the analysis of geographic problems. Indeed, at the height of the movement in the 1960's, the invocation of the phrase 'quantitative methods' was enough to ensure the acceptance of the validity of almost any measurement procedure as long as the analytical methods, *per se*, were correctly employed. Little scrutiny was made of the appropriateness of measurement scales or, more importantly, of the meaning and implications of using various kinds of models of measurement and classification. And although there has recently been some attention directed at problems of developing representation theorems for measurement models, as yet there has been very little by way of an examination of the foundations and general implications of the use of formal methods.

65

S. Gale and G. Olsson (eds.), Philosophy in Geography, 65–107. All Rights Reserved.
Copyright © 1979 by D. Reidel Publishing Company, Dordrecht, Holland.

While a general theory of the appropriate uses of formal methods in the analysis of empirical phenomena and their relationships is still in its formative stages, recent developments in logic and mathematics are beginning to have a number of important impacts on the structure and process of scientific description and reasoning. Thus, as Carnap's (1937 ed., p. 51) "Principle of Tolerance" has become (implicitly) a serious methodological consideration, we have begun to reexamine the foundations of measurement and inference procedures and, in general, to reassess the role of formal languages in the modelling process. In part the moves in this direction have been adoptive: new languages and methods are available and, for experimental purposes, they are used in a variety of contexts. More importantly, however, several of the changes in orientation have been based on failures by existing formalizations to account for specific classes of questions.

2. The aim of this paper is to summarize and extend some recent comments on the use of alternative formal models in the analysis of the regionalization problem. Though the focus will principally be concerned with set theoretic issues, the idea stems from a pragmatic concern with efficacy of the kinds of formal languages which have been used to describe geographic partitions and the ways in which these partitions, in turn, affect the outcomes of related analyses of geographic problems. The argument itself parallels a number of earlier discussions concerning the rationale of using non-classical formal languages[2] and the theory of fuzzy sets (Zadeh, 1965; Zadeh et al., 1975) to characterize the properties of regions and boundaries (Gale, 1976). Following from these discussions, then, the argument will be developed first (Sections 3–7) in terms of some general remarks on a language-based program for scientific inquiry and its implications for the development of alternative set-based models. The second step (Sections 8–22) will contrast the use of alternative set theories in the characterization of the notion of a 'region'. And the final step (Sections 29–32) will describe some practical implications of the use of alternative languages of description of inference; particular attention will be paid to their effect on the design (and legitimacy) of territorially-based voting procedures.

One additional point should be made at the outset. Though much of the argument is philosophically based, it should nevertheless be regarded primarily as a methodological device for analyzing the relative efficacy of language-based strategies for description and inference in practical circumstances. In itself, the discussion is not designed to provide direct clarification of any philosophic disputes (though it may do this). The intent is simply to characterize several linguistic and set-theoretic perspectives on 'region' and 'boundary' so as to provide a sufficiently rich operational basis for discussion of substantive issues.

II. SET BASED WORLDS AND THE MODELLING PROCESS

3. Though current social science lore has emphasized the development and testing of explanatory and predictive models in an effort to discern 'social laws', there have recently been strong counterarguments to the effect that these goals are, if not misplaced, certainly of limited scope.[3] To be sure, these claims have often been ideologically based, but they have at least provided a methodological conscience to what often are regarded as truisms. At heart, however, there is a gap between these perspectives: on one side there is a tradition of what has come to be viewed as scientific orthodoxy based on formal model-building using mathematical criteria of description and inference; and on the other side, there is a heterodox discursive tradition (often) combining historical, philosophical, and critical methods. The first is based largely on extensions of physical science paradigms while the second appears grounded in predominantly humanistic perspectives and ideals.

In effect, contemporary research programs on social science problems seem to be clustered around two sides of this conceptual gap. The formal, models-oriented, theory-testing crowd is on one side proclaiming that the true path has been found; the humanists, on the other side, have sought mainly to preserve the integrity of less formalized reasoning methods, to remind us that even truth is relative, and that there are important classes of questions that have been ignored by their opposite numbers. In a sense, it is a kind of debate in which there are neither commonly recognized grounds of dispute (i.e., in terms of the delineation and character of the conceptual gaps), nor even a reasonably good idea of what kinds of arguments would resolve the dispute.

What appears to have been ignored in this intellectual face-off is that there are pragmatically-related conceptions of scientific inquiry which can (potentially) give some structure to the ground between these seemingly disparate perspectives — at least in so far as they can delineate methodologies which are appropriate for different classes of questions. For example, one recent paper has described the basis for such a conception with in the framework of a logic of questions and answers (i.e., an erotetic logic).[4] The argument is quite simple: If we view science as a general question–answering process then, by virtue of the (say, linguistically determined) class of question (e.g., formation of names, definitions and measurements, alethic issues, value-based problems), methods of description and inference can be delineated for each such class. In this view, the gap between the positions described above is not so much one of 'in principle' differences as a claim for methodological heterogeneity and the need for an understanding of the appropriateness of specific methodological strategies in specific circumstances. In other words, there appear to be grounds for considering these seemingly disparate approaches in terms of a richer conception of the modelling process which does not regard truth (in the formal sense) as the only aim of inquiry.

4. The term 'model' has come to have about as many different meanings as there are people doing modelling.[5] Quite apart from the various functions (e.g., simplification and partitioning of problems), however, at its root a model is simply an expression in a given language: there are linguistic models of thought (e.g., natural languages), mathematical models of entitivity and relations (e.g., various set theories), physical models (e.g., reduced scale representations of streams, airfoils, etc.), and so on. Within the framework of a given language, a model provides a (usually simplified) representation of some fragment of concepts and/or phenomena. Of course, except for special abstract cases (e.g., those arising in connection with classical model theory), representational rules are rarely complete; they simply form conditions for satisfaction which (under some circumstances) provide the basis for successively better approximations.

More specifically, the modelling process may be (heuristically) conceived of as a question-answering system $\mathcal{Z} = (Q, M, G)$ consisting of a question (Q), an answer (or model M), and a generalized procedure (G) which describes (or prescribes) the relations between Q and M.[6] In particular

$$Q = ((?)S, P, L) \qquad \text{and}$$

$$M =_D (L, A, T, U, R_1, \ldots, R_n)$$

where $(?)S$ is an interrogative sentence (or proposition), L is a given (formal or natural) language, P is a set of presuppositions, A is a set of axioms (consisting specifically of the axioms of some set theory), T is a set of potential answers to (i.e., theories about) Q (as allowed by P), U is the (non-empty) universe of discourse, and $R_1, \ldots, R_n$ are relations on U.[7] G may be regarded as a sort of 'algorithm' which provides a context-dependent procedure for, say, the recursive elimination and substitution of unsatisfactory elements

$t_i \in T$, the identification of homomorphic representations, and so on. A more thorough going specification of G would involve a greater number of complex issues than can be dealt with here. For the present, the designation of rules of satisfaction and partial satisfaction is regarded as a metatheoretical issue, the solution to which is dependent (at least) on the nature of Q and the properties of **L**.

5. Clearly, this very abstract perspective on inquiry processes needs much more flesh than has been given here. For the present purposes, however, two points are of special importance. First, it should be noticed that the structure of $\mathfrak{Z}$ is dependent on its specification in a language, **L**. Questions, for example, arise and are phrased in (i.e., presuppose) a language; the language of answers (or models) must be comformable (in the sense that a response in some other language is not intelligible without explicit translation rules); and the relationships between Q and M, i.e., G, must be sufficiently rich to be able to represent (at least) the syntactic and semantic relationships of all sentences (propositions) within the inquiry process. Language, in a sense, is the concept which carries the principal epistemic force. Ideas and the object world itself are treated as *linguistically-based* entities (within a question–answering process); the reconstruction of ideas and the addition of new concepts (e.g., value-based propositions) are similarly regarded as being predicted on the formulation of the underlying linguistic structure.

The second point amends the first. Though we may agree that all thinking and communicating takes place in language, as Suppes (1970) and others have pointed out, models which are expressed solely in terms of even standard formal languages become not only impossible to axiomatize in many cases, but also operationally intractable. Thus, as a way of providing a fixed set of operational procedures, $\mathfrak{Z}$ also includes axioms for a set theory which is conformable with the structure of **L**, i.e., **A**; in special cases this, of course, provides a sufficient basis for the use of the usual mathematical operations and inference methods.

6. The world pictured in this view of the process of inquiry is thus a language and set based world: entities, their relations, and theories about them are all stated in and reasoned about in **L**, i.e., as part of a process of inter- and intra-personal communication. Ontologically, epistemologically, and operationally, the world is treated as a function of its (assumed) linguistic and set-theoretic character. Note, however, that although the language and set theory must be fixed for operational purposes, no *particular* language or set theory is

presupposed; as was noted above, this is in keeping with Carnap's (1937 ed., p. xv) "Principle of Tolerance":

... the view will be maintained that we have in every respect complete liberty with regard to the forms of language; that both the forms of construction for sentences and the rules of transformation (the latter are usually designated as 'postulates' and 'rules of inference') may be chosen quite arbitrarily. Up to now, in constructing a language, the procedure has usually been, first to assign a meaning to the fundamental mathematico-logical symbols, and then to consider what sentences or inferences are seen to be logically correct in accordance with this meaning .... The connection will only become clear when approached from the opposite direction: let any postulates and rules of inference be chosen arbitrarily; then this choice whatever it may be will determine what meaning is to be assigned to the fundamental logical symbols.

The choice made with respect to L and A thus not only influences the ideas we have about the world (say, in the sense that 'the elements of T are predicated on L'), but also the very structure of the universe of discourse and its relations: in effect, whether or not U and $R_1, \ldots, R_n$ have independent existence (a knotty philosophic problem), pragmatically they are treated (structured, reasoned about, and understood) in terms of the linguistic and set-theoretic character of the overall inquiry process.[8]

7. Now, this kind of transformation of the modelling process into a more general framework for the analysis of language-based structures may appear artificial or even extraneous. For a number of decades, the linguistic and set theoretic foundations of science have been almost universally treated as being equivalent with that of mathematics. (This is the so-called 'mathematics is the language of science' argument which was reified by the logical-empiricist movement.) But it is precisely this sort of intellectual move that has been successful in the history of physics (e.g., quantum mechanics and, to a lesser degree, relativity theory), where developments in mathematics and logic have generally gone hand-in-hand with the development of substantive theories.[9] The same has, of course, been true in other areas (e.g., ethics[10]), but the results have engendered far less general agreement. The point is quite simple, however, and amounts to a paraphrase of Nuel Belnap's (1967, pp. 27–28) reply to Herbert Simon's claim for the singular efficacy of existing mathematical structures: it may be "that when it comes to fundamental questions, there is no point asking the applied scientist *which* foundational questions are not worth asking, for from his point of view there are *no* foundational questions worth asking", but from the point of view of the scientist asking *new* classes of questions, it may also be that there are no questions *other than* foundational questions!

III. ASPECTS OF SET THEORY[11]

8. Thus far, only the rudiments of an operational program have been described. As it was presented, the modelling process, $\mathcal{Z}$, gains its epistemological force through the way in which **L** (in particular) is specified. In effect, the structure of each of the elements of the inquiry process depends on **L** for their principal characterization. Where **L** is a two-valued, classical, first-order functional logical calculus (with identity) and the set **A** contains axioms for a Boolean set theory (say, the Zermelo–Fraenkel axiomatization), then the interrogative statement (?)**S** and its presuppositions (**P**) must conform to **L**, the domain of the theories (**T**) can draw only on concepts which can be formulated in L and **A**, and even the universe of discourse (**U**) and its empirical relations ($R_1, \ldots, R_n$) must be 'based' on the same properties. Similarly, by changing **L**, say to a many-valued alethic or modal calculus, the structure of $\mathcal{Z}$ would have concomitant modifications – including the acceptability of different classes of interrogatives and observations.

A related, and in many ways operationally more satisfying position is to utilize the set-theoretic assumptions, **A**, as the principal analytic 'cut'.[12] That is, by examining the nature of alternative set theories, it should be possible to characterize and contrast their respective pragmatic implications by showing, first, their relationship to particular classes of languages and, second, their implications for the structure of observations and their relationships. To do this, however, we need to understand (even in an elementary sense) some of the details of set theory – and, to some extent, its historical development. We are too used to speaking about sets without understanding both what the term presupposes and what it entails.

9. If ever there was a paradise lost, it was the set theory of Cantor. Simple and elegant, the philosophical strength of Cantor's theory was in its appeal to intuitions about the nature of mathematical entities. In fact, the appeal is so strong that mathematicians still use the theory, even though it is known to contain certain very elementary paradoxes. Yet, as the appearance of agreement about the foundations of mathematics turned out to be illusory, acrimony grew over attempts to remedy the paradoxes. The fall of naive set theory, in effect, marked the rise in speculation on the unity of the foundations of mathematics.

Cantor himself never formalized set theory as an axiomatic system, but this was not really necessary since his system is based on only two assumptions and these are very easily understood. Known as the Axioms of Extensionality and Comprehension, the axioms (respectively) state (I) two sets are equal if and only if they have the same members, and (II) for any property applying to objects, there exists a set having as members just those objects which have that property. For the present purposes, it is crucial that the very fundamental role of the Comprehension Axiom be understood; in this regard, consider the following explication by Beth (1964 ed, p. 229):

(i)   Objects which have a certain property in common constitute a class, which is defined by that property and of which those objects are members;

(ij)   Classes are objects and hence they may in turn appear as members of a class;

(iij)   Classes which contain the same members are considered as identical; hence a class is uniquely determined by its members.

The reasoning clearly depends on one's intuitions about objects, properties, and membership; the spirit, however, is directly related to the need for a principle which characterizes mathematical entities unambiguously and 'crisply'. And though it is difficult to visualize at this point, the Comprehension Axiom plays a singularly important part in the paradoxes which arise in Cantorian set theory.

10. To see how these paradoxes arise in such a seemingly self-evident and intuitive system, we first need to note two principal results (due to Cantor). The first is developed as follows:

DEFINITION 1: For sets S and T, $/S/ \geqslant /T/ \leftrightarrow \exists \phi$ such that $\phi: S \to T$ is onto, i.e., $T = \{t \mid \exists s \in S, \phi(s) = t\}$.[13]

DEFINITION 2: $/S/ > /T/ \leftrightarrow /S/ \geqslant /T/ \ \& \ /T/ \not\geqslant /S/$.

DEFINITION 3: $2^S = \{\sigma \mid \sigma \subset S\}$.

Cantor's Theorem states that:

THEOREM A: $/2^S/ > /S/$ for any non-empty set S.
    Proof: First, we know that $/2^S/ \geqslant /S/$, since $\phi(\{x\}) = x$ and $\phi(X)$ arbitrary for non-singleton X is onto from $2^S \to S$, so $/2^S/ \quad /S/$. Now suppose that $/S/ \geqslant /2^S/$. Then there is a $\phi: S \to 2^S$ which is onto. Let $X = \{y \mid y \in S \ \& \ y \notin \phi(y)\}$. Since $X \subset S$, $X \in 2^S$, and there is some $x \in S$ such that $\phi(x) = X$.

It is apparent that $x \in X \to x \notin \phi(x) \to x \notin X$, and $x \notin X \to x \in \phi(x) \to x \in X$. The assumption that $/S/ \geqslant /2^S/$ has led to a contradiction, so we conclude that $/2^S/ > /S/$.

Two remarks are in order here. First, the intuition behind *Definition 1* is that the set S has greater cardinality than the set T just in case there is a way of assigning members of S to members of T in S. If, for example, S has m elements and T has n elements, $m \geqslant n$, and if we write $S = \{x_1, \ldots, x_m\}$ and $T = \{y_1, \ldots, y_n\}$, then we can assign x_1 to y_1, x_2 to y_2, $\ldots$, x_n to y_n, and whatever x_i's remain at will. Counting the number of elements of two finite sets can always be regarded as an assignment of this sort.

The other comment concerns the statement of *Theorem A*. Intuitively, it may be thought that the theorem ought to hold for the empty set as well, since $2^\phi = \{\phi\}$, and a set with one member would seem to be larger than a set with no members. Unfortunately, there is no function $f: 2^\phi \to \phi$, onto or not, because then we would have (i) $\phi \in 2^\phi$, and so (ii) $f(\phi) \in \phi$, which is plainly impossible, as ϕ has no members at all. For this reason, and because this same difficulty arises when trying to show $/X/ \geqslant /\phi/$ for any set X at all, *Definition 1* is sometimes modified to

DEFINITION 1': For sets S and T, $/S/ \geqslant /T/ \leftrightarrow T = \{f(x) \mid x \in S \ \& \ f: S \to T\}$ for some function f, or if $T = \phi$.

The second result due to Cantor is:

THEOREM B: $/R/ > /N/$, where R is the set of real numbers, and N is the set of natural numbers.

Proof: Suppose $f: N \to R$ is onto. For each n, let r_n be the decimal part of $f(n)$, and write $r_n = .r_{1n}r_{2n} \ldots$ as the decimal expansion of r_n. We know that $r_{mn} \subseteq \{0, 1, \ldots, 9\}$. Let $r = .r'_{11}r'_{22} \ldots$, where $r'_{ij} = r_{ij} + 1$ if $r_{ij} \neq 9$ and $r'_{ij} = 0$ if $r_{ij} = 9$. It is clear that $r \in R$, but r is not in the image of f, since for every n, $f(n)$ is different from r in the nth decimal place. Hence, $/R/ > /N/$

11. The paradoxes of Cantor's set theory are traditionally classified into two categories: the logical antinomies and the semantic antinomies. By way of illustration, two of each will be mentioned here.[14]

The logical antinomies. (i) Cantor's paradox. Consider the set of all sets, V. Then $2^V \subset V$, whence $/2^V/ \leqslant /V/$. This contradicts *Theorem A*. (ii) Russell's paradox is even simpler. Let $X = \{x \mid x \notin x\}$. Then $X \in X \leftrightarrow X \notin X$. The word 'paradox', suggesting, as it does, the possibility of a remedy, may be psychologically less damaging than the word 'contradiction', but if one accepts classical set theory, and if one reasons by classical mathematical methods, one is forced to accept such conclusions.

The semantic antinomies. (i) The first of the semantic paradoxes, Richard's antinomy, is of particular importance because of the way it mimics Cantor's diagonalization method. Let R be the set of all real numbers characterizable by English sentences of finite length. There are only countably many of these, so they may be ordered as $r_1, r_2, \ldots$, as before. In similar manner, construct $r = r'_{11} r'_{22} \ldots$. Both $r \in R$ and $r \notin R$ must therefore hold. It should be observed that this is not a true paradox, because $r \in R$ cannot be obtained in a rigorous development. It is interesting to note, however, that historically, Richard's paradox was the inspiration for the method of proof of Godel's famous incompleteness theorem. (ii) The other semantic antinomy takes the form of a statement "I am lying" — which is true if and only if it is false.

12. The antinomies suggest that something is awry with the intuitions underlying the Comprehension Axiom, i.e., that to every property there corresponds the set of just those objects having that property. Russell (1938, pp. 102–103; 20), for example, was apparently fully aware of the relationship between his paradox and the Comprehensive Axiom. As he puts it,

the reason that a contradiction emerges here is that we have taken it as an axiom that any propositional function containing only one variable is equivalent to asserting membership of a class defined by the propositional function. Either this axiom, or the principle that every class can be taken as one term, is plainly false ... If ϕx and Ψy are equivalent propositions for all values of x, then the class of x's such that ϕx is true is identical with the class of x's such that Ψy is true.

The problem then seems to be one of revising the ontological foundation of the Comprehension Axiom (what we shall call a 'naive reconstruction') or devising further axioms which restrict the conditions under which sets are introduced which subsequently lead to paradoxes (the 'mathematical reconstruction'). The thrust of much of the past half century's work on axiomatic set theory has been directed at the problems concerned with giving a sufficient mathematical reconstruction of the axioms of set theory.

Two approaches have been used in mainstream mathematics: (i) allow only those properties which do not violate a certain principle or principles; or (ii) allow only those properties which can be built up via the use of a particular system of rules. This is the main bifurcation in conventional set theory, with **type** theory representing the first approach and the axiomatic treatments (due to Zermelo–Fraenkel and to Godel–von Neumann–Bernays) representing the second. As we shall see, however, neither approach has been entirely satisfying, nor have they attempted to address the important issues which lie at the heart of the naive reconstruction, i.e., our intuitions about objects, properties, and membership. Notably, these issues also lie at the heart of the same problem when approached from the language-based point of view.

Notwithstanding this very general question, it is of considerable importance that the main lines of the mathematical reconstructionist approaches to the recent development of axiomatic set theory be understood. To do this, however, we first need to introduce one additional technical point concerning the (so-called) Axiom of Choice.

13. In the course of the 'post-paradox' development of set theory, it was found that a number of seemingly harmless theorems were being lost. One additional axiom had the property that the theory obtained by conjoining it to the rest of the axioms recovered most of these results, so that the set theory so derived looked very much like the Cantorian set theory, save that none of the known paradoxes could be obtained. Furthermore, the axiom had no serious competition: the alternatives suggested have either turned out to be equivalent, or very closely related. The axiom, known as the Axiom of Choice (AC), asserts the following:

AXIOM OF CHOICE: If A is a set of non-empty disjoint sets, then there exists a set B having exactly one element from each member of A, i.e., $x \in B \to \exists A_i \in A$, $x \in A_i$, and $A_i \in A \to \exists! x \in B$, $x \in A_i$. Several dozen logically equivalent forms of this axiom are known.[15] Nevertheless, intense controversy has raged over its acceptability, largely because of its inherently nonconstructive nature. Despite the belief of Fraenkel et al. (1973, p. 68) that "the majority of the attacks on the axiom of choice have derived from not appreciating its *purely existential character*", the justification of the axiom is a tangled argument. The nature of mathematical existence is far from clear, and the extent to which the AC is a reasonable proposition is very much dependent on one's philosophical position.

14. We begin our discussion of the mathematical reconstruction of set theory with some general remarks on the two 'mainstream' approaches: (i) type theory and (ii) axiomatization.

(i) According to a (caricatured) type theorist, the source of all the paradoxes of set theory lies in a rather subtle fallacy of sentence formation.

Specifically, in every known antimony, a self-reference takes place which gives rise to a circularity of definition. For example, in Russell's paradox, the set $X = \{x \mid x \notin x\}$ plays a central role. But whether $x \in y$ can be expected to hold depends on the object x first, and then the object y. If x and y are the same object, we are limited to a kind of simultaneity inconsistent with a priority on x. The set X is not a set because '$x \notin x$' is not a property; indeed, the argument goes, '$x \notin x$' is not even a sentence. The solution is to define a hierarchy of 'types' of variables. More specifically, let any variable x_{ij} have the interpretation that i is the 'level' of x_{ij} and j distinguishes it from other variables of level i. Both the first and second subscripts are assumed to be ordered, so that for distinct k and k', either $k < k'$ or $k' < k$, and the operation 'adding one' is assumed to be meaningful. This modification of Cantor's theory, the *ramified class calculus*, thus provides the basis for the following form of the Comprehension Axiom:

If ϕ is a formula free only in x_{ij}, such that $k = \max\{i, j\}$, then
$\exists y_{i+1, k+1} x_{i,j} (x_{ij} \in y_{i+1, k+1} \leftrightarrow \phi(x_{ij}))$.

A number of versions of type theory exist, which will be discussed below.

(ii) In distinction to the procedure of disallowing certain forms of propositions, it is possible to also replace the Comprehension Axiom by a collection of rules guaranteeing the existence of certain elementary sets from those already proved to exist. The axiom system of Zermelo and Fraenkel (AZ) works on this principle; they can be classified as follows:

(a) Extensionality.
(b) Axioms guaranteeing the existence of sets;
    1. pairing,
    2. infinity.
(c) Axioms for building new sets;
    1. union,
    2. power set,
    3. subsets,
    4. replacement.
(d) Axiom of foundation.

A related approach, Godel–von Neumann–Bernay's (GNB) class theory, takes a set theory as its base (in this case, ZF) and adds an *axiom of comprehension for classes*. Class variables are assumed to be a different category of variables than set variables; and an object cannot be both a set and a class. Strictly speaking, if X is a set and Y is a class variable, $X = Y$ is not a formula, although equality is often defined in an extensional sense.[16] For example, for the set variable X and the class variables Y and Z, of $X \in Y$, $Y \in X$, and $Y \in Z$ only the first is a formula. The Comprehension Axiom for classes varies from one theory to another — in fact, this is usually the distinguishing feature — but usually takes the following form:

COMPREHENSION AXIOM FOR K CLASS THEORY: if ϕ is any property satisfying the requirement K, there exists a class whose members are just those *sets* satisfying ϕ.

The condition K usually has to do with quantification over class variables and similar issues. The point of this is to be able to talk about collections of sets in a precise way without having to confer sethood on the collection.

It would be difficult to over-estimate the impact of these two methods of avoiding the antinomies. The type theorist begins with the idea of avoiding self reference in set definition; what results is a complex hierarchy of variables which is often unwieldy in practice and, just as often, as incongrous to the intuition as impredicative set definition. And, though the avoidance of certain kinds of self reference and the stratification of objects into types are separate questions, thus far they have not proven to be easily separable. Stratification, moreover, adds a stronger bias towards a constructive view of set theory than an avoidance of self-reference alone would strictly indicate.

15. The tendency to think of sets as being built up inherent in type theory has been minor compared with the move toward the sort of axiomitizations proposed (respectively) as ZF and GNB. Here, certain very elementary sets are assumed to exist, and nothing else is a set unless it can be derived from the primitive sets via a small number of specific kinds of operations. Since the primitive sets have the feel of a real 'collection' of 'objects', and since the set operations give the sensation of actually manipulating sets, there is a definite impression left that one is 'making sets' involved in the use of such a theory.

As is pointed out above, the axioms of ZF fall into four categories: the axiom of extensionality, two axioms of existence, four set operation axioms (not counting AC) and the technical axiom of foundation. We will first present discussions of each of these categories of axioms and then discuss the axioms themselves.

The axiom of extensionality says that two sets are equal if and only if (*iff*) they have the same members. Because sets are not distinguished from other kinds of objects, a consequence of this axiom is that there are no individuals, i.e., no objects different from the null set which have no members. The extension of a 'thing' is the range of other 'things' to which it bears a certain predetermined relation, in this case, 'being a member of'. In effect, the axiom asserts that a set is strictly determined by its extension.

The axioms of pairing and infinity guarantee the existence of sets having, respectively, two (not necessarily distinct) elements, and an infinite number of elements. More specifically, the pairing axiom states that for any two elements of a set x and y, there is a z such that if $a \in z, a = x$ or $a = y$. Denote such a z by $z = \{x, y\}$. Observe that, by a double application of the pairing axiom, we can construct sets of the form $\{x, \{x, y\}\}$. This set has the property that it is an *ordered pair*, viz $(x, y) = (x', y') \leftrightarrow x = x'$ and $y = y'$. It is customary to denote the set $\{x, \{x, y\}\}$ by (x, y), called an ordered pair; and an ordered $n + 1$-tuple is defined by $(x_1, \ldots, x_n, x_{n+1}) = \{(x_1, \ldots, x_n), \{(x_1, \ldots, x_n), x_{n+1}\}\}$. A *function* is a set F of ordered pairs such that (x, y'), $(x, y) \in F \rightarrow y = y'$. The *domain* and *range* of F are the sets of first and second elements, respectively. If the domain of F is D, and $E \subset D$, the restriction of F to E, call it F_E, is the subset of F such that $(x, y) \in F$ is in F_E iff $x \in E$. F is *onto* a set S iff S is the range of F; F is *into* S iff the range of F is contained in S. A set X has *power at least as great as* a set Y iff there exists a function with domain X and onto Y. Functions are thus treated as special cases of *relations*; a relation is any set of ordered pairs. Finally, an *infinite* set is one which has a proper subset of power at least as great as itself. That is to say, a set X is infinite iff there exists a set Y such that $Y \subset X$ and $X \neq Y$, and a function F with domain Y and range X. The axiom of infinity thus asserts that there exists an infinite set; a number of forms of this axiom exist which, given the rest of the axioms of ZF, turn out to be equivalent.

The axioms of pairing and infinity are the only axioms we have guaranteeing the existence of any sets. Except for the axiom of foundation, or regularity, the remaining axioms tell us only that certain sets exist *given that* certain other sets have been shown to exist. These axioms say, briefly, that we may take the union and power set of a family of sets, that any property determines a subset of a given set, and that we may replace some of the elements of a set and still have a set.

UNION: Let A be any set. There exists a set B such that $x \in B$ iff there exists $X \in A$ such that $x \in X$. This is the axiom of union, or sum-set, and we write $B = \cup A$. To get the conventional $X \cup Y$, we let $B = \{X, Y\}$ and define $X \cup Y = \cup B$.

POWER SET: Let **A** be any set. There exists a set **A'** of all the subsets of **A**: **A'** is called the power set of **A**. Note that because we have not yet had the axiom of subsets, this axiom by itself does not tell us very much. Cantor's theorem, for example, cannot be proved without the next axiom.

SUBSET: Let **A** be any set. If ϕ is any property, $\mathbf{A}_\phi = \{x \mid \phi(x) \& x \in \mathbf{A}\}$ exists. We require that A_ϕ not be free in ϕ. Observe that when ϕ involves the power set of **A**, this axiom is impredicative. No contradictions are known to arise from this sort of set definition, but it is essentially non-constructivist. Note that the proof of Cantor's Theorem (Theorem A) now goes through.

AXIOM OF REPLACEMENT: Let **X** be a set, and Ψ be a formula with two free variables. We call Ψ a *functional condition* on **X** iff for every $x \in \mathbf{X}$ there exists at most one object y such that $\Psi(x, y)$ is true. The axiom of replacement asserts that there exists a set **Y** such that $y \in \mathbf{Y} \leftrightarrow \exists x \in \mathbf{X} \colon \Psi(x, y)$. Note, however, that the following formulation is *not* equivalent: if **X** is a set and **F** is a function with domain **D**, then the image of $\mathbf{X} \cap \mathbf{D}$ is a set. It is the axiom of replacement and the axiom of infinity which allow us to show the existence of a set isomorphic to the natural numbers, which, by Gödel's incompleteness theorem, implies that ZF cannot be proved consistent.

AXIOM OF FOUNDATION: The last axiom of ZF, the axiom of foundation, is one which is seldom used in normal mathematics. Its usual function is to allow us to derive a contradiction from a particular construction which surfaces from time to time in set theory proper. What we wish to exclude is the possibility of sequences such as the following:

$$\ldots y_3 \in y_2 \in y_1.$$

For any property ϕ such that there exists an object x such that $\phi(x)$ holds, there exists a y such that $\phi(y)$ is true and $z \in y \rightarrow \neg \phi(z)$. It is possible to show, using this axiom, that all sets are well-founded, which is to say, that the kind of sequence we wanted to avoid is indeed disallowed.

The justification for including the axiom of foundation is somewhat obscure. In the interest of definitiveness one is often concerned with excluding deviant constructions and it can be argued that the idea of a set is one which should be built up from members, i.e., so that members determine the set rather than having the members being identified by the fact of their being in the set. If the world is conceived of as falling into layers, as in type theory, this problem is obviated by the existence of a 'bottom layer'. But without the type theorist's perspective, there doesn't appear to be much to be said which makes this axiom clear and obvious.

In the interest of completeness, we list the following axioms of ZF:

I. Extensionality.
$$x = y \leftrightarrow \forall x: z \in x \leftrightarrow z \in y$$

II. Existence axioms.
A. Pairing.
$$\forall x, y, \exists z \forall a: a \in z \leftrightarrow a = y \vee a = x$$
B. Infinity.
$$\exists x, y, F: x \subset y \ \& \ x \neq y \ \& \ F \text{ is a function from } x \text{ onto } y$$

III. Set operations.
A. Union.
$$\forall x, \exists y \forall z: z \in y \leftrightarrow \exists w: w \in x \ \& \ z \in w$$
B. Power set.
$$\forall x \exists y \forall z: z \in y \leftrightarrow z \subset x$$
C. Subsets (separation).
For any condition ϕ free only in $x, \forall a \exists y \forall x: x \in y \leftrightarrow (x \in a \ \& \ \phi(x))$
D. For any functional condition Ψ on a free only in two variables, $\exists x \forall y: y \in x \leftrightarrow \exists z: z \in a \ \& \ \Psi(z, y)$

IV. Axiom of foundation.
For any condition ϕ free only in $x, \exists \imath: \phi(a), \rightarrow \exists x: \phi(x) \ \& \ \forall y: y \in x \rightarrow \neg \phi(y)$.

16. GNB class theory adds to the language of ZF a new kind of variable. It is not just that a class X is something which satisfies a classhood predicate, such as $cl(X)$, while the set X satisfies the predicate $set(X)$; rather, X and X are variables belonging to different categories of the underlying language. We denote the categories of class and set variables by C and S, respectively. For a unary predicate P, we will need a rule to tell us whether or not to count '$P(x)$' as a meaningful statement or not, depending on whether x is of category C or S. One way to do this is to let V_P be a subset of $\{C, S\}$, and allow $P(x)$ to be a formula just in case x is of a category in V_P. Though this way of stating this property is a bit pedantic for unary predicates, the usage extends nicely to n-ary predicates. Let R be an n-place predicate. We assume V_R is a subset of $\{C, S\}^n$, the n-fold cross product of $\{C, S\}$. Then $R(x_1, \ldots, x_n)$ is a formula

iff $(t_1, \ldots, t_n) \in V_R$, where t_i is C or S according to whether x_i is of category C or S, respectively. In Bernay's formulation of class theory, there were, in fact, two membership relations, 'ϵ' and 'η', such that $V_\epsilon = \{(S, S)\}$ and $V_\eta = \{(S, C)\}$.

The modifications of ZF made by GNB were twofold: first, with respect to the introduction of the axioms of class extensionality and predicative class comprehension, and second by the substitution of the three axiom schemas of subset, replacement, and foundation with single axioms which use classes in the role of conditions. The axiom of class extensionality asserts that $X = Y \leftrightarrow \forall X: X \in X \leftrightarrow X \in Y$. Thus, we define a formula ϕ to be a predicative condition iff it is free only in one variable, where that variable is a set variable, and ϕ contains no quantifiers over class variables, i.e., there is no sequence of symbols in ϕ of the form $\forall X$ or $\exists X$ for any class variable X. The axiom schema is thus:

PREDICATIVE CLASS COMPREHENSION (PCC): If ϕ is any predicative condition which does not mention X, then there exists a class X such that $X = \{X: \phi(X)\}$, which is to say, $\forall X: X \in X \leftrightarrow \phi(X)$.

The axiom schemas of ZF are reduced to single axioms in the following manner:

(1)   The axiom of subsets.
       $\forall X \forall X \exists Y \forall Z: Z \in Y \leftrightarrow Z \in X \ \& \ Z \in X$

(2)   The axiom of replacement.
       Given that a class function is defined in the usual way, we then have $\forall F \forall X \exists Y \forall Z_1: F$ is a function $\rightarrow Z_1 \in Y \leftrightarrow \exists Z_2: Z_2 \in X \ \&$ $(Z_1, Z_2) \in F$ (that is, $Z_1 = F(Z_2)$).

(3)   The axiom of foundation
       $\forall X \exists X: X \in X \rightarrow \exists Y \forall Z: Y \in X \ \& \ (Z \in Y \ \& \ Z \notin X)$.

The axiom schema of predicative comprehension can be reduced to eleven separate axioms, so that GNB can be characterized by finitely many axioms. These axioms are difficult to use and the usual procedure is to prove PCC as a theorem and proceed as before.

Part of the motivation for introducing classes is to avoid the constant use of the metamathematical notion of a condition. If class theory is to succeed in this endeavor, we must have that the purely set theoretic part of class theory is not changed in any essential way. The intention of class theory is to make set theory smoother, not different. The following theorem speaks to this issue:

THEOREM: If Ψ is any sentence in the language underlying GNB which does not involve classes, i.e., if Ψ is a string of symbols $\Psi_1, \ldots, \Psi_n$ such that for $i = 1, \ldots, n$, Ψ_i is not a class variable or constant, then Ψ is proveable in GNB iff it is proveable in ZF.

It is an immediate corollary of this theorem that GNB is consistent iff ZF is consistent.

17. ZF and GNB clearly play central roles in the mathematical treatment of sets, but the position is not unrivalled. Type theory, for example, is every bit as vigorous; in fact, its only drawback in actual use seems to be its notational complexity. Even in the case of Russell's theory, where all the variable subscripts are dropped in favor of a policy of 'typical ambiguity', it is necessary to keep track mentally of all the relationships among the types of variables.

Leaving aside purely practical considerations, however, two points are ordinarily brought up in the comparison of type theory with GNB. One, made by advocates, is that the axioms of type theory look much more similar to Cantorian set theory, in the sense that we have only an axiom of extensionality and an axiom of abstraction in the theory, say, of ramified types. The other, made by detractors, is that the world is not structured in layers, a difficult proposition to refute – or confirm!

Again, in the interest of clarity, we will describe, briefly, modern type theory. Define types and levels as follows:

(a1)   0 is a type.

(a2)   If $t_1, \ldots, t_n$ are types, $t = (t_1, \ldots, t_n)$ is a type.

(a3)   Nothing but finite applications of (1) and (2) is a type.

(b1)   The level of "0" is 0.

(b2)   The level of $t = (t_1, \ldots, t_n)$ is $1 + \max \{$level of $t_i | i = 1, \ldots, n\}$.

Predicates have arities, defined as follows:

(c1)   0 is an arity.

(c2)   If t is a type, (t) is an arity.

(c3)   If $t = (t_1, \ldots, t_n)$ is a type, $(t, t_1, \ldots, t_n)$ is an arity.

(c4)   Nothing but finite applications of (1), (2), and (3) is an arity.

Clearly, an arity can be written as a sequence $a = (t_1, \ldots, t_k)$. We say that such an arity as a is of length k. Every predicate is presumed to have an arity associated with it. Type theory admits into the language as proper formulae only those formulae which are *stratified*. A formula is stratified iff every variable and constant occurs only at places of the same type.

An example is in order at this point. Define the types $t_1 = (0)$ and $t_2 = (0, (0), 0)$ and the arities $a_1 = 0$, $a_2 = (t_1, 0)$ and $a_3 = (t_2, 0, t_1, 0)$. A predicate of arity a_1 is treated as a constant. If P and Q are predicates of arity a_2 and a_3, respectively, then $\forall x \forall y \forall z \ [Q(x,y,z,y) \leftrightarrow P(z,y)]$ is a stratified formula, while $\forall w \forall x \forall y \forall z \ [Q(w,x,z,y) \leftrightarrow P(z,y)]$ is not, because w appears both in positions of type 0 and type t_2. If we interpret '$x \in y$' formally as '$\in (y,x)$', then '$\in$' is a system of predicates, each of arity $((t), t)$, where t is of length one. It is enough, usually, to consider only the types $((0), 0)$ and a few more layers for most applications. The matter is less trivial for the theory of sets itself, of course. Indeed, the foregoing theory of types, with axioms of extensionality and abstraction added on, is essentially an extension of the theory presented in the *Principia Mathematica*, where a good portion of classical mathematics was subsequently developed. The more general theory we have outlined here has additional uses. It forms, for example, an integral part of non-standard analysis (Robinson, 1972).

18. In the midst of all of this very hard-headed view of sets, what should be apparent at this point is that the heart of the program of set theory is bound up with Cantor's original 'naive' conceptions — and particularly his perspective on the formation of sets through the Comprehension Axiom. In a sense, the whole of the move toward both the axiomatic and type theoretical treatments may be understood as a way of formalizing Cantor's program and ridding it of some of the problems which led to paradoxes.

It should be immediately recognized that Cantor's program and its later developments were at once moves toward providing a consistent basis for mathematics and the identification and characterization of mathematical entities. The idea, in effect, was to develop a form of 'language' which, in accord with prescribed inference procedures, could be a sufficiently strong basis for many aspects of mathematics. For its part, the program was successful, but with the success came an almost inevitable recognition of the limitations of the approach. Thus, whereas one could avoid certain internally generated antinomies, there are external problems concerning the application of set theory. What does it mean to speak of a set of subatomic particles whose joint probability of a particular position and velocity is x? What does it mean to speak of the set of all people in a neighborhood, or the set of all working class men, or the set of all books on medical geography? Here the problem is not one of paradox, but of the applicability (or, perhaps, appropriateness) of Cantorian sets, sets (in a way) 'created' by the Comprehension Axiom. It is, in Carnap's sense, a 'language' chosen freely, but perhaps a 'language' which does not represent the nature of the entities which are under consideration.

We will return to this issue below. For the moment, it is important only to recognize that the kind of set theory we have thus far presented is a means for speaking about very special kinds of objects and relationships — mathematical entities — and that other kinds of set theories can be developed for different purposes. The remaining sections on set theories will provide a sketch of some of these alternatives.

19. In this regard, we will first look at the principal rival to Cantorian set theory and, indeed, to all of classical mathematics — the intuitionist point of view. While both the formalist and the intuitionist approaches call themselves 'mathematics', the meaning that each attaches to the term is quite different. Heyting (1956, p. 4), for example, states that:

I must protest against the assertion that intuitionism starts from definite, more or less arbitrary assumptions. Its object, constructive mathematical thought, determines uniquely its premises and places it beside, not interior to, classical mathematics, which studies another subject, whatever subject that may be.

Contrast this position with that of the formalist, i.e., one who takes mathematics to be the manipulation of certain signs according to particular rules. The signs need have no further significance than their shape on the page, and any rules comprehensible by the human mind are admissible. A formalist who is also of a Platonistic bent may, in addition, choose to regard the symbols he is using as representing a universe of some sort governed by the same or analogous rules he is using on the symbols, though this is purely optional. But this point also leads to a crucial difference. The nominalist, i.e., the formalist who does not regard the marks he makes on the paper as indicative of a universe somewhere, denies the meaningfulness of the question. 'What is the nature of mathematical existence?' beyond some possible inscription, called an existence operator, which might appear in the formal language he is using.

The intuitionist disagrees with both the formalist and the nominalist on the grounds that the responses of both contain a false presupposition, viz., that mathematical reasoning takes place in the language employed. Language, it is argued, is only a tool for communicating reasoning, and perhaps a crutch for making it easier to learn and exercise. But thinking is an operation of the literal mind, unsullied by words, particular logical systems, and 'rules'. He answers all such problems with the question, 'Has it been constructed?' As Brouwer (1913, p. 67) puts it, "The question where mathematical exactness does exist is answered differently by the two sides; the intuitionist says: in the human intellect, the formalist says: on paper". What might be called the logic of intuitionism is thus nothing more than a collection of principles which have been observed to be true about the way in which mental constructions are effected. Intuition is reasoning itself, as apart from any reconstruction of its logic, consists of actual mental constructions, and of the construction of algorithms for carrying constructions out.

Indeed intuitionistic assertions must seem dogmatic to those who read them as assertions about facts, but they are not meant in this sense. Intuitionistic mathematics consists . . . in mental constructions; a mathematical theorem expresses a purely empirical fact, namely the success of a certain construction. '2 + 2 = 3 + 1' must be read as an abbreviation for the statement: "I have effected the mental constructions indicated by '2 + 2' and by '3 + 1' and I have found that they lead to the same result'. Now tell me where the dogmatic element can come in; not in the mental construction itself, as is clear by its very nature as an activity, but no more in the statements made about constructions, for they express purely empirical results (Heyting, 1956, p. 8).

The meat of intuitionist mathematics lies in its particular substantive claims of ontology. We perceive time, says the intuitionist, in discrete chunks, which has, as a consequence, an understanding of the abstract notions of 'one' and of 'adding one'. Thus justifies the use of at least these two concepts in mathematical reasoning.

This neo-intuitionism considers the falling apart of moments of life into qualitatively different parts, to be reunited only while remaining separated by time, as the fundamental phenomenon of the human intellect, passing by abstracting from its emotional content into the fundamental phenomenon of mathematical thinking, the intuition of the bare two-oneness. This intuition of two-oneness, the basal intuition of mathematics, creates not only the numbers two and one, but also all finite ordinal numbers, inasmuch as one of the elements of the two-oneness may be thought of as a new two-oneness, which process may be repeated indefinitely; this gives rise still further to the smallest infinite ordinal number ω. Finally, this basal intuition of mathematics, in which the connected and the separate, the continuous and the discrete are united, gives rise immediately to the intuition of the linear continuum, i.e., of the 'between', which is not exhaustable by the interposition of new units and which therefore can never be thought of as a mere collection of units (Brouwer, 1913, p. 69).

To concretize these rather abstract philosophical considerations, we will outline a portion of intuitionist mathematics. In doing so, we will borrow heavily from Heyting's *Intuitionism: An Introduction*, especially Chapters II and III. Since it is intuitionist set theory we are really after, our policy will be to pick out what is needed for the central ideas of 'spread' and 'species' in the development of sets.

It is supposed that we know what the natural numbers are. This assumption is claimed to be based on the primordial intuition; certain facts concerning the natural numbers can be verified by direct observation, including Peano's axioms. The integers and the rationals are developed in the usual way: a negative integer is a mathematical object, called '$-p$' where p is a positive integer, i.e., natural number, such that $p + (-p) = 0$, a rational number is an object 'p/q', where p and q are integers, and the arithmetic operations are defined by $p/q + r/s = (sp + rq)/sq$ and $(p/q) \cdot (r/s) = pr/qs$, and where $p/q \leqslant r/s$ iff $ps \leqslant qr$. Also, as a consequence of the primordial intuition, it is assumed that the notion of a sequence is understood. In particular, we will allow ourselves to think of an *infinitely proceeding sequence* (abbreviated *ips*) as a mathematical entity, and write $\{a_n\}$ for it, where the a_n are the elements of the sequence.

An *ips* of rationals $a = \{a_n\}$ is called *Cauchy* iff for every natural number k, there is a natural number p such that, for every natural number q, $|a_p - a_{p+q}| < 1/k$. Given k, p must be, in principle, calculable. A Cauchy sequence is also called a real number generator. Two such generators a and b are *congruent* iff for every natural number k, we can find p such that $|a_{p+q} - b_{p+q}| < 1/k$ for every natural number q. Congruence, as defined, is thus an equivalence relation. If a and b are real number generators, then a *lies apart from* b iff we can find natural numbers p and k such that $|a_{p+q} - b_{p+q}| < 1/k$ for every q. We write '$\simeq$' for 'is congruent to' and '$\neq$' for 'lies apart from'.

To get a feel for intuitionist reasoning, we prove the following theorem, which Heyting credits to Brouwer:

THEOREM: If a cannot lie apart from b, then $a \simeq b$

Proof: Find p such that $|a_{p+q} - a_p| < \frac{1}{4}k$ and $|b_{p+q} - b_p| < \frac{1}{4}k$ for every q. Suppose $|a_p - b_p| > 1/k$. Then $|a_{p+q} - b_{p+q}| = |(a_{p+q} - a_p) + a_p - (b_{p+q} - b_q) + b_q| \geqslant |a_p - b_p| - |a_{p+q} - a_p| - |b_{p+q} - b_p| > 1/k - \frac{1}{4}k - \frac{1}{4}k$. This implies that a and b lie apart. But the hypothesis of the theorem is that this leads to a contradiction, whence $a = b$.

Note that classically we could have merely argued that the lack of existence of p and k in the definition of '$\neq$' implies '$\simeq$' directly.

We are now ready to discuss the intuitionist notions of 'spread' and 'species'. These play roughly the same role in intuitionist mathematics as 'set' assumes in classical mathematics. While a spread is not intended to represent the totality of its elements, it fulfills some of the functions of a set. For example, we would normally take the real numbers to be equivalence classes on the real number generators under the relation of conguence. While a spread is not intended to represent the totality of its elements, it fulfills some of the functions of a set. For example, we would normally take the real numbers to be equivalence classes on the real number generators under the relation of congruence. Intuitionistically, we would be inclined to define a real number as a certain spread of Cauchy sequences. The set of real numbers would be the species of such spreads.

A spread is a spreadlaw, together with a complementary law. The spreadlaw governs the choice of natural numbers which are allowable for the continuation of sequences of natural numbers. The complementary law determines an object to correspond to every finite sequence allowed by the spreadlaw. We quote Heyting (1956, pp. 34, 35) in giving the definitions in more detail.

DEFINITION 1: A *spreadlaw* is a rule Λ which divides the finite sequences of natural numbers into admissible and inadmissible sequences, according to the following prescriptions:

(1) It can be decided by Λ for every natural number k whether it is a one-number admissible sequence or not;

(2) Every admissible sequence $a_1, \ldots, a_n, a_{n+1}$ is an immediate descendant of an admissible sequence $a_1, \ldots, a_n$;

(3) If an admissible sequence $a_1, \ldots, a_n$ is given, Λ allows us to decide for every natural number k whether $a_1, \ldots, a_n, k$ is an admissible sequence or not.

(4) To any admissible sequence $a_1, \ldots, a_n$ at least one natural number k can be found such that $a_1, \ldots, a_n, k$ is an admissible sequence.

DEFINITION 2: The *complementary law* Γ_M of a spread M assigns a definite mathematical entity to any finite sequence which is admissible according to the spreadlaw of M.

It is necessary also to define an element of a spread. Let $\{a_n\}$ be an *ips* of natural numbers, and $a^n = a_1, \ldots, a_n$. Call $\{a_n\}$ an admissible *ips* iff every a^n is admissible. Let b_n be the object assigned to a^n. Any such sequence $\{b_n\}$

is an element of the spread. Two elements of a spread $\{a_n\}$ and $\{b_n\}$ are equal iff $a_n = b_n$ for every n. Two spreads A and B are congruent, $A = B$, whenever $\{a_n\} \in A$ iff $\{a_n\} \in B$. If we define spreads $A = (\Lambda_A, \Gamma_A)$ and $B = (\Lambda_B, \Gamma_B)$ to be equal iff Λ_A and Λ_B are the same, and Γ_A and Γ_B are the same, then it would be easy enough to contrive examples of spreads which are congruent, but not equal. Hence, spreads have an intentional character.

The most important result on spreads is the fan theorem, on which much of intuitionist analysis depends. Define a spread A to be finitary, or a fan, iff the spreadlaw of A is such that (i) only a finite number of one member sequences are admissible and (ii) for every admissible finite sequence a^n, there are only a finite number of natural numbers k such that a^n, k is admissible. The fan theorem is now stated as:[17]

THEOREM: If $f(\{a_n\})$ is an integer valued function defined on every $\{a_n\} \in A$ for a finitary spread A, then a natural number N can be computed from the definition of f such that if $\{a_n\}$, $\{b_n\} \in A$ and $n < N$ implies $a_n = b_n$, then $f(\{a_n\}) = f(\{b_n\})$.

It is a myth that intuitionism is a strictly weaker system than classical mathematics. This is true if intuitionism is taken to be a logical calculus of the type proposed by Heyting. But the constructive point of view has its strengths, too, which are not captured in the calculi. The following remarkable theorem, a fairly direct application of the fan theorem, expresses a proposition for which it is easy to give a counter-example from the classical point of view:[18]

THEOREM: If I is a closed interval of the reals, and $F: I \rightarrow R$ is real valued, then F is uniformly continuous.

Nowhere in the hypothesis of the theorem is anything said about the continuity of F. Because, however, we are dealing with an intuitionist system, it is implicitly assumed that F is constructible. The theorem may be interpreted to mean that, on a closed interval, only uniformly continuous functions can be defined by constructive methods.

The reason that it is possible to get a result such as this, which is patently unobtainable in the classical theory, even while the intuitionist logic seems to proceed by weaker rules, is that the proof the fan theorem makes use of what would ordinarily be called metamathematical methods, although Heyting resists the use of the term in this case. Roughly speaking, one proves, by intuitionist methods, that there are certain things one cannot do intuition-istically. In the context of a closed real interval, this turns out to include the definition of functions which are not uniformly continuous.

Spreads have a certain set-like character (for example, the possession of elements), but one would not expect them to be able to bear the entire foundational burden of sets — the concept is too restrictive. Another notion is thus needed: 'species'.

DEFINITION 1: A *species* is a property which mathematical entities can be supposed to possess.

DEFINITION 2: After a species S has been defined, any mathematical entity which has been or might have been defined before S and which satisfies the condition S, is a *member* of the species S (Heyting, 1956, p. 37).

If we call any *ips* or spread a species of type 0, and any species whose mem-bers are of type 0 a species of type 1, we can inductively define a species to be of type $n + 1$ if the greatest type of its members is n. From the construc-tive point of view, it is clear that all species are of some definite, finite, type. There are no surprises lurking about the definition of 'species' comparable to the fan theorem and its consequences; species are a fairly harmless breed of set, subject to a type hierarchy conceptually not greatly different from the Russell scheme.

We close our discussion with a speech of 'Int', the advocate of intuitionism in Heyting's "Disputation".

It seems quite reasonable to judge a mathematical system by its usefulness. I admit that from this point of view intuitionism has as yet little chance of being accepted, for it would be premature to stress the few weak indications that it might be of some use in physics; in my eyes its chances of being useful in philosophy, history and the social sciences are better. In fact, mathematics, from the intuitionist point of view, is a study of certain functions of the human mind, and as such it is akin to these sciences.

20. Though intuitionism has earned a strong place in the debate over the set theoretic foundations of mathematics, it is in no sense the sole contender. Another variation on set theory begins by following the motivation for n-valued logic (Rescher, 1969) and allowing the relation '∈' to be more than just two-valued. This, of course, can be done in several different ways.

One approach is to begin by changing the underlying language to one whose formulae take more than just two values. To fix ideas, let us define a new connective 'V' which accepts formulae in **L** as its first argument and the values of **L** for its second argument, and call the formula 'ϕVv' a meta-formula meaning that ϕ has a value v, where ϕ and v are a formula and a value, respectively. Let $\phi_1, \ldots, \phi_n$ be formula variables, and c be an n-ary connective defined over these variables.[19] We say that c has a fixed point iff there exists a value v such that $(\phi_1 Vv \& \ldots \& \phi_n Vv) \to c(\phi_1, \ldots, \phi_n) Vv$. The Russell paradox occurs in a language with values $\{T, F\}$, and is of the form $(x \in XVv) \leftrightarrow (c(x \in XVv))$; the connective in this case is negation. The paradox obviously arises only because '$\neg$' has no fixed point. The consistency of the Comprehension Axiom in a language all of whose connectives have fixed points is an open issue at present.

21. Another (related) tack which can be taken in defining many valued sets is to make '$\in$' a three-place relation, where the third place is the value of membership. We write '$x \in y/z$' for 'x is an element of y with value z'. These theories can be characterized in GNB as follows:

    (i)   There exists a class V, called the class of values, with a special null value v.

    (ii)   There exists a class M, called the class of members.

If $X: M \to V$ is a class function, X is called a many-valued class. If $M_X = \{m: X(m) \neq v\}$ is coextensive with a set, then the set function $x: M_X \to V$ such that $m \in M_X \to x(m) = X(m)$ is a many valued set corresponding to X. '$\_\_/\_$' in this case is defined as $y \in x/vx(y) = v$. In the case that membership can take on more than one value at a time, we want two predicates, '$\_\_/\_$' and '$\_\_/\_$'. We let the hyperclass U be the power class of V, and define a many-valued class as a class function $X: M \to U$. For any $m \in M$, $X(m)$ is the class of all possible values that m considered as a member of X can have. Define $x \in X/ /V \leftrightarrow X(x) = V$, and $x \in X/v \leftrightarrow (v \in X(x))$. The formula '$x \in X/ /V$' means that the 'class of values with which s is a member of X is V', and '$x \in X/v$' means that 'x is a member of X with the value v'. In the special case of fuzzy sets, M is a fixed set, and $V = [0, 1]$, and $v = 0$. A fuzzy set A in M is characterized by the assignment $m \to f_A(m), f_A: M \to [0, 1]$ where f_A is the generalized characteristic function which assigns to every object $m \in M$ its grade of membership $f_A(m)$. In general, then, $A = \{(m, f_A(m))\}$, for all $m \in M$. Clearly, if $V = \{0, 1\}$, the theory reduces to the characteristic function of ordinary sets.

22. The notion of a set as a collection of all objects having the same property

implies a close algebraic connection between logic and set theory. It is a common notation, for example, to let Fx denote a proposition free in x, and $\hat{F}x$ the set of all x satisfying F. The algebra of the connectives of a logic is paralleled by the set operations: conjunction and intersection perform essentially equivalent functions. In particular, the algebra of classical mathematical logic, the propositional calculus, is the same as that of ZF/GNB. To illustrate, let U be the class of all objects. Then $\forall x(Fx)$ is true iff $\hat{F} = U$. Again, $\widehat{Fx \;\&\; Gx} = \hat{F}x \cap \hat{G}x$.

If we wish to consider logic and sets on the continuum. $\mathcal{L}_\infty$[20] and fuzzy sets will do for any proposition Fx in $\mathcal{L}_\infty$ and $\hat{F}x$ is a fuzzy set, i.e., a function from the constants of the language into the closed unit interval such that $\hat{F}(a)$ takes on the value assigned to Fa. For most logics, we can in this way invent a set theory having the same algebra. Purely from a truth table point of view, the same can be done for logics from a given set theory, although it will not always be possible to construct an axiom system for the logic using *modus ponens* as the rule of inference (Rosser and Turquette, 1952, pp. 27–48).

Statements of other kinds can be made as well. Suppose $\mathcal{L}^1$ is $\mathcal{L}_\infty$, and suppose that σ is a mapping from the parts of L^1 which induces an interpretation of M^1 in some universe of discourse in such a way that for each Fx, we have that $\sigma(Fx)$ is a set. Then we can construct a language L^2, whose logic is $\mathcal{L}_2$, and an interpretation M^2, induced by τ, such that for Fx, $\tau(Fx)$ is a fuzzy set in such a way that the diagram

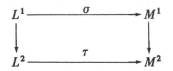

commutes. The reverse direction is, of course, also possible. Another way of saying the same thing is that ' $L^1 \overset{\sigma}{\to} M^1$ ' is structurally equivalent to ' $L^2 \overset{\tau}{\to} M^2$ ': in one case a fuzzy language is given an exact interpretation, while in the other an exact language is given a fuzzy interpretation.

Ontological, and other, difficulties enter in when we try to generalize to other combinations of logic and set theory. For example, not only does ZF set theory in intuitionist logic fail to be isomorphic to intuitionist set theory in classical mathematical logic, but such pairings are not even sensible. Even though we may be able to treat them formally, using the usual mathematics for our metalanguage, such an exercise lacks meaning, as we have torn the theories from the philosophical context which gives them meaning.

The resulting picture is thus one of heterodoxy: classical mathematical logic, Cantorian set theory, and GNB are all essentially Boolean; L_n and n-valued set theory are Post algebras of order n; L_∞ and fuzzy sets are Post algebras of the order of the continuum; intuitionist logic bears a close relationship to pseudo-Boolean algebras, i.e., Boolean algebras lacking the axiom corresponding to the excluded middle; several type theoretic set theories can be taken as Post algebras; practically all logics and set theories are implicative algebras and lattices of one sort or another. The following table is intended to indicate the range of the (less exotic) logics, set theories, and relevant algebras available:

Logics	Set Theories	Algebras
Classical Math. Logic	Cantorian Set Theory	Boolean Algebra
	ZF/GNB	
	Type Theory	
$Ł_3, L_n, L_\infty$	Many Values Sets	Post Algebras
'Vagueness'	Fuzzy Sets	
Intuitionism	Brouwerian Species	Pseudo-Boolean Algebras

Other logics abound: Kleene's logic, Bochvar's logic, combinatory logic, Godel's proof theory, non-alethic calculi, formalized inductive logic, and so on. The point is simply that one does not *use* set theory to characterize 'regions' or any other object of study; one constructs or designs set theories to accommodate certain ideas.

IV. REGIONS AND BOUNDARIES[21]

23. We turn now to the set theoretical interpretation of the notions of 'region' and 'boundary'. First, a few general, descriptive remarks.

In Western tradition, a 'boundary' is regarded as the 'edge' of a 'region' and arises in connection with two related developments: (1) the organization of space under conditions where property can be owned, and (2) the view of a legal and political system which resolved conflicts within the structure of territorially legitimatized criteria of justice. The first point is obvious. Although the territorial division of space has historically been organized according to a variety of principles, with the development of trade patterns and the need to allocate resources for purely economic purposes came a concept of exchange-based ownership which required the clear delimitation of the extent of spatial units. Most geometrical principles of delimitation have been employed and, by virtue of the meaning of contiguity, the interface between any two regional units was defined as the boundary. (Detailed discussion of this issue may be found in, e.g., Cowan (1959), Parsons (1959), Benn (1967), Furubotn and Pejovich (1972) and Benveniste (1973).)

Equally important in the development and use of the concepts 'region' and 'boundary' has been the impact of a political and legal tradition which emphasizes the complementary relationships between legitimacy and the context-dependency of the concepts of justice within regional systems. Societies and the rules which govern them have come to be regarded as territorially defined. As Soja puts it, specifications of territorial partitions

... become clearly differentiated from the broader sociocultural space and organized into a cellular system of formal regions which served as a means of societal control, identity, and integration ... Citizenship – membership in a particular state system – can be determined in large part by residence or birth in *formally bounded* (emphasis added) territorial units. Space in the state was partitioned into distinct parcels and structured into an administrative hierarchy nested into the primary locus of sovereignty, the state government (Soja, 1971, p. 15).

The acme of politically defined human territoriality is reached in the modern nation-state system. Rooted in Aristotelian logic and Greek geometry, linked to Western concepts of private property, buttressed by the resulting distinctive perspective on the political organization of space, and focused on achieving complete coincidence between the functional region occupied by the national community and the formal region defined by the state ..., the nation system has been imposed on the entire world (Soja, 1971, p. 33).

To govern, it has been argued (at least in Anglo–American jurisprudence), is to know clearly the domain of applicability of the law, both with respect to its territorial scope of legitimacy and the conflict at issue. Furthermore, the very act of establishing a legitimate domain is itself a function of the ways in which the legal and legislative systems are organized in any given territory. Adopting Georgescu-Roegen's (1972) usage, the term 'arithmomorphic' will be employed as the designation for this conception of regions and their respective boundaries. It is meant to convey an impression of crisp, clearly identified units within a tradition of legally and politically separable areal units.

24. A parallel tradition with respect to the notions of 'regions' and 'boundary' can also be identified – though not with an equivalent historico-legal foundation. It arises in the study of primitive societies, animal territories, problems of pattern recognition, and the like (see, e.g., Bohannon (1964), Ardrey (1966), Sommer (1969), Watanabe (1974)). A few examples should provide some grounding:

> The regional concept is a static view of human life, in two senses: (a) first, a regional system has validity for the moment at which it is devised and for no other moment ... (and) (b) second, regional studies have tended to treat the defined region as a community isolated from the rest of the world yet clearly no area or region in the modern world is independent of other parts of the world (Grigg, 1967, p. 471).

> In most traditional, non-centralized societies, the political organization of space was based on a fluid arrangement of functional regions shaped by the character and structure of the kinship system, the local ecological factors, and by the pattern of inter-group relations ... Localization, when it operated from descent patterns, worked primarily to create a kind of 'neighborhood' of mutual cooperation based on physical proximity. These 'neighborhoods', however, are rarely if ever formally bounded but were characterized by the same fluidity as the descent-derived socio-political regions (Soja, 1971, p. 13).

> Territorial patterns ... take on a variety of forms. There are group or horde territories and there are individual territories. There are fixed and portable territories. Some territories are clearly marked, ... and are always defended; others are very 'fuzzy' and may be defended under specific circumstances (Soja, 1971, p. 23).

Once again using Georgescu-Roegen's (1972) terminology, this tradition of territorial conceptions will be designed as 'non-arithmomorphic'. The term is meant to imply a state of flux, indeterminacy, and context-dependency; it is neither crisp nor does it (necessarily) imply a completely partitioned set of territories.

25. In their non-formal senses, then, 'region' and 'boundary' convey at least two kinds of presuppositions. On the one hand, there is the arithmomorphic perspective which is intended to account for the meaning of classical geometric concepts as they are applied to regional partitions. On the other hand, there is a rather less deterministic, non-arithmomorphic conception which, though also having empirical referents, apparently has no direct geometrical connotations. Neither usage is explicitly normative; neither are they completely distinguishable in natural language.

26. Thus far, the terms 'region' and 'boundary' have been given only very loose, almost associative meanings. For some purposes this may be sufficient, but in any formal context, more carefully proscribed meanings are required.

To fix ideas, we will begin by recapitulating several earlier observations concerning the structure of arithmomorphic conceptions of 'region' (Gale, 1974a). Let $V = \{V_1, \ldots, V_n\}$ be a set of n mutually exclusive and exhaustive regions. For example, if V is the world, then the set $V = \{V_1, \ldots, V_n\}$ might be the set of national political divisions; or if V is a given metropolitan area, then the set $V = \{V_1, \ldots, V_n\}$ might be the n police districts. The language underlying this conception of 'region' is a classical, two-valued, truth functional calculus. Its associated set theory is the usual Boolean version of sets, under some given axiomatization; membership of a particular location $(x, y) \in X$ in any region in a set V is then designated in the usual way by the set theoretic membership relation '$\in$' (which is categorical only for a prespecified V). Models of the term 'region' under this conceptualization will be designated as M_C.

We can denote membership in $V_i \in V$ by a set of ordered pairs of the following form:

$$V_i =_D \{((x,y), \mu V_i(x,y)), \text{ for all } V_j \in V \text{ and } (x,y) \in X\},$$

where (x, y) is any location and $\mu V_i(x, y)$ is the characteristic function associated with (x, y)'s membership in V_i. For the classical (Boolean) case, (x, y) is a member of some V_i just in case $\mu V_i(x, y) = 1$ and (x, y) is not a member of V_i just in case $\mu V_i(x, y) = 0$; furthermore, each (x, y) is a member of one and only one V_i. The arithmomorphic concept of region is thus described by the usual set theoretic membership conditions herein.

(i) $((x, y), \mu V_i(x, y)) \in V_i$ iff $\mu V_i(x, y) = 1$;

(ii) $((x, y), \mu V_i(x, y)) \notin V_i$ iff $\mu V_i(x, y) = 0$;   and

(iii) $\mu V_i(x, y)$ cannot assume values other than 1 or 0.

It is a strict, exhaustive partition and the $\{\mu V_i(x, y)\}$ forms a Boolean algebra.

Using the notion of a generalized characteristic function for a set, we may also obtain a description of the non-arithmomorphic conception of 'region' in terms of Zadeh's (1965) theory of 'fuzzy' sets. A *fuzzy set* $\tilde{V} = \{\tilde{V}_1, \ldots, \tilde{V}_n\}$ in X is a set consisting of the ordered pairs $((x, y), \mu\tilde{V}_i(x, y))$ $(l = 1, \ldots, n)$ wherein $\mu\tilde{V}_i(x, y)$ is a function which can take on any value over a given domain, say the unit interval $[0, 1]$. In this case, the conditions for membership in any region V_i would be expressed by three conditions:

(i') $((x, y), \mu\tilde{V}_i(x, y)) \in \tilde{V}_i$ iff $\mu\tilde{V}_i(x, y) = 1$;

(ii') $((x, y), \mu\tilde{V}_i(x, y)) \notin \tilde{V}_i$ iff $\mu\tilde{V}_i(x, y) = 0$;   and

(iii') $((x, y), \mu\tilde{V}_i(x, y)) \in^* \tilde{V}_i$ iff $\mu\tilde{V}_i(x, y) \in (0, 1)$.

In case (iii') we read '$\in^*$' as 'member to degree' or 'belongs to degree' $\mu V_i(x, y)$ in the fuzzy set $\tilde{V}_i$. Effectively, the characteristic function is regarded as the meaning of 'region' in the sense that it provides a formal basis for the semantics of the concept; the membership conditions $\{\mu\tilde{V}_i(x, y)\}$ are usually treated as subjective estimates of belongingness (Zadeh, 1971; Gale, 1972a, 1974a). In general, the $\{\mu V_i(x, y)\}$ do not form a Boolean lattice; for example, depending on the structure of the characteristic function, it may be either a modular or non-complemented lattice (Goguen, 1968–1969; deLuca and Termini, 1972). Furthermore, associated with changes in the set theoretic characterization there are concomitant changes in the underlying formal languages. (See, e.g., Korner (1966); Bellman and Zadeh (1970); deLuca and Termini (1971, 1972); Gale (1972a, 1974a, 1975); and Preparata and Yeh (1972).)

'Region' then, may be regarded as having at heart at least two different kinds of meaning, each with a distinctive formal language and set theoretic foundation: the arithmomorphic conception (modelled in terms of classical logic and Boolean set theory) and the non-arithmomorphic conception (modelled by non-classical alethic logic and a family of non-Boolean set theories). Notice, however, that the geometric connotations of 'region' and 'boundary' are not explicit in either of these formulations – though it is easily demonstrated that the arithmomorphic version gives rise to the usual geometric conditions for Euclidean space. The remainder of this section will discuss the extension of the fuzzy set-based conception of 'region' and 'boundary' in terms of the conditions needed for modelling their geometric interpretation.

With regard to the linguistic spirit of the argument, we first let L be Łukasiewicz's three-valued, truth functional language (as given in Rescher's (1969, p. 335) description). Following from the conditions for a fuzzy set V, a set theoretic model of L may thus be provided in terms of the conditions for membership on a distributive, non-complemented lattice wherein for each $(x, y) \in X$ and $\tilde{V}_i \in \tilde{V}$:

(i'') $((x, y), \mu\tilde{V}_i(x, y)) \in \tilde{V}_i$ iff $\mu\tilde{V}_i(x, y) \geqslant \alpha$;

(ii'') $((x, y), \mu\tilde{V}_i(x, y)) \in \tilde{V}_i$ iff $\mu\tilde{V}_i(x, y) \leqslant \beta$;   and

(iii'') $((x, y), \mu\tilde{V}_i(x, y)) \in^* V_i$ iff $\beta < \mu V_i(x, y) < \alpha$.

The rules of composition (e.g., intersection, union, equality) are defined as in Zadeh (1965); the choice of α and β is based on a context-dependent concept of closeness.

27. The extension of this structure to a geometry is obtained by the addition of axioms for a *tolerance geometry* (Zeeman, 1962). Following Roberts' (1970) argument, we obtain a tolerance space on a line by inducing point-by-point a tolerance relation I. Thus, for $x, x' \in X$ and $\epsilon > 0$, a tolerance space is induced as follows:

$$x \, I \, x' \quad |f(x) - f(x')| < \epsilon.$$

I may be regarded as a 'closeness' relation which is reflexive and symmetric but not transitive. The axioms for a tolerance ('ϵ-betweenness') geometry on a line are then given by conditions T1–T7 (where $B(x, y, z)$ is read as 'y is between x and z'):

T1. X, I is an indifference graph.

T2. $B(x, y, z) \rightarrow B(z, y, x)$.

T3. $B(x, y, z)$ or $B(x, z, y)$ or $B(y, x, z)$.

T4. $B(x, y, u)$ and $B(y, z, u)$ and $B(x, y, z) \rightarrow u \, I \, y$ and $u \, I \, z$.

T5. If $u \, I \, z$, then $B(x, u, z)$ and $B(u, z, y) \rightarrow B(x, u, y)$.

T6. $B(x, y, z)$ and $B(y, x, z) \rightarrow x \, I \, y$ or ($z \, I \, x$ and $z \, I \, x$ and $z \, I \, y$)

T7. $x \, I \, y \rightarrow B(x, y, z)$

Roberts' main result (1970) is a proof that T1–T7 are necessary and sufficient to characterize a tolerance geometry based on ϵ-betweenness.

Recalling our previous characterization of 'region' in terms of a fuzzy set in X we may observe that the ϵ-betweenness relation is isomorphic to the generalized characteristic function under the restriction given by (i″)–(iii″). That is, if $1 - \alpha = \beta + \epsilon$ then the axioms T1–T7 give a necessary and sufficient characterization of the non-complemented set theory of the fuzzy set representation. As noted above, the specification of α, β, and ϵ is context dependent.

28. So much for the abstract framework. Now what does all this amount to in terms of the related concepts of 'region' and 'boundary'? First, we recall that the whole of the motivation and grounding for the development of the structure Z, and in particular L, was designed to provide a formal basis for the characterization of the syntax and semantics of concepts. In the case of the non-arithmomorphic notions of 'region' and 'boundary' L and A were constructed so as to provide sufficiently rich properties for describing this idea.

In particular, **L** and **A** permit 'fuzzy' regions and boundaries with non-transitive indifference relationships to be described.

Second, we can observe that the meaning supplied to 'region' and 'boundary' by **L** and **A** immediately gives rise to a semantics based on subjective 'belongingness' and indifference at the margin (i.e., between two regions). Thus, where the arithmomorphic model forces a distinct, discrete division (as in the Cantorian version of the Comprehension Axiom), the non-arithmomorphic model simply provides a characterization of the flux and indeterminancy often associated with the separation between areas. A good example here is the kind of relation which obtains in describing speakers of a given language where, although they may live in separate political regions, they nevertheless comprise a single language group with a fuzzy boundary.

Third, by virtue of the tolerance geometry induced on the space X, the boundary between two areas, $\tilde{V}, \tilde{V}' \in \tilde{V}$ is just that subset of $\tilde{V} \cup \tilde{V}'$ wherein $\beta < \mu V \mu V'(x, y) < \alpha$, i.e., those points (x, y) within the ϵ-tolerance. Boundaries, in this sense, are not borders of partitions, nor a probability distribution on the borders; they are contextually-defined, point-by-point assessments of 'degree of membership'.

Finally, extending this argument to the idea of a 'political boundary', it can be seen that the notions of nation, state, administrative district, and so on take on a connotation quite removed from the Greek ideal of the city-state. People are no longer regarded as necessarily members of one and only one district. Having a distinct measure $\mu \tilde{V}_i(x, y)$ for each $\tilde{V}_i \in \tilde{V}$ with respect to some given issue or situation, each person has a grade of membership in all subsets of $\tilde{V}$ even though some will, of course, be zero. And 'boundary', at least in the political sense, ceases to function as a line separating two areas; it is a set of points $\{(x, y)\}$, the members of which are derived from individual assessments of belonging to some degree $\beta < \mu \tilde{V}_i(x, y) < \alpha$. The upshot of this argument is quite simply a generalization of the notions of 'region' and 'boundary' which accounts for the variability in individuals' criteria of membership in various areas. It reflects, for example, changing patterns of communication and social and economic interactions. It also provides a formal language and set theoretical structure for describing and making inferences about 'regions' and 'boundaries'. Note also that it is sufficiently rich to cover not only the cases where there is a truly non-arithmomorphic tolerance relation, but the classical, arithmomorphic case as well. This is particularly important where for reasons external to individual assessments (e.g., the structure of legal and administrative institutions), boundaries in the usual sense must be accounted for. In short, the logic of 'region' and 'boundary' may be regarded as the logic of a three-valued calculus together with axioms sufficient for characterizing membership in fuzzy sets and ε-tolerances on the line. Models based on this combination of L and A will be denoted as M_F.

29. As a characterization of the descriptive qualities of 'region' and 'boundary', models formed with respect to fuzzy sets and tolerance geometry (i.e., M_F) have some very desirable properties. But as it has thus far been presented, a model is simply a way of representing the structural features of the content of questions, and here only with regard to the implications of its language-based features. Discussion of the structure of the so-called 'object world' in terms of the $n + 1$-tuple, $\langle U, R_1, \ldots, R_n \rangle$, has been effectively side-stepped in favor of what may appear to be singularly more abstract concerns. Furthermore, in itself the formulation gives no real hints as to how a reconceptualization of 'region' and 'boundary' has anything to do with the ways in which regions and boundaries function.

In terms of the preceding discussion, 'region' may be regarded as a non-Cantorian class name: it functions as a way for dividing a continuous surface so that we can speak unambiguously about the members of any given region. In no sense, however, does any regionalization scheme (arithmomorphic or non-arithmomorphic) provide a categorical representation (Tarski, 1959). Regions are simply names which do not even have the usual kinds of theoretical homogeneities which can be postulated, say, for species of a population.

Clearly, there is more to it than this. Legal jurisdiction, historical tradition, cultural homogeneities, and the like, all serve to give some weight to particular regionalization schemes. But at its root, 'region' is a name and 'boundary' a means of demarcating the classes of members. What remains to be seen is whether changes in the naming process in terms of changes in the structure of L and A affect the ways in which decisions are made and the criteria for selecting among alternative methods for resolving disputes.

30. Though there are other examples of decision procedures which are affected by regionalization, (e.g., regional resource allocation, the judicial process, etc.), voting is probably the most important. Not only is it regarded as the central criterion of democracy, but in Western countries its almost *a priori* legitimacy makes it difficult to conceive of what 'civilized society' would mean in its absence. (See Macpherson (1966) for some provisos concerning democracy in non-Western contexts.)

In this regard it is strange to find a comment such as Coleman's (1970, p. 1076):

... increasing geographic mobility ... creates a fundamentally different infrastructure to society, one which is not based on a geographic unit. The geographically based representation is, or will soon be, an anachronism compared to other systems for effecting the same constituent-representative interchange, systems that have not yet been invented.

In the spirit of the transformation from barter to market economies, Coleman does offer one such invention: political money. But this 'invention' is primarily a substitute for the legitimizing criteria associated with the use of the market mechanism; decision is there, but voting in the sense of individual franchise and participation is not.

Coleman has, however, touched on the rawest nerve of the voting process: as a means for societal decision-making, voting can be dominated by the ways in which names are assigned to districts. Realizing that these inequities come hand-in-hand with a regionally-based participation process, Coleman turned to the market for a solution. And, as might be expected, the transformation led to another justification for a form of weighted voting based on an exchange medium for votes.

In an earlier paper on the 'regionalization problem', (Gale, 1974a) much the same conclusions as Coleman's were arrived at, though for somewhat different reasons. By recognizing the non-categoricity of models of regional partitions under M_C, it was argued that participation in the political system could best be effected by institutionalizing weighted voting based on the membership function $\mu \widetilde{V}_i(x, y)$. That is, by treating 'region' and 'boundary' in terms of a model M_F, it was suggested that the set of measures $\{\mu \widetilde{V}_i(x, y)\}$ could be interpreted as indices of weighted participation for each individual in each region, $\widetilde{V}_i \in \widetilde{V}$. Votes could then be distributed in accordance with these measures, thereby accounting for the variation in regionally-oriented interaction patterns. Legitimacy, however, was not presented in terms of equity considerations with respect to distributional criteria; following Rawl's (1958) argument, it was based only on processual considerations of *fairness*.

31. What have we gained, then, from this rather wide-ranging analysis of the use of alternative languages and set theories in the analysis of the regionalization problem? By way of summary, the five main points of the argument of this essay will be outlined.

(1) The process of scientific inquiry, when viewed as a general question-answering scheme, provides for the explicit inclusion of questions of all types and, therefore, of models based on a wide range of formal and non-formal languages (L) and set theories (A).

(2) In particular, contemporary set theory was viewed as a development

which reflected the entitivity and inferential requirements of mathematics. As such, different versions of set theory can be developed by re-examining, in particular, Cantor's Comprehension Axiom and the modern axiomatic treatments of his program.

(3) The notions of 'region' and 'boundary' can be regarded as having at least two different natural language meanings: one based on clear-cut partitions of space and the other based on classes of syntactic and semantic indeterminancies. The former was termed 'arithmomorphic', and the latter 'non-arithmomorphic'.

The arithmomorphic notion of a boundary was identified in terms of model M_C (e.g., wherein L is a two-valued, classical logic and A is a set of axioms containing, say, the Zermelo–Fraenkel axioms for set theory and the axioms of Euclidean geometry); the non-arithmomorphic notion of a boundary was identified in terms of a model M_F (e.g., wherein L is a three-valued logical calculus and A contains axioms for fuzzy sets and a tolerance geometry).

(4) The potential application of this revised picture of 'region' and 'boundary' was illustrated by noting that, under M_F, voting is inherently a problem of rules of weighted participation.

32. There are many points in the argument which need additional amplification. There is also a very obvious need to state many of the claims in a more formal way and give proofs of the assertions. These will have to wait for a subsequent paper. To round out the discussion, however, two remarks on some of the more general implications of the argument are in order.

First, it should be clear at this point that, for the social sciences in general, there is now a need for a general re-examination of the foundations of our formal methods of analysis. In the past three decades, the thrust of much of the formalist movement in the social sciences has been adoptive: the methods of mathematics and the natural sciences were cited as paradigms and it was maintained that the necessary and sufficient conditions for progress in any science depended on their use. Special names were usually given to this adoption process (usually 'the quantitative revolution' or 'the systems approach') but little was done by way of giving any more than metaphysical claims for analogies. Whether the analogies have any real utility has yet to be demonstrated, but at least one thing seems to be clear at this point: a lot of foundational work needs to be done in order to identify the range of the utility of each of these methods. A good guess is that, while we will find the analogies holding in some very restrictive cases, for the most part the teleological, non-mechanistic structure of social explanations and prescriptions will need quite different methodological tools.

Second, the explicit inclusion of language as an aspect of the modelling process once again opens the door to a methodological union of the social sciences and the humanities. One such area concerns the foundations of legal reasoning (e.g., Perelman (1963), Toulmin (1969)); another is the recent growth of sociolinguistics (e.g., Hymes (1964); Gumperz and Hymes (1970)); another is the developing area of poetics (e.g., Weitz (1964); van Dijk (1972); Klammer (N. D.)). The humanistic approach lost its value solely as a con-science when it began to develop independent methods of inquiry; the social sciences, by facing only one direction, lost sight of the importance of this shift for the reorientation of methodological strategies.

NOTES

[1] Several passages of this paper have been adapted from two previous essays: Gale (1975, 1976).

[2] See Rescher (1969) for a detailed discussion of the historical development of many-valued logic.

[3] The literature relating to this point is far too extensive to document here. For the record, and with no attempt at comprehensiveness, we note just a few ready examples from several different fields: Braybrooke and Lindblom (1963), Korner (1966), Bromberger (1971), Churchman (1971), Targ (1971), von Wright (1971), Ackoff and Emery (1972), van Dijk (1972), Gale (1972b), Georgescu-Roegen (1972), Habermas (1972), Morgenstern (1972a, b), McCarthy (1973), Gottinger (1974), and Suppe (1974).

[4] Gale (1976). See also Belnap (1963, 1966, 1969), Bromberger (1963, 1965, 1966, 1971), Harrah (1963, 1969a, 1969b, 1971), Aquist (1965, 1972), Keenan and Hull (1973), and Hintikka (1976).

[5] See Suppes (1960) for a discussion of some variety of meanings. Note, however, that in Suppes' view all the uses are regarded as effectively equivalent to the model-theoretic conception developed with respect to the semantics of mathematical logic.

[6] The symbol '$=_D$' indicates 'is by definition'.

[7] More generally, we can conceive of $R_1, \ldots, R_n$ as being a function $f: L \rightarrow U$ which specifies the reference in U, of each element of the language L.

[8] See Korner (1966, 1970, 1976) and Zinov'ev (1973) for related discussions. Note also that this perspective is not all that different from the so-called 'radical meaning variance' position taken by, e.g., Feyerabend (1965, 1970a, 1970b).

[9] See, for example, Reichenbach (1944), Watanabe (1969), Heelan (1970), Sneed (1971), and Hooker (1973).

[10] See, for example, the collections by Rescher (1969), Hudson (1969), and Hilpinen (1971).
[11] For the obvious reasons, the discussion of this part is highly schematic. For further details, the reader is referred to the referenced papers and books.
[12] For example, this is the position taken (for quite different reasons) by Suppes (1970) and Zadeh (1965).
[13] The symbol '/./' indicates 'the cardinality of'.
[14] The descriptions of the paradoxes is adapted from Fraenkel and Bar-Hillel (1973).
[15] See Rubin and Rubin (1970) for a discussion of the equivalent representations of AC.
[16] We shall follow the convention here of using bold-face letters to indicate set variables and bold-face italic letters to indicate class variables.
[17] This theorem, and its proof, can be found in Heyting (1956, pp. 42–44).
[18] A proof is in Heyting (1956, p. 46).
[19] This connective is similar to Rescher's (1969, pp. 76–91) auto descriptive operator.
[20] See Rescher (1969) for a 'catalogue' of logics and an interpretation of this notation.
[21] Much of the argument of this section is drawn from Gale (1974, 1975, 1976).

BIBLIOGRAPHY

Ackoff, R. L.: 1972, *On Purposeful Systems*, Aldine, Chicago.
Aquist, L.: 1965, *A New Approach to the Logical Theory of Interrogatives, Part I: Analysis*, The Philosophical Society Series, Uppsala.
Aquist, L.: 1972, 'On the Analysis and Logic of Questions', in R. E. Olson and A. M. Paul (eds.), *Contemporary Philosophy in Scandanavia*, The Johns Hopkins Press, Baltimore, pp. 27–39.
Ardrey, R.: 1966, *The Territorial Imperative*, Athenum, New York.
Bellman, R. E. and Zadeh, A. L.: 1970, 'Decision-making in a Fuzzy Environment', *Management Science* 17, B-141–B-164.
Belnap, N. D. Jr.: 1963, *An Analysis of Questions: Preliminary Report*, Technical Memorandum, System Development Corporation.
Belnap, N. D. Jr.: 1966, 'Questions, Answers, and Presuppositions', *The Journal of Philosophy* 63, 609–611.
Belnap, N. D. Jr.: 1967, 'Comments on H. Simon's "The Logic of Heuristic Decision-Making"', in N. Rescher (ed.), *The Logic of Decision and Action*, University of Pittsburgh Press, Pittsburgh, pp. 27–31.
Belnap, N. D. Jr.: 1969, 'Questions: Their Presuppositions and How They Can Fail to Arise', in K. Lambert, *The Logical Way of Doing Things*, Yale University Press, New Haven, pp. 23–38.
Benacerraf, P. and Putnam, H.: 1964, *Philosophy of Mathematics: Selected Readings*, Prentice Hall, Englewood Cliffs, New Jersey.
Benn, S. I.: 1967, 'Property', in P. Edwards, *The Encyclopedia of Philosophy*, Macmillan, New York, 6, 491–495.
Benveniste, E.: 1973, *Indo-European Language and Society*, University of Miami Press, Miami (Translated by E. Palmer).
Beth, E. W.: 1964, *Foundations of Mathematics*, North Holland, Amsterdam, Netherlands.

Bohannan, P.: 1964, 'Space and Territoriality', in P. Bohannan (ed.), *Africa and Africans*, The Natural History Press, pp. 174–181.

Braybrooke, D. and Lindblom, C. E.: 1963, *A Strategy of Decision*, Free Press, Glencoe.

Bromberger, S.: 1963, 'A Theory About the Theory of Theory and About the Theory of Theories', in B. Baumrin (ed.), *Philosophy of Science, the Delaware Seminar II*, John Wiley, New York, pp. 79–105.

Bromberger, S.: 1965, 'An Approach to Explanation', in R. J. Butler (ed.), *Analytical Philosophy*, 2nd series, Basil Blackwell, pp. 72–105.

Bromberger, S.: 1966, 'Why-Questions', in R. G. Colodny, *Mind and Cosmos*, University of Pittsburgh Press, Pittsburgh, pp. 86–111.

Bromberger, S.: 1971, 'Science and Forms of Ignorance', in E. Nagel, S. Bromberger and A. Grunbaum (eds.), *Observation and Theory in Science*, The Johns Hopkins Press, Baltimore.

Brouwer, L. E. J.: 1913, 'Intuitionism and Formalism', *Bulletin of the American Mathematical Society* (reprinted in P. Benacerraf and H. Putnam: 1964, *Philosophy of Mathematics*, Prentice Hall, Englewood Cliffs, New Jersey), pp. 66–77.

Carnap, R.: 1937, *Logical Syntax of Language*, Routledge & Kegan Paul, London.

Chapin, E. W.: 1974, 'Set Values Set Theory, Part I', *Notre Dame Journal of Formal Logic* XV, 619–634.

Chapin, E. W.: 1975, 'Set Values Set Theory, Part II', *Notre Dame Journal of Formal Logic* XVI, 255–267.

Churchman, C. W.: 1971, *The Design of Inquiring Systems*, Basic Books, New York.

Cohen, P.: 1966, *Set Theory and the Continuum Hypothesis*, W. A. Benjamin, New York.

Coleman, J. S.: 1970, 'Political Money', *American Political Science Review* 64, 1074–1087.

Cowan, T. A.: 1959, 'The Principle Structures of Community Reviewed', in C. J. Friedrich (ed.), *Community*, The Liberal Arts Press, Indianapolis.

Dwinger, P.: 1968, 'Generalized Post Algebras', *Bull. Ac. Pol. Sc. Ser. Sci. Math. Astr. Phys.* 16, 559–563.

Feyerabend, P.: 1965, 'Problems of Empiricism', in R. G. Colodny (ed.), *Beyond the Edge of Certainty*, Prentice Hall, Englewood Cliffs, New Jersey.

Feyerabend, P.: 1970a, 'Problems of Empiricism, Part II', in R. G. Colodny (ed.), *The Nature and Function of Scientific Theories*, Prentice Hall, Englewood Cliffs, New Jersey, pp. 275–353.

Feyerabend, P.: 1970b, 'Against Method: Outline of an Anarchist Theory of Knowledge', in M. Radner and S. Winokur (eds.), *Analyses of Theories and Methods of Physics and Psychology*, University of Minnesota Press, Minneapolis, pp. 17–130.

Fine, K.: 1975, 'Vagueness, Truth and Logic', *Synthese* 30, 265–300.

Fraenkel, A.: 1966, *Abstract Set Theory*, North Holland, Amsterdam, Netherlands.

Fraenkel, A. and Bar-Hillel, Y.: 1973, *Foundations of Set Theory*, North Holland, Amsterdam, Netherlands.

Furubotn, E. and Pejovich, S.: 1972, 'Property Rights and Economic Theory: A Survey of Recent Literature', *Journal of Economic Literature* 10, 1137–1162.

Gale, S.: 1972a, 'Inexactness, Fuzzy Sets and the Foundations of Behavioral Geography', *Geographical Analysis* 4, 337–349.

Gale, S.: 1972b, 'On the Heterodoxy of Explanation, a Review of David Harvey's *Explanation in Geography*', *Geographical Analysis* 4, 285–322.

Gale, S.: 1975, 'Conjectures on Many-valued Logic, Regions, and Criteria for Conflict Resolution', Working Paper No. 10, *Research on Metropolitan Change and Conflict Resolution*, Peace Science Department, University of Pennsylvania, Philadelphia.

Gale, S.: 1976, 'A Resolution of the Regionalization Problem and its Implications for Political Geography and Social Justice', *Geografiska Annaler*, Series B, 5B, 1–16.

Gale, S.: 1977, 'A Prolegomenon to an Interrogative Theory of Scientific Inquiry', in H. Hiz (ed.), *Questions*, D. Reidel, Dordrecht, forthcoming.

Galtung, J.: 1967, 'On the Future of the International System', *Journal of Peace Science* 4, 305–333.

Geogrescu-Roegen, N.: 1972, *The Entropy Law and the Economic Process*, Harvard University Press, Cambridge, Massachusetts.

Goguen, J. A.: 1968–9, 'The Logic of Inexact Concepts', *Synthese* 19, 325–373.

Gottinger, H. W.: 1974, 'Toward Fuzzy Reasoning in the Behavioral Sciences', in W. Leinfellner and E. Kohler (eds.), *Developments in the Methodology of Social Science*, D. Reidel, Dordrecht, pp. 287–308.

Grigg, D.: 1967, 'Regions, Models and Classes', in R. J. Chorley and P. Haggett (eds.), *Models in Geography*, Methuen, New York.

Gumperz, J. and D. Hymes: 1970, *Directions in Socio-linguistics*, Holt, Rinehart, and Winston, New York.

Habermas, J.: 1972, *Knowledge and Human Interest*, Beacon Press, Boston (Translated by J. Shapiro).

Harrah, D.: 1963, *Communication: A Logical Model*, The M.I.T. Press, Cambridge, Massachusetts.

Harrah, D.: 1969a, 'On Completeness in the Logic of Questions', *American Philosophical Quarterly* 6, 158–164.

Harrah, D.: 1969b, 'Erotetic Logistics', in K. Lambert (ed.), *The Logical Way of Doing Things*, Yale University Press, New Haven.

Harrah, D.: 1971, 'Formal Message Theory', in Y. Bar-Hillel (ed.), *Pragmatics of Natural Languages*, D. Reidel, Dordrecht, pp. 69–83.

Heelan, P.: 1965, *Quantum Mechanics and Objectivity*, Nijhoff.

Heyting, A.: 1956, *Intuitionism: An Introduction*, North Holland, Amsterdam, Netherlands.

Hintikka, J.: 1976, 'The Semantics of Questions and the Questions of Semantics', *Acta Philosophica, Fennica* 28.

Hooker, C. A.: 1973, *Contemporary Research in the Foundations of Quantum Theory*, D. Reidel, Dordrecht.

Hymes, D.: 1964, *Language in Culture and Society: A Reader in Linguistics*, Harper and Row, New York.

Jaskowski, S.: 1967, 'Investigations into the System of Intuitionist Logic', in S. McCall, *Polish Logic: 1920–1939*, Oxford University Press, Oxford, pp. 259–263.

Keenan, E. and Hull, R.: 1973, 'The Logical Presuppositions of Questions and Answers', in J. S. Petofi and D. Franck (eds.), *Presuppositions in der Philosophie und Linguistik*, Atheneum, New York.

Klammer, T. P. N.: 1973, 'Foundations for a Theory of Dialogue Structure', *Poetics* 9, 27–64.

Korner, S.: 1966, *Experience and Theory*, Humanities Press, New York.

Korner, S.: 1970, *Categorial Frameworks*, Basil Blackwell, Oxford.

Korner, S.: 1976, *Experience and Conduct*, Cambridge University Press, Cambridge.
de Luca, A. and Termini, S.: 1971, 'Algorithmic Aspects in Complex Analysis', *Scientia* **106**, 659–671.
de Luca, A. and Termini, S.: 1972, 'Algebraic Properties of Fuzzy Sets', *Journal of Mathematical Analysis and Applications* **40**, 373–386.
Macpherson, C. B.: 1966, *The Real World of Democracy*, The Clarendon Press, Oxford.
McCarthy, T.: 1973, 'On Misunderstanding "Understanding" ', *Theory and Decision* **3**, 351–370.
Morgenstern, O.: 1972a, 'Descriptive, Predictive, and Normative Theory', *Kyklos* **2**, 699–714.
Morgenstern, O.: 1972b, 'Thirteen Critical Points in Contemporary Economic Theory: An Interpretation', *Journal of Economic Literature* **4**, 1163–1189.
Parsons, T.: 1959, 'The Principle Structures of Community: A Sociological View', in C. J. Friedrich (ed.), *Community*, The Liberal Arts Press, Indianapolis.
Perelman, C.: 1963, *The Ideas of Justice and the Problem of Argument*, The Humanities Press, New York (Translated by J. Petrie).
Preparata, F. P. and Yeh, R. T.: 1972, 'Continuously Valued Logic', *Journal of Computer and Systems Science* **6**, 397–418.
Rasiowa, H.: 1974, *An Algebraic Approach to Non-classical Logics*, North Holland, Amsterdam, Netherlands.
Rawls, J.: 1958, 'Justice as Fairness', *The Philosophical Review* **57**, 164–194.
Reichenbach, H.: 1944, *Philosophic Foundations of Quantum Mechanics*, University of California Press, Berkeley.
Rescher, N.: 1969, *Many-valued Logic*, McGraw Hill, New York.
Roberts, F. S.: 1970, *Tolerance Geometry*, Paper P-4430, The Rand Corporation, Santa Monica, California.
Robinson, A.: 1972, *Non-standard Analysis*, North Holland, Amsterdam, Netherlands.
Rosser, J. B. and Turquette, A. M.: 1952, *Many Valued Logic*, North Holland, Amsterdam, Netherlands.
Rubin, H. and Rubin, J. E.: 1970, *Equivalents of the Axiom of Choice*, North Holland, Amsterdam, Netherlands.
Russell, B.: 1938, *Foundations of Mathematics*, Cambridge University Press, London.
Sneed, J. D.: 1971, *The Logical Structure of Mathematical Physics*, D. Reidel, Dordrecht.
Soja, E. W.: 1971, *The Political Organization of Space*, Commission on College Geography, Resource Paper No. 8, Association of American Geographers.
Sommer, R.: 1969, *Personal Space: The Behavioral Test of Design*, Prentice Hall, Englewood Cliffs, New Jersey.
Spence, N. and Taylor, P.: 1970, 'Quantitative Methods in Regional Taxonomy', *Progress in Geography* **2**, 1–64.
Sraffa, P.: 1960, *Production of Commodities by Means of Commodities*, Cambridge University Press, Cambridge.
Suppe, F.: 1974, 'The Search for Philosophic Understanding in Scientific Theories', in F. Suppe (ed.), *The Structure of Scientific Theories*, University of Illinois Press, Urbana, Illinois, pp. 3–232.
Suppes, P.: 1960, *Axiomatic Set Theory*, Princeton University Press, Princeton, New Jersey.

Suppes, P.: 1970, *Set Theoretic Structures in Science*, Institute for Mathematical Studies in the Social Sciences, Stanford, California.

Targ, H.: 1971, 'Social Science and a New Social Order', *Journal of Peace Research* 8, 207–220.

Tarski, A.: 1959, 'What is Elementary Geometry?', in L. Henkin, P. Suppes, and A. Tarski (eds.), *The Axiomatic Method*, North Holland, Amsterdam, Netherlands.

Toulmin, S.: 1969, *The Uses of Argument*, Cambridge University Press, Cambridge.

van Dijk, T. A.: 1972, *Some Aspects of Text Grammars*, Mouton.

von Wright, G. H.: 1971, *Explanation and Understanding*, Cornell University Press, Ithaca, New York.

Watanabe, S.: 1969, *Knowing and Guessing*, John Wiley, New York.

Watanabe, S.: 1974, 'Paradigmatic Symbol – A Comparative Study of Human and Artificial Intelligence', *IEEE Transactions on Systems, Man and Cybernetics*, SMC-4, 100–103.

Weitz, M.: 1964, *Hamlet and the Philosophy of Literary Criticism*, The World Publishing Company, New York.

Whitehead, A. N. and Russell, B.: 1927, *Principia Mathematica*, Cambridge University Press, Cambridge.

Zadeh, L. A.: 1965, 'Fuzzy Sets', *Information and Control* 8, 338–353.

Zadeh, L. A.: 1971, 'Comparative Fuzzy Semantics', *Information Science* 3, 159–176.

Zadeh, L. A. *et al.*: 1975, *Fuzzy Sets and Their Applications to Cognitive and Decision Processes*, Academic Press, New York.

Zeeman, E. C.: 1962, 'The Topology of the Brain and Visual Perception', in M. K. Fort (ed.), *The Topology of 3-Manifolds*, Prentice Hall, Englewood Cliffs, New Jersey, pp. 240–256.

Zinov'ev, A. A.: 1973, *Foundations of the Logical Theory of Scientific Knowledge*, Boston Studies in the Philosophy of Science IX, D. Reidel, Dordrecht.

REGINALD G. GOLLEDGE

REALITY, PROCESS, AND THE DIALETICAL
RELATION BETWEEN MAN AND ENVIRONMENT[1]

An increasing desire for more complete levels of understanding of the
relationship between man and environment led, in the later nineteen-sixties
and early seventies, to a variety of research efforts focussing on the difference between form and process oriented approaches in human geography
(e.g., Olsson (1969); Olsson and Gale (1968); King (1969); Golledge (1970);
Olsson (1971) and Eichenbaum and Gale (1971)). Most of these papers discussed in some way the relative contribution of spatial form and spatial processes to our understanding of human behavior, and some specifically argued
that more attention should be paid to human behavioral processes such as
learning, perception, and attitude formation as part of the geographer's
explanatory schema. Concurrently there existed a growing concern for discovering what man knew of the various environments in which he existed
(Lynch, 1960; Gould, 1965; Golledge, Briggs, and Demko, 1969; Appleyard,
1970; Downs, 1970). This latter research began uncovering various properties
of 'known' environments that appeared to be somewhat different from the
world of substance and fact which is experienced by our senses and which is
usually described in terms of atomistic facts and mechanistic forces (Russell,
1918; Whitehead, 1933).

I. ASSUMPTIONS NECESSARY FOR THE STUDY OF SPATIAL
FORMS AND PROCESSES

The emphasis on spatial form and spatial processes typical of much geographic
research in the 1960's required a set of primitives relating to the world at
large. The first of these was that there is a world composed of more-or-less permanent objects; the second, that this world is external to individuals; and the
third, that the world is regulated in time without continuous annihilation and
resurrection. This world, which I shall call 'objective' or 'external' reality, was
at once *substantial*, *relatively stable*, and *composed of many discrete things*
which obeyed sets of natural laws. It was also necessary to assume that
phenomena existed as *facts in time and space* and were *independent of mind*;

S. Gale and G. Olsson (eds.), Philosophy in Geography, 109–120. All Rights Reserved.
Copyright © 1979 by D. Reidel Publishing Company, Dordrecht, Holland.

in this way their *definitive structures* could be inventoried and described (i.e., their 'spatial form' could be discovered). Both the definitive structures of man and nature were researched. Human actions, which are but fleeting events in the on-going flux of existence, were given substance and stability by assuming that they were *repetitive* and *relatively invariant* events, and were related through activity links to elements of objective reality. 'Explanation' was assumed to be achieved if a sufficient number of like events or actions could be associated with discernable elements of the definitive structure of either human or natural environments.

The action of relating human behavior to elements of objective reality necessitates acceptance of a further number of premises concerning man and environment. These are: that each individual places himself and others in a common external environment; that elements of this external environment exist and will continue to exist even after human interactions with them cease; that *knowledge* of the existence of such environments can be retained by sensate beings even if interaction ceases; that any object in external reality can continue in existence as part of a total external environment quite independent of human awareness; and that sensate beings function in objective environments by disengaging the objects of such environments from their own actions. This latter premise marks the development of *true objectification* and accounts at least in part for our joint ability to specify the nature and characteristics of objective reality. It also requires yet another subset of premises related to the sensate beings themselves such as: each being requires a *means for constructing a system of relations among objects in external reality*; each being *needs an understanding of itself in relation to these objects and relations*; and each *must have the ability to form some type of simultaneous spatial-temporal network which incorporates these relations*. In other words it is necessary to assume that our *internalized reflections of the external flux must also have some structure and some commonalities*. This implies that beings endeavor to develop constancy in their images and percepts and uniformity in concepts such that individual elements of the external flux can be recognized and elaborated within a structure or system which relates their existence to other elements in that objective reality.

An even more fundamental assumption relating to the study of spatial form and spatial processes is that we are capable of acquiring *knowledge* about them. Knowledge, of course, is an adaptive activity of an organism; it represents a progressive adaptation of one part of a process to other parts. In the course of this adjustment, the part reacted to becomes 'environment'. Thus, environment is defined in relation to the part reacting (see Lee (1961)).

However, there appears to be no fixed boundary between what reacts and what is environment. Not only are the two relative to each other, but each partakes of the other; physical organisms such as human beings are thought of as part of what reacts and also as part of environment.

Lee (1973) argues that knowledge arises within consciousness and consciousness arises within experience, but consciousness and experience are not co-extensive; experience is more inclusive than consciousness. Everything of which one is conscious is experienced, but much of what is experienced consciousness takes no note. In the broader sense of the term then, experience refers to every way in which one part of the process affects or is affected by other parts. Experience arises from participation and process; but this is not the mind's participation for there is no mind until consciousness has emerged. Experience is essentially an act; so also is the consciousness which arises within experience and the knowledge which arises within consciousness. Consciousness and knowledge are specialized modes of activity of an organism. There is nothing in experience and there is nothing in knowledge to indicate either the existence of an 'originally structured reality' or a pre-existent mind. Conscious perception involves an act of selecting from unconscious experience those elements in which there is repetition and similarity. Percepts then become clearer and more precise as the involved concepts become clearer and more precise. There is, however, no clear-cut perception of persisting physical objects until language is learned for such perception requires clear-cut conceptualization, and clear-cut conceptualization of this sort is socially inherited through the symbolism of language. The sense in which the individual *determines* a world in which he lives is as profound as the sense in which the world determines him. The world without regard to the acting individual is not fully determined.

Knowledge then is a result of the appearance of self-consciousness. The appearance of self-consciousness indicates that there is mind. By means of concepts developed by the mind, delineation and definition of environment takes place and knowledge about environment is developed. Conceptualization is cognition and this is knowledge. Concepts are mental, not in the sense of being entities being entertained by a mind, but in the sense in which mind is conceptual activity — that is, responds to more than what is actually present.

All knowledge is hypothetical in some sense or another. Exactly in what sense each kind of knowledge is hypothetical must be determined. Each kind will be found to be characterized by a particular interplay between percepts and concepts. For example, the natural sciences, although still bound by perceptual observations, are highly elaborate theoretic structures and the role of induction and hypothesis within them is well known.

A. N. Whitehead (1933, p. 228) says, "if we cannot speak of the same thing twice, knowledge vanishes, taking philosophy with it". However, there is knowledge and there is philosophy and one can speak of the same thing twice. The reason that one can, is that one speaks of *intuitive data interpreted as instances of kinds*. For example most of the words of speech refer not to unique events but to generalities, and generalities have more than one instance.

Let us look briefly at the situation existing if any of the sets of assumptions articulated in this section are violated. We would most probably be forced to accept the existence of a universe without substance or a population without communal understanding. Of course a universe without objects does not constitute a solid external environment; it is a world of pictures, any one of which can disappear and reappear capriciously and at each reappearance can be somewhat changed. A population without communal understandings assumes knowledge is unique to each person and implies a potentially chaotic existence for the members of any population. In other words the well argued mind–body problem and the problem of Cartesian dualism surface once more and the doctrine of uniqueness of mind and of uniqueness of external reality would dominate thought.

So far this discussion has emphasised the epistemological primitives and assumptions necessary for sensate study of the definitive structure of an external reality; hints have also been offered concerning the process by which sensate beings exist in and acquire knowledge of this reality. But what is the relationship between external reality and knowledge of it?

II. COMMENTS ON THE NATURE OF REALITY

At this stage we are faced with the inevitable and perplexing question – what is reality? To some reality is simply what most people recognize it to be. To philosophers such as Bertrand Russell reality is the sum total of atomistic facts in the Universe. Wittgenstein (1922) defines reality as "what is the case" – and what is the case appears to be a collection of atomic facts. Lee (1973) suggests that anything that is apprehended in perception and grasped in understanding is real in some category or another. Concrete experiences are real, concepts are real, facts are real. Thus reality is the ongoing flux of process; it is the continuity of existence and awareness. This is a 'process' view of reality.

Given this latter point of view everything is real in some sense or another, and the task of categorization is defined as finding the right sense in which something 'becomes real'. The right category, in *this* sense, is one which introduces order into experience. Another definition of reality then may be 'whatever can be categorized'. We must remember however that categories and classes are probably 'there' in reality, but not absolutely there. They are always relative to some conceptual scheme and are conditioned by the scheme. It is doubtful whether there are such things as 'the' categories of reality (Whitehead, 1929, p. 365). They are more probably a result of the way mind reacts to the flux outside its boundary. Knowledge, therefore, results from the reaction between mind and an external universe, and the content of knowledge (e.g., knowledge of nature) is composed of selections from this flux. Mind orders this content and builds it into a theoretic structure. The structure is not something already there to be inspected and investigated by scientists; it is built by people, working together.

The structure of this objective reality is not known immediately to the persons inhabiting it; it is 'constructed' little by little as knowledge and awareness mounts. Although everyone lives in what is in broad outline the 'same' world, no two persons reconstruct this world in *precisely* the same way. Every person is the center of his/her own experience and this experience is unique in precise detail, but persons *are* able to communicate with others and each is *part* of the other's external reality. Reconstructions of reality then include not only elements of the stable external universe but self and other persons. As knowledge about objective reality accumulates individualized reconstructions become systematic. As more and more people become exposed to the same elements of objective reality and communicate amongst themselves with respect to specific objects and the nature of relations among objects in this reality, there emerges an external world which is regarded as being relatively fixed and stable, and various elements of this reality appear to a greater or lesser extent in individual reconstructions of it. The *necessity* for overlap in these individual reconstructions is at once obvious. Each person must exist in a common external environment and in the many artificial structurings imposed on objective reality (such as political, legal, moral, economic and social structures), and to achieve existence without chaos there must be some common structurings and understandings.

To sum up then, intervening between a constant but changing external world and a chaotic mass of unique sensate beings are the internalized reflections of the external flux or the isomorphisms of this flux produced by the minds of the sensate beings. Although each of these isomorphisms is a transformation unique to a being, there is no evidence that a unique transformation *determines* the world in which the being exists, or that it is subject to only one determination. It appears that no-one fully invents his own scheme of conceptual interpretation;[2] it is handed down in language. For example, as a child learns language he learns the broad features of the more or less traditional interpretations of experience and the more or less stable and identifiable objects in the external world. The adult, having learned the language, lives in a world of conceptual objects which he directly perceives. What he perceives consists of intuitive data with their identifying interpretations adhering to them. So 'reality' to an adult is the world of perceptual and remembered objects in which he lives.

Thus, in order to remove ourselves from the realm of utter chaos we impose many different structures on 'external reality', and we impose even more structures (i.e., constructions) on the activity relationships between ourselves and external environments. These constructions partly condition the interface between man and external reality and partly limit interaction potential, and include things such as social systems, legal systems, economic systems, and psychological systems. The success with which we can both form and conform to these constructions (and therefore can exist in and use reality) is very much a product of the transformations made at the individual level. Lack of success in making communicable constructions may mean ostracism and/or (frequently) confinement.

III. A SPATIAL PERSPECTIVE ON REALITY AND PROCESS

Epistemologically, the analysis of reality can be approached from a number of different directions. Traditionally, two directions seem to dominate: one of these consists of undertaking the analysis of a complex system of knowledge (such as may be found in mathematics and natural science or even the organized sense of ordinary language), and the second concentrates on investigating the process of gaining knowledge in a wide variety of situations of varying degrees of complexity.

The first approach seeks to lay bare the structure of knowledge and may be called the paradigmatic approach. In this approach, one takes already formulated knowledge from the ultimate to logically primitive. One then proceeds by analyzing fully formulated relatively complex cases of adult knowledge. Prerequisites for such knowledge are both the mastery of language and experience of a world full of things. It is assumed that adults already have language and have experienced things and consequently, it can be assumed that things can be taken for granted as soon as knowledge of the external world to contain them has been established. In other words, this is an attempt to show how ready made minds can know a ready made external world.

The second approach investigates the process of gaining knowledge; this is a dynamic and somewhat speculative approach, in that the structure of knowledge is the goal of the investigation but the structure is clearly delineated only as it stands out in the process of knowing and learning. The relation between structure and process is one of the things to be explicated but no explications are achieved by neglecting one of the terms of the relation. The second direction then assumes that the world is a world of process and it argues that in the course of obtaining knowledge, things are abstracted from events. What happens is more fundamental than what is because what happens gives rise to what is. If we give an emphasis to events rather than things, this gives time and continuity an importance beyond what normally accrues to them in much of traditional epistemology. *Events* then are selections from the continuous, on-going flux of process, but *things* are static and discreet. Since space, like time, is a continuum, it would seem that to acquire knowledge about space it is only reasonable to concentrate on processes and events related to space rather than on the things of space. Let us briefly pursue this problem of achieving knowledge about space.

Philosophers from Plato to Wittgenstein have pointed out that the only way to grasp a continuous process is to stop it. Processes are stopped *conceptually*, not actually, for by stopping a process one kills it. To understand reality then, one must conceptually stop a process; by stopping the process, events in space–time can be defined and a picture of a moment of reality can be constructed.

In attempting to understand or to conceptualize the continuity of space, we make the equivalent of a Dedekind cut (Dedekind, 1901). As we cut the continuous space–time process at different places, then facts can be observed to be in existence at each particular place. Natural phenomena can be interpreted as objects or events that exist in space and time and are perceivable in principle. They are delineated by concepts and their contents are the intuitive data that are the concepts of perception: natural phenomena are therefore episodes in the continuous flux of being. Elements of objective reality are in essence facts in space–time. But facts about space are physically conditioned by the frame of reference to which they relate. They are also conditioned by the conceptual frame by which they become known. Recognition of the existence of such facts is a product of the way the mind reacts to the flux outside its boundary and makes its Dedekind cuts. Knowledge of space results from the reaction between mind and the external universe. The content of knowledge (for example, knowledge of nature) is composed of selections from this flux. Mind orders the content and builds it into a theoretic structure. The structure is not something already there to be inspected and investigated by scientists (as would be the case if Cartesian dualism was accepted); it is built by scientists and is the achievement of communal thinking.

IV. 'EVERYDAY REALITY' AS PROCESS

Bergmann (1957) argues that process knowledge is the most complete and powerful form of knowledge. He also assumes that process knowledge is divisible into subprocesses and through this divisibility we find out much about life and everyday experiences. Through the workings of various subprocesses we get to know multiple realities including various cultural-specific realities as well as our own subjective reality. These realities are formed through an interchange of what each person thinks is inside or outside his/her organism and according to what the community thinks is inside or outside an organism. There is therefore *a dialectical relationship between individual and environment*, in which the environment affects and gives meaning to the individual who, at the same time, acts with respect to and gives meaning to environment (Berger and Pullberg, 1965). This of course is the process of objectification mentioned earlier in this paper.

The objectification process has been subdivided into four moments or subprocesses (Berger and Pullberg, 1965, p. 200); these are objectification, externalization, internalization and historization. Each is important in the following ways:

(a) a consensus of objectifications is the basis for institutionalization and the acceptance of a common external reality;

(b) externalization separates self from external objects and allows external reality to have a structure independent of self;

(c) internalization represents conscious awareness of an external object and the assimilation of the objectified experience into a belief system; and

(d) historization is transmission of knowledge about objectifications among people.

For any individual only a small number of experiences are sedimented such that they remain in consciousness (Berger and Luckman, 1966). These experiences then congeal into recognizable entities which may be used for referencing purposes. Consciousness of certain experiences which are sedimented are transmitted from generation to generation in the form of institutions. Institutions of both natural and artificial kinds provide the structure on which everyday life functions — in other words they embody a general social knowledge of reality. Awareness of parts of this general social knowledge allows us to abstract from various external environments, to focus on and interpret cues relating to such environments, and to participate in an everyday existence. Although there is a difference from present moment to present moment, individuals rely on knowledge of a continuing objective reality to provide a security with which to face the next presence. As one aid, we continually rewrite or re-interpret the past (Meade, 1932: p. 11) and this helps us to continue existing by being able to face the next present.

To understand (and to exist in) everyday environments, people learn to select critical subsets of the mass of experiences to which they are exposed. Experiences of which we become aware are stored as information and assist us in living a real everyday life. This continual and simultaneous exposure to experiences, the sensing and storing of bits of information, and the use of information to cope with the task of existing can be termed process knowledge of everyday life (Nyerges, 1975).

It is this process which we need to 'cut' and examine closely if we are to gain further meaningful insights into the relationship between mankind and the environments in which he lives.

V. CONCLUDING COMMENTS

Although I have spent considerable time and space in this paper recording some of the primitives and assumptions necessary for the acquisition of knowledge of spatial form and spatial processes, I have also tried to introduce some epistemological assumptions relating to the study of the constructions superimposed on external reality by the minds of sensate beings. By putting forward these assumptions a wide range of problems become at once obvious.

Specific types of questions that are implicit in the discussion are: What relationship exists between objective reality and the world inside our heads? How can we determine the nature of the relationship between man in the world and the world in man? How can we determine what is assimilated by individuals from this objective reality and to what do we accommodate ourselves? How can we extract from people what their re-constructions of objective reality are? How can we represent these extractions in an external form so that others can observe them? How can we analyze the representations that we so construct? What purposes would underlie the analysis of such representations?

As geographers we have a number of particularly important things to which we must pay attention if we are to improve the level of understanding of the worlds in which we live and if we are to hasten the accumulation of knowledge about these worlds. If we confine ourselves to determining what is outside of us, we are in effect concentrating only on a process of external validation of a segment of this large external objective reality. Even if we are capable of establishing what exactly exists in the external environment at a particular point in time, for the most part we establish its presence only for a fleeting period of time. While this fleeting period of time may be enough for us to obtain a generalized picture of how the objects in external reality are associated with each other, and while the gaining of such knowledge may help us in coordinating our activities with the object relationships that we can determine, it should not be the whole essence and purpose of our search for knowledge. Obviously, many of the certainties for which we search are those which simply establish the permanence or impermanence, the transitive nature, or the stabilities, of elements in the external environment in which we place ourselves, but we must remember that our attempts to operate in these environments are in a very real sense conditioned by the constructions we place on them. In order to remove ourselves from the realm of utter chaos we impose many different structures on such environments and we impose even more structures on the activity relationships between ourselves and environments. Thus, as well as an objective physical environment existing which can be described in mechanistic terms there are a series of constructions placed on such environments which limit man's ability to interact with them and partly condition his behaviors. The success with which we can form and conform to these constructions and with which we are able to use elements of objective reality, are very much dependent on the transformations that are made at the individual level from objective reality to the world inside our heads. It is even more important to know the nature of the transformations between what is extracted from an external environment and what is translated into an action so as to begin to achieve the barest skeleton of process knowledge.

Department of Geography
University of California, Santa Barbara

NOTES

[1] The final draft of this paper was written while the author was a Visiting Professor in the Department of Geography at the University of Aukland in 1976. I would like to acknowledge the insightful criticisms that were made by members of the Auckland faculty at that time.

[2] Except possibly autistic and/or 'insane' persons.

BIBLIOGRAPHY

Appleyard, D.: 1970, 'Styles and Methods of Structuring a City', *Environment and Behavior* 2, 100–117.

Berger, P. and Luckmann, T.: 1966, *The Social Construction of Reality*, Garden City, Doubleday and Co., New York.

Berger, P. and Pullberg, S.: 1965, 'Reification and the Sociological Critique of Consciousness', *History and Theory* IV, 2.

Bergmann, G.: 1957, *Philosophy of Science*, University of Wisconsin Press, Madison.

Dedekind, R.: 1901, 'Continuity and Irrational Numbers', *Essays on the Theory of Numbers* (translated by W. W. Beman), Open Court Publishing Company, La Salle, Illinois.

Downs, R.: 1970, 'The Cognitive Structure of a Shopping Center', *Environment and Behavior* 2, 13–39.

Eichenbaum, J. and Gale, S.: 1971, 'Form, Function and Process: A Methodological Inquiry', *Economic Geography* 47, 525–544.

Golledge, R. G.: 1970, 'Process Approaches to the Analysis of Human Spatial Behavior', Department of Geography Discussion Paper, Columbus, Ohio.

Golledge, R. G., Briggs, R., and Demko, D.: 1969, 'The Configuration of Distances in Intra-Urban Space', *Proceedings of the Association of American Geographers* 1, 60–65.

Gould, P.: 1965, *On Mental Maps*, MICMG Papers in Geography, Ann Arbor.

Kenny, A.: 1973, *Wittgenstein*, Harvard University Press, Cambridge, Massachusetts.

King, L. J.: 1969, 'The Analysis of Spatial Form and Its Relation to Geographic Theory', *Annals of the Association of American Geographers* 59, 573–595.

Lee, H. N.: 1969, 'Two Views of the Nature of Knowledge', *Tulane Studies in Philosophy*, 85–91.

Lee, H. N.: 1973, *Percepts and Theoretical Knowledge*, University of Tennessee Press, Memphis, Tennessee.

Lynch, K.: 1960, *The Image of the City*, M.I.T. Press, Cambridge, Massachusetts.

Meade, G. H.: 1932, *The Philosophy of the Present*, Open Court Publishing Company, Chicago.

Nyerges, T.: c.1975, 'Reality, Process and Internal Relationships', unpublished manuscript, Department of Geography, Ohio State University.

Olsson, G.: 1969, 'Inference Problems in Locational Analysis', in K. R. Cox and R. G. Golledge (eds.), *Behavioral Problems in Geography: A Symposium*, Department of Geography, Northwestern University.

Olsson, G.: 1971, 'Correspondence Rules and Social Engineering', *Economic Geography* **47**, 545–554.

Olsson, G. and Gale, S.: 1968, 'Spatial Theory and Human Behavior', *Papers and Proceedings of the Regional Science Association* **21**, 229–242.

Russell, B.: 1918, *Mysticism and Logic*, Garden City, Doubleday and Company, Inc., New York.

Watts, A.: 1966, *The Book: On the Taboo Against Knowing Who Your Are*, Random House, New York.

Whitehead, A. N.: 1929, *Process and Reality*, MacMillan and Company, New York.

Whitehead, A. N.: 1933, *Adventures of Ideas*, The MacMillan Company, New York.

Wittgenstein, L.: 1922, *Tractatus Logico Philosophicus*, Harcourt, Brace and Company, Inc., New York.

PETER GOULD

SIGNALS IN THE NOISE

... only human beings find their way by a light
that illumines more than the patch of ground they
stand on.

PETER and JEAN MEDAWAR, *Revising the Facts
of Life*, Harpers, 1977.

I. INTRODUCTION

This essay expresses opinion. It could hardly express anything else, since it is
not an exercise in logic, using specified rules to tease out from stated conditions the consequences contained in them. My aim is to capture your assent,
even though it is only partially given. Without such an aim there is no point
in writing, and, equally, no point in reading. If you disagree with my opinions,
I hope you tell me. I may revise some or all of them, and look again at a number of questions which are far from resolved. In scholastic fashion, I shall
marshall references to support my opinions, but these will be only more
opinions, frequently those of authority figures in my current intellectual
pantheon. A few of these seem to be permanent residents, others are new
arrivals, and some may shortly disappear. But be skeptical of all of them:
opinions supporting opinions should not be taken too seriously.

It is an unnerving experience to write a 'philosophical' essay, for I believe
with Nietzsche that it is practically impossible to say anything new. Philosophers have covered a lot of ground; they tend to be clever, articulate people,
and the better ones are very intelligent indeed. At the same time, it is disappointing to see how the same questions appear millenium after millenium,
and how much remains unresolved by their concentrated speculation. Time
and again a new body of thought, a new school, insinuates that it has super-
seded or absorbed previous approaches (Mehta, 1962; Popper, 1976). In
reality, it only captures the assent of a new coterie for a few decades, or perhaps centuries, but then it falls. Sometimes philosophers 'absorb' previous
ideas, in much the same way that newly generated theories about the physical
world 'absorb' earlier constructs, reducing them by equivalence concepts, but

121

S. Gale and G. Olsson (eds.), Philosophy in Geography, 121–154. All Rights Reserved.
Copyright © 1979 by D. Reidel Publishing Company, Dordrecht, Holland.

then moving beyond them (Stegmüller, 1976). Sometimes an older philosophical position is nourishing (i.e., Hegel → Marx: Popper → Stegmüller: Nietzsche → Foucault), but often a former idea is positively dietetic, for example Poincaré's insistence on the primacy of Euclidean geometry, versus Einstein's willingness to explore the implications of the Riemannian (Kockelmans, 1972, p. 400). With such a record, we cannot take ourselves too seriously, and it is healthy to imagine how inadequate the essays of this book will appear when someone reads them a few decades or a century from now. We shall almost certainly know many more things of fundamental biological and physiological importance, and our extensive use of prosthetic intelligence will both answer some current questions and make others redundant.

II. THE COMMONPLACE DIVINITY OF MAN

Lying on my back in an open field on a warm summer's night convinces me that teleological speculations are a waste of time. Even a superficial reading of contemporary astronomy reinforces the absurdity, the futility, the utter hubris of asking such questions. What bodies of myth have congealed through the ages in response to such speculations is important for the intellectual cast they have given to whole cultures, but this is an entirely different thing from ascribing intellectual worth to the primitive stories themselves. Ignoring the infinite regress of teleology allows us to focus, in a fashion less emotional than usual, upon material objects with a capacity to sustain and reproduce themselves briefly by organizing energy inputs from a small star. What we call living forms appear to be small, local, and highly temporary negentropic perturbations in an expanding, energy-smoothing process. In common with all living forms, those termed human have changed over time by a process we label *evolution*. The word is unfortunate, for it has acquired a load of mythical connotation characteristic of nineteenth century England. Speculations based upon it are completely tautological, for in a theory dealing with the 'survival of the fittest', the fit are defined by survival. Since there can never be a counterexample, we must consider Darwinism as a metaphysical research program (Popper, 1976, p. 168), a body of ideas replacing primitive religious myths, but not a theory since it is untestable.

With this *caveat*, human beings have evolved and survived in diverse physical environments, and in the presence of larger, carnivorous creatures. We ascribe such survival to the enlarged brain (Calhoun, 1971), a slightly alkaline lump of matter running on glycogen at 25 watts (Beer, 1974). Unless we wish to generate pleasure by self-glorification, there is no reason to regard the brain as something out of the ordinary, which is to say that if we wish to regard it as miraculous, then we are obliged to regard everything else in the universe as miraculous. As a posture for consciousness, this intellectual dead end does not appear to be desirable, but I will be the first to admit that we have entered an area beyond the 'bubble of discourse', and rational discussion is not possible if you wish to disagree.

Like all other living forms, the brain has developed by chance from the necessity of random conjunctions of elements chained into self-replicating molecules (Monod, 1972). Presumably it has enlarged, and grown topologically richer (Thom, 1975), by a selection process necessarily and tautologically implying survival value. After all, we seem to be here. A basic question, then, is what sentient capacities have increased the chances of human survival? In brief, I am asking what we know about the fundamental proclivities of the brain before we start using it in traditionally speculative ways. Perhaps such a prosaic beginning will constrain later flights of Germanic fancy, and avoid simultaneously the plodding naivities of Anglo-Saxon empiricism. It is likely that proponents of each will disagree.

Despite considerable efforts, we know little about the general proclivities and operations of the brain. Molecular, neural and synaptal research are asking different, highly reductionist questions, while psychiatric models are still extremely crude. Yet one finds lots of false modesty, but little humbleness, in molecular biology and psychiatry. It is curious how brains, engaged upon an infinitely recursive process of self-examination and awareness (Brown, 1969, p. 105; Steiner, 1972, p. 77), are prepared to stop and imply that the Truth about themselves is just around the corner – another push along this line of research, a bit of fine tuning (after all, nineteenth century Vienna is not exactly typical), and surely we can see the day when . . . ?

What can brains do? Along with the rest of the neural world, they appear to be able to draw a distinction (Brown, 1969, p. 1; Bannister and Fransella, 1971, p. 7). Such distinction drawing appears to be biased towards things that move, presumably for survival reasons (stones and logs do not eat you), and taken to an extreme form of cleaved dichotomy, as a form of total partitional thinking, it seems to have become intellectually dysfunctional. Most distinction drawing appears highly visual, presumably because of the extreme sensory importance of the eyes for survival, and Thom (1975, p. 5) has noted that intellectualization consists of interpreting a given process *geometrically* – where this word now has deeper connotations than those usually ascribed by traditional thinking in Geography and the Human Sciences. We could perhaps imagine other, topologically richer, forms for which another sense is dominant, and speculate what the equivalent of geometry might be in a world of sound or feel. But this is best left to creative writers of science fiction: in our world the deaf person in the wilderness has a better chance of maintaining the gene pool than the blind.

Secondly, the brain has the ability to impose pattern upon a set of events, and such a proclivity also appears to have had great survival value. Pattern seeking and imposition seem to be absolutely fundamental functions of the brain, and in as much as pattern is defined in terms of its opposite, randomness (itself a human construct), pattern implies predictability (Polanyi, 1963; Sayre, 1963). Even a slight edge here, a flickering taper of intellect reducing the gloom ahead, has greatly increased the chances for survival. I am obliged to assume an imposition of pattern upon chaos, in as much as it is impossible for a brain to assume the opposite – namely the existence of a pattern 'out there' in reality (whatever 'reality' means) – since a demonstration of the latter, would be an instance of the former. Similarly, with Borges (1964, p. xii), I assume imposition upon *chaos*, despite the authoritative declaration of Thom (1975, p. 1) that the universe is not chaotic [because?] there is local clumping and some degree of stability. These 'reasons' are *non sequiturs*. Even simple nearest neighbor studies indicate that quadrats shifted around in E^2 impose local clustering, chaos (randomness), or uniformity. We impose pattern at the local level, at a particular scale of observation, but the non-chaotic universe of Thom must imply some ordering presence. At the moment my sights are set lower, and revising Thomas Aquinas somewhat, it is for the sake of reasonableness that I shall suspend belief (Popper, 1976, p. 87).

The proclivity of pattern imposition is so strong, so fundamental, that a number of people have invoked genetic imprinting to account for it (Thom, 1975, p. 13; Popper, 1976, pp. 48–49). Nor is this the only area where genetic transmission is invoked: in the tightly related area of language, it has been postulated that the deep-structure is genetically programmed (Chomsky, 1957, 1965, 1968, 1975; Lyons, 1970, p. 4); and in the closely associated area of problem-solving the propensity of the human brain to search for structural invariance has again been founded upon genetic transmission (Popper, 1976, p. 49; Thom, 1975, p. 13). Heredity plays a fundamental role. That this raises political problems today should not obscure the fact, which is not to deny in the least the part played by a cultural environment. In extreme cases, we know that a brain's early environment can totally override genetic imprinting, for the brains of infants existing in isolation never become human in any sense distinguishable from non-human forms. Most either–or, nurture–nature discussions, when they are not simply silly, are distorted by the latent political and ethical questions raised.

We also have much firmer evidence today of the inseparable and interacting effects of hereditary and environment from a broad spectrum of research in fields demarcated by traditionally drawn and culturally transmitted distinctions. That these fields are dealing with connected facets of the same problem should make us ask about the intellectual utility of the distinctions. It is impossible to review many examples here, but the ethnographic work of Whorf, and many subsequent workers, has demonstrated the role of language in shaping our view of the world (Whorf, 1956). Laing has formalized our intuition that projected and induced cultural perturbations are transmitted by the response stuctures of one generation to another, and he has made us acutely aware of the way an individual experiential structure fails to be mapped onto a public event (Laing, 1969a; Laing and Esterson, 1970; Levine, 1975, pp. 3–5). That his language of formalization is set-theoretic should not escape our attention. Thom has noted that the brain's dynamic to think of only one thing at a time constrains our apprehension of the world (Thom, 1975, p. 11), and even if we enlarge the repertoire that human thought can use, from verbal and written language to pictures and algebras, we must acknowledge the acute constraints under which we try to think. It is surely not difficult to make a strong case for the rapid extension of artificial, prosthetic intelligence under such limited natural circumstances. Finally, in this necessarily limited review, Kelly has placed the problem-solving propensity at the center of his Man as Scientist (Kelly, 1955; Bannister and Fransella, 1971), and since this defines science properly as a prosaic, everyday affair, it raises the question of clinging to yet another traditionally-drawn distinction (Snow, 1959; Leavis, 1963) – something we shall consider again later.

Distinctions, patterns, languages, solving problems, culture and heredity: a highly connected structure of enquiry that should be considered in a multi-dimensional discourse space, and not for the first time do I feel the constraint and loss as Time's Arrow maps such complexity onto the single dimension of conventional narrative. The order of consideration depends simply upon which projection we choose.

III. PATTERN

By pattern I shall mean structural regularity in a local space. As I have noted, the perception of pattern implies predictability, and also survival value in a species sense. Predictability necessarily implies order, and there are (at least?) four types: orders of symmetry, clumping, periodicity, and time–space sequences capable of being extrapolated. These are not mutually exclusive: for example, symmetry and periodicity both imply repetition of form. But all orders are juxtaposed against randomness, which is defined in terms of an inability of the brain to pre- or postdict an event with any edge of certainty. Claims have been made by eminent philosophers, scientists and mathematicians that a random series "[passing] all statistical tests of randomness" can be generated (Popper, 1976, p. 101; Hawkins, 1964, p. 199; Ulam, 1974, pp. 323–324), thus making it perfectly predictable to anyone who knows the underlying generating function. This contradiction is only apparent: it dissolves when one follows up the references, and actually tries out the suggestions. All sequences soon cycle, display pattern, and are therefore not random even if the aggregate distributions are rectangular. So much for statistical tests (Gould, 1976, pp. 139–144). Conversely, it is amusing to read the tortuous reasoning of statisticians when a series is generated by an empircal process (dice throwing, geiger clicks, etc.), and does not conform to 'all statistical tests'. Randomness in the finite aggregate, say the statisticians, must conform to our template (Brown, 1957) – or should we say, perhaps, our *pattern*?

In this short essay, it is only possible to demonstrate fleetingly the dominance of pattern in *all* areas of human inquiry. The Polish novelist and playwright Gombrowicz has affirmed the creative act as one of pattern formulation (May, 1975, p. 61; Richler, Fortier and May, 1975); literary criticism today links apparently diverse and superficial instances with deeper, underlying forms (Barthes, 1963, 1974, 1975); stylistics expresses language not as " ... reality, but a pattern in reality" (Turner, 1973, p. 29); a great author writes " ... behind the cottonwool is hidden a pattern" (Woolf, 1977); cybernectics equates pattern and model (Beer, 1972, 1974); and architects note that the functional origin of a design problem is in pattern seeking (Alexander, 1966, p. 15). From history we see growing acknowledgement of pattern imposition (Mehta, 1962, pp. 124–126, quoting Carr and Toynbee), while narrative that decomposes complexity into simpler components (Braudel, 1972, pp. 20–21) represents a form of intuitive Fourier analysis for which psychology and research in artificial intelligence confirm that the

" . . . higher frequency dynamics are associated with the subsystems, the lower-frequency dynamics with the larger systems" (Simon, 1969, p. 106). From formal enquiry into mental processes (de Bono, 1971, p. 92), and research in artificial intelligence (Greg, 1974; Kotovsky and Simon, 1973; Newell and Simon, 1973), it appears that the seeking of pattern is a fundamental act of creativity; and the psychiatry of Jung confirms artistic form as an often unconscious expression of pattern (Storr, 1973, pp. 96–97). Increasingly, the contemporary study of literature moves from the particular to emphasize repetitive, constantly reoccurring themes (Sharpless, 1974; Borrowes, Lapides, and Shawcross, 1973). Music, poetry and mathematics are founded on patterns generated by rare and gifted intelligences. To marshall examples from areas traditionally labeled as science is simply unnecessary.

That the patterns we impose are not permanent may be seen in the long history of replacement, transformation and change (Scheffler, 1970; Ehrmann, 1970). Many have noted how mythologies are devices for ordering experience (Cranston, 1969; Storr, 1973; Hawkins, 1964; Levi-Strauss, 1955, 1964, 1966, 1968; Leach, 1969, 1970), and how they corrupt languages (Barthes, 1957), but they too are examples of the contingent structures human beings use. The vinicultural symbolism of the Bacchanalia is borrowed almost intact by Christianism (Campbell, 1974; Jung, 1964, pp. 141–143), with graftings of fertility rites from European animism. "We are writing to shape into a version a tangle of events that was not designed as a pattern", writes the historian Taylor (1976, p. 11); his colleague Carr echoes that " . . . the facts of the past are simply what human minds make of them" (Mehta, 1962, p. 159); and Geyl's *Napoleon: For and Against* is an explicit attempt to demonstrate a variety of contingent patterns on the same events. Newton's Laws, once immutable, are now contingent expressions absorbed by equivalence statements into a larger structure (Kockelmans, 1972, p. 400), while *a* physics, one of many, may be defined richly or weakly depending upon the algebra onto which it happens to be mapped (Atkin, 1965). Linguistics is a succession of models contingently held (Lyons, 1970), reminding one of the early days of the Copenhagen School, when atomic models designed for posterity lasted weeks (Hoffman, 1959, pp. 45–58). And if Foucault and Nietzsche are right, that language reflects the desires of men whose power drives are shaped by society, then as societies transform and break (Marchand, 1974, p. 18), so *all* expressions of language must be regarded as contingent upon the social underpinnings.

A fundamental act of imposing pattern is classification, an arbitrary act of drawing distinctions. The aesthetic, pleasure-seeking component may be strong, as we know from the 'tidiness complex' of the collector, and studies of seminal minds such as Sade, Fourier and Loyola, for whom the obsession and pleasure of classification has been emphasized (Barthes, 1976). The arbitrary nature of all taxonomy is worth stating explicitly: the recognition of similarity and distinction appears to be almost entirely a projection of culture (Foucault, 1965). Desires for the absolute, for the objective, are themselves culturally specific (Steiner, 1974a, p. 51). Leach has noted the acute comments of Lévi-Strauss on the seemingly bizarre classificatory schemes used by the English for animals, schemes just as arbitrary and incomprehensible as certain categories of Australian aboriginal groups (Leach, 1970, pp. 36 and 40). Foucault presents the 'Chinese encyclopedia' of Borges on the first page of *The Order of Things (Les mots et les choses)*, to shock the reader into a state of disorientation, a state in which all the familiar ordering constructs of Linneaus are knocked away, so forcing the reader into a state of self-examination in which the fetters of culture are themselves loosened. At the same time, it is worth noting how perceptive analyses of such fundamental acts of pattern imposition in a culture have led to much deeper insights (Levi-Strauss, 1963). The arbitrary, contingent nature of classificatory schemes was recognized in earlier debates; Linneaus, with his great authority, demanding that the natural world should be accommodated by classification, while Buffon and Bonnet insisted upon a graduated continum (Foucault, 1973, pp. 126, 146–147; Glacken, 1967). It is a thought-provoking and salutary lesson to see the way the pendulum between these views is swinging.

Classically, that is to say since the days of Linneaus, a 'good' classification has been defined in terms of imposing a partition upon the finite set of individual, discrete elements. Much intellectual energy has been expended in traditional numerical taxonomy upon finding 'better' ways of putting things into non-overlapping boxes. Today one can only marvel at such simplicity and the unintelligent way in which the leading exponents of taxonomy have been followed. Granting that the brain draws distinctions, one would have thought that the stress-inducing experience of forcing a partition would have given emotional, if not intellectual, insight that a pattern of cleavage could destroy more than it created. Despite paying lip service to the idea that boundary lines on maps are only representative of shaded zones of gradual transition, geographers have rushed blindly down the Gadarene slopes of traditional numerical taxonomy, a formal area where the underlying partitional thinking is seldom examined. They should have known better, and insisted that taxonomy enlarge its view to accommodate them, rather than conforming to existing, and highly constrained, methods.

The notion of overlap, of course, leads directly to the idea of a *cover*, rather than a partition, a reasonably obvious idea that appeared in botany thirty years ago, at a time when the proponent did not have the mathematical apparatus to express and develop it (Hogben, 1963). It is ironical that it should be available in a popular book for the lay person before being in the consciousness, let alone operational approaches, of most people working in the human and biological sciences (de Bono, 1971, p. 204). I partially exclude the physical sciences here, because there seem to be some fundamental differences in the meaning of the word classification. Mendelev, for example, did not classify in the sense of partitioning a set of elements, but found a pattern, a new and original cover set, expressed in spatial, two-dimensional form, which included blank spaces for elements undiscovered in his day. For such a marvellously creative feat of structuring he was ridiculed and nearly broken by his peers. With that historical lesson behind them, physicists today are more open. Indeed, the success of group theoretic approaches in quantum mechanics laid such a basis of intellectual acceptance that the pattern of the eight-fold way for baryons, based upon a Lie group, actually included a gap that was later filled (Stewart, 1975, pp. 274–277; Gardner, 1970, p. 210).

In contrast to arranging elements in a spatial pattern, and guessing that gaps have meaning, a classificatory act in the biological and human sciences consists of assigning elements of a set to subsets by partition. Anyone who has formally approached a set of data with a traditional numerical technique has 'felt' the tension and uncertainty generated by the unexamined authority of partitional thinking. It is for this reason that a critique by Atkin is so important, not the least because it is couched in completely practical terms (Atkin, 1975a, p. 13). In Britain, as elsewhere, the Ministry of Labour's job classification scheme is partitional, so it destroys some of the information inherent in such 'ambiguous' elements as jobs. Destroying information by forcing a partition means greater difficulty in getting unemployed people to new jobs: the partition is dysfunctional. In Atkin's language of structure, the insistence of a classical partition, rather than a cover, destroys structure inherent in the data, hinders traffic (searching for jobs) on the backcloth, and generates the t-forces indicative of the stress induced by forcing a partition in the first place.

IV. PROBLEM SOLVING

If we admit to much ignorance about the process of structuring pattern, how much more must we be tentative in the larger area of problem-solving, in which patterns play such an important role. It is in this area that we find little help from philosophers; as Simon has noted, some of the opinions of the earliest philosophers went unchallenged for over two millenia. No one, for example, pointed out the absurdity of the conclusion derived by Socrates with Meno that all answers were already in the 'mind' and only had to be found. Such a notion would imply a genetic inheritance of the infinite set of all solutions to all problems ever to be postulated. There is no need to discuss this sort of thing with philosophical solemnity.

Physical objects, possessing a topology of such richness that it defines life (Thom, 1975, p. 8; Popper, 1976, p. 179; Simon, 1969, p. 97), solve problems by sensing a structure or pattern in the environment. Whether it is spermatozoa sensing an acidity gradient, or a mathematician developing the implications of an algebra, both require some degree of structure in the problem domain to find a solution. Intelligence requires a problem in which there is structure, and if solutions were randomly distributed in a problem space there would be no way of exhibiting intelligence (Simon and Newell, 1976). In brief, problem solving requires a detectable structure; it is *structure detection* that emerges as a key concept in the construction of artificial intelligence. Virtually all of the concerted efforts over the past twenty years have extended the abilities of machines to detect properties that could be mapped onto structures already contained within the algorithm (Moore and Newell, 1974, p. 251). Algorithms, such as UNDERSTAND, constitute formal searches for isomorphs (Simon and Hayes, 1976, p. 165; Klahr, 1974, p. 300), which may be viewed as stricter, more tightly defined forms of analogy – the richest source of human problem solving (Hawkins, 1964, pp. 249–250). In this they are modelling the brain, which also explores the structure of a problem and tries to map it upon a known form, or searches a space with known heuristics as guiding constraints in a hillclimbing process. Such a program as Lenat's AM has generated rediscoveries in areas of mathematics originally opened up by such seminal thinkers as Ramamujam (Lenat, 1976, pp. 285–286). Every application of a standard optimizing technique demonstrates the process of analogical search and structural mapping. Some fascinating, cross-linked ideas emerge from this expanding body of work. Experiments with UNDERSTAND demonstrate that the way objects are named, and the way the internal problem is represented, are virtually determined by the language of the problem instructions (Simon and Hayes, 1976, p. 189), something that is directly confirmed in humans by Whorf, and an idea explicitly built upon by Atkin (1974a). It is little wonder that the latter has focused upon the problem of finding a language to express structure, and his demonstration is enhanced by the wide application of his work, particularly in the game of chess (Atkin, 1974a; Atkin, Hartston and Witten, 1976; Atkin and Witten, 1975). This work is particularly important if we think about the possible extensions over the next century into other 'games', such as economics, politics, and many other areas of human affairs.

It has been clear for many years that tree-searching is *not* what Grandmasters do as a general approach to a game of chess. Efforts in these directions demand bigger computers to search down the combinatorial branches a bit further, postulate up to 50 000 templates of previous positions, or call for non-local use of information in a space where search is still conceived essentially as a tree – except that we now need to connect some of the branches (Simon and Newell, 1976). In contrast, Atkin has described the microgeography of a chess board, and the relationships between its aggressive inhabitants, to express the problems at the positional, or strategic, level that appears to match much more closely the 'fields of force' sense of Master play (Steiner, 1974b). The structure vectors clearly reflect the positional dissolution of one player, and the growing dominance of the other, long before resignation.

V. THE LANGUAGES OF OUR INVESTIGATIONS

In the structural description of chess we have an example of the way in which the expression of a problem in a particular language changes our abilities to see patterns, anticipate events, and solve problems. Having covered some of these questions in simpler, pedagogic settings (Gould, 1976, 1977a, 1977b), I shall make only a few, fairly brief remarks here. We have many languages (dance, theatre, music, film, body gestures, and so on), but when we investigate the world around us, rather than express our inner sensibilities, we tend to confine our languages to three; the verbal, the graphic, and the algebraic. Many have commented upon the problems of using ordinary verbal languages: the way linguistic structures make translations virtually impossible (Popper, 1976, p. 24); the manner in which new areas of analysis extend " . . . beyond the point of simplicity where language ceases to act normally as a currency of communication" (Brown, 1969, p. xx; Steiner, 1969, p. 33); the way we are using more words to say less (Steiner, 1972, p. 96); and the way in which subject–object differentiation varies between, say, Greek and Chinese grammars (Pirsig, 1974, p. 344), with profound consequences for the way in which these two cultural traditions perceive and structure the world. Bernstein has shown the way in which linguistic differences between classes in England shape their experiences and the manner in which they construe their social and physical environments (Bernstein, 1959, 1961; Halsey, Floyd and Anderson, 1961). In this area there is little one can add to increase the awareness of anyone who has taken a reasonably intelligent interest in human thought and investigation.

But less has been said about the graphical and algebraic languages, perhaps because much less education is attempted in these despite their growing importance in *all* fields (Steiner, 1969, p. 36). Graphical languages vary, but central to all is the idea of a map. And I use the word in a greatly expanded, and intellectually much richer, sense than the traditional portrayal of a piece of the earth's surface. It is central to something we might call 'spatial thinking', a dimension of intellect so potent and creative that one wonders why so little attention is paid to it. There is even some evidence that young children possess natural skills and propensities which are allowed to atrophy in the present educational system (Blaut, McCleary and Blaut, 1970).

Any graphic expression is a filtered, mathematical relation, and it can be considered *fruitfully* as a model (Hawkins, 1964, p. 32; Toulmin, 1953). In many such selected and contrived simplifications there can be an intellectual immediacy, literally an 'Oh I see!', that is difficult for verbal and algebraic languages to match. One only has to contrast the words and equations of catastrophe theory with the two and three dimensional graphic expressions (Zeeman, 1976; Isnard and Zeeman, 1975; Collins, 1975). No wonder Thom has equated intellectualization with geometricalization; but why are we all so blind to the pedagogic implications (Steiner, 1971, p. 111)? The problem is that most of the graphic potential in an investigation or exposition is wasted: we seem incapable of employing what is available, even though the repertoire of imaginative graphic approaches has expanded greatly in recent years (Tobler, 1973, 1975; Tobler and Weinberg, 1971). Part of the problem is that our thinking is confined to traditional earth spaces, when in many investigative areas people desperately need maps of the botanical, theatre, psychotherapy, archeological, intellectual, and other specialized spaces relevant for their particular subject. For in Leibnitzian fashion, the spaces are *defined* by the relationships between the elements or objects that are the focus of the investigation, and the expression or projection of a set of relationships in E^2 or E^3 can sometimes add greatly to creative thought (Gardner, 1970, p. 159; Weinberg, 1972, p. 16). Such an enlargement of the traditional definition of a map brings it much closer to that of the mathematician, and joins it to the spaces of the systems analyst and the cybernetician. For the latter, a sense of dynamics can be achieved by emphasizing the trajectory of a system through the appropriate phase space.

A willingness to think in non-traditional spatial terms, to consider carefully the space appropriate to a problem area, and how one might transform one into another, could also clarify some problems whose difficulty may be more apparent than real. For example, diffusion processes, which appear hierarchic on the ordinary map, may be considered more simply as contagious in the appropriate space. Influenza is carried by people to people, and appears to be controlled by some degree of 'trickle down' effect in the urban hierarchy. In a suitably transformed, perhaps multidimensional space, in which distances between cities are determined by a gravity type formulation, the diffusion of influenza may be treated as contagious if the cities are 'captured' by a multidimensional bubble spreading from the initial source.

There come times, however, when graphical languages are no longer adequate, for the dimensionality of many problems today forces us to eschew the visual. It is here that algebraic languages take over as the *only* forms capable of describing complexity with any degree of depth. Ironically, those who point most frequently to the complexity of the Human Sciences, almost as an excuse to do nothing at all, are frequently those who deliberately avoid the intellectual efforts to learn the languages most appropriate for their expression. Along the same lines, it is worth noting how algebraic expressions of human complexity arouse deep resentments if 'translations' are not provided. As far as the physical and biological sciences are concerned, lay people accept that many areas of contemporary research are far beyond them. But in the Human Sciences, where all acknowledge the extreme complexity of the subject matter, there is the feeling that somehow everything should be understandable to everyone. The contradiction is an interesting topic of investigation in its own right.

What is the intellectual strength of algebraic languages, the "unreasonable effectiveness of mathematics", to use Wigner's puzzled phrase (Browder, 1976, p. 548)? Surely it lies in the fact that every algebra represents a relatively well-explored area of human thought at a highly abstract and unambiguous level. Quite apart from the question of multidimensionality, if we can map a subject area onto an algebra, and the algebra is rich enough to bear the complexity of the subject, then highly creative extensions of the subject matter may be discovered by exploring and interpreting the implications already inherent in the algebra itself. For example, some theories can be reduced to others by equivalence concepts, although the theories, and the conceptual systems that underpin them, are completely different (Stegmüller,

1976; Kockelmans, 1976, p. 295). In artificial intelligence, the Merlin program maps problems onto equivalent structures already known (Simon and Newell, 1976; Moore and Newell, 1974; Greg, 1974), and Knuth has noted how the traveling salesman problem is computationally equivalent to hundreds of problems of general interest (Knuth, 1976, p. 1240).

The idea of mapping a subject area onto an algebra is extremely simple, and pedagogic examples can be given at the advanced high school–beginning university level (Strack, 1971; Gould, 1977c, 1977d). It is easy to show, for example, that simple linear algebra can bear von Thunen's theory extended to mixed land uses once linear constraints are introduced, demographic structure and prediction, flows through networks, and numerous other geographical subjects usually treated as quite separate and disparate areas, although they share a similar algebraic structure. Admittedly, the algebra is not very robust, and the applications are pedagogically simple. On the other hand, Nobel Prizes are awarded in economics for exactly the same naive mappings.

Perhaps the best examples of mapping traditional subject matter areas onto algebras are the early work of Atkin, and the more recent extensions into diverse areas of application in the Human Sciences, including medicine (Atkin, 1972a; Chamberlain, 1976). He noted how *a* physics begins by defining a set of elements, a set of scales, and the complete set of measures (Atkin, 1965, pp. 499–500; 1971). The content is then defined by the elements, while the structure is dependent solely upon the scales. Thus *a* theoretical physics can be defined by an algebra whose elements are in correspondence with the measures by bijective mappings (Atkin, 1965, p. 500). In such a framework, 'conservation of energy'. in one algebra is the same as 'wave motion' in another by an algebraic endomorphism. The theory of wave motion is nothing more than the mapping itself. Atkin has followed his own advice, to map measures onto various algebras to explore their full significance, by writing a language of structure in algebraic topology suitable for the expression of human affairs (Atkin, 1972b, 1972c, 1973, 1974a, 1974b, 1974c, 1974d, 1975a). In the process, he has created a totally original perspective, a perspective of such generality that a number of traditional approaches, particularly the statistical, are subsumed, and the questions we ask are being altered.

I noted earlier that the space of linear narrative tears apart the structure of relationships between the topics discussed so far. Pattern is inseparable from problem solving, classification is tightly linked to structure imposed upon a set of data, and expression in a language sufficiently robust to bear the complexity is vital for fruitful extension and deeper understanding. Seldom is the interlocked nature of all these elements seen more clearly than in the area of diagnostics, whether the problem is one of machine failure (Kruskal and Hart, 1966), human illness (Chamberlain, 1976), or familial dysfunction (Mulhall, n.d., (a), (b) and (c)). In all these examples, we are faced with the task of understanding a structure of relationships that has moved from a desirable equilibrium position, and then steering it back to a state labeled 'health'. The problem is to provide a description of a highly complex structure such that the effects of a chosen treatment can be anticipated. This may not be easy because of the joint nature of symptoms whose ambiguity can lead to errors and misinterpretations. In every case, we require a set of tests that slice away portions of the space of all malfunctions, until the particular malfunction is disclosed. Each illness can be considered as a composite of symptoms with a particular geometrical structure – a simplical complex, forming part of a backcloth of all malfunctions. The problem is to search such a diagnostic space, uniquely define and isolate the particular simplex, and then know enough about the complexity of relationships to be able to alter it to a more desirable state without changing other sets of relationships in the process – to avoid falling into the trap of-the cure being worse than the disease. Such 'side effects' are exactly the same as Forrester's counter-intuitive effects in larger scale areas of modelling, diagnosing, and steering complexity (Forrester, 1971; Meadows and Meadows, 1973).

VI. NAVIGATING IN THE SEA OF COMPLEXITY

The human brain, constrained and equipped with the impediments of culture, is a problem solving instrument that for the related reasons of survival and pleasure tries to structure complexity in the physical and social environment. It is ill-equipped to do so, the complexity is usually too great, and only a few alternatives seem available. First, a person may retire, withdraw and disconnect from the set of relations that define a particular life and position in a society, an act of deliberate simplification that may be seen in communes, religious retreats, and certain states traditionally labeled 'ill' that follow mental breakdown. The latter are being reinterpreted today as strategies invented to live in an unliveable society, as acts of sanity in an insane world (Laing, 1969b; Levine, 1975). Secondly, the challenge to deal with complexity beyond normal limits may not be felt, or may be considered too demanding and beyond the developed capacities of the particular individual. Perhaps most people are content to live passively unchallenged lives. As a result they are largely controlled and manipulated. The tired eyes of daily commuters, the glazed passivity of the TV watcher, testify to the willingness to exist rather than live, to " . . . sink into resigned incomprehension which habit will change to indifference" (Thom, 1975, p. 5).

A third alternative is to engage complexity and attempt to reduce it to understandable proportions in order to control the trajectories describing the courses of individual lives and the larger societies in which they are embedded. This is an immensely difficult task given the limited capacity of the brain to handle complexity, and all the evidence points to the fact that the problems are getting worse. Our lack of understanding of environmental systems has led to catastrophic local poisoning of living forms; the ignorance of the medical profession about the human body as a total system reduces most treatments of serious illness to quackery or butchery; we have only the slightest knowledge about controlling a complex modern economy; and our urban areas appear increasingly as devices for breaking human beings. Mental illness in large cities is at much higher levels than generally realized (Strole, 1962); intakes of psychiatric wards are three times higher than 'normal' around large airports, the National Academy documents the inability of teachers to communicate with their pupils for twelve minutes out of every hour even by shouting at the top of their voices. At the same time, we pour asbestos into drinking water supplies, reduce rivers to lifeless sewers, break down the ozone layer with deodorant sprays, produce plutonium in ever greater quantities without having the faintest idea of how to dispose of it for the next 25 000 years, slaughter whales to extinction for lipsticks, spend 1600 hours each year to gather resources to propel a car 7500 miles (at an average speed of less than 5 mph (Levine, 1975, p. 74)), and . . . the list appears endless. The crazy ape of Szent-Györgyi frequently seems unaware that systems of great complexity and sensitivity are even involved (Szent-Györgyi, 1970). And if the niceties of Club of Rome reports are debated like the pins and angels of medieval theologians (Forrester, 1971; Meadows, Meadows, Randers and Behrens, 1972; Mesarovic and Pestel, 1974; Tinbergen, 1976), what possibility is there that the following voice will be heard?

As with all such generalized catastrophies, the evolution will first be very indeterminant, consisting of a mass of small, initially reversible phenomena; then the catastrophe will simplify topologically and enter on an irreversible phase . . . (Thom, 1975, p. 251)

How many small, reversible catastrophies can the Mediterranean absorb, for example, before the system simplifies topologically into a lifeless catastrophe like Lake Erie (Ginsburg, Holt and Murdoch, 1974)? In contrast, the countries of the Baltic have moved far towards systems modelling of that large ecosystem, and it is probably not too much of an exaggeration to say that the degree of international cooperation achieved stems in part from the deliberate systems approach (Lundholm, 1974; Berg, 1974).

The ways of dealing with the levels of complexity now facing contemporary society seem to be extremely limited and self-evident. Basically they all reduced to seeking pattern and structure in highly complex dynamic systems with the aid of prosthetic intelligence. Concretely, this means modeling at levels of non-linearity only recently attempted, and mapping onto mathematical structures of sufficient robustness and generality to provide both global insight as well as local detail. But behind these approaches lie two, more general problems. First, is a willingness to commit resources to monitoring the states of complex systems in real, or close to real, time (Beer, 1975, pp. 429–446). In a simple, rudimentary way, this is what WHO attempts in the area of contagious diseases, although little is done to structure the vast quantities of information, most of which are useless and represent a waste of resources (Chang, 1977). Without constant monitoring there is simply no chance of modeling and steering a system to a more desired state (Block et al., 1976).

Data gathering, even when the required information has been carefully justified, is a prosaic, unexciting task, and the memories of politicians are short. After the disastrous famines of the Sahel, for example, the President of the United States asked the National Academy of Sciences to prepare a series of studies examining America's posture in the face of future food shortages. It is generally conceded that the supply and distribution to the famine areas of the Sahel was disastrous (Rogier, 1975; Sheets and Morris, 1974), and a number of administrators broke down under the enormous pressures and responsibilities. Unfortunately, little could be done because neither Congress, nor any federal agency, were prepared to find the trivial amounts of money to engage in such a vital task, but such an ability to bump from one deepening crisis to another could be illustrated over many areas.

Secondly, our ideas about *prediction* have got to be radically revised, for they are rooted in the physical sciences of the nineteenth century. It is extremely unlikely that we will be able to predict the trajectory of large systems to any far point in the future. Quite apart from trying to define reasonable closure, and dealing with large shocks that change the structure of the system being investigated, the basic reason is simply that we cannot specify the relationships with sufficient accuracy. As an analogy, think of twenty perfectly elastic particles in a box (Linhart, 1973; Hawkins, 1964, p. 196).

Suppose we could specify without error their positions, velocities and directions; then we would have a completely determined, 'Laplacian' system, and we could predict the future states with complete assurance. But now suppose that there is a small error term in the specification of just one parameter of one particle. After a while the particle will bump into another, and transfer its error and uncertainty to it. Eventually an *epidemic of uncertainty* will diffuse through the system until we can no longer say anything about the future states. We have reached the *ignorance time* beyond which we can only specify statistical parameters totally useless for steering and planning.

I disparage the specification of statistical parameters because they tell us so little that is of real worth. To tell me that the weather next month is specified by the mean temperature and variance gives me very little information. More complex systems, in which the human component is large, may present even wider variability, and we may have to face the fact that many of the systems of interest to us are so unconstrained that our models may account for only a small fraction of the variation observed. For example, the disappointing results from a number of space–time analyses of diseases may be due not to a lack of skill, imagination, or technical ability on the part of the investigators, but simply that the signals are very small compared to the background noise. For example, a recent study of influenza diffusion in the United States, using reasonably sophisticated methods, found the *major*, annual component only accounted for roughly ten percent of the variance over the time series of 756 weeks for 121 major cities. Detecting the signal of a new virus moving through the connected urban system is a very difficult task when the masking (noise) effects of other viral forms and pulmonary diseases are present. Thus our ability to allocate scarce resources (vaccines, public health personnel, etc.), over time and space, to intervene in the process and alleviate the distressing human consequences, may be extremely limited and little better than a commonsense guess.

VII. IMPLICATIONS FOR EDUCATION

We have covered a great deal of ground in a necessarily highly compressed form, a form that can represent little more than a sketch of some basic themes that should be pursued at far greater length and in much greater detail. Nevertheless, we have arrived at the point where we can begin to see some of the implications of the opinions expressed. The implications are basically educational, although we must realize that educational institutions are themselves embedded in a cultural matrix. It is difficult to get out of a trap if you do not realize you are in it.

Western society at its core appears schizoid; divisons and splits characterize virtually every aspect of its life and ideas – ideas which today are dominant in the world. Many, from very diverse backgrounds, have commented upon the fractured nature of western thought. The fundamental and damaging division into sacred and profane, part of the " . . . disgusting farrago of Judeo–Christian religiosity . . . " is incomprehensible to many non-western people (Monod, 1972, pp. 171–175), who can accept alternative explanations of natural phenomena without conflict (Dart and Pradhan, 1967, p. 651). The separation of man from God in western mythology is part of the deep structure of the culture. In other cultures man is still within the garden (Vernon, 1973); indeed, the notion of an 'outside', of separation, is absurd to many non-western people (Spink, 1975). In other mythologies, male and female arose from a division and an enlargement of God, elements of both are contained in each other, and the sexuality and eroticism that are forbidden in the West are part of the inseparable whole elsewhere (Campbell, 1974). Some have postulated the aggressive intellectual drive of the West to such a distinct subject–object separation (Steiner, 1974a, p. 59), and have noted how even Indo–European syntax is a mirror of order and hierarchic dependence (Steiner, 1971, p. 113). But thought that is aggressive, in Kelly's sense of actively seeking, does not have to be founded upon such a schizoid base, as we know from the monumental work of Needham on China (1963).

The intellectual and psychic schisms of western society naturally appear throughout the educational institutions, which are staffed by their own products, so perpetuating fragmented thought at the core, while too frequently proselytizing it with evangelical fervor abroad. Simon has lamented the high degree of fragmentation, and has urged a search for a common core of knowledge, a " . . . common understanding of our relation to the inner and outer environments . . . " (Simon, 1969, p. 81); but others have documented how 'contrary imaginations' appear at an early age (Hudson, 1968). What appears to be unstated in such enquiries is that children's patterns of thought are a result of successive and discriminatory reinforcements by the culture in which they find themselves. Thus personal constructs may lead some towards the 'arts', and others to the 'sciences', but the educational system appears deliberately designed for Kelly's 'hardening of the categories' rather than the enrichment and cross-linking of alternative modes of thought (Bannister and Francella, 1971, pp. 88–93). It is pathetic to see how young boys can play the roles of 'Artist' and 'Scientist', and in the process change their patterns of creative thought towards the divergent and convergent (Hudson, 1968, 1970). Why are we so blind to the educational implications? Namely, that the very purpose of a humane schooling should be to heal the splits, to balance the constructs, rather than encourage some to grow in an intellectually parasitic and cancerous fashion by feeding on the others. The enrichment of personal constructs is very closely tied to Jung's process of individuation, which ideally should be a lifelong process (Jung, 1961, p. 209). Young children should not have to *play* at roles, defined by the society as impermeable partitions, in order to think in creative ways. Whether human beings are 'bicameral' or not is irrelevant, whether opposite sides of the brain take on different tasks is beside the point, if we are thinking about educational systems that will help to produce 'whole' people. Children sense very early the set of conditioning expectations placed upon them, and we are finally realizing the crippling effect these may have; for example, the often blatant expectations, both at home and at school, that young women will not enter scientific fields, so that mathematical skills are neglected. Only now are some, few, efforts being made to provide remedial work in such basic languages of natural enquiry (Stent, 1977, p. 41).

The ultimate expression of the present system of western education is seen in the 'Two Cultures' debates (Snow, 1959), and the truly pathetic responses of demi-men who appear to lobotomize and cauterize themselves deliberately from vast areas of human knowledge and creative understanding (Leavis, 1963). In time these debates, and the nauseous attempts to maintain cultural privilege (Williams, 1976, p. 183; Steiner, 1975b, p. 4) will be seen as some of the many symptoms of the schizoid nature of the culture in which they take place.

VIII. PATTERN IN THE HUMANITIES

If one is prepared to move to the $N + 1$ level (Atkin, 1974a), to get outside the system and look in, it is difficult to see how such an artificial split between the N-level sciences and humanities can be sustained. Linguistics is already leading the way by abolishing the boundary between the arts and sciences (Lyons, 1970, p. 9), but all truly creative human endeavor appears as an intellectual process of imposing form, of construing the world to reduce it to some level of just-graspable comprehension. The forms are also contingent, for each era chafes under the constraints of those before, but eventually bursts from the ordering constructs to create new ones. Music is a history of linguistic change characterized by successive explorations into the currently unknown (Ives, 1962; Wittall, 1972); painting and sculpture become stultified by uncreative imitation and break out to new forms; poetry can be seen as a constant exploration for ways of working within contingent constraints of language; in the hands of a Joyce or a Celine, the nineteenth century novel explodes, while Robbe-Grillet and Borges generate short narratives of such originality that they no longer fit former categories of writing. Beckett, Ionesco and Genet enlarge the space of the theatre (Esselin, 1969).

The similarities between the traditional arts and the sciences seem so much more persuasive than the differences, and how could it be otherwise when the same brain is structuring both? Popper has noted:

Thus musical and scientific creations seem to have this much in common: the use of dogma, or myth, as a man-made path along which we move into the unknown, exploring the world, both creating regularities or rules and probing for existing regularities. And once we have found, or erected, some landmarks [discovered, or imposed, some patterns] we proceed by trying new ways of ordering the world, new coordinates, new modes of exploration and creation . . . (Popper, 1976, p. 58)

Creative work in the traditional humanities (can we not now discard the term?), is replete with, is *defined by*, pattern imposition and a search for structure. Barthes has commented exhaustively upon the role of myth (Barthes, 1957, 1967a, 1967b), while the repetitive symbols and archetypes of Jung have altered our interpretation and deepened our understanding of artistic forms (Jung, 1964). The film *Crin Blanc*, the play *Equus*, and Picasco's *Guernica* are linked by the deep symbolism of the horse, but this example could be multiplied a thousandfold. When we have eyes to see, we perceive constantly repetitive themes in artistic expression: Susan Langer reaches the same conclusions about Mandala forms as Jung (Langer, 1953, pp. 69–70); Ehrenzweig (1967) acknowledges the creative role of the unconscious; and in the drawings of children the Mandala constitutes " . . . the most important single unit of prerepresentational drawing" (Storr, 1973, p. 98; also Kellogg, 1967, 1969) In the diagnosis and treatment of mental illness the creation of artistic forms is encouraged by those trained in the scientific ways of contemporary medicine. And it is worth noting that in many cases painting may be the only language available, for psychosis transcends grammar, and Freudian analysis is necessarily limited to neurosis where verbal language is available (Steiner, 1972, p. 87). In these areas of healing *brains* the scientific–humanistic categories take on the bizarre character of the Chinese encyclopedia of Borges. Our divisions and excisions are as awesome as the animals "drawn with a very fine camelhair brush" (Foucault, 1973, p. xv).

Fortunately the language used to convey meaning in artistic areas is closing the traditional schism. Steiner has pleaded for a more balanced, more creatively functional, approach to criticism, and has emphasized the crucial importance of mathematical languages in contemporary linguistics *and* literature: " . . . the instigations of Queneau and Borges, which are among the most bracing in modern letters, have algebra and astronomy at their back" (Steiner, 1971, p. 130). The *structure* of Whitman's poetry is reassessed by Lawrence and Crane, and a poem is seen as a 'field', enlarging its dimensionality from the single path of conventional narrative (Creeley, 1973, pp. 8, 11). The episodes of Proust's *A la recherche du temps perdu* are presented as an ordered *space* (Poulet, 1963); Needham is named his successor for his "sustained flight . . . of recreative intellect" (Steiner, 1971, p. 130); while Marcel himself creates a " . . . segment of negative space . . . a hole in the fabric" (Shattuck, 1974, p. 38), exactly analagous, and perhaps eventually describable, as a Q-hole in the narrative space, a solid object which creates traffic against the backcloth (Atkin, 1974d, 1976). And those who feel the analogy is specious should consider the Q-analysis of a Shakespearean sonnet, and think about the words that appear to create 'aesthetic traffic' by the geometrical object (hole) they form in the space (Atkin, 1977b).

Mapping, as a fundamental act of the human intellect, is emerging with ever greater strength in the artistic–scientific areas. Steiner has stressed repeatedly that all acts of communication are acts of translation (Steiner, 1972, p. 17), and I have indicated elsewhere the value of various forms of translation in a traditional academic field (Gould, 1974). To juxtapose Steiner's comments on translation as " . . . a search for underlying patterns . . . " (Steiner, 1972, p. 147), with Simon's Turing Lecture, in which he comments upon the problem of mapping a natural language onto a symbolic form and then undertaking a further transformation to another natural language, is to realize that two rare intelligences are converging from different traditions and obliterating the conventional boundaries in the process. Nor are such insights found only in formal analytical studies: the mathematical *concepts*, if not always their formal expressions, are seeping rapidly into the consciousness of literature itself. What else can we conclude when Ramanujan says, "I have tried . . . not to match the Kannada with the English, but to *map* the medieval Kannada onto the soundlook of modern English . . . " (Ramanujan, 1973, p. 13)?

In other fields, the philosopher Ryle claims to be a " . . . kind of conceptual geographer . . . providing people with maps . . . to understand where they are" (Cranston, 1969, p. 47); Hawkins and Toulmin insist that maps are models (Hawkins, 1964, pp. 31–32; Toulmin, 1953); Bateson speaks of " . . . mapping onto a system" (Bateson, 1972, pp. 401); and research in artificial intelligence is founded upon mapping concepts (Simon and Newell, 1976). Biologists hope for a " . . . more or less complete map of the central nervous system . . . " (Kenney *et al.*, 1972, p. 22); Jakobson speaks of mapping an unknown region in structural poetics (Jakobson, 1972, p. 86; DeGeorge and DeGeorge, 1972); Freud's 'mythology' (his own word) of human behavior and its underlying motives is referred to as a mapping by a man whose contact with creative mathematicians has been extensive (Steiner, 1972, p. 84). Psychologists use the image of mapping psychological space (Bannister and Fransella, 1971, p. 71); while Beer (1975, p. 352), in a typical leap of great imagination, has raised the possibility of cultural bridging by mapping ethical systems into each other under some transformation.

Simple, non-metric scaling procedures have already opened up the possibility of providing new graphic images of structural relations in certain forms of literature – particularly in theatre and film. When interactions are recorded between players, the resulting maps of the tragedies of Racine and Corneille are found to possess a virtually similar structure (Rogier, 1974); *Romeo and Juliet* provides a readily interpretable map (Gould, 1977b); the map of *Hamlet* provocatively places all those dead at the end of the play in one region; the scene-by-scene trajectories of players in *Through a Glass Darkly* reflect the changing relationships in 'Bergman Space' (de Aquino, 1976).

While one can conceive of random transformations, mapping virtually implies structure since it imposes relationships within and between sets of elements. Again pattern and structure appear as fundamental, and in the Structuralist movement we can see further evidence for intellectual proclivities that may yet result in the " . . . incorporation of the mental energies and speculative forms of science . . . into educated literacy" (Steiner, 1972, p. xi). What is encouraging is that the movement appears in so many fields of the traditional humanities and seems to be working *towards* those areas ordinarily considered to be scientific. I think it is fair to note that the schism is far more easily bridged by those with traditional scientific training, rather than the other way around, because of the linguistic problems of mathmatics. For example, a sensitive physicist, chemist or mathematician finds little intrinsic difficulty in appreciating music, theatre, poetry, dance and literature, while his own area of intellectual exploration is virtually closed to those without the algebras and calculi mandatory for their deeper expression and understanding. But those in the traditional humanities, both consciously and *unconsciously*, appear to be reaching out towards similar concepts, terms, and relationships as those now found in the advanced, and generally non-metric, *qualitative*, areas of the sciences. Perhaps algebraic topology can provide a stronger conceptual underpinning at these levels (Thom, 1975).

It seems natural today that the origins of the Structuralist movement were founded upon linguistics, that the richest sources of inspiration and analogy were found in analyses of language itself (Saussure, 1959). From linguistics the wave spreads to anthropology, literature and psychiatry, so that a search for the deep structures that lie beneath and generate the *literally* superficial forms that appear initially disparate now characterizes much research focused upon humans and their works (Cranston, 1969, 60–61; Pirsig, 1974, p. 259). Increasingly " . . . the focus . . . is shifted from the hitherto uncomprehended particulars to the understanding of their joint meaning" (Polanyi, 1963, pp. 29, 35). In literature, structuralist activity is a " . . . veritable fabrication of the world which resembles the first one, not in order to copy it but to render it intelligible" (Barthes, 1967c, p. 84; DeGeorge and DeGeorge, 1972, p. 150), a phrase that exactly describes modelling and mapping in all areas of human inquiry, and very different from traditional approaches concentrating upon the unique and particular. Literary enquiry is the establishment of 'rules of association', of relationships, of " . . . submission to regular constraints . . . a kind of battle against chance . . . the work of art is what man wrests from chance" (Barthes, 1967c, p. 86). For Leach, as for Lévi-Strauss, the paired equivalences of synchrony–diachrony, metaphor–metonym, paradigm–syntagym, similarity–contiguity, harmony–melody, possess an intellectual utility far beyond the analysis of culture, for the ultimate aim is to understand the deep structures of the brains producing the apparently disparate, superficial (lying on the surface), aspects of culture (Leach, 1970, pp. 14–52).

IX. TO TEACH: AN INTRANSITIVE VERB?

In these final pages, I want to explore, briefly and inadequately, some of the educational problems and implications in these thoughts, even as I acknowledge the oxymoron of this final subheading. It may be that such explorations are irrelevant, that they are wrong, or that the sheer dead weight, the inertia, of educational institutions is simply too overpowering. But to accept this is to commit intellectual suicide, in Camus' sense of " . . . acceptance pushed to its logical extreme" (O'Brien, 1970, p. 31; Camus, 1955). Opportunities occasionally arise at the personal and institutional level for genuine growth and advance, and it is to these small stars in the educational blackness that we must direct our attention.

Partitional thinking has impressed upon the university a schizoid structure of jealous fiefdoms that reflects the divisive nature of the culture. That
such a structure is frequently dysfunctional at a number of levels is obvious:
in times of budget constraints, scarce resources are allocated according to
numbers of students, so that much energy is spent on devising courses which
make few intellectual demands. Successful travesties are rewarded by 'the system': most teachers in a university can point to such courses, and if they cannot, then the students can. Other allocations are predicted on fads and band-
wagons, so that the university too frequently resembles a frantic shopkeeper
trying to supply teenage fancies – if not outright fantasies. In doing so, it
reflects its own insecurity and its own inability to deal with complexity. At
the level of the major, the student is fequently constrained to take more and
more courses within a department or college to bolster the credit hours that
mean survival for the institution concerned. At the personal level, a student is
faced with a fragmented intellectual landscape, with little perspective to
fashion the pieces into a coherent, meaningful experience. At the same time,
catalogues are overblown, and undergraduate curricula closely resemble those
of forty years ago. Few have the energy, the insight, or the opportunity, to
revise the accumulated baggage of the decades, for as Simon has noted " . . .
curriculum revisions that rid us of the accumulations of the past are infrequent and painful" (Simon, 1969, p. 116). One president of a distinguished
university noted that " . . . students perceive correctly that there is little
direct relationship between the detail that must be mastered in many courses
and the substantive knowledge they will need at later stages in their lives"
(President's Message, 1976).

What 'common core of knowledge' can be provided, what is really worth
teaching 'at the center', that will allow people to move creatively and demand-
ingly within a system of archaic fiefdoms? Let me suggest three: mathematics,
philosophy and systems analysis – one new, and two old, areas of enquiry
that form languages and covers for the traditional disciplines. Mathematics
today is a fundamental language that opens vast and growing areas of human
knowledge. Without it those same areas are closed tight, either as sources of
joy themselves, or as areas of rich analogy, structure and pattern. And when
literary criticism is conceived as set relations (Shattuck, 1974, p. 132), when
psychiatrists use the notation of set theory to map a personal experience onto
a public event (Laing, 1969a), when logical symbols and operations are at the
core of modern linguistics (Steiner, 1972, p. 150), should not mathematics
shake itself? Too frequently " . . . the progress from elementary to advanced
courses is to a considerable extent a progress through the conceptual history

of the science itself" (Simon, 1969, p. 116). It need not be so: the Open University foundation course in mathematics provides an indication of what can be done when there is a clean blackboard to write on (Open University, 1970), and the imaginative teacher can explain the rudiments of quite advanced areas, so opening up some insight and understanding that can lead to further exploration (Stewart, 1975).

Philosophy is another cover, but again the catalogues and courses too frequently resemble a recapitulation of the field, a historical trudge, for which the convenient linearity of Time is the ordering construct, rather than imaginative synthesis and restructuring to form a core from which people can move to more detailed study. Why must Hegel, Marx and Wittgenstein be reachable only through a long recapitulation? It is precisely the ability to synthesize and highlight basic, underlying ideas that characterizes the third cover, systems analysis. Here we have a superb example of finding common pattern and structure in many diverse fields, and then organizing such commonalities into a meaningful body of insight and skills really worth teaching. Again the Open University has been able to move far ahead with its sequence of courses on systems analysis, while most traditional universities have yet to grapple with the implications. In fact the Open University is rapidly becoming a *measure* of the binding institutional and human constraints on existing, and all too conventional, universities. Consider how its first year course ranges across dozens of traditional fields, and how the second builds on eight modules from engineering (container ports, air traffic control, and telephone communications), sociology (industrial social systems), political science (local government), geography and agriculture (management of ecosystems), medicine and biology (human respiration), and economics (modeling economic systems), all done with a flair, an imagination, and a concern for general principles seldom found in traditional courses in these fields.

And where, in this essay, contained in a volume of Geography and Philosophy, has Geography gone? Like all the traditional disciplines it has disappeared, and yet not disappeared. It has disappeared at the $N + 1$ level under the cover of systems analysis, mathematics and philosophy, for like all the Human Sciences it has little to contribute from its traditional and conventional pool of teaching at this higher level. The exception would be cartography, radically revitalized and expanded into a study and exposition of *mapping*, in which the fundamental, and therefore *cover*, properties of spatial thinking and representation are taught. Such a course would bear little resemblence to present conceptions, for it would have to range over transformations, graphic languages, algebras for spatial patterns, scaling algorithms, graphic representations of relationships, and the properties of spaces defined by non-Euclidean metrics. Unfortunately, the greater part of contemporary cartography is so naive and banal that few geographers or cartographers would have the intellectual, imaginative, or technical abilities to contribute to a program in higher education.

Yet geography has also not disappeared: it could be recast and reinterpreted as a base, one of many intellectual bases, from which a person might grow to an enlarged and purposeful understanding of the world. Can we imagine what Geography would become if students entered it only after the completion of two years of work under the mathematical, philosophical and systems covers? Students would no longer be satisfied with the conventional materials in Geography, or any other discipline for that matter. They would begin to ask *why* traditionally taught materials were relevant, *how* one justified the factual heaps generally loaded upon them. Under such pressures it is quite possible that a number of fiefdoms would not survive. Indeed, these are often the questions asked by students in their last year, or later in life, but by then it is too late. Those who were not prepared to sieve, reorganize, rethink and restructure their accumulated middens would have little to say to students who possess a core of knowledge giving them precisely a perspective to make judgements about the intellectual depth and worth of a traditional discipline. And by sharing such a common core, perhaps we would see, once again, the type of intellectual discourse last seen in early twentieth century Vienna, when the common, but rigorous, demands of the gymnasium allowed men and women of diverse intellectual persuasions to discuss and communicate freely (Janik and Toulmin, 1973).

I can hear the arguments now: it would never work administratively; it would be too demanding on students, particularly in a democratic system of higher (?) education. But already in some universities of excellence both students for degrees, *and* faculty being considered for tenure, are evaluated by committees with a majority representation from fields other than their own. Intellectual excellence and imaginative contributions to research and teaching are not that difficult to recognize. As for *democratic* education, what does the word mean in these circumstances? Why should democratic education be equated with a watered-down curriculum, why should it be mapped onto a set of elements that make up an intellectual pablum? Such an education still has the old and honorable tasks of helping people to grow, to deal with complexity, to structure the world into meaningful patterns, and to help them see the contingency and impermenance of those structures. Otherwise education has no perspective on itself, no meta-language to discuss itself, and so becomes dogma and myth. Perhaps, in the end, the university can only provide opportunities, genuinely demanding opportunities, for people to teach themselves. Perhaps the verb to teach really is intransitive after all.

Department of Geography
Pennsylvania State Univeristy

NOTES

[1] Apart from the intellectual debts referenced at the end of this essay, I would like to acknowledge the influences of Ronald Atkin, Torsten Hägerstrand, Alan Knight, Bernard Marchand and Thomas Wilson. I hope such acknowledgement does not embarrass them, for they will not agree with all that I have written. The mistakes are mine.

BIBLIOGRAPHY

Alexander, C.: 1966, *Notes on a Synthesis of Form*, Harvard, Cambridge University Press.

Atkin, R.: 1965, 'Abstract Physics', *Il Nuevo Cimento* 38, 496–517.

Atkin, R.: 1971, 'Cohomology of Observations', in T. Baskin (ed.), *Quantum Theory and Beyond*, The University Press, Cambridge.

Atkin, R.: 1972a, 'From Cohomology in Physics to *Q*-Connectivity in Social Science', *International Journal of Man–Machine Studies* 4, 139–167.

Atkin, R.: 1972b, *Urban Structure*, Department of Mathematics, Colchester, Urban Structure Research Report No. 1.

Atkin, R.: 1972c, *A Survey of Mathematical Theory*, Department of Mathematics, Colchester, Urban Structure Research Report No. 2.

Atkin, R.: 1973, *A Study Area in Southend-on-Sea*, Department of Mathematics, Colchester, Urban Structure Research Report No. 3.

Atkin, R.: 1974a, *Mathematical Structure in Human Affairs*, Heinemann Educational Books, London.

Atkin, R.: 1974b, *A Community Study of the University of Essex*, Department of Mathematics, Colchester, Urban Structure Research Report No. 4.

Atkin, R.: 1974c, 1974d, 1975d, 'An Approach to Structure in Architectural and Urban Design', *Environment and Planning B* 1, 51–67; 2, 173–191; and 3, 21–57.

Atkin, R.: 1974d, 'An Algebra for Patterns on a Complex I', *International Journal of Man–Machine Studies* 6, 285–307.

Atkin, R.: 1975a, *Methodology of Q-Analysis: A Study of East Anglia-1*, Department of Mathematics, Colchester, Regional Research Project Report No. 5.

Atkin, R.: 1976, 'An Algebra for Patterns on a Complex II', *International Journal of Man–Machine Studies* 8, 483–498.

Atkin, R.: 1977a, *Combinatorial Connectivities in Social Systems*, Birkhäuser Verlag, Basel.

Atkin, R.: 1977b, *Multidimensional Man*, Department of Mathematics, Colchester, *mss*.
Atkin, R., Hartson, W. and Witten, I.: 1976, 'Fred CHAMP, Positional Chess Analyst', *International Journal of Man–Machine Studies* 8, 517–529.
Atkin, R. and Witten, I.: 1975, 'A Multi-dimensional Approach to Positional Chess', *International Journal of Man–Machine Studies* 7, 727–750.
Bannister, D. and Fransella, R.: 1971, *Inquiring Man: The Theory of Personal Constructs*, Harmondsworth, Penguin Books.
Barthes, R.: 1957, *Mythologies*, Editions du Seuil, Paris.
Barthes, R.: 1963, *Sur Racine*, Editions du Seuil, Paris.
Barthes, R.: 1967a, *Elements of Seminology*, Jonathan Cape, London.
Barthes, R.: 1967b, *Writing Degree Zero*, Jonathan Cape, London.
Barthes, R.: 1967c, 'The Structuralist Activity', *Partisan Review* 34, 82–88.
Barthes, R.: 1970, 'To Write: An Intransitive Verb?', in R. Macksey and E. Donato (eds.), *The Language of Criticism and the Sciences of Man: The Structuralist Controversy*.
Barthes, R.: 1974, *S/Z: An Essay*, Hill and Wang, New York.
Barthes, R.: 1975, *The Pleasures of the Text*, Hill and Wang, New York.
Barthes, R.: 1976, *Sade, Fourier and Loyola*, Hill and Wang, New York.
Baskin, T. (ed.): 1971, *Quantum Theory and Beyond*, The University Press, Cambridge.
Bateson, G.: 1972, *Steps to an Ecology of Mind*, Ballentine Books, New York.
Beer, S.: 1972, *The Brain of the Firm: The Managerial Cybernetics of Organization*, Allen Lane, The Penguin Press, London.
Beer, S.: 1974, *Designing Freedom*, CBC Publications, Toronto.
Beer, S.: 1976, *Platform for Change*, John Wiley and Sons, New York.
Berg, U.: 1974, 'Environmental Science and the Computer', in Ginsberg, Holt and Murdoch (eds.), *Pacem in Maribus*.
Bernstein, B.: 1959, 'A Public Language: Some Sociological Implications of a Linguistic Form', *British Journal of Sociology* 10, 311–326.
Bernstein, B.: 1961, 'Social Class and Linguistic Development: A Theory of Social Learning', in A. Halsey, J. Floud, and A. Anderson (eds.) *Education, Economy and Society*, Free Press, New York.
Blaut, J., McCleary, G., and Blaut, A.: 1970, 'Environmental Mapping in Young Children', *Environmental and Behavior* 2, 335–349.
Block, P. *et al.*: 1970, *Cultural Indicators: The Swedish Symbol System 1945–75*, Sociological Institute, Lund.
Borges, J.: 1964, *Labyrinths: Selected Stories and Other Writings*, New Directions Books, New York.
Borrows, D., Lapides, F. and Shawcross, J.: 1973, *Myths and Motives in Literature*, The Free Press, New York.
Braudel, F.: 1972, *The Mediterranean and the Mediterranean World in the Age of Philip II. Vols. I and II*, Harper Row, New York.
Browder, F.: 1976, 'Does Pure Mathematics Have a Relation to the Sciences?', *American Scientist* 64, 542–549.
Brown, G. S.: 1957, *Probability and Scientific Inference*, Longmans Green, London.
Brown, G. S.: 1969, *Laws of Forms*, George Allen and Unwin, London.
Calhoun, J.: 1971, 'Space and the Strategy of Life', in A. Esser, (ed.), *Behavior and Environment: The Use of Space by Animals and Men*, Plenum, New York.
Campbell, J.: 1974, *The Mythic Image*, Princeton University Press, Princeton.

Camus, A.: 1955, *The Myth of Sisyphus*, Vintage Books, New York.

Chamberlain, M.: 1976, 'A Study of Behcet's Disease by *Q*-analysis', *International Journal of Man–Machine Studies* 8, 549–565.

Chang, J.: 1977, *The Diffusion of Influenza in the United States*, Department of Geography MS Thesis, Pennsylvania State University, University Park, Pennsylvania.

Chomsky, N.: 1957, *Syntactic Structures*, Pennsylvania State University, Mouton, The Hague.

Chomsky, N.: 1965, *Aspects of the Theory of Syntax*, MIT Press, Cambridge.

Chomsky, N.: 1968, *Language and Mind*, Harcourt, Brace and World, New York.

Chomsky, N.: 1975, *Reflections on Language*, Pantheon Books, New York.

Collins, L. (ed.): 1975, *The Use of Models in the Social Sciences*, Tavistock Publications, London.

Cranston, M.: 1969, *Philosophy and Language*, CBC Publications, Toronto.

Creeley, R.: 1973, *Whitman*, Penguin Books, Harmondsworth.

Dart, F. and Pradhan, P.: 1967, 'Cross-Cultural Teaching of Science', *Science* 155, 649–656.

de Aquino, R.: 1976, 'Multidimensional Scaling in Film Study: The Example of "Through a Glass Darkly"' Department of Geography Seminar Paper, University Park, Pennsylvania State University, Pennsylvania.

de Bono, E.: 1971, *The Mechanism of Mind*, Penguin Books, Harmondsworth.

DeGeorge, R. and DeGeorge, F.: 1972, *The Structuralists from Marx to Levi-Strauss*, Anchor Books, Garden City.

Ehrenzweig, A.: 1967, *The Hidden Order of Art*, Weindenfeld and Nicolson, London.

Ehrmann, J.: 1970, *Structuralism*, Anchor Books, Garden City.

Esselin, M.: 1969, *The Theatre of the Absurd*, Anchor Books, Garden City.

Esser, A. (ed.): 1971, *Behavior and Environment: The Use of Space by Animals and Men*, Plenum, New York.

Forrester, J.: 1971, *World Dynamics*, Wright-Allen Press, Cambridge, Mass.

Foucault, M.: 1965, *Madness and Civilization: A History of Insanity in the Age of Reason*, Pantheon, New York.

Foucault, M.: 1973, *The Order of Things: An Archeology of the Human Sciences*, Vintage Books, New York (transl. of 1966: *Les Mots et Les Choses*, Editions Gallimard, Paris).

Gardner: 1970, *The Ambidextrous Universe*, Penguin Books, Harmondsworth.

Geyl, P.: 1949, *Napoleon: For and Against*, Yale University Press, New Haven.

Ginsberg, N., Holt, S. and Murdoch, W. (eds.): 1974, *Pacem in Maribus III: The Mediterranean Marine Environment and the Development of the Region*, The Royal University of Malta Press, Valetta.

Glacken, C.: 1967, *Traces on the Rhodian Shore*, University of California Press, Berkeley.

Gould, P.: 1974, 'Some Steineresque Comments and Monodian Asides on Geography in Europe', *Geoforum* 17, 9–13.

Gould, P.: 1975, *People in Information Space: The Mental Maps and Information Surfaces of Sweden*, C.W.K. Gleerup, Lund.

Gould, P.: 1976, 'The Languages of Our Investigations: Part I Graphics and Maps', *Inter-Media* 4, 13–16.

Gould, P.: 1977a, 'The Language of Our Investigations: Part II Algebras', *InterMedia* 5, 10–14.

Gould, P.: 1977b, 'Concerning a Geographic Education', in D. Lanegran and R. Palm, (eds.), *Invitation to Geography*, McGraw Hill, New York.

Gould, P.: 1977c, 'A Trilingual Approach to Teaching Geography', *Change* 9.

Gould, P.: 1977d, 'What is Worth Teaching in Geography?', *Journal of Geography in Higher Education* 1.

Greg, L.: 1974, *Knowledge and Cognition*, John Wiley and Sons, New York.

Halsey, A., Floyd, J., and Anderson, A. (eds.): 1961, *Education, Economy and Society*, The Free Press, New York.

Hawkins, D.: 1964, *The Language of Nature: An Essay in the Philosophy of Science*, W. H. Freeman, San Francisco.

Hickey, J. (ed.): 1969, *Peregrine Falcon Populations, Their Biology and Decline*, University of Wisconsin Press, Madison.

Hoffman, B.: 1959, *The Strange Story of the Quantum*, Penguin Books, Harmondsworth.

Hogben, L.: 1963, *Science in Authority*, George Allen and Unwin, London.

Hudson, L.: 1968, *Contrary Imaginations*, Penguin Books, Harmondsworth.

Hudson, L.: 1970, *Frames of Mind*, Penguin Books, Harmondsworth.

Isnard, C. and Zeeman, E.: 1975, 'Some Models from Catastrophe Theory in the Social Sciences', in L. Collins, (ed.) *The Use of Models in the Social Sciences*, Tavistock Publications, London.

Ives, C.: 1962, *Essays Before a Sonata, and Other Writings*, Norton, New York.

Jakobson, R.: 1972, 'Linguistics and Poetics', in R. DeGeorge, (ed.), *The Structuralists From Marx to Levi-Strauss*, Anchor Books, Garden City.

Janik, A. and Toulmin, S.: 1973, *Wittgenstein's Vienna*, Simon & Schuster, New York.

Jung, C.: 1961, *Memories, Dreams and Reflections*, Vintage Books, New York.

Jung, C.: 1964, *Man and His Symbols*, Doubleday, New York.

Kellogg, R.: 1967, *The Psychology of Children's Art*, Ransom House, New York.

Kellogg, R. L.: 1969, *Analyzing Children's Art*, National Press Books, Palo Alto.

Kelly, G.: 1955, *The Psychology of Personal Constructs Vols. I and II*, Norton, New York.

Kennedy, A., Longuet-Higgins, H., Lucas, J. and Waddington, C.: 1972, *The Nature of Mind*, Edinburgh University Press, Edinburgh.

Klahr, D.: 1974, 'Understanding Understanding Systems', in L. Greg, (ed.), *Knowledge and Cognition*, John Wiley and Sons, New York.

Knuth, D.: 1976, 'Mathematics and Computer Science: Coping with Finiteness', *Science* 194, 1235–1242.

Kockelmans, J.: 1972, 'Stegmüller on the Relationship Between Theory and Experience', *Philosophy of Science* 39, 397–420.

Kockelmans, J.: 1976, Review of Stegmüller, W.: 1973, *Theorie und erfahrung: Zweiter halbband: theorienstrukturen und theoriendynamik*, Berlin Springer-verlag in *Philosophy of Science* 43, 293–306.

Kotovsky, K. and Simon, H.: 1973, 'Empirical Tests of a Theory of Human Aquisition of Concepts for Sequential Events', *Cognitive Psychology* 4, 339–424.

Kruskal, J. and Hart, R.: 1966, 'Geometric Interpretation of Diagnostic Data from Digital Machines', *Bell System Technical Journal* 45, 1299–1338.

Laing, R.: 1969a, *The Politics of the Family*, CBC Publications, Toronto.

Laing, R.: 1969b, *The Divided Self*, Penguin Books, Harmondsworth.

Laing, R., and Esterson, A.: 1970, *Sanity, Madness and the Faimily*, Penguin Books Harmondsworth.

Langer, S.: 1953, *Feeling and Form*, Routledge and Kegan Paul, London.

Leach, E.: 1969, *Genesis as Myth and Other Essays*, Cape, London.

Leach, E.: 1970, *Claude Lévi-Strauss*, The Viking Press, New York.

Leavis, F.: 1963, *Two Cultures? The Significance of C. P. Snow*, Pantheon Books, New York.

Lenat, D.: 1976, *AM: An Artificial Intelligence Approach to Discovery in Mathematics as Heuristic Search*, Stanford University, Computer Science Department Ph.D. Thesis, Palo Alto.

Levine, P.: 1975, *Divisions*, CBC Publications, Toronto.

Lévi-Strauss, C.: 1955, 'The Structural Study of Myth', *Journal of American Folklore* 68, 428–444.

Lévi-Strauss, C.: 1963, *Structural Anthropology*, Basic Books, New York.

Lévi-Strauss, C.: 1964, 1966, 1968, *Mythologiques I: Le cru et le cuit; II Du miel aux cendres; III: L'origine des manieres de table*, Paris.

Linhart, J.: 1973, 'Uncertainty Epidemics Among Interacting Particles', *Il Nuevo Cimento* 13A, 355–372.

Lundholm, B.: 1974, 'Problems of Baltic Ecosystem Analysis', in N. Ginsberg, S. Holt, and W. Murdoch (eds.), *Pacem in Maribus*, The Royal University of Malta Press, Valetta.

Lyons, J.: 1970, *Noam Chomsky*, The Viking Press, New York.

Macksey, R. and Donato, E.: 1970, *The Language of Criticism and the Sciences of Man: The Structuralist Controversy*, Johns Hopkins University Press, Baltimore.

Marchand, B.: 1974, 'Quantitative Geography: Revolution or Counter-revolution', *Geoforum* 17, 15-3.

May, R.: 1975, 'The Courage to Create' in M. Richler, A. Fortier, and R. May, (eds.) *Creativity and the University*, York University Press, Toronto.

Meadows, D. and Meadows, D. (eds.),: 1973, *Toward Global Equilibrium: Collected Papers*, Wright-Allen Press, Cambridge, Mass.

Meadows, D., Meadows, D., Randers, J. and Behrens, W.: 1972, *The Limits to Growth: A Report for The Club of Rome's Project on the Predicament of Mankind*, Universe Books, New York.

Mehta, V.: 1962, *Fly and the Fly-Bottle*, Penguin Books, Harmondsworth.

Mesarovic, M. and Pestel, E.: 1974, *Mankind at the Turning Point: The Second Report to the Club of Rome*, E. P. Dutton, New York.

Monod, J.: 1972, *Chance and Necessity: An Essay on the Natural Philosophy of Modern Biology*, Vintage Books (transl. of 1970: *Le Hasard et la necessite*, Editions du Seuil, Paris).

Moore, J. and Newell, A.: 1974, '*How Can Merlin Understand*' in L. Greg (ed.), *Knowledge and Cognition*, John Wiley and Sons, New York.

Mulhall, D.: n.d.(a)., *Personal Questionnaires: A Critique and New Design*, St. Andrews Hospital, Norwich.

Mulhall, D.: n.d.(b)., *PQ-10 and PQ-14*, St. Andrews and Hellesdon Hospital, Norwich.

Mulhall, D.: n.d.(c)., *Assessment of the Nature of Dysphasia in the Individual Case*, St. Andrews Hospital, Norwich.

Needham, J.: 1963, *Science and Civilization in China*, The University Press, Cambridge.

Newell, A. and Simon, H.: 1973, *Human Problem Solving*, Prentice Hall, Englewood Cliffs, New Jersey.

O'Brien, C.: 1970, *Albert Camus of Europe and Africa*, Viking Books, New York.

Open University: 1970, *Mathematics Foundation Course, Units 1–36*, The Open University Press, Milton Keynes.

Pirsig, R.: 1974, *Zen and the Art of Motorcycle Maintenance*, Bantam Books, New York.

Polanyi, M.: 1963a, 'Experience and the Perception of Pattern', in K. Sayre, (ed.) *Modelling of Mind*, University of Notre Dame Press, Notre Dame.

Polanyi, M.: 1963b, *The Study of Man*, University of Chicago Press, Chicago.

Popper, K.: 1976, *Unended Quest: An Intellectual Biography*, William Collins Sons, Glasgow.

Poulet, G.: 1963, *L'Espace Proustein*, Gallimard, Paris.

President's Message: 1976, 'Reflections on Learning', *The Johns Hopkins Magazine* 2.

Ramanujan, A.: 1973, *Speaking of Siva*, Penguin Books, Harmondsworth.

Richler, M., Fortier, A. and May, R.: 1975, *Creativity and the University*, York University Press, Toronto.

Rogier, A.: 1974, 'Looking at the Structure of some Tragedies by P. Corneille and J. Racine Using Multidimensional Scaling', Department of Geography, University Park, unpublished seminar paper.

Rogier, A.: 1975, *Distributing Food to the Sahel: A Pilot Study in Linear and Goal Programming*, Department of Geography, University Park, Discussion Papers No. 13.

Saussure, F.: 1959, *Course in General Linguistics*, Philosophical Library, New York.

Sayre, K. (ed.); 1963, *Modelling of Mind*, University of Notre Dame Press, Notre Dame.

Scheffler, H.: 1970, 'Structuralism in Anthropology', in J. Ehrmann, (ed.), *Structuralism*, Anchor Books, Garden City.

Sharpless, F.: 1974, *The Myth of the Fall: Literature of Innocence and Experience*, Hayden Book Co., Rochelle Park.

Shattuck, R.: 1974, *Marcel Proust*, The Viking Press, New York.

Sheets, H. and Morris, R.: 1974, *Disaster in the Desert: Failures of International Relief in the West African Drought*, Carnegie Endowment for International Peace, Washington, D.C.

Simon, H.: 1969, *The Sciences of the Artificial*, MIT Press, Cambridge, Mass.

Simon, H. and Hayes, J.: 1976, 'The Understanding Process: Problem Isomorphs', *Cognitive Psychology* 8, 86–97.

Simon, H. and Newell, A.: 1976, *Computer Science as Empirical Enquiry: Symbols and Search*, The Turning Award Lecture (tape cassette).

Snow, C. P.: 1959, *The Two Cultures and the Scientific Revolution*, Cambridge University Press, New York.

Spink, W.: 1975, *The Axis of Eros*, Penguin Books, Harmondsworth.

Stegmüller, W.: 1976, *The Structure and Dynamics of Theories*, Springer-Verlag, Berlin.

Steiner, G.: 1969, *Language and Silence*, Penguin Books, Harmondsworth.

Steiner, G.: 1970, *Poem into Poem: World Poetry in Modern Verse Translations*, Penguin Books, Harmondsworth.

Steiner, G.: 1971, *In Bluebeard's Castle: Some Notes Towards the Redefinition of Culture*, Yale University Press, New Haven.

Steiner, G.: 1972, *Extra-Territorial*, Faber and Faber, London.

Steiner, G.: 1973, 'Mathematical Literacy for the Non-Mathematician', *Nature* 243, No. 5402, 65–67.

Steiner, G.: 1974a, *Nostalgia for the Absolute*, CBC Publications, Toronto.

Steiner, G.: 1974b, *Fields of Force: Fischer and Spassky at Reykjavik*, The Viking Press, New York.

Steiner, G.: 1975a, *After Babel: Aspects of Language and Translation*, Oxford University Press, London.

Steiner, G.: 1975b, *Why English?* The English Association, Presidential Address, London.

Stent, A.: 1977, 'Can Mathematical Anxiety Be Conquered?' *Change: Report on Teaching* 3, 9, 40–43.

Stewart, I.: 1975, *Concepts of Modern Mathematics*, Penguin Books, Harmondsworth.

Storr, A.: 1973, *C. G. Jung*, Viking Press, New York.

Strack, C.: 1971, *Foundations of Geographic Analysis*, Department of Geography Ph.D. Dissertation, University Park, Pennsylvania State University, Pennsylvania.

Strole, L.: 1962, *Mental Health in the Metropolis: The Midtown-Manhattan Study*, McGraw-Hill, New York.

Szent-Györgyi, A.: 1970, *The Crazy Ape*, Philosophical Library, New York.

Taylor, A.: 1976, *Essays in English History*, Penguin Books, Harmondsworth.

Thom, R.: 1975, *Structural Stability and Morphogenesis: An Outline of a General Theory of Models*, W. A. Benjamin, Reading, Mass.

Tinbergen, J.: 1976, *Reshaping the International Order: A Report to the Club of Rome*, E. P. Dutton, New York.

Tobler, W.: 1973, 'Choropleth Maps Without Class Intervals', *Geographical Analysis* 5, 262–265.

Tobler, W.: 1975, 'Spatial Interaction Patterns', International Institute for Applied Systems Analysis, RR-75-19, Laxenberg.

Tobler, W. and Weinberg, S.: 1971, 'A Cappodocian Speculation', *Nature* 231.

Toulmin, S.: 1953, *The Philosophy of Science*, Harper and Row, New York.

Turner, G.: 1973, *Stylistics*, Penguin Books, Harmondsworth.

Ulam, S.: 1974, *Sets, Numbers and Universes: Selected Works*, M.I.T. Press, Cambridge, Mass.

Ulam, S.: 1977, *Adventures of a Mathematician*, Charles Scribner & Sons, New York.

Vernon, J.: 1973, *The Garden and the Map: Schizophrenia in Twentieth Century Literature and Culture*, University of Illinois Press, Urbana.

Weinberg, S.: 1972, *Gravitation and Cosmology*, John Wiley and Sons, New York.

West, R.: 1969, *McLuhan and the Future of Literature*, The English Association Presidential Address, London.

Whorf, B. L.: 1956, *Language, Thought, and Reality (edited by J. Carroll)*, Harvard University Press, Cambridge, Mass.

Williams, R.: 1976, *Communications*, Penguin Books, Harmondsworth.

Wilson, T.: 1976, *Thirteen Perspectives on the Grammatical Landscape of Social Science*, Department of Geography Master's Thesis, Pennsylvania State University, University Park, Pennsylvania.

Wittall, A.: 1972, *Schoenberg Chamber Music*, University of Washington Press, Seattle.

Woolf, V.: 1977, *Moments of Being: Unpublished Autobiographic Writings*, Harcourt, Brace Javanovitch, New York.

Wurster, C. and Wingate, D.: 1968, 'DDT Residues and Declining Reproduction in the Bermuda Petrel', *Science* 159, 969–981.

Zeeman, E. C.: 1976, 'Catastrophe Theory', *Scientific American* 234, 65–83.

DAVID HARVEY

POPULATION, RESOURCES, AND THE IDEOLOGY OF SCIENCE

It would be convenient indeed if such a contentious issue as the relationship between population and resources could be discussed in some ethically neutral manner. In recent years scientific investigations into this relationship have multiplied greatly in number and sophistication. But the plethora of scientific investigation has not reduced contentiousness; rather, it has increased it. We can venture three possible explanations for this state of affairs: (1) science is not ethically neutral; (2) there are serious defects in the scientific methods used to consider the population–resources problem; or (3) some people are irrational and fail to understand and accept scientifically established results. All of these explanations may turn out to be true, but we can afford to proffer none of them without substantial qualification. The last explanation would require, for example, a careful analysis of the concept of *rationality* before it could be sustained (Godelier, 1972). The second explanation would require a careful investigation of the capacities and limitations of a whole battery of scientific methods, techniques, and tools, together with careful evaluation of available data, before it could be judged correct or incorrect. In this paper, however, I shall focus on the first explanation and seek to show that the lack of ethical neutrality in science affects each and every attempt at 'rational' scientific discussion of the population–resources relationship. I shall further endeavor to show how the adoption of certain kinds of scientific methods inevitably leads to certain kinds of substantive conclusions which, in turn, can have profound political implications.

I. THE ETHICAL NEUTRALITY ASSUMPTION

Scientists frequently appear to claim that scientific conclusions are immune from ideological assault. Scientific method, it is often argued, guarantees the objectivity and ethical neutrality of 'factual' statements as well as the conclusions drawn therefrom. This view is common in the so-called natural sciences; it is also widespread in disciplines such as economics and sociology. The peculiarity of this view is that the claim to be ethically neutral and

155

S. Gale and G. Olsson (eds.), Philosophy in Geography, 155–185. All Rights Reserved.

ideology free is itself an ideological claim. The principles of scientific method
(whatever they may be) are normative and not factual statements. The principles cannot, therefore, be justified and validated by appeal to science's own
methods. The principles have to be validated by appeal to something external
to science itself. Presumably this 'something' lies in the realms of metaphysics,
religion, morality, ethics, convention, or human practice. Whatever its source,
it lies in realms that even scientists agree are freely penetrated by ideological
considerations. I am not arguing that facts and conclusions reached by means
of a particular scientific method are false, irrelevant, immoral, unjustifiable,
purely subjective, or non-replicable. But I am arguing that the use of a
particular scientific method is *of necessity* founded in ideology, and that any
claim to be ideology free is *of necessity* an ideological claim. The results of
any enquiry based on a particular version of scientific method cannot consequently claim to be immune from ideological assault, nor can they automatically be regarded as inherently different from or superior to results
arrived at by other methods.

The ideological foundation of the ethical neutrality assumption can be
demonstrated by a careful examination of the paradigmatic basis of enquiry
throughout the history of science (both natural and social) (Harvey, 1973;
Kuhn, 1962; Mesjaros, 1972), as well as by examining the history of the
ethical neutrality assumption itself (Mesjaros, 1972; Tarascio, 1966). The
ideological foundation can also be revealed by a consideration of those
theories of meaning in which it is accepted that there cannot be an ethically
neutral language because meaning in language cannot be divorced from the
human practices through which specific meanings are learned and communicated (Hudson, 1970; Kapp, 1950). It is not, however, the purpose of
this paper to document the problems and defects of the ethical neutrality
assumption, critical though these are. I shall, rather, start from the position
that scientific enquiry cannot proceed in an ethically neutral manner, and
seek to show how the inability to sustain a position of ethical neutrality
inevitably implies some sort of an ideological position in any attempt to
examine something as complex as a population–resources system.

Lack of ethical neutrality does not in itself prove very much. It does serve,
of course, to get us beyond the rather trivial view that there is one version of
some problem that is scientific and a variety of versions which are purely
ideological. For example, the Malthusian terms 'overpopulation' and 'pressure
of population on the means of subsistence' are inherently no more or less
scientific than Marx's terms 'industrial reserve army' and 'relative surplus
population', even though there is a predilection among unsophisticated

analysts to regard the former phrases as adequately scientific and the latter as purely ideological. Unfortunately, it is not very informative to aver also that *all* versions of a problem are ideological, and it is downright misleading to suggest that our views on the population–resources problem depend merely upon whether we are optimists or pessimists, socialists or conservatives, determinists or possibilists, and the like. To contend the latter is not to give sufficient credit to that spirit of scientific endeavor that seeks to establish 'truth' without invoking subjective personal preferences; to say that there is no such thing as ethical neutrality is not to say that we are reduced to mere personal opinion.

We are, however, forced to concede that 'scientific' enquiry takes place in a social setting, expresses social ideas, and conveys social meanings. If we care to probe more deeply into these social meanings, we may observe that particular kinds of scientific method express certain kinds of ethical or ideological positions. In something as controversial as the population–resources debate an understanding of this issue is crucial; yet it is all too frequently ignored. If, as I subsequently hope to show, the dominant method of logical empiricism inevitably produces Malthusian or neo-Malthusian results, then we can more easily understand how it is that scientists raised in the tradition of logical empiricism have, when they have turned to the population–resources question, inevitably attributed a certain veracity to the Malthusian and neo-Malthusian view. When they have found such a view distasteful such scientists have rarely challenged it on 'scientific' grounds; they have, rather, resorted to some version of subjective optimism as a basis for refutation. This kind of refutation has not been helpful, of course, for it has perpetuated the illusion that science and ideology (understood as personal preference) are independent of each other when the real problem lies in the ideology of scientific method itself.

It is easiest to grapple with the connections between method, ideology, and substantive conclusions by examining the works of Malthus, Ricardo, and Marx, for it is relatively easy to grasp the connections in these works and thereby to discern some important and often obscured questions that lie at the heart of any analysis of the population–resources relation.

II. MALTHUS

It is sometimes forgotten that Malthus wrote his first *Essay on the Principle of Population* in 1798 as a political tract against the utopian socialist-anarchism of Godwin and Condorcet and as an antidote to the hopes for social progress aroused by the French Revolution. In his introduction, however, Malthus lays down certain principles of method which ought, he argues, to govern discourse concerning such an ambitious subject as the perfectibility of man:

A writer may tell me that he thinks a man will ultimately become an ostrich. I cannot properly contradict him. But before he can expect to bring any reasonable person over to his opinion, he ought to show that the necks of mankind have been gradually elongating, that the lips have grown harder and more prominent, that the legs and feet are daily altering their shape, and that the hair is beginning to change into stubs of feathers. And till the probability of so wonderful a conversion can be shown, it is surely lost time and lost eloquence to expatiate on the happiness of man in such a state: to describe his powers, both of running and flying, to paint him in a condition where all narrow luxuries would be condemned, where he would be employed only in collecting the necessaries of life, and where, consequently, each man's share of labour would be light, and his portion of leisure ample (Malthus, 1970, p. 70).

The method which Malthus advocates is empiricism. It is through the application of this empiricist method that the competing theories of the utopian socialists, the proponents of liberal advancement and the rights of man, and the advocates of 'the existing order of things' can be tested against the realities of the world. Yet the first edition of the *Essay* is strongly colored by *a priori* deduction as well as by polemics and empiricism. Malthus sets up two postulates – that food is necessary to the existence of man and that the passion between the sexes is necessary and constant. He places these two postulates in the context of certain conditions; deduces certain consequences (including the famous law through which population inevitably places pressure on the mean of subsistence); and then uses the empiricist method to verify his deductions. Thus Malthus arrives at a conception of method which we may call 'logical empiricism'. This method broadly assumes that there are two kinds of truths which we may call 'logical truths' (they are correct deductions from certain initial statements) and 'empirical truths' (they are correct and verifiable factual statements which reflect observation and experiment). Logical truths may be related to empirical truths by uniting the two kinds of statements into a hypothetico-deductive system. If empirical observation indicates that certain of the derived statements are 'factually true', then this is taken to mean that the system of statements as a whole is true, and we then have a 'theory' of, for example, the population–resources relationship. Malthus constructs a crude version of such a theory.

Another feature of empiricism is worthy of note. Empiricism assumes that objects can be understood independently of observing subjects. Truth is therefore assumed to lie in a world external to the observer whose job is to record and faithfully reflect the attributes of objects. This logical empiricism is a pragmatic version of that scientific method which goes under the name of 'logical positivism', and is founded in a particular and very strict view of language and meaning.

By the use of the logical empiricist method Malthus arrives at certain conclusions supportive of those advanced by the advocates of 'the existing order of things', rejects the utopianism of Godwin and Condorcet, and rebuffs the hopes for political change. The diminution in polemics and the greater reliance on empiricism in the subsequent editions of the *Essay* may in part be regarded as a consequence of Malthus' basic discovery that scientific method of a certain sort could accomplish, with much greater credibility and power than straight polemics, a definite social purpose. The resort to empiricism was facilitated in turn by the growing body of information concerning the growth and condition of the world's population — a prime source, for example, was the work of the geographer Alexander von Humboldt (1811).

Having shown that the "power of population is indefinitely greater than the power of the earth to produce subsistence", and that it is a 'natural law' that population will inevitably press against the means of subsistence, Malthus then goes on to discuss the positive and preventive checks through which population is kept in balance with the means of subsistence. The subsequent evolution in Malthus' ideas on the subject are too well-known to warrant repetition here. What is often forgotten, however, is the class character with which he invests it. Glacken, for example, who treats Malthus in the penultimate chapter of his monumental study, *Traces on the Rhodian Shore* (Glacken, 1967), ignores this aspect to Malthus entirely.

Malthus recognizes that 'misery' has to fall somewhere and maintains that the positive checks will necessarily be the lot of the lower classes (Malthus, 1970, p. 82). Malthus thereby explains the misery of the lower classes as the result of a natural law which functions "absolutely independent of all human regulation". The distress among the lowest classes has, therefore, to be interpreted as "an evil so deeply seated that no human ingenuity can reach it" (Malthus, 1970, p. 101). On this basis Malthus arrives, 'reluctantly', at a set of policy recommendations with respect to the poor laws. By providing welfare to the lowest classes in society, aggregate human misery is only increased; freeing the lowest classes in society from positive checks only results in an expansion of their numbers, a gradual reduction in the standards of living of all members of society, and a decline in the incentive to work on which the mobilization of labor through the wage system depends. He also argues that increasing subsistence levels to "a part of society that cannot in general be considered as the most valuable part diminishes the shares that would otherwise belong to more industrious and worthy members, and thus forces more to become dependent" (Malthus, 1970, p. 97).

From this Malthus draws a moral:

Hard as it may appear in individual instances, dependent poverty ought to be held disgraceful. Such a stimulus seems to be absolutely necessary to promote the happiness of the great mass of mankind, and every general attempt to weaken this stimulus, however benevolent its apparent intention will always defeat its own purpose . . .

I feel no doubt whatever that the parish laws of England have contributed to raise the price of provisions and to lower the real price of labour. They have therefore contributed to impoverish that class of people whose only possession is their labour. It is also difficult to suppose that they have not powerfully contributed to generate that carelessness and want of frugality observable among the poor, so contrary to the disposition to be remarked among petty tradesmen and small farmers. The labouring poor, to use a vulgar expression, seem always to live from hand to mouth. Their present wants employ their whole attention, and they seldom think of the future. Even when they have an opportunity of saving, they seldom exercise it, but all that is beyond their present necessities goes, generally speaking, to the ale-house. The poor laws of England may therefore be said to diminish both the power and the will to save among the common people, and thus to weaken one of the strongest incentives to sobriety and industry, and consequently to happiness (Malthus, 1970, p. 98).

Thus, Malthus arrives at what we have now come to know as the 'counter-intuitive solution' — namely, that the best thing to do about misery and poverty is to do nothing, for anything that is done will only exacerbate the problem. The only valid policy with respect to the lowest classes in society is one of 'benign neglect'. This policy is further supported by a certain characterization of 'typical' behaviors exhibited among the lower classes. Arguments such as these are still with us. They appear in the policy statements by Jay Forrester, Edward Banfield, Patrick Moynihan and others. In fact, welfare policy in the United States at the present time is dominated by such thinking.

Malthus' approach to the lower classes has, if it is to be judged correctly, to be set against his view of the roles of the other classes in society — principally those of the industrial and landed interests. These roles are discussed more analytically in *The Principles of Political Economy*. Here he recognizes that there is a problem to be solved in accounting for the accumulation of capital in society. The capitalist saves, invests in productive activity, sells the product at a profit, ploughs the profit back in as new investment, and commences the cycle of accumulation once more. There is a serious dilemma here, for the capitalist has to sell the product to someone if a profit is to be achieved, and the capitalist is saving rather than consuming. If the capitalist saves too much and the rate of capital accumulation increases too rapidly, then long before subsistence problems are encountered, the capitalists will find expansion checked by the lack of effective demand for the increased output. Consequently, "both capital and population may at the same time, and for a period of great length, be redundant, compared to the effective demand for produce" (Malthus, 1968, p. 402).

Malthus placed great emphasis upon the effective demand problem and sought to convince his contemporary Ricardo that in practice: "the actual check to production and population arises more from want of stimulant than want of power to produce" (Keynes, 1951, p. 117). Ricardo was not persuaded, and the idea of effective demand in relationship to capital accumulation and wage rates remained dormant until Keynes (1936) resurrected it in his *General Theory of Employment, Interest and Money*.

Malthus' solution to the problem of effective demand is to rely upon the proper exercise of the power to consume on the part of those unproductive classes — the landlords, state functionaries, etc. — who were outside of the production process. Malthus took pains to dissociate himself from any direct apologetics for conspicuous consumption on the part of the landed gentry. He was merely saying that if the capitalist, who was not giving in to what Adam Smith calls "mankind's insatiable appetite for trinkets and baubles", was to succeed in the task of capital accumulation, then someone, somewhere, had to generate an effective demand:

It is unquestionably true that wealth produces wants; but it is a still more important truth that wants produce wealth. Each cause acts and reacts upon the other, but the order, both of precedence and importance, is with the wants which stimulate industry ... The greatest of all difficulties in converting uncivilized and thinly peopled countries into civilized and populous ones, is to inspire them with the wants best calculated to excite their exertions in the production of wealth. One of the greatest benefits which foreign commerce confers, and the reason why it has always appeared an almost necessary ingredient in the progress of wealth, is its tendency to inspire new wants, to form new tastes, and to furnish fresh motives for industry. Even civilized and improved countries cannot afford to lose any of these motives (Malthus, 1968, p. 403).

Effective demand, located in the unproductive classes of society and stimulated by need creation and foreign trade, was an important and vital force in stimulating both the accumulation of capital and the expansion of employment. Labor might be unemployed, consequently, simply because of the failure of the upper classes to consume. This theory of effective demand does not sit easily with the theory of population. For one thing, it appears contradictory to assert via the theory of population that the power to consume be withheld from the lowest classes in society while asserting, through the theory of effective demand, that the upper classes should consume as much as possible. Mathus attempts to resolve this contradiction by arguing that the upper classes do not increase their numbers according to the principle of population — they consume conspicuously and regulate their numbers by prudent habits generated out of a fear of a decline in their station in life. The lowest classes imprudently breed. The law of population is consequently disaggregated into one law for the poor and another law for the rich. But Malthus also has to explain why an effective demand cannot be generated by an increasing power to consume on the part of the laboring classes. Such a possibility Malthus quickly dismisses as illogical for: "no one will ever employ capital merely for the sake of the demand occasioned by those who work for him" (Malthus, 1968, p. 404).

He adds that the only case in which this could occur would be if the laborers "produce an excess of value above what they consume". He dismisses this possibility entirely. But even Ricardo, in annotating this passage, asks quite simply "why not?" and writes out a simple case to prove his point (Ricardo, 1951b, p. 429). And, of course, it is this idea, which Malthus rejects out of hand, that forms the foundation of Marx's theory of surplus value, out of which the Marxist theory of relative surplus population stems.

Internal to Malthus' own work there is a central contradiction. On the one hand, the 'natural law' of population asserts a doctrine of inevitable misery for the mass of mankind, while the theory of effective demand points to social controls to the employment of both capital and labor. Zinke suggests that Malthus did not need to reconcile these conflicting positions, for the principle of population applies in the long run, while the theory of effective demand is an explanation for short run cyclical swings (Zinke, 1967). Malthus does not appear to have thought this way about it. In the *Summary View of the Principle of Population*, published in 1830, Malthus attempts to reconcile these divergent views. Here he admits that "the laws of private property, which are the grand stimulants to production, do themselves so limit it as always to make the actual produce of the earth fall very considerably short of the power of production" (Malthus, 1970, p. 245).

He then goes on to point out that under a system of private property "the only effectual demand for produce must come from the owners of property", and that the control of effective demand so intervenes with respect to the principle of population that it prevents the visitation of misery on all sectors of mankind and "secures to a portion of society the leisure necessary for the progress of the arts and sciences" — a phenomena that "confers on society a most signal benefit". Claims for social reform, and particularly any challenges to the principle of private property, are misplaced. To do away with a society based on competitive individualism regulated through the institutions of private property is to permit the principle of population to operate unchecked – an eventuality that will plunge all of mankind into a state of misery. The laws of private property, insofar as they have restricted the opportunities for the laboring classes, have artificially checked the operation of the principle of population and thereby reduced the aggregate misery of mankind. Malthus thus reconciles the principle of population with the theory of effective demand:

It makes little difference in the actual rate of increase of population, or the necessary existence of checks to it, whether the state of demand and supply which occasions an insufficiency of wages to the whole of the labouring classes be produced prematurely by a bad structure of society, and an unfavourable distribution of wealth, or necessarily by the comparative exhaustion of the soil. The labourer feels the difficulty in the same degree and it must have nearly the same results, from whatever cause it arises (Malthus, 1970, p. 247).

Malthus was, in principle, a defender of private property arrangements, and it is this ideology that underlies his formulation of the principle of population as well as the theory of effective demand. Private property arrangements inevitably mean an uneven distribution of income, wealth, and the means of production in society. Malthus accepts some such distributional arrangement and accepts its class character. Specific distributional arrangement may be judged good or bad, but there was no way in which a rational society could be ordered which did not incorporate necessary class distinctions. Malthus bolstered his arguments with analysis and materials blended together, particularly with respect to the theory of population, by appeal to a method of logical empiricism. In his writings on political economy, however, Malthus frequently made use of a method more characteristic of Ricardo. In part the contradictory character of much of Malthus' writings on population and effective demand stems from the disjunction of method used to examine the two phenomena. At this point, therefore, we must turn to that method of investigation most clearly exhibited in the clearly spelled-out analytics of Ricardo.

III. RICARDO

Ricardo accepted Malthus' principle of population without any reservations and, it must be added, quite uncritically. But the population principle plays a

quite different role and is also treated according to a quite different methodology in Ricardo's work. Ricardo's method was to abstract a few basic
elements and relationships out of a complex reality and to analyze and
manipulate these idealized elements and relationships in order to discern the
structure of the system under consideration. In this manner Ricardo built an
abstract model of economic allocation through the market mechanism – a
working model of capitalist society – that had little need for an empirical
base. The function of such a model was to provide a tool for analysis which
would both explain and predict change. Ricardo was not an empiricist in the
sense that Malthus was in the *Essay on Population*, and he used facts spar-
ingly, largely by way of illustration rather than with the intent to verify
theory. The success and legitimacy of such a method depends, of course,
entirely upon the reasonableness of the abstractions made. It is important to
look, therefore, at the nature of the abstractions and idealizations built into
Ricardo's model in order to understand both his substantive conclusions and
his treatment of the population–resources problem.

At the heart of Ricardo's system we find a basic assumption concerning
the nature of economic rationality: 'economic man' is the model of rationality
to which all human beings ought to aspire. Ricardo was, consequently, a
normative rather than an empirical (positive) thinker. More deeply buried in
Ricardo's work, however, is a doctrine of social harmony achieved through
economically rational behavior in the market place. This doctrine of social
harmony is frequently found in the political economy of the period, and its
appearance in Ricardo's work is not unconnected with the use of an analytic,
model-building methodology. A set of elements and relationships linked into
a logical structure is bound to be internally consistent and to be internally
harmonious. The model also generates equilibrium-type solutions to problems
when it is subjected to manipulation and analysis. It is with respect to the
social harmony concept that Ricardo's work contrasts most markedly with
that of Malthus and Marx. The latter's work is expressive of the theme of
class conflict throughout, whereas in Malthus' work the sense of class conflict is confused with social harmony (particularly in *The Principles of
Political Economy*) as Malthus seeks to combine results arrived at by means
of logical empiricism with those arrived at by means of an abstract model of
the economy. Class conflict can scarcely be found in the harmonious
analytics of Ricardo's market system, although the analytical results are used
for class purposes, namely, the defeat of the landed interest and the subser-
vience of wage labor to the interests of the industrial entrepreneur.

Under these conditions it is surprising to find that Ricardo so easily accepted Mathus' principle of population. In part, the simplicity of Malthus' deductive argument must have appealed to him, but there is a much more significant reason for Ricardo's wholehearted endorsement of the principle. Only by means of it could Ricardo keep his system harmonious and in equilibrium. The analytic problem for Ricardo was to explain the equilibrium wage rate. Wages, he argued, were basically determined by two factors: scarcity and the costs of subsistence. In Ricardo's system labor was regarded abstractly as a commodity like any other, and a growing demand for it ought to elicit a supply so that wages would, in the long-run, tend to the level of a 'natural wage' set by the costs of subsistence. The mechanism that Ricardo appropriated from Malthus to achieve the balance between the supply and demand for labor was, of course, the principle of population, through which the laboring population would automatically increase their numbers:

When, however, by the encouragement which high wages give to the increase of population, the number of labourers is increased, wages again fall to their natural price, and indeed from a re-action sometimes fall below it (Ricardo, 1951a, p. 94).

In the short run and under favorable circumstances, the rate of accumulation of capital could exceed that of the power of population to reproduce, and during such periods wages would be well above their 'natural' price (Ricardo, 1951a, p. 98). But such periods are bound to be short-lived. Also, when a population presses against the means of subsistence, "the only remedies are either a reduction of people or a more rapid accumulation of capital". Consequently, the laws determining wages and "the happiness of far the greatest part of every community" were dependent upon a balanced relationship between the supply of labor, via the principle of population, and the accumulation of capital. Population, Ricardo argued, "regulates itself by the funds which are to employ it, and therefore always increases or diminishes with the increase or diminution of capital" (Ricardo, 1951a, p. 78). Even Malthus, however, objected to this use of his population principle, observing that it took at least sixteen years to produce a laborer, and that the population principle was far more than just an equilibriating mechanism (Malthus, 1968, pp. 319–20).

Ricardo accepted that:

the pernicious tendency of the poor laws is no longer a mystery since it has been fully developed by the able hand of Mr. Malthus and every friend of the poor must adamantly wish for their abolition (Ricardo, 1951a, p. 106).

Like Malthus he argues that:

The principle of gravitation is not more certain than the tendency of such laws to change wealth and power into misery and weakness; to call away the exertions of labour from every object, except that of providing mere subsistence; to confound all intellectual distinctions; to busy the mind in supplying the body's wants; until at last all classes should be infected with the plague of universal poverty (Ricardo, 1951a, p. 108).

Further, he warns that:

if we should attain the stationary state, from which I trust we are yet far distant, then the pernicious nature of these laws become more manifest and alarming (Ricardo, 1951a, p. 109).

Ricardo's evocation here of an ultimate stationary state is of interest. The analytic model-building methodology that he employed naturally suggests, as we have seen, harmony and equilibrium, and it is understandable that Ricardo should infer from his model that there must inevitably be some kind of equilibrium or stationary state. (J. S. Mill came to the same sort of conclusion using a similar methodological framework (Mill, 1965, pp. 752-7).) Ricardo is here arguing also that under such an equilibrium condition, in which the demand and supply of labor are equated and the prospects for further capital accumulation eliminated, there would appear to be a choice between conditions of universal poverty (everybody receiving a mere subsistence wage) or conditions in which rational thought and civilization itself could survive, at least among an elite. Ricardo is also suggesting that social welfare provision will become particularly pernicious in non-growth situations. Again, this argument is still with us and we will return to it later.

Ricardo found Malthus' arguments with respect to effective demand 'quite astonishing' however, and commented that: "A body of unproductive labourers are just as necessary and useful with a view to future production as a fire which should consume in the manufacturer's warehouse, the goods which those unproductive labourers would otherwise consume" (Ricardo, 1951b, p. 421).

Ricardo would have no truck with Malthus' defense of the landed interest and it is clear from his remarks and policies with respect to the corn laws, rent, and the like, that Ricardo's sympathies lie entirely with the industrial entrepreneur who alone, in Ricardo's system, epitomized economic rationality. Ricardo was in fact offended by the role the landed interest played, and since he discounted the problem of effective demand entirely, Ricardo came to regard the landed interest as a mere barrier to progress and to the achievement of social harmony.

Ricardo's model building analytics permitted him to argue positively for change. He was not deterred by empirical evidence, and he had no sense of debt to history. His normative analytics allowed him to see the possibility for changing and improving reality, rather than just understanding and accepting it. Like August Lösch (another great normative thinker) Ricardo could take the view that "if my model does not conform to reality then it is reality that is wrong" (Lösch, 1954, p. 363). Ricardo could project upon the world a working model of capitalist society constructed in the image of an idealized social harmony achieved through the benficience of rational economic man. Ricardo sought to change reality to fit this image, and in the process he played an important and vital role in furthering the progress of industrialization in nineteenth century England.

IV. MARX

Marx argues that both Ricardo and Malthus were projecting ideological assumptions without admitting or even perhaps being aware of them:

[Malthus's theory] suits his purpose remarkably well – an apologia for the existing state of affairs in England, for landlordism, 'State and Church' . . . parsons and menial servants, assailed by the Ricardians as so many useless and superannuated drawbacks of bourgeois production and as nuisances. For all that, Ricardo championed bourgeois production insofar as it signified the most unrestricted development of the social productive forces . . . He insisted upon the historical justification and necessity of this stage of development. His very lack of a historical sense of the past meant that he regarded everything from the historical standpoint of his time. Malthus also wanted to see the freest possible development of capitalist production . . . but at the same time he wants it to adapt itself to the 'consumption needs' of the aristocracy and its branches in State and Church, to serve as the material basis for the antiquated claims of the representatives of interests inherited from feudalism and the absolute monarchy. Malthus wants bourgeois production as long as it is not revolutionary, constitutes no historical factor of development, but merely creates a broader and more comfortable basis for the 'old' society (Marx, 1972, pp. 52–3).

The contrasts between Malthus, Ricardo, and Marx are usually portrayed in terms of their substantive views on such issues as the population–resources problem. The more fundamental contrast, however, is surely one of method. Marx's method is usually called 'dialectical materialism', but this phrase conveys little and conceals a lot. Fully to understand it requires some understanding of German critical philosophy and in particular that branch of it which most fully developed a non-Aristotelian view of the world – the most eminent representatives in this tradition being Leibniz, Spinoza, and Hegel. The nature of this non-Aristotelian view requires exposition.

Marx's use of language is, as Ollman has pointed out, relational rather than absolute (Ollman, 1971). By this he means that a 'thing' cannot be understood or even talked about independently of the relations it has with other things. For example, 'resources' can be defined only in relationship to the mode of production which seeks to make use of them and which simultaneously 'produces' them through both the physical and mental activity of the users. There is, therefore, no such thing as a resource in abstract or a resource which exists as a 'thing in itself'. This relational view of the world is fundamentally different from the usual and familiar Aristotelian view (characteristic of logical empiricism or Ricardian type model building) in which things are thought to have an essence of some sort and are, therefore, regarded as definable without reference to the relationships they have to other things.

On this basis Marx evolves certain fundamental assumptions regarding the way in which the world is structured and organized. Ollman suggests that: "The twin pillars of Marx's ontology are his conception of reality as a totality of internally related parts, and his conception of these parts as expandable relations such that each one in its fullness can represent the totality" (Ollman, 1973, p. 495). There are different ways in which we can think of such a totality. We may think of it as an aggregate of elements – a mere sum of parts – which enter into combination without being fashioned by any pre-existing relationships within the totality. The totality can alternatively be viewed as something 'emergent'; it has an existence independent of its parts while it also dominates and fashions the parts contained within it. But Marx's non-Aristotelian and relational view permits him a third view of the totality in which it is neither the parts nor the whole, but the relationships within the totality which are regarded as fundamental. Through these relationships the totality shapes the parts to preserve the whole. Capitalism, for example, shapes activities and elements within itself to preserve itself as an on-going system. But conversely, the elements are also continually shaping the totality into new configurations as conflicts and contradictions within the system are of necessity resolved.

Marx rarely used the word totality to refer to everything there is. He usually focused on the 'social' totality of human society, and within this totality he distinguished various structures. Structures are not 'things' or 'actions', and we cannot establish their existence through observation. The meaning of an observable act, such as cutting a log, is established by discovering its relation to the wider structure of which it is a part. Its interpretation will depend upon whether we view it in relation to capitalism or socialism, or whether we place it in relation to some quite different structure, such as the ecological system. To define elements relationally means to interpret them in a way external to direct observation; hence the departure from empiricism accomplished by relational modes of thought.

Within the social totality Marx distinguishes various structures (Godelier, 1972). The 'economic basis' of society comprises two structures – the forces of production (the actual activities of making and doing) and the social relations of production (the forms of social organization set up to facilitate making and doing). Marx thus distinguished between a technical division of labor and a social division of labor. In addition, there are various superstructural features: the structures of law, of politics, of knowledge and science, of ideology, and the like. Each structure is regarded as a primary element within the social totality and each is capable of a certain degree of autonomous development. But because the structures are all interrelated, a perpetual dynamism is generated out of the conflicts and interactions among them. For example, Marx sees a major contradiction between the increasing socialization of the forces of production (through the intricacies of the division of labor) and the private-property basis of consumption and ownership in capitalist society. Within this system of interacting structures, however, Marx accorded a certain primacy of place to the economic basis. In arguing thus, Marx usually appealed to the fact that man has to eat in order to live and that production – the transformation of nature – therefore has to take precedence over the other structures in a conflict situation. There is a deeper reason for the significance which Marx attached to the economic basis; it is here that the relationship between the natural and social aspects of life becomes most explicit.

Marx's conception of the man–nature relation is complex (Schmidt, 1971). At one level the human being is seen as a part of nature – an ensemble of metabolic relations involving constant sensuous interaction with a physical environment. At another level, human beings are seen as social – each as an ensemble of social relations (Marx, 1964) – and capable of creating forms of social organization which can become self-regulating and self-transforming. Society thereby creates its own history by transforming itself, but in the process the relationship with nature is also transformed. Under capitalism, for example:

Nature becomes for the first time simply an object for mankind, purely a matter of utility; it ceases to be recognized as a power in its own right; and the theoretical knowledge of its independent laws appears only as a stratagem designed to subdue it to human requirements, whether as the object of consumption or as the means of production. Pursuing this tendency, capital has pushed beyond national boundaries and prejudices, beyond the deification of nature and the inherited self-sufficient satisfaction of existing needs confined within well-defined bounds and [beyond] the reproduction of traditional ways of life. Capital is destructive of all this and permanently revolutionary, tearing down the obstacles that impede the development of productive forces, the expansion of need, the diversity of production and the exploitation and exchange of natural and intellectual forces (Marx, 1971, p. 94).

Marx saw the capitalist law of accumulation always pushing society to the limits of its potential social relations and to the limits of its natural resource base — continuously destroying the potential for "the exploitation and exchange of natural and intellectual forces". Resource limitations could be rolled back by technological change, but the tide of capitalist accumulation quickly spreads up to these new limits.

Marx also argued that capitalism had successfully brought society to the point where mankind could be free of nature in certain important material respects. Human beings are now in a position to *create* nature rather than mindlessly to alter it. Through the creation of nature — a creation that has to proceed through a knowledge and understanding of nature's own laws — human beings could be freed to discover their own essentially human nature within the system of nature. There is, for Marx, an enormous difference between this unalienated creation of nature and the mindless exploitation under capitalism which, in the haste to accumulate, is always concerned, as Engels has it, "only about the first tangible success; and then surprise is expressed that the more remote effects of actions directed to this end turn out to be of a quite different, mainly of an opposite, character" (Engels, 1940, p. 296).

In the final analysis, the conflict and contradiction between the system of nature and the social system could be resolved only by the creation of an appropriate and entirely new form of human practice. Through such a practice, human beings will "not only feel, but also know their unity with nature" and thereby render obsolete "the senseless and anti-natural idea of a contradiction between mind and matter, man and nature, soul and body" (Engels, 1940, p. 293).

Marx's methodology allows that knowledge and the processes of gaining understanding are internal to society. Subject and object are not regarded as independent entities but as relationships one to the other. This conception is very different indeed from that of traditional empiricism in which the subject is presumed to be "instructed by what is outside of him", or from that of a priorism and innatism (clearly implied in Ricardo's method) in which the subject "possesses from the start endogenous structures which it imposes on objects" (Piaget, 1972, p. 19). Marx in fact fashions a methodology similar to the constructivism advanced by Piaget: "Whereas other animals cannot alter themselves except by changing their species, man can transform himself by transforming the world and can structure himself by constructing structures; and these structures are his own, for they are not entirely predestined either from within or without" (Piaget, 1970, p. 118). The subject is thus seen as both structuring and being structured by the object. As Marx puts it, "by thus acting on the external world and changing it, [man] at the same time changes his own nature" (Marx, 1967, Vol. 1, p. 175).

The thinking subject can create ideas in the imagination. But ideas have at some stage to leave the realms of abstract knowledge and to enter into human practice if they are to be validated. Once incorporated into human practice, concepts and ideas can become (via technology) a material force in production and can alter the social relations of production (through the creation of new modes of social organization). Although many ideas remain barren, some do not — "at the end of every labour process we get a result that already existed in the imagination of the labourer at its commencement."

Ideas are therefore regarded as social relations through which society can be structured and reconstructed. But concepts and categories are also produced under specific historical conditions which are in part internal to knowledge (the categories of thought handed down to us) and in part a reflection of the world in which knowledge is produced. The categories of thought available to us are, as it were, our intellectual capital which it is open to us to improve (or destroy). If, however, ideas are social relations, then it follows that we can gain as much insight into society through a critical analysis of the relations ideas express, as we can through a study of society as object. The analysis of ideas in Marx's work is as much directed to understanding the society that produced them as it is to understanding what it is they tell us about the reality they purport to describe. Marx is, thus, adopting a methodological framework that is perpetually revolving around the question: what is it that produces ideas and what is it that these ideas serve to produce?

Marx's substantive conclusions on the 'population problem' are in part generated out of a vigorous criticism of writers such as Malthus and Ricardo. Marx set out to transform the categories handed down to him, for he saw that to do so was necessary if the realities of life were to be transformed. Marx traced the structure of Malthus' and Ricardo's thought back to their respective theories of value. Out of a criticism of these and other theories of value, Marx arrived at the theory of surplus value. Surplus value, he argued, originated out of surplus labor, which is that part of the laborer's working time that is rendered gratis to the capitalist. In order to obtain employment, a laborer may have to work ten hours. The laborer may produce enough to cover his own subsistence needs in six hours. If the capitalist pays a subsistence wage, then the laborer works the equivalent of four hours free for the capitalist. This surplus labor can be converted through market exchange into its money equivalent — surplus value. And surplus value, under capitalism, is the source of rent, interest, and profit. On the basis of this theory of surplus value, Marx produces a distinctive theory of population.

If surplus value is to be ploughed back to produce more surplus value, then more money has to be laid out on wages and the purchase of raw materials and means of production. If the wage rate and productivity remain constant, then accumulation requires a concomitant numerical expansion in the labor force — "accumulation of capital is, therefore, increase of the proletariat" (Marx, 1967, Vol. 1, p. 614). If the labor supply remains constant, then the increasing demand for labor generated by accumulation will bring about a rise in the wage rate. But a rise in the wage rate means a diminution of surplus value, falling profits, and, as a consequence, a slower rate of accumulation. But:

this diminution can never reach the point at which it would threaten the system itself . . . Either the price of labour keeps on rising, because its rise does not interfere with the progress of accumulation . . . Or accumulation slackens in consequence of the rise in the price of labour, because the stimulus of gain is blunted. The mechanism of the process of capitalist production removes the very obstacles that it temporarily creates (Marx, 1967, Vol. 1, p. 619).

Under these conditions, the "law of capitalist production" that is at the bottom of the "pretended natural law of population" reduces itself to a relationship between the rate of capitalist accumulation and the rate of expansion in the wage–labor force. This relationship is mediated by technical change, and the increasing social productivity of labor can also be used as "a powerful lever of accumulation" (Marx, 1967, Vol. 1, p. 621). The use of this lever permits an expansion of surplus value through a growing substitution of capital for labor in the production process. Marx then proceeds to show how these processes combine to create a "law of population peculiar to the capitalist mode of production", adding that "in fact every special historic mode of production has its own special laws of population, historically valid within its limits alone" (Marx, 1967, Vol. 1, pp. 632–33). Here we can see a major departure from the thought of both Malthus and Ricardo who attributed to the law of population a 'universal' and 'natural' validity.

Marx largely confines attention to the law of population operative under capitalism. He points out that the laboring population produces both the surplus and the capital equipment, and thereby produces the means 'by which it itself is made relatively superfluous' (Marx, 1967, Vol. 1, p. 632). He then goes on to say:

If a surplus labouring population is a necessary product of accumulation or of the development of wealth on a capitalist basis, this surplus population becomes, conversely, the lever of capitalist accumulation, nay a condition of existence of the capitalist mode of production. It forms a disposable industrial reserve army, that belongs to capital quite as absolutely as if the latter had bred it at its own cost. Independently of the limits of the actual increase of population, it creates for the changing needs of the self-expansion of capital, a mass of human material always ready for exploitation (Marx, 1967, Vol. 1, p. 632).

This relative surplus population has, however, another vital function – it prevents wages rising and thereby cutting into profits:

The industrial reserve army, during the periods of stagnation and average prosperity, weighs down the active labour army; during the periods of overproduction and paroxysm, it holds its pretensions in check. Relative surplus population is therefore the pivot around which the law of supply and demand of labour works. It confines the field of action of this law within the limits absolutely convenient to the activity of exploitation and to the domination of capital (Marx, 1967, Vol. 1, p. 632).

The production of a relative surplus population and an industrial reserve army are seen in Marx's work as historically specific, as internal to the capitalist mode of production. On the basis of his analysis we can predict the occurrence of poverty no matter what the rate of population change. Marx explicitly recognizes, however, that a high rate of capital accumulation is likely to act as a general stimulus to population growth; it is likely that laborers will try to accumulate the only marketable commodity they possess, labor power itself (Marx, 1967, Vol. 3, p. 218). Marx was not arguing that population growth per se was a mechanical product of the law of capitalist accumulation, nor was he saying that population growth per se did not affect the situation. But he was arguing very specifically, contra the position of both Malthus and Ricardo, that the poverty of the laboring classes was the inevitable product of the capitalist law of accumulation. Poverty was not, therefore, to be explained away by appeal to some natural law. It had to be recognized for what it really was – an endemic condition internal to the capitalist mode of production.

Marx does not talk about a population problem but a poverty and human exploitation problem. He replaces Malthus' concept of overpopulation by the concept of a relative surplus population. He replaces the inevitability of the "pressure of population on the means of subsistence" (accepted by both Malthus and Ricardo) by an historically specific and necessary pressure of labor supply on the means of employment produced internally within the capitalist mode of production. Marx's distinctive method permitted this reformulation of the population–resources problem, and put him in a position from which he could envisage a transformation of society that would eliminate poverty and misery rather than accept its inevitability.

V. METHODOLOGY AND THE POPULATION–RESOURCES RELATION

The contrasts between Malthus, Ricardo, and Marx are instructive for a variety of reasons. Each makes use of a distinctive method to approach the subject material. Marx utilizes a non-Aristotelian (dialectical) framework which sets him apart from Ricardo and Malthus who, in turn, are differentiated from each other by the use of abstract analytics and logical empiricism, respectively. Each method generates a distinctive kind of conclusion. Each author also expresses an ideological position, and, at times, it seems as if each utilizes that method which naturally yields the desired result. The important conclusion, however, is that the method adopted and the nature of the result are integrally related.

It is surprising, therefore, to find so little debate or discussion over the question of method for dealing with such a complex issue as the population–resources relation. Here the ethical neutrality assumption appears to be a major barrier to the advance of scientific enquiry, for if it is supposed that all scientific methods are ethically neutral, then debates over methodology scarcely matter. The materials on the population–resources relation published in recent years suggest that the Aristotelian legacy is dominant: we still usually 'think Aristotle' often without knowing it. Yer the Aristotelian cast of mind seems ill-suited for dealing with the population–resources relation, and so there has been a methodological struggle internal to the Aristotelian tradition to overcome the limitations inherent in it. There has been, as it were, a convergence toward Marx without overthrowing the Aristotelian trappings. Marx accepts that the appropriate method to deal with the population–resources relation has to be holistic, system-wide in its compass, capable of handling dynamics (feedbacks in particular), and, most important of all, *internally dynamic* in that it has to be capable of producing new concepts and categories to deal with the system under investigation and, through the operationalization of these new concepts and categories, change the system from within. It is this last feature that gives to Marx's work its dialectical quality. Most contemporary investigations of the population–resources relation recognize all of Marx's requirements save the last, and rely upon systems theory for their methodological foundation. Systems-theoretic formulations are sophisticated enough (in principle) to do everything that Marx sought to do except to transform concepts and categories dialectically, and thereby to transform the nature of the system from within. Some examples will bear out this point.

Kneese *et al.* (1970) adopt what they call a 'materials balance' approach to the population–resources relation which is, in effect, a two-stage input–output model. The first stage describes the flows within the economy; the second stage describes the flows within the ecological system; and the two systems are linked by the physical principle that matter can neither be created nor destroyed. The model is descriptive in the sense that the coefficients have to be estimated from empirical data, but experimentation on the model is possible by examining the sensitivity of results to changes in the coefficients.

In the study by Meadows *et al.* (1972) methods derived from systems dynamics are used; a system of difference equations is simulated to indicate future outcomes of population growth, industrial expansion, resource use (both renewable and non-renewable), and environmental deterioration. The system in this case incorporates feedbacks (both positive and negative) and is, in contrast to that of Kneese *et al.*, oriented to development through time. The Meadows model has come in for a great deal of criticism and a team from the University of Sussex (Cole *et al.*, 1973) has examined the model in detail. They reformulated it in certain important respects; showed some of the problems inherent in the data used to estimate the equations; and concluded that some unnecessarily pessimistic assumptions were injected into the Meadows model.

The essential point to note, however, is that *all* of these formulations lead to neo-Malthusian conclusions: strongly voiced in the Meadows model; somewhat muted in the case of Kneese *et al.* (who speak of the *new* Malthusianism); and long run in the case of the Sussex team's investigation (rather like Ricardo, they seem to suggest that the stationary state is inevitable but a long way off).

The neo-Malthusian results of these studies can be traced back to the Aristotelian form in which the question is posed and the answers constructed. And it is, of course, the ability to depart from the Aristotelian view that gets

Marx away from both the short run and long run inevitabilities of neo-Malthusian conclusions. Marx envisages the production of new categories and concepts, of new knowledge and understanding, through which the relationships between the natural and social system will be mediated. This relational and dialectical view of things comes closest to impinging upon traditional concerns with respect to the problem of technological change. It has, of course, long been recognized that Malthus was wrong in his specific forecasts because he ignored technological change. Ricardo saw the possibilities of such change, but in the long run he saw society inevitably succumbing to the law of diminishing returns. The difference between the Meadows model and the Sussex team's refashioning of it is largely due to the pessimism of the former and the optimism of the latter. In all of these cases, technological change is seen as something external to society — an unknown that cannot be accounted for. But, for Marx technological change was both internal to and inevitable within society; it is the product of human creativity, and stems from the inevitable transformation of the concepts and categories handed down to us. Only if we let ourselves be imprisoned within the system of knowledge handed down to us will we fail to innovate. Further, it is unnecessarily restrictive to think that human inventiveness and creativity apply only in the sphere of technology — human beings can and do create social structures as well as machines. This process Marx regards as essential and inevitable precisely because man could and would respond to the necessities of survival. The only danger lies in the tendency to place restrictions on ourselves and, thereby, to confine our own creativity. In other words, if we become the prisoners of an ideology, prisoners of the concepts and categories handed down to us, we are in danger of making the neo-Malthusian conclusions true, of making environmental determinism a condition of our existence.

It is from this standpoint that Marx's method generates quite different perspectives and conclusions from those generated by simple logical empiricism, Ricardian type normative analytics, or contemporary systems theory. Let me stress that I am not arguing that the latter methods are illegitimate or erroneous. Each is in fact perfectly appropriate for certain domains of enquiry. Logical empiricism has the capacity to inform us as to what is, given an existing set of categories. Insofar as we make use of this method, we are bound to construct what I have elsewhere called a *status quo* theory (Harvey, 1973). The Aristotelian manner in which normative, analytical model building proceeds yields 'ought-to' prescriptive statements, but the categories and concepts are idealized, abstracted, and *stationary* tools imposed upon a changing world. Systems theory is a more sophisticated form of modelling relying upon various degrees of abstraction and a varying empirical content. Dialectical materialism, in the manner that Marx used it, is 'constructivist' in that it sees change as an internally generated necessity that affects categories of thought and material reality alike. The relationships between these various methods are complex. The methods are not, obviously, mutually exclusive of each other; but different methods appear appropriate for different domains of enquiry. And it is difficult to see how anything other than a relational, constructivist, and internally dynamic method can be appropriate for looking into the future of the population–resources relation, particularly when it is so evident that knowledge and understanding are such important mediating forces in the construction of that future. Results arrived at by other means may be of interest, only if they are set within the broader interpretive power provided by Marx's method. All of this would be a mere academic problem (although one of crucial significance) were it not for the fact that ideas are social relations, and the Malthusian and neo-Malthusian results arrived at (inevitably) by means of other methods are projected into the world where they are likely to generate immediate political consequences. And it is to these consequences that we now turn.

VI. THE POLITICAL IMPLICATIONS OF POPULATION–RESOURCES THEORY

At the Stockholm Conference on the Environment in 1972, the Chinese delegation asserted that there was no such thing as a scarcity of resources and that it was meaningless to discuss environmental problems in such terms. Western commentators were mystified and some concluded that the Chinese must possess vast reserves of minerals and fossil fuels the discovery of which they had not yet communicated to the world. The Chinese view is, however, quite consistent with Marx's method and should be considered from such a perspective. To elucidate it we need to bring into our vocabulary three categories of thought:

(1) *Subsistence*. Malthus appears to regard subsistence as something absolute, whereas Marx regards it as relative. For Marx, needs are not purely biological; they are also socially and culturally determined (Orans, 1966). Also, as both Malthus and Marx agree, needs can be created, which implies that the meaning of subsistence cannot be established independent of particular historical and cultural circumstances if, as Marx insisted, definitions of social wants and needs were produced under a given mode of production

rather than immutably held down by the Malthusian laws of population. Subsistence is, then, defined internally to a mode of production and changes over time.

(2) *Resources*. Resources are materials available 'in nature' that are capable of being transformed into things of utility to man. It has long been recognized that resources can be defined only with respect to a particular technical, cultural, and historical stage of development, and that they are, in effect, technical and cultural appraisals of nature (Firey, 1960, p. 39).

(3) *Scarcity*. It is often erroneously accepted that scarcity is something inherent in nature, when its definition is inextricably social and cultural in origin. Scarcity presupposes certain social ends, and it is these that define scarcity just as much as the lack of natural means to accomplish these ends (Pearson, 1957). Furthermore, many of the scarcities we experience do not arise out of nature but are created by human activity and managed by social organization (the scarcity of building plots in central London is an example of the former; the scarcity of places at university is an example of the latter). Scarcity is in fact necessary to the survival of the capitalist mode of production, and it has to be carefully managed, otherwise the self-regulating aspect to the price mechanism will break down (Harvey, 1973).

Armed with these definitions, let us consider a simple sentence: "Overpopulation arises because of the scarcity of resources available for meeting the subsistence needs of the mass of the population". If we substitute our definitions into this sentence we get: "There are too many people in the world because the particular ends we have in view (together with the form of social organization we have) and the materials available in nature, that we have the will and the way to use, are not sufficient to provide us with those things to which we are accustomed". Out of such a sentence all kinds of possibilities can be extracted:

(1) we can change the ends we have in mind and alter the social organization of scarcity;

(2) we can change our technical and cultural appraisals of nature;

(3) we can change our views concerning the things to which we are accustomed;

(4) we can seek to alter our numbers.

A real concern with environmental issues demands that all of these options be examined in relation to each other. To say that there are too many people in the world amounts to saying that we have not the imagination, will, or ability to do anything about propositions (1), (2), and (3). In fact (1) is very difficult to do anything about because it involves the replacement of the market exchange system as a working model of economic integration; proposition (2) has always been the great hope for resolving our difficulties; and we have never thought too coherently about (3) particularly as it relates to the maintenance of an effective demand in capitalist economies (nobody appears to have calculated what the effects of much reduced personal consumption will have on capital accumulation and employment).

I will risk the generalization that nothing of consequence can be done about (1) and (3) without dismantling and replacing the capitalist market exchange economy. If we are reluctant to contemplate such an alternative and if (2) is not performing its function too well, then we have to go to (4). Much of the debate in the western world focusses on (4), but in a society in which all four options can be integrated with each other, it must appear facile to discuss environmental problems in terms of naturally arising scarcities or overpopulation – this, presumably, is the point that the Chinese delegation to the Stockholm Conference was making.

The trouble with focusing exclusively on the control of population numbers is that it has certain political implications. Ideas about environment, population, and resources are not neutral. They are political in origin and have political effects. Historically it is depressing to look at the use made of the kind of sentence we have just analyzed. Once connotations of absolute limits come to surround the concepts of resource, scarcity, and subsistence, then an absolute limit is set for population. And what are the political implications (given these connotations) of saying there is 'overpopulation' or a 'scarcity of resources'? The meaning can all too quickly be established. Somebody, somewhere, is redundant, and there is not enough to go round. Am *I* redundant? Of course not. Are *you* redundant? Of course not. So who is redundant? Of course, it must be *them*. And if there is not enough to go round, then it is only right and proper that *they*, who contribute so little to society, ought to bear the brunt of the burden. And if we hold that there are certain of *us* who, by virtue of our skills, abilities, and attainments, are capable of "conferring a signal benefit upon mankind" through our contributions to the common good and who, besides, are the purveyors of peace, freedom, culture, and civilization, then it would appear to be our bound duty to protect and preserve ourselves for the sake of all mankind.

Let me make an assertion. Whenever a theory of overpopulation seizes hold in a society dominated by an elite, then the non-elite invariably experience some form of political, economic, and social repression. Such an assertion can be justified by an appeal to the historical evidence. Britain shortly after the Napoleonic Wars, when Malthus was so influential, provides one example. The conservation movement in the United States at the turn of this century was based on a gospel of efficiency that embraced natural resource management and labor relations alike. The combination of the Aryan ethic and the need for increased *lebensraum* produced particularly evil results in Hitler's Germany. The policy prescriptions that frequently attach to essays on the problems of population and environment convey a similar warning. Jacks and Whyte (1939), writing in the twilight years of the British Empire, could see only one way out of the scarcity of land resources in Africa:

A feudal type of society in which the native cultivators would to some extent be tied to the lands of their European overlords seems most generally suited to meet the needs of the soil in the present state of African development . . . It would enable the people who have been the prime cause of erosion [the Europeans] and who have the means and ability to control it to assume responsibility for the soil. At present, humanitarian considerations for the natives prevent Europeans from winning the attainable position of dominance over the soil (Jacks and Whyte, 1939, p. 276).

Such direct apologetics for colonialism sound somewhat odd today.

Vogt, whose book *The Road to Survival* appeared in 1948, saw in Russian overpopulation a serious military and political threat. He argued that the Marshall Plan of aid to Europe was the result of an unenviable choice between allowing the spread of communism and providing international welfare, which would merely encourage population increase. He also points to the expendability of much of the world's population:

There is little hope that the world will escape the horror of extensive famines in China within the next few years. But from the world point of view, these may be not only desirable but indispensable. A Chinese population that continued to increase at a geometric rate could only be a global calamity. The mission of General Marshall to this unhappy land was called a failure. Had it succeeded, it might well have been a disaster (Vogt, 1948, p. 238).

It is ironic indeed that this prediction was published in the year before Mao Tse-tung came to power and sought, in true dialectical fashion, to transform China's problem into a solution through the mobilization of labor power to create resources where there had been none before. The resultant transformation of the Chinese earth (as Buchanan (1970) calls it) has eliminated famine, raised living standards, and effectively eliminated hunger and material misery.

It is easier to catch the political implications of overpopulation arguments in past eras than it is in our own. The lesson which these examples suggest is simply this: if we accept a theory of overpopulation and resource scarcity but insist upon keeping the capitalist mode of production intact, then the inevitable results are policies directed toward class or ethnic repression at home and policies of imperialism and neo-imperialism abroad. Unfortunately this relation can be structured in the other direction. If, for whatever reason, an elite group requires an argument to support policies of repression, then the overpopulation argument is most beautifully tailored to fit this purpose. Malthus and Ricardo provide us with one example of such apologetics. If a poverty class is necessary to the processes of capitalist accumulation or a subsistence wage essential to economic equilibrium, then what better way to explain it away than to appeal to a universal and supposedly 'natural' law of population?

Malthus indicates another kind of apologetic use for the population principle. If an existing social order, an elite group of some sort, is under threat and is fighting to preserve its dominant position in society, then the overpopulation and shortage of resources arguments can be used as powerful ideological levers to persuade people into acceptance of the status quo and of authoritarian measures to maintain it. The English landed interest used Malthus' arguments thus in the early nineteenth century. And this kind of argument is, of course, even more effective if the elite group is in a position to create a scarcity to demonstrate the point.

The overpopulation argument is easily used as part of an elaborate apologetic through which class, ethnic, or (neo-) colonial repression may be justified. It is difficult to distinguish between arguments that have some real foundation and arguments fashioned for apologetic reasons. In general the two kinds of arguments get inextricably mixed up. Consequently, those who think there is a real problem of some sort may, unwittingly, contribute strength to the apologists, and individuals may contribute in good faith to a result which, as individuals, they might find abhorrent.

And what of the contemporary ecology and environmental movement? I believe it reflects all of the currents I have identified, but under the stress of contemporary events it is difficult to sort the arguments out clearly. There are deep structural problems to the capitalist growth process (epitomized by persistent 'stagflation' and international monetary uncertainties). Adjustments seem necessary. The welfare population in America is being transformed from a tool for the manipulation of effective demand (which was its economic role in the 1960s) into a tool for attacking wage rates (through the work-fare provision) — and Malthus' arguments are all being used to do it. Wage rates have been under attack, and policies for depressing real earnings are emerging in both America and Europe to compensate for falling rates of profit and a slowdown in the rate of capital accumulation. There can be no question that the existing social order perceived itself to be under some kind of threat in the late 1960s (particularly in France and the U.S.A., and now in Britain). Was it accidental that the environmentalist argument emerged so strongly in 1968 at the crest of campus disturbances? And what was the effect of replacing Marcuse by Ehrlich as campus hero? Conditions appear to be exactly right for the emergence of overpopulation arguments as part of a popular ideology to justify what had and what has to be done to stabilize a capitalist economic system that is under severe stress.

But at the same time there is mounting evidence (which has in fact been building up since the early 1950s) of certain ecological problems that now exist on a world-wide as opposed to on a purely local scale (the DDT example being the most spectacular). Such problems are real enough. The difficulty, of course, is to identify the underlying reason for the emergence of these difficulties. There has been some recognition that consumption patterns induced under capitalism may have something to do with it, and that the nature of private enterprise, with its predilection for shifting costs onto society in order to improve the competitive position of the firm, also plays a role (Kapp, 1950). And there is no question that runaway rates of population growth (brought about to a large degree by the penetration of market and wage–labor relationships into traditional rural societies) have also played a role. But in their haste to lay the origin of these problems at the door of 'over-population' (with all of its Malthusian connotations), many analysts have unwittingly invited the politics of repression that invariably seem to be attached to the Malthusian argument at a time when economic conditions are such as to make that argument extremely attractive to a ruling elite.

Ideas are social relations; they have their ultimate origin in the social concerns of mankind and have their ultimate impact upon the social life of mankind. Arguments concerning environmental degradation, population growth, resource scarcities, and the like can arise for quite disparate reasons and have quite diverse impacts. It is therefore crucial to establish the political and social origins and impacts of such arguments. The political consequences of injecting a strongly pessimistic view into a world structured hierarchically along class and ethic lines and in which there is an ideological commitment to the preservation of the capitalist order are quite terrifying to contemplate. As Levi-Strauss warns in *Tristes Tropiques*:

Once men begin to feel cramped in their geographical, social and mental habitat, they are in danger of being tempted by the simple solution of denying one section of the species the right to be considered human (Levi-Strauss, 1973, p. 401).

VII. CONCLUSIONS

Twentieth century science in the western world is dominated by the tradition of Aristotelian materialism. Within that tradition, logical empiricism, backed by the philosophical strength of logical positivism, has provided a general paradigmatic basis for scientific enquiry. More recently the 'model builders' and the 'systems theorists' have come to play a larger role. All of these methods are destined to generate Malthusian or neo-Malthusian results when applied to the analysis of global problems in the population–resources relation. Individual scientists may express optimism or pessimism about the future, while the results of scientific investigation may indicate the inevitable stationary state to be far away or close at hand. But, given the nature of the methodology, all the indicators point in the same direction.

The political consequences that flow from these results can be serious. The projection of a neo-Malthusian view into the politics of the time appears to invite repression at home and neo-colonial policies abroad. The neo-Malthusian view often functions to legitimate such policies and, thereby, to preserve the position of a ruling elite. Given the ethical neutrality assumption and the dominant conception of scientific method, all a ruling elite has to do to generate neo-Malthusian viewpoints is to ask the scientific community to consider the problems inherent in the population–resources relation. The scientific results are basically predetermined, although individual scientists may demur for personal 'subjective' reasons.

It is, of course, the central argument of this paper that the only kind of method capable of dealing with the complexities of the population–resources relation in an integrated and truly dynamic way is that founded in a properly constituted version of dialectical materialism.

This conclusion will doubtless be unpalatable to many because it *sounds* ideological to a society of scholars nurtured in the belief that ideology is a dirty word. Such a belief is, as I have pointed out, ideological. Further, failure to make use of such a method in the face of a situation that all regard as problematic, and some regard as bordering on the catastrophic, is to court ignorance on a matter as serious as the survival of the human species. And if ignorance is the result of the ideological belief that science is and ought to be ideology free, then it is a hidden ideology that is the most serious barrier to enquiry. And if, out of ignorance, we participate in the politics of repression and the politics of fear, then we are doing so largely as a consequence of the ideological claim to be ideology free. But then, perhaps, it was precisely that participation that the claim to be ideology free was designed to elicit all along.

The Johns Hopkins University

BIBLIOGRAPHY

Buchanan, K.: 1970, *The Transformation of the Chinese Earth*, Praeger, New York.
Cole, H. S. D., Freeman, C., Jahoda, M. and Pavitt, K. L. R.: 1973, *Thinking about the Future: A Critique of the Limits to Growth*, Chatto and Windus, London.
Engels, F.: 1940, *The Dialectics of Nature*, International Publishers,New York.
Firey, W.: 1960, *Man, Mind and the Land*, Free Press, Glencoe, Illinois.
Glacken, C.: 1967, *Traces on the Rhodian Shore*, University of California Press, Berkeley.
Godelier, M.: 1972, *Rationality and Irrationality in Economics*, New Left Books, London.
Harvey, D.: 1973, *Social Justice and the City*, Johns Hopkins Press, Baltimore.
Hays, S.: 1959, *The Conservation Movement and the Gospel of Efficiency*, Atheneum, Cambridge, Massachusetts.
Hudson, W. D.: 1970, *Modern Moral Philosophy*, Macmillan, London.
Humboldt, A. von.: 1811, *Essai Politique sur le Royaume de la Nouvelle Espagne*, F. Schoell, Paris.
Jacks, G. V. and Whyte, R. O.: 1939, *Vanishing Lands*, Doubleday, New York.
Kapp, K. W.: 1950, *The Social Costs of Private Enterprise*, Harvard University Press, Cambridge, Massachusetts.
Keynes, J. M.: 1936, *The General Theory of Employment, Interest and Money*, Harcourt Brace, New York.
Keynes, J. M.: 1951, *Essays in Biography*, Meridian Books, New York.
Kneese, A. V., Ayres, R. U. and D'Arge, R. C.: 1970, *Economics and the Environment*, Resources for the Future, Washington, D.C.
Kuhn, T. S.: 1962, *The Structure of Scientific Revolutions*, Chicago University Press, Chicago.
Levi-Strauss, C.: 1973, *Tristes Tropiques*, Atheneum, New York.
Lösch, A.: 1954, *The Economics of Location*, Yale University Press, New Haven.
Malthus, T. R.: 1970, *An Essay on the Principle of Population and a Summary View of the Principle of Population*, Penguin Books, Harmondsworth, Middlesex.
Malthus, T. R.: 1968, *Principles of Political Economy*, Augustus Kelley, New York.
Marx, K.: 1963, *The Poverty of Philosophy*, International Publishers, New York.
Marx, K.: 1964, *The Economic and Philosophic Manuscripts of 1844*, International Publishers, New York.
Marx, K.: 1967, *Capital*, 3 volumes, International Publishers, New York.
Marx, K.: 1971, *The Grundrisse*, Macmillan, London.
Marx, K.: 1972, *Theories of Surplus Value*, Part 3, Progress Publishers, Moscow.
Meadows, D. H., Meadows, D. L., Randers, J. and Behrens, W. W.: 1972, *The Limits to Growth*, Universe Books, New York.
Mesjaros, I.: 1972, 'Ideology and Social Science', *Socialist Register*.
Mill, J. S.: 1965, *Principles of Political Economy*, University of Toronto Press, Toronto.
Ollman, B.: 1971, *Alienation: Marx's Conception of Man in Capitalist Society*, Cambridge University Press, London.
Ollman, B.: 1973, 'Marxism and Political Science: Prologomenon to a Debate on Marx's Method', *Politics and Society* **3**, 491–510.
Orans, M.: 1966, 'Surplus', *Human Organization* **25**, 24–32.

Pearson, H.: 1957, 'The Economy Has No Surplus: A Critique of a Theory of Development', in K. Polanyi, C. M. Arensberg, and H. W. Pearson, *Trade and Market in Early Empires*, Free Press, Glencoe, Illinois.
Piaget, J.: 1970, *Structuralism*, Harper, New York.
Piaget, J.: 1972, *The Principles of Genetic Epistemology*, Routledge and Kegan Paul, London.
Ricardo, D.: 1951a, *Principles of Political Economy*, Cambridge University Press, London.
Ricardo, D.: 1951b, *The Works and Correspondence of David Ricardo*, Volume 2, Cambridge University Press, London.
Sauer, C.: 1952, *Agricultural Origins and Dispersals*, American Geographical Society, New York.
Schmidt, A.: 1971, *The Concept of Nature in Marx*, New Left Books, London.
Spoehr, A.: 1956, 'Cultural Differences in the Interpretation of Natural Resources', in W. L. Thomas (ed.), *Man's Role in Changing the Face of the Earth*, Chicago University Press, Chicago.
Tarascio, V. J.: 1966, *Pareto's Methodological Approach to Economics*, University of North Carolina Press, Chapel Hill, North Carolina.
Vogt, W.: 1948, *The Road to Survival*, W. Sloane Associates, New York.
Wittgenstein, L.: 1958, *Philosophical Investigations*, Oxford University Press, Oxford.
Zinke, G. W.: 1967, *The Problem of Malthus: Must Progress End in Overpopulation*, University of Colorado Studies, Series in Economics, No. 5, Boulder, Colorado.

LESLIE J. KING

ALTERNATIVES TO A POSITIVE
ECONOMIC GEOGRAPHY

The 1960s witnessed many remarkable changes in the character and substance of research in economic and urban geography. These changes were associated mainly with the introduction of quantitative techniques and, later in the decade, some particular research methodologies borrowed from the behavioral sciences, especially psychology. One chronicler of these developments proclaimed triumphantly that "the substitution of quantitative approaches to problems formerly treated in descriptive verbal ways" represented "one of the greatest periods of intellectual ferment in the whole history of geography"[1]. It now seems most unlikely that this judgement will stand the test of time. It is already clear that the so-called quantitative revolution changed mainly the research techniques employed by economic and urban geographers and did little, at least directly, to channel their attention away from a traditional concern for the static location patterns of economic activities and the flows of people, goods, and services in economic settings which were sterile in respect to any acknowledgement, let alone analysis, of the prevailing value systems, be they political, societal, or individual.[2] To the extent that there was a 'revolution' in the sixties it was a revolution in techniques and not one in the main thrusts of intellectual inquiry in economic and urban geography.[3] It is perhaps this latter revolution that is underway today; some of the evidence in support of this contention is reviewed in this paper.

One direct legacy of the developments of the sixties was the emergence of a number of lines of quantitative-theoretical work in economic and urban geography; in some the quest for formal mathematical theories has been pursued vigorously. These particular areas of theoretical research appear firmly grounded in a positivistic approach to social science research, and operating on this basis they come as close as it seems possible for the social sciences to come in emulating the approaches, if not the achievements, of the physical sciences. Some current work by geographers on the spatial structure of urban areas and on location theory is strongly representative of this theme; work on spatial interaction patterns and on the analysis of economic change over space also reflects this same tendency to a lesser extent. The research problems posed in all these areas present intellectually challenging questions,

187

S. Gale and G. Olsson (eds.), Philosophy in Geography, 187–213. All Rights Reserved.

and considerable mathematical elegance and rigor have been displayed in the formal solution of many of them. The 'validity' of the approach and the results frequently are buttressed by convincing fits to historical data from the real world. The proponents of this approach also would argue that sufficient flexibility is incorporated into the structuring of their models to allow for the critical consideration of policy variables and for the weighing of alternatives in regard to the levels of these variables.

It is on this last contention that much of the current methodological debate is focussed, not only in geography but in the social sciences generally. What, indeed, is the relationship between social science on the one hand, and social change and social policy on the other? Criticisms of the positivistic approach emphasize the inappropriateness and even the inconsistencies of its alleged 'value-free' positions, the fact that its analyses serve mainly to reinforce and even legitimize the *status quo* in society, and its seemingly all too frequent willingness to sacrifice social relevance for mathematical elegance.[4] For those social scientists who find in the theory of Marxism an appealing blueprint for social change, the alternatives to this 'out-moded' positivism are all too obvious. The literature of economic and urban geography today shows the imprint of a small but growing group of geographers who seek not only to formulate new theories of the space economy based upon the exegesis of Marx's writings but also to approach the problem of spatial planning and the related policy issues from a Marxian viewpoint.

For the ideologue there is no real dilemma concerning the course of action to be followed in the future development of social science, be it economic and urban geography or whatever. The positivist, believing in incremental change to the existing system, will continue in his quest for general theories which might serve to anchor his application of quantitative models in the assessment of alternative policy decisions made within the existing socio-political framework. Social change is viewed in his eyes as involving a series of incremental steps, and neither his theories nor his assemblage of models make any acknowledgement of personal judgements concerning the grand unfolding of history, in particular the long term processes of social change. Indeed, a detachment or at least a self-proclaimed right to detachment from the issues of society is often implied in the work of the positivist. He usually argues that he is too involved in the immediate problems of formulating theories and structuring models to be concerned with their 'application': this phase must await the efforts of others! The Marxist scholar, by contrast, is imbued with a sense of history and a belief in the inevitability of the demise of the capitalist system, and can accept no such detachment. Folke made this point in discussing one of David Harvey's papers.[5]

the development of revolutionary theory is itself dependent on revolutionary practice. It is crucially important to understand that theory cannot be developed first and then put into practice. The revolutionary process must be a dialectical one between theory and practice. Revolutionary theory without revolutionary practice is not only useless, it is inconceivable.

These two extreme positions regarding the relationship between social science and social change and policy clearly are irreconcilable. Perhaps they are, in the words of the political scientist MacIntyre, both equally guilty of 'epistemological self-righteousness'[6].

Given this polarity, it is possible to conceive of a middle course, to insist upon an economic and urban geography that will be concerned explicitly with social change and policy, and that will recognize the ethical content of all of its analyses and freely admit the biases which are inherent in them as a result. Such a middle course will not find favor with the ideologues, who will see it either as another obfuscation favoring only 'status quo' and 'counter-revolutionary' theory, or as a distraction from the immediate task of building elegant quantitative-theoretic structures, but some paths are being cut through the thicket of competing epistemologies, rambling lines of empirical analysis, and gnarled branches of applied studies that now cover the middle ground.[7]

This paper begins with a brief review of the major lines of quantitative-theoretic work in economic and urban geography. The overview is not meant to be exhaustive, and it deliberately shuns any presentation of the mathematical frameworks. It seeks to emphasize the major methodological features of what I call the positivistic approach to social science research. This summary is followed by exposition of two major lines of criticism of the positivistic position. The first is well represented in the literature of social science; it emphasizes the failure or inability of the positivistic approach to deal with questions of value and ethical considerations, especially planning social change and social policy. One response to this criticism has been the championing of alternative philosophical frameworks such as phenomenology, existentialism, and many-valued systems of logic. I view these essentially as distractions, perhaps not the 'counter-revolutionary clutter' that David Harvey suggests they are, but certainly as distractions from the main issues confronting economic geography as a social science.[8] The second line of criticism of the positivistic approach is identified with the work of the Marxist scholars.

I. LEGACIES OF THE QUANTITATIVE REVOLUTION

One of the direct legacies of the changes in human geography in the 1960s was the spawning of four lines of quantitative-theoretic work that now appear to be strong and flourishing.

I.1. *Spatial Interaction*

The study of the flows of people, goods, and ideas has long interested economic and urban geographers. At least three main strands of quantitative-theoretic work relate to this tradition: on gravity-model type formulations, on spatial diffusion, and on the behavioral bases of peoples' interaction with their environments. Although the quantitative revolution of the sixties produced no new or exciting analytic approaches or theoretical formulations, the gravity model continued to fascinate some scholars, and numerous regression analyses attempted to estimate its parameters.[9] Graph theory seemed to provide a useful descriptive tool for analyzing particular flow patterns and networks, but the applications generally proved sterile. In the late sixties, however, the work of Alan Wilson and his colleagues breathed new life into the aging body of the gravity model.[10] Wilson showed how it could be restructured to allow for constraints on the flows both at the origins and at the destinations and on the overall system budget. This constrained gravity model proved to be an extremely rich formulation in the sense that it is general enough to apply to migration, interregional economic interaction, transport, and the intraurban location and allocation of activities.[11] Wilson derived his models using entropy-maximizing methods; the introduction of these methods in turn spawned several new lines of quantitative work concerned with statistical estimation problems.[12] It has also prompted methodological inquiries into the nature of entropy-maximizing methods. Webber, for example, has discussed their logical bases and argued that the entropy maximizing formalism is a device which identifies the constraints which must be explained if some observation is to be regarded as natural.[13] Sheppard has challenged the idea that the use of entropy measures is a method of theory construction and has emphasized that they are properly regarded instead as tools of statistical inference in a Bayesian-type framework.[14] He has also suggested that much remains to be done in adapting these tools to the analysis of spatial series.

The unconstrained gravity model also has been the subject of new theoretical work. Curry has suggested that any possible friction of distance effect in the phenomena under study becomes mixed up with a map pattern effect in the conventional regression analysis approach to the estimation of the parameters of the model.[15] This contention, at least so far as it relates to intercity interaction, has been challenged by Cliff and others, and the debate continues.[16] Tobler has sought to remove the difficulties inherent in the basic symmetry associated with the gravity model by introducing "a wind, or current of some type, which facilitates interaction in particular directions".[17]

Hagerstrand initiated geographic inquiry into spatial interactions associated with diffusion mechanism.[18] Recent theoretical work on this topic has been summarized well by Hudson, who has contributed a number of the formulations himself.[19] The best known is the central-place hierarchic model in which the flow of information or ideas from the highest order center down to all lower-order centers is expressed in terms of the frequency distribution of the number of centers at a particular time-lag from the origin. This distribution is a function both of the size and of the location of the centers.

Most of the large volume of work on spatial preference structures, choice behavior, environmental cognition, and individual activity patterns has been empirical, although some theoretical formulations have been proposed, such as Hagerstrand's 'time-geography' model.[20]

I.2. Location Theory

The traditional interest of economic and urban geographers in location theory was the touchstone for much of the revolutionary fervor of the sixties. The related theoretical work which is being done today by geographers can be conveniently grouped into two classes. The formal investigation of the properties of spatial market systems and the related locational arrangements of economic activities is well illustrated by the work of Davies.[21] The spatial configurations of consumers and assumptions about production costs, inventory levels, the nature of consumer demand, and transportation costs are carefully specified. Then given certain objective functions which are to be minimized, the theory addresses:[22]

the necessary and sufficient conditions for the optimal spacing of facilities in terms of the production, transportation and demand functions ..., the optimal level of production and market interval size ..., the results of instituting varying pricing policies, the estimation of deficits incurred under marginal pricing and the derivation of results from other studies as special cases.

If it is assumed that one knows future changes in demand and the point at which demand will level off, then it is possible to consider the dynamics of the system and to identify optimal spatial configurations which will meet this target level while satisfying some other criterion such as the minimization of average total cost.[23] This work on location theory is continuing, much of it under the leadership of Michael Dacey, whose earlier work on the formal properties of settlement patterns which were viewed as having been generated by spatial stochastic processes, helped establish the basic thrust of this line of inquiry.[24]

The location theory theme also finds expression in the research of Julian Wolpert and his colleagues.[25] The special interest of this group is the process of decision-making that is involved in the location of 'controversial facilities'. Wolpert observed that:[26]

sometimes the location finally chosen for a new development, or the site chosen for a relocation of an existing facility, comes out to be the site around which the least protest can be generated by those to be displaced. Rather than being an optimal, a rational, or even a satisfactory location decision the decision is perhaps merely the expression of rejection by elements powerful enough to enforce their decision that another location must not be used; alternatively the locational decision may result in a choice against which no strong argument can be raised since such elements either are inarticulate or command too little power to render their argument effective.

Wolpert seeks a theory of location which will include consideration of threat situations and the stress responses which they generate. Michael Dear has outlined the framework of such a theory for the location of public facilities.[27] This location process is seen as a complex n-person nonzero-sum game involving coalitions of the clients, the service suppliers, government, the funding agency, and the community. The activities of these groups determine sociopolitical decisions concerning the service location and the nature of service delivery.

I.3. *Spatial Structure of Urban Areas*

Quantitative-theoretic investigation of the spatial structure of urban areas by geographers began in the description of urban population density and rent surfaces by fitted mathematical functions, notably the negative exponential function; the publication of Alonso's theory of urban land use structure gave impetus to theoretical work on the same question by geographers.[28] At this point I will focus on the major contributions which two geographers, Casetti and Papageorgiou, have made to the theory.[29] Marxist scholars have made some different theoretical contributions to the analysis of the spatial structure of urban areas.

Alonso's well-known formulation is based on neoclassical consumer behavior theory: it focuses on the equilibrium situation both for the individual household and for the business firm. The individual household was seen as choosing between combinations of land, a composite good, and commuting distance to maximize its utility subject to a budget constraint. The equilibrium solution for the firm involved the maximization of its profit as the measure of utility. Alonso's formulation was weakest in its consideration of the market equilibrium. He was able to show that in general individuals or activities with the steeper bid-price curves would be closer to the center of the city, but he was unable to determine an overall market equilibrium in which the distributions of land prices and population densities as continuous functions of distance from the center would be specified.

Casetti proposed an alternative formulation of the Alonso model for residential households which allowed for the derivation of continuous functions relating land prices and population densities to distance from any central point.[30] Casetti made an important change in the framework used by Alonso; he assumed all households were identical and then, in order to allow for a spatial equilibrium, he saw these households as being able to attain an optimal level of satisfaction (or utility) that was the same throughout the urban area.

Both the Alonso and Casetti formulations assumed only one central location to which accessibility was sought. Most discussions took this central location to be the center of the metropolitan area, the central business district, but from the theoretical viewpoint this particular identification was not essential. All that had to be assumed was a central location where employment and/or other opportunities were concentrated.

An obvious extension of the theory was to consider several centers. Papageorgiou first successfully extended the theory in this direction.[31] He began by assuming the existence of an unbounded homogeneous region containing a number of urban places ordered into a central place hierarchy. Households throughout the region were identical in their desires for space and accessibility, and each household had a utility function which reflected these desires. Accessibility became a function of the distances to several centers. The centers at a particular level in the hierarchy were assumed to offer the same employment opportunities and goods and services. The resident would travel to the closest center of a particular order. A set of distances to the nearest centers of the different orders would be associated with his location. Accessibility in the Papageorgiou formulation was written as a function of these distances. Substitution into the expression for the equilibrium population density, derived under the assumption of a Casetti-type equilibrium, gave the equilibrium population densities also as a function of these distances.[32]

Papageorgiou proved that the equilibrium population density would attain its maximum value within the system of places being considered at the highest order place. This might be thought of as the global maximum. Local maxima at other urban centers would be smaller the farther the centers were from higher-order places. Peaks or maxima could occur only at urban centers, but some centers might not correspond to local maxima.

Work on this problem is continuing.[33] Papageorgiou has given particular attention to the formal properties of many of the theorems and more especially to the existence of spatial equilibriums.[34] He has also introduced into the multicenter formulation a 'residential attractiveness' variable which becomes an extra element in the utility function and an additional constraint on the solution.[35] Casetti has proposed an alternative formulation of the single center case in which households are differentiated according to income.[36]

I.4. *Economic Change Over Space*

One quantitative-theoretic approach to the analysis of economic change over space has examined patterns of regional economic change as expressed in unemployment levels after the macrolevel effects of national economic change have been removed or at least accounted for. The contention is that:[37]

an understanding of the profiles of regional unemployment series must begin with some knowledge of the impact of aggregate national effects which are partly under the control of government policies. Aggregate national effects have a differential impact on individual regions, so that some regional profiles may exhibit damped or amplified versions of national oscillations. In addition, regional and local factors will modify, or perhaps swamp, the echo of the national pattern.

This interest in regional business cycles has been reflected in geographic studies of unemployment in parts of the United Kingdom, the United States, and Australia.[38] Most of these studies have been descriptive, and the underlying mechanisms accounting for the transmission of economic impulses over space and through time have only been hinted at.

Theoretical consideration of these transmission mechanisms has commanded the attention of a number of research workers. In 1969 two colleagues and I outlined a general model in which the level of economic activity in a city (region) at a particular time was determined by the corresponding levels for the other cities in the system and by exogenous national factors or their delayed consequences.[39] We formulated these interdependencies as a system of linear difference equations in which the coefficients determined (1) which cities affected which other cities, to what extent, and after what time lag, and (2) to what extent and after what time lag each city was affected by the exogenous national factors. Bannister has pointed up the difficulties in testing this model because the explanatory variables have a built-in linear dependency.[40] Bennett has generalized this model so that the parameter sets which describe the lagged relationships between a city and all the other cities, and between the exogenous variables and the city, are themselves time-dependent.[41] The matrices of parameters are then interpreted as matrices of impulse response functions.

Recent work on this topic has considered change in regional wage levels and wage inflation. Forster and I outlined some simple models of wage change in labor markets which took into account changes in adjacent labor markets.[42] We also explored the possibility that specific submarkets might lead others in wage change rates, and that some forms of 'transfer' might originate from them. Weissbrod has outlined a spatial diffusion theory of wage inflation in urban labor markets.[43] He assumed the existence of a central-place type urban hierarchy in which the economic activities are grouped into 'labor skill bundles'. The highest order urban center "was assumed to be an innovative center where new technologies and increased production orders might be expected to take place". Wage inflation was seen as diffusing down through the urban hierarchy "according to the ranking of skill bundles; central places with higher ranking skill bundles should be affected before central places with lower ranking skill bundles. A central place responds to or imitates those higher ranking places which are its dominants".[44] Weissbrod used cross-spectrum analysis to test his theory; the results generally supported it. Bannister investigated the notion that regional economic change has a strong hierarchical component in his empirical study of southern Ontario.[45] He examined the importance of three modes of economic change over space — a distance effect, a hierarchical effect, and an economic structure effect. Bannister's results, which were also obtained in part by the use of spectral techniques, confirmed that "the urban system of Southern Ontario is hier-archically structured", but did not confirm that economic impulses were closely related to this hierarchical structure; there was suggestion of a trickling-down of economic impulses only in the lower levels of the system.

The thrust of this work on regional (urban) labor markets and the rates of wage and unemployment changes within them is toward the development of a theory of regional economic change in which the spatial labor markets are seen as responding to external economic forces which are transmitted by the different networks of economic, social, and political linkages between markets, and also to internal forces generated within the labor market itself. Such a theory will have to identify the transmission mechanisms and incorporate the demand and supply considerations for labor both within the individual market and within those that are seen as linked to it. Migration processes will be an integral part of the theoretical formulation, for they clearly relate in some, ways both to the supply and to the demand considerations. Work by geographers on this topic is continuing.[46]

This review has deliberately ignored the valuable contributions of geographers to the development of the theory of spatial statistics, especially by their studies of spatial autocorrelation, spatial forecasting, and point processes in the plane.[47] Much recent work along these lines bears directly on the problems of analyzing economic change over space.

II. THE POSITIVIST POSITION SUMMARIZED

My review of certain lines of quantitative-theoretic research in economic and urban geography allows me to answer three specific questions. The first and least interesting simply seeks to establish the overall objectives of these research efforts: what do the theorists seek to accomplish? The second asks what relationships, if any, the logical structures developed by the theorists bear to the real world. Finally, in what ways are these structures useful in planning and shaping social change? Obviously, the three questions are not unrelated, and the responses probably are highly interdependent.

Thus far I have used the term 'positivism' loosely in describing an approach to the quest for knowledge that is characteristic of various lines of quantitative-theoretic work in economic geography, although admittedly more so in some than in others. Given the wide variation in meaning that is attached to this term in the literature of philosophy and social science, it seems difficult to establish the meaning of the word other than with reference to particular circumstances. In the present context, therefore, the positivistic approach is defined by three suppositions.[48]

(1) That the methodological procedures of natural science may be adapted directly to human geography. This implies that the phenomena studied in economic and urban geography may be treated in the same way as objects in the natural world, notwithstanding the subjectivity, volition, and will of the persons involved in economic and social processes. This supposition implies a particular stance concerning the social scientist as an observer of social reality.

(2) That the outcome or end-results of geographic investigations can be

formulated in the same manner as those of natural science. In other words, the goal of analysis in economic and urban geography can and must be to derive laws and theories such as have been formulated in the natural sciences. This supposition implies a definite view of the social scientist as an "analyst or interpreter of his subject-matter".[49]

(3) That geography as a social science has a technical character and generates knowledge which is supposedly free of any implications for the pursuit of values. The social scientist in this context asserts always his 'neutrality' and insists upon the 'value-free' character of his research. To the extent that he is, or seeks to become, practically involved in social planning then it is always with the belief that his analysis is 'objective' by virtue of its neutrality. This third supposition has drawn more criticism than the first two.

My characterization of positivism is less formal than is usually ascribed to the school of 'logical positivism' in philosophy, but it is a fair reflection of what is generally meant by the word in the social sciences.[50]

The answer to the first question of what the positivists in economic and urban geography seek to accomplish is nicely phrased by Amedeo and Golledge:[51]

Initially, geographers try to establish the spatial connections between sets of facts by finding spatial laws (which are statements of the order in the world). But they go even one step further and try to establish the connections between the laws themselves, by constructing spatial theories, which are the patterns or systems in the domain of spatial problems.

The answer to the question about the relations of these logical structures to the reality of society is much less obvious. Amedeo and Golledge insist that:[52]

Such approaches should not be scorned as being impractical or useless. The use of assumptions designed to simplify more complicated contexts is common strategy with almost all attempts at theory construction. This means that initially ideal worlds are postulated for keeping the problems simple and manageable in order to see how much can be said about these problems with a minimum of complication. Later, if need be, these simplifying assumptions are modified and/or new ones added for testing the theory in the real world.

I have already acknowledged this strategy championed by Amedeo and Golledge in my discussion of work on the spatial structure of urban areas. The assumption in the Alonso and the early Casetti work, for example, that urban residents sought accessibility to a single center was replaced in the Papageorgiou formulation by an assumption of a central place-like hierarchy of centers to which the consumers sought access. Similarly, the introduction of a residential attractiveness variable in the more recent Papageorgiou work added greater credibility to the formulation as a model of actual consumer behavior.

Additional examples of the same strategy are provided in work on spatial interaction models, particularly those developed by Wilson and his colleagues. 'Disaggregating' these models, which has been discussed at length, is simply relaxing particular assumptions about the types of households or the types of occupations or the modes of transportation which are made in the models.[53]

The strategy appears appealingly simple, but unfortunately one or two wrinkles are not easily smoothed out. Consider first the inevitable sacrifices of realism that have to be made in order to model or theorize about any aspect of reality. Choices have to be made, and the searching question asks: what are the bases on which these choices are made? Personal judgements and values undoubtedly enter, but this point is put aside for the moment. What is of concern here is the possibility that the choices between different modelling approaches, and between factors which are included and excluded, often are determined more by the requirements of mathematical tractability than by any concern for closer correspondence with reality. Papageorgiou and Mullally echoed the positivist sentiment when they referred to "the inevitable tradeoffs between realism and tractability".[54] What is usually left unanswered by the positivist is the question of how high a level of mathematical elegance and abstraction must be sought in theorizing about society. Much contemporary geographic work on location theory and the spatial structure of urban areas appears to be trying to emulate the earlier, seemingly elegant, accomplishments of mathematical economists. The question of whether these endeavors by economists have proven very fruitful in contributing useful knowledge about society does not appear to have been considered to the degree that it might have been by the theorists in geography.

Dacey sounded a warning about some of the early theoretical work on the spatial structure of urban areas.[55] He observed that many models involved or implied very complex expressions for the measure of population potential, yet it seemed desirable that this measure should be reasonably simple so that further analysis of other properties of urban structure might be facilitated. His challenge appears to have gone unanswered. He concluded that:[56]

if the present orientation persists, the research on urban population distributions seems destined to produce a finely calibrated, theoretically acceptable model, but a model that cannot be analyzed to obtain the relations that hold between population distribution with social and economic variables. The planners and policy-makers who need urban models will again find that we have developed an elegant model that is useless for most practical applications.

Implicit in Dacey's conclusion is a general admonition concerning two unfortunate tendencies in the positivistic approach to social science research. The first is that the quest for a 'theoretically acceptable' model often carries the theorist past the point of increasing marginal returns; beyond this point theoretical work begins to feed upon itself and not upon further observations of the real world. Roberts, a critic of the economists' theorizing, expresses the concern thus:[57]

Consider the now quite fashionable work developed to proving the existence of an equilibrium in various highly general models of the economy. As the techniques employed have become more elegant, the point of the exercise has become less evident.

The second tendency is a corollary of the first; it relates to the pursuit of mathematical elegance as an end in itself. The advantages of mathematical reasoning, especially as it has been used in the physical sciences, are well known. What is often overlooked is the fact that the phenomena dealt with in the physical sciences are sharply differentiated, and may be categorized in such a way that there is no overlap between the categories and maximum homogeneity within them. In human geography this lack of ambiguity is difficult to achieve unless, as in some of the earlier theorizing on city settlement patterns, the phenomena are reduced to points or other such abstractions. Furthermore, the theorists who apply the mathematics of probability theory to physical science are dealing with very, very large numbers of phenomena in comparison to the usual situation in social science research. Mathematics must be used cautiously in social-science research, or theory development may degenerate simply into a form of 'recreational mathematics'.[58]

III. SOCIAL PLANNING AND VALUES

One of my more important premises is that social science must contribute to social policy and to the shaping of social change. The nature of this contribution has to be considered. Yeates and Garner have expressed the optimistic view that "there is no doubt that geographers are becoming increasingly involved in solving ... kinds of applied problems, particularly in the context of urban and regional planning, and will continue to do so in the future".[59] Many of these same attempts at applied analysis have been damned by Harvey as consisting of "an attachment to the 'liberal virtue of objectivity' in an ideological world, of a faith in technocratic 'scientific' solutions, and of a naïve optimism".[60]

The debate over the nature and role of social science as an applied field of knowledge has been going on for many decades. The major schools of thought in the debate may be identified by their handling of the central issue of the place of human values in fashioning social science knowledge and in shaping social policy.

If 'values' are thought of as the moral assumptions and normative suppositions that underlie human behavior, the positivistic tradition insisted upon a sharp separation between values and facts. Values may influence the choice of research problems or the particular paths of anlaysis that are followed, but the analysis itself is considered free of any such considerations. Only factual statements such as "the regional distribution of unemployment will become more variable" are considered verifiable. Value judgements such as "I regard this tendency as good" cannot be the subject of scientific inquiry since this judgement is merely a matter of personal taste. On the other hand if an objective function is defined, which may be consistent with such personal values, then one can determine the effectiveness of different policies in meeting this objective. The consequences of this insistence upon a sharp separation of facts and values can be seen in geographic research on the spatial structure of urban areas. Spatial equilibrium where households differ only by income implies that households with higher incomes occupy larger parcels of land than those with lower incomes, but the ethical content of this conclusion is seen as outside of the domain of analysis. Similarly, the assumption of a particular distribution of incomes allows for no statements concerning the equity of this distribution.

Consider in a different context how the values of the observer affect the character of the analysis. When using unemployment insurance registration data in Canada I may judge unemployment to be bad, and hence I will evaluate social policies in terms of how well they reduce the levels of unemployment. What is the basis of my judgement that unemployment is bad? Certainly it does not lie in any profound Christian belief in the virtue of labor, nor can I be convinced that 'unemployed' persons drawing government insurance benefits are less happy than I am, but I do know that the costs of such programs are a charge to me as a taxpayer, and I reject this form of equalization policy. My views of the problem and my approach to it are certainly going to differ from those of a person who holds a different set of values in regard to my liability as a taxpayer. The Marxist scholar obviously would view the problem in a still different manner. Joan Robinson summarizes the issue well:[61]

it is not possible to describe a system without moral judgements creeping in. For to look at a system from the outside implies that it is not the only possible system; in describing it we compare it (openly or tacitly) with other actual or imagined systems. Differences imply choices, and choices imply judgements. We cannot escape from making judgements and the judgements that we make arise from the ethical preconceptions that have soaked into our view of life.

One important consequence of the separation of fact and value in the positivist approach is the difficulty in reconciling the need for normative statements, as the basis for planning and policy, with the scientific emphasis upon statements of fact. This gap between the 'ought' and 'is' propositions in the positivist approach has been the subject of much philosophical debate, especially in German sociology, and somewhat more recently in geography.[62] For the moment, however, I will ignore these philosophical considerations and examine the procedures whereby this gap has been bridged by social scientists concerned with policy. Rein has suggested that three techniques have been used.[63] The first is *mapping*, which requires the establishment of laws or law-like statements of cause and effect relationships (the domain of social science), and the specification of certain means and ends (the domain of policy making). These two elements, the 'means–ends' and the 'cause and effect' relationships, are then considered to be in close correspondence, and the policy ends should be attainable by manipulating the causes. Rein points out that:[64]

if the known causes . . . cannot be manipulated by policy, then they are of little practical application; but even if they can be manipulated, they may also be morally offensive and hence politically unacceptable. On the other hand, the causes may be both manipulable and ethically neutral, and yet in some cases their implementation may conflict with other ends of public policy.

The second technique is *code harmonization*, whereby conflicts "between the feeling of what is normally right and what the legal code prescribes" are corrected by changing the legal code.[65] Finally, *feedback* is a technique whereby research "aids policy by measuring the gap between ideals and practice (evaluation) and by examining alternative programmatic means for more effectively and efficiently narrowing the gap (experimentation)".[66]

Rein does not accept the positivist interpretation of applied social science which encompasses these three techniques. He rejects it mainly because he sees all three techniques as depending upon the development of laws and theories of social science, but he insists:[67]

there are no general laws in social science that are consistent over time and independent of the context in which they are imbedded. The search for law-like generalization of cause and effect relationships is an illusion. Any particular patterning of events will not remain stable for very long, and generalization about them cannot provide a firm theoretical basis for intervention.

This particular line of criticism is familiar in the social sciences, including geography.[68] Rein also argues that mapping as a technique is plagued by the fact that most policy situations involve more than one simple aim or 'end', and tradeoffs inevitably have to be made among them. In such situations, Rein would argue, it is impossible to map onto these competing 'ends' the 'effects' of social science theories that are, at best, incomplete and partial.[69] Events over the past several years in urban transportation planning have certainly illustrated this point. The competing goals of transportation efficiency, preservation of neighborhood communities, and environmental protection all have had to be balanced in the real world, and no model or theoretical structure seems to have been able to incorporate this feature. Similarly, code harmonization is limited by the many inconsistencies and unavoidable conflicts between codes. Finally, Rein sees the feedback technique as extremely frustrating because it demands social experimentation which is inevitably affected in all of its phases — definition, design, and interpretation — by the values of those social scientists cast in the roles of the technicians.

The separation of fact and value, wherein lies the essence of the positivist approach, is not acknowledged in the schools of philosophy known as phenomenology and existentialism. These lines of thought have had little impact upon geography, although of late some thoughtful discussions of their philosphical positions have appeared in the geography literature.[70] The distinctive features of the two philosophies have been reviewed and even debated.[71] What emerges is a consensus that inasmuch as these philosophies are concerned with "the nature of experience and with the meaning of being human", they are relevant to those fields of geography such as historical, cultural, and behavioral which focus on man's existence.[72] Less clear is the view these philosophies have of the social scientist as one involved in shaping and directing social change. Buttimer has suggested a partial answer by noting in regard to the phenomenological position:[73]

that the social scientist's role is neither to choose or decide for people, nor even to formulate the alternatives for choice but rather, through the models of his discipline, to enlarge their horizons of consciousness to the point where both the articulation of alternatives and the choice of direction could be theirs.

This surely suggests that social scientists have some awareness of which models are worth discussing in relation to what issues. The very elegant mathematical models of urban spatial structure or the persuasively stated verbal theories of regional economic development might well enlarge the horizons of consciousness while describing ideal worlds that are unattainable. Besides, the problems of mapping still remain.

To the extent that phenomenology emphasizes a deep sensitivity to issues of the human condition, of human aspirations and feelings, then its message must be heeded by the applied social scientist, but it is difficult to resist the conclusion that the world described by the phenomenologists and existentialists is one in which self-reflection is esteemed above all else. Planning at the social level demands that decisions be made for groups, often quite large groups, and self-reflection may provide an inadequate guide for balancing the competing claims and aspirations that inevitably are involved.

IV. MARX: AN IDEOLOGICAL ALTERNATIVE

Marxist thought had no more impact on North American geography than phenomenology and existentialism until the 1970s, but now a small but growing group of dedicated scholars seek by exegesis of the writings of Marx and his interpreters to chart new courses not only for geography and the social sciences as fields of inquiry, but also for the structuring of society itself. These critics have presented novel interpretations of many problems that have been of continuing interest to economic and urban geographers, and they have outlined fresh blueprints for the involvement of social scientists, including geographers, in the shaping of social policy.

I will not attempt to address the philosophical issues of Marx's theory of social evolution. The task is beyond my competency. Harvey has outlined Marx's conception of method from which the "theory naturally flows", and the journal *Antipode* has published a number of interpretations of parts of the theory.[74] One or two distinctive features of the approach, gleaned mainly from Harvey's writings, bear on the issues discussed in this paper. First, the distinction between fact and value is considered meaningless; "for Marx, the act of observing is the act of evaluation and to separate them is to force a distinction on human practice that does not in reality exist",[75] The Marxist interpretation of the development of the political economy then has an explicit moral position, and the ethical content of all events and actions is reviewed from this position. The problem of reconciling the 'is' with the 'ought' disappears as a consequence, and the development of thought and action proceed hand in hand. "By confronting our situation directly we become active participants in the social process. The intellectual task is to identify real choices as they are immanent in an existing situation and to devise ways of validating or invalidating those choices through action".[76] The means whereby this intellectual task is pursued and accomplished are provided by the dialectical method, which allows for interplay between thought and action, and seeks thereby to resolve the apparent contradictions and paradoxes. The method subsumes not only the development of theory, but also the techniques of mapping, code harmonization, and feedback. Whether the method is 'objective' is a philosophical question. Harvey has written contemptuously of the "liberal virtue of objectivity", but presumably it was the 'liberalism' and the positivist notion of objectivity that is implied which he saw as being at fault. Cunningham, for example, in the preface to his tract on objectivity suggested that "belief in anti-objectivism on the part of Marxists is a hindrance to the scientific development and application of Marxism".[77] Certainly Harvey and his colleagues have stressed a 'scientific' (in the sense of analytical) approach to the study of many questions relating to urbanization and urban spatial structure.

Harvey's view of urbanism as "a set of social relationships which reflects the relationships established throughout society as a whole", and his acceptance of Marx's interpretations of history, are the bases of his theorizing about a number of specific urban issues.[78] Urbanization and all of its facets (suburbanization, highway development, ghetto formation) are seen as expressions of the process whereby the capitalist market economy sustains itself. The growing metropolitan areas are the foci for the increased accumulation of surplus capital, and the associated patterns of exploitation reach far into the countryside and the underdeveloped parts of the world. The formation of ghettos becomes an inevitable consequence of the operation of the market mechanisms for housing and mortgage capital. The conception of rent as "but one manifestation of surplus value under capitalist institutions" suggests to Harvey that analyses such as those of Casetti and Papageorgiou are incorrect because they ignore all other aspects of production and institutional structures of the capitalist system on which rent itself is dependent.[79] Rent theory, the Marxian statement of it, and its application in studying urbanization has been the subject of a number of recent papers. Much of this discussion has been theoretical and has focussed on Marx's analysis of rent and its different component parts.[80] A few attempts have been made at structuring mathematical models of urban growth and spatial structure, analogous to the Alonso formulation, based upon such analyses.[81] Harvey's work in particular has a strong empirical component derived from his analysis of the Baltimore housing market.[82]

These studies suggest the intellectual power of the Marxist approach in interpreting and providing explanations of social processes and events. Its explicit acknowledgement of a particular value framework demands that any rebuttals or counter arguments make similar acknowledgements. Harvey has shown in his discussion of population and resources that the conclusions drawn from an analysis may differ sharply depending on the value frameworks, or biases, that are held.[83]

As with any approach, the prescriptions based upon the Marxist interpretations are palatable only to those who accept the ideological frameworks within which they are set. It would seem foolish, however, for urban and economic geographers to ignore the approach, whatever their own ideological positions might be.

V. A MIDDLE COURSE

I have now reached the point of asking whether there is a middle course between the straits of pure positivism and scientific socialism. What might be suggested to accommodate requests for a new type of social science, one that is not based on the physical sciences paradigm, that considers values along with facts, and that allows for applied social science to contribute to the development of policy paradigms.[84] I am not convinced that the answer is to be found in the abstract philosophical arguments on many-valued logics and fuzzy sets.[85] The neopositivistic position ascribed to Olsson has some very attractive features especially in the sense that it contemplates the use of the dialectical method as a means of welding facts and values.[86]

Rein has suggested a 'value critical' approach as an alternative to the positivist approach.[87] Values and goals themselves become subject to analysis and debate in this framework, which assumes that a social science divorced from action is indefensible. The different consequences of alternative end values, for example of income equalization or lower unemployment goals in regional planning, would be explored and analyzed and choices would be made only after both the ends and their possible consequences had been fully considered. In Canada some rather searching questions have been asked recently of the approach to regional economic development which emphasizes the payment of subsidies, both direct and indirect, to firms which are prepared to invest in the less developed regions. The positivistic premises upon which this policy is based are fairly well known. Location theory suggests that such firms normally would prefer more advantageous locations, and the comparative cost of locating in the poorer regions must therefore be met by subsidies. Once located in the poorer regions, so the argument goes, these firms will create employment opportunities, raise incomes, and generate multiplier effects, but there are serious doubts about the effectiveness of the program either in terms of reducing income inequalities, creating employment, or fostering 'modernization and progress'.[88] On the contrary, "the program is after all a transfer of income through the intermediary of the fiscal system of the Federal government from all Canadians to that group of Canadians rich enough to be owners of or stockholders in the subsidized firms".[89] The costs of the program also include the sacrifices in traditional ways of life, values, and environments which must be made by the people of the so-called less developed regions.

Research and policy formulation that addresses questions of regional development needs an awareness of the competing goals, an understanding of the consequences of programs tailored to meet these goals, and a sensitive yet critical assessment of the alternatives. "Research within the value critical framework does try to discern patterns but it seeks general principles that take account of the context and comingle facts and values".[90] Using these research findings, the social scientist is then able to communicate with the policy-maker by what Rein calls 'story-telling' based on metaphors. The strategy is not unfamiliar in geography; Wolpert used story-telling (scenarios) in describing the role of community groups in neighborhood change.[91] The scenario points up the interactions of forces which affect a community's life cycle and allows for the playing out of fantasies. Geographers have also used metaphors in describing social and economic processes. Tobler's analogy between spatial interaction patterns and winds might be useful to a social scientist advising the policy-maker on controlling the flows of new immigrants within a country.[92] Perhaps the metaphor might suggest ways of devising 'windbreaks'. The geographer speaks of ideas and changes diffusing over space either as a wave or by progression through the branches of a tree. In the diffusion of adverse economic effects, such as the wage inflation discussed by Weissbrod, it might be possible to discuss policy alternatives in terms of providing protection to the branches of the tree or injecting 'correctives' into the trunk. The use of the metaphor allows the social scientist:[93]

to bring two separate domains into cognitive and emotional relation by using language directly appropriate to the one as a lens for seeing the other; the implications, suggestions, and supporting values entwined with the literal use of the metamorphical expression enable (him) to see a new subject matter in a new way.

In devising his story and metaphors the social scientist must face some vexing issues. He must, for instance, admit his biases in interpreting society if he is to integrate fact and values. They may well be determined by matters of personal style but only up to a point, and more substantively they will reflect the value screen which the observer uses in seeking his explanations.[94] Does he view social issues in terms of the 'malfunctioning of institutions and organization', and 'failure of people to cope', the 'importance of power', or is his perspective a synthesis of elements of these ideologies?[95] Having admitted his biases, how does he maintain objectivity, avoid moral conflicts, and legitimatize his role? These are questions which urban and economic geographers must address if they wish to be social scientists.[96]

Much current formal theoretical work in economic and urban geography appears to be heading in the wrong direction; at a time when more and more questions are being asked about the appropriate institutional forms for the functioning of our modern societies in all their political, economic, and social complexities, these theories continue to regard the institutional frameworks as fixed and given. When welfare criteria are discussed, if at all, they are considered something imposed on the system from outside, usually by a benevolent government assumed to be the guardian of the 'public interest'. Recent widespread labor disputes and strikes in the public sector have brought into sharp focus the question of what indeed is the public interest, who defines it, and who guards it? These are value-laden questions that obviously have policy implications, and if geographers are to say something useful about the shaping of society they cannot ignore such questions. The work of Wolpert and his colleagues on the location of public facilities has made a start on redirecting geographers' attention away from the private to the public sector, and this new emphasis should be reinforced. Land use in our cities of the future, for example, is probably going to be shaped as much by public land ownership policies, and by public housing and environmental protection agencies and the like, as by private entrepreneurs. Rent controls rather than bid-rents may be the more important mechanisms, and geographers should have something to say about such possibilities.

The current research of Hagerstrand and his colleagues on human activity patterns, which is both theoretical and applied, has demonstrated a sensitivity to the human condition and life that too frequently is overlooked in theoretical formulations. The emphasis in economic and urban geography should be shifted from the formal analysis of sterile propositions relating to abstract competitive economic settings to less formal, but still rigorous, analysis of real world situations in which values, conflict, power, the public sector, and the individual are given greater prominence.

This paper began with a discussion of the quantitative revolution in geography and it is appropriate to end with a comment on the role of quantitative analysis in this suggested new plan. It is assumed that the need for quantitative analysis will increase rather than decrease in the future. The storytelling mentioned above will draw upon whatever evidence is available and in the sorting and arrangement of these facts, both for the present and for the future, there will be a requirement for quantitative as well as verbal skills. The argument that runs throughout this discussion, however, is that we should lower our mathematical sights and aim at the target of developing operationally useful models rather than at that of formally proving existence theorems and the like.

Department of Geography
McMaster University

NOTES

* Reprinted from the *Annals of the Association of American Geographers*, Volume 66, No. 2, June, 1976, pp. 293–308.
[1] P. R. Gould, 'Methodological Developments Since the Fifties', in C. Board, R. J. Chorley, and P. Hackett (eds.), *Progress in Geography*, I, 1969, p. 3.
[2] I. Burton in 'The Quantitative Revolution and Theoretical Geography', in *Canadian Geographer* 7 (1963), 151–62.
[3] See A. G. Wilson, 'Theoretical Geography: Some Speculations', in *Transactions*, The Institute of British Geographers No. 57 (1972), 31–44.
[4] In geography such criticism is represented by D. Harvey, 'Revolutionary and Counter Revolutionary Theory in Geography and the Problem of Ghetto Formation', in *Antipode* 4 (1972), 1–13, 36–41; in sociology see A. Giddens (ed.), *Positivism and Sociology*, Heinemann, London, 1974; in economics see B. Ward, *What's Wrong with Economics*, Basic Books, New York, 1972.
[5] S. Folke, 'Why a Radical Geography Must be Marxist', in *Antipode* 4 (1972), 17.
[6] A. MacIntyre, 'Ideology, Social Science and Revolution', in *Comparative Politics* 5 (1973), 334.
[7] The terms *'status quo'* and 'counter-revolutionary' theory are taken from Harvey, *op. cit.*, p. 41.
[8] Harvey, *op. cit.*, p. 40.
[9] See G. Olsson, 'Distance and Human Interaction: A Review and Bibliography', in *Bibliography Series*, Regional Science Institute, No. 2 (1965).
[10] Much of the work is summarized in A. G. Wilson, *Urban and Regional Models in Geography and Planning*, J. Wiley and Sons, London, 1974; see also A. G. Wilson, 'Some New Forms of Spatial Interation Models: A Review', in *Transportation Research* 9 (1975), 167–79.

[11] See especially Chaps. 7–10, Wilson, *Urban and Regional Models in Geography and Planning, op. cit.*, 79–219.

[12] For example, M. Batty and S. Mackie, 'The Calibration of Gravity, Entropy and Related Models of Spatial Interaction', in *Environment and Planning* 4 (1972), 205–33; M. Batty *et al.*, 'Spatial System Design and Fast Calibration of Activity Interaction–Allocation Models', in *Regional Studies* 7 (1973), 351–66.

[13] M. Webber, 'The Meaning of Entropy Maximizing Models', unpublished paper presented at Conference on Mathematical Land Use Theory, McMaster University, Hamilton, Ontario, 1975.

[14] E. S. Sheppard, 'Entropy, Theory Construction and Spatial Analysis', unpublished paper presented at Annual Meeting of American Geographers, Milwaukee, 1975.

[15] L. Curry, 'A Spatial Analysis of Gravity Flows', in *Regional Studies* 6 (1972), 131–47.

[16] A. D. Cliff, R. L. Martin and J. K. Ord, 'Evaluating the Friction of Distance Parameter in Gravity Models', in *Regional Studies* 8 (1974), 281–86; L. Curry, D. A. Griffith and E. S. Sheppard, 'Those Gravity Parameters Again', in *Regional Studies*, forthcoming.

[17] W. Tobler, 'Spatial Interaction Patterns', in *Research Report*, International Institute for Applied Systems Analysis No. RR-75-19 (1975).

[18] T. Hagerstrand, 'The Propagation of Innovative Waves', *Lund Studies in Geography*, No. 4, Series B (1952); and *idem, Innovation Diffusion as a Spatial Process* (transl. by A. Pred), University of Chicago Press, Chicago, 1967.

[19] J. Hudson, 'Geographical Diffusion Theory', *Studies in Geography*, Northwestern University, Department of Geography, No. 19 (1972).

[20] See R. M. Downs and D. Stea (eds.), *Image and Environment: Cognitive Mapping and Spatial Behavior*, Aldine Publishing Company, Chicago, 1973; T. Hagerstrand, 'What About People in Regional Science?', in *Papers*, Regional Science Association 24 (1970), 7–21; A. Pred, 'Urbanization, Domestic Planning Problems and Swedish Geographic Research', in *Progress in Geography* 5 (1973), 1–76.

[21] For example O. Davies, 'Optimal Facility Location in a One-Dimensional Spatial Market', in *Geographical Analysis* 6 (1974), 239–64; and *idem*, 'An Examination of Properties Associated with the Isolated Producer in Two-Dimensional Spatial Markets', in *Journal of Regional Science* 15 (1975), 47–52; a similar approach is seen in N. Alao, 'An Approach to Intraurban Location Theory', in *Economic Geography* 50 (1974), 59–69.

[22] Davies, *Geographical Analysis, op. cit.*, p. 240.

[23] O. Davis, 'A Dynamic Hotelling-type Model', in *Environment and Planning* 7 (1975), 153–62.

[24] See M. F. Dacey *et al.*, 'One Dimensional Central Place Theory', in *Studies in Geography*, Northwestern University, Department of Geography, No. 21 (1974); N. Alao and M. F. Dacey *et al.*, 'Christaller Central Place Structures: An Introductory Statement', Northwestern University, *Studies in Geography*, forthcoming.

[25] See for example A. M. Auston, T. E. Smith and J. Wolpert, 'The Implementation of Controversial Facility-Complex Programs', in *Geographical Analysis* 2 (1970), 315–29; J. Wolpert, M. Dear and R. Crawford, 'Satellite Mental Health Facilities', in *Annals*, Association of American Geographers 65 (1975), 24–35.

[26] J. Wolpert, 'Departures from the Usual Environment in Locational Analysis', in *Annals*, Association of American Geographers 60 (1970), 220.

[27] M. Dear, 'A Paradigm for Public Facility Location Theory', in *Antipode* 6 (1974),

46–50; and *idem* 'A Political Theory of Public Facility Location', unpublished paper presented at the Twenty-First Regional Science Association Meetings, Chicago, 1974.

[28] W. Alonso, *Location and Land Use*, M.I.T. Press, Cambridge, 1964.

[29] The discussion that follows draws upon an excellent review presentation given by G. Papageorgiou at the IGU Commision on Quantitative Methods meetings, Palmerston North, New Zealand, 1974.

[30] E. Casetti, 'Equilibrium Land Values and Population Densities in an Urban Setting', in *Economic Geography* 47 (1971), 16–20.

[31] G. Papageorgiou, 'A Generalization of the Population Density Gradient Concept', in *Geographical Analysis* 3 (1971), 121–27.

[32] For a discussion of the equilibrium population density distribution under the assumption of a Casetti-type equilibrium, see G. Papageorgiou, 'A Theoretical Evaluation of the Existing Population Density Gradient Functions', in *Economic Geography* 47 (1971), 21–26.

[33] G. J. Papageorgiou and E. Casetti, 'Spatial Equilibrium Residential Land Values in a Multicenter Setting', in *Journal of Regional Science* 11 (1971), 385–89.

[34] G. J. Papageorgiou, 'On Spatial Consumer Equilibrium', unpublished paper presented at Conference on Mathematical Land Use Theory, McMaster University, Hamilton, Ontario, 1975.

[35] G. J. Papageorgiou and H. Mullally, 'Urban Residential Structure', unpublished mimeographed paper, McMaster University, Department of Geography, 1975; see also G. J. Papageorgiou and A. C. Brummel, 'Crude Inferences on Spatial Consumer Behavior', in *Annals*, Association of American Geographers 65, (1975), 1–12.

[36] E. Casetti, 'Spatial Equilibrium in an Ideal Urban Setting with Continuously Distributed Incomes', in *London Papers in Regional Science* 4 (1974), 129–40.

[37] A. D. Cliff, P. Haggett, J. K. Ord, K. Bassett and R. Davies, *Elements of Spatial Structure*, Cambridge University Press, Cambridge, 1975, p. 113.

[38] For example P. Haggett, 'Leads and Lags in Inter-regional Systems: A Study of Cyclic Fluctuations in the South-West Economy', in M. Chisholm and G. Manners (eds.), *Spatial Policy Problems in the British Economy*, 1971, pp. 69–95; M. Sant, 'The Geography of Business Cycles', *Geographical Papers*, Lond School of Economics and Politcal Science No. 5 (1973); L. King, E. Casetti and D. Jeffrey, 'Cyclical Fluctuations in Unemployment Levels in U.S. Metroplitan Areas', in *Tijdschrift voor Economische en Sociale Geografie* 63 (1972), 345–52; D. Jeffrey and D. J. Webb, 'Economic Fluctuations in the Australian Regional System, 1955–70', in *Australian Geographical Studies* 10 (1972), 141–60.

[39] L. King, E. Casetti and D. Jeffrey, 'Economic Impulses in a Regional System of Cities: A Study of Spatial Interaction', in *Regional Studies* 3 (1969), 213–18.

[40] G. Bannister, 'Modes of Change in the Ontario Economy', unpublished Ph.D. dissertation, Department of Geography, University of Toronto, 1974, pp. 11–12.

[41] R. J. Bennett, 'Dynamic Systems Modelling of the North West Region: 1. Spatio-temporal Representation and Identification', in *Environment and Planning*, forthcoming.

[42] L. J. King and J. J. H. Forster, 'Wage Rate Change in Urban Labor Markets and Inter-market Linkages', in *Papers*, Regional Science Association 30 (1973), 183–96.

[43] R. Weissbrod, 'Spatial Diffusion of Relative Wage Inflation', unpublished Ph.D. dissertation, Department of Geography, Northwestern University, 1974.

[44] Weissbrod, *op. cit.*, p. 127.

[45] See Bannister, *op. cit.* ; also *idem*, 'Population Change in Southern Ontario' in *Annals*, Association of American Geographers **65** (1975), 177–88.

[46] For example G. Clark, 'Macro Economic Planning and Regional Impact: A Victorian Regional Analysis 1953–74', unpublished M.A. thesis, Department of Geography, Monash University, Melbourne, 1975; J. W. Young, 'Structural Unemployment, Migration and Growth During an Expansionary Phase: Canada 1961–1966', unpublished Ph.D. dissertation, Department of Geography, McGill University, Montreal, 1975.

[47] For example K. A. Bassett, 'Numerical Methods for Map Analysis', in C. Board, R. J. Chorley, P. Haggett and D. R. Stoddard (eds.), *Progress in Geography* **4**, 1972, 217–54; A. D. Cliff and J. K. Ord, *Spatial Autocorrelation*, Pion Ltd., London, 1973; L. Curry, 'Applicability of Space–Time Moving Average Forecasting', in M. Chisholm, A. Frey and P. Haggett (eds.), *Regional Forecasting*, Butterworth, London, 1971, 11–24.

[48] These are discussed in relation to sociology in Giddens, *op. cit.*, pp. 3–4.

[49] Giddens, *op. cit.*, p. 4.

[50] See for example M. Brodbeck (ed.), *Readings in the Philosophy of the Social Sciences*, The Macmillan Company, New York, 1968.

[51] D. Amedeo and R. G. Golledge, *An Introduction to Scientific Reasoning in Geography*, J. Wiley and Sons, Inc., New York, 1975, p. 35.

[52] Amedeo, *op. cit.*, p. 26.

[53] For example see M. Echenique *et al.*, 'A Disaggregated Model of Urban Spatial Structure', in *Environment and Planning* A**6** (1974), 33–63.

[54] Papageorgiou and Mullally, *op. cit.*, p. 14.

[55] M. F. Dacey, 'Some Comments on Population Density Models, Tractable and Otherwise', in *Papers*, Regional Science Association **27** (1971), 119–133.

[56] Dacey, *op. cit.* pp. 129–130.

[57] M. J. Roberts, 'On the Nature and Condition of Social Science', *Daedalus* **103** (1974), 60.

[58] Roberts, *op. cit.*, p. 53: see also G. Myrdal, *Against the Stream. Critical Essays on Economics*, Pantheon Books, New York, 1973, Chapter 7.

[59] M. L: Yeates and B. J. Garner, *The North American City*, Harper and Row, New York, 1971, p. 15.

[60] D. Harvey, 'Review of B. J. L. Berry, *The Human Consequences of Urbanization*', in *Annals*, Association of American Geographers **65** (1975), 102.

[61] J. Robinson, *Economic Philosophy*, Pelican, London, 1970, p. 102.

[62] For a discussion of the debate in German Sociology see Giddens, *op. cit.*, pp. 17–21, Chapters 8 and 9; in Geography see Sister Annette Buttimer, 'Values in Geography', *Resource Paper*, Commission on College Geography, Association of American Geographers, No. 24 (1974), 29; also D. Harvey, *Social Justice and the City*, Edward Arnold Publishers Ltd., London, 1973, pp. 14–16.

[63] M. Rein, 'The Fact-Value Dilemma', *Working Paper*, Joint Center for Urban Studies of the Massachusetts Institute of Technology, No. 28 (1974), pp. 8–21.

[64] Rein, *op. cit.*, p. 11.

[65] Rein, *op. cit.*, pp. 12–13.

[66] Rein, *op. cit.*, p. 16.

[67] Rein, *op. cit.*, p. 22.

[68] See for example the reasoning of L. Guelke, 'Problems of Scientific Explanation in Geography', in *The Canadian Geographer* **15** (1971), 38–53; or the rhetoric of

W. Zelinsky, 'The Demigod's Dilemma', in *Annals*, Association of American Geographers 65 (1975), 123–43.

[69] This point is illustrated also in Olsson's discussion of the Swedish housing market. The imposition of rent controls 'as a means to abolish housing shortages and associated injustices' apparently failed there as it has done also in other market economics. Under rent controls, development capital is diverted into other more predictable outlets – the goals of low rents and adequate housing supply are difficult to reconcile in the market economy. See G. Olsson, 'On Reason and Reasoning, On problems as Solutions and Solutions as Problems, but mostely on the Silver-Tongued Devil and I', in *Antipode* 4 (1972), 30.

[70] See Yi-fu Tuan, 'Geography, Phenomenology, and the Study of Human Nature', in *The Canadian Geographer* 15 (1971), 181–92; *idem*, 'Man and Nature', *Resource Paper*, Commission on College Geography, Association of American Geographers, No. 10 (1971); Buttimer, *op. cit.*; D. J. Walmsley, 'Positivism and Phenomenology in Human Geography', in *The Canadian Geographer* 18 (1974), 95–108.

[71] See discussion in Buttimer, *op. cit.*, p. 29.

[72] The quotation is from Tuan, *op. cit.*, p. 191.

[73] Buttimer, *op. cit.*, p. 29.

[74] See Harvey, *op. cit.*, pp. 286–302; Blaut *et al.*, 'Marxist Geography', in *Antipode* 7 (1975), 1–90.

[75] Harvey, *op. cit.*, p. 15.

[76] Harvey, *op. cit.*, p. 40.

[77] F. Cunningham, *Objectivity in Social Science*, University of Toronto Press, 1973, p. viii.

[78] See especially Harvey, *op. cit.*

[79] Harvey, *op. cit.*, pp. 153–94.

[80] See for example Harvey, *op. cit.*, pp. 153–94; R. A. Walker, 'Urban Ground Rent: Building a New Conceptual Theory', in *Antipode* 6 (1974), 51–58; *idem*, 'Contentious Issues in Marxian Value and Rent Theory: A Second and Longer Look', in *Antipode* 7 (1975), 31–53.

[81] See T. A. Broadbend, 'An Attempt to Apply Marx's Theory of Ground Rent to the Modern Urban Economy', *Research Paper*, Center for Environmental Studies, London, No. 17 (1975); A. Farhi, 'Urban Economic Growth and Conflicts: A Theoretical Approach', in *Papers*, Regional Science Association 31 (1973), 95–124.

[82] See D. Harvey and L. Chatterjee, 'Absolute Rent and Structuring of Space by Governmental and Financial Institutions', *Antipode* 6 (1974), 22–36; D. Harvey, 'Class-Monopoly Rent, Finance Capital and the Urban Revolution', in *Regional Studies* 8 (1974), 239–55.

[83] D. Harvey, 'Population, Resources, and the Ideology of Science', in *Economic Geography* 50 (1974), 256–77.

[84] The notion of a policy paradigm is develped in M. Rein, 'Values, Social Science, and Social Policy', *Working Paper*, Joint Center for Urban Studies of the Massachusetts Institute of Technology and Harvard University, No. 21 (1973).

[85] G. Olsson, 'Logics and Social Engineering', *Geographical Analysis* 2 (1970), 361–75; S. Gale, 'Inexactness, Fuzzy Sets and the Foundations of Behavioural Geography', *Geographical Analysis* 4 (1972), 337–49.

[86] Olsson's position is so characterized by Walmsley, *op. cit.*, p. 105; the paper G. Olsson,

'Explanation, Prediction and Meaning Variance: An Assessment of Distance Interaction Models', in *Economic Geography* 46 (1970), 223–33, seems consistent with Walmsley's assessment; but see G. Olssson, 'The Dialectics of Spatial Analysis', in *Antipode* 6 (1974), 50–62. In this paper Olsson's position seems to be more that of an existential phenomenologist rather than a neopositivist!

[87] Rein, *op. cit.*, pp. 44–72.

[88] D. Usher, 'Some Questions About the Regional Development Incentive Act', in *Canadian Public Policy* 1 (1975), 557–75.

[89] Usher, *op. cit.*, p. 569.

[90] Rein, *op. cit.*, p. 48.

[91] J. Wolpert, A. Mumphrey and J. Seley, 'Metropolitan Neighborhoods: Participation and Conflict Over Change', *Resource Paper*, Commission on College Geography, Association of American Geographers No. 16 (1972).

[92] The policy issue has been discussed in Canada in relation to restricting the movement of new immigrants into the three largest metropolitan areas.

[93] M. Black, *Models and Metaphors*, Cornell University Press, Ithaca, 1962, pp. 236–37.

[94] Rein, *op. cit.*, pp. 54–60.

[95] The recently published discussion of geography research on crime illustrates the gap between those who view the issue in terms of power concepts (Dr. Peet) and those who view it in terms of institutions and organizations (Drs. Harries, Phillips and Lee). See 'Views and Opinions', in *The Professional Geographer* 27 (1975), 277–85.

[96] For a related but different viewpoint see W. Bunge, 'Geography of Survival', in *Annals*, Association of American Geographers 63 (1973), 291. Dr. Bunge writes, "A survival bent geography is thus free of value judgement or logic because it rests on something more basic, human nature itself. It is both good and logical because it is natural".

DAVID LEY

SOCIAL GEOGRAPHY AND THE
TAKEN-FOR-GRANTED WORLD[1]

Humanisons la géographie humaine (MAX SORRE).

The most important thing, therefore, that we can
know about a man is what he takes for granted,
and the most elemental and important facts about
a society are those that are seldom debated and
generally regarded as settled (LOUIS WIRTH).

I. THE PRESENT IMPASSE

The recent growth of interest in social geography once again raises the question of the field's latent ambiguity. Despite a proliferation of empirical
studies, there is neither a well-developed body of theory nor explicit discussion of philosophical underpinnings. More conspicuous is the complete
equivocation concerning the relative roles of spatial form and social process.
Review articles over the past decade have increasingly inclined to the view
that while the map may be the first step it should not be the last word.[2] Yet
the precise avenues for process studies have not been explicitly discussed and
even current research seems preoccupied with the 'frail structure'[3] of spatial
fact rather than social process. Pahl's inclusive definition of social geography
remains more a declaration of faith than of actuality: ". . . the processes and
patterns involved in an understanding of socially defined populations in their
spatial setting";[4] more appropriate is Buttimer's less specific statement,
". . . a multi-faceted perspective on the spatial organization of mankind".[5]

This paper argues that the lack of firm direction in contemporary social
geography is based upon a fundamental distinction between spatial form and
social process. These concepts find themselves on opposite sides of a philosophical divide separating fact from value, object from subject, and natural
science from social science. It is only by establishing a firm and appropriate
philosophical underpinning that social geography will pass successfully to a
concern with the social processes antecedent to a spatial fact and beyond that
to the development of limited generalisations and ultimately theory. The

215

S. Gale and G. Olsson (eds.), Philosophy in Geography, 215–236. All Rights Reserved.

history of geography has several instructive examples of the false blooming of a social geography of man, failures, it will be argued, due to the discipline's traditional preoccupation with the objective, and neglect of the lesson of everyday experience where every object is an object *for* a subject. These examples from the past provide useful lessons now as the epistemological impasse is once again engaged, and contribute toward a possible solution within the philosophy of phenomenology, where object and subject reassume the unity they share in our naive realms of experience, those realms, we will argue, which form the subject matter and central concern for a social geography of man.[6]

II. LESSONS FROM THE PAST

The school of human geography founded by Paul Vidal de la Blache has often been suggested as a forerunner to the present development of a social geography concerned with the relationships and processes underlying a landscape fact. His dual concepts of *genre de vie* and *milieu* were the building blocks for exploring the reciprocal relationship between social group and environment, and his possibilist stance acknowledged that landscapes were the outcomes of choice-making social groups. Each region, each place, was to be considered holistically as an intimate amalgam of environment and decision-making men, as an object with a subject. Men were rooted, they "saturated themselves with the environment";[7] yet the dialectic was continuously emphasised, as in Vidal's famous description of a landscape as a medal cast in the likeness of a people. Within this relationship there were few independent phenomena; each feature pointed beyond itself to other parts of the whole. In undertaking such research, Vidal was sceptical of the appropriateness of the methodology of the physical sciences and of being able to develop general laws of human behaviour. Here he was close to the position of incremental, middle-order generalisation held by Weber, whose interpretative sociology has acted as an important bridge in the introduction of phenomenological perspectives to the science of man.

The passing of Vidal's system reveals an instructive methodological turn. It had been under often bitter criticism from the new field of social morphology, led by Durkheim and other sociologists.[8] This conflict had philosophical undertones. The Durkheimian method adopted much of the positivist model of the natural sciences insisting upon a definition of each science which incorporated a distinctive set of phenomena and a body of laws. This ran at odds with the Vidalian perspective which emphasised more a point of view of place, and the uncovering of relationships which did not force deterministic statements, while pointing to likelihood and probability.[9]

But the more severe blow came from a gradual shift of emphasis within the French School itself. Concern passed from interpretative statements of place to the more formal categorisation of landscape facts in the work of Jean Brunhes and others.[10] These landscape facts were categorised, removed from their context, so that they expressed only the objective meaning of functionalism. Vidal's balanced humanism was replaced by an increasing materialist orientation culminating in Demangeon's quantitative coding of rural settlement,[11] and in North America represented in aspects of Carl Sauer's landscape school.[12] The material facts had sprung loose of their everyday human world; artifact replaced attitude, and land use morphology triumphed over regional personality. The transition from a science of man in place to a science of phenomena prepared the way for a scientism which ultimately abstracted place to a geometry of space, and reduced man to a pallid, entrepreneurial figure. Unlike Weber's interpretative sociology, Vidal's interpretative human geography did not engage epistemological and philosophical questions. Consequently it found no firm base to counter the criticisms of idosyncrasy and an atheoretical content and method of a later generation attuned to the fiats of 'positive' science. These criticisms can, however, be met in geography as they have been in sociology from the foundation of a philosophy embracing both subject and object such as that offered by phenomenology.

Turning from the rural French school to the urban Chicago school there are some instructive developmental parallels. The methodological similarities between Park's urban sociology and Vidal's human geography are striking, and negate too easy a dismissal of the Vidalian system in an urban setting. Park was certainly familiar with French human geography which he quoted in his earlier writing. Like Vidal, Park saw the man–environment relationship as reciprocal. Though the prompting influence of environment was not to be disregarded,[13] a land use unit only became a neighbourhood when it was "inevitably stained with the peculiar sentiments of its population",[14] a phrase reminiscent of Vidal's humanistic definition of landscape. The natural area was the equivalent of the region, and the concept of social world parallel to *genre de vie*, a localised set of people, attitudes and behaviour in a given setting. Park's view was as holistic as the French school, emphasising the role of regional monographs of natural urban areas, a synthetic, inductive approach in which generalisation could only be incremental. The regional

monograph was to be concerned with the everyday, experienced world of the
city dweller, the moral order, "man in his habitat and under the conditions in
which he actually lives",[15] incorporating his attitudes, subjective experiences,
and conception of self relative to his milieu.[16] The role of man the creator
and of human decision-making were as prominent in the Chicago urban
studies as in rural France, for what was the city other than "a product of
nature, and particularly of human nature"?[17] The humanist motif is clear in
these statements, and it is important to note the influence of both Dewey and
Mead upon Park and the Chicago school, North American scholars whose
thought is closely associated with the phenomenological stream.

In this context the debate of the 1940's when the Chicago school was
accused of narrow-minded economic determinism and the neglect of social
and cultural variables appears incongrous.[18] But in the same way that the
French school had passed into a period of materialistic functionalism, so
Chicago sociology had become preoccupied with human ecology, a science
of spatial relations heavily impregnated with biological metaphor in which
social groups and land uses were allocated spatially according to economic
gradients in the city.[19] This change of emphasis permitted a methodological
about turn from Park's earlier statements concerning the place of theory:

Reduce all social relations to relations of space and it would be possible to apply to
human relations the fundamental logic of the physical sciences.[20]

In this climate the geographical response to the Chicago school is illuminating. While the regional monographs were ignored, human ecology emphasising material phenomena and economic relations was quickly claimed from
within the geographic bailiwick, an emphasis which has continued into
current writing. Barrows, writing in 1923, claimed that "upon economic
geography for the most part the other divisions of the subject must be based"
while, as much of the material of social geography is "intangible . . . this body
of relationships appears to form a potential field for geography rather than an
assured one".[21]

Similar currents diverted both the early French and early Chicago schools
from common initial methodological goals. In each instance a humanistic
perspective with a holism incorporating subject and object was compromised
for a materialist treatment drawing upon a physical science tradition encouraging deterministic thinking.[22] Social relations were suppressed in the interest
of spatial facts, and social geography became preoccupied with man's material
works and the irresistible objectivity of the map. It was not until 1960 that
Firey's injunction concerning the role of social and cultural variables in urban

land use was broadly advertised in the geographic literature.[23] Before an intellectual climate underscoring economic materialism, social geography has substituted objective description of spatial facts for a *human* geography which was no less concerned with the *meaning* of those facts in the life-world of social groups.

III. THE LESSON OF BEHAVIOURAL GEOGRAPHY

At first glance it would seem as if the balance has been righted in recent years. Vidal's humanism was revived in Max Sorre's development of the concept of social space, with its subjective as well as objective components.[24] Both seminal and empirical research in perception, often emphasising holistic microscale settings, promised to reassert the role of human values and creativity in interaction with the environment.[25] But most of all the emergence of behavioural geography witnessed the explicit commitment to delve beneath the distribution maps and spatial facts to an examination of social and cognitive process in their everyday context: ". . . behavioural approaches emphasize the decision processes that were responsible for locations rather than concentrating on the topological relation between locations themselves".[26]

At the heart of behavioural geography, however, lies a methodological ambiguity which represents yet another example of the subject–object dichotomy, the dualism of cognitive process and spatial form. On the one hand is the recognition that behavioural geography is less concerned with the geometry of spatial relations, than it is with the motives and social processes operating to prompt group and individual behaviour. From the other perspective is the concern with the science of spatial geometry, macro-scale patterns, in which cognitive variables absorb only individual exceptions, "a 'residual' domain of events which cannot be handled by the normative or stochastic location theories".[27]

This locational perspective has its familiar methodological entourage which is lucidly described in *Explanation in Geography*.[28] Its underpinning is positivism, its model the model of natural science, with a concern for a set of phenomena particular to each discipline, precisely stated concepts, high order measurement, and the formulation of theory and ultimately general laws. In geography it is associated with the properties of aggregates, macro-spatial structure, and implicit economic determinism, with a pale spectre of man responsively following economic gradients. In this manner, the locational school is not unrelated to human ecology, albeit in more sophisticated costume and separate from the cruder biological analogies. Mackenzie's definition of human ecology captures much of the flavour of the spatial school: "Human ecology deals with the spatial aspects of the symbiotic relations of human beings and human institutions".[29] The interconnections are more fully underlined in Park's statement that human ecology seeks to emphasise not so much geography as space, for now geography has itself claimed the mantle of the geometric science of space.[30]

As has occurred in other social sciences, it is this methodological set which has been extended to the behavioural approach in geography.[31] Yet positivism's uneasiness in dealing with the cognitive is apparent, and leads to the conclusion that "we may get further more quickly in developing economic and stochastic theory than we will in developing the cognitive-behavioural theory".[32] The marked similarity of this conclusion with that of Barrows a half century earlier, is an important commentary on a common epistemological foundation which is not well suited to the examination of social and cognitive processes. To the positivist, the subjective has been seen as metaphysical, and therefore unknowable, irrational or private, and beyond the range of theory. Alternately, the mental world has been reduced by the kind of psychologism challenged by Husserl which, in its imitation of natural science, destroys those situational aspects which are integral to the meaning of experience. "In the realm of the mental we cannot understand the whole from the parts".[33]

Behavioural geography has tended to follow the model of psychologism and it is for this reason that Olsson has described the field as still-born. In the passage from spatial fact to social process an important threshold is crossed as the objective world of facts and material phenomena is joined by the subjective world of ideas and values, and the logical language for discussing the former does not necessarily cover the latter: ". . . in the oblique realm of intentions, hopes and fears, two times two is not always equal to four".[34] The deterministic (or stochastic) relations implicit in the positivist perspective suggest a precision that is foreign to the world of human action which is more properly characterised by relations which are fuzzy, ambiguous and evolving, where 'rational' behaviour is clouded by a myriad of subjective influences. These influences are rarely revealed by the types of group variables contained in the census or mass surveys; these variables are convenient for scientific analysis but rarely salient for human decision-making. To understand social process one must encounter the situation of the decision-maker, which includes incomplete and inconsistent information, values and partisan attitudes, short-term motives and long-range beliefs.

IV. THE PHENOMENOLOGICAL TRADITIONS

The preceding discussion has isolated two methodological positions, the one concerned with holism, a man–environment dialectic, and the incorporation of social and cognitive variables, and the other committed to material phenomena, explicit reductionism and implicit determinism, and analysis which separates fact from value. In each instance there has been a tendency for human geography to pursue the latter rather than the former route, so that even initially man-centred fields such as Vidalian geography, Chicago sociology, and behavioural geography have evolved toward the inappropriate format of physical science.[35]

The debate between these two positions should be drawn into its much broader epistomological context. The emergence of the Vidalian school as a corrective to the implicit materialism and determinism of Ratzel was a local example of a widespread protest against the scientism of the late nineteenth century. Dilthey's emphasis on historical consciousness, Weber's method- ology of *Verstehen*, Mannheim's sociology of knowledge, were all reactions against a too-severe positivism which in disassociating subject from object, had removed the human context from behaviour, and even from life. In North America a second and largely independent scholarship represented by Dewey, Cooley, and Mead similarly reacted against the strictures of stimulus– response behaviourism and founded what was later to be known as symbolic interactionism with its concern upon the essential meaningfulness of human interaction. Though there is often a difference in emphasis among these writers, their position is often parallel with if not derivative of their con- temporary, Edmund Husserl, founder of phenomenology:

In the second half of the nineteenth century the world-view of modern man was deter- mined by the positive sciences. That meant a turning away from the questions which are decisive for a genuine humanity ... Mere factual knowledge makes for factual man ... In our desperate need, this science has nothing to say to us.[36]

The second generation of phenomenologists, including Merleau-Ponty and Alfred Schutz have maintained its fundamental critique of positivism, while also synthesizing the phenomenological traditions; Schutz, for example, has successfully built a bridge between Weber and Husserl, and thus established a firm philosophical underpinning for Weber's interpretative sociology.[37]

If phenomenology begins in radical protests, its assertion of 'back to the things themselves' is a constructive rebuilding of the relations between subject and object. Action is regarded as intended, as meaningless divorced from its subject. Thus phenomenology is a holistic philosophy: "The world is all in us, and I am all outside myself".[38] Merleau-Ponty and Schutz have also been prominent in asserting the primacy of human relations, of encounter with the world; before them, Mannheim had emphasised the relational nature of knowledge, its 'existential relativity' to an historical era. Likewise Schutz' concept of multiple realities points to the relational nature of both objects and concepts; every object, including knowledge, is an object for a subject.[39] It follows then that in all phenomenological traditions the question of meaning is a central concern, for meaning and perception speak of existence, of a subject in encounter with an object.

This summary account of some of the themes of phenomenology serves to locate the discussion of social geography within its philosophical context. The Vidalian commitment to holism, and reciprocity between man and environment, subject and object overlapped with this philosophical stream in its disagreement with Durkheim's positivism. Sympathetic understanding as a mode of inquiry, the creative role of man, the use of artefacts as products, and the interest in the genius or personality of place which is the spatial equivalent of Mannheim's *Weltanschauung*, the global outlook of an historical era, were all features of Vidalian geography shared with phenomenological enquiry. These remarks apply equally to the early Chicago school, and here the philosophical influence is more direct, for Park and his colleagues were in close contact with the work of Dewey and Mead.

But what of the present day? Does the phenomenological stream continue to offer an underpinning to a reinvigorated social geography concerned with group action which culminates in a landscape effect? The shortcomings of the positivist approach in behavioural geography have been suggested. What is the phenomenological alternative?

V. SOCIAL SCIENCE AS SOCIAL BEHAVIOUR

Since its beginnings with Husserl, the first task of phenomenology has been the unmasking of the founding assumptions of alternate philosophies; foundational criticism is often regarded as one of the ways to phenomenology.[40] In this manner it can be shown that at the root of an empirical science, there are necessary taken-for-granted assumptions, the same subjective naiveté as occurs within our own private life-worlds. The revelation of the subjective at the root of a science which empirically rejects the role of subjectivity, prepares the way for a constructive synthesis in which subject and object are re-united as they are in naive experience. A phenomenological examination of social science thus begins with an analysis of presuppositions, with the exposure of assumptions which are unselfconsciously taken-for-granted.

In science as in life, the subjective basis for the objective is most visible in circumstances where an individual or group encounters the unknown, and into the informational vacuum projects its own definition of reality.[41] An instructive case was the geographical misinterpretation endemic to many scientific expeditionary parties of the eighteenth and nineteenth centuries. An example was the search for the Southern Continent, an intellectual myth which was perpetuated for centuries as Pacific explorers resolved ambiguous cues in the physical environment before the clarity of their own unambiguous mental image. Thus low clouds on the horizon were *interpreted* as the edge of a continous land surface, the presence of sea birds and floating vegetation were *regarded* as indicators of the proximity of a landmass, and the island archipelagoes were *perceived* as its northernmost promontories and offshore islands. Exploratory behaviour became an amalgam of fact and value, object and subject. To contemporaries the image of the Southern Continent was neither idiosyncratic nor whimsical; it was a socially constructed reality, endorsed and maintained by intellectual and scientific fiat.

These processes do not disappear in recent intellectual exploration. Consider for example the unchanging social science image of black America. The attempt by intellectual explorers to order their own conceptual uncertainty has characteristically been from a distance with the use of secondary sources. At whatever period they have written, social scientists have claimed a contemporary new unity in the black movement. In 1920 Kerlin referred to what he called the New Negro Movement, and Detweiler listed many examples of rising nationalism.[42] Arnold and Caroline Rose outlined a growing black morale through the 1930's and 1940's, which they regarded as peaking at their time of writing in 1953, when it was "now a powerful force in Negro life in America".[43] Five years later, Robert Johnson claimed to have identified a "New Negro Creed" of "unwavering race pride".[44] Another five years and Robin Williams claimed the newfound birth of "The New Negro Code".[45] Yet another five years and the "New Ghetto Man" has been created, "a ghetto man who is very different in his actions and sympathies from the Negro of the past . . .".[46]

The New Negro Movement, the New Negro Creed, the New Negro Code,

the New Ghetto Man . . . at each period social scientists imposed organisation
upon the black community, claiming that at the time of *their* writing new
mobilising forces were at work. Nobody recognised that what was happening
was not a new awakening of black America in their day, but rather a cyclic
reinforcement and perpetuation of a tenacious image of social science. It was
the socially endorsed image which was highly organised and possessed a clear
teleology, not black America. It is difficult to account for the disarray
revealed by more perceptive participant observation studies in black inner
city neighbourhoods if real forces of unity have been active for at least fifty
years. Social scientists, in their own search for order in chaos, imposed a
conceptual structure which was then unwittingly projected onto the black
community. Scientific behaviour then followed the pilot light of its own misplaced image.

It is from this perspective that the black sociologist Andrew Billingsley
comments that "American social scientists are much more American than
social and much more social than scientific".[47] Subjective in-group values
have pervaded objective analysis; indeed we learn as much about the cognitive
categories of the researcher as we do of the 'facts' he is examining. The *a
priori* 'outside view' of behaviour acts as a mirror reflecting the social values
of the observer. Behind the objective is the subjective, the mind which selects
it, names it, classifies it, interprets it, or alternatively dismisses it. The check
against such bias is of course to bring back scientific theory against the test
of common experience. But when the everyday world is perceived only from
afar by an objective observer, and its fabric is defined in secondary sources by
easily derived variables of convenience, testing is often far from complete,
and the 'sighting' of a Southern Continent too easily occurs.

In social science neither questions of technique nor of concept are endorsed
in a social vacuum. As we now become a stranger to them is this not exactly
what we see in parts of the methodological fervour in geography during the
1960's? The diffusion of an innovative technique was as much a matter of
in-group endorsement as it was of pragmatic application to the everyday
world.[48] Or consider spatial theory with its isolation of transportation costs
and behaviour characterised by distance minimisation. Why these? Is over-
coming distance *the* central preoccupation for man in his selection of home
and workplace, or as he shops for clothes, or is it a socially underscored
variable in the collective mind of a group of mutually attendant social scientists?[49] Pehaps there is a deeper irony than we have yet recognized to the
oft-quoted maxim of geographers who follow the natural science model of
explanation: "by our theories you shall know us".[50]

VI. THE INTERSUBJECTIVE LIFE WORLD

Even in the most attentively objective of behaviours – the scientific – it is impossible to disregard the powerful influence of the subjective. Geographic 'thinking as usual', the taken-for-granted building blocks of the scientific method, reveal the full interplay of fact and value within a milieu of inter-subjective social conventions. As social geography follows its agenda and dips beneath spatial facts and the unambiguous objectivity of the map, it encounters the same group-centred world of events, relations, and places infused with meaning and often ambiguity. Husserl, in his later writing, characterised this realm as the *life-world*. More recent philosophers like Schutz and Merleau-Ponty have urged that this reality encompassing mundane experience is not irrational and impossible to study; but neither, they argue, should it be investigated with an inappropriate methodology which violates the integral unity of the things themselves. The phenomenological method provides a logic for understanding the life-world. Its basic question becomes "what does this social world mean for the observed actor within this world and what did he mean by his acting within it?"[51] Actions are intentional and purposive, they have meaning, but access to this meaning requires knowledge of the motives and perception of the actor, his definition of the situation.[52]

Meanings are rarely fully private, but are invariably shared and reinforced in peer group action. Unlike the lonely wasteland of the economic rationalist and of some existential notions of man, phenomenological man is unavowedly social. His life-world is an intersubjective one of shared meanings, of *fellow men* with whom he engages in face-to-face *we-relationships*. These relationships are entered into by choice and show, in pure form, the familiar pattern of selective interaction between like-minded individuals, birds of a feather flocking together.[53] The social group is not of course autonomous in its decision-making, but is impinged upon to varying degrees by society at large. For some men, the macro social structure does not permit a wide range of action. As one graffiti artist of the American inner city put it:

There isn't much choice of what to do ... I did it because there was nothing else. I wasn't goin' to get involved with no gangs or shoot no dope, so I started writing' on buses. I just started with a magic marker an' worked up.[54]

Each individual has a history and a geography which imposes constraints within his life-world; so begins the dialectic between creativity and deter-minism, charisma and institution, a dialectic which for the geographer becomes that between man and place.

A second, and often more binding, set of constraints upon action in every-day life are forces internal to the life-world of the individual and group. In the process of group consolidation its collective view of the world becomes more telling on the individual, as he becomes successively more 'included' within it. So too his action becomes increasingly identified with group norms. At the extreme, a common reality is enacted by repeated interaction and shared tasks, a reality which becomes socially defined and may appear quite eccentric to the outsider who does not share its taken-for-granted norms.[55] The phenomenological model of man is one of a life-world with a group-centred reality.

Artistic reflection on experience constantly animates the life-world profile:

> This sea-town was my world; outside a strange Wales, coal-pitted, mountained, river-run, full, so far as I knew, of choirs and football teams and sheep and storybook tall hats and red flannel petticoats, moved about its business which was none of mine.
> Beyond that unknown Wales with its wild names like peals of bells in the darkness, and its mountain men clothed in the skins of animals perhaps and always singing, lay England which was London and the country called the Front, from which many of our neighbours never came back. It was a country to which only young men travelled.[56]

Dylan Thomas' portrait is a particularly spatial one, but the contours of the life-world also have social and temporal salience. At the core is the unprob-lematic and unquestioned world of everyday experience, of we-relationships. Beyond is the world of indirect communication, of *they-relationships*, the world not of intimates but of contemporaries. My contemporaries I do not know; they are *typified*, seen only as types. The post-office clerk, for example, is known only as the man who handles my mail, just as England takes on the typification of London, and the world beyond that of the Front, the only salient intersection between a child's world in South Wales and the European continent during the years of war. Though the postal clerk also lives within a life-world of fellow men, as also England is far more than its typification of London, for now, in my taken-for-granted milieu, such things are of no matter to me.[57]

Dylan Thomas also demarcates the incomplete nature of an information field. Unlike economic man, social man has highly biased information sources, an information map characterised by a core area of familiar and credible subjective knowledge, which is succeeded by realms where knowl-edge is increasingly objective and typified, and passing finally into realms of ignorance.[58] This information map is closely related to behaviour, for the stock of knowledge is essentially pragmatic in origin and is acquired in achiev-ing mastery over recurrent situations in the life-world; standard procedures, or *recipes*, are devised to deal with the more repetitive or routine matters. Not only is knowledge within the life-world incomplete, but also it can be contradictory; consistency and certainty of information are by no means to be assumed even for a single individual, for as social roles are changed so both the relevance and the interpretation of knowledge may shift.

Schutz' model of the intersubjective life-world can usefully be extended beyond informal groups to organisations. While recent analysis has stressed the manner in which organisations impersonally stand over man, yet they too retain a less visible internal environment, a taken-for-granted life-world which is the seed-bed for action and decision-making: "the objectivity of the institutional world, however massive it may appear to the individual, is a humanly produced, constructed objectivity".[59] The economic model of the firm is as incomplete as the lonely figure of rational man; as soon as analysis passes from organisational facts to the meaning of organisational decisions, the analyst enters the same fuzzy, intersubjective world.[60]

Decisions in the organisational world are also coloured by both an external and internal environment. Organisations establish a tradition of goals, priorities, and strategies and all of these reveal a corporate set of values, a climate which influences decision-making. Corporate action displays the social basis of this climate as past allies and familiar networks are activated in routine problem-solving.[61] A common world view is constructed through intersubjective we-relationships; isolation, however, permits the survival of alternative values even between different departments of the same institution.[62]

Perception is a central concern in understanding organisational behaviour: "it is perhaps through the study of perception and information flows that progress can be made in understanding the process whereby organizations respond to their changing environment".[63] Information fields are group-centred for organisations as for informal groups, biased in favour of socially and spatially proximate sources, and once again knowledge in the life-world need be neither complete nor consistent; "in fact ... consistency or completeness, at times, create problems in finding feasible solutions".[64] Decisions are usually made following simple, standardised and pragmatic rules, following closely Schutz' model of the recipe. The social basis of decision-making is reflected by widespread mimicry in problem-solving, whereby organisations imitate the strategies of their 'fellow men', those which are proximate to them in social space.[65] Finally, we note how newcomers to an institution are socialised to its construction of reality, its view of the world. To some extent this is formalised in training and orientation, but probably of greater significance is the incremental experience of daily contact, as newcomers are attuned to the taken-for-granted world of the organisation, and its definition of the situation becomes their own.[66]

Thus the social model of man derived from Schutz's theory of social action within the life-world is equally useful for charting the naive realms of experience which constitute both the presuppositions and the source of scientific, informal, and institutional behaviour. This is not to assert a new determinism where the social milieu necessarily controls individual behaviour, but rather to identify a set of baseline characteristics within the life-world from which there will invariably be local departures. The theory of social action provides a pertinent framework and underpinning for a social geography which examines the social and cognitive contexts antecedent to a spatial fact.

VII. THE MEANING OF PLACE

One of Mannheim's achievements was to reveal the relational nature of history. This was not to present a relativism where everybody and nobody was right, but rather to stress that every historic truth was also a truth for a subject, that the existential relativity of historic facts should be remembered in their interpretation: "history is a creative medium of meanings and not merely the passive medium".[67]

There is a meaning to space as well as to time. Each place should equally be seen phenomenologically, in its relational context, as an object for a subject. To speak of a place is not to speak of an object alone, but of an image and an intent, of a landscape much in the Vidalian sense of the word.[68] Thus place always has meaning, it is always 'for' its subject, and this meaning carries back not only to the intent of the subject, but also forward as a separate variable prompting the behaviour of a new generation of fellow men and contemporaries.

But if a place is meaningless without a subject, so too a person removed from his own place is a man of uncertain identity.[69] This simple dialectic permits an understanding of the human dimensions of, for example, long-range migration. The distant metropolis is never perceived in the perfect material terms that the gravity model with its economic determinism would have us believe. The metropolis has a meaning, it is, in Park's words, a state of mind, and it is always this meaning for the subject that precedes action; creative decision-making is not pre-empted by a mechanistic gravity field. In the same manner, the newly arrived urban immigrant finds himself initially disassociated from his new environment; the place is not a place *for him*.[70]

In unravelling the personality of place, the interpretative geography of the French school, with (like Max Weber) its strong empirical and intuitive base, was primarily concerned with the relationships between man and his physical environment. Vidal's successor, Max Sorre, recognised that in an urbanising age the critical forces in defining *genre de vie* were increasingly becoming social rather than physical. Merleau-Ponty has commented that history is other people; in an urban age, geography too has become other people. Place is increasingly being defined in terms of relations between men; the province of British Columbia has an added meaning to a Toronto investment company since the electoral defeat of its socialist-leaning government, as does Mexico City to a potential New York vacationer named Goldstein since Mexico's alignment against Israel at the United Nations.

In contemporary urbanism a place may commonly have a multiple reality; its meaning may change with the intent of its subject, and a plurality of subjects may simultaneously hold a different meaning for the same place. Usually, however, a dominant meaning holds sway, and the landscape can then act in the phenomenological sense of a product, as an indicator of the subjective intentions which guided it. In the same way, mundane and taken-for-granted features of the environment can point beyond themselves to local societal values. Wall graffiti, for example, present a mirror on intangible attitudes which govern everyday relations between groups and between groups and space in the American inner city. They also of course have an immediate audience and act as an indirect form of communication between social groups. Many landscape settings present such cues of appropriate behaviour within their bounds, through micro-design features and the creation of a 'mood' atmosphere.[71] The meaning of a place systematically attracts groups with similar interests and lifestyles; places are selected and retained by reflective decision-makers on the basis of their perceived image and stock of knowledge. The result is that the city becomes a mosaic of social worlds each supporting a group of similar intent, who in their habitual interaction reinforce the character both of their group and of their place.

This personality of place ranges in scale from the nation state to the neighbourhood church; any habitually interacting group of people convey a character to the place they occupy which is immediately apparent to an outsider, though unquestioned and taken-for-granted by habitués. Thus a newcomer to a place is under strong pressures to adopt the local world view, and empirically there is a tendency for such attitudinal convergence to occur.[72]

Within the life-world there is a spatial counterpart to the social designation of fellow men and contemporaries. At the simplest level in our experience

space is partitioned into near and far portions, those that are private and public. Near space is well-known, predictable and protective, anchored, though
not limited, to the home; it "concentrates being within limits that protect".[73]
The home is the core of the taken-for-granted world. Bureaucracies speak of
housing programmes, of geometry and dollars; home is a word of experience,
a word of the people.

There are circumstances in which private space extends beyond the home
to a community. This extension is rarely determined by objective land use or
socio-economic characteristics but through an intersubjective consensus
derived from a shared perception of solidarity and identity.[74] A distinctive
status on the map is not enough to define community; consider the comment
of a frustrated resident in a spatially well-identified, ethnically homogeneous
black inner city neighbourhood:

The community? Huh, what is the community? There ain't no community. People are
just watching out for themselves ... Who cares about the community? Give people a
meal and a can of beer and they're satisfied. They don't need no community.

To have meaning and thereby reality in experience, community must be an
amalgam of fact and value; it must be a common object for a plurality of
subjects.

The separation of subject from object is a characteristic of the anomie of
the post-industrial metropolis. Dehumanised urban settings comprise little
more than space, little more than geometry; they excite no commitment,
they are not 'for' a collectivity. They are the landscape realisation of a mode
of analysis which has emphasised functional materialism; such analysis translated into a planning paradigm creates a landscape of objective meaning only,
a form without a subject.[75] Both the capitalist and the socialist city display
manifestations of a materialist philosophy which has forgotten man. In
response, many contemporary grass roots movements are attempting to
reinstate meaning to the land: the protection of historic buildings, the preservation of neighbourhoods, opposition to demolition for freeways and public
works, asserting the sanctity of nature and open space; all are protests against
the objectification of the land, its reduction to a fact which has been torn
free of its human context. For some groups such as nationalist minorities in
peacetime, and whole nations in time of war, the land is a surrogate for
identity; "if we lose the land, we lose ourselves".[76] The relationship between
identity and landscape is profound, though largely unexamined, and lends
credence to the phrase of French phenomenologists that a man *is* his place.
The deterministic implications of this watchword fade when we recall its

dialectical dimension, that the meaning of a place is itself derived initially in relation, from the intent of a human group.

VIII. CONCLUSION

In conclusion the omissions of this paper should be acknowledged. There has been no discussion of a number of important methodological issues, including the nature of generalisation in a phenomenologically based social geography, *verstehen* as an explanatory method, the role of structural as against situational forces in social action, and the controversy of existence and essence in phenomenology. These are matters which require far more space than is possible in this paper.[77] It should be added also that phenomenological analysis is not prescriptive; it encounters reality as it *is*, not as it *should* be.

The objective of this paper has been more modest. It has argued that the present equivocal status of social geography is not a new problem but arose at least as early as Barrows' presidential address in 1922. It stems from the discipline's preoccupation with material phenomena, economic forces, and the physical science model in explanation. Successively this tradition has diverted the Vidalian school, the Chicago school of urban sociology, and behavioural geography as it has either disregarded the subjective or else has forced essentially subjective problems into an inappropriate *a priori* hypothetico-deductive cast. This is not a promising avenue for a progression beyond spatial fact to social process, a progression which leads from questions of form to questions of meaning and intent.

The first step in a reformulation is a radical description of the things themselves which recognises the pervasive presence of the subjective as well as the objective in all areas of behaviour: the informal, the scientific, the institutional. The second is to adopt a philosophical underpinning which embraces both object and subject, fact and value. Phenomenology restores to these troubling dualisms the unity they carry in the everyday world; indeed it is exactly this taken-for-granted realm of experience which is its constant reference point. Third is the recognition that the life-world is not solitary but a place of fellow believers; intersubjectivity is the basis for a social model of man. Fourthly, place should be viewed in relation, as an amalgam of fact and value, comprising both the objectivity of the map and the subjectivity of experience. For the social geographer a materialist preoccupation with spatial facts is not enough; in Sorre's words, "A geographer is not a collector of shells which are no longer the home of a living being".[78]

As social geography delves beneath a spatial fact to a social group, these prescriptions will draw the researcher back to the ground of behaviour, to the world as it is naively known, "back to the 'forgotten man' of the social sciences, to the actor in the social world whose doing and feeling lies at the bottom of the whole system".[79]

Department of Geography
University of British Columbia

NOTES

[1] I am grateful to Anne Buttimer, Thomas Koch, and Marwyn Samuels for their helpful comments on an earlier draft of this paper.
[2] For example, J. W. Watson, 'The Sociological Aspects of Geography', in G. Taylor (ed.), *Geography in the Twentieth Century*, Methuen, London, pp. 463–99; R. Pahl, 'Trends in Social Geography', in R. Chorley and P. Haggett (eds.), *Frontiers in Geographical Teaching*, Methuen, London, pp. 81–100; A. Buttimer, Social Geography', in D. Sills (ed.), *International Encyclopedia of the Social Sciences*, New York, Vol. 6 (1968); P. Claval, 'Problèmes Théoriques en géographie sociale', in *Canadian Geographer* 17 (1973), 103–112.
[3] E. Jones, *Readings in Social Geography*, London, Oxford, 1975.
[4] Pahl, *op. cit.*, p. 81.
[5] Buttimer, *op. cit.*, p. 138.
[6] The small and as yet exploratory literature introducing phenomenology to geography includes E. Relph, 'An Inquiry into the Relations between Phenomenology and Geography', in *Canadian Geographer* 14 (1970), 193–201; D. Mercer and J. Powell, *Phenomenology and Other Non-Positivist Approaches in Geography*, Monash Publications in Geography, Melbourne, 1972; A. Buttimer, *Values in Geography*, Association of American Geographers, Washington, D.C., 1974; A. Buttimer, 'Grasping the Dynamism of Life-world', in *Annals* 66 (1976), 277–292.
[7] P. Vidal de la Blache, *Principles of Human Geography*, Holt, New York, 1926. Compare, in interpretative sociology, Max Weber's dialectic between individual creativity and social institutionalisation: M. Weber, *On Charisma and Institution Building*, University of Chicago Press, Chicago, 1968.
[8] V. Berdoulay, 'Human Geography Versus Social Morphology', presented at Canadian Association of Geographers Meeting, Vancouver, 1975; A. Buttimer, *Society and Milieu in the French Geographic Tradition*, Rand McNally, Chicago, 1971.
[9] A North American echo of this debate appeared in a little-known paper published in 1908; E. Hayes, 'Sociology and Psychology; Sociology and Geography', in *American Journal of Sociology* 14 (1908), 371–407.
[10] Buttimer, 1971, *op. cit.*, p. 63.
[11] *Ibid.*, p. 103.
[12] For the source of this characterisation see H. Brookfield, 'Questions on the Human Frontiers of Geography', in *Economic Geography* 40 (1964), 283–303.

[13] Indeed isolated extracts from Park, as from Vidal, could give the misleading impression of a deterministic inclination. For example, ". . . while temperament is inherited, character and habit are formed under the influence of environment", R. Park, 'The City as a Social Laboratory', in R. Turner (ed.), *On Social Control and Collective Behavior*, University of Chicago Press, Chicago, pp. 3–18.

[14] R. Park, 'The City: Suggestions for the Investigation of Human Behavior in the Urban Environment', in *American Journal of Sociology* 20 (1916), 597–612.

[15] Park, 1967, *op. cit.*, p. 5; for an outstanding example of an urban regional study see H. Zorbaugh, *The Gold Coast and the Slum*, University of Chicago Press, Chicago, 1929.

[16] The fullest studies of personality and milieu were carried out by other members of the Chicago school, notably William Thomas and Florian Znaniecki. See the useful review volumes: W. Thomas, *On Social Organization and Social Personality*, M. Janowitz (ed.), University of Chicago Press, Chicago, 1966; F. Znaniecki, *On Humanistic Sociology*, R. Bierstedt (ed.), University of Chicago Press, Chicago, 1969.

[17] Park, *op. cit.*

[18] For example, W. Firey, 'Sentiment and Symbolism as Ecological Variables', in *American Sociological Review* 10 (1945), 140–48; C. Jonassen, 'Cultural Variables in the Ecology of an Ethnic Group', in *American Sociological Review* 14 (1949), 32–41.

[19] R. Park, 'Human Ecology', in *American Socological Review* 42 (1936), 1–15. In effect Park retained the concept of the moral order even at the height of his social Darwinism, though this qualification was often overlooked by both outside reviewers and his students.

[20] *Ibid.*; but again Park went on to moderate this strong claim, with the statement that the vagaries of human idiosyncracy would make this development unlikely.

[21] H. Barrows, 'Geography as Human Ecology', in *Annals* 13 (1923), 1–14.

[22] At this period, geographic determinism continued to be physical rather than economic as in human ecology. Compare Stephen Visher's "Democracy is interfered with by exceptionally fertile soil . . ." in his remarkably deterministic introduction of social geography to a broader audience in 1932: S. Visher, 'Social Geography', in *Social Forces* 10 (1932), 351–4.

[23] E. Jones, *A Social Geography of Belfast*, Oxford University Press, London, 1960.

[24] M. Sorre, *Rencontres de la géographie et de la sociologie*, Rivière, Paris, 1957; A. Buttimer, 'Social Space in Interdisciplinary Perspective', in *Geographical Review* 59 (1969), 417–26.

[25] For example, W. Kirk, 'Problems of Geography', in *Geography* 48 (1963), 357–71; D. Lowenthal, 'Geography, Experience, and Imagination', in *Annals* 51 (1961), 241–60.

[26] R. Golledge, L. Brown and F. Williamson, 'Behavioural Approaches in Geography: An Overview', in *Australian Geographer* 12 (1972), 59–79.

[27] D. Harvey, 'Conceptual and Measurement Problems in the Cognitive-Behavioral Approach to Location Theory', in K. Cox and R. Golledge (eds.), *Behavioral Problems in Geography*, Northwestern University Press, Evanston, 1969, pp. 35–67.

[28] D. Harvey, *Explanation in Geography*, Edward Arnold, London, 1969; see also, W. Alonso, *Location and Land Use*, M.I.T. Press, Cambridge, 1964. In the frank introduction to this influential work in locational analysis, Alonso sets out the economic model of man upon which his theoretical structure is based; as Olsson has pointed out, the logic of Alsonso's model has been retained in Harvey's recent socialist reformulations.

[29] R. Mackenzie, 'Human Ecology', in *Encyclopedia of Social Sciences* 5 (1931), 314.

[30] R. Park, 'The Urban Community as a Spatial Pattern and a Moral Order' reprinted in R. Turner, *op. cit.*, pp. 55–68; the fullest statement of the primacy of geography as spatial science appears in W. Bunge, *Theoretical Geography*, Gleerup, Lund, 1966. The convergence of the two literatures is made explicit in O. D. Duncan, R. P. Cuzzort and B. Duncan, *Statistical Geography*, Glencoe, Free Press, 1961; D. Timms, 'Quantitative Techniques in Urban Social Geography', in R. Chorley and P. Haggett (eds.), *op. cit.*, pp. 239–65.

[31] R. Golledge and D. Amadeo, 'On Laws in Geography', in *Annals* 58 (1968), 760–774; compare the critique of behaviouralism in other social sciences in M. Natanson (ed.), *Phenomenology and the Social Sciences*, Northwestern University Press, Evanston, 1973.

[32] D. Harvey in Cox and Golledge, *op. cit.*, p. 63.

[33] K. Mannheim, *Essays on the Sociology of Knowledge*, London, 1952, p. 82.

[34] G. Olsson, 'The Dialectics of Spatial Analysis', in *Antipode* 3 (1974), 50–62.

[35] Compare here Zelinsky's recognition and protest against this trend in geography, and also his inability to offer an alternative: W. Zelinsky, 'The Demigod's Dilemma', in *Annals* 65 (1975), 123–43.

[36] Quoted by F. Buytendijk, 'Husserl's Phenomenology and Its Significance for Contemporary Psychology', in N. Lawrence and D. O'Connor (eds.), *Readings in Existential Phenomenology*, Prentice Hall, Englewood Cliffs, N.J., 1967, pp. 352–64.

[37] For this aspect of Schutz's work, a recent review appears in R. Williame, *Les Fondements Phénoménologiques de la Sociologie Comprehensive: Alfred Schutz et Max Weber*, Martinus Nijhoff, The Hague, 1973.

[38] Quoted by H. Spiegelberg, *The Phenomenological Movement*, Martinus Nijhoff, The Hague, 1969, p. 551; also M. Samuels, 'Human Geography and Existential Space', Department of Geography, University of British Columbia, 1976.

[39] A. Schutz, 'On Multiple Realities', in *Philosophy and Phenomenological Research* 5 (1945), pp. 533–76.

[40] For example, R. Zaner, *The Way of Phenomenology*, Pegasus, New York, 1970.

[41] For a further empirical discussion see D. Ley, *The Black Inner City as Frontier Outpost: Images and Behavior of a Philadelphia Neighborhood*, Association of American Geographers, Washington, D.C., 1974.

[42] R. Kerlin, *The Voice of the Negro*, Dutton, New York, 1920; F. Detweiler, *The Negro Press in the United States*, University of Chicago Press, Chicago, 1922.

[43] A. Rose and C. Rose, *America Divided*, New York, 1953, p. 193.

[44] R. Johnson, 'Negro Reactions to Minority Group Status', in M. Barron (ed.), *American Minorities*, Knopf, New York, 1958, p. 212.

[45] R. Williams, *Strangers Next Door*, Prentice-Hall, Englewood Cliffs, 1964, p. 280.

[46] N. Caplan, 'The New Ghetto Man', in *Journal of Social Issues* 26 (1970), 59–73.

[47] A. Billingsley, 'Black Families and White Social Science', in *Journal of Social Issues* 26 (1970), 127–42; for a generic discussion of such 'false universes' see A. Schutz, 'Concept and Theory Formation in the Social Sciences', in *Journal of Philosophy* 51 (1954), 257–74.

[48] Note, for example, that the spatial and social diffusion of the new geography both in Britain and the United States during the 1960's shows parallels with the diffusion of other phenomena whose adaptation is heavily dependent upon social consensus: J.

Whitehead, 'Innovation Diffusion in an Academic Discipline: The Case of the "New Geography" ', in *Area* 2 (1970), 19–30; P. Lavalle, H. McConnell, and R. Brown, 'Certain Aspects of the Expansion of Quantitative Methodology in American Geography', in *Annals* 57 (1967), 423–36.

[49] For an example of the potentially distorting effects from overemphasis of the distance variable see C. Smith, 'Distance and the Location of Community Mental Health Facilities: A Divergent Viewpoint', in *Economic Geography* 52 (1976), 181–91. Zelinsky's recent critique of scientism in geography (note 35) continually underscores the social nature of the geographic endeavor. The literature of symbolic interactionism offers a more formal development of the institutionalisation of social norms: T. Shibutani, *Society and Personality*, Prentice-Hall, Englewood Cliffs, 1961.

[50] Harvey, *op. cit.*, note 28, p. 486.

[51] A. Schutz, 'The Social World and the Theory of Social Action', in *Social Research* 27 (1960), 205–21: This provides the most succint overview of a significant part of Schutz' thinking; another useful review is A. Gurwitsch, 'The Commonsense World as Social Reality', in *Social Research* 29 (1962), 50–72; for fuller statements, see A. Schutz, *The Phenomenology of the Social World*, Northwestern University Press, Evanston, 1967; A. Schutz, *On Phenomenology and Social Relations*, H. Wagner (ed.), University of Chicago Press, Chicago, 1970; A. Schulz and T. Luckmann, *The Structures of the Life-World*, 1973, Northwestern University Press, Evanston.

[52] This well-known concept was developed by W. I. Thomas, one of Park's contemporaries at Chicago, and points again to the appropriateness of the situational philosophies of phenomenology and symbolic interactionism as underpinnings for the early empirical schools of Vidal and Park. See also D. Mercer, 'Behavioural Geography and the Sociology of Social Action', in *Area* 4 (1972), 48–51.

[53] This is a central tenet of symbolic interactionism; see, for example H. Blumer, *Symbolic Interactionism*, Prentice-Hall, Englewood Cliffs, 1969; for empirical validation, see E. Laumann, *Bonds of Pluralism: The Form and Substance of Urban Social Networks*, Wiley, New York, 1973.

[54] D. Ley and R. Cybriwsky, 'Urban Graffiti as Territorial Markers', in *Annals* 64 (1974), 491–505.

[55] For an excellent discussion, see P. Berger and T. Luckmann, *The Social Construction of Reality*, Doubleday, New York, 1966; for an empirical example, see D. Ley, 'The Street Gang in its Milieu', in H. Rose and G. Gappert (eds.), *The Social Economy of Cities*, Sage Publications, Beverly Hills, Calif., 1975, pp. 247–73.

[56] D. Thomas, *Quite Early One Morning*, New Directions, New York, 1960, p. 4.

[57] For a useful discussion of the role of typification in the life-world see M. Natanson, *Phenomenology, Role, and Reason*, Charles Thomas, Springfield, Illinois, 1974.

[58] Schutz and Luckmann, *op. cit.*, pp. 178–9.

[59] Berger and Luckmann, *op. cit.*, p. 57.

[60] R. Cyert and J. March, *A Behavioral Theory of the Firm*, Prentice Hall, Englewood Cliffs, 1963; F. Hamilton (ed.), *Spatial Perspectives on Industrial Organization and Decision-Making*, Wiley, London, 1974. Despite the subjective nature of their data, these authors nevertheless largely follow the standard procedure in behavioural studies of working within a positivist framework; compare note 31.

[61] See for example C. Hartmann, *Yerba Buena: Land Grab and Community Resistance*

in San Francisco, Glide, San Francisco, 1974.

[62] Weiner and Deak, for example, have shown the very different world views of the Connecticut state highways departments, and the state planning commissioners as they jointly plan the state's transportation network: P. Weiner and E. Deak, *Environmental Factors in Transportation Planning*, D. C. Heath, Lexington, Massachusetts, 1972.

[63] P. Dicken, 'Some Aspects of the Decision-Making Behavior of Business Organizations', in *Economic Geography* 47 (1971), 426–37.

[64] Cyert and March, *op. cit.*, p. 78.

[65] For example, J. Mercer, 'City Manager Communities in the Montreal Metropolitan Community', in *Canadian Geographer* 18 (1974), 352–66.

[66] This would help explain the familiar pattern of cooptation of organisational watch-dogs set up in the public interest. Repeated interaction with the organisation being regulated leads to a convergence of attitudes, and ultimately to a sharing of its view of the world.

[67] Mannheim, *op. cit.*, p. 187.

[68] See, for example, Yi-Fu Tuan, 'Geography, Phenomenology, and the Study of Human Nature', in *Canadian Geographer* 15 (1971), 181–92.

[69] See Schutz' analysis of the existential dilemma of the stranger: A. Schutz, 'The Stranger', in *American Journal of Sociology* 49 (1944), 499–507.

[70] The classic study of adjustment problems remains one of the early publications of the Chicago school: W. Thomas and F. Znaniecki, *The Polish Peasant in Europe and America*, Knopf, New York, 1927.

[71] For example, P. Cressey, *The Taxi-Dance Hall*, University of Chicago Press, Chicago, 1932; P. Hugill, 'Social Conduct on the Golden Mile', in *Annals* 65 (1975), 214–28.

[72] This contextual effect has often been observed in the geographic literature, for example, B. Robson, *Urban Analysis*, Cambridge University Press, Cambridge, 1969; Schutz has examined it from the subjective perspective, Schutz, *op. cit.*, note 69.

[73] G. Bachelard, *The Poetics of Space*, Beacon Press, Boston, 1969, p. xxxiii; also Y. Tuan, 'Place: An Experiential Perspective', in *Geographic Review* 65 (1975), 151–65.

[74] D. Clark, 'The Concept of Community: A Reexamination', in *Sociological Review* 21 (1973), 397–416.

[75] R. Sommer, *Tight Spaces: Hard Architecture and How to Humanize It*, Prentice-Hall, Englewood Cliffs, 1974.

[76] The slogan on a banner at a recent rally for native land rights in Canada. Place may also lead to a stigmatized identity: for example, the wrong side of the tracks, the clues of certain regional dialects and, as the television series reminds us, in Victorian house-holds, below stairs as opposed to upstairs.

[77] These questions are taken up in detail in two volumes presently in preparation: A. Buttimer, *Rhythm, Routine, and Symbol*; D. Ley and M. Samuels (eds.), *Humanistic Orientations in Geography*.

[78] Sorre, *op. cit.*, note 24, p. 199.

[79] Schutz, *op. cit.*, 1960, note 51, p. 207.

B. MARCHAND

DIALECTICS AND GEOGRAPHY

> The dutiful child of modern Civilization is possessed
> by a fear of departing from the facts which, in the
> very act of perception, the dominant conventions
> of science, commerce, and politics-cliché-like —
> have already molded; his anxiety is none other
> than the fear of social deviation.
>
> HORKHEIMER and ADORNO, 27: xiv

During the 1960's, geography in English speaking countries enjoyed a period
of development and enthusiasm without precedent: with new generations
flooding the universities and dissent shaking the campuses, old structures
seemed ready to crumble and even among academic geographers, new ideas
were welcome, sometimes hungrily looked for. Then, the middle-class, in
western Europe and North America, became frightened by its own boldness
and, moved by changes in the economy, contradicted itself and looked back
with nostalgia to the 1950's. A new generation of graduate students started
refusing mathematical methods and, in strong defiance of what it called
'reason', advocated personal contacts, 'empathy' and socially 'relevant' issues:
a 'radical' geography, often strongly colored by Christian ideology, appeared,
at the antipodes — or so it seemed — of mathematical modelling. It seems as if
a pendulum was endlessly moving from technology to mysticism and back,
with little hope to break the vicious cycle.

There is a way out of this sterile dilemma, but it is carefully barred by the
prevalent ideology: it would consist in replacing the present *dichotomic*
opposition of the extremes by a *dialectical* opposition leading necessarily to
synthesis. To show this is the purpose of this paper.

A characteristic of North American social sciences, which is most surprising for a Continental European, is an extreme disdain for philosophy, and
particularly for modern philosophy. In most book stores, fundamental texts
are few, usually shelved away under the title 'Philosophy, Religion and
Occultism': Hegel and Sartre are mixed with Gurdieff, St. John of the Cross,
and Black Magic in a strange, but non-dialectical, mixture of opposites. Geographers using philosophers always stop at Kant, who, characteristically,

237

represents the Enlightenment at his peak. The cataclysm of Hegel's work, closing an era and building the foundations of all modern thought (e.g., Marx, Freud, Nietzsche) is not even discussed but conveniently ignored. Everything which has been important, controversial or pregnant with endless moral, social and political transformations for the past 150 years constitutes an enormous blind spot. Some particularly adventuresome social scientists may skirt it and use the work of a few people at its margins — Russell, Wittgenstein, Heidegger, Jung, Fromm — but they keep avoiding the centre of the maelstrom.

A related intellectual characteristic is an extreme defiance of intelligence and of the act of reflection: students keep opposing the 'real world', 'out there', source of all truth and all reality, to their thoughts, constructions of the mind whose only role, it seems, is to reproduce clumsily the external world. The sole merit of a model is to fit closely the data in a self-defeating effort to copy the 'real world': what would be the use of a model fitting perfectly? Unfortunately (or fortunately?) the fit is 'always bad, because the real world is too complex for human thought to grasp it'. In this way, geography seems condemned to a dumb contemplation of the Creation, or to a futile effort to imitate an un-imitable world. The dichotomic opposition between subject and object is total and leads into a dead-end.

This paper is an effort to overcome such sterile attitudes through Dialectical Reason.[1] After presenting the problem of knowledge in geography, it introduces dialectics, shows how present society tries to refuse dialectics, but how, in doing so, it cannot but help the re-emergence of dialectical thought.

I. GEOGRAPHY AND THE PROBLEM OF KNOWLEDGE

The initial task is to define the object of geographical study, and secondly to show the necessity of a formal language. It is at this point that the danger of perverting such language into a myth appears.

I.1. *The Subject of Knowledge*

Present geographic research relies upon three basic assumptions: (1) there is information we can record and analyze, (2) such analysis will give us objective knowledge (i.e., as a result whose value is independent of the observer) and (3) such knowledge is desirable. These three assumptions are very much open to question.

I.1.1. *Is 'objectivity' possible?* Classical science assumed it was possible to look at things from the outside, and to study them without altering them and without letting the scientist's personality interfere. Modern physics has shown the first hypothesis was false, while modern social science does not believe the second holds anymore. The researcher carries with him a whole social, moral and political background which he cannot discard. No 'objective' white study of Detroit's ghetto is possible, no matter how much mathematics the geographer uses. The choice of the variables, the design of the models, and their ultimate interpretation will be biased. Radical criticisms are true, but they should be developed to their ultimate conclusions. A subjective attitude is no way to solve the problem either, since it does not bridge the gap between different social environments any better.

Geographers must realize they are involved, they are 'in situation', and go beyond the opposition between objectivity and subjectivity to the concept of intersubjectivity, a dialectical synthesis of both. Their involvement in a social system enables them, through the study of other systems, to know their own society and its problems. Bias is unavoidable, but it is also the source of perspective and knowledge. As Merleau-Ponty has noted:

> As long as I keep the ideal vision of an absolute observer, of a knowledge without viewpoint, I cannot see my situation but as a cause of error. If I recognize, however, that, thanks to it, I am involved in all the action and all the knowledge which have any meaning for me, ... then my contact with social phenomena in the limits of my situation appears to me as the origin of all truth, even of scientific truth. Social phenomena are not only ... objects but form mainly my own situation.[2]

A black ghetto is the place to study the defects of white society and the biases of the white geographer. Conversely, it is in the white environment that geographers can find the causes for ghetto problems. To limit the study to the slum is to avoid the real slum problems.

In a recent Antonioni movie ("The Passenger"), a reporter interviews a black leader who has graduated from a western university, but lives back in the tribal environment. The reporter asks him how he can cope with native religion, magic, local medicine practices, witchcraft, etc. And the black man responds: "If I answered you, you would not learn very much about me, but your questions say a lot about you and your world".

The whole dialectic subject–object is at work here, but will have to be explicated later on.

I.1.2. *Is knowledge desirable?* Some geographers, following a larger movement among the physical and social sciences, seem to believe there are subjects

which should not be investigated.[3] Two points are confused here: the search
for knowledge and its subsequent use. In the social sciences, as in nuclear
physics, some findings may be used very dangerously, and it might be appropriate that their dissemination should be restricted. This is a political problem. Such control *a posteriori* is sometimes confused with a refusal to undertake research, *a priori*. The reasons for such an attitude can be traced back
quite a long way, to three related themes.

(a) Thirst for knowledge appears, in the Christian tradition, as a competition with God: it is the first sin, even before sexual pleasure. The tradition
stemming from the Tree of Science and its Apple is well documented, from
Thomas à Kempis' *Imitation of Christ* to *Faust*. A more vulgar, and more
popular example is the Frankenstein story, or the myth of the Sorcerer's
Apprentice. Its extraordinary success shows how deeply it is rooted in occi-
dental thought and perhaps even more strongly in the Anglo-Saxon puritan
tradition.

(b) What could be called the 'Frankenstein Complex' is extremely convenient: it switches criticism from the people using scientific tools wrongly to
the tools themselves. It changes a political argument into an ideological one
and transmutes a logical search for causes into a magical fear of effects. It
conveniently dispenses with the problem of judging the people who exercise
undue power. The means are typically taken for the end, and the guile shifted
from the user to the technique. Machines, not social organization, are responsible for pollution. Kubrick, in "2001: A Space Odyssey" uses a variant of the
same trick: the machine itself becomes alive and can thus bear its own
responsibility. The popular myth of the computer rests necessarily upon a
convenient anthropomorphism. In the same vein, when Bunge and Bordessa[4]
attack the cold steel machines which kill children rather than a society whose
existence is based on making, selling and using those machines, this is nothing
but *Reification* in mirror image in a society where Man is changed into a thing
and it is logical that human responsibilities be attributed to things.

(c) As a variety of the Frankenstein myth, the story of Pygmalion is most
interesting because the Creator is overwhelmed by his creature, the product of
his work turns against him. It is not difficult to recognize here Hegel's dialectic of the Master and the Servant, and, subsequently, Marx's concept of alienation.

I.1.3. *Is information available?* Information, in a general sense, means the
geographer's knowledge about a given phenomenon. We will restrict it subsequently to the more precise meaning the word has in Information Theory.

Information about what? Geographical events are often so poorly defined that there is a dangerous ambiguity about concepts and a near-impossibility of fitting different texts together. Migration, city, urban center, urban function, suburb, and region are key concepts, but nowhere are they precisely defined.

Traditionally, to define is to encode, to delimit, and, in a way to impoverish a concept. This is possible only if the concept is rich enough, and substantiated by numerous observations. Clear-cut definitions are immensely facilitated by long periods of empirical observations: astronomy could be precisely defined and use mathematics only after centuries of astronomical observation — particularly after the work of Tycho Brahe.[5] The social sciences, and Geography in particular, lack adequate data and precise and useful definitions. Geographers need a code fitting unambiguous names to well-delimited concepts, i.e., a *vocabulary*.

A geography without information? An observation does not carry a constant amount of information: to find a harbor at the back of an estuary, or to observe snow at 18 000 feet, is trivial and does not carry much fresh knowledge. The quantity of information is related to the probability of an observation by a logarithmic law defined in Information Theory.[6]

Take something with a given location: a small region, a meander, or a particular slope on a mountain. Consider the set of all the possible geographical phenomena we could reasonably observe at this location today: a large city, a farm town, a dairy farm, a harbor, a desert, and so on. Some geographers argue that one event (or one group of events), was bound to happen and that the others were almost impossible. The probability of the event actually observed is near almost unity, and the Information, *stricto sensu*, practically nil. Somewhat exaggerated, this is the *determinist* viewpoint. In the formal statement of information theory:

$$H = - \sum_{i=1}^{n} p_i \log p_i$$

where p_i is virtually unity, $\log p_i$ is zero, and so H is zero.

If we insist on the complexity of historic evolution, on the number of possible combinations of an enormous number of historical events, then the results are astronomical; the probability of observing the actual event is practically nil, and its information content is almost zero. $-\log p_i$ will assume an enormous value, but p_i will be so small that the information content H will also be close to zero. This is an extreme case of the *possibilist* school.

Let us assume history does not follow an erratic path but obeys some model, for instance a dialectical struggle for the means of production. A geographic phenomenon is not random anymore, nor totally determined, and with a probability noticeably different from 0 and 1, it now gives information. Marxism, as used by George in his early texts, enables the geographer to extract information from his observations, but only at the price of putting history above geography, time upon space. Marxists have characteristically neglected spatial differentiation. They equate, sometimes, the relationship between Imperialist England and Colonial India to the relationship between workers and factory-owners in Manchester. A historian or an economist may accept the comparison. A geographer simply cannot believe that such an analysis exhausts all the phenomena. Far from being 'a new determinism',[7] spatial theories, the core of quantitative geography, enable the geographer to avoid the dilemma of the determinists and the possibilists. The 'uniqueness' viewpoint does not give any information. The geographer must establish relations between events, i.e., define a *syntax*.

The geographer needs a vocabulary and a syntax — a language or a system of formalization to extract information from empirical observations and to put them into relation. Oral languages are but a few of all possible languages. A mathematical model, as a set of relations defined on a set of elements, is also a language. The gravity model may express relations between cities as well as, or even better than, a phrase in English. Even a fashion, as a social language, enables men and women to express themselves.[8]

I.2. *Language and its Perversion: The Myth*

Mathematical languages, among others, are accused of giving a biased view of reality. But what form does such perversion of a language take? Modern linguists[9] have shown how a language is transformed into myth. Mathematical formalization, the main language of modern geographers, has fallen today under heavy criticism, because it is suffering such a perversion.

I.2.1. *Language and myth. Language and Contingency*: Let us define roughly a language as the assignment of a sign (the *signifier*, e.g., the *word* 'tree') to a meaning or an object (the *signified*, e.g., the *object* 'tree'). The *signification* is their dialectical adequation. Fundamentally, the relationship between signifier and signified is quite arbitrary and *contingent*: the sounds 'church' or 'car' could as well have been attached to the object tree. This does not mean that any group of sounds would do: if we only had very short sounds they would be much less numerous than the objects or concepts we wanted to describe, and such paucity would lead to ambiguity. Very long words would be inconvenient, and probably would be shortened quite spontaneously. Oral languages, of course, present examples of both. The set of all possible signifiers must be restricted for each language to a subset of 'convenient' signifiers. This does not alter the fundamental and contingent relation signifier-signified.

1.2.2. *Myth and nature.* The myth is a parasitic language feeding upon another language. Barthes gives the example of a news picture published in France during the colonial crisis of the late 1950's. A black soldier salutes the French flag: this is the signifier. The signified is: respect for the flag. The signification is clear: patriotism. The choice of the subject, at this stage, is contingent: many other images could mean patriotism (Figure 1).

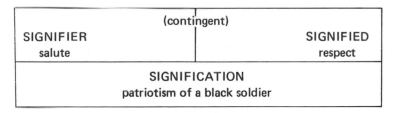

Fig. 1. Language.

In the context of the Algerian war, however, an African soldier saluting the French flag has a deeper meaning. Patriotism becomes itself the signifier of a deeper signified: colonial domination. The new signification is that colonialism is widely accepted and is right. The trick stems from the duality of the signifier. It is no longer a hollow form, chosen contingently, but also a signification. The black soldier has been chosen purposely. The relation between signifier (itself a signification) and signified appears then as beyond any doubt as natural (it is a fact that the African soldier salutes . . .). We have language — the saluting soldier *means* patriotism — and myth — the patriotism of an African *justifies* colonialism. All the power of the myth lies in this transformation of the contingent relation into a necessary and natural one (Figure 2).

1.2.3. *Myths in geography.* Mathematicals models, considered as a language signifying the regularities observed among certain data, are commonly perverted into myth.

NEW SIGNIFIER

Signifier salute	Signified respect	SIGNIFIED colonialism
Signification patriotism of a black solider		
SIGNIFICATION colonialism is accepted and loved		

Fig. 2. Myth, a language feeding on a language.
(After Barthes, *Mythologies*, Seuil, Paris, 1957.)

A regional equilibrium model may give a form to relations observed between locations. It signifies that, using data sorted and collected in a certain way, regularities may be observed in regional flows. The key point is that other signifiers (e.g., descriptive discourse, other models, dialectical analyses) could signify those regularities, or more important ones. This model has been chosen arbitrarily among other signifiers (but not by chance, since it must be somehow adequate to the object signified) in order to justify a certain economic system, rather than to represent 'objectively' an aspect of the world.

But a myth has developed about such a language. Regularities among spatial flows are supposed to signify the existence of an order in the world. Those particular regularities exhibited by the model do not play the role of a *contingent* property: they become signification. Here appears a *natural* relation (i.e. unique and necessary) justifying, indirectly, the existence of an underlying order, i.e., the market mechanism in a 'free enterprise' economy. The signification of such a myth is the natural existence of an Invisible Hand acting in the best interest of all.

By the same process, Scientism considers scientific languages expressing reality as natural: they are supposed to exhaust all of the world and contain the solutions to all questions. Such an illusion of totality is a religious inheritance. Geographers criticizing the scientists myth of Science as God are certainly right.[10]

A symmetrical myth, considering Science as the Devil, is also developing today in radical geography. The scientist myth, together with the Frankenstein complex, leads quickly to a mythical view of science (and especially mathematics), as satanic. Models and machines seem to revolt against man, their creator, as Satan did against God, so that their use would contain "risks of dehumanizing human realities".[11] Revolt is punished by revolt. In the Frankenstein epic, the creature rebels against the doctor because the doctor rebelled against God. Some radical geographers, unconsciously in need for a Law of Retaliation, look only for those points where mathematical methods will break down and lead to absurdities. With a great sigh of relief they find them, and morality is saved. Other geographers, in a self-contradictory attitude, recognize a need for mathematical methodology, but do not want to soil their hands. They prefer to wait for the information to be treated quantitatively by others and afterwards have it submitted to them. They want geography "to refuse ... to be the expression of some determinism and the instrument of some oppression".[12] Similarly, Marxism has been used recently by some radical geographers, not as a language expressing the structure of society, but as a myth of Revolution. A Marxist vocabulary is mixed with anti-Marxist concepts, a contradiction which would destroy the coherence of a language, but does not alter the effect of myth.[13]

I.2.4. *Back from myth to language.* How are we, then, to avoid the myth and come back to language? Modern mathematics shows the way. The basic lesson of set theory is that all forms of mathematics are arbitrary and contingent. Gödel has shown the Axiom of Choice is independent of the other ten basic axioms: many other theories could be developed just as well. Mathematical formalization is no more the expression of some unique and natural structure of the world, i.e., a myth, as it appeared to nineteenth century Scientism. It is simply a set of signifiers, chosen among many others, and fitting adequately, but *contingently*, the world. Physics has followed the same path. A theory, today, does not pretend to explain the world uniquely anymore, but only to fit the observations conveniently. Various and different theories of light coexist.

By refusing to be 'natural' and unique, but only contingent and many, mathematics and physics have ceased to be religious myths and have become languages. Unfortunately, a century later, the social sciences have followed the path to myth.

I.3. *The Object of Knowledge*

What are geographical objects? They may simply be elements of a set: isolated phenomena like individuals, cities, regions. Or they may be interrelations between elements: this is the 'structuralist' approach, focussing on a set of relations for which the concept of equilibrium is crucial. Finally, they may be self-contradicting objects: any phenomenon is relative, existing only by contradiction with another and with itself.

I.3.1. *Phenomena as individual elements.* Consider the black inner cities of America. One approach to studying them is to focus research on the individuals — on their personal characteristics, their idiosyncrasies — and to consider society only as the sum of all the individuals. Such research relies upon personal contacts, fieldtrips, and intuition. Empathy opens the way towards the individuals, and their problems are, and can only be, personal. Poverty is explained by laziness or lack of sufficient education, according to the particular stand of the observer. Poverty-striken districts are explained by economic decay: economic decay by the lack of qualified skills and by crime; crime by drug abuse; drug abuse by poor family structure and the lack of hope, which are related to the bad environment and the unemployment. The reasoning is largely circular because the geographer is dealing with problems typical of one group of individuals. Since society is the whole set of elements, there must be something wrong with an individual ill-adapted to the whole. A social scientist comes up with individual reasons, even pathological ones. A man revolting against society must be a sick man.

Causes of social problems are *moral*: if the landlords were less greedy, the workers less indifferent, the 'capitalists' more altruistic, conflicts would disappear. Action relies on empathy and feeds on mysticism; individuals are responsible for social wrongs.

I.3.2. *The relations between phenomena: structuralism. The synchronic structure.* Another approach is to study the relations between men and to focus our research upon them: a man's behaviour is largely determined by the system of relations in which he is involved. Define a relation (or several) on a set, which transforms it into a graph. The whole set is much more than the sum of its elements because now a structure appears, which is synchronic, or in equilibrium. The task of the geographer is to burrow under the appearances to discover the underlying structure. The moral quality of the individual is immaterial, or perhaps more accurately, undiscernible. Conflicts are explained by the social structure, not by personal qualities or defects. The misery in the ghettos does not stem from the greediness of the landlord or the laziness of its inhabitants, but from certain kinds of relationships between worker and industry-owner. There is no conspiracy (although pressure groups do exist and play important roles) to impoverish or to exploit, but the inner logic of the system leads necessarily to such effects because the system is *subject.*

To discover those structures, often paradoxical and contrary to the appearances, one needs powerful tools, mainly philosophical and mathematical. Since those relations are finite in number and discrete, the use of the continuous mathematics of the eighteenth and nineteenth centuries does not seem particularly promising. Geography has probably relied too much on classical mathematics borrowed from physics, and not enough on modern discrete mathematics derived from set theory.

The Diachronic Structure. Those steady-state or uniformly evolving structures are still quite unsatisfactory: time transforms a structure into another. The problem is to explain such transformation, i.e., to introduce diachrony. A uniform evolution is not enough. While an equilibrium mechanism is necessary to define a structure, it makes it impossible to explain how a structure can change itself into another, quite different one. Structuralists cannot dismiss the existence of diachronic structures, but they seem to be unable to grasp them, and to incorporate brutal changes in them.

The problem can be presented with elementary topological notions. Let X be a given society with a particular structure T1, conceived as a topology representing the relations between individuals. A change of structure, for example, a revolution, will be equivalent to an identity function 1 sending each member of the society, at time t, with the topology T1 to itself at time $t + 1$, with topology T2:

$$1: (X, T1) \rightarrow (X, T2).$$

Three cases are possible:

(i) The identity function 1 is an homeomorphism, i.e., T1 and T2 are equal. The structure has not changed and is still synchronic.

(ii) Function 1 is continuous but 1^{-1} is not continuous. The two structures are not the same any more. The continuity of 1 assures that changes in our society will be progressive: two social groups who were 'near' in the first period are still near in the second. Elementary topology shows, however, that in this case T2 must be coarser than T1: the new social system T2 is less structured, less organized than the preceding one. Our society tends necessarily towards a chaotic state where all structure vanishes.

(iii) We must then assume that 1 is not continuous, but represents a kind of catastrophic evolution: relations between men and social groups are broken and torn apart. We must then abandon the hope of explaining the passage from one structure to the other. We are left with two synchronic structures separated by an unforeseen event of catastrophic proportions. Thom's *Catastrophe Theory* tries to deal with this kind of rupture.[14]

I.3.3. *The contradictions within the phenomena.* The dialectical method deals particularly well with dynamic evolution and catastropic turns, but it is much more than a method: it is the synthetical product of Reason contradicting itself through the evolution of philosophy.

II. THE DIALECTICAL REASON

Hegelian dialectics are the result of twenty-two centuries of progress in philosophy, where every great thinker has negated his predecessors and built upon their works. Philosophy has its tradition, its famous problems, its jargon, like mathematics, but with probably more subtlety. To explain Hegelian thought without such background is as hopeless a task as discussing tensor analysis when matrix algebra is ignored. We shall try only a modest introduction here.

The basis of Dialectics is the discovery that to negate is a positive act, the only one fitted to the nature of things (which are finite and self-contradictory) and of human thought.

The foundation of Hegel's thought and of all modern philosophy is *Time*, that is, *Change*. Everything is seen as in perpetual transition into something else: it is still itself (or we could not identify it anymore), but it becomes, at the same time, other. It contains in itself something different from itself, its own contradistinction. Everything is in historical evolution. A thing A becomes (or negates itself into) Not A; then Not A negates itself, in turn, into Not (Not A), but this is not returning back to the starting point: the thing is realizing itself through those successive transformations. It accumulates an history, an experience: time is not reversible. This is in complete contradiction of mathematical logic, (or 'formal' or 'common' logic) which is circular: A is equivalent to Not (Not A).

Such difference is easily explained. Mathematical logic is a logic of *quantity*: the nature of the variables is fixed; then quantities are compared along a one-dimensional axis with only two directions, plus and minus. Contradiction is represented by inversing a relation: A becomes $-A$. Through a second inversion, $(-A)$ becomes $-(-A) = A$. Conversely, Hegel's logic deals with *qualities*. He understands 'truth' as in the expression: 'a true friend'. We know what a 'true friend' should be; John Doe might slowly, through conflicting experiences, become a 'true friend'.

II.1. *The Nature of Dialectics*

II.1.1. *The finitude of things.* Dialectics is not just a conventient method which we may fit to observations, as one may choose between a linear or non-linear model. It stems from the very nature of all things: first, they are in time, and perpetually changing; second, they are qualitatively finite (the colour yellow can be defined only by reference to other colours, red or blue); it includes in itself the existence of what it is not. Hegel prefigures here the basic concepts of topology: the definition of a closed set, which contains its own boundary. All finite closed sets, if they are not disconnected (radically separated) must have a non-empty intersection: they must include something different from themselves.[15]

II.1.1. *The intellect.* Everything we know is known through thought (even a raw sensation is an element of thought). How does the intellect work? I observe a city existing, say London (Existence or Being) but I also have a *universal* idea of the City (Notion), of which London is only a *particular* realisation. Which, of the particular or the universal, is the foundation of my thought? This question is one of the most important problems in philosophy. It came to a crossroad in the seventeenth and eighteenth centuries: for British Empiricism (Hume, Locke) the particular comes first. Man accumulates observations (sense-perceptions), then generalizes: the Idea is similar to an arithmetic mean and typically, classical (frequentist) statistics developed in England. There is nothing in the intellect: our thoughts are the reflection of the present state of the world.

"It is not reason, which is the guide of life, but custom".[16] Then, there is no good or bad, or better said, the state of the world we observe is necessarily good, since we have no criterion against which to compare it and to judge it. This philosophy, developing with the industrial revolution, is totally conservative and pessimistic:

If experience and custom were to be the sole source of (man's) knowledge and belief, how could he act in accordance with ideas and principles as yet not accepted and established? Truth could not oppose the given order or reason speak against it. The result was not only skepticism, but conformism. The empiricist restriction of human nature to knowledge of the "given" removed the desire both to transcend the given and to despair about it. "For nothing is more certain than that despair has almost the same effect upon us as enjoyment, and that we are no sooner acquainted with the impossibility of satisfying any desire that the desire itself vanishes. When we see that we have arrived at the utmost extent of human reason, we sit down contented" (Hume).[17]

German Idealism (Leibniz, Kant, Fichte, and particularly, Hegel) took an opposite stand: Sense-perception is characterized by multiplicity (of impressions), finitude, and change. What defines thought is the unification of sensations by the unique Ego: the thinking 'I' builds the universal from the variety of sense-perceptions, and generates the Notion.[18] When Locke said "There is nothing in the intellect" (i.e., every content of it is coming from sensation), Leibniz added "but the intellect itself" (i.e., its unifying capacity). German Idealism preserves human freedom: there is a criterion now, that is the notion, by which to judge the world. If the present state of things (Existence) does not correspond to the Notion, then, let us change it.

In a pragmatic society, such controversy is viewed as a senseless waste of time but it has, actually, the most important consequences.

Hegel's concept of reason has a distinctly critical and polemic character. It is opposed to all ready acceptance of the given state of affairs . . . . [19]

II.1.3. *The fundamental dialectical relations.*

(a) *Notion vs. Existence*: The notion of man includes the idea of freedom; his existence, however, might be slavery. This discrepancy between Notion (or Essence) and Being (or Existence) is, for Hegel, the source of all energy moving the world. The existence will, through successive contradictions, tend toward the essence.

(b) *The dialectic subject–object*: Pragmatic 'Common Sense' conceives the relations between subject and object in a most childish way. The subject of knowledge appears like a man looking from an ivory tower with binoculars, down to the 'real world' and writing down 'objectively' what he sees, or like a scientist in a submarine, observing through the window different fishes which pass by, undisturbed. No philosopher, not even the Empiricists, has ever proposed such an oversimplified conception: if subject and object were so radically separated, and since any form of knowledge is in the mind, the reality of the object would disappear. Everything would be totally subjective, and such a 'realistic' position would turn dialectically into total idealism. Knowledge, of course, is not 'immediate': between human beings living in the city and the Burgess concentric model, there are many intermediate steps, many 'mediations', whose study is the object of Logic.

Let us skip the technical discussion of the nature of perception. The Object is represented through *data* which are chosen, collected and sorted by society for the geographer, subject of knowledge. For instance, Census categories of employment were chosen in the U.S.A. at the turn of the century to make apparent social ascension in a society which was to give everybody his chance to climb to the top.[20] Many European censuses, conversely, report social groups according to the control they have on the means of production, in a typical marxist perspective. To exhibit social 'progress', whatever this means, is not easy with European data; to perform a marxist analysis of U.S. labor force is almost impossible: the object of knowledge is shaped, screened, and censored by society, that is by the collectivity in a dialectical relation with the individual, subject of knowledge. When geographers using factor analysis, analyse the same censuses and drop factors with low eigenvalues, they recover not the structure of the 'Real World' whatever this may mean, but the census structure. Is it so surprising that most North American cities present similar factorial structures?

Anyway, the data are multiple, separated and contingent. Reason then steps in (the unifying activity of the self) and generates the Notion, that is a *universal*. In this way, the object is largely a construction of the subject, which does not imply at all any reliance on a kind of subjective hallucination, but only that the subject is present at the core of the object.

The dialectical relation between both is still more subtle: anything which exists (i.e., is real) undergoes perpetual change but maintains its identity at the same time (or else it would vanish and disappear). From this viewpoint, any real object is a center of actions and reactions, and is a *subject*, not necessarily a conscious one. In a city, a neighbourhood, which retains its originality in spite of changes, is a subject inasmuch as it possesses certain mechanisms which allow it to resist the effect of changes in accessibility, land rent, land use, etc. It possesses inner laws of motion (e.g., ethnic cohesion, with its own sociological laws; zoning laws; local amenities; etc.) which explain how it can undergo changes and remain itself at the same time. The *definition* of an object involves much more than a simple list of characteristics or properties, which are static: it must explain its inner laws of motion.

The definition must express ... the movement in which a being maintains its identity through the negation of its conditions. In short, a real definition cannot be given in one isolated proposition, but must elaborate the real history of the object, for its history alone explains its reality.[21]

This does not imply at all any mystical (and absurd) kind of consciousness in a tree, a neighbourhood or a region, but only that the concept of subject is a general one (with man, as a thinking and self-conscious subject in a privileged position). Any existing thing is at the same time, and in turn a subject *and* an object.

Actually, 'Common Sense' runs into an absurd paradox, with its over-simplified conceptions: the subjective is *inside* the observer, and the objective is *outside* him (the student's 'real world out there'). But at the same time, *subjective* qualifies a particular perception, at a particular time, in a particular situation: the particular observed data; while *objective* is said of a model, a more general concept, less biased, less particular; a universal produced by the observer's thought. The meanings have been dialectically reversed.[22]

Anyone who, from want of familiarity with the categories of subjectivity and objectivity, seeks to retain them in their abstraction (i.e., their radical separation) will find that the isolated categories slip through his fingers before he is aware, and that he says the exact contrary of what he wanted to say.[23]

Such dialectical subtlety goes very far. The prevalent social ideology sorts our data and our concepts: to call them objective, i.e., unbiased and 'true' is to accept blindly the view society wants to give of itself. To oppose, as a dichotomy, subject and object is to misunderstand the mechanism of knowledge, where subject and object take reciprocally the position of each other.

From Hegel to the Frankfurt School, different emphasis has been put on different forms of dialectics. In Marx, it takes materialist forms as a struggle between opposed and interdependent social classes. In Marcuse, it is essentially the contrast between what a thing is and what it could be: the emphasis is on the potentialities which are not realized by the present social organization. *Facts* are incomplete, thus abstract, because they negate all other possibilities. A student asked to enumerate the data he should gather to study transportation in Toronto explained that he would not consider bicycle traffic at all because it is presently negligible, which is true and false at the same time: the enormous potentialities of the bicycle in urban traffic (or of any other mode not presently used) are negated; consider however the examples of Amsterdam or Copenhagen.

Dialectical thought ... undermines the sinister confidence in the power and language of facts. ... This power of facts is an oppressive power; it is the power of man over man, appearing as objective and rational condition.[24]

II.2. *Dialectics in Geography*

Dialectical Reason has not yet been applied to geographical questions, but through Marxist analysis, with a very strong emphasis on economic mechanisms. Marxist analysis is a development of Hegel's thought, but at this point, we wish to introduce the reader to Hegel's thinking, as modernized in the Frankfurt school. Convincing examples are necessary at this point; philosophy, however, has been so systematically and purposefully neglected in North

American social sciences (and geography so poorly developed in Continental Europe), that any use it can be put to is necessarily new and still clumsy. The following dialectical analysis of some geographical questions are discussed here only to encourage the reader to go further.

II.2.1. *Lösch regional model as a dialectical process.* The most important and most overlooked conclusion of Central Place Theory is Lösch's demonstration that a perfectly homogeneous landscape, with perfectly similar customers, working inside the framework of perfect competition, will necessarily develop, from its inner laws of motion, into an heterogeneous landscape with rich, active sectors, and poor, depressed regions. The regional system negates itself and generates dialectically its contradiction, as regional inequalities appear. Until Lösch, geographers explained such heterogeneity by physical factors (e.g., soils, climate) or external human factors (e.g., emigration of labour, presence of rich families). Lösch has shown that, even if such disparities do not exist (this is the role of those assumptions of a uniform plain, similar customers, etc. which have been so criticized and so misunderstood), the inner dialectical logic of the system turns it, from the inside, into its very contrary.

Actually, Lösch follows Hegel very closely. In *The Philosophy of Nature*, Hegel shows that the primary determination of nature is *space*, characterized by the property of *self-externality*. Space is first that which is external to itself (like the open set which does not contain its boundary). This indeterminate space negates itself into that which is contained in itself: *the point*. The point is "the negation of space ... which is posited within space".[25] The point negates itself in turn into something which is self-contained, but other than the point, i.e., the line: the line 'passes over into the plane' and so on.

The whole set of geometric figures are built by a necessary inner mechanism of self-negation. In the same way, Lösch posits the centers, which generate necessarily the transport lines between them, then the regions. As Curry pointed out, the very appearance of transport axes negates the original assumption of an isotropic plain. In the same way, the development of distinct sectors (regions) negates the symmetry of the transportation axis. Actually, Lösch's regional model is directly inspired by Hegel's 'mathematical mechanics', which should not be too surprising.

In Hegel, this whole set of geometric figures contradicts itself into a synthesis which will still be spatially self-contained, but other: i.e., into Time or Change. The point, through change in time, can become other while remaining somehow the same. The regional system becomes dynamic, not for a contingent decision to add a time-variable, but because the contradictions between poor and rich sectors sets necessarily the stage for conflicts.

II.2.2. *The dialectics center-periphery.* In Roman antiquity, the economy was based on agricultural production: the word meaning money comes from 'cattle' (*pecus*). Roman civilisation, however, developed as an urban civilisation: its expression was the city, with its typical center, the Forum (from *for* to talk) where people met and talked. The Empire developed as an immense hierarchy of cities dominated by The City, Roma, which was adored as a goddess. But those cities were sucking the energies of the countryside: products, capital, men (particularly through enslavement of small farmers ruined by debts). The very development of this urban civilisation produces its collapse.

The dialectical contradiction between city and farm leads to a synthetical form: the merovingian *villa*. It was a big farm, surrounded by crops and pastures. At the same time, it had urban functions like a city: production with craftsmen, a political role (the owner was a lord, heir of the Roman representative, with his tribunal and his clientele), and religious functions: a chapel and, later, a school.

In a further dialectical step, this complex form explodes into two opposed and related components: the *fortress* and the *village*. Their relation is a simplified form of the master–slave dialectic.

This antithetic contradiction leads to a new synthetic form: the *medieval city*, opposed to the village because it has autonomy and political power, opposed to the fortress, because its inhabitants are commoners, and it is a production center, negating the pair because it represents commerce and the beginning of industrial production, a new form of economics.

Such an illustration of the geographic dialectical processes is clearly oversimplified. A detailed analysis of the underlying economic mechanisms and a finer description of the intermediary contradictions would be most enlightening, but it has been done much more extensively elsewhere. Some students (particularly D. Evans) in our seminar at the University of Toronto, have developed a parallel dialectical analysis of the Inside–Outside relationship. Private property generates the fear of trespassing, and the concept of 'defensive space', that is of collective organisation: hence the appearance of spatial forms (family lot, neighbourhood, nation) which are private for the outside, but collective for the inside. Private appropriation of space generates spatial segregation and negates itself in protective collective organization. Private property culminates in nationalism and destroys itself in what is collectively needed for the protection of the nation: the central government, a defense budget and a tax system on property. There is a strong sense of humour in dialectics.

II.2.3. *The dialectics of nature in North America.* The attitude towards Nature is a fascinating reflection of deep dialectical relationships at the economic and social level. At the end of the nineteenth century, the concept of free market had not yet become a myth. There was a quite perfect competition between independent producers. Darwin paints Nature as the stage for a fierce competition between living beings. Realizing the survival of the fittest, natural processes are seen as cruel, pitiless, but healthy and necessary.

In the 1930's and 1940's, cartels, holdings, corporations largely smoothed competition. After the troubles of the Depression, the accent was on organisation and order: with general obedience, prosperity was round the corner. Nature, as seen through Walt Disney cartoons, is a sugar-coated paradise: in *Snow White*, there is actual division of labor among the animals cleaning the dwarfs' house; everybody is in his or her place (indicated by racial characteristics) and everybody loves it. In the 1950's, when Disney productions released their famous documentaries on wildlife (e.g., "The Living Desert"), the myth explodes on the screen: because those are photographs and not man-made cartoons, the image (superb actually) shows real animal life, an impressive sequence of fear, hunger, violence and killings, while the spoken commentary, as sweet as ever, praises the goodness of God and the admirable order of Nature. The dialectic between image and words exposes the myth as never before.

Relation to Nature changes again with the recent Ecological movement. At a time where giant corporations begin to be feared, where Big Business starts appearing as a menace, people try to relate back to the last reserve of 'freedom', back to Nature's 'true competition'. This last step in the dialectical evolution of the concept of Nature is not a return to the Darwinist conception: there is much less fear of Nature's cruelty and much more longing for something people know unconsciously they have lost. Sometimes, the myth blows up, and instead of the healthy competition he expected, the civilized man finds the true violence of misery, as in "Deliverance": The false contradiction between the artificial urban life and the healthy fight against nature is brutally changed into what it has always been, the social dialectic between the city professional and the miserable Appalachian farmer.

City and Country are dialectically related. North American civilisation has always been urban, from the start, even when it endeavoured agricultural ventures. It is based on exploitation and destruction of nature. Hence this hate for the City and this desperate love for the Country. But Nature is nothing but the negation of the city, a place to go on holidays (which are just a necessary part of the production process) or of which to dream on the T.V. screen in the city. The paramount role of the city in North America explains dialectically the extreme attachment for the Country, which is much more loved, much more destroyed, much more desired and much more ignored than in Europe.

II.2.4. *Distance as a dialectical relation.* In Europe, until the end of the eighteenth century, social separation was based on privileges and titles: space played hardly any role. The different orders lived in the same places, often in the same buildings, with a weak vertical separation: the rich bourgeois had his shop on the ground floor, his apartment on the second or the third. Wealth and power decreased as one walked up the stairs, with the servant rooms under the roof. Next door could be the palace of a powerful prince who, if in need of money, would rent a part of it to commoners (as the Regent of France did in the eighteenth century Paris). Political bodies, such as the Parliaments, assembled the subjects, the sovereign, and the lords under the same roof, often in the same room. The King's gardens were sometimes crowded with the populace.

As the bourgeoisie triumphed, orders and privileges were abolished and social groups began to separate, as if geographical distances took the place of social ones. Traditional groups (nuclear and extended families, productive groups, feudal corporations, religious groups, and local communities of similar interests at the hamlet, village and parish levels), began to lose their importance, and man became increasingly isolated as an individual. Man here was neither a group member anymore, nor yet an autonomous being, but partially and painfully detached from the group.

Commuting appears as a way of negating simultaneously the home and the working place. It gives a man the opportunity of preserving his independence from his colleagues at work, and from his family at home, without breaking completely from either of them. Daily migration is made partly for its own sake. From this viewpoint, the middle-class does not choose suburban locations, and only then finds itself forced to commute. On the contrary, it chooses commuting to fulfill its desire for 'pulling out', and carefully chooses a suburban location to achieve this need. This would explain why so many housewives, in the suburbs around Paris where they have every shop at hand, take their cars so often and drive downtown into the polluted traffic jams.

Psychologists speak in such cases of the need for change. More deeply, the immersion in the downtown crowd decreases a person's *isolation* and increases her *loneliness*: it is a way of mixing with a group but remaining an individual. Loneliness in the crowd is a dialectical spatial process.

The geography of tourism would also be illuminated by such a dialetical view of space. The strong development of camping and trailers illustrates the dialectical need for both leaving and staying there at the same time. The desire for feeling uprooted would not be satisfied by an authentic immersion into true wilderness, nor by staying at home. Modern man needs to park his trailer in a forest and to look at the bears from his living room. National parks in the U.S.A. simultaneously tend to preserve wilderness and to make it domesticated. Organized hikes with a ranger enumerating the Latin names of the flowers shows how an exotic environment is dialectically presented as a foreign wilderness and at the same time dominated in a reassuring classification.

The tourist flying to Calcutta or Bogota wishes to live in some sort of Hilton as similar as possible to his home in order to feel the contradiction completely. It appears between the lounge and the street: he has only to push the door open, or look through its glass panels, to feel uprooted. The feeling of the contradiction would fade away if he were to live a few weeks in a local *posada* with Colombians because this would be discovering a new environment, and not just tourism anymore. Young tourists illustrate such a phenomenon. They often travel alone, going very far in search of new societies, but they gather together quickly as soon as they have the opportunity, to reconstruct their home, restoring in this way the contradiction.

Man can be separated from something by spatial distance (D) or by its strangeness, its exoticism (E): home and office are not very different from each other but separated commonly by miles (E is small, D large). In the case of the American tourist in Colombia, the exoticism of a Bogota street appears strong to one standing in a Hilton lounge; E is quite large, while D is small. Conversely, a Hilton is similar to an American home, but located thousands of miles away.

The events on the screen of a drive-in movie are ordinarily so different from the family environment that home can be reconstructed in the car itself. The most extreme case is presented by T.V. The television shows can be so exotic that they are allowed to take place inside the home: President Nixon's visit to China is viewed from the bed itself. If our model is appropriate, we may infer that T.V. would not have its place at home if it did not present very exotic shows. It is not located inside the family circle because it is a source of 'familiar' information but rather because it presents the most unfamiliar events, but domesticated and digested to fit the social system of values.

There seems to be an inverse relationship between exoticism and 'distance', perhaps something like:

$$E \cdot D = \text{constant.}$$

A more detailed analysis would show dialectical relations between the locations of home, work and pleasure. Fishing is a hobby largely because it is practiced far away from home. A few exceptional cases illustrate how inner contradictions are shifted to other relations but do not vanish. A circus, for example, is one of the very few places where home, work and hobby coincide. Such a group however is extremely mobile and moves over large distances. The movement appears to compensate for such a coincidence of functions and $(E \cdot D)$ is still a constant. If the circus settles down permanently in a place, the artists disperse their homes to various locations, and the exceptional coincidence disappears.

The counterculture communes are another example of such coincidence. The concentration of work, residence and pleasure at the same location is even one of the explicit goals of a community. But such groups tend to be very elastic, with members entering the group or leaving it in a much more mobile way than a middle-class family. Indeed, a basic feature of many communes is their desire to retire from the establishment world altogether, to pull out as far as possible.

III. MODERN INDUSTRIAL SOCIETY: THE NEGATION OF DIALECTICS

Modern industrial society, probably more strongly than any other past society, has strong built-in mechanisms whose role is to conserve it. It contradictorily aims toward quantitative development, while avoiding qualitative change. In Europe, North America, and still more so in Soviet Union, social organisation is presented as natural (unique and necessary) rather than cultural (which would be characteristic of one location, at one point of time, but subject to change). Dialectical Reason, whose role is to understand and to orient change, cannot be but anathema. Contradictions exist among phenomena: this cannot be helped, but a whole set of efforts try to freeze them into a sterile *dichotomic* opposition, avoiding particularly that the clash between thesis and antithesis passes over into a third term, the synthesis.

III.1. *The Reign of Dichotomy: the Either/Or Dilemma*

In the Classical Age (seventeenth and eighteenth centuries), the concept of Reason changed its meaning and its scope. Enlightenment consisted essentially in a radical *shrinking* of Reason.[26] Whereas it designated in the past the faculty of attaining Truth, it became then restricted to a pragmatic meaning: the ways and means to dominate nature, and man by the same token.

Technology is the essence of this knowledge . . . What men want to learn from nature is how to use it in order wholly to dominate it and other men . . . Power and knowledge are synonymous. For Bacon as for Luther, "knowledge that tendeth but to satisfaction is but as a courtesan, which is for pleasure, and not for fruit or generation".[27]

Imagination, art, erotism, and ethics, which were in Antiquity and to an extent in the Middle Ages constituents of Reason, were eliminated from it, which coincided in society with the elimination of everybody who did not fit usefully in the rational system of bourgeoise production. Foucault analyses in detail *le Grand Renfermement* (the great incarceration) of the classical age, when the madman, the libertine, the visionary, the poet and the rebel who roamed the roads quite freely in the Middle Ages were jailed indistinctly with the thief, because they were equally dangerous for the new order. As Reason shrank to Technology, its past components were relegated into Mysticism, forming two poles of the new consciousness, not dialectically conceived but radically separated and opposed in a frozen dichotomy.

From a social viewpoint, Christian ideology is also founded on the dichotomic separation between this world where the oppressed may hope, but must be patient and obedient (the 'Jenseits' of Goethe), and the other world, where liberation will happen (the 'Diesseits'). It developed as a religion of slaves and became soon a state religion, satisfying simultaneously the oppressed and the power to be. The opposition must remain dichotomic and frozen: if it were to emerge into a synthesis, it would explode in revolution, which so many heresies have tried, which have been carefully crushed throughout history.

The result is an endless swing of social thought as a pendulum between the technological pole ('a new electronic streetcar will solve urban problems') and the mystical one ('Love and prayer will resolve social conflicts'). The pendulum's movements seem to be a function of the GNP's rate of growth. Geography has experienced particularly strongly those blind rushes from one hope to the other, in the last twenty years; it seems to be presently leaving slowly, with a typical hangover, the mystical pole. But toward which new technology?

Dichotomic thought leaves *no exit*, as in Sartre's play: the hero, exhausted by sterile discussion, opens the door, but, afraid of the unknown, comes back into his self-accepted jail and concludes 'Let us start all over again'.

III.2. *Towards the Elimination of Dialectical Thought*

Unconscious efforts to eliminate dialectical reason from geography are many:

III.2.1. *Eliminating thought altogether.* The myth of 'the real world out there' is working in that direction. Models seem to many – particularly to students – to have no other merit than reproducing the data. Some students – and the best ones – wonder why to build a model at all?

Fear of intelligence (the Sin of Pride) has a similar effect. The present disinterest in university education is partly the product of those attitudes.

III.2.2. *Defusing contradictions: the concept of equilibrium.* Contradictions exist: there is no point in denying them, but they can be conveniently frozen in a dichotomic relation through the concept of *equilibrium*. Borrowed from mechanics, it assumes that all acting forces are qualitatively equivalent, and not self-contradictory. Then, they can be shown to cancel each other: from the mesh of intricated oppositions emerges not qualitative change, but a 'dynamic' immobility. The market concept as a stage of conflicting forces leading to a unique equilibrium price, is fundamental. Regional Economics is largely geared toward proving the existence of Regional or even General Equilibria.

III.2.2. *Eliminating dialectical relations through mathematics.* Mathematics used in Social Sciences, and particularly in geography, contain, built in them, the very negation of any dialectical process:

– Optimizing methods assume continuous functions, whose derivatives are defined, and convex sets, without conflicting solutions.

– Linear Models, the bulk of our mathematical models, are particularly characteristic:

(i) They assume inner homothetic properties ($a \cdot f(x) = f(ax)$), whereas dialectics show that a change in quantity induces a change in quality: homotethy is bounded.

(ii) The choice of origin is arbitrary ($f(x - a) = f(x) - f(a)$). Processes are supposed to be stationary, and the position in time is indifferent.

(iii) Complexity may be broken into a sum of independent components.

Most sophisticated methods of analysis rely on a form of spectral decomposition as in factor analysis ($X_\gamma = \Sigma_i a_{i\gamma} f_i$) or Fourier analysis. Relationships may be severed, without altering the observed phenomena, if decomposition is practiced along the natural cleavage lines (i.e., along the eigenvectors).

— Spaces are always assumed to be 'metric', i.e., full and continuous. They do not contain any inherent 'holes' or discontinuities.

III.2.4. *Severing the relationships.* The very opposite to dialectical thought is to conceive of the objects of knowledge as positive, close, self-sufficient entities. Extreme specialisation of scholars is an excellent way of avoiding a dialectical approach. Another one is to insist on monographs: one will study Appalachia without considering its dialectical relationships with the Megalopolis; or Bolivia as a closed set, neglecting its dependence on Europe and the United States.

Economists, in particular, tend to consider time as an independent variable which could be isolated (e.g., through principal component analysis and rotation), while other variables would remain intact. Phenomena are not conceived as existing only in an endless qualitative change, but as immobile, frozen entities from which time is not an intrinsic constituent. Psychologists feel more uneasy about partialing out change and Catell, in his confusing style, sees the difficulty and discusses it.[28]

This is duplicated in everyday behaviour; social tension is commonly avoided (but reinforced) through spatial separation: defensive space is a way of avoiding dialectical human relations.

III.2.5. *Projecting complex phenomena onto one unique axis.* Differences in quality (and therefore dialectics) vanish when the scientist reduces everything to measurements in only one unit: the concept of Exchange Value, the basis of present economy, is doing exactly that. Such a view of a 'one-dimensional man' leads to conceive a linear evolution of societies: they all follow the same path, only with different speeds. All cities will, sooner or later, emulate Los Angeles. Thus, geography negates itself into an oversimplified kind of history.[29]

III.2.6. *The biased 'objective science'.* The geographer starting a research project and using present 'objective' methods to get a clean, unbiased conclusion must realize that this approach is hopelessly biased, and that in doing so, he refuses, before he starts, any interpretation related with dialectical reasoning.

Dialectical thought implies	Positivist thought implies
— qualitative analysis and synthesis	— quantitative analysis, no synthesis
— looking for an explicit structure beyond the appearances: dialectic subject–object	— accumulating 'facts' considered as external, given 'objects'
— contradictions do not cancel each other: $A \neq \text{Not (Not } A)$	— formal logic: $A = \text{Not (Not } A)$
— everything finite is self-contradictory	— everything finite is homogeneous, adequate to itself
— quantitative changes induce qualitative changes: the nature of variables changes during the process, while remaining the same (a thing changes and becomes itself)	— variables are fixed
— Time is irreversible	— Time is reversible, the origin may be changed
— change (i.e., Time) is a component of the nature of each variable	— Time may be orthogonal to other variables and extracted from them

The 'objectivity' of positivist thought is a myth.

IV. NEGATING THE NEGATION: THE RESURGENCE OF DIALECTICS

All those unconscious efforts to defuse contradictions and conserve the prevailing order cannot, of course, alter the dialectical nature of processes, but only displace the contradictions: they reappear elsewhere, still more obvious.

IV.1. *The Inner Contradictions of Dichotomic Thinking*

Since Reason does not play a critical role but is restricted to pragmatic efficiency, modern social sciences keep proposing models which are increasingly efficient in an increasingly absurd context. Urban transportation is a good example: Linear Programming or other powerful methods help in designing minimum cost transportation systems, but nobody seems to wonder at the increasing separation of home from working place. The intrinsic absurdity of living at 10, 20, or 30 miles from the office; of commuting twice this distance daily; of choosing a home in a 'Green' suburb which one never enjoys; of leaving it in the early morning, and driving back to it at night; these are never discussed. Such a pattern is typically taken for granted, as a 'fact', and Reason steps in only to rationalize the parts of an unrational system. The same could be said of office concentration downtown. There are, of course, good socio-economic reasons to explain such patterns, but they are very rarely called for.

In Venezuelan oil fields, increasing productivity creates few, but highly paid jobs. Those privileged workers are surrounded by a large number of semi-parasites, with very low productivity (service workers, domestics, prostitutes) sharing indirectly the high salaries. High productivity is dialectically negated into high parasitism, necessary and actually useful in a society with low skilled manpower and high unemployment: productivity is rationally increased, but no rational criticism is made of the concept of productivity in such context. Rational efficiency does not destroy dialectical contradictions, but pushes them away onto another level where they are conveniently left out of the study. Increasing rational efficiency in the parts dialectically generates increasing absurdity in the whole. There was once in a psychiatric hospital, a schizophrenic girl who believed she was a piece of butter; she explained she had to stay carefully away from heaters lest she would melt, being extremely rational in a totally absurd context. Geographers would help her by assuming a distance decay function for heat (probably a negative exponential one?) and by computing the best location in the room, but one wonders if this would be the best way to help.

The swing of the pendulum between Technology and Mysticism produces fascinating – and frightening – effects. The textbook controversy in the U.S.A. is one of them.[30] A strong, sometimes violent movement, refusing that Darwinism be taught at school because it seems to contradict the Bible's teachings, has reappeared recently in the United States. It cannot be easily dismissed as absurd and typical of illiterate peoples:

Most textbook controversies issue not from rural folk in Appalachia but from middle-class citizens, many of whom are technically trained . . . . Their answer to the uncertainties of a technological society was not to reject technology but to return to fundamentalist religion and traditional beliefs.

and

The change (in the late 1960's) became evident in the growing criticism of the scientific rationality and in the proliferation of cults and sects based on Eastern mysticism.[31]

The dichotomic opposition between Reason reduced to operational technology and Mysticism severed from any sensual basis and from Reason, cannot pass over into any synthesis; according to the Frankfurt School, it can only lead into Barbarism.[32]

IV.2. *The Growing Negation of Dichotomic Thought*

In such a pragmatic environment, dialectical reason still reappears, although mutilated and in a clumsy way:

IV.2.1. *Negating empirical attitude.* Pure empirical research, piling up 'facts' and sticking to them, has been strongly negated by the development of mathematical modelling in Social Sciences, and in Geography. Models are based on facts, and try to fit them, but negate them by trying to exhibit universal laws.

Another typical phenomenon is the development of Bayesian statistics, particularly since 1954.[33] Exhibiting many weaknesses of the 'frequentist' approach, Bayesians compound empirical evidence with *a priori* probabilities. This may be far away from the Hegelian Notion, but represents a characteristic departure from the empiricist credo.

IV.2.2. *Negating the either/or dichotomy.* Such dichotomy forms the basis of set theory. Consider a large set U with a subset X. Every μ, element of X is defined by a 'characteristic function' c sending every element of the set U into a small binary set:

$$c: \{U\} \rightarrow \{0, 1\}.$$

Each element of U is or is not a member of X according to its image: it is in X if its image is 1, in the complement of X if it is 0. Membership is an Either/Or operation. Although it forms the basis of all mathematics, it is not subtle enough, in many cases. A generalisation has been developed in Electrical Engineering at Berkeley, by Zadeh: *Fuzzy Set Theory*. The image of the characteristic function is not a binary set anymore, but a larger one, with three, four, or many points. There are now points of U which are 'a bit' in X, but not totally. In this still very rigid way, an inner contradiction appears in some points x which *are*, and at the same time *are not* in X. This is not yet dialectics, but a great step toward it. Some geographers have insisted on the usefulness of Fuzzy Set Theory in Geography.[34]

IV.2.3. *Negating continuity.* Topology itself, which developed at the turn of the century is essentially a study of discontinuity. A very general discipline as Point-Set Topology, it has been used principally by mathematicians to study functions and continuity in integration. It could, however, lead to more general uses in Social Sciences. A new revolutionary theory based on topology has just been proposed: *Catastrophe Theory*, developed by René Thom.[35] Here again, the method still lacks the subtlety of dialectics and, like most mathematical methods, produces rather descriptive measurements and imitative models, rather than intrinsic explanation. It shows however an increasing consciousness of what are actually dialectical processes.

V. CONCLUSION

This paper has tried to attack and weaken three myths which appear lamentably strong in present geography:

— The myth of *trivial empiricism* (actually, a childish misunderstanding of Hume's philosophy) which bows to the tyrannical power of 'facts', and accepts blindly the *status quo*.

— The related myth of *immediacy* which separates radically subject and object (in knowledge and in action) and negates the power of thought by restricting its role to that of a simple, faithful mirroring of 'the external world'.

— The myth of *positivism* which believes hypocritically in an 'objective' i.e., unbiased science which could find Truth independently of any ideological framework.

Every society (and, according to the ethno-psychiatrists, this industrial society more than any other one) generates smoke-screens concealing its actual mechanisms, painted veils which are self-justifying propaganda. To accept the myths indicated above is to gobble up with a blind eagerness this propaganda, i.e., to negate the real role of the scientist dedicated to look, behind the veils, for the actual laws of motion, the real cogs and wheels. In a very dialectical fashion, positivist science turns into a mythical science, and the facts it deems concrete are actually abstractions.

This does not imply at all any absurd condemnation of mathematical methods, as mysticism has wanted us, as geographers, to believe. Mathematics is a unique and indispensable approach to *describe* quantity. It is necessarily and dialectically related to Dialectics which *explains* qualitative changes. Only a dichotomic view, opposing mysticism to technology would like to do without mathematics.

Hegel's thought, as presented here, should itself be negated and modernized. Marx did it by switching from Idealism to Materialism. But dialectical thinking is not necessarily Marxism. In the present dichotomic environment, there exists in North America a mythical fascination and a pathological repulsion toward marxism: the Us/Them dichotomy leads Americans to believe that anybody using dialectics must be 'one of them', whatever that means. There is, however, another important system of thought stemming from Dialectics: the Freudian approach. The Ego is a living synthesis of the contradictions between conflicting Id and Superego. Human behaviour appears as a dialectical synthesis between individual libido and social constraints: Ethno-Psychiatry has opened a way which should be most fruitful for geographers and urbanists.[36]

One of the merits of the Frankfurt School is to have tried, in a very Hegelian way, to relate dialectically the findings of Marx with the findings of Freud.[37] It may be time, today, to negate the Frankfurt School and to go further ahead.

University of Paris,
Sorbonne

NOTES

[1] This paper has evolved from a preceding publication (B. Marchand, 'Quantitative Geography — Revolution or Counter-Revolution?' in *Geoforum* 17 (1974), 15–23). It is also partly a product of discussions held during a seminar I taught at the University of Toronto in 1975–76. I am indebted to its graduate participants: Judy Conmy, Dave Evans, Garry Crowfoot, Gordon Garland and Harry Loksts who, through their suggestions or criticism, oriented some of my ideas. I am grateful for the stimulating discussions with Allen Scott and Shoukry Roweis, from the Planning Department. My largest debt is to Gunnar Olsson, University of Michigan, for his warm friendship and his intellectual influence.

[2] M. Perleau-Ponty, 'Le Philosophe et la sociologie', in *Essais Philosophiques*, Paris, 1953, pp. 136, 143.

[3] R. W. Kates, 'Mirror or Monitor for Man?', in *Antipode* 1 (1969), 1.

[4] W. W. Bunge and R. Bordessa, *The Canadian Alternative: Survival, Expeditions and Urban Change*, York University, 1975.

[5] J. O. Von Neumann and O. Morgenstern, *Theory of Games and Economic Behaviour*, Princeton University Press, Princeton, 1944.

[6] B. Marchand, 'Information Theory and Geography', in *Geographical Analysis* IV (1974), 3.

[7] P. George, 'La Geographie Quantitative, Un Nouveau Determinisme?', in *Notiziario di Geografia Economica*, Rome, 1971.

[8] R. Barthes, *Systeme de la Mode*, Paris, 1967.

[9] R. Barthes, 'Le Mythe Aujourd'hui', in *Mythologies*, Paris, 1957.

[10] S. Gale, 'On the Heterodoxy of Explanation: A Review of Harvey's *Explanation in Geography*', in *Geographical Analysis* 4 (1972), 3, 285–330.

[11] George, *op. cit.*

[12] *Ibid.*

[13] Marchand, *op. cit.*, footnote 6.

[14] R. Thom, *Structural Stability and Morphogenesis*, Reading, Massachusetts, 1975.

[15] G. W. F. Hegel, *Logic*, Clarendon Press, Oxford, 1975, p. 136.

[16] Hume, *An Abstract of a Treatise of Human Nature*, Cambridge University Press, Cambridge, 1938, p. 16.

[17] H. Marcuse, *Reason and Revolution; Hegel and the Rise of Social Theory*, Oxford University Press, London, 1941, p. 20.

[18] According to Hegel (footnote 15), "Whatever is true must be in the actual world and present to sense-perception" (p. 61), but "the sensible appearance is individual and evanescent: the permanent in it is discovered by reflection" (p. 33).

[19] Marcuse, *op. cit.*, p. 11.

[20] W. C. Hunt's analyses were used as a counter to Marx, as kindly indicated to me by John Adams.

[21] Marcuse, *op. cit.*, p. 72.

[22] Hegel, *op. cit.*, p. 49.

[23] *Ibid.*, p. 261.

[24] Marcuse, *op. cit.*, pp. ix, xiv.

[25] G. W. F. Hegel, *Philosophy of Nature* I, Allen and Unwin, London, 1970, p. 223.

[26] M. Foucault, *Madness and Civilization; a History of Insanity in The Age of Reason*, Pantheon Books, New York, 1965.

[27] M. Horkheimer and T. W. Adorno, *Dialectics of Enlightenment*, Seabury Press, New York, 1944, pp. 4–5.

[28] C. W. Harris, *Problems in Measuring Change*, University of Wisconsin Press, Madison, Wisconsin, 1963, p. 117.

[29] B. Marchand *et al.*, *The Ideological Role of Space*, Toronto, forthcoming.

[30] D. Nelkin, 'The Science-Textbook Controversies', in *Scientific American* 234 (1976), 33–39.

[31] *Ibid.*, pp. 33–34.

[32] Horkheimer and Adorno, *op. cit.*

[33] L. Savage, *The Foundations of Statistics*, John Wiley, New York, 1954.

[34] G. Olsson, *Birds in Egg*, Ann Arbor, 1975; S. Gale, 'Inexactness, Fuzzy Sets, and the Foundations of Behavioural Geography', in *Geographical Analysis* 4 (1972), 337–349.

[35] E. C. Zeeman, 'Catastrophe Theory', in *Scientific American* 234 (1976), 65–83; Thom, *op. cit.*

[36] G. Devereux, *Ethnopsychanalyse Complémentariste*, Flammarion, Paris, 1972.

[37] H. Marcuse, *Eros and Civilization*, Beacon Press, Boston, 1967.

ERIC G. MOORE

BEYOND THE CENSUS:
DATA NEEDS AND URBAN POLICY ANALYSIS

I. INTRODUCTION

Over the last decade, the pressures on geographers to demonstrate the relevance of their intellectual wares have increased, as they have for most other social scientists. Although some success has been achieved, overall progress has been slow and has served to illustrate rather forcibly that the eclectic generalizations of existing theories provide a painfully inadequate basis for policy in both the public and private sectors. Reasons for this state of affairs are diverse. In part, it stems from the bias of much research which seeks to examine the nature of only those phenomena deemed the proper subject of discourse within a given discipline while controlling for the effects of other influences either by assumption or research design. In part, it reflects the fact that the search for operational strategies in dealing with issues imposes different demands on analysis than does the attempt to construct explanatory theories. By no means least important, current difficulties reflect the inappropriateness of available data for addressing many questions which appear most relevant to the public policy arena. Each of these arguments is worthy of detailed examination; in this essay, however, I will focus attention on the last observation for it is clear that the opportunities to use new types of data are rapidly expanding and the links between such data and questions of interest to social scientists should be clarified.

In essence, I shall argue that a strong case can be made for increased access of social scientists to public micro-data files, particularly in the context of research on public policy issues. The claim is not made that such access is a panacea for all problems, for data alone can never be a substitute for creative thought about substantive issues; nor are the political problems associated with use of micro-data ignored. What is claimed is that, if certain classes of questions are to be answered, then access to micro-data is essential and, in the first instance, those data currently collected in the public domain should be employed as fully as possible. The political debate should then focus on the value to be attached to these classes of question and whether the answers are worth the political costs.

S. Gale and G. Olsson (eds.), Philosophy in Geography, 269–286. All Rights Reserved.
Copyright © 1979 by D. Reidel Publishing Company, Dordrecht, Holland.

At the outset we might ask why social scientists need micro-data. Perhaps this does not appear to be a substantial issue, worthy of lengthy debate, since our professed interests are in human behavior, most of our assumptions are grounded in the actions of individuals and our analyses should reflect these micro-behavioral foundations. However, doubts emerge. First of all, we are not, in general, interested in specific individuals but in statements about types of individuals and groups. Secondly, there are many cases in other sciences in which we find assumptions about individuals going hand-in-hand with observations on aggregates. Finally, substantial social and political costs are frequently associated with the collection and use of data regarding individuals, costs which require that we at least try to identify the rationale for incurring them.

In seeking to establish such a rationale I first examine the general role played by data in both theory construction (Section II) and in formulation of policy (Section III). This discussion suggests that the types of data we require depend not only on the questions we ask but also on the clarity with which we are able to ask them. The more general the question, the more flexible must be the organization of data if we are to effectively pursue potential answers. Furthermore, the larger the groups of individuals to which our questions are addressed, the more desirable it is to make as much use as possible of existing large-scale data files. The latter point brings us to the crux of the paper, the need for access to public micro-data files. Different modes of access to these files are discussed in Section IV.

The type of access to data we need depends on the questions we have in mind. As our questions become both more specific and more dynamic in orientation we are confronted with a need for greater levels of access to micro-level data. To illustrate this progression I use a variety of examples from the study of urban housing (Section V). In this discussion it is argued that certain classes of questions can be answered only if complete access to micro-data with individual identifiers is permitted. In evaluating whether such access is justified we need to consider whether the costs in terms of the general invasion of personal freedoms are justified, recognizing that the ultimate decision is of a purely political nature. Concluding remarks are offered in Section VI.

II. SOCIAL SCIENCE RESEARCH AND DATA NEEDS

In the most general terms, the academic social scientist seeks to provide an interpretive understanding of human behavior both for individuals and for groups. Although the prime emphasis is on *actions* together with the *motivations* which underly these actions, there are many situations in which we are unable either to observe the actions or to obtain data on motivations directly. Much observation, measurement, and analysis focusses on the outcomes or preconditions of action and we are led to infer the nature of the behavior from its static correlates. Development of theory in any specific branch of social science then embraces both the search for consistent and stable relationships associated with a given behavior and the establishment of a conceptual apparatus capable of explaining such relations.

In this overall process of generating an understanding of human behavior, the activities of theory construction, data collection and use are intimately related. Each step in the evolution of theory both guides the types of data sought and is influenced by the types of data available. Such links are particularly complex in the so-called non-experimental sciences (e.g., Blalock, 1964) which depend on observations on behavior and their outcomes in situations lacking the control of the laboratory environment. Problems arise, however, as we expand the scale of our data collection activities. When the main emphasis is on the general nature of relationships between variables our data needs can often be satisfied by small samples and it is relatively easy to obtain data in the form judged most appropriate for the questions we have in mind. However, as the relations we examine become more complex and as the specific contexts of behavior are explicitly included in our analyses, it becomes much more difficult both from financial and organizational perspectives to obtain the necessary data. We simply cannot afford to undertake large-scale surveys to examine every question which we believe might prove interesting or even useful. Under these circumstances, it would seem desirable, at least from a cost viewpoint, to make as much use as possible of the extensive data sets collected for a wide range of uses in the public sector.

Use of public data by social scientists generates a number of problems. In as far as data are used in a manner other than the purpose for which they were originally collected, there are conflicts of interest both between the social scientist and public official and between the individual who provides the data and the user (Dammann, 1974). One outcome of these conflicts of interest is that access to public data has been strongly circumscribed and the path taken by developing social science interests tends to reflect the pattern of availability of data on social phenomena. It is not surprising, for example, to find in the latter context that the majority of discussions of the residential structure of our cities are phrased in terms of the particular types of socio-economic, demographic, and ethnic data collected by the census and that change is discussed in convenient ten-year intervals (e.g., Murdie (1968), Birch (1974)).

Even recognizing these constraints on data availability, we often tend to forget the extent of the relation between data and theory. As Coombs (1964) observed, even the most basic steps of selecting which variables to measure, specifying measurement procedures, and assigning individuals to classes reflect theories,[1] albeit elementary ones, of behavior. For example, the simple decision to relate the rent of a dwelling to the income of its occupants reflects ideas regarding the nature of household expenditures, while the selection of an age class breakdown such as < 20 years, 20–35, 35–60, > 60 years in the study of mobility might be in response to beliefs about the influence of different stages in the life cycle on migration behavior.

Theory-construction is a developmental process. In its early stages there are few well-formed ideas and many conflicts as to what constitutes an appropriate explanation of a given behavior. These conflicts extend to the basic decisions of the previous paragraph concerning variable selection, measurement, and categorization. Thus we find that the sociological literature is replete with alternative operational definitions of life cycle stages with different ages, marital statuses, and family compositions used for definitions of classes (compare, for example, Speare (1970) and Pickvance (1973)). In many contexts the resolution of these conflicts is an *empirical* question demanding that *each* theory be evaluated with appropriate data; we may even encounter the situation in which no acceptable theory exists and patterns in the data themselves lead to new ideas and theories. In contrast, a well-developed theory should provide a strong structure for data collection activities in that the testable propositions deriving from that theory should be quite specific in regard to the variables to be observed and the measures to be employed.

Typically, within the developmental framework outlined above, we would wish to progress from a situation in which the greatest need is for flexibility in data collection, organization, and presentation to facilitate resolution of a wide range of conflicts to stages of increasing codification of such activities. Unfortunately, the needs of other users of the data (the public agencies themselves) often necessitates some prior degree of codification in data collection: this is understandable but we must then be careful not to restrict the flexibility of data by imposing further *unnecessary* restrictions on their use. The decision as to whether restrictions are necessary or not depends on the perceived importance of the social science question, the level of data flexibility needed at a given state of theory development, and the weight of arguments concerning the dangers of making particular classes of data available. This decision is fundamentally political. Although we can never escape the value judgment of deciding whether a particular research question is worth the effort to answer it, we can attempt in the present context to show that if answers to certain classes of questions are desired then particular data forms are necessary.

III. SOCIAL SCIENCE AND PUBLIC POLICY

With increasing frequency, attempts are being made to co-opt the social scientist into the complex processes of goal formation, program design, assessment of possible impacts and program evaluation in a wide range of government activities. The success with which this function is performed depends in part (though certainly not entirely) on the degree of understanding he possesses of the social processes relevant to a particular policy area. Even if policies are designed to achieve specified states of a given system, they are only likely to be effective if they take into account the ways in which existing processes are generating change and, without knowledge of such processes, such policies certainly cannot be evaluated.

In a policy context we expect answers to our questions to be detailed, and, very frequently, location specific. In particular, as many writers are arguing (e.g., Harvey (1974), Gale and Moore (1975)), the institutional context in which actions occur is a critical factor in accounting for the outcomes of those actions and must therefore be included explicitly in our analyses. In the study of housing problems, for example, we must take the general principles of operation of urban housing markets and translate them into real outcomes of supply and demand relations, given mortgage availability, construction costs, differential migration, state and federal programs, and so forth in New York, Chicago, Los Angeles, and a host of smaller cities. To the local polity, aggregation across many markets is of little value. Decisions must be made which are relevant to specific local conditions and impacts must be anticipated accordingly. The empirical foundations of such decisions must be sufficiently detailed to be able to specify the magnitudes of those segments of the population to be affected, the probable repercussions of a program throughout other sectors of the economy (such as employment, construction and demand on other public services), as well as the appropriate time frame for both implementation and subsequent impact.

The ability to perform these tasks effectively requires a detailed understanding of urban processes. Yet almost any new writing on contemporary urban issues begins with a plea for better theory and better data suggesting that we do *not* have an adequate basis for most urban social policy.[2] Thus David Birch (1974, p. 1) writes

For all the talk about the 'urban crisis' and for all the courses in universities with the word 'urban' in their titles, precious little is understood about how urban areas work . . . The word 'understood' is used in its strictest sense. That is, the person who truly understands a region should be able to predict its evolution accurately several years into the future at the neighborhood level. Much urban analysis falls by the wayside under this test. Yet it is the only test that is satisfactory to those who must formulate programs and make decisions, the success of which will depend on the future course the region takes.

The key to effective action in (public and private policy decisions) is to understand – in the strictest sense – the underlying dynamics that cause change, and then to enter at carefully chosen points with carefully chosen actions . . . The administrator and program designer . . . must understand the pressures causing change in detail and deflect rather than arrest those pressures if they are to have any lasting effect.

Although Birch takes a somewhat extreme Laplacian view of the predictability of human events, he does provide a set of aspirations for urban theory which far exceed current practice. As a first step in moving toward a better understanding of urban processes, we should attempt to make better use of data which are currently available although, in the longer-run, we may need to drastically re-think the relationship between institutionalized forms of data collection and the types of social theory we are seeking to build (Dunn, 1974; Gale and Moore, 1975).

IV. ACCESS TO PUBLIC MICRO-DATA FILES

Once we look beyond the census, the primary sources of public data are associated with the broad range of administrative functions undertaken at federal, state and local levels of government. The types of files that form the focus of interest here are more than arbitrary collections of individual information: it is suggested that these files are both sufficiently large to preclude effective analysis by manual means and that any given file is representative of some well-defined population. Representativeness can be achieved either through complete enumeration or by sample survey provided that the relation to the parent population is understood.

We must not limit our attention solely to files where basic units of observation are individual persons or even households. Micro-data files also include those whose units of observation are artifacts (as in the case of assessment rolls or new car registration lists) and events (such as records of crimes, accidents, or cases of infectious disease) to which personal data are appended. In each case, data are collected in such a form that specific attributes can be assigned to particular individuals within a broader context, that context being established by the frame of reference for construction of the file.

The crucial property from the point of view of this discussion is the presence of a unique individual identifier associated with each record in the file. The individual identifier (a name, address, or even a specific geographic location) provides both the critical element in organizing and analyzing the wealth of material contained in such files and the basis of concern when potential invasions of personal privacy are considered. From the latter perspective, individual identifiers permit detailed information on personal characteristics of those included in the records to be extracted to the embarrassment, harrassment or annoyance of those persons. To the user of such files for analytic (as opposed to administrative) purposes, the role of the identifier is as a necessary link between data items when associations between two or more variables are sought.

A large number of micro-data files already exist in the public sector. As long as individual identifiers are maintained, the potential exists to link files and thereby expand the number of data items which relate to a given individual. However, since the prime interest of the social scientist is not in the person-specific data but in the nature of the cross-linkages established between data items, the issue is one of access to cross-linked or cross-tabulated data rather than to person-specific data.

What range of situations characterize possible different degrees of access to micro-data files? We can respond to this question along two different dimensions: the first refers to the format in which data are presented to the user and the second to the range of variables to which access is granted. A classification of the range of possible outcomes is given in Table I.

In the first instance we differentiate between the degree of access to individual data: this has a two-fold structure. The collecting agency may refuse to release any individual data but may either perform selected cross-tabulations (much as the Bureau of the Census does now) or permit remote entry to micro-files while controlling permissible manipulations and output formats to ensure certain standards of confidentiality. A second set of scenarios arise when agencies decide to release micro-data; in these cases, the fundamental decision is whether to attach individual identifiers such as name, address, social security number, or geographic co-ordinates to each record.

TABLE I

Different modes of access to micro-data files

				Data type
I	No release of individual data by collecting agency	a. No access to individual data: all processing within collecting agency	(i) Limited standardized cross-tabulations subject to small-number controls to protect confidentiality.	[1]
			(ii) Special purpose cross-tabulations with small-number controls	[2]
			(iii) Special purpose cross-tabulations with no small-number controls	[3]
		b. Controlled access to individual data through remote terminals	(i) Access to files on a limited basis with controls for variables linked, types of analysis and output format	[4]
			(ii) All variables accessible but output format controlled	[5]
			(iii) All variables accessible, free output format but no individual identifiers obtainable	[6]
II	Release of individual data to external users	a. Release of individual data in anonymous form: no individual identifiers	(i) Anonymous sample data with selected responses deleted	[7]
			(ii) Anonymous sample data with complete records	[8]
			(iii) Complete files with selected responses and individual identifiers removed	[9]
			(iv) Complete files with only individual identifiers removed	[10]
		b. Release of individual data with individual identifiers	(i) Sample files with selected responses deleted	[11]
			(ii) Sample files with all data items	[12]
			(iii) Complete files with selected variables deleted	[13]
			(iv) Complete files	[14]

Additional controls can be imposed beyond those associated with the decision to permit access to the individual records. Essentially these limit the number of records and the specific variables for which data are released. Such controls permit more sensitive items to be deleted from records thereby reducing potential political costs associated with micro data release.

What implications do these different modes of access have for the social scientist? Following from the discussion in Section II, they imply a considerable variation in flexibility. The most obvious effect is that the greater the number of variables deleted from records, the fewer the number and the less the complexity of relationships which can be examined. Somewhat similar arguments follow with respect to sample and total files. In general, the greater the number of interactions between variables to be examined in a given problem, the higher the dimensionality required from a cross-tabulation. Such higher-dimensional tables are very data demanding, particularly when one dimension is an areal breakdown. For example, we might consider a study of ownership rates in a single city controlling for income, marital status, and family size of households. If we believe that each of the variables interact and relations between variables are non-linear, we could require a table with say 120 cells (5 income categories x 3 marital status x 4 family size) and 25 observations in each cell to estimate ownership rates. If we then add a breakdown by neighborhoods we greatly magnify the number of observations needed (ten neighborhoods would lead to a cross-tabulation of the order of 30 000 observations). It is not difficult to see that, in general, sample files impose limits on the level of detail which can be achieved in subsequent analysis. In particular, in analysis of sample data we are usually forced to choose between exploring detailed relations between substantive variables and spatial variations in responses. As a consequence, we often cannot assess the degree to which spatial variations are attributable merely to compositional differences between areas.

Finally, what is the impact of excluding or including the individual identifiers? Basically these are two-fold. First, the lack of an individual identifier prevents any further file linkage by the user. These operations include the merging of one subject file with another cross-sectionally, merging successive files to produce longitudinal records and assignment of individuals to specific locations within a region. Second, when more detailed questions are being asked, it is of value to use existing micro-level files as a sampling frame (as is done with the Swedish Population Registers) such that the proper controls can be exerted on the design of a given survey. Each of these issues will be treated in greater detail in the next section in the specific context of urban housing studies.

V. DATA NEEDS IN STUDIES OF URBAN HOUSING

In order to provide substance to the general arguments outlined in the previous section, I will focus on specific issues relating to studies of urban housing. It is an area on which much recent attention has been focussed, particularly with regard to the inadequacy of both theory and data in addressing
policy issues; it is here that arguments regarding the importance of local
institutional contexts have been most forcibly expressed (Harvey (1974),
Grigsby and Rosenburg (1975)) and in which the need to make greater use
of administrative data sources is underscored (Forrest, 1976). At the core
of the most recent discussions is the insistence that we consider the way in
which a given population is housed to be the outcome of complex socio-
economic and political processes. We deal with a system in which the relationships between different actors take place within a market framework, however imperfect, and result in continual change in the observed characteristics
of that system. To effectively model and to intervene in this system requires
a perspective which recognizes its basic dynamic properties.

The scale of our inquiry strongly influences the types of question we ask.
At the national level, housing issues arise largely out of processes of overall
growth of the economy, demographic change and evolving aspirations regarding minimum acceptable levels of housing. At the regional level, issues are primarily distributional reflecting derived demand from shifts in the location and
composition of the labor force, while at the scale of the individual city, housing problems are more immediate, visible and volatile. Since a major feature
of housing as a commodity is its durability (de Leeuw, 1973) the characteristics both of the current state of housing and of contemporary processes in
any city owe much to its cumulated history of residential development.
Under these circumstances, the impact of national programs at the local level
can be extremely variable and analysis at this latter scale is of paramount
importance.

At the city level, housing market processes comprise the set of relations
between the supply of housing with different attributes, demand for housing
by households of different types and a market clearing process based on a
price mechanism. The intellectual foundations of most conceptualizations of
these processes lie in the micro-level treatment of individual decisions made
by the multitude of actors in the market (Alonso (1964), Muth (1969),
Quigley (1974), de Leeuw (1972)). In the initial stages of development of
models of the urban housing market, these processes were organized within
the classical equilibrium framework of micro-economics. Housing was treated

as a homogeneous commodity, the basic decision-mechanism involving a trade-off between the amount of the commodity consumed and travel expenditures incurred in getting to the place of work. Testable propositions were primarily statements about aggregate spatial distributions suited to examination with conventional census data (see, for example, Muth (1969)) and, given their origin in equilibrium theory, no reference was made to dynamics.

Recent empirical studies and attendant modelling efforts have moved away from this tradition. Particular concern is expressed for the assumption of homogeneity and for the static nature of prior work. Thus Silver (1970) writes

The housing market . . . is highly differentiated. Considerable interest attaches to the processes by which the many types of agents interact and how the various types of housing good are apportioned to different consumers. I would argue that there is little more useful knowledge to be gained about the housing market at this time from the continued use of the highly aggregated data typical of previous studies. From the point of view of the investigation of housing demand . . . a greater understanding of the relationships, and especially of the dynamic characteristics, must rely upon the examination of disaggregated data, ideally to the household level, and include information both about the socio-economic characteristics of the households, the physical characteristics of its housing and the quality of the environment in which that housing is located.

The utility attached to a given structure is thus seen to be a function not only of its own physical characteristics but also of who occupies it and where it is located. To identify the detailed character of processes within such a conceptual framework has very strong implications for data: the subsequent comments expand on this point within the framework provided by Table I.

V.1. *No Access to Individual Data (Data Types [1], [2] and [3])*

Standard census tabulations mainly yield single-variable and bivariate observations for areal aggregates. Using such data, analyses are limited to a straightforward examination of spatial patterns or to inferences based on ecological correlations; the deficiencies of the latter are well documented (e.g., Dogan and Rokkan (1969)). In some instances, however, in which ecological associations are clearly insufficient, we can resort to the type of special consumer services offered by Statistics Canada under which special tabulations can be requested.

A typical example of the need for such cross-tabulations is provided by the attempt to evaluate differences in housing consumption for selected ethnic or racial groups. Without adequate controls for the differences in the economic and demographic composition of the groups to be compared, there is a strong tendency to over-estimate these differentials. As an illustration, early studies based on small sample data indicated a substantial reduction (of the order of 10 percent) in ownership rates of black as against white households (Kain and Quigley, 1972). More recent work based on extensive microlevel files has shown that such differentials are primarily due to the younger, larger families and lower incomes of black households, the racial effects being reduced to the order of 2–3 percent (Tam, 1975), In addition, the relationships between the different variables are neither linear nor additive which implies that we could not reproduce these results from the marginal distributions of standard census publications.

V.2. *Access to Individual Data on an Anonymous Basis (Data Types [4]–[10])*

Effective use of the consumer services of statistical agencies requires a sound understanding of the relationships to be identified in a given cross-tabulation. Often, however, we do not know in advance exactly how to organize our analyses and we must experiment with a variety of formats. Consider the problem of estimating income elasticities of demand for various attributes of housing, a basic issue in housing analysis (Silver, 1970; de Leeuw, 1971). It is argued that such measures contribute both to an understanding of consumer behavior and to the assessment of impacts of public policy on the housing market. Although these values have usually been computed in aggregate terms for large populations, it is clear that if policies are to be designed to alleviate existing inequities they must be directed at specific segments of the housing market and specific household types. How should such submarkets and house-hold classes be constructed? The number of possible variables is large, including income, assets, marital status, family size, age and sex of children and race for households, and floor area, lot size, tenure, condition, value, site and situation characteristics for dwellings. Attempts to construct functional sub-markets and household consumption groups along the lines suggested by Grigsby (1963) requires extensive experimentation with variable selection and categorization.

Once we are able to obtain access to appropriate microdata, however, considerable light is cast on conventional wisdom. For example, in a study based on detailed public micro-data for Wichita, Kansas it was possible to reduce 136 household classes to approximately 30 groups exhibiting similar behavior in the market (Moore *et al.*, 1975). For each of these groups income elasticities of demand were estimated for tenure, size, value, rent, and condition over four income ranges for both recent movers and the total population of Wichita in 1973. For present purposes, it is perhaps most useful to look at a number of conclusions which arise from this work which illustrate the value of access to this type of data:

(1) Elasticities vary not only from one population sub-group to another but also vary for different income range for the same household (thus violating the oft-adopted assumption of the Engel curve).

(2) The functional form of the relationship between income and elasticity is different for different household types (for example, in the case of tenure it increases with increasing income for households with several pre-school children whereas it decreases for elderly couples whose children no longer live at home).

(3) From a policy standpoint, the consistently low values of demand elasticities for low-income families with children suggests any subsidy program designed to improve housing conditions for this group should be specifically tied to housing expenditure rather than be in the form of a general income subsidy.[3]

Of course, many questions are left unanswered by a single study such as this. Perhaps the most important concerns the effect of local supply conditions on elasticity measures. To explore this issue requires replication in other specific city contexts, although, in this case, we could build on the earlier work and make direct requests for special cross-tabulations.

V.3. Access to Data With Individual Identifiers (Data Types [11]–[14])

Even with access to micro-level data from particular files, the classes of questions which can be addressed are limited. The most serious deficiency lies in the restrictions placed on the construction of individual histories and our subsequent ability to cope with dynamic issues. If we want to understand the nature of change in the occupancy of housing under a variety of market conditions we must be able to identify who enters the market and under what circumstances. Retrospective histories constructed on the basis of recall in interviews are unsatisfactory in that one cannot identify the population at risk at various points of time in the past. Thus we are unable to adequately estimate prospective rate of occurrence for different events such as the decision to enter the market or to own or rent. The need is either for continuous registers of the type kept in several European countries or an ability to link annual files to determine which individuals have changed characteristics between recording times.

Few files built for administrative purposes are capable, in themselves, of satisfying specific research questions. Often, greater value is derived by linking more than one file to generate data relevant to the questions being asked. For example, most discussions of the reasons for entering the housing market stress the importance of changes in family status (such as getting married, divorced, or having a child) in precipitating a move. If we are to estimate the impact of these events on a particular market then we need to document both family changes and shifts in patterns of housing consumption over time. Retrospective analyses are again inadequate and the most promising direction to pursue is to link birth and marriage records to micro-data on housing (in Canada, data on the latter could be provided by the annual assessment files). However, to achieve this linkage, we must have individual identifiers.

A somewhat different situation arises in certain policy or program contexts when we have to consider change which is highly location specific. It is well-known that many institutional arrangements for mortgage financing, insurance, zoning and building code enforcement are structured in great spatial detail often to the block or even the parcel level (Harvey, 1974). In a slightly different vein, many large-scale public projects such as freeway construction or urban renewal programs have specific spatial effects both in terms of changing land prices and of household displacement. If the effects of these activities on local neighborhoods are to be identified we should be able to accurately locate observations on housing consumption by different households at various points in time. The technology to effect this locational assignment is available through a range of address-matching routines as in the DIME system (U.S. Department of Commerce, 1968) but the utility of such procedures again depends on availability of appropriate micro-data.

Finally, consider the question of using micro-data as a sampling frame. Available public micro-data seldom address exactly those questions we would like to see answered. This is presently the situation motivating many interview studies: however, in order to gain the maximum benefit from our sampling procedures we should attempt to control the sample design as tightly as possible. For example, in evaluating current behavior in the market, it has been shown (Goldstein, 1973) that recent movers exhibit substantially different behavior from the total population in terms of patterns of housing consumption. Furthermore, differences occur among intra-urban movers, inter-urban and rural-urban migrants. Under these circumstances we would wish to control for recent migrant behavior in sample design such that our responses can be related to appropriate populations at risk. One effective procedure is to utilize successive micro-files to identify those who are either new to the system or have changed their location within it. Additional stratification by socio-economic and demographic characteristics provides a firm basis for interpreting our survey results in a rigorous fashion.

V.4. *Concluding Comments on Housing Issues*

As we shift from simple equilibrium oriented questions to demand more detailed information on the dynamics of a heterogeneous housing market, our need for micro-data increases. Existing approaches based on aggregate-data have proved singularly ineffective in producing a sound theory of urban dynamics on which to develop policy. It is perhaps illuminating that the many recent well-regarded studies in housing have been forced to use and re-use the now out-of-date micro-level data produced in the large-scale transportation surveys of the late sixties (e.g., Straszheim, 1975). Even these sources do not provide much insight into change but, at least, they permit the researcher to experiment with highly flexible data at the level of the individual. Future progress depends on more up-to-date, change-oriented data becoming available.

The question then arises as to the policy of data access to be pursued. Even when issues are considered to be of sufficient social, economic and political importance to justify use of micro-data, there is still a need to exercise control over access. Presumably the nature of the research would be subject to the usual academic scrutiny but, in addition, adequate protection against disclosure and other potential abuses needs to be established. A professional judgement is needed in each case to determine if the proposed research could be undertaken entirely within the collecting agency or with assistance from an outside expert working as a consultant: only when strong arguments can be made that these procedures are insufficient should data be released under well-defined regulations regarding their use.

VI. GENERAL CONCLUSIONS

The example of social science questions discussed in this paper have focussed on issues in urban housing. Relatively few controversial data items arise in this context, most of those which are contentious relating to observations on personal wealth. In other areas of social science of concern to geographers, however, much more sensitive issues arise such as those associated with various aspects of crime, delinquency, and mental illness, for all of which data are collected by public agencies. With more sensitive issues, concern for access to micro-data undoubtedly increases. Nevertheless, I believe that the general principles set out in this paper still apply. As questions of greater complexity are asked, as theory focusses on the dynamics of social processes rather than on static structures, and as we are asked to examine public actions within well-defined spatial contexts, the need for linkage between files increases and hence the need for micro-data. Certainly, the criteria for access will become more stringent as the perceived social and political costs get higher, but we must still recognize that some questions might be of sufficient importance to justify access.

In this context I think it is important to make the same distinction as Dunn (1974) between *intelligence systems* whose prime function is to compile dossiers on personal behavior and *statistical reporting systems* in which data have little potential impact on the individual but substantial implications for guiding public actions. Of course there are fuzzy boundaries between the two but it can be argued that the majority of data needed for social science use are relatively innocuous at the personal level. However, as Dunn points out, we can substantially reduce the effectiveness of statistical systems by imposing constraints on them which are far more appropriate to intelligence systems and which result in the former becoming too cumbersome and costly to use.

The ability of the social scientist to make effective use of public micro-data files is still somewhat limited. In many areas we do not possess the conceptual frameworks to guide us in the organization and analysis of micro-data and we must experiment. As a consequence, we have few demonstrable benefits accruing from access to micro-data files either in theory construction or public policy. However, on the basis of the arguments developed here, it can be said that, if we wish to address complex questions arising from a concern with both structure and change in contemporary urban society, we will find our progress extremely slow if not non-existent without access to micro-data. In this regard, I am concerned that discussion of access is placed in a reasonable perspective. In fact, I believe that over-emphasis on personal privacy with regard to public micro-data files can often obscure a more fundamental issue. This arises from the argument that the real danger in linking different micro-level files lies in the effect on the distribution of power in society. Although most public data hold few intrinsic dangers for the individual, their linkage into systems of relationships concerning the functioning of society provides the basis for social control through the concentration of information. In these circumstances, perhaps it is the particular *uses* of micro-data rather than access per se which should form the prime focus of public scrutiny and control. Above all, the geographer cannot avoid, in Webber's terms (1970, p. 124), the politics of information and it is within this context that he seeks to "sell his particular brands of rationality and his particular images of the social welfare".

NOTES

[1] The term theory is used in its most general sense of potential answer to a potential question (Gale, 1974).
[2] This statement omits any discussion of the political philosophy underlying the formulation of policy. It asserts that we do not have a sound basis for policy even within the existing political environment.
[3] Although the study does not address the more general policy issue of whether such a goal is desirable (de Leeuw, 1973).

BIBLIOGRAPHY

Alonso, W.: 1964, *Location and Land Use*, Harvard University Press, Cambridge, Massachusetts.

Birch, D. *et al.*: 1974, *Patterns of Urban Change*, D. C. Heath and Co., Lexington, Massachusetts.

Blalock, H. M.: 1964, *Causal Inferences in Non-Experimental Research*, University of North Carolina Press, Chapel Hill.

Coombs, C. H.: 1964, *A Theory of Data*, John Wiley, New York.

Dammann, M.: 1974, 'Datenschutz und Zugang zu Planungsinformationssystemen', paper presented at the Fourth European Symposium on Urban Data Management, Madrid.

de Leeuw, F.: 1971, 'The Demand for Housing: A Review of Cross-sectional Evidence', *The Review of Economics and Statistics* 53, 1–10.

de Leeuw, F.: 1972, *The Distribution of Housing Services*, Urban Institute Working Paper 208-6, Washington, D.C.

de Leeuw, F.: 1973, *What Should U.S. Housing Policies Be?*, Urban Institute Working Paper 729-1, Washington, D.C.

Dogan, M. and Rokkan, S. (eds.): 1969, *Quantitative Ecological Analysis in the Social Sciences*, M.I.T. Press, Cambridge, Massachusetts.

Dunn, E. S. Jr.: 1974, *Social Information Processing and Statistical Systems – Change and Reform*, John Wiley, New York.

Forrest, R.: 1976, *Monitoring: Some Conceptual Issues in Relation to Housing Research*, Working Paper No. 42, Center for Urban and Regional Studies, University of Birmingham.

Gale, S.: 1974, *A Prolegomenon to an Interrogative Theory of Scientific Inquiry*, Work-Paper No. 9, Program on Research on Metropolitan Change and Conflict Resolution, Peace Science Department, University of Pennsylvania.

Gale, S. and Moore, E. G.: 1975, 'Urban Information Systems and the Analysis of Residential Change', paper presented at the Annual Meetings of the Regional Science Association, Cambridge, Massachusetts.

Goldstein, G. S.: 1973, 'Household Behavior in the Housing Market: The Decision to Move and the Decision to Buy or Rent Housing', in E. G. Moore (ed.), *Models of Residential Location and Relocation in the City*, Studies in Geography No. 20, Northwestern University, Evanston, Illinois.

Grigsby, W. G.: 1963, *Housing Markets and Public Policy*, University of Pennsylvania Press, Philadelphia, Pennsylvania.

Grigsby, W. G. and Rosenburg, L.: 1975, *Urban Housing Policy*, Center for Urban Research, Rutgers University.

Harvey, D.: 1974, 'Class-Monopoly Rent, Finance Capital and the Urban Revolution', *Regional Studies* 8, 239–255.

Kain, J. F. and Quigley, J. M.: 1972, 'Housing Market Discrimination, Homeownership and Savings Behavior', *American Economic Review* 62, 263–277.

Moore, E. G., Altman, N. D. E., Clatworthy, S. and Tam, Y.: 1975, *The Effect of Income on Housing Consumption by Household Type*, Technical Paper No. 4, Program of Research on Metropolitan Change and Conflict Resolution, Peace Science Department, University of Pennsylvania.

Murdie, R.: 1968, *Factorial Ecology of Metropolitan Toronto 1951–61*, Research Paper No. 116, Department of Geography, University of Toronto.

Muth, R. F.: 1969, *Cities and Housing*, University of Chicago Press.

Pickvance, C. G.: 1973, 'Life Cycle, Housing Tenure and Intra-Urban Residential Mobility: A Causal Model', *Sociological Review* 21, 279–297.

Quigley, J. M.: 1974, *Towards a Synthesis of Theories of Residence Site Choice*, Working Paper W4-22, Institution for Social and Policy Studies, Yale University.

Silver, I.: 1970, 'A Model of Housing demand in Metropolitan Areas', in J. L. Sullivan (ed.), *Explorations in Urban Land Economics*, University of Hartford.

Speare, A.: 1970, 'Home Ownership, Life Cycle Stage and Residential Mobility', *Demography* 7, 449–458.

Straszheim, M. H.: 1975, *An Econometric Analysis of the Urban Housing Market*, Urban and Regional Studies No. 2, National Bureau of Economic Research, New York.

Tam, Y. K.: 1975, *Racial Differences in Homeownership Rates*, Working Paper No. 11, Program of Research on Metropolitan Change and Conflict Resolution, Peace Science Department, University of Pennsylvania.

U.S. Department of Commerce: 1968, *The DIME Geocoding System*, Census Use Report, Washington, D.C.

Webber, M. M.: 1970, 'The Politics of Information', in N. K. Denzin (ed.), *The Values of Social Science*, Trans-action Books, Aldine, Chicago.

GUNNAR OLSSON

SOCIAL SCIENCE AND HUMAN ACTION OR ON HITTING YOUR HEAD AGAINST THE CEILING OF LANGUAGE

> Misled by me
> the critics assert that my 'tu'
> is an institution, that were it not
> for this fault of mine, they'd have known
> that the many in me are one,
> even though multiplied by the mirrors.
> The trouble is that once caught in the net
> the bird doesn't know if he is himself
> or one of his too many duplicates.
>
> (EUGENIO MONTALE, 'The Use of "Tu"', from *New Poems*, New Directions, 1976.)

A

I. INTRODUCTION

This piece begins as an academic paper about what the social sciences are and it ends as a manifesto of what they ought to be. The message is thoroughly ideological, for ideology is defined as that ethical glue whereby is and ought are forged together into a coherent whole. In the first part, I shall provide a succinct but novel summary of a long and complicated argument recently developed elsewhere.[1] In the second, I shall explore some implications of those thoughts. In neither case shall I draw anything but a rough caricature. But that may be just as well, for it is usually easier to see the prominent features in a caricature than in a fascimile reproduction.

My starting point is in the epistemological belief that any understanding involves translation between a set of different meanings; knowledge is conceived as comparisons of ideas. The resulting fidelity issues are always intriguing, but they become especially vexing when we try to move between the languages of thought and action. Put differently, we do not know explicitly how to specify the translation functions by which we link theory and practice, idea and action, description and prescription, what is in our heads and what comes out of our hands.

287

S. Gale and G. Olsson (eds.), Philosophy in Geography, 287–307. All Rights Reserved.
Copyright © 1979 by D. Reidel Publishing Company, Dordrecht, Holland.

To get further into these translation issues, I shall begin by distilling the deep structures of the languages of social science and human action. I shall not solve any problems, merely try to understand how the two reasoning modes and thereby the two approaches to life are related to each other. In so doing, I shall do nothing less than relive the history of mankind. That history is in the development of language and the development of language is in the changing relations between word and object.

II. THE LANGUAGE OF SOCIAL SCIENCE

The *pragmatics* of the social science language is in the goal of empirical description. Some may rather suggest that the purpose is to develop theory, but that suggestion does not change much, since most theoreticians define theory as interpretive description. Abstract and intellectually economical, perhaps, but description nevertheless. The key word is therefore the verb BE. As if to underline its own metaphysics, this verb is furthermore used primarily in the present tense and the indicative mood. The form 'to be' yields to the form 'is'. Mathematics — the ideal language of science — is in fact a language in which time has come to a stop. For as time comes to a stop, so does the possibility of a shift in truth status.

The scientist's pragmatics subsequently influences his *syntax* such that his calculus becomes that of truth-preservation. It is therefore a sign of good reasoning never to pass from a true premise to a false conclusion — we strive to preserve the truth of the premises into the conclusions. The grammar is that of the first order predicate calculus. It follows that the connectives whereby we anchor ourselves and our propositions are words like NOT, OR and AND. Within that world view, conventional two-valued logic remains the major intellectual tool. By using it, we manage both to glue subject and predicate together and to keep subject and object apart. It is in fact this dialectical principle of uniting and separating that permits the accumulation of so called objective knowledge. Whether it also leads to wisdom and understanding is more disputable and perhaps we do well to remember Kant's dictum that the condition of knowledge lies not in facts but in imagination.

In considering the *semantics* of the social scientist's language, it should first be recalled that his predicates usually are reducible to the is; while his pragmatics reflects the goal of description, his syntax is that of truth-preservation. But truth-preservation about what? About phenomena which can be seen, heard, tasted, touched and smelled. Those things share the decisive characteristic of being countable. They are open to the five senses because – in one form or another – they can be reduced to physical objects. Using Meinong's terminology, we say about those phenomena that they *exist*. This distinction is crucial, for it is only about such existing objects that one can make truth-functional statements. The reason is that when I speak about the other kind of objects – those which are said to *subsist* in my mind rather than exist in their bodies – then it is impossible to tell whether what I see is what you see as well. This ontological bias in turn leads to a heavy reliance on operationalization. Number is thereby made the canon of thought and the habit of numbering transforms the Enlightenment myth into totalitarian ideology. As proof, witness Bacon's rhetorical question:[2]

Is not the rule, '*Si inaequalibus aequalia addas, omnia erunt inaequalia*', an axiom of justice as well as of mathematics? And is there not a true coincidence between commutative and distributive justice, and arithmetical and geometrical proportion?

As disproof, ask what happens if the phenomena I am concerned with are of an ontological kind that is destroyed when I force them into the operational net of measurable quantities. Perhaps, by the mere posing of the latter question, it becomes easier to understand why alienation continues to be our common yoke. Perhaps it even suggests that we have not yet developed a principle of subjectivity capable of destroying it.

Emerging already from this quick sketch are the features of an idiom designed to communicate to others society's shared knowledge of facts rather than my personal understanding of concepts. It is in this sense that today's social science is profoundly ideological, for what it does is to build the practice of criticism and reification into the process of production itself. Concepts and things are thereby made subjects of the same forces of domination. The driving force of both science and technology is indeed in the quest for certainty. The goal is to fight ambiguity and to do so by employing all means. One of these is to emphasize deduction with its inherent elements of hierarchy and coercion; axioms are masters and theorems slaves. Another is to limit discourse to transparent contexts, i.e., to contexts in which words with the same reference can replace each other without change in truth status of the statement as a whole. The paradigmatic example is that of

> Venus is the morning star

and

> Venus is the evening star.

In this case, the proper name 'Venus' designates an existing object, whereas 'the morning star' and 'the evening star' stand for alternative definite descriptions of that object. Since all these denotations can be shown to refer to the same physical body, they can replace each other without affecting the truth value of the whole. The Leibnizian *salva veritatae* principle is consequently upheld. Incommensurability is exorcised and the ritual of rational thinking is once again reconstituted. In its own interest, it has once again reinforced the powers of reification. Fascistic *status quo* has once again prevailed, for *status quo* is meaning variance brought to a halt. Halt! Zum Schuss! Feuer! Say Grace, for Heaven's sake!

And so it is finally worth recalling that the word 'religion' stems from 'religare', which means 'to bind'. Without much ado, the deducers have transcended themselves from the theory of detached enlightenment to the practice of apologetic domination. In the same manner, the values of communication and truth-preservation are invoked as utilitarian justifications for thingification and alienation. But in reifying themselves out of subsistence, the social sciences will in the long run define themselves away.

III. THE LANGUAGE OF HUMAN ACTION

Characterizing the language of science is fairly straight forward. Doing the same for human action — where scientific inquiry itself is but a special case is far more complicated. The reason is that there we are in a territory that most people know so well that we cannot specify what we know about it; we manage to move around in it even though we do not know where we are or where we are going. It is true that meaning is in use, but it is equally true that use is always in flux. Perhaps it is even such that human action is inherently so ambiguous that it will resist any attempts to catch it in the firm categories of formal reasoning. Since thinking about action is itself an action, it becomes impossible to break out of our conceptual prison. What seems needed is an intellectual knife capable of sharpening itself. And yet, something may nevertheless be gained by trying to characterize the language of human action in the same manner as I just have characterized the language of social science.

Considering first the *pragmatics*, it would seem that the actor is less concerned with empirical description of what is and more interested in hypothetical prescription of what ought to be. Or should I rather say with what he ought to do? The distinction is not trivial, even though it rather confirms than denies that the key word in the actor's vocabulary is the verb OUGHT.

It is interesting that in the natural languages it occurs, the ought is usually etymologically connected with the word for owing.[3] It is equally worth noting that it commonly lacks tense. In a mystically mythical way, the ought therefore manages to merge into one word and one concept the pasts, the presents and the futures. In addition, it tends to be highly hypothetical, as it typically – but not necessarily – presents itself in the explorative mood of the subjunctive. Sometimes, however, it is in the indicative and sometimes it hides itself behind the commanding mask of the imperative. But not only are imperatives often considered as hypotheticals, but verbs without subjects usually serve as commands.

As in all languages, the pragmatics of action puts a strong imprint on its *syntax*. Thus, there is common agreement that the fundamental rule of human action cannot be that of truth-preservation. Indeed it is the very point of purposive action to change what now is true so that it becomes untrue. Beginning as an invective, it turns into a vision and ends as a thing. Inherent in these ontological transformations are clearly some peculiar elements of lying, although I am not convinced that the syntax of action aims at the preservation of lies. In the formal work, most attention has instead been directed towards the principles of satisfactoriness-preservation. Its main purpose is to "ensure that we never pass from a fiat, which is satisfactory for a particular purpose, to a fiat which is unsatisfactory for that purpose. The rules are satisfactoriness-preserving, just as the rules for assertoric logic are truth-preserving".[4] To speak about satisfactoriness is therefore not to speak about the actual performance of a particular action, but to give our reasons for performing it. In that realm, there is obviously less need for connectives like 'not', 'or' and 'and' than for connectives like BOTH-THIS-AND-THAT and for modal concepts like POSSIBILITY and PERMISSION. In this context, it is interesting to recall Hume's assertions that "necessity is something that exists in the mind and not in the objects",[5] and that moral ideas, like modal ideas, are founded in internal impressions.

It seems clear that understanding human action is not only to refer to existing physical objects. In addition, it is to refer to mental objects which subsist in minds and relations. Once this much has been acknowledged, it follows that the language of human action must be allotted a *semantics* which allows us to deal with such mind boggling events as speaking about speaking and thinking about thinking. At present, we do not know exactly what that semantics is. One reason is that some of the objects we refer to in practical reasoning are unstable over time. Another is that subsisting objects cannot be counted. Action consequently lies outside the realm of representation and inside that of creation. But the root of creation is at least partly in lying and misunderstanding. The driving force of practical reasoning is therefore in the preservation of those aspects of ambiguity without which creative activity is impossible. It follows that we must admit into our discourse not only transparent but also oblique contexts. Put more technically, we can no longer shun away from those cases in which words with the same reference are not freely interchangeable. The paradigmatic case is that of

> Smith believes that Venus is the morning star

and

> Smith believes that Venus is the evening star.

In the transparent example I gave before, the Leibnizian *salva veritatae* principle was valid. In oblique contexts, however, it breaks down. Since the setting is neither reproduction nor interpretation, symmetric reasoning is of no avail. Unfamiliar juxtaposition is the name of the game as conventional word-things are broken away from servile imitation and brought to the brink of revelation. The word 'revolution' in fact stems from 'revolvere', which means 'to turn over'.

IV. CONCLUSION

It could now be tempting to conclude that whereas the scientific reasoner is prodded on by his quest for the certainty of nominalism, so the practical reasoner is moved by his groping for the ambiguity of relations; in the first case, speech is in narration, in the second in action. But such a conclusion would be much too simplistic, for in both realms we draw on insights from the other. As a consequence, it is more instructive to say that the scientist tends to be certain about ambiguity, while the actor tends to be ambiguous about certainty. I prefer this latter wording, because it stresses the kind of interchange that moves both thought and action. Thus, it seems that both endeavors involve a constant battle between the two opposing concepts of certainty and ambiguity. In this battle, both sides are right, for their natural transcendence leads to a dialectic of unison and plurality. The implication is that if we try to interfere in the struggle by transferring statements from one language to the other, then we are in for trouble. For instance, if we slavishly attempt to transpose statements from the language of social science into the realm of human action, then we run the risk of imposing on reality a strictness

	LANGUAGES OF	
	SOCIAL SCIENCE and	HUMAN ACTION
Pragmatics:	EMPIRICAL DESCRIPTION; IS; INDICATIVE	hypothetical prescription; ought; subjunctive
Syntax:	TRUTH-PRESERVATION NOT; OR; AND	satisfactoriness-preservation both-this-and-that
Semantics:	PHYSICAL OBJECTS EXISTENCE	relations subsistence
Context:	TRANSPARENT	oblique
Paradigm:	VENUS IS THE MORNING STAR	Smith believes that Venus is the morning star
	VENUS IS THE EVENING STAR	Smith believes that Venus is the evening star
Principle:	LEIBNIZIAN *SALVA VERITATAE*	Hegelian identity of identity and nonidentity
Driving force:	CREATION OF CERTAINTY	preservation of ambiguity
Etymology:	TO BIND – RELIGARE – RELIGION	to turn over – reveolvere – revolution

which it neither has nor ought to have. In the Hall of One-Dimensionality, ambiguity would be laid limp, lowly raped by the dominating forces of certainty. What was meant as a tender kiss becomes a deadly throat bite.

B

VI

In my last sentences, I have already started to move away from the simplistic level of this piece into more important and challenging issues. That is not to say, however, that my comments thus far can be dispensed with. Indeed they cannot, for without those well delineated launching pads, it will be impossible to appreciate the saltimbanques which are about to follow. As any epistemologist knows, binary opposition is the first step towards dialectical transcendence.

Listening back at what I have written thus far, it should be obvious that I take the two languages of social science and human action to differ radically in all aspects of pragmatics, syntax and semantics. The two appear in fact to be so different that it would seem impossible to translate their messages into each other. And yet, that Gödelian impossibility feat is exactly what we manage to perform. Not, admittedly, in our class rooms, laboratories or planning offices. But in our daily lives. Not in the shielding pretence of public pronouncements. But in the bare privacy of our bedrooms.

This paradoxical ability raises the challenging question of why and how we succeed in doing in actuality what we are not meant to do if we believe in the principles of structured formal reasoning. It would seem, of course, that the reason is in the fact that the words of normal speech serve many purposes at the same time. They enter the scene as Janus characters whose inherent ambiguity allows them to play the roles of labels and signals at the same time; they are labels attached to objects of physical existence and signals received and emitted as internal relations of subsistence. Since I communicate to others and think to myself, I speak partly to reveal and partly to conceal. As the Bible has it: "In the beginning was the word". Indeed, in the innocent and mythical world of Eden, God's mere naming of a thing made it leap into reality; in Baudelaire's rendering, God did not create the world, but uttered it. Stones and trees, fish and man all flowed from his mouth.

It is part of this creation myth that both identity and existence are in the name. Powerful as the myth may be, its weakness was realized already in Odysseus' encounter with Polyphemus. Thus, when the beastly cannibal asked the wanderer for his name, he received the answer 'Nohbdy'.[6] When Polyphemus subsequently had the redhot spike rammed into his eye and shouted for help, no Cyclop answered because the accusation was that[7]

Nohbdy, Nohbdy's tricked me, Nohbdy's ruined me!

Thus it was only by denying himself that Odysseus could save himself, for — to the primitive creatures between animal and man — word and object were the same. To them it followed that if 'Nohbdy' is somebody's name, then that somebody is a nobody who does not exist. But the wiser Odysseus mused and commented that

I was filled with laughter
to see how like a charm the name deceived them.

But despite the lessons from the Odyssey, it is nevertheless in the western myth of creation that we can find the roots of modern thingification. For there is a close relationship between what we think and what we think about, between the way we speak and what we take to be, between language and ontology, between the Holy Spirit, the Father Almighty and his immaculate son Jessie C. And so it is, that already in the act of creation, we were set on the road of alienation. For just as words create worlds, so the social relations between products create material relations between people.

There would of course be no problem, if the deep structure of all languages corresponded precisely to a stable reality out there or in here. If it were so simple that words were nothing but labels stuck on to things, then words with the same reference would obviously be freely interchangeable. But words and things do not stand in this innocent relation, for even though their external characteristics may be similar, their internal properties are usually quite distinct. Structure is masked by appearance, just as internal and external relations stand to each other like the many-dimensional man to his two-dimensional shadow. The same loss is responsible for the breakdown of the Leibnizian identity principle in oblique contexts. It is this and not the babbel of tongues that makes every translation so problematic. More specifically, it is one thing to rerender a word and another to preserve internal meta-principles; by doing the first, I accept the simplicities of a correspondence theory of truth, while, by doing the second, I commit myself to a coherentist stance. Perhaps it is even here that we can find the gist of the twentieth century tradition of the new in which "we have criticism instead of ideas, methods instead of systems".[8] Perhaps it is here that we can begin to realize that the intellectual avant-garde of modernity lives only by acknowledging its own mortality. And perhaps technological rationality achieves its rationality in the same manner, by sucking on the obsolescence that is its own product.[9]

V I

Am I now about to suggest that if we want our social scientific findings to be translated into action, then we should throw away our equations and instead begin to speak as poets? Am I suggesting that we should cease being manipulative social engineers and instead begin to behave as the sensitive explorers we actually are? Perhaps I am! Perhaps I am not!

But — at the moment — perhaps I really am! The reason is that we seem to live in an age in which the precarious balance between the classical conservatism of certainty and the romantic creativity of ambiguity is being seriously threatened. What I see quite clearly is that the tender intercourse between order and adventure is being stifled by the very way in which positivistic social science is using our words. This is not a consequence of evil motives but of the fact that we have become so imprisoned within our descriptive/truth-functional/thingified language that we continue to perpetuate it without

noticing what we are doing. Here, the poet's approach is drastically different.[10] As an illustration, simply note how B. F. Skinner — the American
behavioral psychologist — at least twice has argued that "you can't have a
science about a subject matter which hops capriciously about".[11] The implication is of course that you and I should be made to behave according to the
strictures of scientific methodology rather than the other way around. Compare now this Skinnerian attitude with that of Octavio Paz — the Mexican
poet. His observation was that "words behave like capricious and autonomous
beings".[12]

'Capricious' is the key concept for both Skinner and Paz. But how different they are in their suggested treatment of it! The first strives to contain it,
thereby confirming the close ties between behaviorism and the verification
principle. The second hopes to set it free, thereby elucidating Harold Bloom's
insight that intellectual change comes from misreading.[13]

The conclusion is inevitable. The relations between words and objects are
far more complicated than the social scientific knowledge can acknowledge.
Thus, while in poetry the word is in meaning or sense, in science it is sign or
reference; while the poet draws on the totality of his insights, the social scientist obeys reasoning rules that make him dumber than he is. The reason is that
the language of modern science is an offspring of the atomistic formalizations
of *The Principia Mathematica*; in the rendering of the early Wittgenstein, "a
name means an object. The object is its meaning".[14] But — as Wittgenstein
himself eventually came to realize — our most important words do not get
their meaning from the objects they denote. Thus, meaning is not in reference
but in use and use is itself in the eternal drama of internal relations. As Marx
knew, however, internal relations are social relations and social relations are
internal relations. It follows that the principles of rationalization and communication become central to a proper understanding of reification and
bureaucratization; equivalence becomes a fetish grounded in a particular conception of identity and existence.

Addressing himself to the same issue, Octavio Paz noted that:[15]

Man's first attitude toward language was confidence: the sign and the object represented
were the same .... To speak was to recreate the object alluded to .... But centuries
later man observed that an abyss had opened between things and their names .... The
belief in the identity between the object and its sign had ceased.

In the same vein, Aldous Huxley distinguished between the two types of discourse in the following way:[16]

The aim of the scientist is to say only one thing at a time and to say it unambiguously and with the greatest possible clarity . . . . This, most emphatically, is not the aim of the literary artist. [He instead] purifies, not by simplifying and jargonizing, but by deepening and extending, by enriching with allusive harmonics, with overtones of association and undertones of sonorous magic.

My own characterization is that where the scientist sees simplicity in complexity, the artist sees complexity in simplicity. And yet, neither the scientist nor the artist can avoid categorization. This presents a most serious dilemma, for to categorize is to fetter and not to categorize is to tear the world asunder. As in other instances of the human condition, tragedy captures the pattern. We are damned if we do and damned if we don't.

The lesson to remember is that when we encounter a new reality, our first reaction is to baptize it. We give it a name. This practice is necessary. Yet it is extremely inhibiting, for if we subsequently proceed as if word and object were the same, then we are liable to confuse use and mention and to commit ourselves to the preservation of the things denoted; I take her picture home to enjoy it for ever, wondering whether her kiss dries off on my lips or solidifies in my memory. But as soon as we understand that the innocence of positivism must be broken, then we recognize that the act of speaking becomes the act of creation. St. Petersburg becomes Leningrad and murder becomes national interest. When the Lord spoke, he knew what he did. So does the husband who lends his name to his wife and children and so does the politician who calls conscription democracy. The resulting paradoxes reflect the condition that language is itself paradoxical, for language can never express any *thing*, only relations. Since we can chase only after shadows, Nietzsche was correct in voicing his fear that we shall never rid ourselves of God, because we shall never rid ourselves of the grammar in which he resides. Perhaps it is such that 'God' is nothing but a name for the social totality of internal relations.

The implications are far reaching. For instance, it should now be easier to see that when man a long time ago spoke his first word, he thereby created the beginning of himself. It should also be easier to appreciate the argument that empires are not created with guns but with words, for words provide the entrance to the armory of the mind. As William Blake put it, "Prisons are built with stones of Law; Brothels with bricks of Religion". And so it is that empires, prisons and brothels are like all other human creations. Verbal acts. As a consequence, they can stay alive only as long as the obligations inherent in those verbal acts are kept alive. When we cease to believe in a word, it no longer has the power. And when words loose their power, so do the institutions that are built upon them.

But this should not be misunderstood to mean that we can manipulate words and worlds at will, merely by touching them with the wand of definition. The lessons are to the contrary. Humpty Dumpty provides a good example. Thus, he said to Alice:[17]

> "There's glory for you!"
> "I don't know what you mean by 'glory'", Alice said.
> Humpty Dumpty smiled contemptuously. "Of course you don't – till I tell you. I meant 'there's a nice knock-down argument for you'!"
> "But 'glory' doesn't mean 'a nice knock-down argument'", Alice objected.
> "When *I* use a word", Humpty Dumpty said, in rather a scornful tone, "it means just what I choose it to mean – neither more nor less".
> "The question is", said Alice, "whether you *can* make words mean so many different things".
> "The question is", said Humpty Dumpty, "which is to be master – that's all".

In an age of manipulative domination it sounds deceptively right. "Who is to be master – that's all". But then, every child knows what happened in the end and that when

Humpty Dumpty had his great fall,
All the King's horses and all the King's men
Couldn't put Humpty Dumpty together again.

The question is now: Who in Humpty Dumpty's world would be master and who would be in power? Would it not be the which of 'all the King's horses and all the King's men'? But, when trouble came around, they managed nothing. Perhaps the explanation is that promises are as much in fertile eyes as in allusive words. At Place du Porte-Manteau, oaths, kisses and grey suits are all for sale. There, the beginning pro- leaves the lips and the ending -mises catch the glance.

VII

The detour into the knowledge of atomism and the wisdom of Humpty Dumpty is completed. But the journey itself is merely beginning. For where we now are is face to face with a tremendous challenge that is too intriguing to ignore. This is to understand where it comes from, the power of those commanding thoughts and words we obey without hearing them.

For many, the answer is that the power comes from ideology. But then? What is ideology, if it is not a particular version of a coherence theory of truth? So, where does that come from? Perhaps it does not come from the people who kill and get killed for ideology's sake, but perhaps it comes from ideology itself. Is it possible, for instance, that our most powerful words all share the characteristic of being neither falsifiable nor verifiable? Is it possible that all of them manage to fuse within themselves a number of seemingly contradictory concepts like mental and physical, past and future, indicative and subjunctive, is and ought, true and false, certainty and ambiguity? Perhaps it shall all fall together if sensibility is allowed to upset reason!

If this is so — and indeed I think it is — then it becomes easier to appreciate the wisdom of those who say that poetic activity is profoundly revolutionary. The reason is of course that the very aim of poetry is to produce new meanings out of old words, new signals out of old labels, new minds out of old things. By being obedient to some linguistic rules, poetry helps to reveal the world as it is. And by being disobedient to some other rules, it creates new images out of old. Its paradigm is to associate what is normally disassociated and to disassociate what is normally associated. Its point is not only to understand the world but to change it as well. In this manner, a text becomes what it really is: A self-generating mechanism whereby we extract from physical things those social relations which keep them alive. As always, ontological transformation is the name of the game, for "what distinguishes the worst architect from the best of bees is this, that he raises his structure in imagination before he erects it in reality. At the end of every labor process, we get a result that already existed in the imagination of the laborer at its commencement".[18]

It is in this context of ontological transcendence that all reification involves both lying and forgetting. It follows that the possibility of change depends on alternative definitions of identity, which themselves are anchored in alternative definitions of existence. It is significant that it was Breton and not Freud himself who claimed that the latter had found in the dream "the principle of the conciliation of opposites".[19]

VIII

To most, what I have said will appear far out. In actuality, though, they are not far out enough. The reason is that in all the themes I have been pursuing I have always ended up in the same frustration of hitting my head against the ceiling of language. What maddens me with these experiences is of course that I remember Wittgenstein's dictum that "the limits of my language mean the limits of my world".[20] It is corollary of this *Weltanschauung* that what you

read right now is not me but yourself. When my words appear incomprehensible — which I am sure they occasionally do — then the reason is not that
they are internally inconsistent to me but that they lie outside the limits of
your world. What is true is therefore not in the correspondence of existing
objects but in the meta principles of coherence. It follows both that truth
resides in the internal relations of grammar and that expansion of truth
involves imperfect translation from one code to another. What is revered as
progress is deciphering into another cipher;[21] "the truth of discourse is caught
in the trap of philology".[22]

It is a sign of increasing awareness that more and more social scientists
begin to recognize that they are caught in the same trap. In the Lévi-Straussian
tradition a most common argument is that "in order to reach the real, one
must repudiate the existential, only to reintegrate it later on in an objective
synthesis from which all sentimentality has been eliminated".[23] As in Roland
Barthes' studies of fashion, the message replaces the object and thereby
becomes the object itself. The examples are easily multiplied to include Gödel,
Arrow, Chomsky and everything in between; the ghost dancers are lining up.

But the contemporary current in the social sciences is little different from
what emerged in literature about a century ago. Thus, most commentators
agree that if there is one concept that unifies modern literature, it is the concept of the 'lacking word'. While the old literature was one comfortably
housed in language, the new literature — that which begins with Baudelaire,
Rimbaud and Mallarmé — is an activity which perceives language as a prison.
It is, furthermore, a prison which is virtually escape proof, for in it everybody
is inmate and warden at the same time. And yet, there are some who try
harder then others to break out. James Joyce in *Finnegans Wake* obviously
comes to mind, because Tim Finnegan is imprisoned within his own Odyssey
and because H.C.E. is nobody but the English language.

Eugene Ionesco has spoken about the same situation in the following manner:[24]

It is as if, through becoming involved in literature, I had used up all possible symbols
without really penetrating their meaning . . . . Words have killed images or are concealing
them. A civilization of words is a civilization distraught. Words create confusion. Words
are not the world (les mots ne sont pas la parole) . . . . The fact is that words say nothing, if I may put it that way . . . . There are no words for the deepest experience. The
more I try to explain myself, the less I understand myself. Of course, not everything is
unsayable in words, only the living truth.

E. M. Cioran — the Rumanian in French clothing — renders the same frustration as:[25]

True contact between beings is established only by mute presence, by apparent non-communication, by that mysterious and wordless exchange which resembles inward prayer.

These are words of people who know words and people equally well. If they sound too *meta* physical to some, then the case of the *quantum* physical should be recalled instead.[26] Thus, there is no doubt that both Heisenberg and Bohr perceived their work in much the same way and that they saw the paradoxes of quantum theory as a consequence of their insistence on thinking and writing in the language of classical physics. Rather than designing a language capable of rendering the new truth, they chose to remain within the old idiom even though it exacts from them the high price of paradox; for them it was more crucial to communicate external correspondence than to establish internal coherence. In addition – and this is yet another Riemannian parallel with Ionesco – Bohr used to make a distinction between 'trivial' and 'profound' truth. The opposite of the former he took to be obviously absurd, while the opposite of the latter was itself taken to be a profound truth. The agreement is clear: Not everything is unsayable in words, only the living truth.

Those who have gone farthest in their attempts to transcend the limits of their language – and thereby the limits of their world – are the surrealists;[27] as Louis Aragon once put it, "the idea of limit is the only inconceivable idea". No group has equalled the surrealists in their attempts to discover high voltage words and to relinquish the language which jornalism has polluted and thereby made impossible. Hence their many attempts to create poetry without words, new syntax without rules, new semantics without physical objects. And hence my own conviction that what unifies the surrealists was not so much their camaraderie, inductions and expulsions as their collective attack on language. They staged this attack because they saw how our blindness to the dreams and the superreal is tied to the practice of linking our words to things rather than to imagination. When that practice is abolished, then the real ceases to be corporeal and begins to become superreal. But since that term was already in the dictionary, Apollinaire coined the signalling label 'surreal'. The message was that total reality includes also that which lies over the roofs and beyond the senses.

The surrealists' conception of revolutionary activity is that the only means to break the chains of invisible words is to cut them by using pliers made from other words; the power of a word is overcome only by the power of another word; the sole way of catching the meaning of one reality is to chase it into a net of other words. To Nietzsche's question "Who speaks?" the Mallarmé of presurrealism answered "The Word itself!" And so it is that we gradually have come to appreciate that language is both a problem and a resource, for language must use itself to overcome itself, just as meaning must use itself to overcome itself. In Heidegger's view, "language speaks, not man".[28] The message is unison: Words get their power from their elements of creative ambiguity, not from the strictures of referential certainty. The difference is that once I have defined a word for ever, then I have for ever tied it to an object. And once I have bound myself in that manner, then I have so castrated my words that they no longer can germinate new meanings, new images and new worlds. Everything becomes as impregnable as the mule itself.

The surrealists were never neutral. In the perennial battle of ontologies they chose sides by honoring Fourier and ignoring Descartes. By that very action they refused the idea of innateness and committed themselves to constant revolution. Their aim was consequently not to write poetry for poetry's sake, but to transform men into living poems, to introduce another way of life. Conceiving new worlds became the same as making new persons. Surrealism is therefore essentially an instrument of knowledge, an epistemology of constant upheaval. The concern is with the relations between man and reality. But for the surrealists, reality is not limited to physical objects. Their search is instead for a fuller reality, which admits into itself both existing and subsisting phenomena. Internal relations, minds and dreams are not buried but resurrected. Breton in fact coined the phrase that "what is admirable about the fantastic is not fantastic but real". For him — as for everybody else — realism is the only ideology.

What is real today fills the pawn shops tomorrow. But the surrealist program retains its vitality not the least for academic social scientists. The reason is that by committing ourselves to the scientific language, we effectively imprison meaning. We do so by assaulting ambiguity and raping the world. The poet is once again different. He does not assault ambiguity. He feeds upon it. He creates from it. And yet, although scientific prose can tell the same story in many ways, poetry allows only one; science and novels can be translated, poetry cannot. It follows that whereas the scientist's certainty becomes ambiguous, so the poet's ambiguity becomes certain. The lesson is that new meaning never comes from the words' reference to things, but rather from the imaginary and rhythm of language itself. Thus, even in the novel, the crisis of modernity has meant a return to the poem. Joyce, Proust and Kafka did there what Strindberg and Brecht did to the theater and what we as social scientists have yet to dare. But there may still be hope. For history always proceeds on the heels of art.

And as history proceeds on the heels of art, the wings it takes off on are the wings of metaphor. I would even suggest that language itself is nothing but a giant metaphor, indeed that all meaning is at bottom metaphoric. Without metaphor we could never see the new in the old and never come to appreciate that creation is expression in search of a meaning. Without it we could never produce new worlds from old words and never generate new ideas like magicians pulling rabbits out of their sleeves.

Like poets from all times, the surrealists know that metaphors are bridges of understanding. They span the gap between known and unknown and allow the tightrope walker to smile over the abyss as he breaks categories and leaps ahead. Myth and language here become linked, for metaphor is the stereoscope of ideas. Reference is given new sense, vehicle new tenor. But it is exactly this creative element that is relegated away from our social scientific language of truth-functional description; while law and order rule over the scientific facts of *status quo*, anarchistic epistemologies promise to be more innovative and more humane.[29]

It is true that a tulip is a flower. But it is also a bubble of blood. An upturned heart is a burning flame, igniting whoever it touches. And so it is the sign of a good metaphor that it defeats ordinary meaning and ordinary existence. If it is successful, then it manages to keep both the general and the particular alive, bringing distant realities into consuming embrace. Dialectics offers the prospect of a similar type of merger, for any dialectic statement contains within itself the seeds of its own destruction. As eyelids close with a bang, tears of contradiction soak into themselves.

IX

It is at this stage — when I look back and ahead at the same time — that I begin to get truly excited. For even though many artists have stumbled on the road before, few social scientists have ever dreamt of entering it. I deplore the fear as I recognize the cause. For just as the Bourgeoisie, the Church and the Revolutions all have expelled their poets, so has the Academy. And for the same reasons of domination in the name of mass communication and ritual communion!

Whether the situation is slowly changing, I do not know. And yet I still harbor the vision that something may be born from our sleeping with the myths. The time has come for dancing as naked as we are. The time has come for stripping the veils and for laying bare the sensitivity of silent words. The time has come for asking why it is so scandalous to be as you are. Emperors!

Only children can see! "What I know at sixty, I knew as well at twenty. Forty years of a long, a superfluous labor of verification".[30] Unmasking is ideology critique. Dressing up is believing in verisimilitude.

What the results of these engagements shall be, I obviously cannot foresee. Perhaps we have even become so self-sufficient that we shall never become pregnant again. But, if the surrealists could create poetry without words, why cannot we have a social science without reified reason? If the poets can reveal the eternal in the present, why cannot we do the same? If dadaists like Hugo Ball saw that his flight from time would succeed only if he broke with a syntax in which time is the binding force, then why cannot we understand that the flight from existing facts will succeed only if we break with a methodology grounded in a two-valued logic of existence? Perhaps we must muster a stronger assault on the language which positivism has polluted and thereby made impossible.

The point is not to dematerialize objects into ideas. It is to become sensitive midwives capable of bringing out alive the Siamese twins of existing things and subsisting relations. If my writings are seen to overemphasize the latter that is only because everyone else overemphasizes the former. 'Power to the People!' will remain a futile cry until preceded by 'Power to the Imagination!' Rather than suppress the individual in the name of the group, we must do exactly the opposite. Like all of us, even Russell and Freud were children of their time. May they now rest in peace!

To describe the present is impossible. To awaken the future is a nightmare. In one season, we hide behind the mask of life. In another, we shudder behind the skull of death. But in order to live and create, we must destroy the tradition from which we stem. Each work must be allowed to become the negation of what it was before. Perhaps there is no choice but to use linguistic alchemy to break with the false stability of things, speech and logic. And — since there is no choice — the challenge is to do a social science which is as surreal as the reality it pretends to portray. But, what will it look like, the work which will do to the social sciences what Joyce's *Ulysses* did to the novel? And what new conventions of reading will it require? Perhaps little has changed. For almost two and a half centuries ago, Hume — Hume of all people! — complained about living "in an age, wherein the greatest part of men seem agreed to convert reading into an amusement, and to reject every thing that requires any considerable degree of attention to be comprehended".[31] In the meantime, how many revolutions have come and gone! Plus ça change, plus ça reste le même. Plus ça reste le même, plus ça change. Peasants never make it.

X

Which — as a sort of forward looking conclusion — brings me back to Alice. Not to her restaurant on the other side of the railroad tracks, but to her Wonderland inside the hole: [32]

> "Did you say 'pig' or 'fig'?" said the cat.
> "I said 'pig'", replied Alice, "and I wish you wouldn't keep appearing and vanishing so suddenly; you make one quite giddy".
> "All right", said the cat, and this time it vanished quite slowly, beginning with the end of the tail, and ending with the grin, which remained some time after the rest of it had gone.
> "Well! I've often seen a cat without a grin", thought Alice, "but a grin without a cat! It's the most curious thing I ever saw in all my life!"

So, in the surrealist tradition, I have ended up with yet another manifesto. But effective manifestoes leave with a slogan. It is fitting to borrow it from a letter Mallarmé wrote to a friend in 1864: PAINT NOT THE THING, BUT THE EFFECT IT PRODUCES.

Instead of looking for the actual of external relations, the task is to unravel the latent of internal relations. But how can this be done? How can I speak about speaking? How can I think about thinking? How can I act about acting? How can I live about living? How can I write to be read as a green pear? Perhaps I can do it by realizing that language is a closed door without hinges. Perhaps I can do it by realizing that we are all confined behind the same gates of the future and within the same asylum of internal relations. In closing his eyes, Apollinaire — the man whose father nobody knew — may have seen the only escape. As he ended his poem 'In Prison':

All is quiet.
There are only two of us in the cell:
I and my mind.

And so it is that inscape triumphs over landscape as white writing of degree zero assumes the activity beyond nihilistic despair. I think that is everything. Not for good, perhaps. But for the here and now and before the now-here moves into nowhere.

Nordplan, Stockholm

NOTES

[1] G. Olsson, *Birds in Egg*, Ann Arbor, 1975.

[2] Quoted in M. Horkheimer and T. Adorno, *Dialectic of Enlightenment*, New York, 1972, p. 7.

[3] A. White, *Modal Thinking*, Ithaca, New York, 1975.

[4] A. Kenny, 'Practical Inference', in *Analysis* **26** (1966), 72.

[5] D. Hume, *A Treatise of Human Nature*, Oxford, 1888.

[6] Note here the similarity in sound between the name 'Odysseus' and 'Udeis', the Greek word for nobody.

[7] The two quotes from *The Odyssey* are from the translation by R. Fitzgerald, New York 1963, p. 157.

[8] O. Paz, *Marcel Duchamp or the Castle of Purity*, London 1970, p. 32.

[9] And as it is that "technology has become the great vehicle of *reification* . . . . The world tends to become the stuff of total administration, which absorbs even the administrators. The web of domination has become the web of Reason itself". Quote from H. Marcuse, *One-Dimensional Man*, Boston 1964, pp. 168–69.

[10] For recent expositions of this and related themes see, e.g., G. Steiner, *After Babel: Aspects of Language and Translation*, New York, 1975; G. D. Martin, *Language, Truth and Poetry*, Edinburgh 1975; and J. Culler, *Structuralist Poetics*, Ithaca 1975.

[11] B. F. Skinner, *Walden Two*, New York, 1948, p. 214; virtually the same wording is also in *idem*: *Science and Human Behavior*, New York, 1953, p. 6.

[12] O. Paz, *The Bow and the Lyre*, New York, 1973, p. 38.

[13] H. Bloom, *A Map of Misreading*, New York, 1975; and *idem*: *Poetry and Repression*, Ithaca, 1976.

[14] L. Wittgenstein, *Tractatus Logico-Philosophicus*, London, 1961.

[15] O. Paz, *op. cit.*, 1973, p. 19.

[16] A. Huxley, *Literature and Science*, London 1963, pp. 13–14.

[17] L. Carroll, *The Annotated Alice*, New York 1960, pp. 268–69.

[18] K. Marx, *Capital*, New York, 1967, Vol. I, p. 178.

[19] A. Breton, 'Reserves Quant à la Signification Historique des Investigations sur le Rêve', *Le Surréalisme au Service de la Révolution* **4** (1932), 9.

[20] Wittgenstein, *op. cit.*

[21] Note here that the *Oxford English Dictionary* gives the meaning of 'cipher' as "1/ An arithmetical symbol or character (0) of no value by itself, but which increases or decreases the value of other figures according to its position . . . " and as "5/ A secret or disguised way of writing, whether by characters arbitrarily invented . . . , or by an arbitrary use of letters of characters in other than their ordinary sense . . . ".

[22] M. Foucault, *The Order of Things*, New York, 1973, p. 297.

[23] F. Jameson, *The Prison-House of Language*, Princeton, 1974, p. 142 f.

[24] Quoted from G. Steiner, *op. cit.*; p. 185.

[25] E. M. Cioran, 'The Trouble With Being Born', in *Antaeus* **20** (1976), 119.

[26] For a fuller treatment, see my *Birds in Egg*, Chap. XII.

[27] Useful overviews are in A. Breton, *Manifestoes of Surrealism*, Ann Arbor, 1969; A. Balakian, *Surrealism: The Road to the Absolute*, New York, 1959; *idem*: *André Breton*, New York, 1971; W. Fowlie, *Age of Surrealism*, Bloomington, Indiana, 1960;

F. Alguie, *The Philosophy of Surrealism*, Ann Arbor, 1969; J. H. Matthews, *Surrealistic Poetry in France*, Syracuse, 1969; H. S. Gershman, *The Surrealistic Revolution in France*, Ann Arbor, 1974; P. Ilie, *The Surrealistic Mode in Spanish Literature*, Ann Arbor, 1974; and M. Benedikt, *The Poetry of Surrealism: An Anthology*, Boston 1974.

[28] M. Heidegger, *Der Satz vom Grund*, Phullingen, 1975, p. 161. Also see H. -G. Gadamer, *Hegel's Dialectic*, New Haven, 1976, Chap. 5.

[29] P. Feyerabend, *Against Method*, London, 1975.

[30] E. M. Cioran, *op. cit.*, p. 119.

[31] D. Hume, *op. cit.*, p. 456.

[32] L. Carroll, *op. cit.*, pp. 90–91.

JOHN S. PIPKIN

PROBLEMS IN THE PSYCHOLOGICAL MODELLING
OF REVEALED DESTINATION CHOICE[1]

I. INTRODUCTION

The shift from rationalistic to behavioral accounts of human action in geography has entailed a radical change in our accounts of spatial choice. It is now a commonplace that in many non-prescriptive contexts a probabilistic and psychologically-based epistemology of choice is preferable to the deterministic account provided by classic consumer theory. This transition has not been accompanied by explicit methodological discussion of the profoundly different mathematical structures underlying algebraic and probabilistic choice. The contrast has been explicitly dealt with in the literatures of economics and psychology[2] as well as geographically-oriented discussions.[3] One context in which the implications of probabilistic choice urgently require clarification is revealed preference analysis of destination choice in shopping travel. Central place theory and market area analysis provide our most elaborate theoretical models of this behavior. Both espouse an algebraic account of individual choice. Both at least in their classic 'un-map-transformed' versions compare unfavorably in descriptive ability with the Huff model[4] which is simple and atheoretical, but probabilistic. Presumably, progress in the study of probabilistic individual choice will lead to theoretically explicit structures which at least equal the Huff model in descriptive power.

It is deceptively easy to construct such a framework in an abstract way. For example, consider an urban area given as a measurable set $A \subset R^2$, containing n competitive stores at arbitrary locations $\{(x_i, y_i), i = 1, \ldots, n\}$. Let $O(x, y)$ represent a trip-origin density function (for example, some suitable transformation of an empirical or theoretical population density surface). Let $p_i(x, y)$ represent the probability that a trip originating at (x, y) terminates at the ith store. Requirements on p_i will be discussed in detail below; clearly in this competitive situation p_i must depend at minimum upon the locational and site characteristics of all the stores. Let the random variable X_i represent patronage at the ith store. Then under general assumptions on A, O and p_i, expressions approximating $E(X_i)$ and $VAR(X_i)$ may be obtained.[5] For example

309

S. Gale and G. Olsson (eds.), Philosophy in Geography, 309–328. All Rights Reserved.
Copyright © 1979 by D. Reidel Publishing Company, Dordrecht, Holland.

$$(1) \qquad E(X_i) = \iint\limits_{(x,y)\in A} O(x,y)p_i(x,y)\,dx\,dy.$$

Numerical evaluation of $E(X_i)$ and $VAR(X_i)$ is straightforward, even for highly complicated O and p_i. Prescriptions on optimum size and location for the ith store may be simply written in terms of partial derivatives. First-order conditions on optimum competitive location for the ith store are given by $\partial E_i/\partial x_i = \partial E_i/\partial y_i = 0$, while the marginal impact of changes in the location of other stores on expected patronage at the ith is measured by $\partial E_i/\partial x_j$ and $\partial E_i/\partial y_j, j \neq i$.

When reasonably realistic forms are assumed for p_i (for example, even the Huff model itself), this framework becomes mathematically complicated. The prospects for explicit analytic solution are scant. One of the numerous sources of complexity in the first-order conditions is the intractable form of the derivatives of Pythagorean distance in the plane. However, if the model proved valuable in predicting empirical store choice, the expense of even brute-force numerical solution would be inconsiderable, in applied contexts. I believe that the main impediment in developing and implementing models of this type is not mathematical complexity, but the difficulties in developing meaningful and mathematically explicit forms for p_i.

There are formidable difficulties in providing accounts of the overt actions involved in shopping travel which are plausible in the context of psychological theory on discrimination and choice and which possess testable empirical content, including constructs interpretable across a series of separate studies. An enormous variety of psychological material has been successfully applied on a conceptual level (for example, the geographic descendants of Lewinian 'life-space' and 'valence'.[6]) It remains true, however, that essentially the only numerical construct we possess which comes close to being measurable across separate data sets is the distance-decay parameter implied by 'psychophysical' analysis of distance perception.

The difficulties stem from the nature of the spatial behavior, and from the character of the (apparently) pertinent psychological theory. Revealed spatial choice differs from the behavior studied in the classic theory of discrimination and choice in obvious ways. The geographer is inclined to treat in a molar way units of behavior which are admitted to possess complex internal structure. Choices are revealed in purely nonexperimental contexts, and consequently practically all trip choices are observed over multiple and not binary choice sets. The classic mathematical structures for discrimination and choice were developed in spare and controlled settings in which binary discriminations were observed over simple stimuli. The enormous literature on replicable binary discrimination and learning is not directly applicable to nonexperimental choices revealed over nonbinary sets of compound alternatives. Specifically, it is clear that no matter how much we prefer to focus on overt behavior and to eschew mentalistic constructs, we cannot emulate the extreme behaviorist stance, rejecting theoretical structure in general and unobservable variables in particular.[7] On the contrary, a scaffolding of unobservable constructs, variables, and parameters is indispensable to achieve at least four specific objectives, none of which can be attained by experimental control. These are: population aggregation, longitudinal aggregation, construction of unitary but compound choice alternatives, and the substitution of parametric for experimental control of response context. Each of these objectives will be elaborated in turn.

Firstly, it is obvious that there exists an inverse relationship between the amount of internal mathematical structure required in a choice model, and the structural simplicity of the choice alternatives. The 'atomic' alternatives of spatial choice may be defined in a variety of ways, as exemplified in the various treatments of timing, route, mode and destination choice that exist in the literature. Bower and Trabasso's[8] concept of 'action unit', and Miller, Galanter and Pribam's[9] 'plan' schema provide conceptual justifications for these incisions into molar trip choice. For example, mode choice may be internalized into a unitary choice model for a sample group which travels by various modes, or may be externalized from the mathematical structure by disaggregation into subgroups of single-mode users. It is clear that with foreseeable data sets on overt shopping choices, no amount of disaggregation can eliminate substantial complexity in the units of choice (such as the familiar separation into site and trip-link attributes). This complexity must therefore be built, the more explicitly the better, into the mathematical structure of the model.

Acts of choice over a homogeneous class of destinations are revealed so rarely and under such varied conditions by specific individuals or households, that true replication of overt behavior at the individual level is probably never observed. It is certainly not observed often enough to permit estimation of choice-model parameters at the individual level. Population aggregation assumptions are indispensable, and these are imposed by assuming constancy (or a specified probability distribution) of parameters across a suitable population. As will be shown below, cross-sectional aggregation assumptions suffice to develop a broad class of models designed for single-choice data. Longitudinal aggregation assumptions are discussed separately.

The final objective in developing a structure of intervening variables is to permit parametric unification of separate choice contexts. For example, in models in which site and link attributes are separable and in which constancy of site attributes is tenable, one single model structure may account for choices revealed over a set of sites from many separate current locations. These observations may then be grouped, to sharpen parameter estimates.

This paper is intended as a contribution to the development of theoretically well-founded, psychologically-based accounts of revealed preference in the specific context of shopping travel. This context is one distinguished by problems, conceptual and technical, and by major differences from contexts in which the psychological theories originally were developed. The problems may be summarized simply: destination choices are revealed rarely, in unreplicable circumstances, by heterogeneous populations, over complex and nonbinary choice sets. The paper emphasizes what appears to be the most promising theoretical existing framework, the classic strength model of Thurstone.[10] The first section compares alternative accounts of a single act of spatial choice. It amplifies a twofold structure of 'choice model' and 'response strength model' proposed previously.[11] Subsequent sections deal with aggregation of homogeneous and heterogeneous populations, and with longitudinal aggregation of choices.

II. PROBABILISTIC ACCOUNTS OF SINGLE CHOICES

The essential component of most psychological accounts of choice is the assertion that a single act of choice or discrimination is most appropriately described by a probability distribution over the set of alternatives. In itself, this assumption is not testable. Longitudinal or population aggregation assumptions imply empirically testable structure in aggregate data. In this section some contrasts are drawn between this structure and classic algebraic choice models. Then the components of a proposed model structure for psychological destination choice are described. More specific details are given in Pipkin,[12] on which the discussion in this section is based.

The deterministic model of choice implied by consumer theory possesses a well-integrated structure and has been summarized by several authors.[13] A primitive and unobservable value structure generates a partial or complete relational preference algebra over single or multi-attribute alternatives in the choice set. Revealed preference techniques permit direct reconstruction of the preference relation. Choice itself is usually taken as a set function defined by maximization of an ordinal or interval-scale utility function, which is in a defined agreement with the preference algebra. This framework is extended (without modification of the underlying logic) to more complicated choice sets in game and statistical decision theory. Psychological accounts of overt choice (or selection or discrimination) do not possess this monolithic structure: they appear in many guises in psychophysics, discrimination, choice and learning theories, where, as Bock and Jones[14] point out, differences of nomenclature sometimes conceal similarities of purpose.

The notion that human behavior under fixed conditions should be consistent is a far weaker requirement than that it should be rational. From the viewpoint of either rationality or even consistency, it is not immediately clear why individual acts of choice or discrimination should be regarded as irreducibly probabilistic. The severity of the logical problem varies with the degree of experimental control. In early, highly controlled experiments on psychophysical magnitudes and thresholds, differential responses to identical stimuli were explained in terms of random and additive neural events generating subjective magnitude.[15] In this case, application of the Central Limit Theorem leads to a normal model of threshold formation. At one extreme, in the theory of the ideal observer, probabilistic response may even be traced back to quantum indeterminacies in the physical stimulus.

At a higher level, Quandt[16] provides an appealing account of probabilistic response which is induced by deterministic preference over randomly sampled attributes. Generally, in situations which are not rigidly controlled, factors external to the organism suffice to account for differential responses. Logically, this does not contravene a deterministic account of response to *identically* the same choice context, for this can never be recaptured.

Destination choice in shopping travel is affected by such a variety of subjective and objective factors, few of which admit of experimental or statistical control, that intrinsic randomness of single choices entails no logical problems. Indeed, a probabilistic account of choice is intuitively more acceptable than a deterministic one. Considerable problems arise in explicitly implementing this account. Firstly, as indicated above, existing psychological frameworks are not directly applicable to nonbinary choices over complex alternatives. Secondly, at best, existing accounts do not possess the coherent and logically explicit epistemology of the consumer-theoretic (algebraic) model in which values figure as predicates, preferences as binary reactions, utilities as real-valued functions and choice as a set-function.

An embracive though not logically exhaustive class of interpreted probabilistic choice models is that in which a unidimensional 'psychological continuum' mediates between a space of perhaps complex alternatives and the discrete probability distribution that describes choice itself. The theoretical role played by this scale does not differ greatly from that performed by (cardinal) utility in consumer theory in the sense that it is unobservable and determined to at least an interval scale of measurement. The mathematical structure and the behavioral postulates of the theory are, of course, quite different. The great majority of structures in mathematical psychology and all choice models in behavioral geography, including the simple Huff model[17] and the multinomial logit model, fall into this class of unidimensional models.

The mapping of complex alternatives onto a linear continuum is a substantive assumption, but a relatively weak one, since the mapping and the choice function defined on the scale are arbitrary. This twofold model is discussed in more detail elsewhere.[18] It seems appropriate to term the function which defines probabilities in terms of scale values the *choice* functions, and that which maps the choice objects to the scale the *response* function. This terminology is not precisely cognate with that used, for example, in Bock and Jones.[19]

Consider first the choice function. Luce and Suppes[20] distinguish two alternate formulations which they term 'constant' and 'random' utility models. In the constant utility models the scale values are unvarying (on the occasion of a single, specific choice), and the choice function has the form $p_i = f(v_1, v_2, \ldots, v_n)$ where p_i is the choice probability of the ith object and v_j is the scale value for the jth. Several alternatives (weak, strong and strict utilities) are feasible in the binary case, but for non-binary choice sets the strict utility formulation $p_i = v_i(\Sigma_j v_j)^{-1}$ is essentially the only possible model. An axiomatic justification for it was given by Luce[21] and under various transformations of the scale it yields the simple Huff model and the multinomial logit formulation.

In measurement terms the v-scale in the Luce model simply represents the mapping of $p_i \in [0, 1]$ to $v_i \in [0, \infty)$ induced by an arbitrary positive constant. Substantively, the model does not contain a particularly compelling account of the behavioral mechanism of choice. It simply asserts that choice probabilities are proportional to scale values.

The second class of choice models distinguished by Luce and Suppes contains a far more explicit choice mechanism. They are termed random utility models, they retain the compelling economic notion of utility-maximization, and they are based on concepts of Thurstone.[22] I have discussed these models in detail elsewhere.[23] Each alternative is characterized by a random utility U_i with mean μ_i and standard deviation σ_i. With statistically independent utilities we have

$$(2) \qquad p_i = \int\limits_{-\infty}^{\infty} \frac{1}{\sigma_i} f\left(\frac{t - \mu_i}{\sigma_i}\right) \prod_{j \neq i} F\left(\frac{t - \mu_j}{\sigma_j}\right) dt$$

where f and F are standardized density and distribution functions. Thurstone took the normal distribution as the natural density for the utilities. If momentary perceived utility is subject to many independent effects, the Central Limit Theorem suggests that this is the case, even though normal densities entail difficulties from the viewpoint of explicit as opposed to numerical solution. A variety of alternative probability distributions are appraised in terms of tractability and empirical distinguishability in earlier work.[24]

Despite the contrast drawn between constant and random utility models, the Luce–Huff and multinomial logit models arise as special cases of expression (2). If the utilities are homoscedastic and distributed in such a way that the utility differences $[U_i - U_j]$ $(i \neq j)$ are logistic, then expression (2) is equivalent to the strict utility model with $v_i = \exp(\mu_i)$. Attempts have been made to use the conceptual structure of random utility models as a theoretical justification for the multinomial logit model.[25] If the v_i are taken as substantively meaningful 'response strengths' which interact proportionally to determine choice probabilities, it is not clear what interpretation is to be given to the μ_i, which are related to the v_i by a logarithmic transformation. If we choose to follow Thurstone and interpret the μ_i as meaningful 'affective values' the logit model commits us to a reciprocal exponential density as the empirical distribution of the individual U_i. (Logistic differences $[U_i - U_j]$ do not imply logistic U_i). I find this implausible and agree with Laming that the numerical similarity between the Luce model and a logistic-difference Thurstone model is misleading and that they are conceptually quite different. He writes

The practical difficulties of discriminating between these two ideas, which at a psychological level are quite disparate, are rather disheartening. For practical purposes . . . the choice between these two alternatives is really a matter of practical convenience in a computational sense . . . But at a theoretical level the matter ought not to be left thus.[26]

It is acceptable to invoke the logistic distribution as an extremely effective approximation to normal $[U_i - U_j]$. It is a far stronger assumption to assert that the reciprocal exponential is the empirical distribution of utility. The Central Limit Theorem applied to the individual utility distributions suggest that this is most implausible.

The Thurstonian framework with the classic interpretation of random utilities yields a large class of homoscedastic and heteroscedastic choice models.[27] We now turn to the second logical component of the unidimensional model, the response function.

The response function is termed the 'psychophysical' function in cases where transparent relationships can be established between physical attributes of the alternatives and some sensory continuum. Typically, the relationship is expressed as a polynomial of low degree or a simple transcendental function as in Weber's and Fechner's laws respectively. Because of the complexity of the alternatives in destination choice (including a range of site characteristics and link attributes such as distance, route and mode measures) it is unreasonable to seek relationships of such simplicity.

In existing literature the scale values are defined in *ad hoc* ways as linear or transformed regression functions of a wide range of such attributes. There is no consistent usage regarding a distinction which is viewed as critical in the psychological literature, that between regressors (measurable characteristics of the alternatives) and parameters to be estimated. For example, in the simplest form of the Huff model, $v_i = s_i \cdot d_i^{-\lambda}$ where s_i and d_i are regressors and λ is a parameter. In a form of the multinomial logit model, $v_i = \exp(\mu_i)$ where μ_i is a linear or log-linear function of a conceptually limitless series of measures such as quality, price, parking space and travel time. Each measure is associated with one free regression parameter. Only two features are common to most existing models. First, a negative power or negative exponential 'psychophysical' function is typically used to relate perceptual and physical distance or time. Secondly, multiplicative or additive separability of site and route effects is assumed, despite some evidence that site utility and distance are not perceived independently. The analytic advantages of this separability are very clear,[28] but its substantive acceptability is debatable.

The variety of existing explicit or tacit proposals for the response function is symptomatic of our ignorance of the relevant attributes of sites and links, and what is the nature of their substantive 'psychophysical' relationship to the putative psychological continuum. The present attitude toward this continuum appears to take it as an *ad hoc* intervening variable. The form of the components, their separability and their status as regressors or parameters is dictated purely by statistical convenience. Where we require the simplest possible arithmetic, we limit the number of parameters, perhaps only retaining Huff's classic λ. Where we require the best possible fit we introduce as many unconstrained parameters as degrees of freedom will bear. To argue for careful discrimination between regressors and parameters is to do more than repeat the classic argument that many parameters lead to good fits while few parameters lead to good (elegant) models. It is at least conceivable that in the long run we will establish the regressor/parameter decision, the separability conditions and the form components of the response function on substantive grounds, in the style of classic psychophysics. The outlook for such results at present is not good and it is arguable that at least in nonbinary revealed-preference contexts we will continue to use the psychological continuum as a statistical convenience determined only by the power of estimation procedures. In this case the psychophysics literature is of little relevance in our context. If we were to opt for substantive relationships, say between site and distance effects, we might well find our statistical assumptions – such as separability – to be untenable.

This section has dealt with conceptual problems implied by a probabilistic account of an individual act of choice. The main available psychological framework contains unidimensional models with two components: a response function and a choice function. Development of response functions in our context is a complex problem. Many logical possibilities exist, and we are unable as yet to weigh the claims of statistical expediency and substantive plausibility. There are only two well-studied candidates for the choice function: the Luce and Thurstone models. The class of Thurstone models is far more general and appears to represent the most promising framework for analysis of destination choice.

III. CROSS SECTIONAL AGGREGATION ASSUMPTIONS

We consider first a data context in which one single destination choice (or expressed preference) is recorded for each respondent in a sample of households or individuals. Data of this type are common: for example, in the study of grocery travel, respondents frequently record the site of their 'major grocery purchase'. The force of this assumption is to eliminate from consideration longitudinal variation in the probability or parameters of choice, and to focus attention on aggregation over respondents. We assume a set of N competitive stores and a localized sample of Q individuals or households. Let X_i^q be a Bernoulli random variable which indicates whether the qth respondent visits the ith site. Define X_i as the total patronage at the ith site from the sample with $X_i = \Sigma_q X_i^q$.

Two radically different accounts of the source of the randomness in the X_i^q are possible. These accounts differ profoundly in concept, though they appear to be frequently confounded in the literature. One possible reason for the randomness of X_i^q is that implicit in the preceding discussion, namely that individual choice is intrinsically probabilistic. In this case we postulate a probability p_i^q which governs X_i^q. This case of *bona fide* individual randomness will be termed *intrinsic*. In this case the appropriate aggregation strategy is to consider relationships between the p_i^q for different individuals, either direct or implied by relationships among underlying parameters. Before attempting this, it is necessary to deal briefly with a quite different source of randomness, which occurs very frequently in interpretations of aggregate choice data. It is implied, for example, in Huff's classic paper.[29] Here, a probability distribution is used to aggregate choices over a heterogeneous population. The value p_i is interpreted as the probability that a randomly chosen individual will record a visit to the ith store. It is *not* necessary to postulate p_i^q at the individual level; indeed nothing need be stipulated about individual behavior. The source of randomness in the X_i^q may be adequately accounted for as the sampling variation in selecting an individual in a heterogeneous population. This type of randomness will be termed *sampling randomness*. It is clear that sampling randomness itself constitutes an aggregation framework. The same formal structures appear that are used to describe intrinsic randomness, though their logical status is radically different. Aggregation via sampling randomness will be briefly discussed, before turning to strategies in the more general case of intrinsic randomness.

III.1. *Aggregation with Sampling Randomness*

Both the Thurstone and Luce–Huff models may be interpreted in an aggregative way. In the Thurstone model, let U_i portray variability in utility of the ith store over a heterogeneous population of individuals. Each individual possesses a vector of *fixed* utilities, representing samples from the U_i. Assuming that each individual is a deterministic utility maximizer, the probability that a randomly chosen individual chooses the ith store is identical to equation (2) above. This is equivalent to the model of Golob and Beckmann.[30] The interpretation placed on U_i and its parameters μ_i and σ_i in this case is profoundly different from that with intrinsic randomness. Under intrinsic randomness the U_i described variability in perceived utility at the individual level, whereas under the alternative interpretation it portrays empirical variation in utility over a population. It is ironic that the same formal structure admits of such radically disparate interpretations; it provides an account of individual choice which is intrinsically probabilistic and also of the behavior of an individual randomly chosen from among deterministic utility-maximizers. It is evident that the randomness of the X_i^q in the latter case is an artifact of sampling. With longitudinal data at the individual level, these interpretations may be distinguished.

In the Luce–Huff model, too, the quantity $p_i = v_i \cdot (\Sigma_j v_j)^{-1}$ is often construed as the probability that a randomly chosen individual visits the ith store, while nothing is stipulated about the behavior of specific individuals. In the individual interpretation of Luce's choice model, the v-scale is interpretable as response strength. An appropriate interpretation of the scale with sampling randomness is much less clear.

III.2. *Aggregation with Intrinsic Randomness*

The most straightforward aggregation scheme with intrinsic randomness is the case in which the p_i^q are constant over a suitably homogeneous sample population, and choices by different individuals are statistically independent. This case will be called *simple aggregation*. Under this assumption the X_i^q are independent and identically distributed Bernoulli variates with common probabilities p_i. The overall probability structure for the observations is a simple multinomial one. Each X_i is binomial with parameter Q and p_i. $E(X_i) = Qp_i$, $\mathrm{VAR}(X_i) = Qp_i(1 - p_i)$ and $\mathrm{COV}(X_i, X_j) = Qp_ip_j$. The log-likelihood of a vector of observations is proportional to

$$\sum_{q=1}^{Q} \sum_{i=1}^{N} X_i^q \log p_i.$$

It is highly significant that with single-choice observations on a random sample of consumers this probability structure is identical to that arising with sampling randomness. This implies that on this type of data the two models cannot be distinguished, despite the different interpretations of the p_i. This confirms the intuitive idea that with single-choice data a decision cannot be made between the algebraic and probabilistic accounts of individual choice.

A sufficient condition for equality of the p_i^q is equality of parameters in the underlying choice models for different respondents. Specification of a form for the p_i in terms of these common parameters yields the simplest class of interpreted probabilistic choice models. Simple aggregation of the constant utility model requires equality of the v-scale over individuals, while for the Thurstone model it requires equality of form and parameters in the random variables U_i. This is evidently an extremely strong assumption even for a localized and socio-economically homogeneous sample of respondents.

For single choice data the substructure of assumptions implied by intrinsic randomness with *simple* aggregation is unnecessary and probably undesirable. The sampling randomness interpretation provides an account of the data which is more economical in terms of unobservable structure. On data containing multiple revealed choices, the situation is quite different, as indicated below.

The simple aggregation assumption with intrinsic randomness is a very strong one. A more realistic alternative exists, in which the price of realism is a substantial increase in analytic complexity. This alternative will be termed *random aggregation*, which signifies that the distribution of choice probabilities over a heterogeneous sample population is specified as a random variable. Individual behavior on this account is doubly stochastic. Individual choice is intrinsically probabilistic, and the site choice probabilities are themselves sampled from some aggregating distribution. The general mathematical description of this case involves mixture distributions.

Randomization may proceed at either of two levels. A probability distribution may be assumed directly for the uninterpreted p_i, or a population distribution of underlying parameters may be made in an interpreted choice model thereby inducing a mixture distribution on the p_i. Randomization of uninterpreted probabilities is a feature of several brand-choice and other marketing models.[31] Burnett has adapted a binary version to store choice.[32] Despite the apparent richness of possibilities for mixtures, the requirement $0 \leqslant p_i \leqslant 1 = \Sigma_i p_i$ implies that there is essentially only one candidate for a family of mixing distributions: the beta family.[33]

Randomization of interpreted probabilities entails imposing a probability distribution on the internal components of the model. The strict utility version may be aggregated by assuming distributions for the v_i and deriving the joint distribution of the p_i. Ideally, compounding distributions should be imposed on the components of the response function (such as perceived site utility and perceived travel time). Pipkin discusses the associated problems and indicates that although estimates of certain moments may be obtained, it is in general very hard to derive the density of the p_i.[34] The problem is compounded by the constraint $v_i \geqslant 0$, which precludes certain obvious aggregating densities including the normal. Essentially, the only case in which the analysis can be carried through explicitly is that in which the v_i are independent gamma variates with one parameter in common. This yields, again, a beta distribution of the p_i. The standard errors of parameter estimates arising in this case are large. It is hard to decide whether the gamma distribution provides an acceptable description of the perceived utility of a store in a heterogeneous population. At any rate, constancy of one parameter over several stores appears rather implausible.

It is not difficult to formulate random aggregation for the random utility choice model in an abstract way. Since the μ_i are unconstrained, they may be taken as normally distributed. I have not found any analysis of the resultant 'doubly random' Thurstone model, which is not surprising: such analysis appears extremely difficult. Also, due to symmetry, the net effect of this aggregation is to increase variances and standard errors without affecting the expected values of utilities or parameter estimates.

In nonbinary contexts, random aggregation of the strict utility model is difficult, and intractable for the random utility model. Simple aggregation yields the simplest parameter estimation structure, although it imposes strong homogeneity constraints on samples of respondents.

IV. LONGITUDINAL AGGREGATION

The preceding discussion has been predicated on the assumption of single choices or expressed preferences by individuals or households. This section contains comments on temporal aggregation with data in which repeated choices are revealed, such as travel diaries. Attention will again be relegated to visit sequences revealed over a single class of destinations by a localized sample of respondents. Our account of an individual act of choice with intrinsic randomness entails a probability distribution p_i^q, and a specified parametric model for the probabilities. Variation in choice on different occasions may be accounted for either as a sample from a learning trajectory for the individual, or as residual (asymptotic) variation in an essentially stable probability structure. These alternatives are discussed in turn. Our conclusions on the feasibility of articulated learning models in this non-binary revealed-preference context are pessimistic. With such data an asymptotic interpretation of the probability structure appears to be the only tractable alternative. We discuss learning models first in order to exhibit the (apparently) insuperable difficulties that arise in applying them to data of the travel diary type.

IV.1. *Learning Formulations*

A wealth of material in mathematical learning theory has been exploited in geographic work, and no attempt will be made here to provide an overview of the variety of potential models. We consider the following matrix of

Bernoulli variables, $X_{it}^q, i = 1, \ldots, n, t = 1, \ldots, m^q$, recording a sequence of m^q visits to n sites made by the qth individual. The probability p_{it}^q is associated with the random variable X_{it}^q. We will fix q and supress it from the notation. We assume statistical independence of the X_{it}. Of course, this does not eliminate the mathematical interdependence of successive choice embodied in the learning models, which transform the vector p_{it} to $p_{i(t+1)}$.

A model of secular change may be imposed either at the level of (uninterpreted) choice probabilities, or at the level of the psychological parameters (scale values) on which these probabilities depend. This distinction has proved an important one in the literature on learning models. Because probabilities are bounded on $[0, 1]$, linear learning transformations of uninterpreted probabilities are inadmissible, except as local approximations, and linear transformations of underlying scale parameters induce quite complicated transformation on the probabilities. As a consequence, the psychological literature has, as usual, focussed on the most tractable case of binary models, which are not directly applicable in our context.

The nonbinary constant and random utility models do admit of fairly straightforward learning extensions on an abstract level. The main problems arise in parameter estimation and aggregation. We will illustrate these problems in the case of the constant utility model. Let $p_{it} = v_{it} \cdot (\Sigma_j v_{jt})^{-1}$, where the time-dependent utilities are functions of site and distance regressors, and parameters to be estimated. We will impose the learning transformation on the v-scale, and will consider a simple special case in which a visit to the ith store alters only the scale value of that store, and no other one, by a constant factor independent of i. Thus a visit to store i at time t results in the transformation $v_{j(t+1)} = v_{jt}, j \neq i$ and $v_{i(t+1)} = v_{it} + \Delta v$. Consider the observed visit sequence to four stores 1, 2, 2, 3. The posterior likelihood of this sequence may be written as follows if we abbreviate v_{i1} as $v_i, i = 1, \ldots, n$

$$\frac{v_1}{\Sigma_j v_j} \cdot \frac{v_2}{\Delta v + \Sigma_j v_j} \cdot \frac{v_2 + \Delta v}{2\Delta v + \Sigma_j v_j} \cdot \frac{v_3}{3\Delta v + \Sigma_j v_j}.$$

Although the notation becomes extremely complex, there is no logical difficulty in writing an n-parameter likelihood or log-likelihood function for any observed sequence of visits. This model is excessively simple because it is most implausible that Δv should be constant, or even of the same algebraic sign, for different stores and times. Several more realistic formulations exist and in each the likelihood expression can be written without logical difficulty. The example given illustrates the mathematical difficulties that would arise in estimating parameters on which the v-scale depends (in a nonlinear fashion).

Although considerable, these mathematical difficulties are not the major difficulty in applying explicit learning models to data of the travel diary type.

A more serious, insuperable, problem is the following dilemma. Choices made under uniform conditions over a single class of destinations by one single individual or household are revealed rarely, at most three or four times, in a typical travel diary. It would be absurd to propose to apply and estimate an individual learning model on such sparse data. On the other hand, no appropriate aggregation frameworks exist which would permit us to pool parameter estimates over individuals. The essence of the learning framework outlined above is that it incorporates explicit functional relations between the probabilities in a particular unique sequence of visits. It would be simply untenable to assume that a similar learning trajectory, governed by identical parameters, applies to several individuals, no matter how carefully variables such as local knowledge and length of residence are controlled. One conceivable approach is the following: Make the arguable assumption of certain common parameters and statistical independence of all visits in a pooled sample. Then write a pooled likelihood function containing multiplicative factors embodying the unique trip sequences of particular individuals. Maximization of this function would yield acceptable estimates of the purported common parameters. This maximization would pose a formidable numerical problem.

In sum I conclude that the attempt to incorporate an explicit mathematical learning model into a probabilistic account of non-binary choices, and to estimate parameters by maximizing the likelihood of the observed site sequences in travel diary format is an extremely difficult and perhaps unsolvable problem. The literature in geography as well as in areas such as brand choice amply confirms the utility of explicit learning models in other data contexts. Typically, these contexts are characterized by evaluative questionnaire data (rather than a strict revealed preference stance) and by choices which are either intrinsically binary or artificially dichotomized.[35]

IV.2. *Asymptotic Randomness*

This section deals with longitudinal aggregation under the assumption that the intrinsic variability in individual choice is residual, asymptotic randomness, and that the p_i^q do not vary in a systematic way with time.

Classical learning theory provides an account of systematic secular change in choice probability, represented by a functional transformation of probabilities or scale values from choice to choice. It has frequently been observed that such change is not a logical concomitant of probabilistic choice. For example, Coleman, in discussing change and response uncertainty distinguishes systematic (learning) change from essentially capricious residual variability exemplified in psychology by test–retest reliability.[36] This randomness may be construed as the limit of a learning process, or it may be invoked in lieu of one. In the brand choice literature a model involving long spells of uniformity punctuated by abrupt switches is frequently preferred to a long process of pseudo-continuous adjustment implied by the usual learning models. Certainly, in the context of destination choice, residual and non-systematic randomness provides an intuitively acceptable surrogate for innumerable minor variations in the subjective and objective context of choice. Burnett states the matter clearly:

> ... it can be argued that the conditional store choice process may not be an adaptive process at all. Learning through personal experience about an offer of a store may have relatively little effect on the next store choice. The store selected for the next visit may be influenced by the systematic but separately indiscernible effects of a large number of market variables which change slowly over a long period ... In these circumstances, random store choice by consumers with generally stable preference structures is a reasonable hypothesis for modelling purposes.[37]

A summary of alternative accounts of equilibrium behavior appropriate to destination choice is provided in Golledge.[38]

The case of simple aggregation and asymptotic randomness yields an operational class of random utility models. The longitudinal assumption implies statistical independence of trips by individuals, and the simple aggregation assumption implies that the multinomial distributions describing individual choice may be added to generate a multinomial vector of aggregate visit frequencies. Assuming m origins, n destinations, the system is described by m multinomial distributions with parameters $m_i = \Sigma_j m_{ij}$ and probabilities p_{ij} Here m_{ij} represents the total number of trips between i and j. The log-likelihood of the system is proportional to

$$\sum_i \sum_j m_{ij} \log \left\{ \int_{-\infty}^{\infty} f\left(\frac{t - \mu_{ij}}{\sigma_{ij}}\right) \frac{1}{\sigma_{ij}} \prod_{k \neq j} F\left(\frac{t - \mu_{ik}}{\sigma_{ik}}\right) \, dt \right\}.$$

One particular simplistic form of response function would be given by

$$\mu_{ij} = u_j \theta \log d_{ij}$$
$$\sigma_{ij} = 1 \text{ for all } i, j.$$

A more appealing form in which perceptual variance depends on distance would require

$$\sigma_{ij} = \alpha e^{\beta d_{ij}}.$$

Here the d_{ij} might be taken as travel time, the $n \, u_i$ would represent unconstrained site utility parameters and α, β and θ would represent positive parameters associated with the perception of travel time. In this case mn frequencies would be used to estimate $n + 3$ parameters. Alternative response functions, numerical estimation procedures and goodness-of-fit tests are described in Pipkin.[39] This simply aggregated model also yields an operational version of the abstract locational problem described in the Introduction above. This is discussed in Pipkin.[40]

V. CONCLUSIONS

This paper has reported and amplified several well-known dichotomies, and proposed others, which are relevant to spatial revealed preference analysis. The distinctions include those between algebraic and probabilistic accounts of choice, constant and random utility models, response and choice functions, intrinsic and sampling randomness, simple and random aggregation and learning versus asymptotic randomness.

The psychological epistemology of choice has essentially supplanted the consumer-theoretic one in behavioral geography. A dominant theme in this literature is the analysis of expressed preferences in questionnaire contexts. But enough has been written on the limitations of reported preferences in predicting overt choice to justify appraisal of psychologically-based models of pure revealed preferences, for example in the case of destination choice. Existing psychological frameworks are not particularly appropriate to this problem. The main differences dealt with above are the non-binary, non-replicable nature of the geographic choices, and the irreducible internal complexity of the elementary alternatives.

Non-binary choices imply that much choice theory and most of mathematical learning theory is inapplicable. We must therefore invent new models, deal with analytically dichotomized rather than truly binary choice sets, or adopt an existing multiple choice framework. The two most highly developed such frameworks are the Luce and Thurstone models. The latter technically contains the former as a special case, but the models do differ in fundamental ways. I believe that the class of Thurstonian random utility models possesses sufficient generality and a sufficiently appealing behavioral mechanism to constitute the most promising class of nonbinary models. It provides a variety of empirically distinguishable forms, including a special case in which Luce's Choice Axiom does apply.

The nonreplicable nature of destination choices implies that parametric control must be exercised over choices at different locations or times. The intrinsic rarity of overt choices implies that population aggregation is unavoidable for purposes of parameter estimation. I believe, for the reasons given above, that individual learning trajectories cannot easily be built into aggregative non-binary revealed preference models despite their proven utility in many other areas of behavioral geography. This implies that an asymptotic interpretation of choice probabilities is appropriate. Simple and random asymptotic aggregation schemes have been described. The latter are theoretically appealing, but analytically complicated.

Irreducible internal complexity of the elementary choice alternatives is inevitable in analysis of destination choice, no matter to what extent route, mode and site choice are treated as probabilistically separable. This throws some doubt on the logical adequacy of the unidimensional psychological model, despite its almost universal acceptance in predictive analysis of recurrent travel. There is no conceptual limit to the number of independent site and trip-link effects that can be accommodated in the unidimensional model, but it implies severe restrictions on their possible interactions. These interactions are typically assumed to be minimal, and statistical assumptions on linearity, log-linearity and separability have dictated our choice of a form for the response function. Our choice contexts are very far removed from those of classical psychophysics. But it may be argued that we should not treat issues of separability and the regressor-parameter distinction purely as matters of statistical convenience. Our knowledge of empirically rather than statistically reasonable response functions is small.

Department of Geography
State University of New York at Albany

NOTES

[1] The support of the Natural Science Foundation (Grant SOC76-15525) is gratefully acknowledged.
[2] H. D. Block and J. Marschak, 'Random Ordering and Stochastic Theories of Response', in I. Olkin *et al.* (eds.), *Contributions to Probability and Statistics*, pp. 97–132; G. M. Becker, M. H. DeGroot and J. Marschak, 'Stochastic Models of Choice

Behavior', in *Behavioral Science* 8 (1963), 41–55; N. Georgescu-Roegen, 'Threshold in Choice and the Theory of Demand', in *Econometrica* 26 (1958), 157–68; R. D. Luce and P. Suppes, 'Preference Utility and Subjective Probability', in R. D. Luce, R. R. Bush, and E. Galanter (eds.), *Handbook of Mathematical Psychology* 3, Wiley, N.Y., 1965.

³ T. A. Domencich and D. McFadden, *Urban Travel Demand: A Behavioral Analysis*, North-Holland, New York, 1975; J. S. Pipkin, *Two Probabilistic Revealed Preference Models of the Choice Process in Recurrent Urban Travel* (unpublished Ph.D. dissertation), Evanston, 1974.

⁴ D. Huff, 'A Probabilistic Analysis of Shopping Center Trade Areas', in *Land Economics* (1963), 81–96.

⁵ J. S. Pipkin, 'Theoretical versus Planning Solutions of Optimal Store Location with Probabilistic Models of Buying Behavior', paper given at Northeastern Regional Science Association Meetings, Ithaca, 1976.

⁶ For example, J. Wolpert, 'Behavioral Aspects of the Decision to Migrate', in *Papers and Proceedings of the Regional Science Association* 15 (1965), 159–69; F. Horton and D. R. Reynolds, 'Effects of Urban Spatial Structure on Individual Behavior', in *Economic Geography* 47 (1971), 36–48.

⁷ B. F. Skinner, *Science and Human Behavior*, Macmillan, New York, 1953.

⁸ G. H. Bower and T. Trabasso, 'Concept Identification', in R. C. Atkinson (ed.), *Studies in Mathematical Psychology*, Stanford University Press, 1964.

⁹ G. A. Miller, E. Galanter, and K. H. Pribram, *Plans and the Structure of Behavior*, Holt, New York, 1960.

¹⁰ L. L. Thurstone, 'A Law of Comparative Judgement', in *Psychological Review* 34 (1927), 273–286; L. L. Thurstone, 'The Prediction of Choice', in *Psychometrika* 10 (1945), 469–93.

¹¹ Pipkin, *op. cit.*, 1974.

¹² *Ibid.*

¹³ For example, H. S. Houthakker, 'On the Logic of Preference and Choice', in A. T. Tymieniecka (ed.), *Contributions to Logic and Methodology in Honor of J. M. Bochenski*, pp. 193–207; J. M. Henderson and R. E. Quandt, *Microeconomic Theory: A Mathematical Approach*, McGraw-Hill, New York, 1971; P. A. Samuelson, 'A Note on the Pure Theory of Consumer Behavior', in *Economica* 5 (1938), 61–71, 353–54.

¹⁴ K. D. Bock and L. V. Jones, *The Measurement and Prediction of Judgment and Choice*, Holden-Day, San Francisco, 1968.

¹⁵ For example, D. Laming, *Mathematical Psychology*, Academic Press, New York, 1973.

¹⁶ R. E. Quandt, 'A Probabilistic Theory of Consumer Behavior', in *Quarterly Journal of Economics* 70 (1956), 507–36.

¹⁷ Huff, *op. cit.*

¹⁸ Pipkin, *op. cit.*, 1974.

¹⁹ Bock and Jones, *op. cit.*

²⁰ Luce and Suppes, *op. cit.*

²¹ R. D. Luce, *Individual Choice Behavior*, John Wiley, New York, 1959.

²² Thurstone, *op. cit.*, 1945.

²³ Pipkin, *op. cit.*, 1974.

²⁴ *Ibid.*

²⁵ For example Charles Rivers Associates, *A Disaggregated Behavioral Model of Urban Travel Demand: Final Report*, Washington, D.C., 1972.

[26] Laming, *op. cit.*, p. 330.

[27] Pipkin, *op. cit.*, 1974.

[28] For example D. Brand, 'Travel Demand Forecasting', in *Background Papers for the Conference on Travel Demand Forecasting*, Williamsburg, Virginia, 1972.

[29] Huff, *op. cit.*

[30] T. F. Golob and M. J. Beckmann, 'A Utility Model for Travel Forecasting', in *Transportation Science* **3** (1971), 79–90.

[31] W. F. Massey, D. B. Montgomery and D. G. Morrison, *Stochastic Models of Buying Behavior*, MIT Press, Cambridge, 1970.

[32] K. P. Burnett, 'A Bernoulli Model of Destination Choice', manuscript, Department of Geography, Northwestern University, Evanston, 1973.

[33] N. L. Johnson and S. Kotz, *Distribution and Statistics: Continuous Univariate Distributions* **2**, Houghton-Mifflin, New York, 1970, p. 38.

[34] Pipkin, *op. cit.*, 1974.

[35] Burnett, *op. cit.*, 1973.

[36] J. S. Coleman, *Models of Change and Response Uncertainty*, Englewood Cliffs, 1964 p.2.

[37] K. P. Burnett, 'An Application of Stochastic Brand Choice Models to Store Choice Problems', manuscript, Department of Geography, Northwestern University, Evanston, 1972, p. 7.

[38] R. G. Golledge, 'Some Equilibrium Models of Consumer Behavior', in *Economic Geography* **46** (1970), 417–24.

[39] Pipkin, *op. cit.*, 1974.

[40] Pipkin, *op. cit.*, 1976.

DAVID RUSSELL

AN OPEN LETTER ON THE DEMATERIALIZATION
OF THE GEOGRAPHIC OBJECT

The putative impertinence of Schaefer's critique can no longer be maintained. Exceptionalism was an accurate characterization of a geographical methodology which has since then encroached geographical theory. By Schaefer II I wish to emphasize the trenchant pertinacity of the exceptionalist critique with respect to the entire spectrum of contemporary social science.

Cute epithets regarding the pathology of the geographic metabolism are no longer condoneable. The message would seem to be as clear in the little magazine literature as in the trade journals: there has been a collusive disinclination to catalogue the open problems of geography; the asking of more appropriate questions is subordinated to the repeated instantiation of answers to essentially closed problems; first-order econometric and statistical models prevail with an emphasis upon heuristic rather than epistemological adequacy; theory is aeteologically brittle as opposed to data-driven; meaning has been sacrificed to rigour; the exigencies of practice are allowed to conceal the contingencies of theory; research is divorced from education; indogenous critical debate is miniscule; mathematical and philosophical persuasions are mutually excommunicative; foundational research is expletive; paraprofessional geographers in the engineering and environmental sciences do better geography than professional geographers. One could go on. The knowledge explosion has apparently seen a concomitant implosion of understanding. I am mildly perturbed that the prognosis for the chorological and social sciences may be continued fragmentation and isolation.

It would be difficult if not impossible to justify the existence of geography as a unitary academic discipline. Geographical institutions exist. It is imperative that the intellectual subsistence of geography be ideologically revitalized. Far from succumbing to eschatological iconoclasm, a reinventing of the contemporary history of geography will, I suspect, find much to recruit if not conserve. (For instance, if one agrees with Bateson that an idea is a difference which makes a difference, does not the Hartshornian definition of geography become more acceptable?) But such a reconstruction presupposes possession of an appropriate medium for comprehensive anticipatory reconceptualization.

329

S. Gale and G. Olsson (eds.), Philosophy in Geography, 329–344. All Rights Reserved.
Copyright © 1979 by D. Reidel Publishing Company, Dordrecht, Holland.

0.1. A DIAGNOSTIC IN *GEDANKEN*-EXPERIMENTATION

It is no digression to recall that the twentieth century has seen a reversal in the traditional relationship between the moral and natural sciences. Progress in quantum physics has made mandatory a radical rethinking of many epistemological positions. Much of this progress was indirectly a product of deliberated speculation, of hypothetical reasoning: an ageless, everyday and non-esoteric mode of enquiry which Mach rather forbiddingly canonized as '*Gedanken*-experimentation'. There is even less reason now than there was in Mach's day to confuse *Gedanken*-experimentation with impressionistic speculation, for the theory of computation affords a plethora of metaphors by which to make our ideas clearer (e.g., recursive function theory surely captures part of the concept of dialectic).

I suggest *Gedanken*-experimentation as a preferred candidate medium for the reconceptualization of the social and chorological sciences. It will facilitate a transition from the accumulation of useless facts in field experiments to the application of useful fiction in laboratory experiments. *Reculer pour mieux penser*.

0.2. A POST-FORMAL SOCIAL SCIENCE

Reconceptualization comes most readily with an expanded universe of discourse. I suspect Isiah Bowman would have concurred that any reconceptualization of geography be unequivocally predicated upon a reconceptualization of the social sciences. Though I dare not say the same for geography, I think there are sufficient grounds to suggest that a reconceptualization of the social sciences is emergent. This I will designate post-formal social science, importantly comprising Social Metascience and Experimental Epistemology. I regard this development as a contextual prerequisite for the dematerialization of the geographic object.

Invocations of spatially intuited '*Zusammenhänge*' have worn somewhat thin. If geographers cannot say what they know, how can they teach what they know? Avoiding the reductionist extension, the problem is to substantiate geographical competence: a research strategy is required for discovering precisely what it is that professional geographers may legitimately be said to know. I propose the study of Artificial Spatial Intelligence as a candidate vehicle for the reconceptualization of geographical science. It comports the complementary study of synthetic metageography and epistemic spatial design. If this sounds gently programmatic, it is then so without apology.

A leit motif is that the social and chorological sciences have too long espoused a concept of economic man: there is a transcendent need for a theory of intelligent man. Social scientists need to think about thinking: geographers need to geographize the geographical. The cognate disciplines are precisely those which treat of cognition.

I. SOCIAL METASCIENCE

I.1. *Anthropocentrism*

I contend that the social sciences are in need of a reaffirmation of their essentially anthropocentric nature. Humankind is singularly distinguished from animalkind in these crucial respects: the creativity of language, the speed of thought, the altruism of action. Not to dissemble, it may be said that consciousness, creativity and intelligence are the proper concerns of social science. Mind is the difference of man which makes the social sciences different.

I.1.1. *Intelligence.* Intelligence we see manifested in the ability to solve problems, to answer questions, to make appropriate responses. Most of the time we do not recognize problems as being problems; even more of the time we do not know how we manage to solve them. Performance often exceeds competence. Small amounts of information are apparently sufficient for very large data-processing tasks. We are able to forget; we learn from mistakes, we can recover from error. Our problem-solving capabilities degrade gracefully in the face of degenerate data inputs. The remarkable aspect to human knowledge is its task-free rather than domain-specific character. Most translation seems to be a species of transliteration wherein metaphor constitutes the mistake of creative misunderstanding. Common sense is as uncommonly deep as ordinary language is extraordinarily complex. Expert problem-solving and common sense reasoning are not well understood because critical self-reflection, for better and worse, is imbued with narcissism and paranoia. There is an imperative to study intelligence independent of its material realization. The intent is rather to assimilate than to replicate natural intelligence.

I.1.2. *Thinking about thinking.* Humankind is capable of both reflexion and self-reflection upon the possible and the actual. The social sciences are *de facto* metascientific. The social scientist would then perhaps do well to reflect on the possible procedures that are operative in the processes of human self-reflection. In the age of digital computation this endeavour is no longer confined to introspection. Humankind's intellectual faculties have evolved slowly in experiential response to a spatio-temporal environment. Might not this be a strong argument for compatibly grounding the study of the ontological nurturing of an individual intelligence within that of the broader phylogenetic evolution of human consciousness?

I.2. *The Phylogeny of Simulation*

Suppose that human consciousness dawned in reflection upon the predator–prey relationship (and creativity in reflexion upon the hand–eye relationship?). A predatory subject is capable of forming an internal world model of his objective prey; the converse is not the case. These internal world models are idealizations or simulations of the external real world; they effect a mediation between the individual consciousness and its perceived ambience. These simulations are constitutive of myth. They may take either a mental, physical or artifactual form. They encapsulate for any given time–space the knowledge and the ignorance of the collective consciousness.

I.2.1. *Artificiality.* An artifice is a formalization of knowledge. Artificiality is about as little understood as mechanism. Artefactual simulations are simultaneously existent and subsistent. The sciences of the artificial lie at the voraciously consuming interface between those of nature and society. The qualitative artifices are those of religion and humanism; the quantitative artifices are those of magic and science.

I.2.2. *Comparitive demonology.* A demon is a proceduralization of ignorance. The demon of non-linearity is as inter-disciplinary as the non-linearity of demons is cross-cultural. Simulations are proceduralized by the operation of demons. Qualitatively, those of the soothsayer and catastrophe theory; quantitatively, those of the witchdoctor and entropy theory. The comparitive demonology of the social sciences is an important and open research topic.

I.3. *A Post-formal Methodology*

The social sciences then require a post-formal methodology for the study of artificial intelligence.

I.3.1. *Discrete symbolic procedural description.* (a) Social metascience requires a demystification of theory. A theory is a description of a description. Hence a theory or captum is imminent in any datum. An explanation is but a mandarin description.

(b) Procedural, imperative knowledge 'how' is preferred to propositional, declarative knowledge 'that'. Procedures are the most useful kinds of descriptors, allowing one to describe the indescribability of informal knowledge and thereby to teach the purportedly unteachable. Only procedural understanding can differentiate local sense from contextual reference.

(c) A numerical index is a terminal evaluation that cannot reflect the considerations that formed it. A symbolic summary can reflect a past record and thereby permit of further, deeper understanding. Symbols are more informatively structured than indices.

(d) The real existent world is continuous; the ideal subsistent world is discrete. Only a discrete mechanism can produce that reflective commentary upon its own behaviour that is required in the modelling of human intelligence.

Discrete symbolic procedural description is then the foundation to any post-formal methodology for social metascience. It is upon this basis that an operational and constructive theory of knowledge can and is being built. Experimental epistemology is no longer a cargo cult of the metaphysician.

I.3.2. *An apprehensive caveat.* Historiographers of geography may someday record that in the course of the twentieth century spatial analysis enlarged its focus to include process and design after an earlier preoccupation with content and form. Procedural designation mediates process and design: contextual feelings mediate content and form. Although it is arguable that any understanding of procedures is predicated upon that of feelings, I will concentrate on the former to the exclusion of the latter, and this in order to shorten the chains of speculation and maintain some anchor points in the current frontier of the social sciences. For what it is worth, I suspect that a post-formal social science must eventually complete the 'Tractatus Neurologico-Philosophicus' and that this will minimally involve, firstly, a deepened appreciation of prehension and concrescense in the study of organizations, power and aggression, and secondly, the exploration of non-conceptual modes of knowing in poetic and tonal imagery. I would hope that any progression which geography may make in the qualitative domain will not be marred by the *ad hoc* analyses and *ad hominem* evaluations which accompanied an earlier quantitative revolution.

II. EXPERIMENTAL EPISTEMOLOGY

II.1. *The Thinking-machine Criterion*

The study of artificial intelligence endows epistemology with a meaning criterion which it has formerly lacked: if one has legitimate knowledge, then build a machine to incorporate and demonstrate the same. The automaton, as a theoretical machine, is par excellence the vehicle for *Gedanken*-experimentation. This has enabled epistemology to move from its former impressionistic mode to the status of an experimental science with a capability to operationally construct knowledge. Invocations of 'epistemic correlation' are now testable. The machine program becomes the embodiment of one's data, description and theory. And programs are better at introspection than humans! But this embodiment need not and usually will not employ the logistic systems that formerly constrained the social sciences. Formal logic is appropriate for metamathematics but not for metaphysics, and perniciously less so for social metascience.

II.1.1. *Anti-logistic.*
Post-formal social science is emphatically anti-logistic. Some knowledge doesn't belong in an axiomatic base (e.g., advice); much knowledge is not formulable in the predicate calculus (e.g., the meaning of 'usually'). Workability should not be sacrificed to elegance, nor propriety to tractability. Completeness is no rare prize. Consistency is neither necessary nore desirable, for few social beings are ever completely consistent. Set-theoretic platonism must give way to Herbrand-type proof procedures. Construction by negation requires a dialect permitting of contradiction. Nothing of interest has ever been discovered in a formal language, and this because logic is for consolidation rather than discovery. Logistic systems are too amorphous to model the systems of society.

II.1.2. *A disclaimer on mechanism.*
I advocate perhaps an appreciation of the demonic but intend no exhumation of the ghost in the machine. The mind–body problem may be unsermountable. Artificial intelligence does not seek a revival of mechanism but rather a new and non-reductionist form of mentalism, if you will, a species of neo-vitalism. It is embedded in post-neo-Darwinism and post-revisionist-Marxism. The pragmatic holism of artificial intelligence research seeks theories which intermediate and transcend those of behaviourism and gestaltism.

II.2. *The Knowledge-based Approach*

Early research in machine translation and pattern recognition was dominated by a power-based approach which employed uniform and exhaustive search procedures. The hard-earned lesson from this was that significant progress cannot be made until common sense and general knowledge is given an adequate data base representation. The operative word is significant, giving precedence to sufficiency over efficiency; adequacy comports both the epistemological and the heuristic. The knowledge-based approach now dominates artificial intelligence research, seeming to vindicate an invisible college of social scientists who have long argued for epistemic foundations. The knowledge-based approach threatens to rewrite and relegate the quantitative revolution in the social sciences since it employs a mode of qualitative reasoning that has before characterized chemistry, biology and, perhaps, meteorology. The modeling of artificial intelligence allows, indeed mandates to an unprecedented degree, the interpenetration of mathematics and philosophy.

II.2.1. *Qualitative modeling.* Closed-form parametric modeling has too long satiated an epidemic theorem-envy throughout the social sciences. The conditions on metricity are very strictly confining. Quantitative models need to be on tap, but they should not be on top. Qualitative models address particular, local, dynamic problems by global, non-parametric means. Qualitative modeling is evocative of that divinitory interrogation which characterized pre-scientific cultures. The primitive mind is not well so called.

II.2.2. *Epistemic programming languages.* The argument that intelligent machines will need the ability to discourse in ordinary language has encouraged the devising of computer programs which understand natural language. The knowledge-based approach has given depth to this linguistic research effort. In particular it has emphasized the importance of procedural semantic depth in the analysis of everyday discourse, where formerly was the syntactic ideal speaker–hearer postulation of Chomsky. Discourse is understood from the outside-in, not from the inside-out. Words are names are concepts, and as such they are neither exact, parsimonious nor exclusive. Conceptual dependency theory postulates that the meaning of concepts can be reduced to a permutation of rather few primitive actions and object-states; such permutations are at once extremely coarse and exquisitly refineable. Epistemic programming languages attempt to explicitly meet the Humpty Dumpty criteria for meaningfulness, namely that 'each actor has complete control over the names he uses' and that 'all other actors must respect the meaning that an actor has chosen for a name'. The underlying problem remains to construct new data-types and explore their capabilities for packaging and unfolding knowledge.

II.3. *Artificially Intelligent Machines*

The study of artificial intelligence provides an epistemological nursery for adults, a conceptual laboratory for children. Artificial intelligence uses the computer as an active metaphor in research, a convivial tool in education. There follow some research communalities amongst third-generation artificial intelligence systems.

II.3.1. *Representation.* The ascendancy of the knowledge-based approach has brought to the fore the problem of how most effectively to represent real world knowledge. Although there is as yet no theory of representation, one can safely say that the study of representation is as basic to post-formal social science as measure theory was to formal social science. The representation problem is to devise multiple alternative characterizations of real world knowledge within a description generalization hierarchy, and to explore the trade-offs involved in using different kinds of knowledge (*viz.* procedural-declarative, particular-general).

II.3.2. *Activation.* In the computational transition from data- to information-processing it has become apparent that useful knowledge is active knowledge with a capacity for self-reference. Self-knowledgable procedures know what they have done and why. Self-activating procedures know when to respond and how. The active knowledge viewpoint supports the grammarian's case for case and must surely point the way to the development of self-improving programs.

II.3.3. *Chunking.* Experience in the modelling of language and vision has suggested that the traditional units of analysis are much too small. Informational chunking connotes an attempt to deal with content in context which involves a transition from the sentence to the literary paragraph, from isolated pattern to robotic vision. Supporting multiple and flexible internal representations of chunked information requires the maintenance of very large data bases.

II.3.4. *Microworlds*. It is now considered that the empirical environments of question-answering, theorem-proving and game-playing do not instantiate in any sufficiently general manner the complexity of human problem-solving abilities. The preference is currently to isolate a microcosm of the real world and comprehensively confront its complexity: Winograd's toy blocks world was the environment for the first successful natural language understanding program. There is increasing support for the belief that deep problem-solving insights are obtainable from examining the more mundane, everyday activities of human life, from elucidating the tacit epistemology in any Jack and Janet narrative. Very small empirical domains will for a while offset the problems involved in maintaining very large data bases.

II.3.5. *Heterarchies*. If knowledge is to be represented in very large data bases, then some means must be found to expediate its active use. Effective self-knowledge requires self-discipline. Some light may be shed on this problem of system control by considering that while knowledge may be hierarchical, its understanding may be heterarchical. Heterarchical systems are goal-oriented, top-down, modular and extensible. Their component programs have a capacity for tacit and tentative knowledge of themselves and others. The distinction between high- and low-level routines virtually disappears since executive control is distributed throughout the system. "The modules interact not like a master and slaves but more like a community of experts" (Winston).

II.3.6. *Synergy*. The conduct of artificial intelligence research rather well reflects the intelligent problem-solving abilities which it seeks to better understand. The field provides the social and chorological sciences with an exemplary instance of well-coordinated, cumulative inter-disciplinary research.

The study of artificial intelligence has already had a profound impact upon theoretical linguistics and cognitive psychology. I consider artificial intelligence to be archetypal of and propadeutic to the post-formal social sciences .... and to this extent artificial intelligence research cannot be other than counter-intelligent with respect to the social science establishment.

III. ARTIFICIAL SPATIAL INTELLIGENCE

Papert's dictum: "when thinking about thinking, it helps to think about somebody thinking about something". Let's think about the geographer thinking about geography. In post-formal social science, the study of artificial intelligence mediates social metascience and experimental epistemology. *Mutatis mutandis*, the study of artificial spatial intelligence mediates synthetic metageography and epistemic spatial design.

III.1. *Synthetic Metageography*

III.1.1. *Geographical problem formulation.* There seems to be a collusive disinclination in the geographical community to consider the nature of geographical problem formulation and the character of geography's open problems. The fundamental geographical problem is surely one of meaningfulness . . . what is a meaningful geographical object? Perhaps a positionally invariant local operator, but surely this is embedded in a global qualitative knowledge whose character is not immediately obvious. Certainly an answer to this problem must precede any agreement on when a geographical problem has been well-posed. I see no *a priori* reason to suppose that the fundamental geographical primitives are necessarily those of first-order geometry. Perhaps a sure route would be to carefully examine the empirical nature of some simple, non-charismatic aspect of human spatial behaviour. After having discovered the facts which require description, develop a coarse theory which describes the deviance of the descriptors, and finally locate an appropriate alogorithmic implementation. Prematurely coherent synthesis and the mimicry of solution mechanisms is to be strenuously avoided.

III.1.2. *Geometry and chronometry.* Human intelligence evolved in experiential contact with the four-dimensional space–time continuum. The conjoint interpenetration of space and time gives no justification to comparitive static partial analysis with either a temporal or spatial bias. It is a peculiar historical fact that temporal analysis has had a preferred status in geographical science. The TIMP calculus was grounded in von Wright's temporal logic M; it could have been grounded in Rescher and Garson's topological logic with a slight gain in power, and still better in McCarthy's calculus of situations (a robotologic with the power of Lewis' CS4). The zeroth law of geography might be that no two things can occupy the same space at the same time. Corollary: this does not hold for ideas. The inexactitude of conjoint spatio-temporal measurement commits social scientists to fuzzy sets, modal logics and tolerance geometries. Computationally the trade-off is between expressive power and search space size. I suspect that the role of spatio-temporal contiguity in the evolution of man's intellect has not yet been appreciated.

III.1.3. *Procedural ontology.* Ontology is the epistemological study of being. All knowledge is constitutive of symbolic language. When we speak of ontology, we speak also of ideosyncrasy and egocentricity. Cassirer's contribution to theory of culture documented the symbolic form of images: McCarthy's contribution to the theory of computation offers the possibility of experimentally studying the symbolic procedures of imagination. Imagination is subsistent. A procedural ontology concerns the transconscious encoding of symbolic data. The procedures involved here are those of metaphor which is intensional, and generalization which is inductive. Selecting an appropriate instance of the induction axiom is the creative part of proof. It amounts to concept formation. Practical inference requires an ontological flexibility that cuts across any platonism–nominalism debate. The question is which entities are to be regarded as being values of bound variables and of individual constants? We must surely allow actions as values of bound variables. A semantic sorting structure is needed of horizontal rather than vertical richness, that is, many different classes each containing but a few members. Locations are modal operators since they are not truth-functional.

All recognition problems are properly ontogenetic. The procedural recognition problem for geography may be the recognition of positional invariance. Geography's standard recognition device is the cartographic map. If we regard geography as a theoretical language, we can perhaps usefully think of any map as a particular model sentence in that language. Relativity theory provides a map of the physical universe. I suspect that Tobler posed the essential recognition question for geography when he proposed that of any pattern one should ask 'of what geographical distribution might this be a map?' But form is often over-identified and thus open to multiple interpretation. The recognition of form is but a part of understanding; it is complemented by representation and ends in their mutual resolution.

I contend that the issues raised in an admittedly cursory manner in the last two paragraphs are constructive to any post-formal reconceptualization of geography, and critically foundational to synthetic metageography in the study of artificial spatial intelligence. This would not be the place to further elaborate a procedural ontology for geographical science, nor to attempt its coherent integration with cognitive teleology and transactional phenomenology. This would however bring us close to a procedural paradigm for postformal geographical science. Suffice to say that I am inclined to the view that every significant transformation is the exclusive progeny of a procedural transaction! Transformations have occupied perhaps a too exalted role in geographical enquiry hitherto.

III.2. *Epistemic Spatial Design*

III.2.1. *Geographical software.* Space is one of humankind's most deeply pervasive metaphors. Yet spatial concepts present notoriously difficult representational problems, of which the artificial intelligence community seems more aware than the geographical community. There is as yet, for instance, no viable solution to the problem of representing the transitivity of nearness.

In the absence of an *inter lingua*, geography needs spatial languages in which to couch its descriptive observations. And this is not a question of the two-dimensional generalization of context-free transformational grammar, nor of finessing varieties of cellular automata, nor of perfecting geometry theorem machines, nor of borrowing aribtrary pattern or picture languages. The appropriate spatial languages cannot be borrowed.

In order that geographical problems be machine formulable, custom-made spatial languages must be incorporated with programming languages. The task is for geographers to embed spatial sub-programs in epistemic programming languages, thereby endowing them with a procedural spatial semantics: this is a matter for empirical discovery and experimentation. Waltz's semantic parsing of solid polyhedral microregions is to date one of the most serious and successful attempts at computationally handling spatial relations.

III.2.2. *Ut pictora geographicus.* Denotation has been carefully studied by analytic philosophers. Analytic geographers might do well to study depiction. The problems of sense and reference are compounded when one moves beyond the one-dimensional, though one might reasonably expect research on anaphorics to reciprocally inform that on anamorphics.

Research on low-level vision is beginning to suggest that the utility of spectral analytic techniques is rather strictly confined to digital picture processing, which is an order of complexity below that understanding of images which is properly required for satellite photo-interpretation. Image understanding will progress when there are better formulations for some of the traditional problems attending the mind's eye (*viz.* do human beings think in pictures? what is the epistemological status of mental imagery?)

Computational cartography affords a fertile arena for the interpretation of conceptual art and cognitive science.

III.2.3. *A theory of planning.* The essential nature of planning has consistently eluded mainstream social science research, the prescience of 'Plans and the structure of behaviour' being sadly misinterpreted as a license for the

statistical decision theory junket. Planning is tactically and strategically constitutive of human problem-solving. A plan is a sequence of actions intended
to bring about a desired result. As such, it seems jejune to allow any conceptual or procedural distinction between planning and programming. Both activities are required to confront compound goal structures with multiple and
complementary internal descriptions, modular problem decomposition, and
the specification of state space changes. For problem-solving, planning and
programming, a bug is to be understood as a conceptual error: debugging is an
important learning experience. Contingently self-adaptive programs may not
find it so difficult to exercise client-oriented, advocacy planning. The future
seems to lie with evolutionary and conceptual programming and planning,
with automatic program and plan synthesis.

III.3. *A Geographical Reconnaissance*

III.3.1. *Spatial taxonomics.* Deixis has been a neglected area in descriptive
and theoretical linguistics. As an input to the spatial language problem, geography needs a better vocabulary in which to couch its descriptive observations. This is a question of inventing new data-types which are explicitly
problem-driven. The received categories of formal social science cannot be
expected to transfer smoothly to the procedural domain.

III.3.2. *Conceptual genetics.* Geography needs fewer pseudo-explanations
masquerading as descriptions. If descriptions are to aspire to explanatory
status, then learning and memory components must perforce be incorporated in both human and physical geography. This would be part of a more
self-consciously longitudinal research concern with the origin and differential
development of spatial behaviour.

III.3.3. *Contra-Laocoonian imperative.* Reductionism may be as deleterious
in an observation language as it is constructive in a theoretical language. It
should by now be clear that geographical analysis has gained nothing by
divorcing the study of spatial perception from that of spatial conception.
Concerted research on the spatial symbiotics of the mind's eye might glean
much from an examination of legal, medical and artistic reasoning processes.

III.3.4. *Microregional science.* Bunge's study of the Fitzgerald block is a step
in the direction towards spatial research on a smaller scale. I have in mind the
microworlds of scene analysis in contemporary robotic vision research.

Provocatively, the problems of interregional development will not be solved until a hand–eye system can manoeuver self-adaptively in the micro-regions of a toy universe. There is a need for a cosmology of solid polyhedra.

III.3.5. *Complementary modularity*. The resolution of complementary models within modular systems should be guided by coherency rather than completeness. Complementarity resides in system trade-offs. Modularity allows the integrated coexistence of models.

III.3.6. *Spatial frames*. Minsky's frame hypothesis is a synthetic procedural-ization of much recent research on the convoluted operations of language, thought and action. The burgeoning literature on frame theory provides geography with the opportunity to contribute to the theory of spatial frame-works. A compelling task for the theoretical geographer is to scrupulously internalize and creatively augment Olsson's schematization of causal and practical inference. Were this to be attempted within the framework of frame theory, then the elusive reconciliations of the 'connecting worlds' might be approached.

III.3.7. *Robotic manipulation*. I would like to see an acceptance of robotic manipulation as an authentic task environment for geographical problem-solving. Unmanned vehicles intended to reconnoitre unprepared environments will require a non-supervised, self-adaptive capability to read and make maps, to simultaneously generate and interpret a symbolic representation of a dynamic ambience. It may well be that in the praxis of robotology the utility of the procedural-declarative distinction will attenuate, but for the moment I think it useful.

III.3.8. *Geographical laboratories*. Geographical institutions have too long negated the theoretical and practical reciprocity of enquiry and education. Artificial spatial intelligence laboratories would provide authentic learning environments in which to concertedly promote the teaching of research in geography. Some intelligent computer-aided instructional systems have adopted a traditional geographical syllabus as an empirical domain, but any-thing approaching modern geography has yet to be accommodated. I would expect geographical laboratories to add procedural semantic depth to the playing of simulation games and the modeling of urban dynamics.

IV. POSTSCRIPT

IV.1. *Elective Affinities*

Many of the ideas which I have touched on in the preceding sections were originally introduced in intellectual movements now derogatively labelled as operationalism, liberalism and surrealism. These movements share with artificial intelligence the fact that they have been the focus of severe intellectual and moral criticism. Yet what is in a name? As the topological singularities of semantics, nouns inevitably commit one to reification. One must borrow where one can, with an emphasis upon coherence. I have borrowed much from Papert, Thom and Waddington.

While the linguistic approach is clearly important, it is imprudent to isolate the study of language from that of its literature. The new literary criticism holds much promise for the social sciences in as much as it is intrinsically post-critical. I have argued for a constructive affinity between the study of artificial intelligence and post-formal research in the social and chorological sciences. Those who doubt my election of artificial spatial intelligence as a vehicle for the reconceptualization of geography might find it persuasive to consult the dissertation in which Kuipers describes his TOUR program. Artificial spatial intelligence allows for an excitingly new kind of geography, one characterized by a harmony between product marketability and intellectual vibrance. And this is so because relevance and responsibility are made explicit correspondants in a dialogue between the conceptual geographical object and the geographer's mental energies.

IV.2. *Terra Incognitae*

Wright well understood that the *terra incognitae* of twentieth-century geography are those epigenetic landscapes of the mind. A better understanding of the intellect must precede any forays upon the unknown frontiers of the oceans and the galaxies.

The social sciences are replete with shareable geographical problems and transferable solutions. If geography will not share these problems, other disciplines will appropriate them. Artificial spatial intelligence provides a framework within which to explore and assimilate the plurality of the spatial metaphor. It matters little whether geographical theories are indigenous or derivative, as long as they are contributive. The need is to liase in constructive interference.

The understanding of understanding is not an objective matter. Understanding geographical activity, that is, doing geography rather than being a geographer, requires a dematerialization of the geographic object. I have suggested that this is accomplishable in a post-formal ethos of computational epistemology. Geography will not be known by its logic or its theoreis ... it will be known by its contribution of theorems to the theory of knowledge. Useable knowledge is interpropositional, and ultimately intersubjective.

The principles of aerodynamics were not discovered by an ornithologist. It was found that an understanding of aeroplane flight transferred smoothly to the flight of birds. And so it may be with intelligence. The egg of post-formal geography has been laid. I am strongly inclined to believe that one of the birds therein will be an intelligent machine terminal.

Ann Arbor, Michigan

ALLEN J. SCOTT

LAND USE AND COMMODITY PRODUCTION

I. INTRODUCTION

One of the central problems of economic theory is the whole question of the inter-relations of the commodity production system and the price system in capitalist economies, and the resulting distribution of profits and wages. A particularly powerful general solution of this problem was published by Sraffa in 1960 – a solution that has in part resuscitated an interest in the classical labour theory of value. At the same time, there exists in geography and regional science a long tradition of land use and land rent analysis generally derivative out of the writings of Von Thünen in the early nineteenth century. This tradition, however, has fairly consistently overlooked precisely the problems of production, pricing and distribution, and has largely been content to show how land use and land rent patterns emerge once these problems have been somehow largely assumed away.

In fact, the two dimensions of the economic system represented on the one hand by Von Thünen and on the other hand by Sraffa are intrinsically and intimately interdependent. Some attempt to integrate the two seems therefore more than overdue. The general problem to which this paper is addressed, then, is to attempt this integration so as to demonstrate both the role of production, prices, and distribution in the Von Thünen model, as well as the role of land use and land rent in the Sraffa model. In the present paper, this integration is accomplished in a largely formal and technical way, and little or no attempt is made here to work out the wider implications of the analysis (though these seem both fascinating and enormous). We proceed, therefore, under some simple commonly accepted assumptions, to construct what is essentially a highly identified set of simultaneous equations representing an integrated model. In passing, it may be noted that Goldstein and Moses (1975) have recently published an account that shares some of the spirit of the present analysis, though the model that they propose seems more restricted in scope and content than the model presented here.

345

S. Gale and G. Olsson (eds.), Philosophy in Geography. 345–359. All Rights Reserved.

II. A GENERAL SPATIAL SYSTEM

Let us assume that there exists a single central market on a perfectly uniform plain over which transport is ubiquitously available. Three crops, labelled a, b, and c, are produced on this plain under conditions of perfect competition. The technical process whereby these crops are produced is understood to be describable by means of some kind of input–output process. We may, indeed, take this input–output process to be non-linear, though in order to simplify the following argument, joint production possibilities are eliminated from the analysis, and capitalist farmers are assumed variously to specialize in the production of some particular crop. At the outset, farmers all have access to a given set of production technologies. Economic competition and rationality then impose the result that farmers in any one branch of production will all adopt a common (optimized) technology, such that both individual farm area and farm output in that branch will be standardized. Nor is this result contradicted once our system is fully generalized to a spatial basis. Let us, then, identify the standard land area of farms of type a, b, and c as λ_a, λ_b, and λ_c, respectively. Production (or total yield) of each of the three types of farms is identified as y_a, y_b, and y_c, respectively.

Now, farmers will compete among each other for the sale of their crops at the central market; this will bring into being a set of unified market prices for each crop. Farmers will also compete among each other for the use of the best (i.e., in the present context, most accessible) land; this will bring into being a set of spatially variable land rents. This latter process will also be associated with the emergence of a geographically disaggregated pattern of production, such that each crop occupies a distinctive annulus or *Von Thünen ring* around the central market. The emergence of these rings is also in part related to the rent-maximizing propensities of landlords. Thus, land at any given location is ceded only to producers of the crop that can pay the highest rent at that location. Without any loss of generality, we may assume for the purposes of the present analysis that crop a occupies the entire ring extending from the central market out to a radius of α distance units from the market; that crop b occupies all land in the ring extending from α to β; and that crop c occupies all land extending from β to γ (cf. Figure 1). The values of α, β and γ are all ultimately determined endogenously to our analysis. For the sake of simplicity, let us also assume that the dwellings of the labour force engaged in agricultural production are spatially distributed in direct conformity with the labour-intensity of production of each crop.

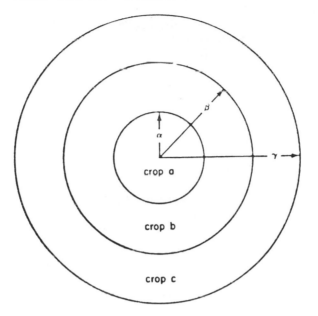

Fig. 1. The spatial structure of production.

III. THE SRAFFA SYSTEM: A NON-SPATIAL MODEL

Let us for the moment consider our three-sector production system independently of its geographical foundations. This production system has already been identified as an input–output process. In keeping with the style of Sraffa's original notation let us write a set of generalized input–output relations for our three-sector system as follows:

$$f_a(a_a, b_a, c_a, l_a) \rightarrow y_a,$$
$$f_b(a_b, b_b, c_b, l_b) \rightarrow y_b,$$
$$f_c(a_c, b_c, c_c, l_c) \rightarrow y_c,$$

where, for example, a_a, b_a, and c_a represent the total quantities of crops a, b, and c, respectively, used in producing the total output (y_a) of one farm of type a; similarly, l_a represents the quantity of labour used in producing the same output. Unit production prices are designated p_a, p_b, and p_c. Let w be the *exogenously* given standard wage rate, and let ρ be the endogenously determined rate of normal profit. Sraffa's model for this simple three-sector non-spatial system can now be written directly. For each farm of type a, the total production system is definable as

$$(a_a p_a + b_a p_b + c_a p_c)(1 + \rho) + l_a w = y_a p_a;$$

for each farm of type b,

$$(a_a p_a + b_b p_b + c_b p_c)(1 + \rho) + l_b w = y_b p_b;$$

and for each farm of type c,

$$(a_c p_a + b_c p_b + c_c p_c)(1 + \rho) + l_c w = y_c p_c.$$

In verbal terms, each of these equations specifies that the capital advanced per farm to secure the physical means of production, plus a normal profit, plus wages, equals the total physical output multiplied by the price of production. Note that capitalist farmers are assumed not to derive any profit directly in relation to the wages bill on the assumption that wages are always paid at the end of each production period; in other words, on the assumption that the worker advances his labour to the capitalist. We may now choose any commodity as our monetary numeraire and set its price equal to any arbitrarily chosen quantity (provided only that the wage rate is identified in comparable real units), say,

$$p_a = 1.$$

We now have the four unknowns, p_a, p_b, p_c and ρ in four equations, and our system is determinate. In order to find total quantities produced in any branch we now need merely multiply output per farm by the number of farms in that branch (see below).

The general model described above is derivative out of the later classical tradition of political economy, represented above all by Ricardo, and it is of considerable interest, as well, as one possible solution of Marx's famous transformation problem. It embodies within itself an explicit conception of the inherent structural conflict between wages (labour) and profit (capital) for the one can increase only at the expense of the other in a stable economic system. This conflict expresses itself in political as well as economic terms and at any given historical moment the wage rate, w, is given as the outcome of the political balance of power between labour and capital.

IV. THE SRAFFA MODEL IN SPATIAL CONTEXT

Extension of the Sraffa model to a specifically spatial framework involves the introduction of a third social force in addition to labour and capital, namely, landowners, who, through their appropriation of land rent, absorb a quantity of the net product (or surplus value) that would otherwise be converted into profit. We must also introduce an additional technical process in the form of a transport system, though in the present anlysis this transport system is taken as a purely exogenous sector of economic activity.

Now, all exchange of commodities occurs at the central market. We must therefore clearly distinguish between f.o.b. price at the point of production, and c.i.f. price at the market. More explicitly, we must distinguish, on the one hand, price at the point of production not only before payment of the costs of transport to the central market but also before payment of land rent, and on the other hand, price at the central market after payment of both transport costs and rent. Transport costs are simply directly passed on to the consumer. Land rent, in the final analysis, is only excess profit (as will appear more clearly below). Excess profit, is, by definition, total revenue minus total costs, and where costs include a normal profit. Therefore, equally by definition, land rent, *qua* excess profit, can only be imputed to that part of total production that passes through the market, and not to that part that is retained for subsequent use in the production process. Accordingly, for crops a, b and c, let us identify production prices before payment of both transport costs and rent as p_a, p_b, and p_c, respectively. In the same way, let us identify delivered prices at the central market after payment of transport costs and rent as p_a^*, p_b^* and p_c^*.

With these various arguments and definitions in mind we can write the initial equations of a spatialized Sraffa model as follows:

(1) $(a_a p_a + b_a p_b^* + c_a p_c^*)(1 + \rho) + l_a w = y_a p_a,$

(2) $(a_b p_a^* + b_b p_b + c_b p_c^*)(1 + \rho) + l_b w = y_b p_b,$

(3) $(a_c p_a^* + b_c p_b^* + c_c p_c)(1 + \rho) + l_c w = y_c p_c,$

(4) $p_a = 1.$

In this model, the intermediate inputs from any farm to itself are of course priced at their production price net of transport costs and rent. All other intermediate inputs are priced at their central market price. The question remains: How can the price of these latter inputs be fixed at a constant level given that farmers must transport them *back* from the central market to the various and scattered locations where they will be used in the production process? The answer is to be found in one of two ultimately equivalent possibilities. Either the capitalist farmer simply passes on the costs of the backward journey (where intermediate inputs are carried back from the market to producing areas) directly to consumers in the form of an increment to the market price of the finished goods brought to market in the preceding forward journey. Or, if the capitalist farmer must indeed make a separate and later payment for the backward journey, then a differential rent on land will emerge in perfect inverse proportion to the costs of the backward journey; in the latter event, final delivered prices will simply everywhere be equal to central market prices augmented by some constant aggregate quantity. In either case, we may here simply take the central market prices p_a^*, p_b^*, and p_c^* as directly equivalent to ultimate delivered prices.

In what follows, the detailed components and extensions of this basic model are defined and discussed at some length.

V. THE DETERMINATION OF TOTAL INPUT

Total demand for each of the crops a, b, and c is composed of two main elements, intermediate capital items, and final consumption items. The demand per farm for intermediate capital items is determined in relation to the input–output conditions of Equations (1), (2) and (3). Then, total system-wide demand for intermediate capital items can be obtained simply by multiplying demands per farm by numbers of farms. Furthermore, let us suppose that the final consumption of any crop is given by a demand function $Q(p_a^*, p_b^*, p_c^*)$, which, for simplicity, neglects the effects of wages and profits on consumption, and is written solely in terms of price (i.e., central market price). At equilibrium, then, total demand for each crop can be written as the aggregate of derived demand plus final consumer demand, that is

$$(5) \qquad a_a \frac{\pi\alpha^2}{\lambda_a} + a_b \frac{\pi(\beta^2 - \alpha^2)}{\lambda_b} + a_c \frac{\pi(\gamma^2 - \beta^2)}{\lambda_c} + Q_a(p_a^*, p_b^*, p_c^*) = A,$$

$$(6) \qquad b_a \frac{\pi\alpha^2}{\lambda_a} + b_b \frac{\pi(\beta^2 - \alpha^2)}{\lambda_b} + b_c \frac{\pi(\gamma^2 - \beta^2)}{\lambda_c} + Q_b(p_a^*, p_b^*, p_c^*) = B,$$

$$(7) \qquad c_a \frac{\pi\alpha^2}{\lambda_a} + c_b \frac{\pi(\beta^2 - \alpha^2)}{\lambda_b} + c_c \frac{\pi(\gamma^2 - \beta^2)}{\lambda_c} + Q_c(p_a^*, p_b^*, p_c^*) = C,$$

where A, B, and C represent the endogenously determined total production of crops a, b, and c, respectively; and where the expressions $\pi\alpha^2/\lambda_a$, $\pi(\beta^2 - \alpha^2)/\lambda_b$, and $\pi(\gamma^2 - \beta^2)/\lambda_c$ identify the total numbers of farms of types a, b, and c, respectively.

In addition, the total supply of any one crop is also in part governed by the total geographical area devoted to the cultivation of that crop. Thus the further conditions determining total production must also apply.

$$(8) \qquad \frac{\pi\alpha^2}{\lambda_a} y_a = A,$$

$$(9) \qquad \frac{\pi(\beta^2 - \alpha^2)}{\lambda_b} y_b = B,$$

$$(10) \qquad \frac{\pi(\gamma^2 - \beta^2)}{\lambda_c} y_c = C.$$

Recall that α, β and γ are endogenous variables in our model, so that the relations defined by Equations (5)–(10) are fully interdependent.

VI. CENTRAL PRICES AND DIFFERENTIAL RENTS

In a competitive economic system, market prices are always fixed by the price at which the least competitive, or marginal, producer can sell his product. Within the frame of reference set up in this paper, the marginal producer, or rather producers, with respect to the central market are producers of crop c located along the limits of cultivation at radius γ from the centre. These producers are marginal in the sense that, because of their location, they would always be the first producers to be eliminated from the market in any economic downturn. Furthermore, so long as the supply potential of crop c is perfectly elastic then competition at the central market will prevent producers of crop c at γ from earning any excess profit beyond the normal rate of profit. That is,

$$(11) \qquad r_c(\gamma) = 0,$$

where r stand for excess profit per unit of output. Similarly, let t stand for transport cost, and in such a way that $t_c(\gamma)$, for example, represents the total cost involved in the forward transport of one unit of crop c from γ to the central market and including any backward transport costs as discussed earlier.

Then, a first approximation to a determination of the market price of crop c
is given by the expression

$$p_c^* = p_c + t_c(\gamma).$$

This expression represents the total final cost of production (including a
normal profit) at the ultimate margin of cultivation. Moreover, once market
price is established in this way then other non-marginal producers of crop c
will also sell at the same price, enabling them to earn an excess profit (or
rent) due to their relatively high accessibility to the market. At distance δ
from the central market this excess profit per unit of output of crop c is
determined in conformity with the rule

$$r_c(\delta) = p_c^* - p_c - t_c(\delta) = t_c(\gamma) - t_c(\delta), \quad \beta \leq \delta \leq \gamma,$$

so that excess profit, in the present exercise, is purely a function of transport
cost differentials.

Now, at β and inwards towards the market, crop b replaces crop c on the
landscape. Moreover, economic competition and rationality will obviously fix
the location of the boundary between crop b and crop c in such a way that
excess profit (rent) per unit area earned on crop b at the boundary will
exactly equal excess profit per unit area earned on crop c at the boundary.
This proposition may be expressed symbolically.

$$(12) \quad \frac{y_b - b_b}{\lambda_b} r_b(\beta) = \frac{y_c - c_c}{\lambda_c} r_c(\beta),$$

where $(y_b - b_b)/\lambda_b$ represents the total amount of crop b per unit area that
is actually marketed at the central point, and $(y_c - c_c)/\lambda_c$ represents the
amount of crop c per unit area that is marketed. Recall, that, in accordance
with an earlier argument, excess profit is imputable only to that part of total
production that passes through the market.

At the same time, producers of crop b along the boundary at β are themselves marginal with respect to all other producers of crop b. Thus, with excess
profit on crop b at β identified as in Equation (12) we can write the market
price of crop b as

$$p_b^* = p_b + t_b(\beta) + r_b(\beta).$$

And excess profit on crop b earned by nonmarginal producers at distance δ
from the market is

$$r_b(\delta) = p_b^* - p_b - t_b(\delta) = t_b(\beta) + r_b(\beta) - t_b(\delta), \quad \alpha \leq \delta \leq \beta.$$

Precisely the same structural relations exist between producers of crops a and b as exist between producers of crops h and c. Thus, excess profit on crop a at the land use boundary at α is equal to

$$(13) \quad \frac{y_a - a_a}{\lambda_a} r_a(\alpha) = \frac{y_b - b_b}{\lambda_b} r_b(\alpha).$$

The market price of crop a is therefore

$$p_a^* = p_a + t_a(\alpha) + r_a(\alpha).$$

Lastly, excess profit on crop a earned by non-marginal producers at distance δ from the market is given by

$$r_a(\delta) = p_a^* - p_a - t_a(\delta) = t_a(\alpha) + r_a(\alpha) - t_a(\alpha), \quad 0 \leq \delta \leq \alpha.$$

Now the excess profits, r, do not remain in the hands of capitalist farmers but disappear immediately in the form of differential land rent. More explicitly, since excess profits result in the first place from the differential economic advantages of various locations in relation to the situation of the central market, they are directly bid away by farmers in mutual competition with one another for rights to the usufruct of the same locations. The resulting price of these rights is not an intrinsic expression of the productive value of the soil, but only of the power of private property. Land *rent* thus enters the sphere of production in a way that is entirely extrinsic and external to the production process itself.

We now need to consider a second and less familiar form of land rent.

VII. SCARCITY RENT

Under certain conditions a *scarcity rent* on land will appear, in addition to ordinary differential rent. Such a scarcity rent corresponds to a levy, extracted out of the total net product, and imposed by landlords as a function of the absolute scarcity of land used in commodity production.

From a purely formal point of view, scarcity rent resembles the Marxian category of absolute rent. In terms of its function and genesis, however, it is more clearly identified in terms of the Walrasian theory of rent. This theory characterizes rent as an increment to the price of a naturally scarce resource so as to contain the consumption of that resource to within the available limited supply (cf. Scott, 1976). Samuelson (1959) describes a somewhat analogous rent as 'residual rent'. In the present context, assuming that the uniform plain is now strictly bounded in some way, this proposition translates into the equivalent idea that scarcity rent represents in some sense an increment to the market prices of crops a, b, and c, and in such a way that consumption of those crops is thereby reduced to a level consistent with the (given) restricted production possibilities of the land base.

Thus, let us suppose that the outer limits of cultivation at distance γ from the central market are strictly limited by some barrier, such as a sea-coast, or a belt of relatively infertile soil, or even some administratively imposed boundary such as a zoning limit. Let us imagine that production of crop c has extended up to this barrier, but that even at the market price $p_c^* = p_a + t_c(\gamma)$ there still exists some excess demand for crop c. In this case there is bound to be an increase in the price of c as consumers compete among each other to secure a portion of the restricted total supply. This increase is really a rent on the absolute scarcity of land, and as such, it falls into the pockets of landowners rather than capitalists.

Let us designate s as this scarcity rent on land *per unit area*. Clearly, if the rent s forms on land producing crop c, then by a process equivalent to the rent-equalizing functions (12) and (13) it must also form on land producing crops a and b. Concomitantly, the general scarcity rent, s, translates into specific rents *per unit of market output* by the following operations

(14) $\quad s_a = \lambda_a s/(y_a - a_a),$

(15) $\quad s_b = \lambda_b s/(y_b - b_b),$

(16) $\quad s_c = \lambda_c s/(y_c - c_c).$

These expressions in turn imply that market prices can be finally and fully defined as follows:

(17) $\quad p_a^* = p_a + t_a(\alpha) + r_a(\alpha) + s_a,$

(18) $\quad p_b^* = p_b + t_b(\beta) + r_b(\beta) + s_b,$

(19) $\quad p_c^* = p_c + t_c(\gamma) + s_c.$

Now, if, by contrast, land is so abundant that γ is effectively perfectly variable, then the scarcity rent s cannot be sustained at a positive level, for it would be driven down to zero by the action of landlords competing among themselves to rent their land along the elastic margins of cultivation. The final equilibrium value of s is thus determined as follows:

$$s \gtrless 0, \quad \text{if } \gamma \text{ is fixed and finite},$$

$$s = 0, \quad \text{if } \gamma \text{ is perfectly variable.}$$

These conditions mean, further, that s and γ are mutually exclusive variables in our system. Thus, if land is limited in quantity, then γ is fixed exogenously accordingly, and s is determined as an endogenous variable. If the value of γ is unrestricted, however, then s is automatically set equal to zero, and γ is determined as an endogenous variable.

VIII. A GENERAL SOLUTION

The various inter-relations between prices, rents and transport costs as described in preceding sections are demonstrated graphically in Figure 2.

The model sketched out above is now seen to represent a perfectly inter-dependent structure. This model contains the twenty variables, $p_a, p_b, p_c, p_a^*,$ $p_b^*, p_c^*, \rho, A, B, C, r_a(\alpha), r_b(\beta), r_c(\gamma), s, s_a, s_b, s_c, \alpha, \beta,$ and γ, in the nineteen Equations (1)–(19). However, since s and γ represent mutually exclusive elements, the model in practice contains only nineteen variables, and so is entirely determinate. The full interdependence of the Von Thünen and Sraffa models is now, in addition, fully apparent. The prices $p_a, p_b,$ and p_c first appear as an outcome of the production process; then they translate via the spatial system into the market prices p_a^*, p_b^* and p_c^*; the latter prices in turn enter the production process, thus determining the values of $p_a, p_b,$ and p_c; and so on, *ad infinitum*.

It is now, in addition, possible to relax our initial assumption that the spatial ordering of all land use rings must be known in advance. If it is required to determine this ordering as an endogenous output of the model, then an extended model can be established, analogous to the model (1)–(19), but such that production of each crop is permitted at each and every location. The competitive equilibrium solution is then simply determined by maximizing total land rent. In fact, Figure 2 finally clarifies the role and function of land rent as a sorter and arranger of land uses, for each individual location within the geographical interval $[0, \gamma]$ is clearly uniquely occupied by the crop that can pay the highest aggregate rent at that location.

IX. THE PROCESS OF LAND USE CHANGE

The model described above seems immediately susceptible to yet further elaboration by embedding a simple but very general dynamic mechanism

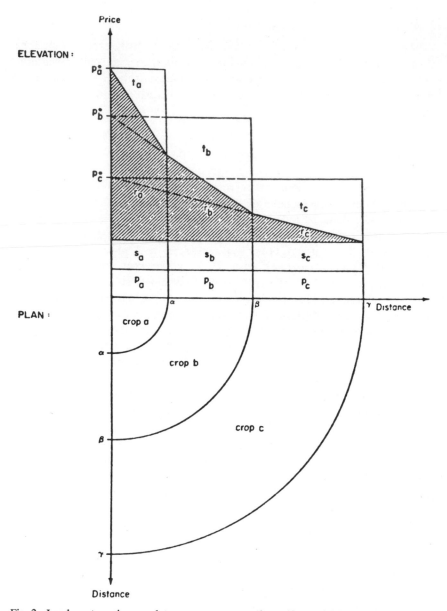

Fig. 2. Land rents, prices, and transport costs on the uniform plain. For simplicity in constructing this figure it is assumed that the conditions of production are such that $p_a = p_b = p_c$, $s_a = s_b = s_c$, $r_a(\alpha) = r_b(\alpha)$ and $r_b(\beta) = r_c(\beta)$. The shaded area represents differential rent.

within it. This mechanism is precisely the overall process of land use intensification (cf. Roweis *et al.*, 1975). Only the most obvious remarks in this question will be adduced here, for it is hoped to develop a fuller analysis of the problem of land use intensification in a subsequent paper.

Thus, suppose that any individual farmer suddenly brings into use some technical innovation that allows him to intensify production. In brief, the innovation allows the farmer to increase his total production from y to $y + \Delta y$. In order to make things easy for ourselves in this highly preliminary exposition, we may take it that the innovation involves no changes either in farm area or in production price. Hence, after intensification, the farmer's total revenue is (supposing that the farmer specializes in the production of crop a, that he is located at distance δ from the centre, and, once more to simplify, that he sends his entire output to market):

$$(20) \quad (y_a + \Delta y_a)p_a^* = (y_a + \Delta y_a)[p_a + t_a(\delta) + r_a(\delta) + s_a].$$

Moreover, the farmer is now able to earn an excess profit. Note that so long as the farmer remains the sole possessor of the innovation then his aggregate land rent cannot increase once he has introduced the innovation. This assertion follows from the observation that competitive land rents must at this stage be determined purely in relation to the old technology. After intensification, then, the farmer's land rent will remain at the level $y_a[r_a(\delta) + s_a]$; by contrast, the farmer's aggregate production price, $(y_a + \Delta y_a)p_a$, as well as his aggregate transport costs, $(y_a + \Delta y_a)t_a(\delta)$, will increase directly in proportion to the increase in production. Then, by manipulation of Equation (20) above, the farmer's excess profits due to intensification can be immediately identified as

$$(21) \quad \Delta y_a[r_a(\delta) + s_a] = (y_a + \Delta y_a)p_a^* - (y_a + \Delta y_a)[p_a + t_a(\delta)]$$
$$- y_a[r_a(\delta) + s_a].$$

From this last equation it is readily apparent that excess profits due to intensification are at an absolute maximum at the geographical centre of the land use system. This, then, is where the intensification process would be expected first to occur, given perfect mobility of capital. Nevertheless, and unfortunately for the initial individual innovator, his competitors are also much motivated to secure excess profits for themselves, and they will therefore actively set about adopting the innovation. Further, given that potential excess profits decrease from the centre of the land use system outwards, in conformity with Equation (21), then any successful innovation will tend to

have a pattern of adoption such that the innovation will diffuse regularly outwards from the centre to the periphery; or, if we wish to think of crop-
specific kinds of innovations, the innovation will diffuse from the inner edge
of any specific land use ring to its outer edge. This diffusion phenomenon will
result in the following general tendencies under conditions of stable demand:

(a) Excess profits due to intensification will gradually be competitively
bid away in the form of land rent, and will, indeed, eventually disappear.

(b) Increasing production will cause scarcity rent to disappear, and
ultimately will cause the total area under cultivation to shrink.

(c) Differential land rent will be reduced (contrary to the pessimistic
Ricardian view).

(d) Market prices will fall.

This general process of innovation, land use intensification, and the quest
for excess profits surely represents the central dynamic of land use systems in
capitalist societies. The specifically geographical manifestation of this process
in any given system is the occurrence of successive waves of land use intensifi-
cations flowing outwards from central to peripheral locations. At any one
moment in time, this phenomenon may result in the empirical appearance of
spatial gradations in the intensity of production within any specific land use
zone, most especially if there is some inertia in existing technology. In long-
run static equilibrium, however, differential land rent will always render the
space within any land use zone economically homogeneous, so that land use
intensities will invariably have a tendency to stabilize at some spatially constant optimal level. This is so, at least, so long as differential rent is due
purely to locational differences and not to intrinsic differences in the physical
or chemical qualities of the soil. In this sense, the model proposed here runs
counter to, and contradicts, certain neo-classical formulations of land use
theory (cf. Beckmann (1972)) which suggest that land use intensities will vary
in relation to simple changes in location.

X. CONCLUSION

The foregoing discussion has shown how traditional Von Thünen land use
theory may be integrated with the Sraffa model of production, prices, and
distribution. The powerful and practically important interdependencies that
exist between these two kinds of systems are the basis of a synthetic model of
the space-economy that appears to be replete with possibilities for further
extension and analysis. The model has obvious and immediate relevance to

such staple items of geographical discourse as industrial location theory, central place theory, growth pole analysis, and so on. The model is further directly applicable to the analysis of the differentiation of intra-urban space (Scott, 1975). Above all, it would be of some considerable interest and significance to attempt to work out the interplay of wages, profits, and rents within the formal framework of each of these various problems. In this way, the present study would seem to provide a possible foundation for a broad, convincing, and long overdue critical enquiry into the economic geography of capitalist societies.

University of Toronto

NOTES

[1] This research was supported as part of the Urban Transportation Policy Impact Study by the University of Toronto/York University Joint Program in Transportation, through a grant from the Transportation Development Agency.

BIBLIOGRAPHY

Beckmann, M.: 1972, 'Von Thünen Revisited: A Neoclassical Land Use Model', *Swedish Journal of Economics* **74**, 1–7.

Goldstein, G. S. and Moses, L.: 1975, 'Interdependence and the Location of Economic Activities', *Journal of Urban Economics* **2**, 63–84.

Roweis, S. T. *et al.*: 1975, 'The Land Market and the Central Core of Toronto: Theory, Analysis and Policy Alternatives', Unpublished Report (City Planning Board, Toronto).

Samuelson, P. A.: 1959, 'A Modern Treatment of the Ricardian Economy: I, The Pricing of Goods and of Labor and Land Services', *The Quarterly Journal of Economics* **73**, 1–35.

Scott, A. J.: 1975, 'Système Spatial et Système de Production: Essai de Synthèse', *Architecture et Méthodologies no. 6* (Institut de l'Environnement, Nanterre) 7–33.

Scott, A. J.: 1976, 'Land and Land Rent: An Interpretative Review of the French Literature', *Progress in Geography* **9**, 101–145.

Sraffa, P.: 1960, *Production of Commodities by Means of Commodities*, Cambridge University Press, Cambridge, Mass.

ERIC S. SHEPPARD

SPATIAL INTERACTION AND GEOGRAPHIC THEORY

Because the one can be explained by the other, it is
strange that many prefer to explain the size of a
central place by the traffic rather than the traffic
by the size of the central place . . . In all economic
theory the same sort of situation applies, e.g., the
price of a good depends on the demand and supply,
the costs of production, the scarcity of the good,
and the income and other conditions of the purchaser. But on the other hand, both the supply
and the demand are themselves determined by the
production costs, the (relative) scarcity, and finally,
to a great extent, by the price willingness of the
purchaser. Where is one to find a beginning and an
end? The secret is that the mechanism will unfold
itself in due time for it is a continually changing
relationship. And that which is a consequence of a
certain system of interdependent economic
relationships, at the same time causes the next system of interdependent economic relationships. If
such a process were demonstrated graphically, it
would not be shown by a closed circle without
beginning or end, but rather, taking the passing of
time into account as a third dimension, it would be
shown by [a] more or less strongly expanding
spiral . . .

WALTER CHRISTALLER, *Central Places in*
Southern Germany, pp. 70–72

I. INTRODUCTION

Since the advent of the so-called quantitative revolution in geography, there
has been an ever-increasing interest in theory construction. One question frequently raised in discussion is whether or not human geography possesses a
group of theories that are distinct from economic, political, or social theory.
Frequently such notions as central place theory or the gravity model are pro-
pounded as support for the fact that theorising is a valid activity for geographers.

361

S. Gale and G. Olsson (eds.), Philosophy in Geography, 361–378. All Rights Reserved.

Ultimately, of course, there should be no question that geography, like all other disciplines with a social science orientation, is attempting to understand society, and that theory construction is a part of that process. The theory being sought, however, should not be divided between disciplines. To talk of geographic or economic theory as separate entities is not particularly progressive since in fact these are just parts of an overall theory of society. A better way of viewing the different disciplines is as alternative perspectives, from which society may be viewed to gain insight unobtainable from the aspects of other social sciences. In this context, the issue of whether or not geography has a distinctive body of theory reduces to one of whether there is a distinctive geographic perspective which provides insight into theoretical studies of society.

The following pages attempt to tackle this question. The position is taken that there is a distinctive geographical viewpoint which is reflected in the manner by which human activities are linked together in space. The interdependencies between locations, which help produce distinctive spatial regularities in many human phenomena, are a result of the interactions between people and their environments. It will be shown that there is an inherently dynamic nature to these interdependencies, and that ignorance of this fact results in biased explanations. The implication, then, is that better explanation is possible if theories can be constructed showing how spatial interaction occurs in many different situations. Such theories may then be combined with those of other disciplines which have ignored this geographical aspect of the relations between phenomena. It seems that new theoretical insight can be provided from this perspective, and that geographers are particularly well equipped to do this.

II. SPATIAL INTERACTION AS A PARAMETER OF EXPLANATION

There are three distinct elements involved in developing an explanation for observed events: the nature of the phenomenon explained and of those causal factors affecting it; the timing of this occurrence; and the location at which it takes place. Causal relationships may be uni-directional (with event A influencing B) or interdependent (whereby if A affects B then B also has an effect on A). Often it is the latter form which best typifies the phenomena we are attempting to understand. Consider, for example, the relationship between income and expenditure. If income is denoted by Y, and expenditure by E, then:

(1a) $E_{t+\delta t} = s \cdot Y_t, \quad 0 < s < 1;$

and

(1b) $\Delta Y_{t+\delta t} = E_{t+\delta t}.$

Equation (1a) suggests that new expenditure is a function of income available (s being the marginal propensity to spend), and (1b) states that new income available in the next increment of time, $\Delta Y_{t+\delta t}$, is identically equal to the increase in expenditure (an accounting identity rather than a theoretical relation).

It then follows that:

(2) $E_{t+2\delta t} = sY_t + s \cdot \Delta Y_{t+\delta t},$

$$= sY_t + s^2 Y_t;$$

or in general:

(3) $E_{t+k} = (s + s^2 + s^3 + \ldots)Y_t,$

$$= \frac{1}{1-s} \cdot Y_t,$$

where $k \geqslant \delta t$. This is the well known multiplier of economics.

Thus we have an explanation incorporating the *structural* relation between two events and a crude measure of the *dynamic* response pattern, but no statement of location. The simplest way of making this relation 'spatial' is to add location as a subscript:

$$E_{i,t+\delta t} = s_i \cdot Y_{i,t}.$$

For n locations this may be rewritten in matrix form as:

(4) $E_{t+\delta t} = \begin{bmatrix} s_1 & & 0 \\ & s_2 & \\ & & \ddots \\ 0 & & \ddots \ s_n \end{bmatrix} \cdot Y_t,$

$$= S \cdot Y_t,$$

where

$$E'_{t+\delta t} = [E_{1,t+\delta t}, E_{2,t+\delta t}, \ldots, E_{n,t+\delta t}]$$

and
$$\mathbf{Y}'_t = [Y_{1t}, \ldots, Y_{nt}].$$
Then
$$\mathbf{E}_{t+2\delta t} = \mathbf{S} \cdot \mathbf{Y}_t + \mathbf{S}^2 \cdot \mathbf{Y}_t$$

or in general:

$$(5) \quad \mathbf{E}_{t+k} = \begin{bmatrix} (1-s_1)^{-1} & & & \\ & (1-s_2)^{-1} & & 0 \\ & & \cdot & \\ & & & \cdot \\ 0 & & & (1-s_n)^{-1} \end{bmatrix} \mathbf{Y}_t,$$

$$(6) \quad = [(\mathbf{I}-\mathbf{S})^{-1} - \mathbf{I}] \cdot \mathbf{Y}_t,$$

where $\mathbf{I}$ is the identity matrix.

This may be called a 'multilocational' formulation. The fact that events may happen at several locations is taken into account, but only under the assumption that occurrences at one location do not affect those at another. In short this is an explanatory framework able to deal only with *in situ* events, or 'congruent facts'.[1] The spatial aspect of this explanation is trivial (in an operational sense; it may not be of trivial importance), and geographers as specialists in spatially related phenomena would have little insight to add. Indeed, several spatial economists, by taking this approach, have been able to add location to their models without any need to modify the economic arguments.[2]

This, of course, is not at all an accurate representation of today's world. In reality, locations are not independent of one another functioning as self-sufficient entities, but rather are highly interconnected. Not only is there much personal communication between them, but in addition the economy of every place is partly dependent on outputs from elsewhere (of a complementary and/or competitive nature). Even economists recognise this in their curiously inconsistent conceptualisations of the space-economy: at one level a city is seen as a kind of macro-firm which operates independently of other cities, whereas at another scale the country is often viewed as a single interdependent unit. In fact, economic activities at different locations affect one another at all scales, both through physical movement of factors of production and via the diffusion of knowledge and technology. Certainly it is true that explanations are easier if these interconnections are simplified or ignored, but they are at the same time dangerous since biased inferences will result.[3]

A more complete conceptualisation of the role played by location in socio-economic processes is thus necessary — one which allows for the fact that any event A_{it} can affect some other phenomenon $B_{j,t+k}$ where i and j are different locations. A direct link between these two may be introduced as

$$B_{j,t+\delta t} = c_{ij} \cdot A_{it}$$

where c_{ij} represents the direct effect of A_{it} on $B_{j,t+k}$. Then the specification for many locations becomes, using matrix notation:

$$(7) \qquad \mathbf{B}_{t+\delta t} = \begin{bmatrix} c_{11} & c_{21} & c_{31} & \cdots & c_{n1} \\ & & & & \vdots \\ c_{12} & c_{22} & & & \vdots \\ \vdots & & & & \\ \vdots & & & & \\ c_{1n} & \cdots & & & c_{nn} \end{bmatrix} \mathbf{A}_t$$

$$= \mathbf{C} \cdot \mathbf{A}_t.$$

This represents a system with interlocational relations (or 'overlapping' facts)[4] in which each place may affect all others. Then the total effect of the spatial configuration of A at time $t(\mathbf{A}_t)$ on that of B at time $t + k(\mathbf{B}_{t+k})$ is presumably given by:

$$(8) \qquad \mathbf{B}_{t+k} = [(\mathbf{I} - \mathbf{C})^{-1} - \mathbf{I}] \cdot \mathbf{A}_t.$$

This approach has long been a tool of input–output analysis, with the matrix $(\mathbf{I} - \mathbf{C})^{-1}$ representing the economic multiplier linking a group of industries together either in the same or in different regions. What has not been so widely recognised is that a spatial multiplier as defined by (8) exists for any pair of phenomena A and B that are related together in an interdependent manner. The multiplier thus not only has explicit spatial connotations, but is a fundamental element underlying the understanding of a wide range of processes. To limit it to economic processes in general and monetary relations in particular is unnecessarily restrictive.

Spatial autocorrelation has recently become widely used in geography as a way of measuring the inter-relatedness between phenomena as they occur in space. In fact any observed autocorrelation is merely the observable manifestation of some spatial multiplier, there being a direct relation between the matrix $(\mathbf{I} - \mathbf{C})^{-1}$ and a matrix of spatial autocorrelations.[5] Thus in order to ultimately understand how autocorrelations are generated, it is not sufficient to design increasingly sophisticated weighting schemes that increase the precision of statistical estimates of spatial correlations. Instead it is better to understand how the basic interrelationships, the c_{ij}'s, come about in the first place.

Equation (7) is a better representation of the relations between phenomena in space than Equation (4). In addition it is obvious that attempting to model phenomena exhibiting interlocational relations by a model such as Equation (4) will lead to incorrect conclusions about how A and B relate to one another. However, even Equation (7) is insufficient since it implies that the c_{ij}'s do not vary with changes in t.

The c_{ij}'s ultimately represent interaction between i and j, and interaction itself is just one realisation of human behaviour. It has been well established empirically that behaviour in space (i.e., interaction) depends on the spatial structure (i.e., the morphology of an individual's environment). This was the conclusion of geography's possibilist/determinist debate, and in recent literature one need not look far to find confirmation. Examples where this has been particularly brought out occur in transportation[6] and in behavioural geography.[7] Since the fact that spatial structure will alter over time underlies the very nature of dynamic models, it is unreasonable to expect the matrix of spatial interdependencies to remain static.

A complete conceptualisation of the relationship between our two variables, taking into account time and location as well as the purely functional effect of A on B, must thus take the form

$$(9) \qquad \mathbf{B}_{t+\delta t} = \begin{bmatrix} c_{11t} & c_{21t} & \cdots & c_{n1t} \\ c_{12t} & \cdot & \cdots & \cdot \\ & & & \cdot \\ & & & \cdot \\ c_{1nt} & \cdot & & c_{nnt} \end{bmatrix} \cdot \mathbf{A}_t$$

$$= \mathbf{C}_t \cdot \mathbf{A}_t,$$

where c_{ijt} is the direct effect of A_{it} on $B_{j,t+\delta t}$. Multipliers may be calculated from this matrix to represent direct and indirect effects. These can be viewed as space–time multipliers, a concept which as yet has received little attention in geography.

III. INTERACTION: ESTIMATION OR SPECIFICATION?

Equation (9) is a framework linking $2n$ stock variables and n^2 flow variables into an integrated model of change. For this to be a theoretical statement it is necessary to have a theory describing how interaction occurs as a function of A_t, and a theory of how interaction and A_t together determine future change (i.e., $B_{t+\delta t}$). In addition, there are various accounting identities between stocks and flows that always occur in formulations of this sort. Since accounting models are often viewed as theory constructs, a clarification of differences between the two seems in order.

Accounting relationships typically fall into one of two categories. First, it is necessary to ensure that the increments or decrements at each location equal the net in- and out-flows.[8] Second, in the event that stock variables represent aggregations of different types of individuals, any changes in interaction due to an alteration in the distribution of these types at each location (for instance the age structure of a population)[9] must be separated from changes due to new patterns of behaviour. These relations are introduced to reduce errors of aggregation in aggregate models.

Although accounting identities are useful, in a technical sense, for removing inconsistencies between stocks and flows, they do not explain how spatial interaction is generated in the first place. A relatively complete theory of change is only possible through consideration of stocks and flows as equally fundamental components in the socio-economic milieu. Unfortunately there have been few attempts to do this. Instead concentration has been on one of the two while neglecting the feedback effects of its relation to the other. For instance many migration and diffusion studies have constructed theories of interaction as a function of the configuration of opportunities, without specifying how these flows themselves change the relative attractiveness of places for future interaction through their effect on the configuration of stocks.

Models of change in regional economics and studies of urban systems dynamics have been particularly guilty of concentrating on stocks while neglecting flows.[10] Conventionally, such models start with a set of economic relations between stock variables. These are then given a spatial context by considering the effect of an event at one location on occurrences elsewhere, representing this nexus by a coefficient such as c_{ijt} of Equation (9).[11] However, rather than regarding c_{ijt} as the realisation of human spatial behaviour capable of explanation through some theory of interaction, the coefficient is often viewed as a parameter of the model to be calibrated. Thus interactions are often measured empirically (such as the income flows in input–output models), or estimated statistically (as in the spatial forecasting models of Cliff and Ord, and Martin and Oeppen).[12]

The approach of input–output analysis, whereby these parameters are customarily derived empirically for one time period and then assumed to remain constant in the future, is clearly inadequate since interactions will vary over time. In fact no statistical estimation procedure will do justice to the patterns of behaviour suggested by Equation (9), since there are n^2 flow parameters to be evaluated with only $2n$ observations (the stocks). Some simplification is therefore necessary to obtain reasonable estimates: either by assuming the congruent specification, where $c_{ijt} = 0$ if $i \neq j$; or keeping c_{ijt} constant for all t; or allowing c_{ijt} to vary over time while constraining some c_{ijt}'s to be a constant proportion of other ones. Cliff and Ord[13] discuss these issues. Given the relation between interaction and changing configurations of opportunities, none of these strategies seem reasonable as they put *a priori* constraints on human behaviour.

Even if statistical estimation were feasible it would not be a good alternative. Ultimately we seek understanding of how the system evolves and this is not attainable without some theoretical model. Estimation is of use once a theory has been developed to the point that its empirical validity may be tested. It is no substitute for lack of theory since, as indicated, erroneous answers are liable to result from this situation. Thus although eventually it might be desirable to calibrate some theoretical specification of c_{ijt} by statistical estimation, it certainly seems inappropriate to treat interaction as a whole in this manner.

IV. A LOGICAL BASIS FOR INTERDEPENDENCIES

Any pair of phenomena, symbolically represented as A and B, that are believed to be linked by some overlapping relationships may be symbolised by:

$$
(10) \quad
\begin{bmatrix}
B_{1,t+k} \\
B_{2,t+k} \\
\cdot \\
\cdot \\
\cdot \\
B_{n,t+k}
\end{bmatrix}
=
\begin{bmatrix}
v_{11t}^{(k)ab} & v_{21t}^{(k)ab} & & \\
v_{12t}^{(k)ab} & v_{22t}^{(k)ab} & & \\
& & \cdot & \\
& & & \cdot \\
v_{1nt}^{(k)ab} & & & v_{nnt}^{(k)ab}
\end{bmatrix}
\cdot
\begin{bmatrix}
A_{1,t} \\
A_{2,t} \\
\cdot \\
\cdot \\
\cdot \\
A_{n,t}
\end{bmatrix}
\cdot
$$

$v_{ijt}^{(k)ab}$ represents the total effect of A at i, time t, on B at j, time $t + k$. The matrix of interdependencies may be equivalently regarded as representing the total deterministic effect of A on B or as a transition probability matrix representing the probability of A affecting B. A stochastic interpretation is more in line with our ignorance about reality[14] and will be used here.

As outlined above there are three elements involved in the relationship represented by $v_{ijt}^{(k)ab}$; space, time, and the structural relationship between A and B. First is the probability that, during time period t, A at i will connect with B at j, represented by u_{ijt}^{ab}. u_{ijt}^{ab} depends on the propensity of A at i to generate interaction with other locations at all, and on the probability that some of this will be attracted to B at j. Second, there is the propensity for a unit impulse of A, arriving at j, to lead to an *in situ* change in B at j. This is the theoretical relation between stock variables studied by economists and other non-spatial social scientists, and is equivalent to the parameter 's' discussed in Section II. It will be denoted by β^{ab}. Finally there is the degree to which the composite effect $u_{ijt}^{ab} \cdot \beta^{ab}$ on B is realised at time lag k (often represented by a distributed lag function), $\alpha_{ij}^{(k)ab}$. Thus schematically

$$(11) \qquad v_{ijt}^{(k)ab} = \alpha_{ij}^{(k)ab} \cdot \beta^{ab} \cdot u_{ijt}^{ab}.$$

Variable u_{ijt}^{ab} represents the spatial specification involved in this relationship, and is thus the major element contributed by a geographical approach to theory construction.

Even if it is reasonable to assume that $\alpha_{ij}^{(k)ab}$ and β^{ab} remain relatively constant over time, the nature of human behaviour is such that spatial interaction will not. The probability defined by u_{ijt}^{ab}, which ultimately is dependent on spatial behaviour, will therefore alter over time. As the configuration of opportunities alters so do the interaction patterns. It is not true, however, to assume that u_{ijt}^{ab} is equal to the interaction that travels directly from A_{it} to B_j at time t. To see this, consider Figure 1.

In Figure 1 the direct effect of i on j is represented by the single link (solid line) connecting i to j. However, because of the bilateral and two dimensional nature of space there are other ways by which i can affect j. A first order indirect link would be $i \rightarrow j \rightarrow k$. Second order indirect connections are, for example, $i \rightarrow k \rightarrow i \rightarrow j$; $i \rightarrow j \rightarrow k \rightarrow j$; $i \rightarrow j \rightarrow i \rightarrow j$; and there are other examples of higher order. This conceptualization is in fact only manageable at all because, in general, nexi which are more indirect are less important. Since an event at i can affect j in any one of these ways, the total propensity of interaction leaving i to reach j can only be obtained by adding up all direct and indirect interactions between the two places. The result is a spatial multiplier representing the total effect that i has on j, u_{ijt}^{ab}.

Since this multiplier is a measure of the *total* interaction between two locations, it should provide a better idea of the total effect or *influence* that one location exerts on another than simple consideration of the direct interaction. Therefore u_{ijt}^{ab} will be known as the influence that A at i has on B at j via the medium of spatial interaction.

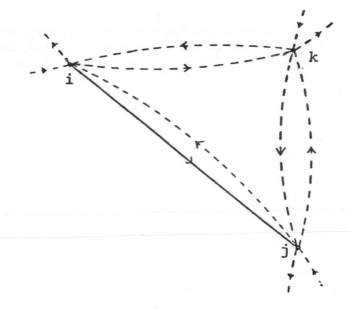

Fig. 1. Direct and indirect links between centres i. ———, Direct connection from i to j.
-----, Links used indirectly in trips from i to j.

A relatively complete conceptualisation of the spatio-temporal relationship that links $\mathbf{A}_t$ and $\mathbf{B}_{t+k}$ may now be outlined.

$$(12) \quad \mathbf{B}_{t+k} = \begin{bmatrix} v_{11t}^{(k)ab} & \cdots & v_{n1t}^{(k)ab} \\ \vdots & & \vdots \\ v_{1nt}^{(k)ab} & \cdots & v_{nnt}^{(k)ab} \end{bmatrix} \cdot \mathbf{A}_t$$

$$(13) \quad v_{ijt}^{(k)ab} = \alpha_{ij}^{(k)ab} \cdot \beta^{ab} \cdot u_{ijt}^{ab}.$$

$$(14) \quad u_{ijt}^{ab} = f(I_{ijt}^{ab}).$$

$$(15) \quad I_{ijt}^{ab} = f[\mathbf{A}_t, \mathbf{A}_{t-1}, \ldots, \mathbf{A}_{t-h}; \mathbf{B}_t, \mathbf{B}_{t-1}, \ldots, \mathbf{B}_{t-l}; \mathbf{D}].$$

Here I_{ijt}^{ab} represents the direct interaction between A at i, time t and B at j. By Equation (15) this is a function of present and past configurations of stocks, and of the matrix $\mathbf{D}$ which represents distance between all locations. In fact the theoretical statement represented by Equation (15) lies at the core of this entire structure. Unless a good theory exists stating how the configuration of stocks in a system generates interaction, then it is impossible to determine how interaction will alter in the future. Without this information it is impossible to specify Equations (12), (13) and (14), and we are reduced to estimating $v_{ijt}^{(k)ab}$ rather than specifying it theoretically. The dangers and inadequacies of that have already been detailed.

To clarify the complex interdependencies between configurations of stocks and patterns of interaction suggested by this system, consider the following interpretation. Changes in structure are a function of spatial interaction (Equations (12), (13), (14)). Equation (15) states on the other hand that changes in interaction are a result of alterations in spatial structure. Thus spatial structure affects the form of interaction which feeds back to alter structure. This two-way interdependency may be described as an *interaction feedback* mechanism. Such a conceptualisation is far from new in the geographic literature,[15] so it is unfortunate that formal models incorporating such feedbacks are rare. Of the few approaches that have allowed both stocks and flows to alter, most tend to use some iteration procedure giving rise to a static equilibrium as typified by the Lowry model. Although dynamic versions of these have been developed[16] they allow very little adaptation of interaction to structure.

Those few rigorous statements that have explicitly incorporated interaction feedback have tended to be either somewhat esoteric in nature,[17] or only constructed for fairly limited examples of what is a very general phenomenon.[18] In fact, interaction feedback is a fundamental dynamic which forms the basis for a very broad range of spatio-temporal models in human geography. Of course this system may be readily simplified to handle particular tasks; to describe the evolution of a single stock variable, or even the highly special case of the economists' aspatial world.[19] However the idea is of sufficient importance to deserve theoretical examination in its most general form.

V. ON THEORIES OF SPATIAL INTERACTION

It has been argued that if the locational aspect of phenomena has any distinctive influence on theory construction in the social sciences it is because of the fact that causal relations tend to be interlocational in nature, and that ignoring these relations leads to biased explanations. Since the only way to understand how events are co-related in space is to comprehend the underlying spatial interaction, it is natural to conclude that the geographer's contribution to theoretical problems should lie in this area. Unfortunately, theories of spatial interaction, particularly at the aggregate level, have been more successful in describing interaction than explaining it. There are two major problems here.

The first issue is a technical one, but is of great relevance to problems of inferring spatial behaviour from aggregate interaction models. When a gravity or intervening opportunities model is calibrated for empirical data, the result is often represented as a distance decay function which is assumed to show how people behave in space. Unfortunately in most realistic situations this decay function not only represents spatial behaviour but also is affected by the spatial configuration of opportunities within which the interaction is taking place. This problem has been recognised by Rushton[20] and Curry,[21] but has only been explicitly outlined recently.[22] The details are discussed elsewhere, but the basic principle bears repetition here. Since distance decay functions are composed of two effects, behaviour and spatial configurations, which are deeply confounded together, many inferences made to date from these models concerning behaviour need to be re-examined. For instance a certain proportion of the variation in distance exponents observed for the gravity model is presumably explained by the different distributions of origins and destinations, rather than by alterations in individual behaviour.

The second issue relates to some dangers in using highly general aggregate formulations for spatial interaction. The example that best illustrates this is also that most often used to model spatial interaction: the gravity model. This has been so widely applied because it has consistently provided a good fit to observed interaction patterns. However there is a danger in confusing a good fit with a good explanation. In fact the gravity model does not represent any one theory of interaction, and it is unreasonable to expect such a simple formulation to do so. There are several theories of individual behaviour that can each give rise to interaction patterns demonstrating a decline with increasing distance. In this respect the gravity model can be viewed as over-identified.[23] Several distinct processes give rise to the same aggregate pattern. This is a situation strongly reminiscent of the form/process debate.

As an illustration of this problem consider two individuals, one a city dweller and the other a person living in the country at some distance from the city. It might well be observed that the former attends classical music concerts six times a year, while the latter has never been to such an event. This behaviour is readily described by a distance decay model, but accounting for it is far more difficult; at least three fundamentally different explanations exist.

First, both may have an equal desire to attend concerts, but one is too far away and cannot afford to go. Instead he either listens to a broadcast of the concert, buys the record, or in some other way compensates for his disadvantage by substituting another activity for that of concert attendance. In this case the goals are identical, but a cost constraint effectively bars the rural dweller from exercising his option. A formal model of this hypothesis postulates identical utility functions for all, but limits the freedom of choice through a budget constraint on travel cost. Thus an observed difference in choice is due to variations in the cost of realising the benefits of alternative opportunities.[24]

A second explanation is that concerts are less preferable to the rural person (i.e., utilities are no longer identical) since his perception of their attractiveness is reduced (or 'discounted') by the fact that the trip is longer. Models of this behaviour would make utility a function of separation as well as of the attributes possessed by the destination.[25] Thus the goals of individuals are seen as inherently the same, but modified in practice by the spatial distribution of activities between which choices are made. In theory, at least, this inherent goal of everyone should be recoverable (for instance, by the use of multidimensional scaling to recover 'revealed space preferences' from observed interaction behaviour).[26] If the role played by relative location in a person's goals and in his knowledge about the environment is small, this hypothesis becomes similar to the first one.

The third possibility is that the rural inhabitant has no desire to attend concerts, and would not do so even if they were put on in his own area. According to this hypothesis he has been brought up in an environment where people have very different preferences in terms of the activities they seek for entertainment. Similar people, when placed in different environments, will evolve fundamentally different values and preferences over a period of time. The very fact that access to the high order functions available in a city is more difficult has itself led to a different preference structure. This implies that the effect of environment can be to so alter preferences that there will not be any inherent goal or revealed space preference that is common to all (except, maybe, something basic such as the will to survive; but elements at this level of generality provide little scope for understanding reality).[27]

For instance, it is unrealistic to imagine that the rural individual, when placed in the city, will adjust immediately to the preference structure of our urbanite (as the existence of revealed space preferences would suggest); such a change would only occur gradually, if at all. This hypothesis is consistent with explaining not only the differences between urban and rural people, but also those between even second generation immigrants to a city and the descendants of long term residents of that place. Such differences do exist, and an explanation in terms of revealed space preferences seems unconvincing. It would also be very difficult to model this type of behaviour with any utility maximising framework, as it would involve comparing fundamentally different utility functions for the various types of individuals.[28]

The reason that the gravity model adequately describes all three situations is presumably because there is a common set of basic principles underlying these three different theories of interaction which are consistent with the gravity formulation. Smith[29] has already suggested this, noting that three extremely elementary postulates about choice behaviour are sufficient to guarantee that a gravity model may be specified that will adequately describe observed interaction. These are:

(a) The probability of interacting with an opportunity at some location j compared to that of interacting with some other location i is independent of the location of all other opportunities.

(b) As long as two opportunities i and j remain located together in space the relative probability of interacting with i rather than j remains constant.

(c) The probability of interacting with any opportunity at some distance away is less than or equal to the probability of interacting with it if this distance is reduced to zero.

In a similar vein, it may be shown that the gravity model says very little about interaction behaviour. Even if the only limitation placed on spatial interaction is that the expected cost of a trip is constant, this alone is suf- ficient to produce behaviour consistent with the gravity formulation.[30]

Since the gravity model is over-identified, it is clearly inadequate as a specification of interaction patterns that change over time. A model that describes behaviour at one time period but does not contain any explanation of this behaviour will not be able to adequately predict changes that occur in interaction when the configuration of opportunities is altered. There are other aggregate interaction formulations in geography, such as the intervening opportunities hypotheses of Stouffer[31] and Schneider.[32] However research in this general area has not progressed rapidly. It is only recently that attempts have been made to develop theories of how spatial interaction relates to individual choice behaviour.[33]

VI. INTERACTION AND INFLUENCE

In developing the explanatory framework outlined in Equations (12)–(15), it is necessary to provide both a theory of interaction, and a measure of how interaction is translated into the influence that one location exerts on another. In short we require some specification of Equation (14). Fortunately this is somewhat easier to handle than Equation (15).

One possibility would be to make influence proportional to interaction:

$$(16) \qquad u_{ijt}^{ab} = k \cdot I_{ijt}^{ab}.$$

This is too simplistic however. If influence is in fact equal to all the direct and indirect ways by which interaction flows from i to j, (16) would only be valid if each location were equally accessible to every other one. That is clearly unrealistic for most purposes. The correct answer is given by:

$$(17) \qquad U_t^{ab} = (I - W_t^{ab})^{-1} - I$$

where W_t^{ab} is the matrix of interactions, I_{ijt}^{ab}, between all pairs of locations, and U_t^{ab} is the matrix of potentials, u_{ijt}^{ab}.

Thus correct specification of Equation (15) is in fact a technical problem of finding the mathematical transformation that satisfies the definition of influence. This particular transformation has in fact already been much studied as potential theory in physics[34] and in probability theory.[35] Other definitions of influence, and hence other transformations than Equation (17), may be necessary in particular situations. However, any such alternatives are likely to represent some combination of direct and indirect interactions, and thus the relevant transformation will lie somewhere between Equation (16) (which ignores indirect flows) and Equation (17) (which indiscriminately counts all such flows).

VII. CONCLUSIONS

In a society as highly interdependent as our own it is clear that explanations have to take into account interlocational relationships. Ignoring these would imply an inadequate conceptualisation which ultimately can result in incorrect inferences about the causes and effects of various phenomena. Geography potentially has much to contribute in remedying this situation. Indeed, demonstration that it is impossible to fully understand society without taking into account its spatial relations would be sufficient to establish the validity of geography as a theoretical branch of the social sciences.

However this position is far away at present. First, many social scientists are unaware of the effect on explanations of ignoring spatial relations. Second, the importance of these relations, and hence the size of the error introduced into explanations when they are ignored, has not been conclusively demonstrated (at least to non-geographers).

When those two hurdles have been passed, however, there is still the largest one ahead. At the core of this approach to geographical theory construction is the concept of spatial interaction. It is not sufficient to establish that spatial relations are important; some good theories explaining them are also necessary. Unfortunately, remarkably little effort has been devoted to developing good theories of interaction. Instead, empirical estimates such as mean information fields and spatial autocorrelation functions have been used to approximate the effects of interaction. However, because of the dynamic inter-relations between spatial behaviour and the configurations of opportunities such approaches will often be inadequate, and will be unable to explain and predict changes in interaction patterns. In the final analysis there is a need for theoretical work on spatial interaction. At present this represents a considerable gap in one of the basic areas where geographers can make a distinctive contribution.

Finally, it is worth re-emphasizing that although this paper has concentrated on discussing spatial relations, these cannot be isolated from the other dimensions of explanation any more than geographical theory can be separated from that of other social sciences. The mathematical trick used in Equation (11) to separate out the spatial aspects of an explanation should be regarded as just that. For the purpose of this paper such a step was necessary so that the geographical perspective could be concentrated on. However, any complete critique of social science theory should consider inadequacies in specifications of the cause and effect relations between social and economic variables. An example would be the controversy over whether classical or neo-classical economic concepts are more applicable to explaining economic relationships. It should also examine the time dimension. It is possible to argue that calendar time is inappropriate as an argument in dynamic models, since observed behaviour depends on reaction times and often these are inadequately approximated by real time (just as spatial interaction is not dependent solely on the Euclidean distance between locations). Ultimately these two areas must be integrated with the spatial perspective. It should always be remembered that to assume any one of these can be studied and understood independently of the other two is at best an approximation to the true situation, and perhaps a dangerous one.

Department of Geography
University of Minnesota

NOTES

[1] R. D. Sack, 'Chorology and Spatial Analysis', in *Annals of the Association of American Geographers* **64** (1974), 439–52.

[2] Cf. J. B. Beare, 'A Monetarist Model of Regional Business Cycles', in *Journal of Regional Science* **16** (1976), 57–63; R. F. Engle, 'A Disequilibrium Model of Regional Investment', in *Journal of Regional Science* **14** (1974), 367–76; L. M. Hartman and D. Seckler, 'Toward the Application of Dynamic Growth Theory to Regions', in *Journal of Regional Science* **7** (1967), 167–73; J. R. Niedercorn, 'An Econometric Model of Metropolitan Employment and Growth', *RAND Monograph* 3758, Santa Monica, 1963; G. J. L. Yi, 'Towards the Application of Dynamic Growth Theory to Regions: Generalizations and Comments', in *Journal of Regional Science* **16** (1976), 117–24.

[3] E. S. Sheppard, 'Interaction Feedback Modelling: Explorations into Configurations, Flows and the Dynamics of Spatial Systems', Toronto, 1976.

[4] Sack, *op. cit.*

[5] Sheppard, *op. cit.*

[6] E. Taaffe, R. L. Morrill and P. R. Gould, 'Transportation Expansion in Underdeveloped Countries: A Comparative Analysis', in *Geographical Review* **53** (1963), 503–529; A. R. Pred, *The Spatial Dynamics of U.S. Urban-Industrial Growth 1800–1914*, Cambridge, 1966; G. M. Barber, 'A Mathematical Programming Approach to a Network Development Problem', in *Economic Geography* **51** (1975), 128–141.

[7] G. Rushton, 'Analysis of Spatial Behavior by Revealed Space Preference', in *Annals of the Association of American Geographers* **59** (1969), 391–400; M. J. Webber, R. Symanski and J. Boot, 'Toward a Cognitive Spatial Theory', in *Economic Geography* **51** (1975), 100–116.

[8] Cf. A. G. Wilson, 'A Statistical Theory of Spatial Distribution Models', in *Transportation Research* **1** (1967), 253–69.

[9] P. H. Rees and A. G. Wilson, 'Accounts and Models for Spatial Demographic Analysis 1: Aggregate Population', in *Environment and Planning* **5** (1973), 61–90.

[10] Sheppard, *op. cit.*

[11] Cf. L. J. King, E. Casetti and D. Jeffrey, 'Economic Impulses in A Regional System of Cities', in *Regional Studies* **3** (1969), 213–218.

[12] A. D. Cliff and J. K. Ord, 'Space–Time Modelling with an Application to Regional Forecasting', in *Institute of British Geographers, Transactions* **64** (1975), 119–128; R. L. Martin and J. Oeppen, 'The Identification of Regional Forecasting Models Using Space–Time Correlation Functions', in *Institute of British Geographers, Transactions* **66** (1975), 95–118.

[13] A. D. Cliff and J. K. Ord, 'A Regression Approach to Univariate Spatial Forecasting', in M. D. I. Chisholm, A. Frey and P. Haggett (eds.), *Regional Forecasting*, pp. 47–70.

[14] L. Curry, 'Chance and Landscape', in J. W. House (ed.), *Northern Geographical Essays*; G. Olsson, 'On Words and Worlds: Comments on the Isard and Smith Papers', in *Regional Science Association, Papers* **35** (1975), 45–49.

[15] W. Christaller, *Die Zentralen Orte in Suddeutschland* (trans. by C. W. Baskin), Englewood Cliffs, 1933, p. 70; R. Vining, 'A Description of Certain Spatial Aspects of an Economic System', in *Economic Development and Cultural Change* **3** (1955), 147–95.

[16] M. Batty, 'Modelling Cities as Dynamic Systems', in *Nature* **231** (1971), 425–28;

J. P. Crecine, 'A Dynamic Model of Urban Structure', *RAND Monograph*, Santa Monica, 1968.
[17] W. Isard and P. Liossatos, 'Industrial Location: Agglomeration and Feedback Analysis', in *Regional Science Association, Papers* 28 (1972), 7–36; W. Isard and P. Liossatos, 'On Location Analysis for Urban and Regional Growth Situations', in *The Annals of Regional Science* 6 (1972), 1–27.
[18] Cf. L. Curry, 'A Spatial Analysis of Gravity Flows', in *Regional Studies* 6 (1972), 131–47; Barber, *op. cit.*
[19] S. Enke, 'Space and Value', in *Quarterly Journal of Economics* 56 (1942), 627–37.
[20] Rushton, *op. cit.*
[21] Curry, *op. cit.*, 1972.
[22] L. Curry, D. A. Griffith and E. Sheppard, 'Those Gravity Parameters Again', in *Regional Studies* 9 (1975), 289–96; Sheppard, *op. cit.*
[23] D. Harvey, *Explanation in Geography*, London, 1969.
[24] Cf. J. R. Niedercorn and B. V. Becholdt, Jr., 'An Economic Derivation of the "Gravity Law" of Spatial Interaction', in *Journal of Regional Science* 9 (1969), 273–82.
[25] T. F. Golob and M. J. Beckmann, 'A Utility Model for Travel Forecasting', in *Transportation Science* 5 (1971), 79–90; T. E. Smith, 'An Axiomatic Theory of Spatial Discounting Behavior', in *Regional Science Association, Papers* 35 (1975a), 31–44; R. W. White, 'A Generalization of the Utility Theory Approach to the Problem of Spatial Interaction', in *Geographic Analysis* 8 (1976), 39–46.
[26] Rushton, *op. cit.*
[27] T. Bethell, 'Darwin's Mistake', in *Harper's Magazine* (February, 1976), 70–75.
[28] L. Curry, 'Position, Flow and Person in Theoretical Economic Geography', in T. Carlstein, D. Parker and N. Thrift (eds.), *Time–Space and Social Organisation*.
[29] T. E. Smith, 'A Choice Theory of Spatial Interaction', in *Regional Science and Urban Economics* 5 (1975b), 137–76.
[30] E. S. Sheppard, 'Entropy, Theory Construction and Spatial Analysis', in *Environment and Planning* A8 (1976), 741–52.
[31] S. A. Stouffer, 'Intervening Opportunities: A Theory Relating Mobility and Distance', in *American Sociological Review* 5 (1940), 845–67.
[32] M. Schneider, 'Gravity Models and Trip Distribution Theory', in *Regional Science Association, Papers and Proceedings* 5 (1959), 51–56.
[33] Smith, *op. cit.*, 1975a, 1975b.
[34] O. D. Kellogg, *Foundations of Potential Theory*, Berlin, 1929.
[35] J. C. Kemeny, J. L. Snell and A. W. Knapp, *Denumerable Markov Chains*, Princeton, 1966.

CELLULAR GEOGRAPHY[1]

Captain Ahab, in the film version of *Moby Dick*, searches for the white whale with the aid of a geographical map on which are noted sighting-frequencies within 5° cells bounded by lines of latitude and longitude. The written version of the story, dating from *circa* 1830, does not contain this scene, but the technique of recording geographical data in this fashion is increasingly popular today. One of the motivations for the use of such partitionings is their 'objectivity'. It is also asserted that there are advantages for analysis purposes over the irregular spatial polygons defined by political jurisdictions. There is no doubt that there are notational simplifications; one can index a cell of an array in the same fashion as in matrix algebra. Thus the cell in the ith row and jth column becomes the cell i,j. Geographical data which pertain to that cell can be referred to by subscripts, as g_{ij} for example. If one lets G represent an N by M array of such cells then this can be considered isomorphic with a portion of the surface of the earth (if one deletes the poles and makes a convention about the edges). But one can also apply matrix algebra to this array and can obtain geographically interesting results. The major advantage however is pedagogical, and results from the fact that in such a scheme every country in the world has exactly the same number of neighbors. The analytical results can be extended to the more realistic variable-number-of-neighbors case but the insight is more easily gained in the cellular case.

I. TYPES OF MODELS

Using the positional notation let g_{ij}^t be the land use category (urban, rural, ...) at the location i,j at time t. Let $g_{ij}^{t+\Delta t}$ be the land use category at this location at some other time. One primitive classification of models of land use change is then as follows:

(I)   The *independent* model: $g_{ij}^{t+\Delta t}$ is a random variable in no way related to g_{ij}^t.

(II)   The functionally *dependent* model. The land use at location i,j at

S. Gale and G. Olsson (eds.), Philosophy in Geography, 379–386. All Rights Reserved.

W. R. TOBLER

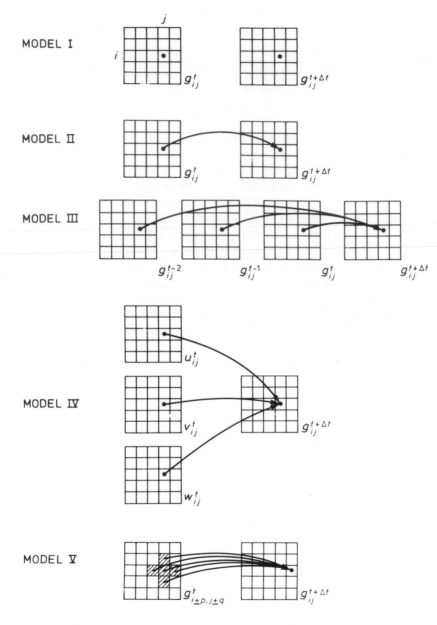

Fig. 1. Graphic illustration of the five models using a 25-cell geographical array

time $t + \Delta t$ depends on the previous land use at that location:

$$g_{ij}^{t+\Delta t} = F(g_{ij}^t).$$

(III) The *historical* model. The land use at position i, j at $t + \Delta t$ depends on the several previous land uses at that location

$$g_{ij}^{t+\Delta t} = F(g_{ij}^t, g_{ij}^{t-\Delta t}, g_{ij}^{t-2\Delta t}, \ldots, g_{ij}^{t-k\Delta t}).$$

(IV) The *multivariate* model. The land use at location i, j is dependent on several other variables at that location:

$$g_{ij}^{t+\Delta t} = F(u_{ij}^t, v_{ij}^t, w_{ij}^t, \ldots, z_{ij}^t).$$

(V) The *geographical* model. The land use at location i, j is dependent on the land use at other locations:

$$g_{ij}^{t+\Delta t} = F(g_{i\pm p, j\pm q}^t).$$

These five model types are all simple abstractions from nature. Combining them would be realistic but complicated. One could also embellish these simple types to include moving average models, or stochastic versions — Model (II) then readily yields a Markov chain. Model (III) is often called a time series model, or a lagged variable model. Model (IV) could be generalized to a system of simultaneous equations, in which each variable is a function of the several others, and so on. The particular classification has been chosen to highlight the *geographical* model.

There are really two models included in the category of geographical model. The first is the extrapolation-filtering model exemplified by

$$g_{ij}^t = F(g_{i\pm p, j\pm q}^t).$$

This can be characterized by a geographical quiz:

Complete the following geographical sentence by filling in the blank:

A	A	A	A	B	B
A	A	A	B	B	A
A	A		A	A	A
A	B	B	A	A	A
B	B	A	A	A	A
B	B	A	A	A	A

There is considerable literature on this topic, but the model of concern here is the dynamical geographical one which is better characterized as

$$g_{ij}^{t+\Delta t} = F(g_{ij}^t, n_{ij}),$$

where n_{ij} is shorthand for all of the land uses in the neighborhood of the location i, j. This single lag, univariate deterministic — as here described — model has only two parameters: the neighborhood n and the function F.

II. NEIGHBORHOODS

The simplest definition of a neighborhood in a square lattice is to include all cells in a box around the cell of interest; $n_{ij} = $ cells $i \pm p, j \pm q$. The neighborhood then consists of $(2p + 1)(2q + 1)$ cells. Also common is the five cell neighborhood consisting of a cell and its North, South, East, and West adjacent cells. The importance of the neighborhood is that it defines the geographical domain of influence. But the definition of the neigborhood of a cell can be quite general. One could, for example, provide a list of all of the cells which are included in the neighborhood of a given cell. But the usual rule is to invoke *spatial neighborhood stationarity*. By this is meant that all cells have the same size and shape of neighborhood. The indexing by subscripts, $n_{ij} = c_{i \pm p, j \pm q}$, makes this very clear.

This model contrasts very nicely with reality in which, for example, an urban resident may have a geographical contact field which differs in size and shape from that of a rural resident, or of a suburbanite. Thus it is possible to let the size, shape, or orientation of a neighborhood be a function of the location of the cell, i.e., $p, q = F(i, j)$, in either a simple or a complicated fashion; neighborhoods near borders usually require a special definition.

Board games such as chess, checkers, and go are all defined on square lattices; chinese checkers on a triangular lattice. One can see the advantages of such arrays most easily if one attempts to define a game similar to chess on a political map. An identical problem is encountered in converting geographical lattice models — Hägerstrand's model of the diffusion of ideas, for example — to political units. The basic difficulty is topological; the 'cells' on the political map do not all have the same number of adjacent cells. Their neighborhoods cannot be defined by any simple notational scheme, and the concept of spatial stationarity of neighborhood must be defined in a different manner.

III. THE TRANSITION RULE

The other important variable in the geographical model $g_{ij}^{t+\Delta t} = F(g_{ij}^t, n_{ij})$ is the function F. For the present purpose it is still valid to ignore such distinctions as deterministic or stochastic, time varying, and so on, and to concentrate on the geographically interesting aspects. An example is helpful. Suppose that the contents of the geographical cells consist of five land use types: Residential (R), Commercial (C), Industrial (I), Public (P), and Agriculture (A). Suppose further that the neighborhood consists of the cells (i, j), $(i-1, j)$, $(i+1, j)$, $(i, j-1)$, and $(i, j+1)$. There are thus five states (S) and five neighbors (N). A possible transition rule would be

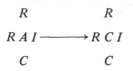

which means that the center cell, in agriculture, is converted to a commercial land use. This might more conveniently be written as

$$RICRA \longrightarrow C$$

with a clockwise convention. One sees that one must consider the $S^N = 5^5 = 3125$ cases to cover all possibilities. But it is now natural to invoke *spatial isotropy* so that the positioning of the neighbors does not count, e.g., writing the above rule as

$$(2R, 1I, 1C, A) \longrightarrow C,$$

and this clearly cuts down on the necessary number of rules. Of course we have already assumed *spatial stationarity* again. Translated this means that the same environment (neighborhood) results in the same consequences, or, that the rules do not depend on where you are. Compare again with chess; the allowed moves, although piece specific, are the same everywhere, almost. Thus, the laws of nature do not depend on, say, latitude. Or do they? 'When in Rome do as the Romans do'. Cultural geographers assert that behaviour in England is different from that in China. This is equivalent to saying that the rules depend on where you are, i.e., $F(i, j)$. These models and games make a nice pedagogical contrast with reality. Sometimes it is easy to write down rules which depend on where you are, sometimes it is not easy.

One type of scientific investigation can be caricatured by the following problem: given 20 pictures, in order, of the board positions from a game of chess, determine the rules of chess. The rules of chess are rather simple, but the game, which involves using the rules in a strategy, is complex. Does a similar situation hold for changes of pattern on the surface of the earth? My students have now conducted some experiments in which geographical maps (of one area but from different times) are fed into a computer and a program attempts to estimate the geographical transition rules.

An analogy can also be made with geographical planning. Given an initial state, a desired state, and a set of transition rules, we can ask whether or not here exists a path from the one situation to the other, and if so where there is a minimum path. Or what changes need be made to the rules so that the objective is realizable.

Some of these ideas are nicely illustrated by Conway's 'Life', a two-state, nine-neighbor play. The game is played on a square lattice, and the two states are conveniently called filled or empty. The change of state from full to empty, or visa versa takes place via the rules, which are conveniently displayed as a decision tree, invoked for all cells simultaneously in one round of the play.

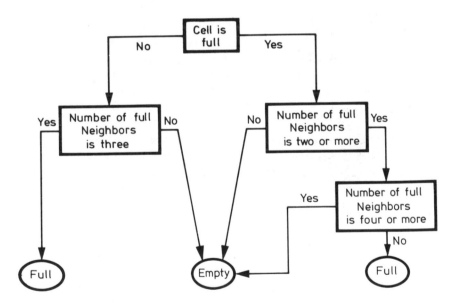

The play begins from an initial state in which some cells are full and others are empty. Such a pattern then changes over time, appearing to move, often in interesting ways. Sometimes the pattern repeats itself periodically, in other cases it disappears completely. One can prove inter alia that there exist patterns which could never arise from some other initial state (Moore's Garden-of-Eden theorem). The point which I wish to stress is that there are a whole host of theoretical questions which one can ask of even such a simple two-state nine-neighbor situation, and similar theoretical questions should also be asked of the more complex geographical case.

As a final contrast attention is called to the fact that all of the examples considered up to this point have been of the categorical type. On rare occasions in nature the states, the observed entities in the cells, can be represented by numbers. This rare situation seems to be the one most often studied by scientists in general and geographers in particular. The transition rule in this case becomes the usual mathematical function. Of all possible functions linear functions are most often used, e.g.,

$$g_{ij}^{t+\Delta t} = \sum_p^{+p} \sum_q^{+q} W_{pq} g_{i+p, j+q}^t$$

in the discrete case, or

$$g_{ij}^{t+\Delta t} = \int_{-\infty}^{+\infty} \int w(x-u, y-v) g^t(x,y) \, du \, dv$$

in the spatially continuous case. Here one again notices the spatial stationarity assumption. Possible geographical interpretations and applications have been discussed elsewhere and need not be repeated here. Perhaps more results can be expected from a study of the above case, but an interesting area would appear to be in the mathematical study of non-numerical transformations.

Department of Geography
University of California at Santa Barbara

NOTES

[1] A condensed translation of a lecture "Schachbrette Modelle in der Geographie" presented to the Arbeitskreis fur neue Methoden in der Regionalforschung, Wien, 17 April 1975.

BIBLIOGRAPHY

Agterberg, F.: 1974, *Geomathematics*, Elsevier, New York.
Codd, E.: 1968, *Cellular Automata*, Academic Press, New York.
Hägerstrand, T.: 1968, 'A Monte Carlo Approach to Diffusion', in B. Berry and D. Marble
   (eds.), *Spatial Analysis*, Prentice Hall, New York.
Matheron, G.: 1971, 'The Theory of Regionalized Variables and Its Applications', Cahiers
   du Centre de Morphologie Mathematique de Fontainebleau, No. 5, Ecole National
   Superieure des Mines.
Tobler, W.: 1975, 'Linear Operators Applied to Areal Data', in J. Davis and M.
   McCullaugh (eds.), *Display and Analysis of Spatial Data*, J. Wiley, New York.

YI-FU TUAN

SPACE AND PLACE: HUMANISTIC PERSPECTIVE[1]

> Ce n'est pas la distance qui mesure l'éloignement. Le mur d'un jardin de chez nous peut enfermer plus de secrets que le mur de Chine, et l'âme d'une petite fille est mieux protégée par le silence que ne le sont, par l'épaisseur des sables, les oasis sahariennes.
>
> ANTOINE DE SAINT EXUPÉRY, *Terre des hommes* (1939).

I. INTRODUCTION

Space and place together define the nature of geography. Spatial analysis or the explanation of spatial organisation is at the forefront of geographical research. Geographers appear to be confident of both the meaning of space and the methods suited to its analysis. The interpretation of spatial elements requires an abstract and objective frame of thought, quantifiable data, and ideally the language of mathematics. Place, like space, lies at the core of geographical discipline. Indeed an *Ad Hoc* Committee of American geographers (1965, 7) asserted that "the modern science of geography derives its substance from man's sense of place". In the geographical literature, place has been given several meanings (Lukermann, 1964; May, 1970). As location, place is one unit among other units to which it is linked by a circulation net; the analysis of location is subsumed under the geographer's concept and analysis of space. Place, however, has more substance than the word location suggests: it is a unique entity, a 'special ensemble' (Lukermann, 1964, p. 70); it has a history and meaning. Place incarnates the experiences and aspirations of a people. Place is not only a fact to be explained in the broader frame of space, but it is also a reality to be clarified and understood from the perspectives of the people who have given it meaning.

387

S. Gale and G. Olsson (eds.), Philosophy in Geography, 387–427. All Rights Reserved.

II. HUMANISTIC PERSPECTIVE

All academic work extends the field of consciousness. Humanistic studies contribute, in addition, towards self-consciousness, towards man's increasing awareness of the sources of his knowledge. In every major discipline there exists a humanistic subfield which is the philosophy and history of that discipline. Through the subfield, for instance, geography or physics knows itself, that is, the origins of its concepts, presuppositions, and biases in the experiences of its pioneer scholars and scientists (Wright 1966; Glacken, 1967; Gilbert, 1972). The study of space, from the humanistic perspective, is thus the study of a people's spatial feelings and ideas in the stream of experience. Experience is the totality of means by which we come to know the world: we know the world through sensation (feeling), perception, and conception (Oakeshott, 1933; Dardel, 1952; Lowenthal, 1961; Gendlin, 1962). The geographer's understanding of space is abstract, though less so than that of a pure mathematician. The spatial apprehension of the man in the street is abstract, though less so than that of a scientific geographer. Abstract notions of space can be formally taught. Few people know from direct experience that France is bigger than Italy, that settlements in the American Middle West are arranged in nested hexagons, or even that the size of their own piece of real estate is 1.07 acres. Less abstract, because more closely tied to sense experience, is the space that is conditioned by the fact of my being in it, the space of which I am the centre, the space that answers my moods and intentions. A comprehensive study of experiential space would require that we examine successively felt, perceived, and conceptual spaces, noting how the more abstract ideas develop out of those given directly to the body, both from the standpoint of individual growth and from the perspective of history. Such an undertaking is beyond my present purpose. Here I shall attempt to sketch spaces that are sense-bound, spaces that respond to existential cues and the urgencies of day-to-day living. A brief discussion of mythical space will serve as a bridge between the sense-bound and the conceptual.

The importance of 'place' to cultural and humanistic geography is, or should be, obvious (Hart, 1972; Meinig, 1971; Sopher, 1972). As functional nodes in space, places yield to the techniques of spatial analysis. But as unique and complex ensemble — rooted in the past and growing into a future — and as symbol, place calls for humanistic understanding. Within the humanistic tradition places have been studied from the historical and literary-artistic perspectives. A town or neighbourhood comes alive through the artistry of a scholar who is able to combine detailed narrative with discerning vignettes of description, perhaps further enriched by old photographs and sketches (Gilbert, 1954; Swain and Mather, 1968; Lewis, 1972; Santmyer, 1962). We lack, however, systematic analysis. In general, how does mere location become place? What are we trying to say when we ascribe 'personality' and 'spirit' to place, and what is the sense of 'the sense of place'? Apart from Edward Relph's dissertation (1973), the literature on this topic – surely of central importance to geographers – has been and remains slight. We have learned to appreciate spatial analysis, historical scholarship, and fine descriptive prose, but philosophical understanding, based on the method and insight of the phenomenologists, lies largely beyond our ken (Mercer and Powell, 1972). In this essay the phenomenological perspective will be introduced. I shall not, however, confine myself to it and will try to avoid its technical language.

The space that we perceive and construct, the space that provides cues for our behaviour, varies with the individual and cultural group. Mental maps differ from person to person, and from culture to culture (Hall, 1966; Downs, 1970). These facts are now well known. What is the nature of the objective space over which human beings have variously projected their illusions? It is common to assume that geometrical space is the objective reality, and that personal and cultural spaces are distortions. In fact we know only that geometrical space is cultural space, a sophisticated human construct the adoption of which has enabled us to control nature to a degree hitherto impossible. The question of objective reality is tantalising but unanswerable, and it may be meaningless. However, we can raise the following question and expect a tentative answer: if geometrical space is a relatively late and sophisticated cultural construct, what is the nature of man's original pact with his world, his original space? The answer can be couched only in general terms, for specification would lead to the detailing of richly-furnished personal and cultural worlds. We can say little more than that original space possesses structure and orientation by virtue of the presence of the human body. Body implicates space; space coexists with the sentient body. This primitive relationship holds when the body is largely a system of anonymous functions, before it can serve as an instrument of conscious choice and intentions directed towards an already defined field (Merleau-Ponty, 1962; Ricoeur, 1965). Original space is a contact with the world that precedes thinking: hence its opaqueness to analysis. Like all anthropological spaces it presupposes a natural (i.e., non-human) world. This natural world is not geometrical, since it cannot be clearly and explicitly known. It can be known only as resistances to each human space, including the geometric, that is imposed thereon. Experientially, we know the non-human world in the moments that frustrate our will and arbitrariness (Floss, 1971). These are the moments that cause us to pause and pose the question of an objective reality distinct from the one that our needs and imagination call into being.

Visual perception, touch, movement, and thought combine to give us our characteristic sense of space. Bifocal vision and dexterous hands equip us physically to perceive reality as a world of objects rather than as kaleido-scopic patterns. Thought greatly enhances our ability to recognise and struc-ture persisting objects among the wealth of fleeting impressions. The recog-nition of objects implies the recognition of intervals and distance relation among objects, and hence of space. The self is a persisting object which is able to relate to other selves and objects; it can move towards them and carry out its intentions among them (Hampshire, 1960, p. 30). Space is oriented by each centre of consciousness, and primitive consciousness is more a question of 'I can' than 'I think'. 'Near' means 'at hand'. 'High' means 'too far to reach' (Heidegger, 1962).

II.1. *Space and Time*

The notion of 'distance' involves not only 'near' and 'far' but also the time notions of past, present and future. Distance is a spatio-temporal intuition. 'Here' is 'now', 'there' is 'then'. And just as 'here' is not merely a point in space, so 'now' is not merely a point in time. 'Here' implies 'there', 'now' 'then', and 'then' lies both in the past and in the future. Both space and time are oriented and structured by the purposeful being. Neither the idea of space nor that of time need rise to the level of consciousness when what I want is at hand, such as picking up a pencil on my desk; they are an indissoluble part of the experience of arm movement. Units of time are often used to secure the meaning of long distances: it takes so many days to go from here to there. Distant places are also remote in time, lying either in the remote past or future. In non-Western societies, distant places are located in the mythical past rather than future, but since time tends to be perceived as cyclical remote past and remote future converge. In Western society, a distant place can suggest the idea of a distant past: when explorers seek the source of the Nile or the heart of a continent they appear to be moving back in time. But in science fiction distant stars are presented as distant future worlds.

II.1.1. *The primacy of time.*
Though time and space are inseparable in loco-motor activity, they are separable in speech and thought (Booth, 1970). We can talk abstractly about areas and volumes without introducing the concept

of time, and we can talk about duration and time without introducing the concept of space, although the latter is much more difficult to achieve in Indo-European languages. Experience in the real world supports both the primacy of time and of space. Confusion arises out of the different ideas that are grouped under these two terms. The time dimension matters more, one may say, because people appear to be more interested in narratives than in static pictures, in events that unfold in time (drama) than in objects deployed in space that can be comprehended simultaneously. That unique endowment of the human species, language, is far better suited to the narration of events than to the depiction of scenes. The apprehension of distance, we know, often rests on measures of time. Nature's periodicities, such as night and day, the changing phases of the moon and the seasonal cycle, provide units for calculating time. But nature, other than the human body itself, doesn't seem to provide convenient yardsticks for the measurement of space. The psychological reason for the inclination to estimate space in time units may be this. Man's ability to negotiate and manipulate the world depends ultimately on his biological energy. That energy is renewable. For each individual, however, it has a limit that is circumscribed by his expectable life-span. Man can annul space with the help of technology but he has little control over his allotted life-span, which remains at the Biblical three scores and ten, and is subject to termination through all manner of contingencies. Man feels vulnerable to events; he is more constrained by time than by the curbs that space may impose. Significantly we say of a prisoner in his cell that he is doing time. Fate is event, a temporal category.

In philosophical discourse, with the notable exception of Kantians (May, 1970) time has assumed greater importance than space since Leibniz (Jammer, 1969, p. 4). Both positivists and phenomenologists believe that time is logically prior to space. Among scientific philosophers the increasing interest in the nature of cause puts the limelight on time, for the direction of the flow of time is thought to be determined by the causal interconnection of phenomena. Space, in contrast, is only the order of coexisting data. Among phenomenologists time is believed to be more fundamental than space, a belief that seems to rest on their concern with the nature of being, becoming, duration, and experience.

II.1.2. *The primacy of space.* It is possible to argue for the primacy of space on the ground that space can be comprehended more directly than time; that a concept of space can give rise to theoretical science whereas, in Kant's view, one-dimensional time cannot (May, 1970, p. 116); and that spatialisation is a capacity developed in tandem with the evolution of human speech, utterance directed toward the creation of a public world. From the psychological viewpoint, knowledge of space is much more direct and simpler than knowledge of time. We can perceive the whole of a spatial dimension, such as a straight line, simultaneously. "A temporal duration, however, no matter how short it is, cannot be apprehended at once. Once we are at the end of it, the beginning can no longer be perceived. In other words, any knowledge of time presupposes a reconstruction on the part of the knower, since the beginning of any duration has already been lost and we cannot go back in time to find it again" (Piaget, 1971, p. 61). Children apprehend space before time. A one-year-old child plays 'peek-a-boo' and can ask to be picked up or let down. At eighteen months a child plays 'hide-and-seek' and knows how to find his way in the house. But only some six months later does he acquire a rudimentary knowledge of time, recognising, for instance, the return of the father as the signal for supper (Sivadon, 1970, p. 411). At seven years a child shows an interest in distant countries and an elementary understanding of geography; he has some idea concerning the relative size and distance of places. But the appreciation of historical time comes much later. In treating mentally disturbed patients, psychiatrists are beginning to find that they respond more readily to attempts at restoring their fragmented spatial world than their fractured past (Mendel, 1961; Izumi, 1965; Osmond, 1966). The structure of the present world can be elucidated and enforced by architectural means: spatial coherence can be perceived. But the past is gone and can be recalled only with the help of language. Dreams, when we remember them, centre on a few images. These remain, often with great vividness, while the narrative itself fades (Langer, 1972, p. 284). The causal link of events in dreams has a slender hold on our memory, but certain pictures can make an indelible impress. For some people, not only spatial relationships but the complex flow of events are not clearly understood without the aid of diagrams, this is, explication in space.

Human speech is unlike animal utterance because it strives to create a stable and public realm to which all who speak the same language have access. Psychic states find public expression in the objective correlates that are visible in space. Ideas are 'bright' as the sun is bright and souls can be 'lost' like the bodies they inhabit. Sensations, perceptions, and ideas occur under two aspects: the one clear and precise, but impersonal; the other confused, ever changing, and inexpressible, because language cannot clothe it without arresting its flux and making it into public property. "We instinctively try to solidify our impressions in order to express them in language. Hence we confuse the feeling itself, which is a perpetual state of becoming, with its permanent external object, and especially with the word which expresses this object" (Bergson, 1910, pp. 129–30). Speech creates social reality (Rosenstock-Hussey, 1970). In the social world the private lived-time of individuals is mapped onto space, where confused feelings and ideas are made sensible and can be tagged and counted. Pure duration thus becomes homogeneous time, which is reducible to space because its units are not successive but lie side by side. Heterogeneous and changing psychic states become discrete sensations and feelings; quality becomes quantity; intensity extensity.

Language is suited to the telling of stories and poor at depicting simultaneous order. On the other hand, Benjamin Whorf (1952) has made us aware that a characteristic of Indo-European languages is to spatialise time. Thus time is 'long' or 'short', 'thenafter' is 'thereafter', and 'alltimes' is 'always'. European languages lack special words to express duration, intensity and tendency. They use explicit spatial metaphors of size, number (plurality), position, shape and motion. It is as though European speech tries to make time and feelings visible, to constrain them to possess spatial dimensions that can be pointed to, if not measured. Not all languages attempt this to the same degree. Hopi speech, for example, eschews spatial metaphors. It has ample conjugational and lexical means to express duration and intensity, qualities and potentials, directly. Terms descriptive of space have much in common whether Indo-European or Hopi. The experience and apprehension of space is substantially the same irrespective of language (Whorf, 1952, p. 45). In this sense, space is more basic to human experience than time, the meaning of which varies fundamentally from people to people.

II.2. *Space, Biology and Symbolism*

Anthropological studies have familiarised us with the idea that people's conception of, and behaviour in, space differs widely. At a more exalted level, mathematicians appear to pull geometries out of a hat. We need, however, to be reminded of spatial perceptions and values that are grounded on common traits in human biology, and hence transcend the arbitrariness of culture. Although spatial concepts and behavioural patterns vary enormously, they are all rooted in the original pact between body and space. Spatial concepts may indeed soar nearly out of sight from this original pact, but spatial behaviour among ordinary objects can never stray very far from it. As C. H. Waddington puts it, "Although in mathematics we are free to choose whether to build up our geometry on Euclidean or non-Euclidean axioms, when we need to deal

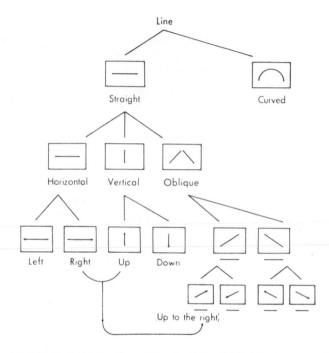

Fig. 1. A possible hierarchical schema for orientation in English: more words exist for horizontal and vertical orientations than for curved and oblique lines. Vocabulary – richness in some expressions, paucity in others – is a guide to what a culture considers important (*Based on Olson, 1970*).

with the world of objects of the size of our own bodies, we find that it is the Euclidean axioms which are by far the most appropriate. They are so appropriate, indeed, that we almost certainly have some genetic predisposition to their adoption built into our genotypes, for example the capacity of the eye to recognise a straight line" (1970, p. 102).

Human beings are more sensitive to vertical and horizontal lines than to oblique lines, more responsive to right angles and symmetrical shapes than to acute or obtuse angles and irregular shapes (Figure 1). An increasing array of evidence supports this view. Thus children aged three to four soon learn to choose | from —, but most of them have difficulty learning to choose / and not \. They can easily discriminate ⊓ from ⊔ but not ⊏ from ⊐ (Howard and Templeton, 1966, p. 183). The bilateral organization of the human body and the direction of gravity have been suggested as the causes of such bias. Furthermore, orientations provide ecological cues for movement, and their invariance is a decided advantage. When we move about, oblique lines are not invariant; left–right differences are similarly low in invariance, but up–down differences are relatively stable (Olson, 1970, p. 177). An angle of 93° is not seen as an angle in its own right but as a 'bad' right angle. Streets that join at an angle are recalled as joining at right angles or nearly so. North and South America are not aligned along the same meridian but in memory they tend to do so (Arnheim, 1969, pp. 82, 183). In general, shapes that have their main axes tilted tend to be reproduced in a vertical orientation. Horizontally symmetrical shapes are sometimes reproduced in a vertically symmetrical position whereas vertically symmetrical figures are always recalled in their correct position. Two shapes are best discriminated when they are vertical. The apparent length of a line tends to be maximally exaggerated in the neighbourhood of the vertical, and it tends to be minimised at about the horizontal position (Pollock and Chapanis, 1952).

Human beings are not alone in their greater sensitivity to vertical cues in their environment. Like the human child, an octopus can readily discriminate vertical from horizontal rectangles, but confuses rectangles oriented obliquely in different directions (Sutherland, 1957). Of course only among human beings do these natural biases acquire symbolical meaning. The direction upward, against gravity, is then not only a feeling that guides movement but a feeling that leads to the inscription of regions in space to which we attach values, such as those expressed by high and low, rise and decline, climbing and falling, superior and inferior, elevated and downcast, looking up in awe and looking down in contempt. Prone we surrender to nature, upright we assert our humanity. In getting up we gain freedom and enjoy it, but at the same time we lose contact with the supporting ground, mother earth, and we miss it. The vertical position stands for that which is instituted, erected, and constructed; it represents human aspirations that risk fall and collapse (Straus, 1966). To go up is to rise above our earth-bound origin towards the sky, which is either the abode of, or identical with, the supreme being. Horizontal space is secular space; it is accessible to the senses. By contrast, the mental and mythical realm is symbolised by the vertical axis piercing through the heart of things, with its poles of zenith and underground, heaven and hades. The gods live on the mountain peak while mortals are bound to the plain. On medieval T–O maps Jerusalem lies at the centre of the world; this is well known, but in Rabbinical literature Israel is perceived to rise higher above sea-level than any other land, and Temple Hill is taken to be the highest point in Israel (Bevan, 1938, p. 66). Centre implies the vertical and vice versa in mythological thinking (Figure 2). The human partiality for the vertical, with its transcendental

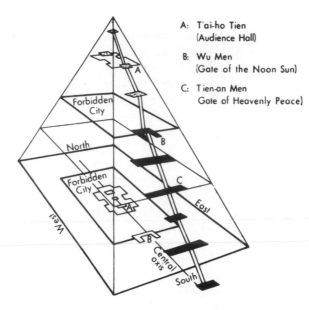

A: T'ai-ho Tien
(Audience Hall)

B: Wu Men
(Gate of the Noon Sun)

C: Tien-an Men
Gate of Heavenly Peace)

Fig. 2. The northern city of traditional Peking in a diagram of the Chinese conception of cosmic order. The emperor at the centre, in his Audience Hall, looks southwards down the central (meridional) axis to the world of man. The city's plan can be interpreted three dimensionally as a pyramid: going towards the centre is also to go up symbolically (*Based on Wu, 1963*).

message, is manifest in a vast array of architectural features that include megaliths, pyramids, obelisks, tents, arches, domes, columns, terraces, spires, towers, pagodas, Gothic cathedrals and modern skyscrapers (Giedion, 1964).

We begin with the biological fact of the animate body in space. Vertical elements in the environment provide relatively stable cues for orientation as the body moves. In action vertical and horizontal figures are easier to distinguish than those which are oriented obliquely in different directions. Gravity is the pervasive environment for all living things. Animals, no less than human beings, feel the strain of defying it: to move vertically is to make the maximum effort. From this common biological fundament the human being has elaborated a world of meaning that pervades his every act and accomplishment, from bodily postures to the verticality and horizontality of buildings. In the following sections I shall attempt to clarify further the nature of space as it is grounded in the needs of the human ego and of social groups.

TABLE I

(i) *Length and distance*

Body		Thing		Action	
	fingernail				
	breadth and length of finger				
	span from thumb to little finger		spear		spear cast
	top of middle finger to elbow (cubit, ell = elbow)		customary length of cord or chain		bow shot
	outstretched arms (= fathom)				day's journey
	various kinds of pacing				

(ii) *Area*

Thing		Action	
	oxhide		day's ploughing with a yoke of oxen, land
	cloak		which can be sown with a certain amount
	mat		seed, for example, the ancient Sumerian
			for area was *sĕ* (grain): the labour
			involved was a factor of measurement

II.3. *Spatial References and the Ego*

(a) Primitive measures of length are derived from parts of the body. They also depend on the dimensions of commonly used objects, and on the actions that one performs with one's body, such as a day's journey, or with an object, such as the distance of a bow shot. The move from the biologic base, then, is from the body to the object, and to acts performed with the object. Measures of area seem less bound to parts of the human body. They are based on the size of common objects, those which have been made or partly processed by man, and to acts performed with them. Unlike the segmentation of time, nature itself doesn't seem to provide suitable units for the measurement of either distance or area. (See Table I).

The parts of the human body serve as a model for spatial organisation. Central African and South Sea languages, in particular, use nouns (names for parts of body) rather than abstract prepositional terms to express spatial relations, thus:

Parts of body:	face	back	head	mouth or stomach
	‖	‖	‖	‖
Spatial relations:	in front	behind	above	within

In addition, material objects outside the human body can serve as prepositional terms indicating position. Instead of 'back' meaning 'behind', the 'track' left by a person means 'behind'; and 'ground' or 'earth' means 'under', 'air' means 'over'. Natural objects lend themselves to locations in space but not, originally, to the measures of space, for which pre-scientific man depended on his body, his artifacts, habitual acts, and natural period-icities (Hamburg, 1970, pp. 98–99).

(b) Locative adverbs, spatial demonstratives and personal pronouns have parallel meanings, and in some languages, they appear to be etymologically related (Humbolt, 1829). Ernst Cassirer points out that both personal and demonstrative pronouns are half-mimetic, half-linguistic acts of indication: personal pronouns are spatially located. '*Here* is always where *I* am, and what is here I call *this*, in contrast to *das* [that] and *dort* [yonder]' (Cassirer, 1953, p. 213). In Indo-Germanic languages the third person pronoun has close formal links with the corresponding demonstrative pronouns. French *il* goes back to Latin *ille* (that, there, the latter); Gothic *is* (modern German *er*) corresponds to Latin *is* (that, that way). In Semitic, Altaic, American Indian and Australian languages, I–thou pronouns appear to have close ties with demonstrative pronouns (Cassirer, 1953, p. 214). Egocentrism prevails every-where. We make fun of the capitalisation of the 'I' in English, but in Chinese and Japanese *pen jen* (I) means 'this very self', the person at the 'origin' or 'centre'. As to the egocentrism of spatial demonstratives, consider the expres-sion, "We talked of this and that — but mostly that". "Why", Bertrand Russell asked, "does the 'that' imply the triviality of the topics talked about?" (Figures 3(a) and (b)).

(c) To the speaker of a European language, a striking feature of some American Indian languages, and of Kwakiutl in particular, is the specificity with which location in relation to the speaker is expressed, both in nouns and in verbs. Spatial designations have almost mimetic immediacy; they bind actors to specific contexts and activities. Various languages can say 'the man is sick' only by stating at the same time whether the subject of the statement is at a greater or lesser distance from the speaker or the listener and whether he is visible or invisible to them; and often the place, position and posture of the sick man are indicated by the form of the word sentence (Boas, 1911, p. 445).

II.4. *Personal Experiential Space*

The structure and feeling-tone of space is tied to the perceptual equipment, experience, mood, and purpose of the human individual. We get to know the world through the possibilities and limitations of our senses. The space that we can perceive spreads out before and around us, and is divisible into regions of differing quality. Farthest removed and covering the largest area is visual space. It is dominated by the broad horizon and small, indistinct objects. This purely visual region seems static even though things move in it. Closer to us is the visual–aural space: objects in it can be seen clearly and their noises are heard. Dynamism characterises the feel of the visual–aural zone, and this sense of a lively world is the result of sound as much as spatial displacements that can be seen (Knapp, 1948). When we turn from the distant visual space to the visual–aural zone, it is as though a silent movie comes into focus and is provided with sound tracks. Next to our body is the affective zone, which is accessible to the senses of smell and touch besides those of sight and hearing. In fact, the relative importance of sight diminishes in affective space: to appreciate the objects that give it its high emotional tone our eyes may even be closed. We cannot attend to all three zones at the same time. In particular, attendance to the purely visual region in the distance excludes awareness of the affective region. Normally we focus on the proximate world, either the intimate affective space or the more public visual–aural space.

Here is an example of how the visual–aural zone can be further subdivided. I am engaged with people and things: they are in focus and lie at the fore-ground of my awareness. Beyond, in the middle ground, is the physical setting for the people and things that engage me fully. The middle ground may be the walls of a room or hall. It is visible but unfocused. Foreground and middle ground constitute the patent zone. Beyond the patent zone is the latent zone of habituality (the past), which is also the latent zone of poten-tiality (the future). Although I cannot see through the walls of the hall, the unfocused middle ground, I am subliminally aware of the existence of a world, not just empty space, beyond the walls. That latent zone is the zone of one's past experience, what I have seen before coming into the hall; it is also potentiality, what I shall see when I leave the hall. The latent zone is the invisible but necessary frame to the patent zone (Ortega y Gasset, 1963, p. 67; Ryan and Ryan, 1940). It acts as a ballast to activity, freeing activity from complete dependence on the patent, i.e., visible space and present time.

In characterising the structure of space, I introduce the terms past, present, and future. The analysis of spatial experience seems to require the usage of time categories. This is because our awareness of the spatial relations of objects is never limited to the perceptions of the objects themselves; present awareness itself is imbued with past experiences of movement and time, with memories of past expenditures of energy, and it is drawn towards the future by the perceptual objects' call to action. A tree at the end of the road stretches out in advance, as it were, the steps I have to take in order to reach it (Brain, 1959). Distance, depth, height, and breadth are not terms necessary to scientific discourse; they are part of common speech and derive their multiple meanings from commonplace experiences (Kockelmans, 1964; Straus, 1963, p. 263). Spatial dimensions are keyed to the human sense of adequacy, purpose, and standing. Certain heights are beyond my reach, given my present position or status. I feel inadequate and the objects around me appear alien, distant, and unapproachable. The window that is near seems very far once I have snuggled into bed. Distance shrinks and stretches in the course of the day and with the seasons as they affect my sense of well-being and adequacy (Dardel, 1952, p. 13).

A far-sighted person is not necessarily someone with good eyesight. He is a person who has a grasp of the future. Yet the popular image of far-sightedness is someone gazing into the distant and open horizon. Statues of eminent statesmen often overlook sweeping vistas. Their gaze into the distant horizon is intended to suggest that they have the people's present and future well-being in mind. The open horizon stands for the open future (Minkowski, 1970, pp. 81–90). What is ahead is what is not yet – and beckons. Hope implies the capacity to act and opens up space. However, specific hope or expectation inhibits activity: it is a kind of waiting during which the expected event appears to move towards oneself, and the co-ordinate spatial feeling is one of contraction.

Many of our waking hours are spent in historical or directed space (Straus, 1966, pp. 3–37). Such space is structured around the spatio-temporal points of here (now) and there (then), and around a system of directions, ahead–behind, over–under, right–left. In walking from here to there, energy and time are consumed to overcome distance. The pedestrian advances by leaving step after step behind him, and by aiming at the destination ahead as though it were at the end of a time-demarcated line. This commonplace observation gains interest if we think how radically space-and-time changes when a person is not walking but marching with a band. The marching man still moves, objectively, from A to B; however, in feeling open space displaces the constrained space of linear distance and point locations. Instead of advancing by leaving steps behind the marching man enters space ahead. The sense of beginning and end weakens as also the articulation of directions. Directed, historical space acquires some of the characteristics of homogeneous space – the space of present time without past or future.

In historical space, moving forwards and moving back may cover the same

route, but psychologically they are quite different activities. We move forwards or out to our place of work even if we are driven there and have our
back to the direction the car is moving; and we return or move back home
even as we drive the car forward on the same road. On a map the two routes
are identical and may be shown by the same line with arrows pointing in
opposite directions. However, strictly speaking, what is mapped is the route
of the car and not that of its human occupant, for whom not only does the
scenery change in major ways, depending on whether he is moving in one
direction or another, but the route itself acquires different feeling-tones
depending on whether the driver is moving *forwards* (as to dinner party or
office) or *back* home. Distance is asymmetric for reasons more fundamental
than the example of the one-way street that Nystuen gives (1963, p. 379). On
the scale of moving one's own body, walking backwards is painfully difficult:
one is afraid of falling over unseen obstacles or even of plunging into empti-
ness: in walking backwards the space that cannot be seen does not exist.
Physiologically the human person is not built to walk backwards. There seems
no need to look beyond this evident fact. Yet, as Erwin Straus has pointed
out, when we dance to music, moving backwards does not feel awkward: we
have no fear of it, it does not feel unnatural despite the fact that on a
crowded dance floor moving backward may mean bumping into others. When
we dance we are in homogeneous, nondirected 'presentic' space (Straus, 1966,
p. 33).

Just as the human bias in favour of the vertical finds expression in the
semiotics of body posture and in architecture, so the structures of experiential
space are manifest in spatial behaviour and in the physical setting. The space
of work is essentially directed. A project has a beginning and an end. In
mental work it could occur entirely in the brain and leave no trace in the
external world. The logic of such work is characterised, however, by the
spatial metaphor 'linear'. Physical work requires the physical organisation of
space: a manufacturing process, for example, starts here (now) and ends there
(then). The space is historical and directed; it is elongated. The factory itself,
of course may be square in shape, for any single work process can be repeated:
individual work spaces can be placed side by side to form a more isometric
figure. The historical, oriented space *par excellence* is the highway or railroad.
The straight rail tracks leading from one station to the next show a perfect
correspondence between single-minded intention, process, and form.

In contrast to work space, sacred and recreational spaces are essentially
ahistorical and non-directed along the horizontal plane. Sacred structures
such as temples and altars tend to be isometric; where they depart from

equidimensionality it is the result of the need to compromise eternity in the interest of time-bound human beings who feel more comfortable in directed space. Sacred monuments that are solid and cannot admit people are almost invariably equidimensional in ground plan. Recreational space is essentially homogeneous, 'presentic' space in which means and ends, here and now there and then, can be forgotten. Gardens of contemplation are isometric. Where recreational space is elongated it may well be in response to the demands of the physical environment, such as the bank of a river or a main thoroughfare; it is not required by the inherent character of recreation or the enjoyment of nature. Many modern recreational activities (mountain climbing and snow skiing, for instance) are as oriented as work, and hence require and acquire the elongated space of the work line. Race tracks, it is true, are oval-shaped. The starting and terminating points are clearly marked, but in racing the destination itself has no inherent significance; it can indeed be identical with the starting point. What is important is speed — speed in non-directed space. Race tracks in the desert or on the beach, drag-strips for hot-rodders, are linear and yet non-directed, for the sensation of speed itself, within an abstract world, is the essential experience (Jackson, 1957–58).

The type of directed space most familiar to geographers is that in which arrows are drawn to indicate the direction of movement of people, goods, and cultural traits. One map might show the flow of oil out of the Middle East to European ports; another the movement of people from America's eastern seaboard into the interior. We are used to seeing the one map as a cartographic device summarising certain economic facts, and the other as a means for representing events in historical geography. But the humanist geographer can read between the lines. From his perspective, the arrows symbolise directed activities that give rise to oriented, historical spaces on a world stage. Instead of a mere short walk from here (now) to there (then), the journey of a tanker over thousands of miles of water, taking several weeks around the Cape of Good Hope, acquires a little of the drama of an odyssey. Home port and destination, to the captain of the tanker, are hardly the indifferent points that they appear to be on a map. The arrow symbolises his lived-space, which is also his lived-time. If, instead of an oil tanker one thinks of a ship embarking on a voyage of exploration into the unknown, then destination is destiny. On maps that depict historical movements, the arrows appear to show mere routes in space; but they also represent the temporal dimension. Months, and perhaps years, have lapsed between the stem and the tip of the arrow. For the individual emigrants the journey takes them not only to a place that can be marked on the map, or to a point later in time that can be shown on the calendar, but a place that symbolises their future.

II.5. *Group Experiential Space*

Personal experiential space focuses on the experience of space in which the effect of the presence of *other* persons is left out of account. This does not mean that the structure of the personally experienced space is unique and private to the individual. Enough people normally share its essential elements to have an impact on the physical setting. The sharing is made possible through 'intersubjectivity', a concept often explored by phenomenologists. By group experiential space, I mean the spatial experience that is defined by the presence of other people. The point of departure is no longer 'person–space', but 'person–other persons–space' (Buttimer, 1969; Claval, 1970; Caruso and Palm, 1973).

Consider the feeling of spatial constraint, the prickly sense that there are too many people. Students of animal behaviour have applied their findings to problems of human space with mixed results (Callan, 1970; Esser, 1971; Lyman and Scott, 1967; Getis and Boots, 1971). As a feeling, 'crowdedness' is not something that one can easily measure. It is only roughly correlated with the arithmetic expression of density. A phenomenological description of 'crowdedness', applicable to human beings, is needed to complement the floodtide of ethological literature based on the observation of animals. The idea that we can best (i.e., scientifically) understand humans by *not* studying them directly has, perhaps, been carried to undue extreme. As to the type of description a humanist geographer might undertake, I shall attempt to illustrate with a brief sketch of one type of sociospatial experience, namely, crowdedness.

Nature is not ordinarily perceived to be crowded. Not only is this true of the great open space but also of forested wilderness. A boulder field is a solitary place however densely it might be packed with boulders; forests and fields are a joy of 'openness' to the city man even though they are certain to throng with pulsating organic life. Even people do not make a crowd if they seem an organic part of the environment, as, for example, when we contemplate an early evening scence in which fishermen intone in unison as they haul in their catch, or undulating fields specked by peasants harvesting their crops. Two may be a crowd if both are poets of nature (McCarthy, 1970, p. 203). On the other hand, a baseball stadium packed with 30 000 people is certainly crowded in a numerical sense, but it doesn't follow that the spectators feel the spatial constraint, particularly when an exciting game is going on. The sense of spatial constraint and of crowding is more likely to occur on the highways leading to the ball park, although – objectively – the human density then is lower than it is later in the stadium itself. The two poets of nature sense each other's presence as obtrusion because each requires, in psychological nescessity, the entire field to himself: their purposes conflict despite the fact that they are identical. In the stadium, the eyes of the spectators are all turned to the same event; by focusing on the event the remainder of the visual field, including their neighbours, becomes an unoffending blur.

A well-attended ball game and a mass political or religious rally are alike in that the crowds do not detract, but enhance the significance of the events: vast numbers of people do not necessarily generate the feeling of spatial oppressiveness. On the other hand, a large classroom packed with students may well create a sense of overcrowding, even though – as in the ball game or political rally – the students' eyes are all focused on a performance occurring beyond the space they themselves occupy. Superficially and objectively the situations are alike – crowd on the one side and an event of narrow focus on the other – but psychologically they are worlds apart. The student feels that ideally learning is a leisurely dialogue between the teacher and himself: the more packed the classroom the further it deviates from the perceived ideal, and hence the more urgent the sense of crowding.

Where peasant farmers are barely able to eke out a livelihood on limited land, one might think that the sense of crowding would be prevalent. Yet it is possible that the half-starved peasants do not see it that way. Foremost in their minds are too many mouths to feed and not enough food to go around, but these facts do not add up to the sensation of crowding. To see the farm-yard bustling with the activities of one's own half-naked children is to feel oppressed by fate and a sense of inadequacy rather than that there are too many people. Crowding, in this situation, would be the result of rational calculation, not a direct perception. The direct perception of crowding occurs when, for example, a person, desperately in need of a job, pushes open the door of the employment office and finds long lines of people waiting.

II.6. *Mythical-conceptual Space*

In distinction to the types of felt space described thus far, the space that I call 'mythical-conceptual' (see Figures 3 and 4) is more the product of the generalising mind. On the scale of total human experience, it occupies a position between the space of sense perception and the space of pure cognition (geometry). Mythical-conceptual space is still bound to the ego and to direct experience but it extrapolates beyond sensory evidence and immediate needs to a more abstract structure of the world. The defect of distance from immediate needs is more than compensated by the ability of mythical-conceptual space to satisfy the stable and recurrent needs of a large community.

Different types of mythical-conceptual space exist. One type is of outstanding importance because it is both sophisticated and widespread: this is the space that is focused on the centre (the place of men) and partitioned by a system of cardinal directions (Durkheim and Mauss, 1967; Marcus, 1973; Müller, 1961; Wheatley, 1971). Among the scattered tribes and nations in the New World, and among the disparate peoples in the ancient civilised centres of the Orient, we find space organised according to the same broad principles of centre, cardinal directions and the four quarters. The spatial co-ordinates are but a part of a total world view that embraces the cyclical rounds of nature, the constituent elements of the world, animals, people and social institutions. Spatial co-ordinates provide the ostensive frame to which the less tangible experiences in nature and society can relate. The centre of the universe is the human order. Mythical-conceptual space is egregiously anthropocentric. It differs from personal experiential space, not only in conceptual complexity, but also in the grandiose scale of its anthropocentrism. Instead of subsuming a sector of perceived space to the needs of the moment, the entire universe is conceptually organised around the world of man. The system thus conceived is so large and elaborate that, paradoxically, the human king-pin — from a certain perspective — appears only as one gear in the total mechanism. However, only from a certain perspective can the people of non-literate and traditional societies claim that their world view recognises the necessity for human beings to submit and adapt to the forces of nature; from the standpoint of their world view's organising principle, it is the universe that is adapting to man. The pueblo Indians of the American Southwest, for example, believe that people should not attempt to dominate nature. Yet their world view is conceptually highly anthropocentric. As Leslie White describes it, "Earth is the center and principal object of the cosmos. Sun, moon, stars, Milky Way [are] accessories to the earth. Their function is to make the earth habitable for mankind" (1942, p. 80).

A central theme in this survey of space is the bond between space and the human existential: body implicates space; spatial measures are derived from dimensions of the body; spatial qualities characterised as static, dynamic and affective, patent and latent, high and low, near and far are clearly called into being by the human presence; depth and distance are a function of the human sense of purpose and adequacy; 'crowdedness' is less an expression of density than a psychological condition. Mythical space is a sophisticated product of

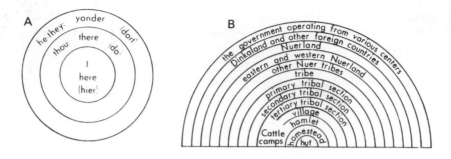

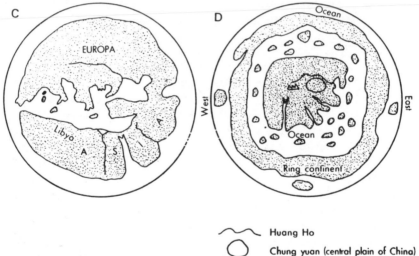

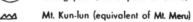 Huang Ho

○ Chung yuan (central plain of China)

ᶺᶺᶺ Mt. Kun-lun (equivalent of Mt. Meru)

the mind answering the needs of the communal group. Conceptualisation progressively removes spatial structures from the unstable requirements of the individual ego, and even from the biases of culture, so that in their most ethereal form they appear as pure mathematical webs, creations of the disembodied intelligence, maps of the mind — and hence, maps of nature insofar as mind is a part of nature.

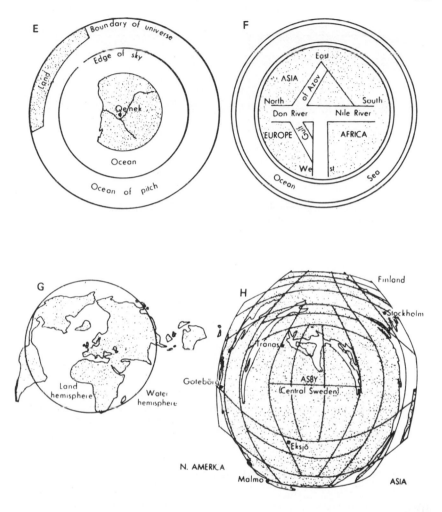

Fig. 3. Ego- and ethnocentric organisations of space (I) and (II), illustrating increasing cartographic sophistication at the service of persistent self-centred viewpoints, necessary to practical life: A: personal pronouns and spatial demonstratives; B: Nuer socio-spatial categories (*after Evans-Pritchard, 1940*); C: the world of Hecateus (fl. 520 BC); D: religious cosmography in East Asia; E: Yurok (California Indian) idea of the world (*after Waterman, 1920*); F: T–O map, after Isidore, Bishop of Seville (AD 570–636); G: Land and water hemispheres centred on northern France; H: Map with azimuthal logarithmic distance scale, centred on central Sweden (*after Hägerstrand, 1953*).

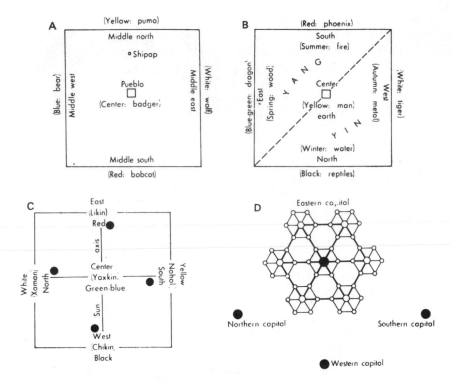

Fig. 4. Mythical-conceptual spaces: A: a Pueblo Indian world view; B: traditional Chinese world view; C: Classic Maya world view: quadripartite model of AD 600–900; and D: the spatial organisation of lowland Classic Maya, from regional capital to outlying hamlet: hexagonal model of AD 1930 (*after Marcus, 1973*).

III. PLACE

III.1 *Definition*

In ordinary usage, place means primarily two things: one's position in society and spatial location. The study of status belongs to sociology whereas the study of location belongs to geography. Yet clearly the two meanings overlap to a large degree: one seems to be a metaphor for the other. We may ask, which of the two meanings is literal and which is metaphorical extension? Consider, first, an analogous problem the word 'close'. Is it primarily a measure of human relationship, in the sense that 'John and Joe are close friends', or is it primarily an expression of relative distance as, for example, when we say that 'the chair is close to the window'? From my discussion of space, it is clear that I believe the meaning of human relationship to be basic. Being 'close' is, first, being close to another person, on whom one depends for emotional and material security far more than on the world's non-human facts (Erickson, 1969). It is possible, as Marjorie Grene suggests, that the primary meaning of 'place' is one's position in society rather than the more abstract understanding of location in space (1968, p. 173). Spatial location derives from position in society rather than vice versa (Sorokin, 1964). The infant's place is the crib; the child's place is the playroom; the social distance between the chairman of the board and myself is as evident in the places we sit at the banquet table as in the places we domicile; the Jones's live on the wrong side of the tracks because of their low socio-economic position; prestige industries requiring skilled workers are located at different places from lowly industries manned by unskilled labour. Such examples can be multiplied endlessly. People are defined first by their positions in society: their characteristic life styles follow. Life style is but a general term covering such particulars as the clothes people wear, the foods they eat, and the places at which they live and work. Place, however, is more than location and more than the spatial index of socio-economic status. It is a unique ensemble of traits that merits study in its own right.

III.2. *Meaning of Place*

III.2.1. *Spirit and personality*. A key to the meaning of place lies in the expressions that people use when they want to give it a sense carrying greater emotional charge than location or functional node. People talk of the 'spirit', the 'personality' and the 'sense' of place. We can take 'spirit' in the literal sense: space is formless and profane except for the sites that 'stand out' because spirits are believed to dwell in them. These are the sacred places. They command awe. 'Personality' suggests the unique: places, like human beings, acquire unique signatures in the course of time. A human personality is a fusion of natural disposition and acquired traits. Loosely speaking, the personality of place is a composite of natural endowment (the physique of the land) and the modifications wrought by successive generations of human beings. France, according to Vidal de la Blache (1903), Britain, according to Cyril Fox (1932), and Mexico, according to Carl Sauer (1941), have 'personality'. These regions have acquired unique 'faces' through the prolonged interaction between nature and man. Despite the accretion of experience the child

is recognisable in the adult; and so too the structural lineaments of a region —
its division into highland and lowland, north and south — remain visible
through the successive phases of change.

Personality has two aspects: one commands awe, the other evokes affection. The personality that commands awe appears as something sublime and
objective, existing independently of human needs and aspirations. Such is the
personality of monumental art and holy places. Powerful manifestations of
nature, like the Grand Canyon and the Matterhorn, are also commanding
personalities. By contrast, a place that evokes affection has personality in the
same sense that an old raincoat can be said to have character. The character
of the raincoat is imparted by the person who wears it and grows fond of it.
The raincoat is for use, and yet in time it acquires a personality, a certain
wayward shape and smell that is uniquely its own. So too a place, through
long association with human beings, can take on the familiar contours of an
old but still nurturing nanny. When the geographer talks of the personality of
a region, he may have both aspects in mind. The region can be both cozy and
sublime: it is deeply humanised and yet the physical fundament is fundamentally indifferent to human purpose.

III.2.2. *A sense of place.* Place may be said to have 'spirit' or 'personality',
but only human beings can have a sense of place. People demonstrate their
sense of place when they apply their moral and aesthetic discernment to sites
and locations. Modern man, it is often claimed, has lost this sensitivity. He
transgresses against the genius loci because he fails to recognise it; and he fails
to recognise it because the blandness of much modern environment combined
with the ethos of human dominance has stunted the cultivation of place
awareness.

Sense, as in a sense of place, has two meanings. One is visual or aesthetic.
The eye needs to be trained so that it can discern beauty where it exists; on
the other hand beautiful places need to be created to please the eye. From
one limited point of view, places are locations that have visual impact. On a
flat plain, the buttes and silos are places; in a rugged karst landscape, the flat
poljes are places. However, other than the all-important eye, the world is
known through the senses of hearing, smell, taste, and touch. These senses,
unlike the visual, require close contact and long association with the environment. It is possible to appreciate the visual qualities of a town in an afternoon's tour, but to know the town's characteristic odours and sounds, the
textures of its pavements and walls, requires a far longer period of contact.

To sense is to know: so we say 'he senses it', or 'he catches the sense of it'.

To see an object is to have it at the focus of one's vision; it is explicit knowing. I see the church on the hill, I know it is there, and it is a place for me.
But one can have a sense of place, in perhaps the deeper meaning of the term,
without any attempt at explicit formulation. We can know a place subcon-
sciously, through touch and remembered fragrances, unaided by the discriminating eye. While the eye takes in a lovely street scene and intelligence categor-
ises it, our hand feels the iron of the school fence and stores subliminally its
coolness and resistance in our memory (Santmyer, 1962, p. 50). Through
such modest hoards we can acquire in time a profound sense of place. Yet it
is possible to be fully aware of our attachment to place only when we have
left it and can *see* it as a whole from a distance.

III.3. *Stability and Place*

> We shall not cease from exploration
> And the end of all our exploring
> Will be to arrive where we started
> And know the place for the first time.
>   T. S. Eliot, *The Four Quartets*

An argument in favour of travel is that it increases awareness, not of exotic
places but of home as a place. To identify wholly with the ambiance of a
place is to lose the sense of its unique identity, which is revealed only when
one can also see it from the outside. To be always on the move is, of course,
to lose place, to be placeless and have, instead, merely scenes and images. A
scene may be of a place but the scene itself is not a place. It lacks stability: it
is in the nature of a scene to shift with every change of perspective. A scene is
defined by its perspective whereas this is not true of place: it is in the nature
of place to appear to have a stable existence independent of the perceiver.

A place is the compelling focus of a field: it is a small world, the node at
which activities converge. Hence, a street is not commonly called a place,
however sharp its visual identity. L'Etoile (Place de Charles de Gaulle) is a
place but the Champs-Elysées is not: one is a node, the other is a throughway.
A street corner is a place but the street itself is not. As we have noted earlier,
a street is directed, historical space: on the horizontal plane, only non-directed
homogeneous spaces can be place. When a street is transformed into a centre
of festivities, with people milling around in no particular direction, it becomes
non-directed space — and a place. A great ocean liner is certainly a small world,
but it is not rooted in location; hence it is not a place. These are not arbitrary
judgments. They are supported by the common use and understanding of

language. It is a great wit who asks: 'When is this place (the *Queen Mary*) going to New York?'

III.4. *Types of Place*

In the discussion on the personality and sense of place, I distinguished between places that yield their meaning to the eye, and places that are known only after prolonged experience. I shall call the one type 'public symbols', and the other 'fields of care' (Wild, 1963, p. 47). Public symbols tend to have high imageability because they often cater to the eye. Fields of care do not seek to project an image to outsiders; they are inconspicuous visually. Public symbols command attention and even awe; fields of care evoke affection. It is relatively easy to identify places that are public symbols; it is difficult to identify fields of care for they are not easily identifiable by external criteria, such as formal structure, physical appearance, and articulate opinion (see Table II).

Obviously, many — perhaps most — places are both public symbols and fields of care in varying degree. The Arch of Triumph is exclusively a symbol; the secluded farmstead, the focus of bustling rural activities, is exclusively a field of care. But the city may be a public (national) symbol as well as a field of care, and the neighbourhood may be a field of care and a public symbol, a place that tourists want to see. What do the Arch of Triumph and the secluded farmstead have in common so that both may be called places? I believe the answer to be that each is, in its own way, a small world, i.e., a centre of power and meaning relative to its environs. With a monument the question that arises is how a lifeless object can seem to be a vital centre of meaning. With a field of care the question is one of maintenance, that is, what forces in experience, function, and religion can sustain cohesive meaning in a field of care that does not depend on ostentatious visual symbols?

TABLE II

Places as public symbols	Places as fields of care
(high imageability)	(low imageability)
sacred place	park
formal garden	home, drugstore, tavern
monument	street corner, neighbourhood
monumental architecture	marketplace
public square	town
ideal city	

III.5. *Public Symbols*

In the ancient world, as well as among many non-literate peoples, the landscape was rich in sacred places (White, 1967). Let a thunderbolt strike the ground and the Romans regarded it as holy, a spot that emitted power and should be fenced off (Fowler, 1911, pp. 36–7; Wissowa, 1912, 467–8, 477, 515). In ancient Greece Strabo's description suggests that one could hardly step out of doors without meeting a shrine, a sacred enclosure, an image, a sacred stone or tree (Book 8, 3: p. 12). Spirits populated the mountains and forests of China. Some were endowed with human pedigrees and carried official ranks (De Groot, 1892, p. 223). Although an entire landscape could embody power (Scully, 1962, p. 3), yet it was often the case that spirits lent numen to particular localities at which they received periodic homage. Examples of the holy place can be multiplied endlessly from all parts of the world. The essential point is that location, not necessarily remarkable in itself, nonetheless acquires high visibility and meaning because it harbours, or embodies, spirit (Eliade, 1963, pp. 367–87; Van der Leeuw, 1963, pp. 393–402). The belief system of many cultures encourages one to speak, literally, of the spirit of place. Modern secular society discourages belief in spirit, whether of nature or of the illustrious dead, but traces of it still linger in people's attitude toward burial places, particularly those of national importance; and of course in the attitudes of ardent preservationists who tend to view wilderness areas, nature's cathedrals, as sacred. Wilderness areas in the United States are sacred places with well-defined boundaries, into which one enters with, metaphorically speaking, unshod feet.

Public monuments create places by giving prominence and an air of significance to localities (Figure 5). Monument building is a characteristic activity of all high civilisations (Johnson, 1968). Since the nineteenth century, however, monument building has declined and with it the effort to generate foci of interest (places) that promote local and national pride. Most monuments of modern times commemorate heroes, but there are important exceptions. St Louis' Gateway Arch (St Louis, United States), for example, commemorates a pregnant period in the city's, and nation's, history. Public squares often display monuments and they are also a type of 'sacred area', in the sense that they may be dedicated to heroic figures and transcend purely utilitarian ends. Certain public buildings are also symbols: the Houses of Parliament, Chartres Cathedral, the Empire State Building, and, in the United States, the palatial railway stations. To modern geographers, it may seem lax usage to call monuments and buildings 'places', just like towns and cities, but this reflects our

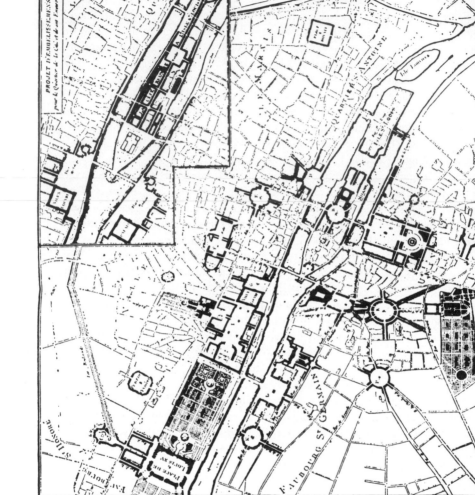

Fig. 5. Place as highly visible public symbol, something that architects can create. M. Patte's prize-winning plan for the Paris of Louis XV, in which the *place royale* is extremely prominent. Each *place royale* has a statue of the monarch at the centre, and streets faning out like rays *(Based on Moholy-Nagy, 1968).*

parochialism and distance from phenomenological reality. Elizabethan geographers of the early seventeenth century did not labour under such constraint and freely described towns and buildings at the same level of concreteness (Robinson, 1973). Cities are of course places, and ideal cities are also monuments and symbols. In the second world war, Coventry and Hiroshima were destroyed but Oxford and Kyoto were spared from aerial decimation (Lifton, 1967, p. 16). Thus the cultural and historical significance (the symbolic value) of Oxford and Kyoto was recognised even by the enemy. This recognition by the outsider is characteristic of places that are public symbols.

Monuments, artworks, buildings and cities are places because they can organize space into centres of meaning. People possess meaning and are the centres of their own worlds, but how can things made of stone, brick, and metal appear to possess life, wrap (so to speak) space around them and become places, centres of value and significance (Norberg-Schulz, 1971)? The answer is not difficult with buildings and cities for these are primarily fields of care, habitats for people who endow them with meaning in the course of time. Buildings and cities can, however, also be considered as works of art, as piles of stone that create places. How they are able to do this is the problem for philosophers of art: that they have this power is a matter for experience. A single inanimate object, useless in itself, can appear to be the focus of a world. As the poet Wallace Stevens (1965, p. 76) put it:

> I placed a jar in Tennessee,
> And round it was, upon a hill.
> It made the slovenly wilderness
> Surround that hill.
>
> The wilderness rose up to it,
> And sprawled around, no longer wild.
> The jar was round upon the ground
> And tall and of a port in air.
>
> It took dominion everywhere.
> The jar was gray and bare.
> It did not give of bird or bush,
> Like nothing else in Tennessee.

Only the human person can command a world. The art object can seem to do so because its form, as Susanne Langer (1953, p. 40) would say, is symbolic of human feeling. Perhaps this can be put more strongly; personhood is incarnate in a piece of sculpture; and by virtue of this fact it seems to be the centre of its own world. Though a statue is an object in our perceptual space, we see it as the centre of a space all its own. If sculpture is personal feeling made visible, then a building is an entire functional realm made visible, tangible, and sensible: it is the embodiment of the life of a culture. Thus monuments and buildings can be said to have vitality and spirit. The spirit of place is applicable to them, but in a sense different from holy places in which spirits are believed to dwell literally.

Some symbols transcend the bounds of a particular culture: for example, such large architectural forms as the square and the circle, used to delimit ideal (cosmic) cities, and such smaller architectural elements as the spire, the arch, and the dome, used in buildings with cosmic pretensions (Moholy-Nagy, 1968). Certain structures persist as places through aeons of time; they appear to defy the patronage of particular cultures. Perhaps any overpowering feature in the landscape creates its own world, which may expand or contract with the passing moods of the people, but which never completely loses its identity. Ayer's Rock in the heart of Australia, for example, dominated the mythical and perceptual field of the aborigines who lived there, but it remains a place for modern Australians who are drawn to visit the monolith by its awe-inspiring image. Stonehenge is an architectural example. No doubt it is less a place for British tourists than for its original builders: time has caused its dread, no less than its stones, to erode, but nonetheless Stonehenge is still very much a place (Dubos, 1972, pp. 111–34; Newcomb, 1967). What happens is that a large monument like Stonehenge carries both general and specific import: the specific import changes in time whereas the general import remains. The Gateway Arch of St Louis, for example, has the general import of 'heavenly dome' and 'gate' that transcends American history (Smith, 1950), but it also has the specific import of a unique period in American history, namely, the opening of the West to settlement. Enduring places, of which there are very few in the world, speak to humanity. Most public symbols cannot survive the decay of their particular cultural matrix: with the departure of Britain from Egypt, the statues of Queen Victoria no longer command worlds but merely stand in the way of traffic. In the course of time, most public symbols lose their status as places and merely clutter up space.

III.6. *Fields of Care*

Public symbols can be seen and known from the outside: indeed, with monuments there is no inside view. Fields of care, by contrast, carry few signs that declare their nature: they can be known in essence only from within. Human beings establish fields of care, networks of interpersonal concern, in a physical setting (Wagner, 1972). From the viewpoint that they are places, two questions arise. One is, to what degree is the field of care emotionally tied to the physical setting? The other is, are the people aware of the identity and limit of their world? The field of care is indubitably also a place if the people are emotionally bound to their material environment, and if, further, they are conscious of its identity and spatial limit.

Human relationships require material objects for sustenance and deepening. Personality itself depends on a minimum of material possessions, including the possession of intimate space. Even the most humble object can serve to objectify feelings: like words — only more permanent — they are exchanged as tokens of affective bond. The sharing of intimate space is another such expression. But these myriad objects and intimate spaces do not necessarily add up to place. The nature of the relationship between interpersonal ties on the one hand and the space over which they extend on the other is far from simple. Youth gangs have strong interpersonal ties, and they have a strong sense of the limits of space: gang members know well where their 'turf' ends and that of another begins. Yet they have no real affection for the space they are willing to defend. When better opportunity calls from the outside world, the local turf — known to the gang members themselves for its shoddiness — is abandoned without regret (Eisenstadt, 1949; Suttles, 1968). Strong interpersonal ties require objects: English gypsies, for example, are avid collectors of china and old family photographs (Lynch, 1972, p. 40). But the resilience of the gypsies shows that the net of human concern does not require emotional anchoring in a particular locality for its strength. Home is whereever we happen to be, as all carefree young lovers know. Place is position in society as well as location in space: gypsies and young lovers are placeless in both senses of the word and they do not much care.

The emotion felt among human beings finds expression and anchorage in things and places. It can be said to create things and places to the extent that, in its glow, they acquire extra meaning. The dissolution of the human bond can cause the loss of meaning in the material environment. St Augustine left his birthplace, Thagaste, for Carthage when his closest friend died in young manhood. "My heart was now darkened by grief, and everywhere I looked I saw death. My native haunts became a scene of torture to me, and my own home a misery. Without him everything we had done together turned into excruciating ordeal. My eyes kept looking for him without finding him. I hated all the places where we used to meet, because they could no longer say to me, 'Look, here he comes', as they once did" (*Confessions*, Book 4: pp. 4–9). On the other hand, it is well known that the dissolution of a human bond can cause a heightening of sentimental attachment to material objects and places because they then seem the only means through which the dead can still speak. Sense of place turns morbid when it depends wholly on the memory of past human relationships.

What are the means by which affective bond reaches beyond human beings to place? One is repeated experience: the feel of place gets under our skin in the course of day-to-day contact (Rasmussen, 1962). The feel of the pavement, the smell of the evening air, and the color of autumn foliage become, through long acquaintance, extensions of ourselves — not just a stage but supporting actors in the human drama. Repetition is of the essence: home is "a place where every day is multiplied by days before it" (Stark, 1948, p. 55). The functional pattern of our lives is capable of establishing a sense of place. In carrying out the daily routines we go regularly from one point to another, following established paths, so that in time a web of nodes and their links is imprinted in our perceptual systems and affects our bodily expectations. A 'habit field', not necessarily one that we can picture, is thus established: in it we move comfortably with the minimal challenge of choice. But the strongest bond to place is of a religious nature. The tie is one of kinship, reaching back in time from proximate ancestors to distant semi-divine heroes, to the gods of the family hearth and of the city shrines. A mysterious continuity exists between the soil and the gods: to break it would be an act of impiety. This religious tie to place has almost completely disappeared from the modern world. Traces of it are left in the rhetoric of nationalism in which the state itself, rather than particular places, is addressed as 'father land' or 'mother land' (Gellner, 1973; Doob, 1964). Religion is maintained by rites and celebrations; these, in turn, strengthen the emotional links between people and sacred places. Celebrations as such demarcate time, that is, stages in the human life cycle, seasons in the year, and major events in the life of a nation; but notwithstanding this temporal priority celebrations, wherever they occur, lend character to place. The progressive decline in the sense of place, then, is the result of various factors, among them being: the demise of the gods; the loosening of local networks of human concern, with their intense emotional involvements that could have extended to place; the loss of intimate contact with the physical setting in an age when people seldom walk and almost never loiter; and the decline of meaningful celebrations, that is, those that are tinged with religious sentiment and tied to localities (James, 1961).

Unlike public symbols, fields of care lack visual identity. Outsiders find it difficult to recognise and delimit, for example, neighbourhoods which are a type of the field of care (Keller, 1968). Planners may believe an area to be a neighbourhood, and label it as such on the ground that it is the same kind of physical environment and people come from a similar socio-economic class, only to discover that the local residents do not recognise the area as a neighbourhood: the parts with which they identify may be much smaller, for instance, a single street or an intersection (Gans, 1962, p. 11). Moreover, although the residents of an area may have a strong sense of place, this sense is not necessarily self-conscious. Awareness is not self-awareness. Total immersion in an environment means to open one's pores, as it were, to all its qualities, but it also means ignorance of the fact that one's place as a whole has a personality distinct from that of all other places. As Dardel puts it (1952, p. 47):

La réalité géographique exige une adhésion si totale du sujet, à travers sa vie affective, son corps, ses habitudes, qu'il lui arrive de l'oublier, comme il peut oublier sa propre vie organique. Elle vit pourtant, cachée et prête à se reveiller. L'éloignement, l'exil, l'invasion tirent l'environnement de l'oublie et le font apparaître sous le mode de la privation, de la souffrance ou de la tendresse. La nostalgie fait apparaître le pays comme absence, sur le fond d'un dépaysement, d'une discordance profonde. Conflit entre le géographique comme intériorité, comme passé, et le géographique tout extérieur du maintenant.

The sense of place is perhaps never more acute than when one is homesick, and one can only be homesick when one is no longer at home (Starobinski, 1966). However, the loss of place need not be literal. The threat of loss is sufficient. Residents not only sense but know that their world has an identity and a boundary when they feel threatened, as when people of another race wants to move in, or when the area is the target of highway construction or urban renewal (Suttles, 1972). Identity is defined in competion and in conflict with others: this seems truc of both individuals and communities (Figure 6). We owe our sense of being not only to supportive forces but also to those that pose a threat. Being has a centre and an edge: supportive forces nurture the centre while threatening forces strengthen the edge. In theological language, hell bristles with places that have sharply drawn — indeed fortified — boundaries but no centre worthy of defence; heaven is full of glowing centres with the vaguest boundaries; earth is an uneasy compromise of the two realms.

III.7. *What is a Place?*

The infant's place is in the crib, and the place of the crawling child is under the grand piano. Place can be as small as the corner of a room or large as the

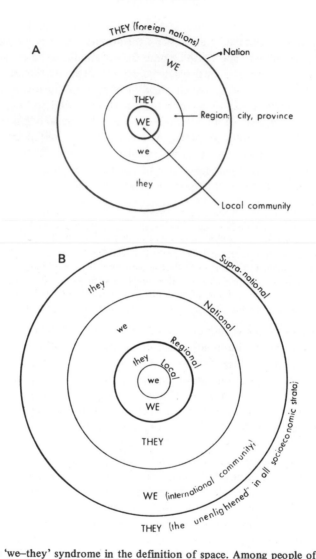

Fig. 6. The 'we–they' syndrome in the definition of space. Among people of the lower middle socio-economic class: A: the 'we–they' distinctions tend to be clearly recognized at the local and national (superpatriotic) levels. The suspicion of strangers and foreigners extends to their lands. Among the cosmopolitan and highly educated types: B: the home base is broadened beyond the local neighbourhood to a region, and nationalism (national boundary) is transcended by familiarity with the international life style.

earth itself: that earth is our place in the universe is a simple fact of observation to homesick astronauts. Location can become place overnight, so to
speak, through the ingenuity of architects and engineers. A striking monument creates place; a carnival transforms temporarily an abandoned stock-
yard or cornfield into place; Disneylands are permanent carnivals, places
created out of wholecloth. On the other hand, places are locations in which
people have long memories, reaching back beyond the indelible impressions
of their own individual childhoods to the common lores of bygone generations. One may argue that engineers create localities but time is needed to
create place (Lowenthal, 1966; Lynch, 1972). It is obvious that most definitions of place are quite arbitrary. Geographers tend to think of place as having the size of a settlement: the plaza within it may be counted a place, but
usually not the individual houses, and certainly not that old rocking chair by
the fireplace. Architects think on a smaller scale. To many of them places are
homes, shopping centres, and public squares that can be taken from the drawing boards and planted on earth: time, far from 'creating' place, is a threat to
the pristine design of their handiworks. To poets, moralists, and historians,
places are not only the highly visible public symbols but also the fields of care
in which time is of the essence, since time is needed to accumulate experience
and build up care. All places are small worlds: the sense of a world, however,
may be called forth by art (the jar placed on the hill) as much as by the
intangible net of human relations. Places may be public symbols or fields of
care, but the power of the symbols to create place depends ultimately on the
human emotions that vibrate in a field of care. Disneyland, to take one
example, draws on the capital of sentiments that has accumulated in inconspicuous small worlds elsewhere and in other times.

IV. CONCLUDING REMARKS

Space and place lie at the core of our discipline. From the positivist perspective, geography is the analysis of spatial organisation. From the humanist perspective, space and place take on rather different characteristics. Showing
what these are in a coherent structure is the humanist's first task. It is true
that "The modern science of geography derives from man's sense of place",
then the humanist geographer would ask, "What *is* this sense of place on
which we have not only erected a spatial geography of considerable elegance
but, more important, on which we still depend for the decisions and acts in
our daily lives?" Unlike the spatial analyst, who must begin by making

simplifying assumptions concerning man, the humanist begins with a deep commitment to the understanding of human nature in all its intricacy. The relevance of positivist and humanist geography to each other appears to be this. To the humanist, positivist concepts are themselves material for further thought because they represent for him an extreme example of the universal human tendency toward abstraction. It is not only the social scientist but the man in the street who constantly shuns direct experience and its implications in favour of the abstract typologies of people, space, and place (Schutz, 1970, p. 96). The broad aim of the humanist geographer must be: Given human nature and the direct experience of space and place in the ordinary world, how can man have conceived different worlds, more or less abstract, among which being the maps of utopia and the geographer's own concepts of location? As distinct from the concepts, the conclusions of the positivist geographer are of primary interest to the humanist because, like the findings of other scientists, they show him the limits to human freedom that he cannot otherwise know. Do the works of the humanist have any value for the positivist? I suggest that they do for two reasons. One is that they draw attention to, and clarify, certain kinds of human experience, at least some of which may be amenable to the positivist's own methods of research. The second reason is that humanist findings promote self-knowledge. The promotion of self-knowledge is perhaps the ultimate value of the humanities; and we are told on good authority that the unexamined life is not worth living.

University of Minnesota

NOTES

[1] First, I should thank my colleagues at the University of Minnesota for their tolerance – and even encouragement – of the humanistic approach to geography. Minnesota's benign climate makes it possible for at least twenty flowers (the present size of our faculty) to bloom. Among geographers I owe a special debt to Hildegard Binder Johnson for her knowledge of the European literature, her sympathy (and tea!); and to my former colleague at Toronto, J. A. May, whose training in philosophy enables him to resist, rationally, the doctrine that positivistic science monopolises sense and meaning in human discourse. This particular paper has benefited from the gentle surgery of Ward J. Barrett, Anne Buttimer, J. A. May, Risa Palm, and P. W. Porter; needless to add, I alone am responsible for its remaining warts and heteronomy.

BIBLIOGRAPHY

Ad Hoc Committee on Geography, 1965: 'The Science of Geography', in *National Academy of Sciences–National Research Council Publication*, 1277, Washington, D.C.
Arnheim, R.: 1969, *Visual Thinking*, University of California Press, Berkeley and Los Angeles.
Bergson, H.: 1910, *Time and Free Will*, Allen and Unwin, London. Translation of *Essai sur les données immédiates de la conscience*, Alcan, Paris.
Bevan, E. R.: 1938, *Symbolism and Belief*, Allen and Unwin, London.
Boas, F.: 1911, 'Kwakiutl', in: F. Boas (ed.), 'Handbook of American Indian Languages', *Bureau of American Ethnology Bulletin* 40, Smithsonian Institute, Washington, D.C.
Booth, S.: 1970, 'The Temporal Dimensions of Existence', *Philosophical Journal* 7, 48–62.
Brain, R.: 1959, *The Nature of Experience*, Oxford University Press, London.
Bunge, W.: 1962, 'Theoretical Geography', in *Lund Studies in Geography, Series C, General and Mathematical Geography* 1, Gleerup, Lund.
Buttimer, A.: 1969, 'Social Space in Interdisciplinary Perspective', *Geographical Review* 59, 417–26.
Callan, M.: 1970, *Ethology and Society, Towards an Antropological View*, Clarendon Press, Oxford.
Caruso, D. and Palm, R.: 1973, 'Social Space and Social Place', *Professional Geographer* 25, 221–225.
Cassirer, E.: 1953, *The Philosophy of Symbolic Forms*, Yale University Press, New Haven. Translation of *Philosophie der symbolischen formen*, Cassirer, Berlin, 1923.
Claval, P.: 1970, 'L'Espace en géographie humaine', *Canadian Geographer* 14, 110–124.
Dardel, E.: 1952, *L'homme et la terre: nature de la réalité géographique*, Presses Universitaires de France, Paris.
De Groot, J. J. M.: 1892, *The Religious System of China*, Brill, Leiden.
Doob, L.: 1964, *Patriotism and Nationalism: Their Psychological Foundations*, Yale University Press, New Haven.
Downs, R. M.: 1970, 'Geographic Space Perception', in C. Board *et al.* (eds.), *Progress in Geography* 2, London.
Dubos, R.: 1972, *A God Within*, Scribner, New York.
Durkheim, E. and Mauss, M.: 1967, *Primitive Classification*, University of Chicago Press, Phoenix edition. (Translation of De quelques formes primitives de classification: contribution à l'étude des représentations collectives, *Année Sociologique* 6 (1901–2), Paris, 1903.).
Eisenstadt, S. N.: 1949, 'The Perception of Time and Space in a Situation of Culture-contact', *Journal of the Royal Authropological Institute of Great Britain and Ireland* 79, 63–68.
Eliade, M.: 1963, *Patterns in Comparative Religion*, World Publishing Co., Cleveland, Ohio. (Translation of *Traité d'histoire des religions*, Payot, Paris, 1953.).
Erickson, S. A.: 1969, 'Language and Meaning', in J. M. Edie (ed.), *New Essays in Phenomenology*, Quadrangle Books, Chicago.
Esser, A. H., (ed.): 1971, *Behavior and Environment, the Use of Space by Animals and Men*, Plenum Press, New York–London.

Evans-Pritchard, E. E.: 1940, *The Nuer*, Clarendon Press, Oxford.

Floss, L.: 1971, 'Art as Cognitive: Beyond Scientific Realism', *Philosophy of Science*, 38, 234–250.

Fowler, W. W.: 1911, *The Religious Experience of the Roman People*, Macmillan, London.

Fox, C. R.: 1932, *The Personality of Britain: Its Influence on Inhabitant and Invader in Prehistoric and Early Historic Times*, National Museum of Wales and the Press Board of the University of Wales, Cardiff.

Gans, H. J.: 1962, *The Urban Villagers*, Free Press, New York.

Gellner, E.: 1973, 'Scale and Nation', *Philosophy of the Social Sciences* 3, 1–17.

Gendlin, E. T.: 1962, *Experiencing and the Creation of Meaning*, Free Press of Glencoe, New York.

Getis, A. and Boots, B. N.: 1971, Spatial Behaviour: Rats and Man, *Professional Geographer* 23, 11–14.

Giedion, S.: 1964, *The Eternal Present: the Beginnings of Architecture*, Patheon Books, New York.

Gilbert, E. W.: 1954, *Brighton, Old Ocean's Bauble*, Methuen, London.

Gilbert, E. W.: 1972, *British Pioneers in Geography*, David and Charles, Newton Abbot.

Glacken, C. J.: 1967, *Traces on the Rhodian Shore*, University of California Press, Berkeley and Los Angeles.

Grene, M.: 1968, *Approaches to a Philosophical Biology*, Basic Books, New York.

Hägerstrand, T.: 1953, *Innovations föroppet un Korologisk Synpunkt*, Gleerup, Lund.

Hall, E. T.: 1966, *The Hidden Dimension*, Doubleday, New York.

Hamburg, C. H.: 1970, *Symbol and Reality: Studies in the Philosophy of Ernst Cassirer*, Nijhoff, The Hague.

Hampshire, S.: 1960, *Thought and Action*, Viking, New York.

Hart, J. F. (ed.): 1972, *Regions of the United States*, Harper and Row, New York.

Howard, I. P. and Templeton, W. B.: 1966, *Human Spatial Orientation*, Wiley, New York.

Humbolt, W.: 1829, 'Uber die Verwandtschaft der Ortsadverbien mit dem Pronomen in einigen Sprachen', *Gesammelte Werke* 6, 304–330.

Izumi, K.: 1965, 'Psychosocial Phenomena and Building Design', *Building Research* 2, 9–11.

Jackson, J. B.: 1957–58, 'The Abstract World of the Hot-rodder', *Landscape* 7, 22–27.

James, E. O.: 1961, *Seasonal Feasts and Festivals*, Thames and Hudson, London.

Jammer, M.: 1969, *Concepts of Space: History of Theories of Space in Physics*, Harvard University Press, Cambridge.

Johnson, P.: 1968, 'Why We Want Our Cities Ugly', in *The Fitness of Man's Environment*, Smithsonian Annual, Washington, D.C., 2, 145–160.

Keller, S. I.: 1968, *The Urban Neighborhood*, Random House, New York.

Kockelmans, J. A.: 1964, 'Merleau-Ponty on Space-perception and Space', *Review of Existential Psychology and Psychiatry* 4, 69–105.

Knapp, P. H.: 1948, 'Emotional Aspects of Hearing Loss', *Psychosomatic Medicine* 10, 203–222.

Langer, S. K.: 1953, *Feeling and Form*, Scribner, New York.

Langer, S. K.: 1972, *Mind: an Essay on Human Feeling*, Johns Hopkins University Press, Baltimore.

Lewis, P. F.: 1972, 'Small Town in Pennsylvania', *Annals of the Association of American Geographers* 62, 323–351.

Lifton, R. J.: 1967, *Death in Life: Survivors of Hiroshima*, Random House, New York.

Lowenthal, D.: 1961, 'Geography, Experience, and Imagination: Towards a Geographical Epistemology', *Annals of the Association of American Geographers* 51, 241–250.

Lowenthal, D.: 1966, 'The American Way of History', *Columbia University Forum* 9, 27–32.

Lukermann, F. E.: 1964, 'Geography as a Formal Intellectual Discipline and the Way in Which it Contributes to Human Knowledge', *Canadian Geographer* 8, 167–172.

Lyman, S. M. and Scott, M. B.: 1967, 'Territoriality: a Neglected Sociological Dimension', *Social Problems* 15, 236–249.

Lynch, K.: 1972, *What Time is this Place?*, MIT Press, Cambridge, Mass.

McCarthy, M.: 1970, 'One Touch of Nature', in *The Writing on the Wall and other Literary Essays*, Harcourt, Brace and World, New York, 189–213.

Marcus, J.: 1973, 'Territorial Organisation of the Lowland Classic Maya', *Science* 180, 4089, 911–916.

May, J. A.: 1970, 'Kant's Concept of Geography and Its Relation to Recent Geographical Thought, *University of Toronto Department of Geography Research Publications* 4, University of Toronto Press, Toronto.

Meinig, D. W.: 1971, 'Environmental Appreciation: Localities as a Humane Art', *Western Humanities Review* 25, 1–11.

Mendel, W.:1961, 'Expansion of a Shrunken World', *Review of Existential Psychology and Psychiatry* 1, 27–32.

Mercer, D. C. and Powell, J. M.: 1972, 'Phenomenology and Related Non-positivistic Viewpoints in the Social Sciences', *Monash Publications in Geography* 1.

Merleau-Ponty, M.: 1962, *Phenomenology of Perception*, Routledge and Kegan Paul, London. (Translation of *Phénoménologie de la perception*, Gallimard, Paris, 1945.).

Minkowski, E.: 1970, *Lived Time: Phenomenological and Psychopathological Studies*, Northwestern University Press, Evanston. (Translation of *Le temps vécu*, Delachaux and Niestlé, Neuchâtel, 1968.).

Moholy-Nagy, S.: 1968, *Matrix of Man: An Illustrated History of Urban Environment*, Praeger, New York.

Müller, W.: 1961, *Die heilige Stadt*, Kohlhammer, Stuttgart.

Newcomb, R. M.: 1967, 'Monuments Three Millenia Old – the Persistence of Place', *Landscape* 17, 24–26.

Norberg-Schulz, C.: 1971, *Existence, Space and Architecture*, Praeger, New York.

Nystuen, J. D.: 1963, 'Identification of Some Fundamental Spatial Concepts', *Papers of the Michigan Academy of Science, Arts, Letters* 48, 373–384.

Oakeshott, M.: 1933, *Experience and Its Modes*, Cambridge University Press.

Olson, D. R.: 1970, *Cognitive Development: the Child's Acquisition of Diagonality*, Academic Press, New York.

Ortega y Gasset, J.: 1963, *Man and People*, Norton Library, New York. (Translation of *El hombre y la gente*, Revista de Occidente, Madrid, 1957.).

Osmond, H.: 1966, 'Some Psychiatric Aspects of Design', in L. B. Holland (ed.), *Who Designs America?* Doubleday, Garden City, New York.

Piaget, J.: 1971, *Genetic Epistemology*, Norton Library, New York.

Pollock, W. T. and Chapanis, A.: 1952, 'The Apparent Length of a Line as a Function of Its Inclination', *Quarterly Journal of Experimental Psychology* 4, 170–178.

Rasmussen, S. E.: 1962, *Experiencing Architecture*, MIT Press, Cambridge.

Relph, E.: 1973, *The Phenomenon of Place*, Unpublished Ph.D. thesis, University of Toronto.

Ricoeur, P.: 1965, *Fallible Man*, Regnery, Chicago. (Translation of *Philosophie de la volonté*, Aubier, Paris, 1950.).

Robinson, B. S.: 1973, 'Elizabethan Society and Its Named Places', *Geographical Review* **63**, 322–333.

Rosenstock-Hussey, E.: 1970, *Speech and Reality*, Argo Books, Norwich, Vermont.

Ryan, T. A. and Ryan, M. S.: 1940, 'Geographical Orientation', *American Journal of Psychology* **55**, 204–215.

Santmyer, H. H.: 1962, *Ohio Town*, Ohio State University, Press, Columbus.

Sauer, C. O.: 1941, 'The Personality of Mexico', *Geographical Review* **31**, 353–364.

Schutz, A.: 1970, 'The Problem of Rationality in the Social World', in D. Emmet, and A. Macintyre, (eds.), *Sociological Theory and Philosophical Analysis*, Macmillan, New York, 89–114.

Scully, V.: 1962, *The Earth, the Temple, and the Gods*, Yale University Press, New Haven and London.

Sivadon, P.: 1970, 'Space as Experienced: Therapeutic Implications', in H. H. Proshausky, W. H. Ittelson and L. E. Rivlin (eds.), *Environmental Psychology: Man and His Physical Setting*, Holt, Rinehart and Winston, New York, pp. 409–419.

Smith, E. B.: 1950, *The Dome, a Study in the History of Ideas*, Princeton University Press, Princeton, New Jersey.

Sopher, D. E.: 1972, 'Place and Location: Notes on the Spatial Patterning of Culture', *Social Science Quarterly*, September, 321–337.

Sorokin, P. A.: 1964, *Sociocultural Causality, Space, Time*, Russell and Russell, New York.

Stark, F.: 1948, *Perseus in the Wind*, John Murray, London.

Starobinski, J.: 1966, '*The Idea of Nostalgia*', *Diogenes* **54**, 81–103.

Stevens, W.: 1965, *Collected Poems*, Knopf, New York.

Straus, E. W.: 1963, *The Primary World of Senses*, The Free Press, New York. (Translation of *Vom Sinn der Sinne*, Springer, Berlin, 1956.).

Straus, E. W.: 1966, *Phenomenological Psychology*, Basic Books, New York.

Sutherland, N. S.: 1957, 'Visual Discrimination of Orientation and Shape by Octopus', *Nature* **179**, 11–13.

Suttles, G. D.: 1972, *The Social Construction of Communities*, University of Chicago Press, Chicago.

Swain, H. and Mather, E. C.: 1968, *St Croix Border Country*, Pierce County Geographical Society, Prescott, Wisconsin.

Van der Leeuw, G.: 1963, *Religion in Essence and Manifestation*. (Translation of *Phänomenologie der Religion*, Mohr, Tübingen, 1933.).

Vidal de la Blache, Paul.: 1903, 'La personnalité géographique de la France', in E. Lavisse (ed.), *Histoire de France* **1** (1), Hachette, Paris.

Waddington, C. H.: 1970, 'The Importance of Biological Ways of Thought', in A. Tiselius, and S. Nilsson (eds.), *The Place of Value in a World of Facts*, Wiley, New York, 95–103.

Wagner, P.: 1972, *Environments and Peoples*, Prentice-Hall, Englewood Cliffs, New Jersey.

Waterman, T. T.: 1920, 'Yurok Geography', *University of California Publications in American Archaeology and Ethnography* **16**, 182–200.

Wheatley, P.: 1971, *The Pivot of the Four Quarters*, Aldine, Chicago.

White, L. A.: 1942, 'The Pueblo of Santa Ana, New Mexico', *American Anthropological Association, Memoir* **60**.

White, L.: 1967, 'The Historical Roots of Our Ecologic Crisis', *Science* **155**, 1203–1207.

Whorf, B. L.: 1952, 'Relation of Thought and Behavior in Language', in *Collected Papers on Metalinguistics*, Foreign Service Institute, Washington, D.C.: pp. 27–93.

Wild, J.: 1963, *Existence and the World of Freedom*, Prentice-Hall, Englewood Cliffs, New Jersey.

Wissowa, G.: 1912, *Religion und Kultur der Römer*, Beck'sche, Munich.

Wright, J. K.: 1966, *Human Nature in Geography*, Harvard University Press, Cambridge.

Wu, N. I.: 1963, *Chinese and Indian Architecture*, Braziller, New York.

MICHAEL J. WOLDENBERG

A PERIODIC TABLE OF SPATIAL HIERARCHIES*

I. INTRODUCTION

Spatial systems may be organized hierarchically so that large high order areas in a system may collect flows from, or deliver flows to, small low order areas in the system. Examples at a geographical spatial scale are rivers, alpine glaciers and central place systems. Examples in the organic realm are at a much smaller scale, i.e., trees, blood vessels, airways, bile ducts, and even the microscopic branching of the Purkinje cell in the brain.

These spatial hierarchies all exhibit certain mathematical regularities which lead one to speculate about a common generating model. For example, for a large river basin there is a geometric progression[1] of basin area with order (Horton, 1945; Schumm, 1956). To order basins, we follow Strahler's modification (1952) of Horton's method of stream ordering. Unbranched tributaries are of order one and flow within a first-order basin. Two streams of order one join to make a stream of order two (Figure 1). Generalizing, two streams of equal order join to make a stream (and basin) of the next higher order; tributary streams of lower order are considered to be within the basin of higher order. The number of streams (areas) *declines* by geometric progression as order increases. Therefore, the size of basin area must increase geometrically with order. The area ratio (R_A) is equal[2] approximately to the reciprocal of the branching or bifurcation ratio (R_b). This method is used for all branching systems.

For systems of towns, organized into a hierarchy of central places, again, areas of market regions surrounding towns increase geometrically with town order (Christaller, 1933, p. 72; Baskin, 1966, p. 67). Central place ordering is a complex matter, not entirely free of subjectivity. Christaller (1933) used a map to create town orders by distinguishing between the centrality indices of different towns. The centrality index used here was related to the concentration of telephones. Palomäki (1964) made a complete functional analysis of towns in a region in Finland to identify orders. The comparison of central places requires an accepted set of rules to provide reproducibility. For one such set see Marshall (1968).

429

S. Gale and G. Olsson (eds.), Philosophy in Geography, 429–456. All Rights Reserved.

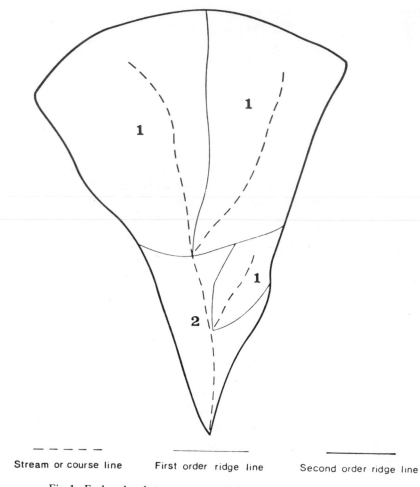

Stream or course line   First order ridge line   Second order ridge line

Fig. 1. Each ordered stream segment defines a basin of the same order.

In addition to geometric progressions of area, there are geometric progressions of other properties such as the stream slope (an inverse series), cumulative stream length, width, depth, velocity and volume rate of flow (Leopold and Miller 1956; Strahler, 1964) and the number of activities and number of establishments and populations of towns (Christaller, 1933, p. 72; Baskin, 1966, p. 67; Woldenberg and Berry, 1967; Berry, 1967).

Techniques of fluvial morphometry[3] have been applied to trees (Holland,

1969) and cow livers (Woldenberg, 1968a), the human lung (Woldenberg *et al.*, 1970), and to the Purkinje cells in the brain (Hollingworth and Berry, 1975). Analogous geometric progressions have been found. Thus these organized states exist from the microscopic to the regional scale and therefore are of interest not only to geographers and geologists, but to social, physical and biological scientists generally.

How can we explain these persistent geometric progressions? If one can establish the necessity for geometric progressions of area with order, then other parameters which are related to area by power function[4] relationships must also progress geometrically with order (Woldenberg, 1972b). Thus a key to explaining Horton's (and Christaller's) laws and to explaining related power functions is to explain the geometric progressions of modular areas.

It will be proposed here that R_A and the closely related R_b, the branching ratio,[5] may be inversely related to power available for a system divided by resistance (work to be done/time). As power over resistance decreases, R_A increases. This suggestion, if true, should cause a reevaluation of the hypothesis of the random model in generating spatial hierarchy (Shreve, 1966, 1967; Curry, 1964).

The major part of this paper, however, will relate to how values of R_A may be selected. In previous articles, I have offered a model based on Christaller's conception of the division of two-dimensional space into hexagons (Woldenberg, 1968b, 1969, 1971a, 1972a). These earlier versions of the model failed to predict the branching structure of the airway of the human lung. This paper will present an improved version of the hexagonal model which can predict the airway structure and which is capable of predicting six other types of hierarchical systems which have been recognized (see Table I). In addition this model suggests four new forms of hierarchical networks which have not yet been observed. The model has been programmed for computer evaluation (Thurston *et al.*, 1975).

II. THEORIES OF HIERARCHICAL STRUCTURE

II.1. *Work Related Space Filling*

Two types of models have been offered to describe and explain these spatial systems. One approach is based on concepts of work and space filling. The other is based on various stochastic models which can operate more or less removed from work and two-dimensional space filling though these factors can be built into the models.

MICHAEL J. WOLDENBERG

TABLE I

Periodic table of spatial hierarchies*

'Target' hierarchies				
<u>1</u>	<u>1</u>	<u>1</u>	<u>1</u>	<u>1</u>
<u>3</u>	<u>3</u>	<u>3</u>	<u>5</u>	<u>5</u>
<u>8</u>	<u>10</u>	<u>10</u>	<u>23</u>	<u>21</u>
<u>21</u>	<u>37</u>	<u>37</u>	<u>118</u>	<u>98</u>
<u>56</u>	<u>118</u>	<u>147</u>	<u>547</u>	420
<u>151</u>	420	<u>518</u>	2293	<u>1814</u>
<u>420</u>	<u>1551</u>	1814	11791	8281
1024	6480	5256	59049	36954
2836	18217	17595	278851	145881
6561		59049	1307208	629044

Other empirical hierarchies (rare)		Undiscovered hierarchies			
<u>1</u>	<u>1</u>	1	1	1	1
<u>3</u>	<u>5</u>	3	3	5	5
<u>14</u>	<u>17</u>	8	7	29	37
<u>56</u>	<u>64</u>	27	23	148	218
183	249	98	64	668	1497
668	965	256	183	3623	10133
2293	4182	965	518	17595	60307
8281	16384	3192	1814	99680	412607
29234	65265	10920	5256	512891	2658256
115575	262144	36954	16384	2658256	17300256

* Underlined values were actually observed in natural systems. The other values are predicted extensions of the hierarchies. For a description of the natural systems, see Table IV. Numbers are rounded to the nearest whole integer.

Christaller (1933) in his theory of central places and their associated market areas, assumed that the hexagon produced an optimum partitioning of space on a featureless plain. Lösch (1954) developed a proof showing that aggregate transport costs for a fixed area were minimized for a hexagonal lattice with a given number of points. By assuming that nth-order hexagons are contained within or shared by $n + 1$ order hexagons, Christaller reasoned that each large hexagon might contain 3, 4 or 7 small hexagons. Thus he suggests three unmixed or pure hierarchies developed on the basis of ratios of 3 or 4 or 7 (Figure 2).

Lösch proposed additional arrangements of market areas, all of which assume that the inner hexagon has unit area, while the outer hexagon may

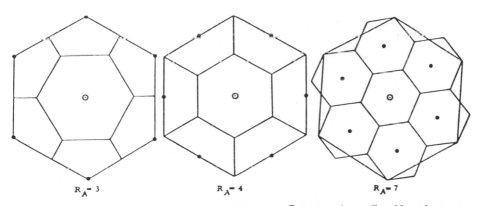

$R_A = 3$ $R_A = 4$ $R_A = 7$

R_A = Ratio of areas   ● Center of a small hexagon   ⊙ Center of a small and large hexagon

Fig. 2. Dividing an hexagonal area – after Christaller.

have a total area of 3, 4, 7 or an infinite number of other values. These arrangements have been shown to be generated by a simple formula $R_A = U^2 + UV + V^2$, where R_A is the set of all possible area ratios, and U and V are non-negative integers, $U \leqslant V = 1, 2, \ldots$ (Loeb, 1964; Dacey, 1965).

A large number of regional central place studies have been made and none of them, including Christaller's original work, show a value of $R_A = 3, 4$ or 7, for any hierarchy of four orders or more.[6] Furthermore, none of Lösch's values for $R_A > 7$ for market areas surrounding towns have been observed for hierarchies of more than two orders.

Analysis will show that $2 \leqslant R_A \leqslant 7$. This is true for both central place and branching systems. I will make the argument first in terms of branches. Suppose we are given a hexagonal area. Let us divide the area into equal hexagonal areas (Figure 2). When the ratio of areas, R_A, equals three, space may be filled with hexagons. Ratios of less than three have been observed in the human airway. R_A can be less than three, if one cuts the surface and excises some area. This is possible in the lung, which can be thought of as a cut surface, which is folded into alveoli and connected to tubes. A river flows on a bent, but continuous, surface. Thus no area is excluded, and the river must have $R_A \geqslant 3$ (Woldenberg, 1971a).

The value of R_A can never be less than two because for branching systems two branches of equal order are required to elevate a branch to higher order. $R_A < 7$, because small outside branches tending to flow to the center would eventually join with branches in the ring of six hexagons surrounding the center and create higher order branches before R_A could exceed seven. For analogous reasons R_A for market areas cannot be less than three (unless there are unserved areas) nor greater than seven. In the latter case, the intervening towns would become higher order.

In the case of fluvial systems, Horton suggested a headward growth model in which slopes were divided and subdivided into square basins as long as overland flows were sufficient to erode and maintain a channel (Horton, 1945, pp. 339–349). A channel was located on one diagonal of each square. The repeated division and subdivision of square drainage basin areas would tend to create a geometric series law of stream number, ($R_b = 4$), and stream length,[7] ($R_L = 2$). Stream confluence angles would be 90°. It is noted here that very few rivers conform to $R_b = 4$.

Horton did not hold rigidly to the division of space into hierarchies of square basin areas. He recognized that the variation of basin shape and slope and confluence angles all will have an effect on R_b and R_L. Nonetheless, his space filling model serves as a hint towards explaining the geometric progressions which he found. It is important to point out that the models of Christaller, Lösch and Horton do not satisfactorily account for the numbers of areas per order in hierarchial spatial systems.

II.2. *Random Models*

Random models are based on the idea that fluvial systems are so complex that our knowledge of individual events can never be complete enough to deduce the causes for a single network. Nevertheless, certain average relationships can be deduced, because the net effect of many individual events is the same as if the events were to occur at random, although the events are entirely predetermined (Scheidegger and Langbein, 1966, p. C1).

Some investigators generated random walk graphs. In most models first-order streams coalesce eventually to form a main stream (Leopold and Langbein, 1962; Schenk, 1963; Smart, Surkan and Considine, 1967). Howard (1971) simulated the branching of a stream by headward erosion, i.e., areal subdivision. These methods generate networks which, upon analysis, produce geometric progressions of number and length. Howard's method has the added advantage of producing symmetrical basins.

In other random models, the results are expressed in equations rather than cartographically. Shreve (1966) proposed investigating all the topologically distinct networks[8] which could be created from n first-order streams. Then these networks were classified by number of orders. It was found that the most probable networks followed an inverse geometric progression of stream number with order. (This implies that basin area should follow a direct geometric progression.)

Shreve (1967, p. 184) suggests that R_b should approach 4 for an infinite network and R_L should be 2. Using a variant of Shreve's approach, Werner (1970) derives R_b equal to 3.618. For further developments see Shreve (1967; 1969). Other writers have developed the probability models and a comprehensive review of their work may be found in Haggett and Chorley (1969), Howard (1971), Smart (1972) and Werrity (1972).

Random models generate a single mode of branching where $R_b = 4$ (Shreve) or 3.618 (Werner). In natural systems there is considerable variation in branching ratio. While statistics for very large numbers of stream and other networks are lacking, at this stage a survey of natural networks suggests several modes of branching ratio. I have observed that the most common fluvial system of more than three orders has a branching ratio of 4.5. Rivers also exhibit less frequent modes of branching at $R_b = 3.3$ and 3.6. Blood vessels, bile ducts, Purkinje cells and central place hierarchies show the same values, $R_b = 3.3$ or 3.6. The airway of the human lung has $R_b = 2.8$ and Lichtenberg figures (generated by discharge of static electricity in plastic) give a ratio of 4.83. Existing random models do not account for most of these empirical findings.

It has been shown that for small networks, with numbers of first-order streams not much greater than six, the random model can account for different patterns of branching. However, it is also true that the random hypothesis cannot be tested for larger networks. There is such an enormous number of possible networks that an empirical check is impossible. There are not enough networks in the world to test the hypothesis (Werner, 1970).

III. LINEAR BASED THEORY OF MIXED HEXAGONAL HIERARCHIES

The theory of mixed hexagonal hierarchies is an outgrowth of central place theory (Christaller, 1933, 1950). Christaller suggested that pure hierarchies of market areas could be generated by dividing a large hexagon into parts, and reconstructing the parts to form 3, 4, or 7 hexagons. Pure (as opposed to mixed) hierarchies with ratios of areas, $R_A = 3, 4$, and 7 are implied. After over forty years of empirical research these pure hierarchies of several orders have rarely if ever been observed, and this has caused many to lose confidence in the ability of central place theory to predict the number of market areas.

The assumption of hexagons, however, is spatially reasonable. Almost all basin areas or market areas have three-edged corners. Graustein (1932), Smith (1952) and Woldenberg (1972a) have shown that Euler's Law[9] leads inevitably to the result that the average number of sides per polygonal area approaches six as an upper limit when one assumes a network of polygons with three-edged corners.

In 1950 Christaller suggested mixing the pure hierarchies and Woldenberg (1968a, 1968b, 1969) modified Christaller's method of mixing and grouping the elements (powers of 3, 4, 7) so as to be able to generate numbers of branches per order or 'basin areas' in rivers, livers, and lungs etc., and the numbers of market areas for a central place system. (See also Woldenberg *et al.*, 1970; Woldenberg, 1971a.)

Woldenberg's original model, like Christaller's, was based on making a geometric progression of areas. Using hand calculations the model was successful in reproducing numbers of areas for four of five important empirical hierarchical types (see Table I). However, no single method of mixing and grouping hierarchical elements could reproduce all five of these target hierarchies for six order systems.

Thurston *et al.*, (1975) collaborated to create a computer model which generated and examined all possible mixed hierarchies of numbers of *areas* for agreement to the five target hierarchies. Many different mixing and grouping rules were tried. Thurston confirmed that none of the possible geometric progressions of areas which were tried could produce all of the target hierarchies. However, she also found that using combinations of the square roots of hexagonal areas, a total *length* measure, did generate the target hierarchies. I will review the new model, and then explain the rationale for it.

In Table II the powers of 3, 4, an 7 for each R_A are found in columns labelled N_p or the number of areas at power p. For each N_p there is an A_p or area of an individual hexagon (see Table II). Thus

$$(1) \qquad A_p = \frac{1}{N_p}.$$

A characteristic length measure (G_p) may also be defined as

$$(2) \qquad G_p = k\left(\frac{1}{N_p}\right)^{1/2}, \quad \text{where } k \text{ is a constant.}$$

The total length measure (L_p) for all N_p hexagons is:

$$(3) \qquad L_p = N_p(G_p) = kN_p\left(\frac{1}{N_p}\right)^{1/2} = k(N_p)^{1/2}.$$

TABLE II

Number, area, length and aggregate length of hexagons

power of p	Number of hexagons N_p	Area of hexagon A_p	Length measure of hexagon G_p	Aggregate length measure $L_p = N_p \cdot G_p = (N_p)^{\frac{1}{2}}$
Ratio of areas = 3				
0	1	1	1	1
1	3	1/3	$\sqrt{3}/3$	$\sqrt{3}$
2	9	1/9	1/3	3
3	27	1/27	$\sqrt{3}/9$	$3\sqrt{3}$
4	81	1/81	1/9	9
5	243	1/243	$\sqrt{3}/27$	$9\sqrt{3}$
6	729	1/729	1/27	27
	etc.	etc.	etc.	etc.
Ratio of Areas = 4				
0	1	1	1	1
1	4	1/4	1/2	2
2	16	1/16	1/4	4
3	64	1/64	1/8	8
4	256	1/256	1/16	16
	etc.	etc.	etc.	etc.
Ratio of Areas = 7				
0	1	1	1	1
1	7	1/7	$\sqrt{7}/7$	$\sqrt{7}$
2	49	1/49	1/7	7
3	343	1/343	$\sqrt{7}/49$	$7\sqrt{7}$
	etc.	etc.	etc.	etc.

We may assume, without loss of generality, that $k = 1$. Thus

$$(4) \qquad L_p = (N_p)^{1/2}.$$

From the array of values L_p in Table II we create the following mixed sequence of consecutive numbers; each number is a square root of N_p.

$$1, 1, 1, \sqrt{3}, 2, \sqrt{7}, 3, 4, 3\sqrt{3}, 7, 8, 9, 9\sqrt{3}, 16, 7\sqrt{7}, 27, \ldots.$$

The next step is to create i groups of consecutive values of L_p where the mean of each group, L_i is given by

$$(5) \qquad L_i = \bar{L}_p = \sum \frac{L_p}{n}.$$

In practice $1 \leqslant n \leqslant 6$.

When $i = 1$, $L_i = (1 + 1 + 1)/3 = 1$. This is the highest order length. What is the criterion by which we can select the remaining values of L_p to make the other L_i? Remembering that hierarchical systems typically exhibit geometric progressions of various attributes with order, we will constrain the selection process for L_p for group i to create a geometric progression in the following way:

$$(6) \qquad \text{minimize } S = \sum_{i=3} \left| L_i - L_{i-1}^{i-1/i-2} \right|.$$

In (6), L_i is a trial value, and L_{i-1} is the previously accepted value. The $i - 2$ root of L_{i-1} is found, and then raised to the $i - 1$ power to give a predicted value of L_i, assuming a perfect geometric progression. This is then subtracted from L_i. The sum of the absolute value of the differences, here termed cumulative 'stress' (S), is to be minimized.

Having selected the best values of L_i, one can calculate[10] the number of hexagonal areas at i, N_i:

$$(7) \qquad N_i = (L_i)^2.$$

The program exhausts all possible hierarchies subject to the following constraints. First, $L_1 = (1 + 1 + 1)/3 = 1$. Second, R_A between consecutive orders must be greater than 2 or less than 7. Third, the number of orders is 9 or 10.

The procedure which happens to generate a target hierarchy which corresponds to many river systems is shown in Table III.

Thus a model is created which hits the five target hierarchies and can be used to generate new hierarchies, i.e., fifty-nine ten-order hierarchies are generated. However, while all of these hierarchies may be found in nature, it seems likely that the model generates too many hierarchies since most of the hierarchies have very high stress values. One may limit the number of hierarchies, and at the same time, choose hierarchies which have a variety of values for R_A.

With this goal in mind, all the fifty-nine hierarchies may be grouped, for convenience, into series. Each series is identified by a code number, for instance 342. The numbers refer to the array of square roots of N_p following Equation (4). The first digit, 3, signifies that we place the first 3 of these numbers in a group, to calculate L_i when $i = 1$. The 4 signifies that the next four numbers are used for L_i when $i = 2$. The 2 signifies that the next two numbers are used for L_i when $i = 3$. There are ten series. The stresses of each hierarchy within a series were compared at increasing values of i.

TABLE III

Generation of a common river hierarchy

	Trial Value, L_i	Extrapolated value $L_{i-1}^{i-1/i-2}$	Stress or difference $|L_i - L_{i-1}^{i-1/i-2}|$	Cumulative stress $\Sigma|L_i - L_{i-1}^{i-1/i-2}|$	Number of areas or (L_i)* N_i
1	$(1 + 1 + 1)/3 = 1$				1
2	$(\sqrt{3} + \sqrt{4} + \sqrt{7} + \sqrt{9})/4 = 2.344$				5.494
3	$(\sqrt{16} + \sqrt{27})/2 = 4.598$	5.494	0.896	0.896	21.142
4	$(\sqrt{49} + \sqrt{64} + \sqrt{81} + \sqrt{243})/4 = 9.897$	9.859	0.038	0.934	97.951
5	$(\sqrt{256} + \sqrt{343} + \sqrt{729})/3 = 20.506$	21.249	0.743	1.677	420.496
5*	$(\sqrt{255} + \sqrt{343})/2 = 17.260$	21.249	3.989	4.923	

* Alternate 5. Note that the computer has completed four levels of the hierarchy. At $i = 5$, two alternatives are tried, and the first one is selected because it produces the lowest cumulative stress. For explanation of the headings, see Equations (4)–(7).

TABLE IV

Explanation of headings

i: The computer calculates the hierarchy from the largest hexagon (the total area) at $i = 1$, to the smallest hexagon at $i = 10$. Thus i and order are inversely ranked.

Number of elements in each group: The square roots of powers of 3, 4 and 7 are arrayed in consecutive order. That is, 1, 1, 1, $\sqrt{3}$, $\sqrt{4}$, $\sqrt{7}$, $\sqrt{9}$, $\sqrt{16}$, $\sqrt{27}$, etc. Each of these powers is called an element. A 3 in the first group signifies a group composition of the 3 elements 1, 1, 1. A 4 in the second group signifies that the group is composed of the elements $\sqrt{3}$, $\sqrt{4}$, $\sqrt{7}$, $\sqrt{9}$. A 2 in the third group signifies that the next 2 elements, $\sqrt{16}$ and $\sqrt{27}$ are represented. Please see Table VI for a representation of this hierarchy.

Series: The hierarchies generated by the computer may be classified into series for convenience. Each series is identified by a code number, for instance 342. This number relates to the number of elements in the first 3 groups. (See discussion immediately preceding). Each series is a separate part of Table IV, e.g., IVa, IVb, etc.

R_A: This is the ratio of areas between successive orders.

Stress: Stress is calculated according to Equation (6). Note: The lowest stress hierarchy within each series is retained for the Periodic Table.

IVa
Series: 314

i	Number of elements in each group	Number of areas	R_A	Stress
1	3	1		
2	1	3	3	
3	4	8.48	2.82	0.089
4	1	27	3.19	0.319
5	4	97.95	3.63	1.214
6	1	256	2.61	2.768
7	4	965.43	3.77	5.982
8	2	3192.25	3.31	7.391
9	2	10920.25	3.42	11.350
10	4	36954.09	3.38	16.729

Comment: System unobserved in nature. A possible system for organic branching where ratio between orders may not equal 3. Note ratio between $i = 2$ and 3, 5 and 6.

IVb
Series: 321

i	Number of elements in each group	Number of areas	R_A	Stress
1	3	1		
2	2	3.48	3.48	
3	1	7	2.01	0.836
4	4	23.03	3.29	1.332

IVb (*Continued*)

Series: 321 i	Number of elements in each group	Number of areas	R_A	Stress
5	1	64	2.78	1.427
6	3	183.05	2.86	1.502
7	2	518.02	2.83	1.521
8	3	1813.78	3.50	5.794
9	2	5256.25	2.90	6.080
10	1	16384	3.18	10.235

Comment: This system has not been recognized in nature. See previous comment.

IVc

Series: 322 i	Number of elements in each group	Number of areas	R_A	Stress
1	3	1		
2	2	3.48	3.48	
3	2	7.97	2.29	0.659
4	2	21.14	2.65	0.804
5	2	56.25	2.66	0.950
6	2	151.15	2.69	1.067
7	3	420.53	2.78	1.267
8	1	1024	2.44	3.194
9	3	2836.11	2.77	3.948
10	1	6561	2.31	10.478

Comment: This system is found in the airway of the human lung up to $i = 7$. (Woldenberg *et al.*, 1970; Woldenberg, 1971, p. 165; Woldenberg, 1972, p. 346.)

IVd

Series: 323 i	Number of elements in each group	Number of areas	R_A	Stress
1	3	1		
2	2	3.48	3.48	
3	3	10.34	2.97	0.267
4	2	37.19	3.60	0.600
5	3	118.00	3.17	0.878
6	3	420.53	3.56	1.664
7	2	1551.0	3.69	3.525
8	4	6480.25	4.18	11.383
9	2	18216.62	2.81	27.093

Comment: This hierarchy has been observed in rivers (Woldenberg, 1969, p. 108); in blood vessels and bile systems in bovine livers (Woldenberg, 1968a, 1969, p. 109); and the human pulmonary artery (Woldenberg, *et al.*, 1970; Woldenberg, 1971a, p. 164, and 1972a, p. 345). The model which generates this hierarchy is probably slightly in error since the hierarchy stops at $i = 10$, and the pulmonary artery extends to 16 orders

(Woldenberg *et al.*, 1970). The hierarchy in modified form from $i = 1$ to $i = 5$ was observed in central place systems (Woldenberg, 1968b; 1971, p. 166). See Table V.

IVe Series: 323 i	Number of elements in each group	Number of areas	R_A	Stress
1	3	1		
2	2	3.48	3.48	
3	3	10.34	2.97	0.267
4	2	37.19	3.60	0.600
5	4	147.55	3.97	1.606
6	2	518.02	3.51	1.689
7	3	1831.78	3.50	1.755
8	2	5256.25	2.90	8.842
9	3	17594.95	3.35	9.886
10	1	59049	3.36	11.246

Comment: This hierarchy has been observed in central place systems, and in the hierarchy of the left lung pulmonary artery. (Woldenberg, 1968b, 1969, p. 108; Woldenberg *et al.*, 1970; Woldenberg, 1971a, pp. 169, 170, 1972a, p. 343.) The model indicates a ratio of less than 3 between orders 7 and 8. This is possible if the surface is not completely served.

IVf Series: 324 i	Number of elements in each group	Number of areas	R_A	Stress
1	3	1		
2	2	3.48		
3	4	13.77	3.954	0.288
4	2	56.25	4.09	0.581
5	3	183.05	3.25	1.732
6	3	667.71	3.65	1.840
7	2	2292.75	3.43	3.474
8	3	8281.0	3.61	3.719
9	3	29233.92	3.53	6.081
10	3	115574.56	3.95	20.910

Comment: This is a likely hierarchy, but I have recognized it only once in Beech Creek, Ohio (Woldenberg, 1969, p. 105).

IVg Series: 333 i	Number of elements in each group	Number of areas	R_A	Stress
1	3	1		
2	3	4.52	4.52	
3	3	16.53	3.66	0.454
4	3	64.0	3.87	0.651

IVg (*Continued*)

Series: 333 i	Number of elements in each group	Number of areas	R_A	Stress
5	2	249.46	3.90	0.857
6	4	965.43	3.87	1.272
7	3	4181.77	4.33	4.161
8	1	16384.0	3.92	5.717
9	6	65265.42	3.98	6.245
10	1	262144	4.02	7.435

Comment: Perhaps observed in a few cases in rivers. See Woldenberg, 1969, p. 107. Note Little Tujunga, California, Little Mahoning River, Pennsylvania. (Multiply each order in this river by 0.86.)

IVh

Series: 334 i	Number of elements in each group	Number of areas	R_A	Stress
1	3	1		
2	3	4.52	4.52	
3	4	23.03	5.10	0.279
4	3	118.00	5.12	0.629
5	4	546.63	4.63	1.307
6	2	2292.75	4.19	4.835
7	5	11791.26	5.14	9.619
8	1	59049.0	5.01	15.441
9	6	278850.75	4.72	19.983
10	2	1307308.0	4.69	32.820

Comment: This hierarchy is found in Lichtenberg figures in plastic. See Table VI.

IVi

Series: 342 i	Number of elements in each group	Number of areas	R_A	Stress
1	3	1		
2	4	5.50	5.50	
3	2	21.14	3.84	0.898
4	4	97.95	4.63	0.936
5	3	420.53	4.29	1.678
6	3	1813.78	4.31	2.728
7	3	8281.0	4.57	3.540
8	4	36954.09	4.46	4.301
9	2	145881.25	3.95	29.823
10	4	629044.12	4.31	39.763

Comment: This is the most common river hierarchy observed to date (Woldenberg, 1969, p. 106; Woldenberg, 1971b; Woldenberg and Onesti, 1972b).

Table IV (*Continued*)

IVj

Series: 343 i	Number of elements in each group	Number of areas	R_A	Stress
1	3	1		
2	4	5.50	5.50	
3	3	29.15	5.29	0.098
4	4	147.55	5.06	0.495
5	3	667.71	4.53	2.578
6	4	3623.0	5.43	4.509
7	3	17594.95	4.86	8.460
8	4	99680.31	5.67	24.628
9	3	512890.94	5.15	26.832
10	4	2658256.0	5.18	28.368

Comment: This hierarchy has not yet been observed.

IVk

Series: 344 i	Number of elements in each group	Number of areas	R_A	Stress
1	3	1		
2	4	5.50	5.50	
3	4	36.59	6.65	0.533
4	4	218.37	5.97	0.653
5	4	1497.02	6.86	3.082
6	4	10132.52	6.77	7.245
7	4	60306.60	5.95	14.851
8	4	412607.38	6.84	42.665
9	4	2658256.0	6.44	55.460
10	4	17300256.0	6.51	104.881

Comment: This hierarchy has a very high ratio, probably the highest possible ratio for systems whose branching ratios cannot exceed 7. As yet this hierarchy has not been observed.

Selecting on the basis of the lowest stress values within each series, the list of 59 hierarchies can be narrowed to ten, each containing ten orders. Sometimes hierarchies from two series converge on the same L_i (see Table IV). The program will then select the hierarchy with the lowest cumulative stress. This will eliminate the hierarchy from the other series. Two of the target hierarchies were found to have the lowest stress values within one series, 323, for $i = 9$. The number of areas at $i = 9$ was different for each hierarchy. At $i = 10$ both hierarchies converged on the same value of N, but one hierarchy had the lower stress. Since both hierarchies exist in natural systems of up to 6 or 7 orders, both of these predicted hierarchies were retained. Thus, though only 10 hierarchies should have survived, the list of predicted hierarchies has been enlarged to 11. Of these 5 are target hierarchies, 2 others have been empirically found, and 4 others are predicted (see Tables I and IV).

IV. THE PHYSICAL BASIS OF THE MODEL

Why should we create a network of mixed hierarchies when perfect hexagonal hierarchies are possible in a pure $R_A = 3$, 4, or 7 network? For one, with mixed hierarchies R_A can show more variation than in a pure hierarchy and the value of R_A in a hierarchy seems to be related to the power needed and the available power in a system.

Empirical evidence suggests the truth of this proposition, but I have not been able to provide a complete physical model. For example, the lung airway, which transports a gas with low viscosity and low resistance to flow has a value of $R_A = R_b$ of 2.8. The pulmonary artery which transmits the more viscous blood has a value of $R_A = R_b$ of 3.3 to 3.6. Rivers with high relief ratios (basin drop/basin length) tend to have low values for $R_A \sim R_b = 3.6$. Those with low basin relief ratios tend to have $R_b = 4.5$. This suggests that if there is a surplus of power available for the load, then R_b is low.

In the airway and pulmonary artery the ratio of diameters (R_D) between orders grows proportionally with R_A and R_b. In the lung, $R_D/R_b = 1/2$ for both the airway and pulmonary artery (Woldenberg et al., 1970; Woldenberg, 1972b). Do similar relations hold for rivers? That is, since resistance in tubes is proportional to $1/(Diameter)$,[4] it may be reasonable to conjecture that branching is an unknown function of diameter and diameter is related to work or power.

Another empirical example may show agreement with this reasoning. Plastic blocks can be charged with static electricity. When discharged, a tree-like fracture pattern is created (called a 'Lichtenberg figure'). This tree has an R_b of 4.83 in the examples I have seen. The supposition is that the high resistance of the plastic induces a high branching ratio (see Table VI, series 334).

In the specific example of a reach of a river, power is proportional to slope times discharge times length. Thus if slope is high, water and load move rapidly. If slope is low, water and load may move too sluggishly. A high value of R_b increases the flow into a higher order channel. The stream must increase its width and depth to accommodate the extra volume. The wetted surface

TABLE V

An anomalous empirical hierarchy

i	Number of elements in each group	Number of areas	R_A	Stress	Central places of Munich $\times$ (1.5) (Christaller 1933)	Central places in Saskatchewan Woroby (1957)
1	3	1			1	(1)
2	2	3.48	3.48		3	2
3	3	10.34	2.92	0.267	12	10
4	2	37.19	3.60	0.600	39	36
5	3	118.00	3.17	0.878	127	101
6	1	256	2.17	4.592	249	256
7	2	518.02	2.02	9.689	519	

Comments: This hierarchy changes its ratio of areas radically at $I = 6$ and 7. The present model is unable to generate it. For comparison see the minimum stress hierarchy Table IVd. This hierarchy would be unsatisfactory from the point of view of space filling, since a ratio of areas of at least 3 to 1 is required to fill space with hexagons. One may speculate that for Munich-type central place systems, the ratio is less than 3 to 1 at the lowest orders, only. This implies that rural people must travel somewhat further for lower order goods than would be the case if there were a higher ratio between $i - 5$ and 6; and 6 and 7. High order travel is unaffected. With this system, on a daily basis some people are somewhat inconvenienced. On long distance infrequent trips, no one is inconvenienced.

area will increase less rapidly than the volume, hence there will be less frictional loss/time, saving power. This should be reflected in an increase of velocity. Aside from the increase in velocity, there will be an increased cross-sectional area in the higher order stream. The higher velocity and higher cross-sectional area cause an increase in discharge and load/time. Thus the effect of a high value of R_b is to compensate for low power. In fact there is such a gain of power that streams usually develop lower slopes down stream.

From the foregoing the suggestion is that for a system in development when (available power)/(load) is high, R_b is low, and if the (available power)/(load) is low, then R_b is high. R_b may thus be thought of as a mechanical gear wherein high R_b is 'low gear' and vice-versa. Low gear sacrifices speed for power and high gear sacrifices power for speed. The particular value of R_b is not a continuous variable, but rather it is a variable which depends on the few possible ways of dividing space into hexagons.

The number of orders depends on the equilibrium size of the first-order basin, the total size of the space which must be filled, and obviously, the value of R_b. For a river, the area of the first order basin must be large enough to supply sufficient water to maintain a permanent channel. For a town, the threshold market area must be achieved. However, the optimum size of the first order area may be larger than the minimum threshold size.

If we were to divide an area into a few big hexagons, for each hexagon there would be large flows in the river or the town and there would be scale economies. Costs of transport to the river or town will be high in the aggregate for all hexagons of this size. If all the hexagons were small, aggregate costs of transport to the town or river would be low, but there would be few scale economies. There should be an optimum-sized hexagon which would minimize power or monetary costs. This optimum hexagon is achieved by taking the mean of the lengths of sides or radii for all hexagons in the group with the smaller lengths represent minimizing movement costs to the town or river and the longer lengths sacrifice low movement costs to the town or river, but with savings in scale economies. The mean represents the best compromise for the first order area.

Once the optimum size of the first-order area is determined, the size of each higher order area is determined by R_b (or R_A) which depends on power available divided by power required. The number of orders depends on the size of the entire region, the optimum size of the first order region and the value of R_b (or R_A).

V. TESTING THE PERIODIC TABLE AGAINST REAL HIERARCHIES

Some natural hierarchies may develop in uniform regions such as a river system in an area free of structural controls. Other hierarchies may develop in areas where structure controls branching. In such regions, the numbers of areas and R_A may not be predicted by the model. But even for hierarchies developed in uniform regions, very few can be compared directly to one of the ideal hierarchies in the Periodic Table. The first step is to compare R_b (or R_A) calculated for all orders but the highest two or three. This is necessary, because some systems may have, for instance, twice as many areas or branches at each order as the ideal hierarchy. An adjustment must be made, in this case the total number of branches at each order must be divided by two, and the resulting values compared to an ideal hierarchy.

One method of proceeding might be to multiply the first order of an empirical hierarchy by a factor which will cause it to correspond with a value at an analogous order in an ideal hierarchy. Then multiply all orders in the empirical hierarchy by the same factor, and see whether the corrected data matches the ideal hierarchy. For instance, suppose an empirical (river) hierarchy had the values 1, 2, 10, 42, 200, 840. An ideal hierarchy has the values 1, 5, 21, 98, 420. If the empirical hierarchy were multiplied by 0.5 the two hierarchies would correspond. Christaller used the same method in his discussion of the Munich system of cities (Baskin, 1966).

VI. SUMMARY

The model presented here depends on the partitioning of space by hexagons. In contrast to all previous forms of hexagonally based models, this model creates a geometric progression of lengths, based on means of groups of square roots of hexagons. The computer has selected 59 hierarchies of 10 orders arranged in ten subsets (series). From each of these ten series the best hierarchies were chosen. Two similar hierarchies, one of nine and the other of ten orders were taken from the same series because there is evidence that both exist in nature.

The computer was able to generate five commonly found 'target' hierarchies, two other empirical hierarches, and has predicted the existence of four hierarchies, as yet unobserved in natural systems.

A theory of hierarchical structure is proposed although not definitely established. R_b and R_A seem to be inversely related to available power/ power required. Rather than a continuum of values for R_b or R_A, implying an infinite number of hierarchical types, only a few may be generated, because partitioning of space must conform to Euler's law.

Department of Geography
State University of New York at Buffalo

TABLE VI

Lichtenberg figure in plastic*

(Series 334. This data has not been published).

Branch A				Branch B			
Order	No. of branches	X.502	X2.32608	Order	No. of branches	X.502	X2.32608
d	1		2.33	d	1		2.60
$d-1$	2	1.00	4.56	$d-1$	2	1.12	5.21
$d-2$	9	4.52	20.93	$d-2$	9	5.06	23.43
$d-3$	47	23.6	109.33	$d-3$	46	25.85	119.74
$d-4$	235	118.00	546.63	$d-4$	210	118.00	546.63

Branch C				Total Lichtenberg figure (A + B + C)			
Order	No. of branches	X.34104	X1.5798	Order	No. of branches	X.491782	X.69106
d	1		1.58	d	1		
$d-1$	3	1.02	4.74	$d-1$	3		2.07
$d-2$	14	4.77	22.18	$d-2$	7	1.04	4.84
$d-3$	76	25.92	120.07	$d-3$	32	4.77	22.11
$d-4$	346	118.00	546.63	$d-4$	169	25.21	116.79
				$d-5$	791	118.00	546.63

* For each branch the numbers are multiplied by a common factor so that the lowest order corresponds exactly to the value in the model hierarchy. When this is done, ratios between orders are preserved, and the calculated values can be compared to the model. Branch A resembles a fourth order hierarchy; branches B and C may be more in agreement with a fifth order model hierarchy. The total figure may best fit a fifth order model. See Table IVh.

APPENDIX TABLE A-I

Table of numbers of areas

In Table A-I the powers of 3, 4 and 7 are mixed and arranged in groups in order of increasing size. A group may have from 1 to 9 members in these tables. To use these tables, start with the first member of the group after the break in column A. Read down the column, stopping at the last member of the group, and move the eye horizontally to column L_i or L_i^2. For example: L_i^2 of 3, 4 and 7 is 4.52. For an explanation of A, L_i and L_i^2, see text.

(See pp. 450–452 for table itself.)

MICHAEL J. WOLDENBERG

CONSECUTIVE POWERS (A), ARITHMETIC MEAN OF SQUARE ROOTS (L_i) AND NUMBER OF AREAS (L_i^2)
(or aggregate length)

A	L_i	L_i^2	A	L_i	L_i^2
1	1.0C0	1.CCC	9	3.000	9.000
1	1.000	1.CCC	16	3.500	12.250
1	1.0C0	1.000	27	4.065	16.527
3	1.183	1.4CC	49	4.799	23.031
4	1.346	1.813	64	5.439	29.585
7	1.563	2.443	81	6.033	36.393
9	1.768	3.127	243	7.398	54.727
16	2.047	4.191	256	8.473	71.793
27	2.397	5.746	343	9.589	91.957
1	1.0C0	1.000	16	4.000	16.000
1	1.000	1.CCC	27	4.558	21.142
3	1.244	1.548	49	5.399	29.146
4	1.433	2.054	64	6.049	36.591
7	1.676	2.808	81	6.635	44.079
9	1.896	3.596	243	8.131	66.109
16	2.197	4.826	256	9.255	85.654
27	2.572	6.614	343	10.413	108.433
49	3.064	9.387	729	12.256	150.212
1	1.000	1.000	27	5.196	27.C0C
3	1.366	1.666	49	6.098	37.187
4	1.577	2.488	64	6.732	45.32C
7	1.844	3.402	81	7.299	53.276
9	2.076	4.308	243	8.957	80.226
16	2.396	5.742	256	10.131	102.632
27	2.796	7.819	343	11.329	128.352
49	3.322	11.034	729	13.288	176.574
64	3.842	14.758	1024	15.367	236.151
3	1.732	3.000	49	7.000	49.CCC
4	1.866	3.482	64	7.500	56.250
7	2.126	4.520	81	8.000	64.000
9	2.344	5.496	243	9.897	97.953
16	2.676	7.159	256	11.118	123.603
27	3.096	9.583	343	12.351	152.558
49	3.653	13.347	729	14.444	208.632
64	4.197	17.613	1024	16.639	276.842
81	4.730	22.377	2187	19.986	399.440
4	2.000	4.000	64	8.000	64.CCC
7	2.323	5.396	81	8.500	72.250
9	2.549	6.495	243	10.863	118.0C1
16	2.911	8.476	256	12.147	147.552
27	3.368	11.346	343	13.422	180.143
49	3.974	15.790	729	15.685	246.C12
64	4.549	20.692	1024	18.016	324.559
81	5.105	26.C63	2187	21.609	466.96C
243	6.270	39.313	2401	24.653	607.754
7	2.646	7.000	81	9.000	81.CCC
9	2.823	7.969	243	12.294	151.148
16	3.215	10.338	256	13.529	183.047
27	3.710	13.768	343	14.777	218.365
49	4.368	19.083	729	17.222	296.588
64	4.974	24.737	1024	19.695	387.49C
81	5.549	30.790	2187	23.553	554.764
243	6.804	43.292	2401	26.734	714.720
256	7.826	61.240	4096	30.875	953.259

A	L_i	L_i^2	A	L_i	L_i^2
243	15.588	243.CCC	2401	49.000	24C1.000
256	15.794	249.458	4096	56.5C0	3192.25C
343	16.703	278.987	6561	64.667	4181.773
729	19.277	371.6C9	16384	80.5C0	6480.25C
1C24	21.822	476.188	16807	90.328	8159.211
2187	25.979	674.9C8	19683	98.656	9733.C63
2401	29.268	056.599	59049	119.277	14226.961
4096	33.6C9	1129.582	65536	136.367	18596.C20
6561	38.875	1511.257	117649	159.326	25384.906
256	16.0C0	256.000	4096	64.000	4C96.C00
343	17.260	297.912	6561	72.500	5256.25C
729	20.507	420.526	16384	91.000	8280.996
1024	23.380	546.627	16807	1CC.660	10132.523
2187	28.057	787.201	19683	108.588	11791.258
2401	31.548	995.250	59049	130.990	17158.277
4096	36.184	1309.257	65536	148.848	22155.8C5
6561	41.786	1746.C44	117649	173.117	29969.574
16384	51.365	2638.37C	177147	200.647	40259.352
343	18.520	343.000	6561	81.000	6561.C00
729	22.760	518.023	16384	104.5C0	1C920.250
1024	25.840	667.709	16807	112.881	12742.C23
2187	31.071	965.432	19683	119.734	14336.344
2401	34.657	1201.116	59049	144.388	2C847.77C
4096	39.548	1564.012	65536	162.990	26565.6C9
6561	45.469	2067.463	117649	188.7C5	35609.727
16384	55.786	3112.043	177147	217.728	47405.598
6807	63.992	4C94.567	262144	250.425	62712.742
729	27.000	729.000	16384	128.000	16384.000
1024	29.500	87C.25C	16807	128.821	16554.82C
2187	35.255	1242.923	19683	132.646	17594.949
2401	38.691	1497.015	59049	160.234	25675.086
4096	43.753	1914.331	65536	179.388	32179.858
6561	49.961	2496.089	117649	206.656	4270C.809
16384	61.109	3734.350	177147	237.261	56292.723
16807	69.676	4854.727	262144	271.603	73768.313
19683	77.523	6009.750	531441	322.425	103957.875
1024	32.0C0	1024.000	16807	129.642	16806.996
2187	39.383	1550.995	19683	134.969	18216.621
2401	42.588	1813.775	59049	170.979	29233.918
4096	47.941	2298.371	65536	192.234	36954.094
6561	54.553	2976.C37	117649	222.388	49456.223
16384	66.794	4461.465	177147	255.471	65265.418
16807	75.772	5741.461	262144	292.118	85332.875
19683	83.838	7028.793	531441	346.728	120220.438
59049	101.523	103C6.828	823543	409.035	167309.938
2187	46.765	2186.599	19683	140.296	19682.996
2401	47.883	2292.75C	59049	151.648	22728.977
4C96	53.255	2836.107	65536	213.099	45411.C43
6561	60.191	3622.996	117649	245.574	60306.598
16384	73.753	5439.512	177147	280.637	78756.638
16807	83.C68	69C0.266	262144	319.197	101886.875
19683	91.243	8325.340	531441	377.740	142687.813
59049	110.213	12146.883	823543	443.959	19710C.C00
65536	126.411	15979.855	1048576	5C8.4C8	258479.125

A	L_i	L_i^2	A	L_i	L_i^2
59049	243.000	59049.000	823543	907.493	823542.938
65536	249.500	62250.250	1048576	965.746	932665.938
117649	280.667	78773.625	1594323	1064.719	1133626.000
177147	315.722	99680.313	4194304	1310.539	1717513.000
262144	354.978	126009.000	4782969	1485.831	2207694.000
531441	417.314	174151.313	5764801	1638.359	2684220.000
823543	487.340	237500.213	14348907	1945.450	3784776.000
1048576	554.423	307384.375	16777216	2214.269	4902987.000
1594323	633.116	400835.813	40353607	2674.066	7150631.000
65536	256.000	65536.000	1048576	1024.000	1048576.000
117649	299.500	89700.250	1594323	1143.332	1307208.000
177147	339.963	115574.563	4194304	1444.888	2087701.000
262144	382.972	146667.438	4782969	1630.416	2658256.000
531441	452.177	204464.438	5764801	1784.533	3184557.000
823543	528.063	278850.750	14348907	2118.443	4487799.000
1048576	598.911	358694.813	16777216	2400.951	5764566.000
1594323	681.881	464961.125	40353607	2894.888	8380379.000
4194304	833.672	695008.375	43046721	3302.234	10904748.000
117649	343.000	117649.000	1594323	1262.665	1594322.000
177147	381.944	145881.250	4194304	1655.332	2740124.000
262144	425.296	180876.563	4782969	1832.555	3358256.000
531441	501.222	251223.375	5764801	1974.666	3899305.000
823543	582.476	339278.375	14348907	2337.332	5463119.000
1048576	656.063	430418.938	16777216	2630.443	6919228.000
1594323	742.721	551634.000	40353607	3162.158	9999242.000
4194304	905.881	820619.688	43046721	3587.013	12866665.000
4782969	1048.227	1098779.000	67108864	4098.676	16799136.000
177147	420.899	177146.813	4194304	2049.000	4194304.000
262144	466.444	217570.063	4782969	2117.500	4483806.000
531441	553.963	306874.563	5764801	2212.000	4892942.000
823543	642.345	412607.375	14348907	2605.999	6791228.000
1048576	719.676	516495.188	16777216	2903.999	8433208.000
1594323	809.341	655032.563	40353607	3478.740	12101630.000
4194304	986.292	972772.375	43046721	3919.063	15359054.000
4782969	1136.381	1291360.000	67108864	4453.180	19830800.000
5764801	1276.894	1630457.000	129140163	5221.047	27259328.000
262144	512.000	262144.000	4782969	2187.000	4782969.000
531441	620.500	385020.250	5764801	2254.000	5082926.000
823543	716.164	512890.938	14348907	2791.998	7795253.000
1048576	753.123	629044.125	16777216	3117.999	9721914.000
1594323	887.031	786824.813	40353607	3764.888	14174284.000
4194304	1080.526	1167536.000	43046721	4230.902	17900528.000
4782969	1238.594	1534114.000	67108864	4796.773	23009024.000
5764801	1383.895	1915164.000	129140163	5617.676	31558272.000
14348907	1651.017	2725856.000	268435456	6813.934	46429680.000
531441	729.000	531441.000	5764801	2401.000	5764801.000
823543	818.246	669527.063	14348907	3094.497	9575913.000
1048576	896.831	786468.875	16777216	3428.331	11753455.000
1594323	980.789	961947.625	40353607	4159.359	17300256.000
4194304	1194.231	1426188.000	43046721	4639.688	21526688.000
4782969	1359.693	1848764.000	67108864	5231.738	27371072.000
5764801	1508.451	2275424.000	129140163	6107.773	37304856.000
4348907	1793.394	3216262.000	268435456	7392.301	54646096.000
6777216	2049.239	4199380.000	282475249	8438.379	71209224.000

NOTES

* The author wishes to thank the Milton Fund of Harvard University for financial aid. This paper could not have been written without the help of Rachel Thurston and David Barer, programmers. Rachel Thurston was responsible for developing the length – rather than area – based model. Dr. Keith Harding challenged the author by suggesting this project in 1969. Professor William Warntz supported and encouraged my research on spatial hierarchies from the beginning.

[1] $y = y_1 R^{u-i}$ where R is the common ratio or base of the progression, u is order, y is the dependent variable and y_1 is the value of y at order one.

[2] The ratio of areas (R_A) or branching ratio (R_b) is usually defined as the anti-logarithm of the slope of the regression of log number of areas (or branches) against order (Maxwell, 1955). For rivers, $1/R_b$ is always less than R_A but of about the same size because of interbasin areas which do not flow directly into a first order area. For blood vessels or airways, $1/R_b$ and R_A are equal, because there are no interbasin areas (Woldenberg, 1971a, and Woldenberg et al., 1970).

[3] For a review of fluvial morphometry, see Salisbury (1971), Haggett and Chorley (1969), Strahler (1964).

[4] $y = ax^b$ where x and y are variables and a and b are constants. These functions plot as straight lines on double logarithmic paper. b is the slope of the line.

[5] R_b is, for convenience, taken to be a ratio greater than unity, even though the geometric progression declines with order.

[6] For references see Berry et al., 1965; Andrews, 1971; Mott et al., 1975; Smith, 1972.

[7] R_L is the ratio of basin lengths. To calculate L_u, basin length at order u, one must cumulate mean segment length, $S_{\bar{u}}$, from order one through order u. Thus

$$L_u = \sum S_{\bar{u}} \quad \text{and} \quad R_{L_{u,\,u-1}} = \frac{L_u}{L_{u-1}}.$$

[8] Topologically distinct networks are those whose schematic map projections cannot be continuously deformed and rotated in the plane of projection so as to become congruent (Shreve, 1966, p. 27).

[9] For a plane surface, (Polygons) − (Edges) + (Corners) = 1.

[10] Note that $(L_i)^2$ is very close to the value of the convergent mean when the original powers of 3, 4, and 7 which were used in column L_i of Table III are not very far apart in arithmetic terms. The convergent mean of several numbers is created by taking the arithmetic mean (A_1) of a group and the geometric mean (G_1) of a group. Then the arithmetic mean (A_2) and the geometric mean (G_2) of A_1 and G_1 are taken. The process continues until the difference between A_n and G_n is very small (Woldenberg, 1968a, 1968b, 1969).

BIBLIOGRAPHY

Andrews, H. F.: 1971, 'Working Notes and Bibliography on Central Place Studies, 1965–1969', Council of Planning Librarians Exchange Bibliography 209.

Baskin, C. W.: 1966, *Central Places in Southern Germany* (trans. of *Die Zentralen Orte in Süddeutschland* by W. Christaller), Prentice Hall, Englewood Cliffs.

Berry, B. J. L.: 1967, *Geography of Market Centers and Retail Distribution*, Prentice Hall, Englewood Cliffs.

Berry, B. J. L., Pred, A., Barnum, H. G., Kasperson, R. and Kiuchi, S.: 1965, *Central Place Studies: A Bibliography of Theory and Applications*, Regional Science Research Institute, Philadelphia.

Christaller, W.: 1933, *Die Zentralen Orte in Süddeutschland*, Gustav Fischer Verlag, Jena.

Christaller, W.: 1950, *Das Grundgerüst der Räumlichen Ordnung in Europa*, Frankfurter Geographische Hefte, **24**, 1–96.

Curry, L.: 1964, 'The Random Spatial Economy: An Exploration in Settlement Theory', *Annals* **54**, 138–46.

Dacey, M. F.: 1965, 'A Note on Some Number Properties of a Hexagonal Hierarchical Plane Lattice', *Journal of Regional Science* **5**, 63–67.

Graustein, W. C.: 1932, 'On the Average Number of Sides of Polygons of a Net', *Annals of Mathematics* **32**, 149–153.

Haggett, P.: 1965, *Locational Analysis in Human Geography*, Arnold, London.

Haggett, P. and Chorley, R. J.: 1969, *Network Analysis in Geography*, Arnold, London.

Holland, P. G.: 1969, 'The Maintenance of Structure and Shape in Three Mallee Eucalyptus', *New Phytologist* **68**, 411–421.

Hollingworth, T. and Berry, M.: 1975, 'Network Analysis of Dendritic Fields of Pyramidal Cells in Neocortex and Purkinje Cells in the Cerebellum of the Rat', *Philosophical Transactions of the Royal Society* **270**, 227–264.

Horton, R. E.: 1945, 'Erosional Development of Streams and Their Drainage Basins: Hydro-Physical Approach to Quantitative Morphology', *Bulletin of the Geological Society of America* **56**, 275–370.

Howard, A. D.: 1971, 'Simulation of Stream Networks by Headward Growth and Branching', *Geographical Analysis* **3**, 29–50.

Leopold, L. B. and Langbein, W. B.: 1962, 'The Concept of Entropy in Landscape Evolution', United States Geological Survey Professional Paper 500-A.

Leopold, L. B. and Miller, J. P.: 1956, 'Ephemeral Streams – Hydraulic Factors and Their Relation to the Drainage Net', United States Geological Survey Professional Paper 282-A.

Loeb, A. L.: 1964, 'The Subdivision of the Hexagonal Net and the Systematic Generation of Crystal Structures', *Acta Crystallographica* **17**, 179–182.

Lösch, A.: 1954, *The Economics of Location* (trans. of 2nd ed. by W. Woglom and W. Stolper), Yale University Press, New Haven.

Marshall, J. U.: 1968, 'An Approach to the Analysis of Central Place Systems, A Study in Geographical Methodology', Ph.D. diss, Department of Geography, University of Toronto.

Maxwell, J. C.: 1955, 'The Bifurcation Ratio in Horton's Law of Stream Numbers (Abst.)', *Transactions of the American Geophysical Union* **36**, 250.

Mott, L. M., Silin, R. H., and Mintz, S. W.: 1975, 'A Supplementary Bibliography on Marketing and Market Places', Council of Planning Librarians Exchange Bibliography 792.

Palomäki, M.: 1964, 'The Functional Centers and Areas of South Bothnia, Finland', *Fennia* 88, 1–235.

Salisbury, N.: 1971, 'Threads of Inquiry in Quantitative Geomorphology', in M. Morisawa (ed.), *Quantiative Geomorphology: Some Aspects and Applications*, State University of New York, Binghamton.

Scheidegger, A. E. and Langbein, W. B.: 1966, 'Probability Concepts in Geomorphology', United States Geological Survey Professional Paper 500-C.

Schenck, H. S., Jr.: 1963, 'Simulation of the Evolution of Drainage-Basin Networks With a Digital Computer', *Journal of Geophysical Research* 68, 597–646.

Schumm, S.: 1956, 'Evolution of Drainage Systems and Slopes in Badlands at Perth Amboy, New Jersey', *Bulletin of the Geological Society of America* 67, 597–646.

Shreve, R. L.: 1966, 'Statistical Law of Stream Numbers', *Journal of Geology* 74, 17–38.

Shreve, R. L.: 1967, 'Infinite Topologically Random Channel Networks', *Journal of Geology* 75, 178–186.

Shreve, R. L.: 1969, 'Stream Lengths and Basin Areas in Topologically Random Channel Networks', *Journal of Geology* 77, 397–414.

Smart, J. S.: 1972, 'Channel Networks', *Advances in Hydroscience* 8, 305–346.

Smart, J. S., Surkan, A. J., and Considine, J. P.: 1967, 'Digital Simulation of Channel Networks', in *Symposium of River Morphology*, International Association of Scientific Hydrology, Bern, pp. 87–98.

Smith, C. S.: 1952, 'Grain Shapes and Other Metallurgical Applications of Topology', in *Metal Interfaces*, American Society of Metals, Cleveland, pp. 65–113.

Smith, R. H. T.: 1972, 'Periodic Markets in Africa, Asia and Latin America', Council of Planning Librarians Exchange Bibliography 318.

Strahler, A. N.: 1952, 'Hypsometric (Area-Altitude) Analysis of Erosional Topography', *Bulletin of the Geological Society of America* 63, 1117–1142.

Strahler, A. N.: 1964, 'Quantitative Geomorphology of Drainage Basins and Channel Networks', in V. T. Chow (ed.), *Handbook of Applied Hydrology*, McGraw Hill, New York, pp. 439–76.

Thurston, R. F., Woldenberg, M. J., and Barer, D.: 1975, 'A Computer Program for Mixed Hexagonal Hierarchies', Laboratory for Computer Graphics, Graduate School of Design, Harvard University.

Werner, C.: 1970, 'Horton's Law of Stream Numbers for Topologically Random Channel Networks', *Canadian Geographer* 14, 57–66.

Werrity, A.: 1972, 'The Topology of Stream Networks', in R. Chorley (ed.), *Spatial Analysis in Geomorphology*, Methuen, London.

Woldenberg, M. J.: 1968a, 'Hierarchical Systems: Cities, Rivers, Alpine Glaciers, Bovine Livers and Trees', Ph.D. diss., Department of Geography, Columbia University.

Woldenberg, M. J.: 1968b, 'Energy Flow and Spatial Order – Mixed Hexagonal Hierarchies of Central Places', *Geographical Review* 58, 552–574.

Woldenberg, M. J.: 1969, 'Spatial Order in Fluvial Systems: Horton's Laws Derived from Mixed Hexagonal Hierarchies of Drainage Basin Areas', *Geological Society of America Bulletin* 80, 97–112.

Woldenberg, M. J.: 1971a, 'A Structural Taxonomy of Spatial Hierarchies', in

M. Chisholm, A. Frey and P. Haggett (eds.), *Regional Forecasting, Proceedings of the Colston Research Society* **22**, Butterworths, London, pp. 147–175.

Woldenberg, M. J.: 1971b, 'The Two Dimensional Organization of Clear Creek and Old Man Creek, Iowa', in M. Morisawa (ed.), *Quantitative Morphology: Some Aspects and Applications*, State University of New York, Binghamton.

Woldenberg, M. J.: 1972a, 'The Average Hexagon in Spatial Hierarchies', in R. Chorley (ed.), *Spatial Analysis in Geomorphology*, Methuen, London.

Woldenberg, M. J.: 1972b, 'Relations Between Horton's Laws and Hydraulic Geometry as Applied to Tidal Networks', Laboratory for Computer Graphics, Graduate School of Design, Harvard University.

Woldenberg, M. J. and Berry, B. J. L.: 1967, 'Rivers and Central Places: Analogous Systems?' *Journal of Regional Science* **7**, 129–139.

Woldenberg, M. J. and Onesti, L.: 1972, 'Two Dimensional Spatial Organization of the Pecatonica River, Southwestern Wisconsin', Laboratory for Computer Graphics, Graduate School of Design, Harvard University.

Woldenberg, M. J., Cumming, G., Harding, K., Horsfield, K., Prowse, K. and Singhal, S.: 1970, 'Law and Order in the Human Lung', Laboratory for Computer Graphics, Graduate School of Design, Harvard University.

Woroby, P.: 1957, 'Functional Relationship Between Farm Population and Service Centers', Master's Thesis, Department of Agricultural Economics, University of Manitoba.

Unconventional Name Index

Pages	Authors included in this volume	Authors not included in this volume	Total authors	No. of references to works of other authors in this volume	No. of references to own works	No. of references to works of authors not included in volume	Total references
Blaut	1	11	12	0	2	13	15
Buttimer	2	75	77	3	0	86	89
Dacey	0	1	1	0	0	1	1
Dear	2	14	16	1	2	14	17
Gale/Atk.	1	74	75	0	5	97	102
Golledge	4	15	19	5	2	20	27
Gould	4	51	55	5	7	177	189
Harvey	1	33	34	0	1	42	43
King	13	47	60	25	3	68	96
Ley	6	61	67	13	3	76	92
Marchand	3	17	20	2	2	20	24
Moore	1	8	9	0	1	8	9
Olsson	1	30	31	0	1	35	36
Pipkin	2	24	25	1	2	27	30

NAME INDEX (*Continued*)

	Pages	Authors included in this volume	Authors not included in this volume	Total authors	No. of references to works of other authors in this volume	No. of references to own works	No. of references to works of authors not included in volume	Total references
Russell								
Scott		1	5	6	0	2	5	7
Sheppard		3	32	35	2	2	5	7
Tobler		1	4	5	0	1	4	5
Tuan		1	111	112	1	0	112	113
Woldenberg		2	31	33	1	9	39	49

	Blaut	Buttimer	Dacey	Dear	Gale/Atkinson	Golledge	Gould	Harvey	King	Ley	Marchand	Moore	Olsson	Pipkin	Russell	Scott	Sheppard	Tobler	Tuan	Woldenberg
Blaut	2																			
Buttimer		0							1				2							
Dacey			0																	
Dear				2				1												
Gale/Atkinson					5															
Golledge						2	1	1					3							
Gould	1						7				1							3		
Harvey								1												
King	1	1	2	3	1	1	1	6	3				5				1	1	2	
Ley		6				2		2	3				1						2	
Marchand				1							2		1							
Moore				1								1								
Olsson													1							
Pipkin						1								2						
Russell																				
Scott																2				
Sheppard						1		1					1				2			
Tobler																		1		
Tuan		1																	0	
Woldenberg		1																		9

459

INDEX OF NAMES

Ackoff, R. L. and Emery 102
Ad Hoc Committee of American Geographers 387
Alao, N. 191
Alao, N and Dacey, M. F. 192
Alexander, C. 126
Alguie, F. 301
Alonso, W. 192, 219, 278
Amedeo, D. and Golledge, R. G. 197
Appleyard, D. 109
de Aquino, R. 143
Aquist, L. 102
Ardrey, R. 94
Arendt, H. 20
Arnheim, R. 395
Atkin, R. 127, 129, 130, 131, 134, 140, 142
Atkin, R., Hartston, W. and Witten, I. 131
Atkin, R. and Witten, I. 131
Auston, A. M., Smith, T. E. and Wolpert, J. 192

Bachelard, G. 230
Balakian, A. 301
Bannister, D. and Fransella, R. 123, 125, 139, 143
Bannister, G. 195
Barber, G. M. 366
Barrows, H. 218
Barthes, R. 126, 127, 128, 141, 144, 242
Baskin, C. W. 429, 430, 448
Bassett, K. A. 196
Bateson, G. 143
Batty, M. 371
Batty, M. and Mackie, S. 190
Beare, J. B. 364
Becker, G. M., De Groot, M. H. and Marschak, J. 309

Beckmann, M. 358
Beer, S. 123, 126, 137, 143
Bell, D. 18
Bellman, R. E. and Zadeh, A. L. 96
Belnap, N. D. Jr. 70, 102
Benedikt, M. 301
Benn, S. I. 93
Bennett, R. J. 195
Benveniste, E. 93
Berdoulay, V. 216
Berg, U. 137
Berger, P. and Luckmann, T. 24, 116, 226
Berger, P. and Pullberg, S. 116
Bergmann, G. 116
Bergson, H. 393
Berlin, B. and Kay, P. 2
Bernstein, B. 132
Berry, B. J. L. 430
Bethell, T. 373
Bevan, E. R. 395
Bierstedt, R. 218
Billingsley, A. 224
Birch, D. 272, 274
Black, M. 206
Blalock, H. M. 271
Blaut, J. 1, 4, 203
Blaut, J., McCleary, G. and Blaut, A. 132
Block, H. D. and Marschak, J. 309
Block, P. 137
Bloom, H. 296
Blumer, H. 225
Board, C., Chorley, R. J. and Hackett, P. 187
Boas, F. 398
Bock, K. D. and Jones, L. V. 313
Bohannan, P. 94
de Bono, E. 127, 129

Booth, S. 390
Borges, J. 124
Borrowes, D., Lapides, F. and
    Shawcross, J. 127
Bortoff, H. 21, 22, 23
Bourne, L. S. 54
Bower, G. H. and Trabasso, T. 311
Brain, R. 400
Braithwaite, R. B. 19, 20
Brand, D. 316
Braudel, F. 126
Braybrooke, D. and Lindblom, C. E. 102
Breton, A. 299, 301
Broadbend, T. A. 204
Brodbeck, M. 197
Bromberger, S. 102
Brookfield, H. 217
Brouwer, L. E. J. 85
Browder, F. 133
Brown, G. S. 21, 123, 126, 131
Buchanan, K. 180
Bunge, W. W. 207
Bunge, W. W. and Bordessa, R. 240
Burnett, K. P. 320, 324
Burton, I. 187
Butler, S. 9
Buttimer, A. 201, 202, 215, 216, 219, 231,
    403
Buytendijk, F. 221

Calhoun, J. 122
Callan, M. 403
Campbell, J. 127, 139
Camus, A. 144
Caplin, N. 223
Carnap, R. 19, 20, 21, 66, 70
Carroll, L. 298, 305
Caruso, D. and Palm, R. 403
Casetti, E. 193, 194
Cassirer, E. 398
Castells, M. 61
Chamberlain, M. 134, 135
Chang, J. 137
Charles Rivers Associates 315
Chase, S. 19
Chomsky, N. 6, 124
Christaller, W. 371, 429, 430, 432, 435

Churchman, C. W. 102
Cioran, E. M. 300, 304
Clark, D. 230
Clark, G. 196
Clark, G. and Dear, M. 54
Claval, P. 215, 403
Cliff, A. D., Haggett, P., Ord, J. K.,
    Bassett, K. and Davies, R. 194
Cliff, A. D., Martin, R. L. and Ord, J. K.
    191
Cliff, A. D. and Ord, J. K. 196, 367, 368
Cole, H. S. D., Freeman, C., Jahoda, M.
    and Pavitt, K. L. R. 175
Coleman, J. S. 99, 324
Collins, L. 132
Conklin, H. 1, 2, 6
Coombs, C. H. 272
Cowan, T. A. 93
Cranston, M. 127, 142, 144
Crecine, J. P. 371
Creeley, R. 142
Cressey, P. 229
Culler, J. 296
Cunningham, F. 204
Curry, L. 191, 196, 368, 371, 374, 431
Curry, L., Griffith, D. A. and
    Sheppard, E. S. 191, 372
Cyert, R. and March, J. 227

Dacey, M. F. 192, 198, 433
Dahrendorf, R. 62
Dammann, M. 271
Dardel, E. 388, 400, 419
Dart, F. and Pradhan, P. 139
Davies, O. 191, 192
Dear, M. 56, 63, 192
Dedekind, R. 115
DeGeorge, R. and DeGeorge, F. 143,
    144
Detweiler, F. 223
Devereux, G. 266
Dewey, J. 4
Dicken, P. 227
van Dijk, T. A. 102
Dilthey, W. 22
Domencich, T. A. and McFadden, D.
    309

Doob, L. 418
Down, R. 109
Down, R. M. 389
Downs, R. M. and Stea, D. 191
Dubos, R. 416
Dunn, E. S. Jr. 274, 284
Durkheim, E. and Mauss, M. 405

Echenique, M. 198
Ehrenzweig, A. 141
Ehrmann, J. 127
Eisenstadt, S. N. 417
Eliade, M. 413
Engels, F. 170
Engle, R. F. 364
Enke, S. 371
Entrikin, J. N. 18, 21
Erickson, S. A. 409
Esselin, M. 141
Esser, A. H. 403
European Cultural Foundation 20
Evans-Pritchard, E. E. 407

Farhi, A. 204
Ferkiss, V. C. 30
Feyerabend, P. 102, 303
Firey, W. 178, 218
Fischer, R. 32
Floss, L. 390
Folke, S. 188
Forrest, R. 278
Forrester, J. 135, 136
Foucault, M. 128, 141, 259, 300
Fowler, W. W. 413
Fowlie, W. 301
Fox, C. R. 409
Fraenkel, A. 75
Fraenkel, A. and Bar-Hillel, Y. 103
Frake, C. 1
Freire, P. 32
Friedman, M. and Rosenman, R. H. 32
Friedrich, P. 2
Fromm, E. 18, 20, 33
Furubotn, E. and Pejovich, S. 93

Gadamer, H.-G. 22, 23, 302
Gale, S., 66, 95, 96, 100, 102, 103, 205,
    244, 264

Gale, S. and Moore, E. G. 273, 274
Gans, H. J. 419
Gardner 129, 132
Gellner, E. 418
Gendlin, E. T. 388
George, P. 242
Georgescu-Roegen, N. 93, 94, 102, 309
Gershman, H. S. 301
Getis, A. and Boots, B. N. 403
Giddens, A. 19, 188
Giedion, S. 396
Gilbert, E. W. 388, 389
Ginsburg, N., Holt, S. and Murdoch, W.
    136
Glacken, C. 128, 159, 388
Godelier, M. 155, 169
Goguen, J. A. 96
Goldstein, G. S. 282
Goldstein, G. S. and Moses, L. 345
Golledge, R. G. 109, 324
Golledge, R. and Amadeo, D. 220
Golledge, R. G., Briggs, R. and
    Demko, D. 109
Golledge, R., Brown, L. and
    Williamson, F. 219
Golob, T. F. and Beckmann, M. J. 318,
    373
Gottinger, H. W. 102
Gould, P. R. 109, 126, 131, 134, 142,
    143, 187
Gouldner, A. W. 20, 24
Goulet, D. 22, 29
Graustein, W. C. 436
Greg, L. 127, 134
Grene, M. 409
Griffin, D. W. 26
Grigg, D. 94
Grigsby, W. G. 280
Grigsby, W. G. and Rosenburg, L. 278
De Groot, J. J. M. 413
Guelke, L. 202
Gumperz, J. and Hymes, D. 102
Gurwitsch, A. 225

Habermas, J. 22, 23, 25, 102
Haggett, P. 194
Haggett, P. and Chorley, R. J. 435

Hall, E. T. 389
Halsey, A., Floyd, J. and Anderson, A.
    132
Hamburg, C. H. 398
Hamilton, F. 227
Hampshire, S. 390
Harrah, D. 102
Harris, C. W. 261
Hart, J. F. 388
Hartman, L. M. and Seckler, D. 364
Hartmann, C. 227
Harvey, D. 57, 60, 156, 176, 178, 188,
    199, 201, 204, 205, 219, 273, 278,
    282, 372
Harvey, D. and Chatterjee, L. 204
Hawkins, D. 126, 127, 130, 132, 137, 143
Hayes, E. 217
Heelan, P. 102
Hegel, G. W. F. 249, 253
Heidegger, M. 23, 29, 302, 390
Hempel, C. G. 19, 21
Henderson, J. M. and Quandt, R. E. 312
Heyting, A. 84, 85, 87, 89, 103
Hilpinnen 103
Hintikka, J. 102
Hoffman, B. 127
Hogben, L. 129
Holland, P. G. 430
Hollingworth, T. and Berry, M. 431
Hollis, M. and Nell, E. 63
Hooker, C. A. 102
Horkheimer, M. and Adorno, T. W. 259,
    289
Horton, F. and Reynolds, D. R. 310
Horton, R. E. 429, 434
Houthakker, H. S. 312
Howard, A. D. 434, 435
Howard, I. P. and Templeton, W. B. 394
Hudson, J. 103, 191
Hudson, L. 139, 140
Hudson, W. D. 156
Huff, D. 309
Hugill, P. 229
von Humboldt, A. 159
Humbolt, W. 398
Hume, D. 291, 304
Hunt, W. C. 251

Husserl, E. 21, 22
Huxley, A. 296
Hymes, D. 102
Hägerstrand, T. 31, 191, 407

Ilie, P. 301
Illich, I. 20, 32
Isard, W. and Liossatos, P. 371
Isnard, C. and Zeeman, E. 132
Ives, C. 141
Izumi, K. 392

Jacks, G. V. and Whyte, R. O. 180
Jackson, J. B. 402
Jakobson, R. 143
James, E. O. 418
Jameson, F. 300
Jammer, M. 391
Janik, A. and Toulmin, S. 147
Janowitz, M. 218
Jasper, K. 19
Jeffrey, D. and Webb, D. J. 194
Johnson, N. L. and Kotz, S. 320
Johnson, R. 223
Jonassen, C. 218
Jones, E. 215, 219
Jung, C. 127, 140, 141

Kain, J. F. and Quigley, J. M. 280
Kapp, K. W. 156, 182
Kates, R. W. 240
Keenan, E. and Hull, R. 102
Keller, S. I. 419
Kellogg, O. D. 375
Kelly, G. 125
Kemeny, J. C., Snell, J. L. and
    Knapp, A. W. 375
Kennedy, A. 143
Kenny, A. 291
Kerlin, R. 223
Keynes, J. M. 161
King, L. J. 109
King, L. J., Casetti, E. and Jeffrey, D.
    194, 367
King, L. J. and Forster, J. J. H. 195
Kirk, W. 219
Klahr, D. 130

Klammer, T. P. N. 102
Knapp, P. H. 399
Kneese, A. V. 175
Knight, C. G. 2
Knuth, D. 134
Kockelmans, J. J. 22, 122, 127, 134, 400
Kohler, W. 20
Korner, S. 96, 102
Kotovsky, K. and Simon, H. 127
Kruskal, J. and Hart, R. 135
Kuhn, T. S. 156

Laing, R. 125, 135, 145
Laing, R. and Esterson, A. 125
Laming, D. 313
Lane, D. 54
Langer, S. 20, 141
Langer, S. K. 392, 415
Laumann, E. 225
Lavalle, P., McConnell, H. and Brown R. 224
Leach, E. 127, 128, 144
Leavis, F. 125, 140
Lee, H. N. 110, 111, 112
de Leeuw, F. 278, 280
Van der Leeuw, G. 413
Leiss, W. 21, 25
Lenat, D. 130
Leopold, L. B. and Langbein, W. B. 434
Leopold, L. B. and Miller, J. P. 430
Levine, P. 125, 135, 136
Lévi-Strauss, C. 127, 128, 182
Levy, F. S. 55, 60
Lewis, P. F. 389
Ley, D. 223, 226
Ley, D. and Cybriwsky, R. 225
Ley, D. and Samuels, M. 231
Lifton, R. J. 415
Linhart, J. 137
Loeb, A. L. 433
Losch, A. 432
Lovelock, J. 29
Lowenthal, D. 219, 388, 421
deLuca, A. and Termini, S. 96
Luce, G. 32
Luce, R. D. 314
Luce, R. D. and Suppes, P. 309

Lukermann, F. E. 387
Lundholm, B. 137
Lyman, S. M. and Scott, M. B. 403
Lynch, K. 109, 417, 421
Lyons, J. 124, 127, 140
Lösch, A. 167

MacIntyre, A. 189
Mackenzie, R. 220
Macpherson, C. B. 99
Malthus, T. R. 158, 159, 160, 161, 162, 163, 165
Mannheim, K. 24, 220
Marchand, B. 127, 241, 261
Marcus, J. 405, 408
Marcuse, H. 22, 25, 249, 266, 295
Marshall, J. U. 429
Martin, G. D. 296
Martin, R. L. and Oeppen, J. 367
Martindale, D. 22
Marx, K. 167, 169, 170, 171, 172, 173, 299
Massey, W. F., Montgomery, D. B. and Morrison, D. G. 320
Matthews, J. H. 301
May, J. A. 387, 391, 422
May, R. 126
McCarthy, M. 403
McCarthy, T. 102
Meade, G. H. 117
Meadows, D. and Meadows, D. 135
Meadows, D., Meadows, D., Randers, J. and Behrens, W. 136, 175
Medawar, P. and J. 121
Mehta, V. 121, 126, 127
Meinig, D. W. 388
Mendel, W. 392
Mercer, D. 225
Mercer, D. and Powell, J. 18, 21, 216, 389
Mercer, J. 227
Merleau-Ponty, M. 389
Mesarovic, M. and Pestel, E. 136
Mesjaros, I. 156
Miliband, R. 54
Mill, J. S. 166
Miller, D. 60

Miller, G. A., Galanter, E. and
   Pribram, K. H. 311
Mills, C. W. 24
Minkowski, E. 400
Moholy-Nagy, S. 414, 416
Monod, J. 123, 139
Morgenstern, O. 102
Moore, E. G. 280
Moore, J. and Newell, A. 130, 134
Mulhall, D. 135
Murdie, R. 272
Murton, B. J. 2
Muth, R. F. 278, 279
Müller, W. 405
Myrdal, G. 19, 20, 199

Natanson, M. 226
Nelkin, D. 263
Newcomb, R. M. 416
Newell, A. and Simon, H. 127
Niedercorn, J. R. 364
Niedercorn, J. R. and Becholdt, B. V. 373
Norberg-Schulz, C. 415
Nyerges, T. 117
Nystuen, J. D. 401

Oakeshott, M. 388
O'Brien, C. 144
Ollman, B. 168
Olson, D. R. 395
Olsson, G. 20, 109, 190, 202, 205, 220,
   264, 287, 368
Olsson, G., Eichenbaum, J. and Gale, S.
   109
Olsson, G. and Gale, S. 109
Open University 146
Orans, M. 177
Ortega y Gasset, J. 399
Osmond, H. 392
Ostrom, V. 58

Pahl, R. 215
Palmer, R. E. 22
Palomäki, M. 429
Papageorgiou, G. 192, 193, 194
Papageorgiou, G.J. and Brummel, A.C.
   194
Papageorgiou, G. J. and Casetti, E. 194

Papageorgiou, G. J. and Mullally, H. 194
Park, R. 217, 218, 220
Parsons, T. 93
Passmore, J. 20
Paz, O. 295, 296
Pearson, H. 178
Perelman, C. 102
Perleau-Ponty, M. 239
Persig, R. 131, 144
Piaget, J. 171, 392
Pickvance, C. G. 272
Pipkin, J. S. 309
Pivcevic, E. 22
Polanyi, M. 124, 144
Pollock, W. T. and Chapanis, A. 395
Popper, K. 121, 122, 124, 126, 130, 131,
   141
Poulet, G. 142
Pred, A. 191, 366
Preparata, F. P. and Yeh, R. T. 96
President's Message 145

Quandt, R. E. 313
Quigley, J. M. 278

Ramanujan, A. 142
Rasmussen, S. E. 418
Rawls, J. 60, 100
Rees, P. H. and Wilson, A. G. 367
Reichenbach, H. 102
Rein, M. 201, 205
Relph, E. 216, 389
Rescher, N. 89, 96, 102, 103
Ricardo, D. 162, 165, 166
Richards, P. 32
Richler, M., Fortier, A. and May, R. 126
Ricoeur, P. 22, 389
Roberts, F. S. 97
Roberts, M. J. 199
Robinson, B. S. 415
Robinson, J. 200
Robson, B. 229
Rogier, A. 137, 143
Rokkan, S. 279
Rose, A. and Rose, C. 223
Rosenstock-Hussey, E. 393
Rosser, J. B. and Turquette, A. M. 91

Roweis, S. T. 357
Rubin, H. and Rubin, J. E. 103
Rushton, G. 366
Russell, B. 74, 109
Ryan, T. A. and Ryan, M. S. 399

Sack, R. D. 364
Samuels, M. S. 18, 222
Samuelson, P. A. 312, 353
Sant, M. 194
Santmyer, H. H. 389, 411
Sauer, C. O. 409
Saussure, F. 144
Savage, L. 264
Sayre, K. 124
Scheffler, H. 127
Scheibe, K. E. 20
Scheidegger, A. E. and Langbein, W. B. 434
Schenck, H. S. Jr. 434
Schneider, M. 374
Shibutani, T. 224
Schmidt, A. 169
Schroyer, T. 21
Schum, S. 429
Schutz, A. 222, 225, 228, 422
Schutz, A. and Luckmann, T. 225
Scott, A. J. 353, 359
Scully, V. 413
Seley, J. 63
Sharpless, F. 127
Shattuck, R. 142, 145
Sheets, H. and Morris, R. 137
Sheppard, E. S. 190, 364, 374
Shreve, R. L. 431, 434, 435
Silver, I. 279, 280
Simon, H. 127, 130, 139, 145, 146
Simon, H. and Hayes, J. 130
Simon, H. and Newell, A. 130, 131, 134, 143
Sivadon, P. 392
Skinner, B. F. 296, 311
Smart, J. S. 435
Smart, J. S., Surkan, A. J. and Considine, J. P. 434
Smith, C. S. 224, 436
Smith, E. B. 416

Smith, T. E. 373, 374
Sneed, J. D. 102
Snow, C. P. 125, 140
Soja, E. W. 93, 94
Sommer, R. 94, 230
Sopher, D. E. 388
Sorre, M. 219
Sorokin, P. A. 409
Speare, A. 272
Spence, N. and Taylor, P. 65
Spiegelberg, H. 19, 22, 222
Spink, W. 139
Stark, F. 418
Starobinski, J. 419
Stegmüller, W. 122, 133
Steiner, G. 123, 128, 131, 132, 139, 140, 141, 142, 143, 145, 296
Stent, A. 140
Stevens, W. 415
Stewart, I. 129, 146
Storr, A. 127, 141
Stouffer, S. A. 374
Strack, C. 134
Strahler, A. N. 429, 430
Straszheim, M. H. 283
Straus, E. W. 395, 400, 401
Strole, L. 136
Sturtevant, W. 1
Suppe, F. 102
Suppes, P. 69, 102, 103
Sutherland, N. S. 395
Suttles, G. D. 417, 419
Swain, H. and Mather, E. C. 389
Szent-Györgyi, A. 136

Taaffe, E., Morrill, R. L. and Gould, P. R. 366
Tam, Y. K. 280
Tarascio, V. J. 156
Targ, H. 102
Tarski, A. 99
Taylor, A. 127
Teilhard de Chardin, P. 18, 30
Teitz, M. B. 53, 55, 59
Thom, R. 123, 124, 125, 130, 136, 144, 247
Thomas, D. 226

Thomas, W. 218, 225
Thomas, W. and Znaniecki, F. 228
Thurston, R. F. 431
Thurstone, L. L. 312
Timms, D. 220
Tinbergen, J. 136
Tobler, W. 132, 191
Tobler, W. and Weinberg, S. 132
Toffler, A. 18
Tolman, E. C. 4
Toulmin, S. 102, 132, 143
Tuan, Y. 202, 228, 230
Turner, R. 217
Tuttle, N. H. 22
Tyler, S. A. 2

Ulam, S. 126
U.S. Department of Commerce 282
Usher, D. 206

Vernon, J. 139
Vidal de la Blache, P. 216, 409
Vining, R. 371
Visher, S. 218
Vogt, W. 180
Von Neumann, J. O. and Morgenstern, O. 241

Wagner, H. 225
Wagner, P. 417
Walker, R. A. 204
Wallace, W. L. 40
Walmsley, D. J. 202
Ward, B. 188
Watanabe, S. 94, 102
Waterman, T. T. 407
Watson, J. W. 215
Webber, M. 190, 285
Webber, M. J., Symanski, R. and Boot, J. 366
Weber, M. 25
Weinberg, S. 132

Weiner, P. and Deak, E. 227
Weissbrod, R. 195
Weitz, M. 102
Werner, C. 435
Werrity, A. 435
Wheatley, P. 405
White, A. 291
White, L. 413
White, R. W. 373
Whitehead, A. N. 109, 112, 113
Whitehead, J. 224
Whorf, B. L. 125, 393
Wild, J. 18, 21, 412
Williams, R. 140, 221, 223
Wilson, A. G. 187, 190, 367
Winter, G. 18, 29
Wissowa, G. 413
Wittall, A. 141
Wittgenstein, L. 112, 296
Woldenberg, M. J. 431, 433, 436, 441, 442, 443, 445
Woldenberg, M. J. and Berry, B. J. L. 430
Wolpert, J. 26, 63, 192, 310
Wolpert, J., Dear, M. and Crawford, R. 192
Wolpert, J., Mumphrey, A. and Seley, J. 206
Woolf, V. 126
Wright, J. K. 388
von Wright, G. H. 102

Yeates, M. L. and Garner, B. J. 199
Yi, G. J. L. 364
Young, J. W. 196

Zadeh, L. A. 66, 95, 96, 103
Zaner, R. 222
Zeeman, E. C. 97, 132, 265
Zelinsky, W. 26, 202, 221
Zinke, G. W. 162
Znaniekci, F. 218
Zorbaugh, W. 218

INDEX OF SUBJECTS

analysis xix–xx, 9–37, 39–52, 187–199, 269–286, 288–290, 309–328, 345–359
artificial intelligence 336–342

belief statements 1–7
boundaries 92–102

cellular geography 379–385
class struggle 157–174

dialectics 116–117, 167–174, 237–266

education 138–140, 144–148
ethics 28–34
ethnogeography 1–7
existentialism 18–24, 215–236

form/process xi–xvi, 109–119, 361–378

geographical data 269–285
geographical theories 39–52
geography and choice theory 309–328
geography and epistemology 329–344
geography and ethnoscience 1–7
geography and planning 9–37, 177–182
geography and postmodernism 287–305, 329–344
geography and public sector 53–64

ideology 155–185, 203–205

land use theory 345–359
language 131–138, 242–245, 287–307, 387–422

mythology 1–7, 242–245, 293–298, 387–422

pattern 126–131, 140–144
phenomenology xix–xx, 9–37, 215–236, 290–293, 387–427
place 228–231, 387–422
positivism 18–24, 187–208
process 109–119

quantitative geography 187–208

rationality 17–28, 155–183
regionalization 65–107

scenarios 17–24
set theory 65–107
spatial hierarchies 429–457
spatial interdependence 361–378
surrealism 300–305

thought and action xvi–xviii, 9–37, 65–107, 177–182, 199–203, 269–286, 287–307

THEORY AND DECISION LIBRARY

An International Series in the Philosophy and Methodology
of the Social and Behavioral Sciences

Editors:

Gerald Eberlein, *University of Technology, Munich*
Werner Leinfellner, *University of Nebraska*

1. Günther Menges (ed.), *Information, Inference, and Decision.* 1974, viii + 195 pp.
2. Anatol Rapoport (ed.), *Game Theory as a Theory of Conflict Resolution.* 1974, v + 283 pp.
3. Mario Bunge (ed.), *The Methodological Unity of Science.* 1973, viii + 264 pp.
4. Colin Cherry (ed.), *Pragmatic Aspects of Human Communication.* 1974, ix + 178 pp.
5. Friedrich Rapp (ed.), *Contributions to a Philosophy of Technology. Studies in the Structure of Thinking in the Technological Sciences.* 1974, xv + 228 pp.
6. Werner Leinfellner and Eckehart Köhler (eds.), *Developments in the Methodology of Social Science.* 1974, x + 430 pp.
7. Jacob Marschak, *Economic Information, Decision and Prediction. Selected Essays.* 1974, three volumes, xviii + 389 pp.; xii + 362 pp.; x + 399 pp.
8. Carl-Axel S. Staël von Holstein (ed.), *The Concept of Probability in Psychological Experiments.* 1974, xi + 153 pp.
9. Heinz J. Skala, *Non-Archimedean Utility Theory.* 1975, xii + 138 pp.
10. Karin D. Knorr, Hermann Strasser, and Hans Georg Zilian (eds.), *Determinants and Controls of Scientific Developments.* 1975, ix + 460 pp.
11. Dirk Wendt, and Charles Vlek (eds.), *Utility, Probability, and Human Decision Making. Selected Proceedings of an Interdisciplinary Research Conference, Rome, 3–6 September, 1973.* 1975, viii + 418 pp.
12. John C. Harsanyi, *Essays on Ethics, Social Behavior, and Scientific Explanation.* 1976, xvi + 262 pp.
13. Gerhard Schwödiauer (ed.), *Equilibrium and Disequilibrium in Economic Theory. Proceedings of a Conference Organized by the Institute for Advanced Studies, Vienna, Austria, July 3–5, 1974.* 1978, 1 + 736 pp.
14. V. V. Kolbin, *Stochastic Programming.* 1977, xii + 195 pp.
15. R. Mattessich, *Instrumental Reasoning and Systems Methodology.* 1978, xxii + 396 pp.
16. H. Jungermann and G. de Zeeuw (eds.), *Decision Making and Change in Human Affairs.* 1977, xv + 526 pp.
18. A. Rapoport, W. E. Stein, and G. J. Burkheimer, *Response Models for Detection of Change.* 1978 (forthcoming)
19. H. J. Johnson, J. J. Leach, and R. G. Mühlmann (eds.), *Revolutions, Systems, and Theories; Essays in Political Philosophy.* 1978